CONTENTS

KU-752-927

CRAFTS

FILM & TELEVISION

National

Regional

Local

Others

HERITAGE, LIBRARIES, GALLERIES, MUSEUMS

EDUCATION & YOUTH

ECONOMIC & SOCIAL DEVELOPMENT

PART TWO - INTERNATIONAL

INFORMATION SOURCES

BRITISH SUPPORT FOR VISITS/EXCHANGES

EUROPEAN FUNDING

FUNDING FROM THE USA

PART THREE - SUPPORT FROM COMPANIES

PART FOUR - CHARITABLE TRUSTS

APPENDICES

INDEXES

ALPHABETICAL LISTS

THE ARTS FUNDING GUIDE
1997/98 EDITION

Susan Forrester

A DIRECTORY OF SOCIAL CHANGE PUBLICATION

THE ARTS FUNDING GUIDE
1997/98 EDITION
Susan Forrester

Copyright ©1996 the Directory of Social Change

First published 1989
Second edition 1991
Third edition 1994
Fourth edition 1996

Published by the Directory of Social Change,
24 Stephenson Way, London NW1 2DP
(tel: 0171 209 5151, fax: 0171 209 5049), from whom further copies and a publications list may be obtained.

The Directory of Social Change is a registered charity no. 800517.

Design by Linda Parker.
Printed and bound by Page Bros, Norwich.

ISBN 1 873860 92 7

British Library Cataloguing-in-Publication Data
A catalogue record for this book is available from the British Library

ACKNOWLEDGEMENTS

I should like to give warm thanks to all those many people who have assisted in supplying information. Most particularly I would like to thank the originating editor, Anne-Marie Doulton, and the editors of the National Lottery Yearbook.

PART ONE

UK Official Sources

INTRODUCTION

This guide concentrates on sources of funds for arts activities of all kinds. Some general advice is given about approaching local authorities, trusts and companies, but the main aim of the guide is to direct readers to appropriate funders rather than advise them how to fundraise.

It has been compiled at a time of dramatic change to arts funding. The massive increase in arts funding from the National Lottery is having a knock-on effect on other arts funding bodies. As its own criteria are likely to broaden, so other official sources of funds may be threatened with further cuts. As these shifts occur, the reorganisation of local authorities with the introduction of new unitary authorities is creating further uncertainty for many arts organisations with a history of support from their local authority.

I am indebted to the National Campaign for the Arts for allowing the reproduction of their "family tree" of official arts funding bodies which clearly illustrates the connections between the Department of National Heritage, other departments and specific arts funding bodies. Readers interested in an overview of total arts funding should obtain the campaign's *"Facts About The Arts"* (£5.00).

National Campaign for the Arts, Francis House, Francis Street, London SW1P 1DE; Tel: 0171-828 4448; Fax: 0171-931 9959

Figure 1

CULTURAL FUNDING THROUGH GOVERNMENT DEPARTMENTS

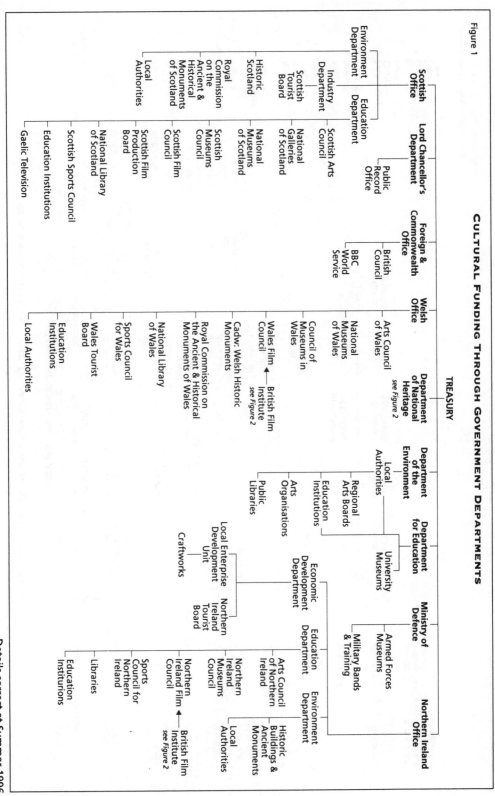

Details correct at Summer 1996

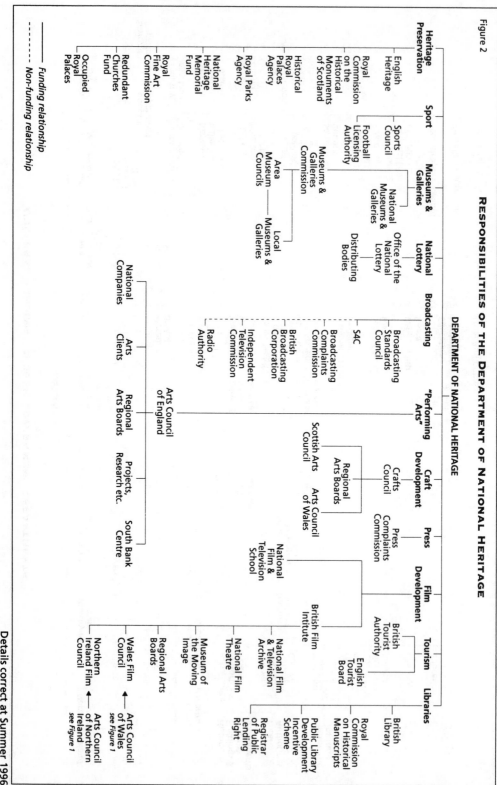

Figure 2

RESPONSIBILITIES OF THE DEPARTMENT OF NATIONAL HERITAGE

DEPARTMENT OF NATIONAL HERITAGE

Details correct at Summer 1996

THE NATIONAL ARTS COUNCILS

The Arts Council of England

The Scottish Arts Council

The Arts Council of Wales

The Arts Council of Northern Ireland

THE ARTS COUNCIL OF ENGLAND

14 Great Peter Street, London SW1P 3NQ
Tel: 0171-333 0100; Fax: 0171-973 6590
Mary Allen, Secretary-General
Grant total: £118,404,000 (1994/95)

The Arts Council of England (ACE) is the national funding body for the arts in England. It is responsible for fostering the arts across the nation through the distribution of public money from central government and revenue generated by the National Lottery.

On 1 April 1994, the responsibilities and functions of the Arts Council of Great Britain (ACGB) were transferred to three new bodies, the Arts Council of England, the Scottish Arts Council and the Arts Council of Wales. The Arts Council of Northern Ireland was already established as a separate body. The Scottish Arts Council, the Arts Council of Wales and the Arts Council of Northern Ireland are accountable to, and receive their funding from the Scottish, Welsh and Northern Ireland Offices respectively.

ACE is responsible for continuing the work of the ACGB in England, and is directly accountable to the Secretary of State for National Heritage. Each year, ACE receives a grant-in-aid from central government, via the Department of National Heritage, with which it supports arts organisations and artists across the country.

ACE has the following objects:

- to develop and improve the knowledge, understanding and practice of the arts,
- to make the arts more accessible to the public,
- to advise and co-operate with central government departments, local authorities, the Arts Councils of Scotland, Wales and Northern Ireland and other bodies on any relevant matters.

The mission of ACE is to enable everyone to enjoy and derive inspiration from the arts. It does so by nurturing creativity, responding to innovation, promoting excellence, sustaining our living traditions, supporting multi-cultural interests, fostering audiences and helping more people to encounter the work of artists.

ACE distributes part of its annual grant-in-aid directly and part through the ten Regional Arts Boards (RABs) with which it works closely. The RABs are independent organisations responsible for developing the arts in their area. Together ACE and the RABs make up the integrated system for arts funding and development in England.

The major part of the council's grant-in-aid (some 90%) is devoted to a group of organisations funded on a regular or fixed-term basis (excluding the funding to the RABs). Of the hundreds of grants made by the council in 1994/95 only 15 were in excess of £1 million but they comprised 68% of total arts expenditure (£80,219,000):

Under "Combined Arts"
South Bank Board £13,330,000
Under "Dance"
Royal Opera House £10,890,000
English National Ballet £3,528,000
Northern Ballet Theatre £1,065,000
Rambert Dance Company £1,125,000
Under "Drama"
Royal National Theatre Board
   £11,167,000
Royal Shakespeare Theatre
   £8,470,000

Under "Music"
English National Opera £11,655,000
Royal Opera House £8,581,000
Opera North £3,815,000
Bournemouth Orchestras £1,570,400
Royal Liverpool Philharmonic Society
   £1,482,800
Hallé Concerts Society £1,251,000
City of Birmingham Orchestra
   £1,149,000
London Symphony Orchestra
   £1,140,000

A wide range of one-off grants known as development funds (see below) are also available throughout the year for specific productions, exhibitions, tours, events, projects, research and training schemes.

ACE supports the following art forms: combined and interdisciplinary arts; dance; drama; film, video and broadcasting; literature; live art; mime; music; puppetry; visual arts including photography and architecture. It also supports touring arts events, education programmes by professional artists and training initiatives for arts professionals. The council's annual reports contain details of organisations and individuals supported and full information on the expenditure of the grant-in-aid.

The Arts Council depends on a network of expert art-form advisers, both formally appointed to panels and boards, and informally providing reports on artistic trends and developments. The network of advisers plays a particularly crucial role in the appraisal of arts organisations.

Grants by Artform 1994/95

	Regularly Funded Organisations £'000s	Project Grants £'000s	Total Grants £'000s
Combined arts	14,359	1,001	15,360
Cross-disciplinary	–	275	275
Dance	20,351	1,272	21,623
Drama & Mime	25,192	1,573	26,765
Film, Video, Broadcasting	13	321	334
International Initiatives	–	517	517
Literature	729	738	1,467
Music	39,949	1,182	36,131
Touring	6,852	3,384	10,236
Education & Training	21	782	803
Visual Arts	2,650	1,588	4,238
Architecture	–	158	158
Arts 2000 (Cities of Culture)	–	275	275
Total	105,292	13,112	118,404

Grants to Regional Arts Boards 1994/95   £58,062,000
Other funded activities   £3,455,000
(including promotion of Contemporary
Music Network, research, consultancies,
publications, conferences, etc.)

The council has agreed the following core attributes of quality to help ensure it
has clear and consistent decision-making.

Criteria	*Core attributes*
Artistic	Vision and imagination; quality of execution; the power to communicate to the target audience.
Managerial	Creativity of approach in securing and using resources; efficiency of operation; efficient use of human resources.
Strategic	Capacity to attract and broaden public involvement in the arts; fulfilment of the appropriate local/regional/national role; commitment to equality of opportunity.

DEVELOPMENT FUNDS 1996/97
(formerly known as Projects, Schemes and Awards)

These funds comprise about 10% of the council's total arts expenditure. This
summary covers funds for the financial year 1996/97. Please check for up-to-date
provisions.

Applications
Application forms should be obtained for all the following funds. Be sure to check
the deadline dates. These may alter. The following list only gives the deadline
months to indicate the frequency of consideration, not the exact dates.

◆ COMBINED ARTS DEPARTMENT
Tel: 0171-973 6573
For all deadlines, except where noted,
contact the department for details.

International Initiatives Fund
Contact: 0171-973 6573
Deadline: Applications are considered
every two months.
To assist promoters in Great Britain to
present a range of arts events and artists
from abroad.

Live Art Development Fund
Contact: 0171-973 6512
To develop the practice, distribution,
awareness and appreciation of Live Art.

Live Art Commissions Fund
Contact: 0171-973 6512
Open to any promoter, partnership of
promoters or artists acting as promoters
with a commitment to Live Art.

Live Art Travel and Research Fund
Contact: 0171-973 6512
To enable practitioners to develop their
work by visits to projects, events, and
appropriate fieldwork.

Live Art in Higher Education Fund
Contact: 0171-973 6512
To support innovative links.

New Collaborations Fund
Contact: 0171-973 6512
To support and encourage innovative collaborations between artists from different artform areas and to assist the development of emerging inter-disciplinary practices.

Notting Hill Carnival Bands Scheme
Contact: 0171-973 6512

◆ DANCE DEPARTMENT
Tel: 0171-973 6489
For all the dance funds listed below, unless otherwise stated -
Contact: 0171-973 6490
Deadlines: November, April.

Making and Touring of Dance Work including Revivals
To support the touring of a range of high quality dance throughout England including the production costs of new work and/or the costs of rehearsing or reworking of existing pieces. A tour involves venues in at least 3 Regional Arts Board regions.

Research and Development
To help artistic development without the pressure of performing/touring. Companies, organisations and individuals who have received RAB or ACE funding within the last three years may apply.

Choreographic Development
Both individuals and organisations can apply and could include a residency at a venue, agency, consortia of organisations, a teaching programme or various commissions. The application must involve the making of new choreographic material.

Promoters/Artists Collaborations including Festivals
Applications are invited from promoters and producers who wish to collaborate with an artist/company or group of artists/companies. This category includes a range of activities – the commissioning of new work, the curation of programmes of work by a number of choreographers and/or work by a number of choreographers and/or the programming of festivals/seasons.

Taped Dance Videos for use in Education
Contact: 0171-973 6491
Deadline: November.
To produce professionally made video tapes, imaginative in approach and suitable for educational use. The proposals can include existing/reworked, specially choreographed dance works or take a documentary approach.

Dance Training
Contact: 0171-973 6485
Deadline: November.
For organisations wishing to provide training opportunities for individuals professionally involved in dance. A training initiative may take the form of a one-off event or programme of activity over a longer period of time.

◆ DRAMA DEPARTMENT
Tel: 0171-973 6479

Drama Projects and Funds
Contact: 0171-973 6484/6496
Deadlines: November, March.

Project Subsidy Funds
To support drama, mime and puppetry companies for a single new production which can be planned and costed in some detail, including reasonable preparation and winding up periods.

Black and Asian Theatre or Mime or Puppetry Encouragement Subsidies
To help both companies and artists with a specific area of work within a project, such as production costs, administration, marketing or the cost of commissioning a director, designer or choreographer.

Mime and Puppetry Festival Subsidies
To support organisers of mime and puppetry festivals of national importance.

Theatre Writing Funds
Contact: 0171-973 6480
Deadlines: April, July, October, January.

Commission or Option Award
To part-fund the cost of paying a writer a commission fee to write a new play or a fee to secure the rights to an unperformed play.

Theatre Translations Fund
To provide support for theatre translators who must be translating directly from the original language. Priority is given to translation of contemporary work.

Theatre Writing Bursaries
To provide experienced playwrights with an opportunity to research and develop a play for the theatre independently of financial pressures and free from the need to write for a particular market.

Resident Dramatist Attachment Award
To part-fund the cost of having a playwright in residence for a continuous period of six months. The company may apply for an extension of six months.

Traineeships for Theatre Directors and Designers
Contact: 0171-973 6481
Deadlines: Schemes advertised April, closing date May.

Arts Council/Calouste Gulbenkian Foundation Scheme A - Residencies for Associate Directors
Two traineeships are available to train promising experienced directors to undertake year-long placements in theatres to learn more about theatre management, producing and programming.

Arts Council/Calouste Gulbenkian Foundation Scheme B - Residencies for Assistant Directors
Four traineeships available for inexperienced directors to spend a year at a theatre.

Black and Asian Trainee Directors
In addition to the above, two traineeships are available for black and Asian directors to spend a year at a theatre.

Residencies for Theatre Designers
Two traineeships are available for aspiring designers to undertake a year-long residency with a theatre design department.

◆ EDUCATION & TRAINING DEPARTMENT
Tel: 0171-973 6450

Creativity and New Technologies
Deadline: January.
To support one-off national training initiatives where there is no other similar provision. Open to individuals, companies or organisations who wish to respond to the creative use of new technologies.

◆ FILM, VIDEO & BROADCASTING DEPARTMENT
Tel: 0171-973 6443
For all deadline dates please contact the department periodically.

Production Funding: Arts Programmes
Contact: 0171-973 6443
To support single and short series of arts programmes on a matching-funding basis

with broadcasters. Professionally made programmes primarily for television distribution. No house style. Dramatisations or fiction, even when adapted from a novel or play, are not eligible.

Dance for Camera
Contact: 0171-973 6443
To support commissions of original dance programmes for television by choreographer/director teams. A joint series with BBC 2.

Sound on Film
Contact: 0171-973 6443
To support commissions of original music programmes for television by composer/director teams. A joint project with BBC 2.

Animate!
Contact: 0171-333 0100 x410
To support animation work which is formally experimental and technically innovative. A joint project with Channel 4.

Midnight Underground
Contact: 0171-333 0100 x410
To support experimental work for television on Hi and Super-8 by experienced film and video artists. A joint project with Channel 4.

Expanding Pictures
Contact: 0171-333 0100 x410
To support commissions of original live/performance art programmes for television.

Artists Film and Video Production Awards
Contact: 0171-333 0100 x410
To provide production funding targeted at artists unlikely to benefit from television funds or gallery-linked commissions.

Artists Film and Video National Distribution Fund: Exhibition and Initiatives
Contact: 0171-333 0100 x410
To provide funding for touring/commissioning/other projects related to artists' film/video.

Black Tracks
Contact: 0171-973 6443
To support commissions of five 15 minute television programmes which bring fresh insights to their theme of black music. A joint series with Channel 4.

Synchro
Contact: 0171-973 6443
To encourage short imaginative and original programmes which present aspects of black arts, music and culture to an ITV audience. A joint commissioning project between the Arts Council and Carlton Television.

Disability Arts Video Project
Contact: 0171-973 6455
To support arts video productions dealing with the practice and availability of disability arts.

◆ LITERATURE DEPARTMENT
Tel: 0171-973 6442

Literature Touring
Contact: 0171-973 6441
Deadlines: Applications can be made at any time.
Writers on Tour
To encourage readings and interest in as wide a range of literature as possible and to give audiences more opportunity to listen to new and exciting live performances.
Writers in Residence
To place overseas writers in residence for at least two months giving various communities in each region in England the opportunity to benefit from having access to a professional writer over an extended period.

Translation Fund
Contact: 0171-973 6542
Deadlines: May, September, January.
Publications
To enable publishers to bring out literature in translation where it would not normally be commercially viable.
Projects
To promote literature in translation, such as a series of events, an exhibition or a tour

based around work in translation, to introduce readers to writing from a particular country.

Writers' Award Fund

Contact: 0171-973 6441
Deadline: September.
To provide fifteen awards of £7,000 each to creative writers who have had at least one book previously published. Awarded annually. Advertised in July.

The Raymond Williams Community Publishing Prize

Contact: 0171-973 6442
Deadline: April 1996.
To commend an outstanding creative and imaginative work which reflects the values of ordinary people and their lives and is submitted by non-profit-making publishers producing books in mutual and co-operative ways. Awarded annually.

Independent Initiative Fund

Contact: 0171-973 6542
Deadlines: October, March.
To allow for applications for funding of literary projects that do not readily fall into the categories of other literature funds listed above. Special note will be taken of applications with a disability aspect.

◆ MUSIC DEPARTMENT

Tel: 0171-973 6495

Artists' Research and Development fund (including Composers in Association Fund)

Contact: 0171-973 6496
To enable creative and performing musicians to prepare new or unusual repertoire, or to explore new techniques. The Composers in Association Scheme enables large-scale arts organisations to develop an association with a creative musician over an extended period and involve them in a range of activity, including education and outreach work and programming, as well as composition.

Early Music Projects

Contact: 0171-973 6493
To encourage new approaches to historically-informed performance by smaller-scale ensembles.

Improvised Music Touring

Contact: 0171-973 6494
To assist touring in England by free improviser, that is music without any pre-determined harmonic or rhythmic structures.

Jazz Touring

Contact: 0171-973 6494
To assist touring in England by large-scale groups of jazz musicians. Each group normally consists of seven or more performers (no upper limit on size).

New Music Commissioning Subsidy

Contact: 0171-973 6496
Deadlines: February, September.
To support a) commissioners who are Arts Council regular clients, b) the commissioning of work for tours in the UK and/or first performances abroad (with subsequent UK performances).

New Music Recording Subsidy

Contact: 0171-973 6494
Deadline: March.
Subsidised recordings of new music.

London-based Chamber Orchestras

Contact: 0171-973 6492
Deadline: October.
To assist these orchestras to develop projects which have a regional emphasis and which aim to develop performances of new work, adventurous programming and wider audiences (through audience development initiatives and education and community projects).

Music and Disability

Contact: 0171-333 0100 x596
Deadline: May.
To support projects which improve access to music. Applications for capital initiatives or

work for audiences at arts events, which are already substantially supported, are not eligible.

African, Caribbean and Asian Music
Contact: 0171-973 6494
Deadlines: February, June.
To assist touring and development in England, especially by British-based artists and organisations.

Opera/Music Theatre Development
Contact: 0171-973 6496
Deadlines: June, October.
To support both its development and presentation and the innovative production of existing repertoire on the small-scale.

◆ TOURING DEPARTMENT
Tel: 0171-973 6500

Drama and Dance Projects
Drama contact: 0171-973 6499
Dance contact: 0171-973 6503
Deadlines: November, February, May, August.
To fund, usually on a guarantee-against-loss basis, tours primarily to large and middle-scale venues by performing arts companies.

International Projects
Contact: 0171-973 6498
Deadlines: November, February, May, August.
To fund tours by incoming international performing arts groups, usually through a British promoter.

Opera/Music Theatre Projects
Contact: 0171-973 6501
Deadlines: June, October.
To support performances and tours by primarily middle-scale opera/music theatre groups.

Contemporary Music Network (CMN) Tours
Contact: 0171-973 6501
Deadlines: Please enquire.
To support new and experimental music, including contemporary classical, jazz, non-Western and improvised music.

Venue Development Fund
Contact: 0171-973 6593
Deadlines: November, February, May, August.
To support programming and audience development plans proposed by presenting venues.

Promoter Development Funds
Contact: 0171-973 6500
Deadlines: Applications can be considered at any time.
To support promoters to see work that re-lates to future programming development.

◆ VISUAL ARTS DEPARTMENT
Tel: 0171-973 6472

Development Grants for Visual Arts Touring Exhibitions and Events .
Contact: 0171-973 6566
Deadline: April.
To extend the range and distribution of visual arts touring exhibitions in England. To be used towards initial research, establishing sources of funding and tour venues, or other costs associated with the development period.

Exhibitions and Events
Contact: 0171-973 6566
Deadline: December.
To provide support primarily for contemporary visual arts exhibitions and events which are originated in England and will take place in more than one region. Work from abroad and historical material, if it is presented within a contemporary context, may be included.

Touring Exhibition and Event Travel Grants

Contact: 0171-973 6566

To provide support for those actively engaged in the curatorship or organisation of touring exhibitions, events or collaborations in England. This can be in the form of visits, meetings with artists, conferences, or with museums or galleries both nationally and internationally.

Publishing

Contact: 0171-333 0100 x425
Deadline: December.

To support the production, promotion and distribution of visual arts publication that feature the work of visual artists or critical, theoretical, educational or historical texts which contribute towards the knowledge, understanding and appreciation of the visual arts.

First Time Publications

Contact: 0171-333 0100 x425
Deadline: October.

To support and assist the development of artists' and photographers' careers through the production of a publication which feature their work for the first time. The publications must be marked by the public presentation of work in the form of an exhibition, commission, or site/event.

Symposia

Contact: 0171-333 0100 x425
Deadline: December.

To provide support for talks, seminars and conferences which contribute to the understanding and appreciation of the visual arts nationally.

Photography Publishing Grants

Contact: 0171-973 6474
Deadline: October, March.

To support the production, promotion and distribution of photography publications (including CD-ROMs) that feature the work of photographers, critical, historical or theoretical texts which contribute to the understanding or appreciation of photography. To support the production of publications intended for education and training.

In addition:

The "WORKING FOR CITIES AWARD" is an award scheme run by the council and British Gas to encourage and reward arts projects which have made the most successful contribution to urban regeneration. It is an annual scheme with eight categories of award. Guidelines and application forms are available from: Arts Council/British Gas "Working for Cities" Award, 2 Portland Road, Holland Park, London W11 4LA (Tel: 0171-221 7883).

National Lottery

ACE is also responsible for distributing National Lottery money to the arts in England. This is dealt with in a separate Lottery Section.

THE SCOTTISH ARTS COUNCIL

12 Manor Place, Edinburgh EH3 7DD
Tel: 0131-226 6051; Fax: 0131-225 9833;
Help Desk: 0131-243 2444
Seona Reid, Director

Total arts expenditure: £21,745,000 (1994/95)

The Scottish Arts Council is one of the principal channels of government funding for the arts in Scotland. It is responsible to and financed by the Scottish Office. Current priorities are education; the indigenous arts of Scotland; the encouragement of international collaborations; artistic innovation; greater access to the arts; improved marketing.

Expenditure by Artform 1994/95

Music	40%	Visual Arts	9%
Drama	21%	Literature	5%
Dance	12%	Crafts	1%
Combined Arts	12%		

Major arts organisations are funded on an ongoing revenue basis and their work is assessed each year. Some 80% of the council's budget was dispersed in revenue funding in 1994/95 to the following organisations: the four national companies (the Royal Scottish National Orchestra, Scottish Chamber Orchestra, Scottish Ballet, and Scottish Opera); 9 arts centres; 6 festivals; 1 dance and 14 theatre companies; 5 music, 7 literary, 21 visual arts and 6 development or service organisations.

In addition the council makes projects funds available to individual artists and arts organisations.

Projects and Schemes 1994/95	£	Number of grants
Crafts	129,000	57
Literature	337,000	182
Dance	389,000	93
Drama	714,000	139
Music	612,000	214
Visual arts	406,000	191
Combined arts	349,000	93
Central funds	319,000	103
TOTAL	3,255,000	

FUNDS AND SCHEMES 1996/97

The following schemes were current for 1996/97 however all schemes are subject to review and details may change.

Applications

Guidelines with full details are available from the relevant department or from the Help Desk: 0131-243 2444. Most schemes have precise closing dates.

◆ CRAFTS

Contact: Crafts Department
Awards for individual development
Exhibitions
Special projects
Start-up grants
Indigenous grants development fund

◆ LITERATURE

Contact: Literature Department
Book awards
Fellowships for translators
Grants to magazines
Grants to publishers
Literary events
SAC/HarperCollins short story
Travel and research grants
Writers' bursaries
Writing Fellowships (awarded jointly with host organisations)
Writers in public/writers in schools

◆ PERFORMING ARTS

Contact: Performing Arts Department
General
Medium-scale venue development fund
Promoters "Go and See" fund
Performing arts promoters fund
Dance
Choreographic development award
Dance bursaries
Dance artist-in-residence
Dance project awards
Touring to small and mid-scale venues by Scottish dance companies
Scottish traditions of dance
Drama and Mime
Mime bursaries
New writing development

Playwrights' bursaries
Playwrights's commissioning scheme
Project awards for Scottish theatre companies
Training and travel bursaries: drama
Touring to small and mid-scale venues by Scottish theatre companies
Touring to small and mid-scale venues by non-Scottish theatre companies
Music
Creative artists' bursaries
Education and outreach projects
Performing material subsidy
Concert series and festivals
Early music projects
Music commission fee subsidy
Traditional and Gaelic music development
Training and travel bursaries
Recordings
Promoters' development fund

◆ VISUAL ARTS

Contact: Visual Arts Department
Individuals
Amsterdam studio residency
Artists' awards
Small assistance grants
British school at Rome SAC scholarship
Organisations/Groups
Artists' placements
Commissioning
Exhibitions and projects
Hiring touring exhibitions
Seeded posts
International exchanges schemes
Training and travel grants
Touring franchise

◆ COMBINED ARTS
Contact: Combined Arts Department
Cross-media collaborations
Development and project fund
Minority ethnic projects

◆ CENTRAL FUNDS
Contact: Planning and Development
Department
Conferences and seminars
Consultancies and research
Marketing
Training in arts management

THE ARTS COUNCIL OF WALES

Museum Place, Cardiff CF1 3NX
Tel: 01222-394711; **Fax:** 01222-221447
Emyr Jenkins, Chief Executive;
◆eth Lawton, Information Manager

Total arts expenditure: £12,901,000 (1994/95)

The Arts Council of Wales is the national organisation with specific responsibility for the funding and development of the arts in Wales. Most of its funds come from the Welsh Office but it also receives funds from local authorities, the Crafts Council and other sources.

From these funds the council provides regular annual and revenue grants to arts organisations which account for the most of its spending. It also operates a number of schemes which provide grants and other forms of financial support on a one-off basis.

SCHEMES DURING 1996/97

A few schemes are open throughout the year as long as funds last but the majority have closing dates, sometimes only a single one, each year. Potential applicants should obtain this information and full guidelines as soon as possible.

◆ CRAFT
Contact: Craft Department ACW Cardiff
Office
Promotion grants (marketing)
Exhibition support grants
Special projects: groups
Craft bursaries and projects

◆ DANCE
Contact: Dance Department
Department ACW Cardiff Office
Project support to dance companies and
individuals
Travel and study bursaries for dance
professionals

◆ DRAMA

Contact: Drama Department, ACW Cardiff Office

Trainee director & associate director bursaries
Training grants to individuals
Group sponsored training initiatives
Personal refreshment/sabbaticals
Playwrighting commissions and writers on attachment
Playwrights bursaries
Step forward (initiation and touring of new, innovative theatre work and styles of presentation)
Venue commissioning scheme
"Seasons of Work" (developing audiences for new work by Wales-based artists, particularly new writing)
Inter-link (to stimulate touring of foreign theatre groups)
Inter-recce (to assist future collaborations with projects outside the UK)

◆ LITERATURE

Contact: Literature Department ACW Office

Writers' bursaries and enabling grants
Writers' critical service
Literature projects fund
Grants to small presses and magazines
Production grants for books
Grants to periodicals: the franchise scheme
Design fund (Contact Literature or Art Department, Cardiff Office)
Writers on Tour (Contact nearest ACW Regional Office)
Literature programme support (Contact nearest ACW Regional Office)

◆ MUSIC

Contact: Music Department, ACW Cardiff Office

Music commissions
Awards for advanced study
Orchestral concerts

◆ VISUAL ARTS

Contact: Visual Arts Department ACW Cardiff Office.

Bursaries for artists
Interest-free loans to artists
Grants towards artists' exhibition fees
Masterclass, industrial experience and travel grants
Collectorplan
Moving pictures
Contact ACW South East Wales
Visual arts projects fund

◆ RESIDENCIES

Contact: nearest Regional Office

Artists, musicians and writers in residence

◆ TOURING AND PRESENTING THE ARTS (MULTI-DISCIPLINARY)

Arts marketing (Contact North Wales Office)
Visual arts and crafts (Contact nearest Regional Office)
Exhibition transport scheme (Contact Visual Art Department Cardiff Office)
Programme support scheme: performing arts (Contact nearest Regional Office)
Presenting the arts: performing arts (Contact nearest Regional Office)
Roundabout – for local community promoting organisations (Contact West Wales Office)
"Night-Out" performing arts touring scheme for community organisations (Contact South East Wales Office)
Transport subsidy-group booking incentive scheme (Contact North Wales Office)

◆ ARTS IN THE COMMUNITY

Arts in the community grants (Contact nearest regional office)
"Creatability" South East Wales (Contact South East Wales Office)
Special Projects - Arts & disability grants North Wales (Contact North Wales offices at Bangor or Mold)
Arts and disability grants - West Wales (Contact: Arts Care, St David's Hospital, Job's Well Road, Carmarthen, Dyfed (01267-223341)

◆ RESEARCH AND TRAINING (MULTI-DISCIPLINARY)

Contact: Planning Department, ACW Cardiff Office

REGIONAL OFFICES

North Wales Office, Wellfield House,
Bangor, Gwynedd LL57 1ER
Tel: 01248-353248; Fax: 01248-351077

North East Wales Office, Daniel Owen
Centre, Earl Road, Mold, Clwyd CH7 1AP
Tel: 01352-758403; Fax: 01352-700236

*NB. The addresses of the North and North
East offices are due to change in early 1997.*

South East Wales Office, Victoria Street,
Cwmbran Gwent NP44 3YT
Tel: 01633-875075; Fax: 01633-875389

West Wales Office, 6 Gardd Llydaw,
Jacksons Lane, Carmarthen, Dyfed SA31 1QD
Tel: 01267-234248; Fax: 01267-233084

THE ARTS COUNCIL OF NORTHERN IRELAND

185 Stranmillis Road, Belfast BT9 5DU
Tel: 01232-381591; Fax: 01232-661715
Brian Ferran, Chief Executive

Grant total: £5,983,000 (1994/95)

The Arts Council of Northern Ireland is a registered charity and company limited by guarantee which receives an annual grant from the Northern Ireland Office through the Arts and Museums Branch of the Department of Education. Major institutions operating all the year round and implementing an artistic and financial policy agreed with the council receive renewable annual grants. These grants which form the major part of the council's funding are negotiated each year. Other applications for more than £5,000 are generally submitted in the January before the new financial year. In addition awards of £5,000 and less are allocated (see details below).

Expenditure by Art Form 1994/95

Visual Arts & Film	£820,292	Traditional Arts	£107,573
Drama & Dance	£1,235,748	Education	£157,617
Grand Opera House	£615,000	Community Arts	£515,777
Music & Opera	£848,871	Regional Projects	£159,411
Ulster Orchestra	£826,000	Belfast Festival at Queen's	£78,000
Literature	£317,013	Cultural Traditions	£250,000

PROJECT GRANTS 1996

Applications for project grants across all art forms are made on one form on which the main six funding areas are listed:

Performing Arts Department (music, opera, drama, dance)
Contact: Philip Hammond, Performing Arts Director

Creative Arts Department (visual arts, photography, crafts, architecture, literature, traditional arts/music)
Contact: Noirin McKinney Creative Arts Director

Strategic Development Department (education, community arts)
Contact: Nick Livingston, Strategic Development Director

Applicants indicate on the application form whether they are seeking grants from one or more departments. Separate applications need not be made. Proposals may range in scope and scale. £5,000 should be regarded as an upper limit. A special bursary of £1,000 in Jazz is available.

Criteria for Funding: "In deciding whether to fund an organisation or activity the Arts Council will bear in mind all relevant considerations. The Arts Council seeks to be as well informed as possible about its client/partners' work and, in considering applications, will ensure that what is proposed is consistent with the objectives and priorities it is pursuing, However, to assist applicants for grant aid in approaching the council, the following criteria should be born in mind as among those influencing the council in its decisions:

♦ Excellence;
♦ Education;
♦ Equity;
♦ Effect;
♦ Economic Benefit;
♦ Efficiency"

For further details of the council's objectives and priorities see "To the Millennium – A Strategy for the Arts in Northern Ireland", 1995

Deadline: Only one closing date in April in 1996 (more dates in previous years). Responsibility for the development of cultural film activity in Northern Ireland was devolved to the Northern Ireland Film Council (see separate entry) from 1996.

Individual visual artists should also enquire about other special awards which the council may assist in administering.

THE NATIONAL LOTTERY

The National Lottery Arts Funds

The Lottery Department, Arts Council of England

The Scottish Arts Council, Lottery Department

The Lottery Unit, Arts Council of Wales

The Lottery Unit, Arts Council of Northern Ireland

The Heritage Lottery Fund

The Millennium Commission

The National Lottery Arts Funds

The four national Arts Councils of England, Scotland, Wales and Northern Ireland are each responsible for distributing lottery proceeds for the arts in their own country. The lottery funds are allocated between the councils in the following proportions:

England   83.3%
Scotland   8.9 %
Wales   5%
Northern Ireland 2.8%

Allocations from Lottery Funds and Arts Councils

	Lottery 1995 £ millions	Arts Councils 1994/95 £ millions
Arts Council of England	228.3	118.4
Scottish Arts Council	14.4	21.7
Arts Council of Wales	9.1	12.9
Arts Council of Northern Ireland	4.3	5.98
Total	256.1	158.9

The above table shows the massive injection of funding for the arts from the Lottery during its first year. The Lottery income for England in 1995 was over double its anticipated income as well as nearly double the Arts Council's own grant-aid in 1994/95. This has introduced a severe imbalance between the Lottery funds for capital projects and the Arts Councils' funds for revenue support.

Changes in Arts Grants from the Lottery

In January 1996 the Department of National Heritage announced that it would be consulting with the distributing bodies about proposals which could widen their funding practice to allow other aspects of arts support in addition to the single capability to fund capital projects. In April 1996 the National Heritage Secretary announced changes in the rules as to how Lottery money can be spent:

♦ talent funds to develop the creative abilities of individual performers and young artists

♦ initiatives which increase access to the arts, for example by supporting touring companies and subsidised ticket schemes for schools and community groups.

It is also believed that the Arts Council of England is considering proposals for some form of endowment funding to give organisations long-term financial stability.

All applicants should check if the creation of new work is an area which can be considered under the definition of capital funding. The Arts Council of Northern Ireland announced it would be issuing new criteria and application forms in mid-

June, 1996, and that funds would be available immediately "to enable organisations to commission new work across all art forms". This is an area of support that could be taken up by other Arts Councils in 1997.

All applicants should be sure to check about the changes in criteria for grants. If decision to support the revenue costs of touring companies is in fact taken up it seems bound to lead to further extensions of types of non-capital projects which may be supported.

GENERAL INFORMATION COVERING EACH OF THE FOUR NATIONAL LOTTERY FUNDS

The four arts councils all have broadly similar policies regarding the types of organisation and project which are eligible for lottery funding. These criteria are described in the next section.

Applicants will be wise to seek advice from the designated lottery officer of their local regional arts board on the preparation of their applications. Many run workshops and advice surgeries. It is also important to talk to the RAB about the project and its relevance to local and regional plans for developing the arts.

KEY POINTS AT A GLANCE

Funding for capital projects
Open to charitable, public and non-profit arts organisations
Minimum grant size normally considered:

- £5,000 - England and Scotland
- £2,000 - Wales and Northern Ireland

Minimum partnership funding normally required for smaller projects:

- 10% - England
- 25% - Scotland (but reduced in some cases), Wales and Northern Ireland

KEY CRITERIA:

- Capital projects
- Widest possible public benefit and maximum access for disabled people
- Long term financial viability
- Amount of partnership funding
- Quality of design and construction
- Quality of planned artistic activity
- Contribution of artists, craftspeople, etc
- Relevance to local regional and national plans for developing the arts
- Quality of plans for education and marketing

WHO CAN APPLY?

Applications to the lottery funds for the arts can be made by: registered charities, non-profit distributing bodies, local authorities, schools, colleges, universities, amateur or voluntary arts groups, and public sector agencies.

In certain circumstances, commercial, or for-profit, organisations will be considered if they are able to show that their proposals will greatly benefit the public. Any profits made by their projects may have to be shared with their national Arts Council. Each Arts Council will usually consider only those applications made by eligible bodies based within their national area; for example, the Arts Council of Wales will normally restrict support to projects and organisations located in Wales.

WHO CANNOT APPLY?

Individuals are not allowed to apply on their own behalf for lottery funds from any of the Arts Councils. Neither are commercial organisations, unless the project is primarily for the benefit of the public.

WHAT WILL BE FUNDED?

In broad terms, lottery funding is available for capital expenditure on arts projects and facilities. Capital projects are defined as including the construction of new buildings, improvement or refurbishment of old buildings, and purchase of equipment, instruments or vehicles, and commissioning works of public art. The Arts Councils will also consider applications relating to: feasibility studies or architectural design competitions as part of larger capital projects; individual film and video production projects; and the commissioning of public works of art. All forms of the arts are covered, including architecture, circus, crafts, dance, drama, film, the moving image, literature, mime, music, photography, video, the visual arts, and any combination of these (such as arts centres and festivals).

KEY CRITERIA TO BE FULFILLED

Smallest grants available: £5,000 (England and Scotland); £2,000 (Wales and Northern Ireland). Whilst stating that projects of all sizes will be considered, each Arts Council will not normally give grants below a certain minimum threshold. For the Arts Council of England and the Scottish Arts Council it is £5,000; for the Arts Councils of Wales and Northern Ireland it is £2,000. The Scottish Arts Council states, however, that the £5,000 limit is flexible to some extent - particularly for feasibility studies, it has awarded several grants below £5,000.

Capital Projects

Lottery funding will normally only be available for capital projects, as defined above. In very exceptional cases, however, the Arts Councils may provide funds to support running costs or set up an endowment but only if a project is of particular significance and has already received lottery funding towards its capital costs. However in January 1996 the Department of National Heritage announced that it would be consulting with the distributing bodies about some widening of its brief to include for instance, talent funds to support young individuals and new initiatives to increase access to the arts.

Public Benefit and Accessibility

Priority will be given to projects which will have the widest possible impact by improving artistic facilities for the public or for artists and others who work in the arts. Full consideration must be given to the needs of people with disabilities, be they attending, performing, participating or working. Accessibility should also be encouraged through adoption of a formal equal opportunities policy and through appropriate education, marketing and outreach activities to increase the potential audience's understanding and enjoyment.

Organisations with restricted membership, including educational bodies such as schools and universities, must provide public access to the project for a substantial part of the time.

Partnership Funding

The Arts Councils are not permitted by government to use lottery funds to provide the total cost of any project. The remainder of the finance should come from at least one other source of partnership or matching funds, and cannot include any other distributor of lottery funds or non-lottery Arts Council budgets.

This partnership funding can consist of financial contributions, support in-kind, or an agreement to support future project running-costs. It can also include any money raised for the project within the last three years, and can include any financial contribution by your own organisation.

National partnership funding requirements:

England
Grant requests below £100,000 - at least 10% of project costs from partnership funding
Grant requests above £100,000 and feasibility studies - at least 25%

Scotland
Projects costing less than £1m - normally 25%, although in some cases a minimum of 10% may be acceptable
Projects costing more than £1m and feasibility studies - at least 50%

Wales
Normal applications - at least 25%
Projects for groups/areas of particular need - at least 10% (at the discretion of the Art Council of Wales)

Northern Ireland
Normal applications - at least 25%
Feasibility studies, design competitions and local authorities - at least 50%

Long-term viability
The project should be financially viable in the long-term, with a clear and comprehensive management plan, controlled by a named manager, which includes budgets and timetables. The management of a lottery-funded facility or project must be effective and able to demonstrate public accountability. The impact that any lottery-funding might have upon your organisation's future finances should be taken into account, as priority will be given to projects which have a positive effect upon long-term financial stability.

England: Applications for more than £100,000 of lottery funding must provide a detailed cashflow forecast and business plan.

Scotland, Wales and Northern Ireland: Applications for between £100,000 and £500,000 of lottery funding must provide a business plan and cashflow forecast (typically covering a three year period after project completion), and those asking for more than £500,000 must provide a fully worked up project and investment appraisal, cash flow forecast and business plan.

QUALITY OF ARCHITECTURE, DESIGN AND CONSTRUCTION

Proposals should show high standards of design, architecture and construction, with regard to factors such as accessibility for people with disabilities, environmental impact, energy efficiency, and costs in use. They should make a significant and lasting positive impact on their surroundings and customers, and complement the nature of the facilities they house. Larger projects should undertake feasibility studies, and those requesting more than £1m of lottery funding are generally expected to have held design competitions:

The Arts Council of England states that for large projects requesting over £100,000, priority is generally given to those based on a successful feasibility study and suitable design competition. Projects requesting more that £1 million are expected to proceed in this way.

The Arts Councils of Scotland, Wales and Northern Ireland employ similar criteria according to project size. When considering applications for more than £100,000, firm preference is given to projects having completed a favourable feasibility study. Any applications for more than £1 million are generally expected to have conducted both a feasibility study and a design competition.

QUALITY OF PLANNED ARTISTIC ACTIVITIES

Projects should enhance the quantity and quality of future artistic activities. The project should also be relevant to, and supported by, any other plans to develop the arts reflected in the policies and priorities of the national Arts Councils, Regional Arts Boards and individual local authorities, and should fit into the appropriate local, regional or national frameworks for arts planning.

Projects should result in the creation of new work and employment in the arts. Artists, craftspeople, and film and video makers should be involved in the project work - they should be consulted about planning and design, employed as part of the design and construction team, or commissioned to create new work as part of a project or to commemorate the opening of new or improved facilities (these commissioning costs can be included in the total project costs).

Projects should address a clear demand for facilities and resources which is not currently being met, both within and outside principal centres of population. This demand will need to be demonstrated by market research, and plans must be made to promote the facility or project effectively through education and outreach.

OTHER INFORMATION

In general, applications for projects which do not involve straightforward capital expenditure on building work (such as funding of feasibility studies or architectural design competitions, film production and art in public places) have additional guidance notes which are available from each Arts Council. In particular, the Arts Council of Northern Ireland has a number of criteria relating to musical bands, including a maximum grant size of £20,000.

WHAT IS EXCLUDED?

The four Arts Councils will not normally provide funding for projects which fail to meet all of the above criteria. In particular: revenue funding will be provided only in very exceptional circumstances where a lottery grant has already been made; grants below £5,000 (England and Scotland in most cases) or £2,000 (Wales and Northern Ireland) will not normally be made; and each Arts Council will not support projects located in other parts of the UK. The Arts Council of Northern Ireland also has a maximum grant size - it will not normally make any grants larger than £2 million.

THE LOTTERY DEPARTMENT, ARTS COUNCIL OF ENGLAND

14 Great Peter Street, London, SW1P 3NQ
Tel: 0171-312 0123; **Fax:** 0171-973 6541
Jeremy Newton, Lottery Director

Grant total: £228.3 million (1995)

During 1995, the first year of its operation, the Arts Council of England made 388 lottery grants totalling £228.3 million. These grants ranged in size between £78.5 million to five grants of £5,000 each and a grant of under £2,000 to a primary school.

Funding in England was dominated by the four largest grants, all to major London organisations (see list below), which together received over half of the year's expenditure (£136.7 million). Almost two thirds of the total lottery arts funding in England was given to organisations within London. (The funding for the new Tate Gallery of Modern Art at the former Bankside Power Station, with its strong element of economic regeneration, is being supported with £50 million of funding as a Millennial "landmark" from the Millennium Commission, not by the Arts Council as is often assumed.)

The four massive grants to London organisations have generated much controversy and have obscured the fact that the following 23 largest grants of £1 million or more are spread widely throughout the country.

TOP GRANTS OF £1 MILLION AND MORE 1995

Royal Opera House, for rebuilding (£78.5 million, £23.5 million of which is subject to further work and conditions);

Sadler's Wells Foundation, to redevelop its theatre (£30 million);
Royal Court Theatre, for renovation (£15.8 million);
Shakespeare's Globe Trust, for reconstruction (£12.4 million).
Cambridge Arts Theatre, for modernisation (£6,640,000)
Tyne & Wear Development Corporation, for National Glass Centre (£5,591,000);
Contact Theatre Company, Manchester, to redevelop theatre (£4,456392);
City of Birmingham Symphony Orchestra, for rehearsal hall (£3,729,305);
Ikon Gallery, Birmingham (£3,676,000);
Hereford City Council, for new arts complex (£3,000,000);
The Hall for Cornwall Trust, Carrick, to convert hall to arts centre (£2,584,521);
Oxford Playhouse Trust, to upgrade theatre (£2,525,000);
Kings Lynn Borough Council, concert venue (£2,236,000);
Liverpool Institute for Performing Arts, for building (£2,000,000);
Northern Contemporary Dance School, Leeds (£1,750,000);
South Holland District Council, for arts centre (£1,698,000);
Wellhouse Community Arts Centre, Wansdyke, for arts centre (£1,680,306);
Music Heritage Popular Music Centre, South Yorkshire, design competition and
    feasibility study (£1,585,000);
Scarborough Theatre, for conversion (£1,480,000);
English National Opera, for rehousing feasibility study (£1,384,000);
Eastleigh District Council, for arts centre (£1,380,000);
Fosmic Charitable Trust, Hastings, for cultural centre (£1,362,263);
Nottingham Media Centre, for development (£1,320,000);
Musicworks Resource Centre, London, new centre for young people (£1,155,885);
River Films, for "The Woodlanders" £1,000,000);
Palace Picture Films, for "The Spire" (£1,000,000);
Film and General Productions, for "True Blue" (£1,000,000).

A large number of the projects were for instrument purchases by brass and silver
bands, vans and coaches for performing groups and building refurbishments and
improvements. About 60 brass bands received lottery support in its first year which
rather counterbalances the notion that it is only interested in supporting music for
and by the "élite".

    In 1995, 80% of the grants were for less than £100,000, but absorbed only
6% of total funding. A third of the grants were for less than £30,000 but absorbed
only 1% of total funds. Smaller grants have included the following examples:

Victoria Dock Company, Hull, towards costs of designing a public park including
    works of art (£100,000);
Robinswood Primary School, Matson, to redevelop the school hall as a centre for
    community use (£80,000);
Aldeburgh Cinema, Suffolk, for renovation (£65,700);
The Dance Xchange, Birmingham, for equipment (£40,500);
Oxford Film and Video Makers, for editing suite (£36,722);

SAMPAD South Asian Arts Development Organisation, study for a new centre
  (£22,903);
Jill Freud and Company, Southwold, minibus (£15,000);
Spirit of Bristol Marching Showband, for van (£15,000);
Sutton Community Music Project, St Helens, to replace instruments (£10,000);
Pudleston Village Hall Management Committee, Herefordshire, for refurbishment
  (£8,863);
Greentop Community Circus Centre, Sheffield (£7,825).

Grants Breakdown by Artform

Artform	No of applications	Award - £	%
Drama	99	55.744m	27
Combined arts	59	39.606m	20
Dance*	22	33.534m	17
Opera*	3	28.950m	14
Music	108	18.780m	9
Visual arts	37	7.272m	4
Film, production	12	6.932m	3
Crafts	10	6.666m	3
Film, other	15	3.759m	2
Broadcasting	6	0.738m	<1
Architecture	7	0.578m	<1
Literature	5	0.484m	<1
Circus	3	0.150m	<1
Other	3	0.124m	<1

HOW TO APPLY

Information is not given in this entry about the detailed requirements of the
application form for several reasons including:

◆ Application forms and accompanying documents were being revised to take in
  the new extended criteria (see beginning of general entry on National Lottery
  Arts Funds) and were not available at the time of finalising this entry;

◆ Applicants need to obtain the full up-to-date information pack themselves,
  acquaint themselves with the eligibility criteria and obtain advice and assistance
  as necessary from their Regional Arts Board.

FIRST STAGES

The first step is to obtain the application pack from the address at the head of this
entry and **carefully check the eligibility criteria** in the Detailed Guidance to
Applicants booklet.

The next step is to fill in the Advance Notice Form contained in the application
pack. This has to be completed by all potential applicants. This asks for basic
details about the organisation and its proposed project, including a brief project
description, total project cost, amount requested from the Arts Council lottery

funds, the other lottery distributors, if any, being approached, and other sources of funding. Figures quoted at this stage can be changed as work on the full application proceeds.

The completed Advance Notice Form should be sent to the Arts Council Lottery Department as soon as possible, at least four weeks before submitting a full application. Once the Arts Council has details on its database and has informed the relevant Regional Arts Board, applicants can then be more easily advised about any additional guidance relevant to their application.

A letter of acknowledgement will sent with the lottery application number for the proposal.

AFTER APPLICATIONS HAVE BEEN SENT

Applications are acknowledged along with an indication of the time lapse before a decision is made.

The application will then be processed by the named lottery officer, who will consult with other relevant bodies (such as other Arts Council departments, the Regional Arts Board, the British Film Institute, the Crafts Council, or specialists in the field of access for people with disabilities). The lottery officer may get in contact if more information is needed about the plans.

Applications for more than £100,000 of lottery funding will usually be assigned one or more independent lottery assessors to discuss the project with the applicant or other relevant bodies, and in the light of this prepare a detailed report.

The lottery officer will then present the details of the application to the Arts Council of England National Lottery Panel, which is an advisory committee of the Arts Council. The panel will make a recommendation to the Arts Council as to whether the proposal should be accepted or rejected. The applicant will be informed of the final decision "as soon as possible". Applications for sums above £100,000 will take at least 6 months to assess. Applicants are given a timing when their application is acknowledged.

Arts Council of England National Lottery Panel

Prudence Skene (chair); Jon Foulds; Lady Patricia Hopkins; Cleo Laine; Ruth Mackenzie; Paddy Masefield; Tony Pender; Dr Nima Poovaya-Smith; Sir David Puttnam

THE SCOTTISH ARTS COUNCIL, LOTTERY DEPARTMENT

12 Manor Place, Edinburgh, EH3 7DD
Tel: 0131-226 6051; Fax 0131-220 2724
David Bonnar, Director of Lottery Department

Grant total: £14.4 million (1995)

In 1995 105 lottery grants were made totalling £14.4 million. They ranged from £3 million to £1,667. The four largest grants of £1 million or higher totalled £7.625 million, more than half the funding allocated during the year. The 18 major grants of £100,000 and over:

Edinburgh Festival Society, to convert Tolbooth to festival centre (£3,000,000);
Royal Scottish Academy of Music, Strathclyde, to build opera school (£2,500,000);
Brunton Theatre Trust, Musselburgh, to upgrade theatre (£1,125,200);
Parallel Pictures, for film production (£1,000,000);
Glasgow University, for theatre/film/TV centre (£900,000);
Glasgow Film Theatre, for refurnishing (£710,000);
Arran Theatre and Arts Trust, for new centre (£609,000);
Scottish Poetry Library, Lothian, for new building (£506,301);
Hi Arts Limited, mobile cinema for the highlands (£380,317);
Newton Steward Cinema Committee, Dumfries, for new auditorium (£341,250);
Monklands District Council, Strathclyde, for sculptures on the M8 (£219,628);
Cumbernauld Theatre Trust, Strathclyde, to develop studio theatre (£176,400);
Hamilton District Council, Strathclyde, eleven artworks for the town centre (£164,250);
Central Regional Council, artworks on roads and paths (£137,300);
Sidewalk Films, to produce "Stella Does Tricks" (£137,138);
Phoenix Films, for film production (£135,507);
Prestwick International Airport, sculptures (£105,000);
Galloway Arts Project, Dumfries, to convert church to theatre (£100,000).
Glasgow received nearly one third of funds in 1995

80% of the grants (88) fell within the range £5,000 to £100,000 but they comprised only 15% of total allocations. 41% of the grants were for £10,000 or less but they received only 2% of the total allocation.

Grants by Artform 1995

Artform	No. of grants	Award - £	%
Combined arts	19	4,951,135	34
Opera	1	2,500,000	17
Drama	18	1,562,927	11

Film, production	6	1,431,225	10
Film, other	5	1,489,530	10
Visual arts	25	1,268,868	9
Literature	3	545,113	4
Music	16	238,585	2
Other	2	119,098	1
Video	3	117,798	1
Crafts	3	93,437	<1
Dance	4	45,140	<1
Total	100	14,362,859	100

How to Apply

Information is not given in this entry about the detailed requirements of the application form/s for several reasons including:

♦ The revisions to the application forms and accompanying documents to take in the new extended criteria (see beginning of general entry on National Lottery Arts Funds) were not available at the time of finalising this entry.

♦ It is important for applicant to obtain the full up-to-date information themselves directly from the Lottery Department rather than use a summarised version.

First Stages

If you want basic information in order to assess whether your organisation or project is eligible, you should ask the Scottish Arts Council to send you their basic information leaflet, which includes a request for an application pack.

You should then request an application pack from the Scottish Arts Council Lottery Department. These packs are not issued as a matter of course, and any enquirer is interrogated to ensure that the appropriate forms are sent.

The application pack contains detailed guidance on applying for lottery funds. If you want to apply for funding for feasibility studies, architectural design competitions, film production or art in public places you will also have to request the relevant, and more specific, guidelines and application forms. You should then **carefully check the eligibility criteria** which are set out in the general information booklet.

If you are going to apply for £100,000 or more of lottery funding from the Scottish Arts Council you should complete the Early Warning Form contained in the application pack, and submit it at the earliest possible opportunity. This form requests brief details about your organisation, the contact person, and the proposed project - in particular its estimated total cost, the amount you are applying for, and the likely date of returning the full application form.

Within one week of the Scottish Arts Council receiving your Early Warning Form you should be sent a letter of acknowledgement which will specify your Lottery Application Number. Any enquiries at this stage should be directed to the department's Administration Officer. The Early Warning Form is for information purposes only, and does not constitute an application.

If you believe your organisation and project to be eligible for funding, the next stage is to complete and submit the application form suitable for the type of project you are proposing.

At time of compiling this entry (Spring 1996) there were five separate application forms available which covered:

- Building projects (including equipment and fixtures)
- Equipment purchase only
- Feasibility studies and architectural design competitions
- Art in public places
- Film production

AFTER AN APPLICATION HAS BEEN MADE

Within one week of the Lottery Department receiving your application form you should be sent a letter of acknowledgement. This will inform you of your application number and named Lottery Officer, and whether you had missed any essential information on your application.

The Lottery Department will then assess your application against its basic criteria. If it fails to meet any of the basic criteria it could be rejected at this stage. The Lottery Department may then consult with various bodies about your application, such as your local authority, the relevant Scottish Arts Council art form department, and disability organisations. An independent assessor may be appointed in certain cases, particularly for applications asking for more than £100,000. Your Lottery Officer will keep you informed of the progress of your application and the likely timescale within which a decision may be reached.

Decisions are made at three levels depending on grant-size. The Director of the National Lottery (David Bonnar) has the power to make decisions in consultation with the Director of the Scottish Arts Council (Seona Reid) for applications asking for £10,000 or less. The Scottish Arts Council National Lottery Committee makes decisions on applications requesting £10,000-£100,000. Above £100,000 the National Lottery Committee makes recommendations to the Scottish Arts Council which makes the final decision. The length of time within which a decision may be reached will vary, depending on the scale and complexity of the application. However, a decision should be made within 6 to 8 weeks for applications of £10,000 or below; within 3 months for applications of between £10,000 and £100,000, and within 4 months for applications in excess of £100,000 - although 'major projects' may take up to 6 months. Once a decision is made, you will be informed in writing within one week, and unsuccessful applicants will be informed of the reason(s) for rejection. If you wish to appeal any decision you should do so within two months of receiving notification of that decision. But an appeal will only be considered if additional information was not included in the initial application which might have materially influenced the decision.

Scottish Arts Council National Lottery Committee
Douglas Connell (chair); Ian Brown; David Bruce; Paul Dowds; William English; Geoffrey Lord; Maud Marshall; Christine May; Shona Powell; Colin Ross; Jenny Wilson

Scottish Arts Council Members
Magnus Linklater (chair); Fiona Walker (vice-chair); Dr Sheila Brock; Douglas Connell; John Denholm; Keith Geddes; Sheriff Peter Hamilton; Robert Love; Dr Rita McAllister; Dr Ian McGowan; Janette Richardson; Professor Eric Spiller; Lesley Thomson

THE LOTTERY UNIT, ARTS COUNCIL OF WALES

Museum Place, Cardiff CF1 3NX
Tel: 01222-388288; Fax: 01222-388288
Jo Weston, Lottery Director

Grant total: £9.1 million (1995)

The Arts Council for Wales is responsible for distributing 5% of the total lottery arts money. By the end of 1995 it had received about £14 million of which it had allocated about 65% – £9.1 million. It distributed this sum in 126 grants ranging between £2 million to only £955. Three major grants dominated and accounted for more than half the money distributed.

THE TOP FIFTEEN GRANTS IN 1995
Cardiff Old Library, rebuilding (£2,000,000);
Powys County Council, theatre in Brecon (£1,677,879);
Welsh College of Music & Drama, South Glamorgan (£1,180,500);
St Donats Arts Centre, South Glamorgan, for buildings (£330,000);
Penrhys Partnership Trust, Mid Glamorgan, for estate arts centre (£326,000);
House of America, feature film (£250,000);
Powys Dance, theatre facilities (£218,700);
Caldicot Male Voice Choir, Gwent, for hall (£162,620);
Y Ganolfan Community Centre, Gwynedd, for refurbishment (£150,000);
Cyngor Llyfrau Cymraeg, Dyfed, Books Council database (£120,000);
Delyn Borough Council, Clwyd, room for Northop Silver Band (£112,500);
Brecon Jazz, Powys, building (£99,750);
Ogwr BC, Pencoed Comprehensive, Mid Glamorgan, to extend sports hall
    (£85,365);
Ucheldre Centre, Gwynedd, for centre development (£83,500);
Mid Border Community Arts, Powys, to refurbish Assembly Rooms (£79,537).

A large proportion of small grants were made, with some 45% of grants for £10,000 or less. Since the minimum grant size is £2,000 (lower than in England and Scotland) over 20 grants were for less than £5,000.

During this first year the spread of grants throughout the country was uneven. This is to be expected with population concentrated in a few urban areas with most of the land area sparsely populated. However the two major cities have made very different use of the lottery at this stage with 22 grants totalling £3.5 million in Cardiff and only a single grant of £2,024 in Swansea. The Welsh love of music showed in the predominance of grants for music.

Grants by Artform

Music	39	Drama	18
Bands	17	Visual	13
Other	16	Craft	4
Choirs	6	Literature, film, dance	2 each
Multi art use	23	Video, media, circus	1 each
Village halls/community centres	17		
Arts centres	6	Total	106

How to Apply

Alternative address to obtain basic information:
North Wales Regional Office of the Arts Council for Wales,
10 Wellfield House, Bangor LL57 1ER
Tel: 01248-371695; Fax: 01248-372382

Detailed information is not given below about the requirements of the application form/s for several reasons including:

◆ applications forms for the new extended criteria (see beginning general entry on the National Lottery Arts Funds) were not available at the time of compiling this entry;

◆ applicants need to obtain the full details about eligibility criteria and information required themselves rather than be tempted to use a summarised guide.

First Stages

The first stage is to obtain the Guidelines for Applicants from the Lottery Unit at the Arts Council of Wales in Cardiff (address given at the top of this entry) or from the alternative address noted above. All documentation is available in both English and Welsh. Check the eligibility of your project.

If you consider your organisation to be eligible you should request the relevant application form from the addresses above. Separate forms are available for different types of projects, such as equipment purchase and construction of new facilities, etc.

If eligible you will receive an application form carrying your Lottery Application Number. The completed application form and all supporting documentation should be sent to the *Lottery Unit in the main Arts Council of Wales office.*

After Your Application

After the Lottery Unit has received your application you will be sent a letter of acknowledgement identifying the Lottery Officer who has been assigned to your application. You should contact your Lottery Officer if you have any enquiries about your application.

The Lottery Unit will then assess your application and consult with appropriate bodies such as art form and regional departments of the Arts Council of Wales, and other external specialist and umbrella bodies. Applications for grants greater than £100,000 will have an independent Project Assessor appointed to compile a detailed report on your plans.

The details of your application will be presented by your Lottery Officer to the Arts Council of Wales Lottery Advisory Board, which will consider the request and make an appropriate recommendation to the full Council, which makes the final decision. You will be informed of the outcome as soon as possible - normally within four months for applications involving less than £100,000, and within six months for larger requests.

Arts Council of Wales Lottery Advisory Board
Alwyn Roberts (chair); Jane Davidson; Hugh Hudson-Davies; Geraint Stanley Jones

THE LOTTERY UNIT, ARTS COUNCIL OF NORTHERN IRELAND

185 Stranmillis Road, Belfast, BT9 5DU
Tel: 01232-667000; **Fax:** 01232-664766
Brian Ferran, Chief Executive Officer

Grant total: £4.3 million (1995)

The Arts Council of Northern Ireland receives 2.8% of lottery funds for the arts. By the end of 1995 about £8 million had been generated of which over half had been allocated in 49 grants ranging between £3 million. The largest grant for a theatre in Armagh absorbed some 70% of total spend. Most to the grants (40 out of 49) were quite small, all for less than £30,000. Whilst they totalled only £468,000 their 11% share of the total spend was a higher proportion given to smaller grants than the other Arts Councils. It is understood that other major proposals were pending.

THE TOP 10 GRANTS - 1995
Armagh District Council, to build theatre (£3,000,000);
Ti Chulainn, Down, to build Gaelic culture centre (£350,000);
Footprint Television, Antrim, for feature film (£200,000);
Northern Visions, Antrim, video and office equipment (£74,853);

Riverside Theatre, Londonderry, to extend disabled access (£58,515);
Grand Opera House, Antrim, box office system (£50,000);
Best Cellars Music Collective, Antrim, recording and office equipment (£48,753);
Drake Music Project, Down, vehicle for disabled people (£48,000);
Queens Film Theatre, Antrim, technical upgrading (£35,050);
Fermanagh District Council, sculpture at Necarne Castle (£30,000).

Grants by Artform 1995

Artform	No of grants	Total - £	%
Combined arts	21	3,684,000	85 (70% in 1 grant)
Film & video	3	309,903	7
Music	13	172,500	4
Drama	4	98,726	2
Dance	2	34,825	1
Visual art	5	24,211	<1
Literature	1	7,500	<1
Total	49	4,332,000	100

How to Apply

Detailed information is not given below about the requirements of the application form/s for several reasons including:

- application forms and accompanying documents for the new extended criteria (see beginning of general entry on the National Lottery Arts Funds) were not available at the time of compiling this entry;
- applicants need to obtain full details about eligibility criteria and information required themselves rather than be tempted to use a summarised guide.

First Stages

The first step is to obtain the Application Guidance Notes from the Arts Council of Northern Ireland Lottery Unit so you can check whether your organisation and project are eligible for funding. The standard information pack also includes application forms for building projects and equipment purchase - if you wish to apply for funding for feasibility studies, design competitions, film production, or commissioning public works of arts, etc., you will have to separately request the relevant guidelines and application forms. When you are satisfied that your project is eligible you should move on to the next stage.

If you are going to ask for £100,000 or more of lottery funding, you should complete and return the Early Warning Form contained in the standard information pack, and return it to the Lottery Unit as soon as possible. This form asks for brief details of your organisation, the type of project you are proposing, its cost, other potential sources of funding, and the date you will be sending your full application. On receiving your Early Warning Form, the Lottery Unit will send you a letter of acknowledgement, which will state your Lottery Application Number to be quoted on all future correspondence (including your full application).

The next stage is to complete and submit the application form which is most appropriate for the type of project you are proposing. (NB: If you are applying for more than £100,000 of lottery funding, you should already have submitted your Early Warning Form.) At the time of compiling this entry separate application forms are available for:

- Building projects (including equipment and fixtures)
- Equipment purchase
- Feasibility studies or design competitions
- Film production.

Further application forms will become available to cover the extended criteria (see beginning of general entry on the National Lottery Arts Funds).

AFTER AN APPLICATION HAS BEEN MADE

When the Lottery Unit receives your full application you will be sent a letter of acknowledgement, which will give your Lottery Application Number (although if you had already sent an Early Warning Form you should already know this and should have used it on your full application).

The Lottery Unit will then assess your application against its criteria, and may consult with any body it considers appropriate (such as your local authority, the most relevant Arts Council art form department, or other specialist advisers and consultants). For larger applications, an independent assessor may be appointed to draw up a detailed report on your plans. You will be informed of the date of the meeting at which your application will be considered by your appointed lottery officer.

Once the consultation process is complete, the details of your application will be considered by the Arts Council of Northern Ireland Lottery Committee, which consults with and reports to the full Council which makes the final decision. You will be notified of its decision as soon as possible. Six of the Lottery Committee members are also members of the full Council.

Arts Council of Northern Ireland Lottery Committee

Sir Charles Brett (chair); Charles Adams; Donnell Deeny; Patrick Donnelly; Jennifer Johnston; William O'Connell; Richard Pierce; Irene Sandford; Aidan Shortt; Richard Taylor

THE HERITAGE LOTTERY FUND

National Heritage Memorial Fund,
10 St James's Street, London, SW1A 1EF
Tel: Enquiry service: 0171-649 1345 (24 hour);
Application helpline: 0171-747 2088
Mrs Anthea Case, Director

Grant total: £96 million (1995)

In 1995 the fund gave 170 grants totalling £96,000 (though it had committed a further £24 million). It has allocated fewer grants and less of its available funds of some £290 million than the arts and sport lottery funds. This must be largely due to the fact that the National Heritage Memorial Fund (NHMF) was not part of an established regional infrastructure for advice and grant-making unlike the arts and sports councils. It has had not only to build up its own staff of seven to 50 people but has had to develop a network of over 20 specialist organisations to help it with advice.

The vast majority of grants in the first year were given in England, particularly the South East.

Grants by country in 1995

England	129
Scotland	25
Wales	12
Northern Ireland	4

Expenditure in categories 1995

	£ million	% of spend	No. of grants
Museums, galleries & collections	35.2	37	44
Manuscripts & archives	13.4	14	3
Industrial, transport & maritime	10.4	11	17
Land	20.2	21	26
Buildings	16.4	17	80

THE TOP 14 GRANTS OVER £1 MILLION 1995

(some 80% of the total spend)

Cambridge University, for Churchill archive (£13,250,000);

National Trust for Scotland, to buy and endow Mar Lodge estate, Grampian (£10,276,993);

National Gallery, London, to buy Seurat painting (£8,000,000);

Scottish National Museum, Lothian, for New Museum of Scotland (£7,250,000);

Imperial War Museum, for US Air Museum, Cambridgeshire (£6,500,000);

National Trust, restore Croome Park landscape, (£4,917,042);

Geffrye Museum, London, to build extension (£3,750,000);

Thackray Medical Museum, West Yorkshire, to convert Leeds Union Workhouse (£3,000,000);

Scottish National Gallery of Modern Art, for the Penrose collection (£3,000,000);

Surrey County Council, to create history centre (£2,740,000);

Christchurch Borough Council, Dorset, for Highcliffe Castle (£2,650,000);Lancaster University, to build Ruskin Library (£2,314,259);

Tameside MBC, Manchester, to restore Central Library (£1,400,000).

In 1995 most grants were given to public-sector organisation (57%) compared with charitable and religious bodies (42%). No grants were given to private sector organisations though applications had been made.

In 1996 the fund issued guidelines to local authorities to stimulate applications from inner city parks. The fund will consider proposals with less than 25% partnership funding in areas of particular social and economic need. It is possible that projects such as training schemes in preservation skills will be added to relax the capability to only support capital schemes. Applications such as those from museum, gallery and library projects for Lottery grants over 1 million will be considered in batches twice a year (see further information below under "Applications").

WHO CAN APPLY?

Eligibility check for Heritage Lottery Fund

If your project satisfies these criteria, you have a good chance of a grant

✔ We are a public sector organisation, a charity or a voluntary organisation involved in preserving buildings or land or important objects or collections

✔ We are based in the UK

✔ Our application covers heritage based in the UK

✔ The project which we want support for has not yet started

✔ It is a capital project for one of the following:

- buying property
- repairing, conserving or restoring
- new building work or improving buildings
- improving the public's access to, and understanding and enjoyment of buildings, land, objects and collections

✔ We will get funding from other sources

✔ The total cost of our project is over £10,000

✔ We have looked into other funding for our project and think it is unlikely to go ahead without the support of lottery funds

✔ Our project will improve the public's access to and enjoyment of our heritage

The Heritage Lottery Fund will consider applications from organisations which are public, charitable or non-profit distributing, based in the UK, and have the preservation or conservation of the heritage in this country as one of their purposes. The National Heritage Memorial Fund (NHMF) lists the following types of bodies which are eligible for lottery funding:

- Any museum, art gallery, library or other similar institution having as one of its purposes the preservation for the public benefit of a collection of historic, artistic or scientific interest.
- Any body having as one of its purposes the provision, improvement or preservation of amenities (including ancient monuments and historic buildings) to be enjoyed by the public or the acquisition of land to be used by the public.
- Any body having nature conservation as one of its purposes.
- The Secretary of State for National Heritage.
- The Department of the Environment for Northern Ireland acting in discharge of its functions relating to the acquisition of historic monuments or listed buildings by agreement.

WHO CANNOT APPLY?

Private individuals are not allowed to apply to the Heritage Lottery Fund, and neither are organisations established or conducted for profit, and any institution located outside the UK.

WHAT WILL BE FUNDED?

The Heritage Lottery Fund aims to secure, conserve, improve, and enhance the public's access to and appreciation of 'tangible heritage assets'. These are buildings, land, objects or collections which are of importance to the heritage in a local, regional or national context. The term 'asset' is used by the NHMF to reflect the nature of these items: they are tangible resources which add to the overall wealth of the national heritage.

Examples of eligible projects

The NHMF gives the following examples of the types of projects which are eligible for support from the Heritage Lottery Fund:

- Acquisition, repair, conservation or restoration of buildings, land or objects of importance to the heritage.
- New buildings, or improvements to existing buildings, designed to house museum or archive collections of importance to the heritage, or to improve public access to any kind of heritage asset.
- Listing or cataloguing of archives or collections of objects, or the recording of sites and buildings, where these can be demonstrated to be finite projects resulting in a significant enhancement of public access to and better preservation of the assets concerned.
- Any other capital project which aims to improve public access to, and understanding and enjoyment of, such buildings, land, objects and collections.

Key criteria used to assess applications

The Heritage Lottery Fund takes account of the following general criteria when assessing applications:

Local, regional or national heritage importance of project
The project should concern heritage assets, falling into one of the above categories, which are of importance on a national, regional or local scale. Projects should bring a tangible benefit to these heritage assets.

Consolidation rather than innovation
The Heritage Lottery Fund will be primarily used in order to enhance and consolidate existing heritage assets and heritage provision, rather than for the creation of new institutions or the reconstruction of past heritage.

Public benefit and access
All applicants must be able to show the public benefit that would result from their proposed project. Projects should enhance public access to, and enjoyment of, heritage assets. New buildings or projects should provide the fullest possible access for people with disabilities, although the NHMF recognises that there may be constraints to full access in certain kinds of projects (such as listed buildings).

Capital projects
In keeping with the Secretary of State's policy directions, the Heritage Lottery Fund will be directed almost exclusively at capital projects. These are projects which involve direct capital expenditure on purchase, improvement, restoration, construction or creation of a tangible asset, including any costs directly connected with these activities.

The Heritage Lottery Fund does have powers to make endowment or revenue funding available for lottery-funded projects, but expects to use this ability 'very sparingly'. Money will only be distributed in revenue grants or for the purposes of endowments where these costs are associated with capital projects already funded by the lottery and whose completion would be prevented by the lack of any other suitable source of revenue or endowment finance.

Project viability
Applicants need to be able to show that sources of funding have been identified which will provide support after lottery funding has ceased. As revenue costs and grants for future maintenance are not available from the Heritage Lottery Fund, applicants should be able to demonstrate how these will be met from other sources. Applicants should also have sound finances and a reasonably secure future.

Partnership funding
The Heritage Lottery Fund will not provide 100% of the costs of any project. It expects applicants to provide a significant element of partnership funding, or contributions in-kind, from non-lottery sources. The NHMF states that it will be flexible in determining what constitutes a significant element as it realises this will vary according to the situation of the applicant and the nature of the project. It does state, however, that it usually expects at least 25% of total project costs to come from other sources, and there should always be some contribution from the applicant's own resources. A lower figure may be accepted in areas of particular

social and economic need. Projects under £100,000 may provide 10% partnership funding.

Minimum project cost £10,000
In general, the Heritage Lottery Fund will only consider applications for projects with a total cost greater than £10,000, although this figure is being kept under revue. (N.B. This is the minimum project size which will be considered, and so actual heritage lottery grants may be considerably smaller.) Projects with a total cost below £10,000 may, however, be eligible where the applicant can show both genuine need, that there are no appropriate sources of public funds, and that the project is of importance to the heritage.

Other criteria
Applicants must show that their project would be unlikely to succeed without the support of the Heritage Lottery Fund. The project, or phase of work, should not yet have commenced, and the work proposed should be realistically costed and of good quality with regard to design, construction, historical integrity, and professional and technical standards.

If the proposed project would normally be eligible for priority funding from other public funding sources, it is likely to be given a lower priority by the Heritage Lottery Fund unless the project would fail without lottery support.

Applicants are also responsible for obtaining the necessary planning or other statutory consents necessary to enable the project to be carried out. No grant offer will be made by the Heritage Lottery Fund without evidence of all such consents being secured.

The NHMF distinguishes between five main types of heritage asset which it will consider for funding, and has produced detailed guidelines and eligibility criteria for each of them:

1. Ancient monuments, historic buildings and their contents and settings
This category covers the acquisition, major repair, conservation, or restoration of: town and country houses, places of worship, civic buildings, domestic, agricultural and garden buildings, monuments, memorials, statues, and sites, buildings and structures important to the archaeological, industrial, transport, maritime or defence heritage. The installation of appropriate visitor facilities to promote the public appreciation of such sites and buildings are also included. These sites and buildings, and their settings, should be of recognised importance to the national heritage, which may be indicated by scheduled, listed, graded or registered status, or location in a Conservation Area.

In April 1996 additional provisions were announced to allow the fund to help Building Preservation Trusts to acquire, restore, conserve, or improve and then dispose of heritage property, or projects which seek to restore, conserve, or improve such property notwithstanding that it is not owned by such organisations.

2. Land of scenic, scientific or historic importance
This category includes the purchase, restoration, preservation, enhancement, and improvement of public access to land of geological, biological, historic or scenic

importance. These may be parks, gardens, and land including archaeological sites, monuments or historic buildings. The land should be of recognised importance to the heritage, either by virtue of officially designated status or other identification as locally or regionally important.

3. Special library collections, books, manuscripts, archives and other records, and the buildings housing them

This covers acquisition and housing of items or collections of artistic, historic or scientific interest and importance, such as manuscripts and archives, special library collections, photograph, sound and film archives. Applicants must be able to show that any items or collections purchased will be appropriately conserved and made available for public study or display. The listing, cataloguing and conservation of collections are only eligible if they could only be achieved with the assistance of lottery funds and are beyond the normal scope of the applicant's budget. New buildings or collections will only be considered if they fill a major gap in present provision, either on a geographical basis or in a specific subject area.

4. Museum and gallery collections

This includes the purchase, conservation, cataloguing, housing and display of collections of importance to the national heritage held in galleries and museums. These may concern: fine and applied art, archaeology, antiquities, ethnography, local and social history, military history, industry, science and technology, biological and geological collections, and collections of historic buildings in open-air museums. Projects should have access to professional staff and meet the minimum standards of operation defined by the Museums and Galleries Commission. Applicants should be able to show that the proposed project is outside the scope of the capital funding provided by the Museums and Galleries Commission and the ten Area Museums Councils covering the UK, and that lottery funding is vital to the project's success.

5. Buildings, sites and objects associated with industrial, transport and maritime history

This category covers the costs of acquisition, removal, repair, conservation, restoration or housing of very large objects of industrial, scientific and technological importance to the national heritage, such as ships, vehicles, aircraft, railway items, and other machinery. Buildings and sites of such importance are covered by the first category. The condition and completeness of any object will usually be one of the factors taken into consideration. Projects involving the return of objects to working order will only be considered if this will not damage the historical integrity of the item and subsequent maintenance is assured. The applicant should also be able to guarantee that any will be met. Any proposals should meet relevant statutory safety standards, and take into account the appropriate best practice outlined by the Museums and Galleries Commission.

EXCLUSIONS

Organisations and projects based outside the UK are not eligible to apply, and the Heritage Lottery Fund will not normally consider requests for revenue funding or applications relating to projects with a total cost under £10,000. The NHMF gives the following examples of some specific project types which are excluded:

- Training programmes
- Temporary exhibitions
- Marketing initiatives
- Educational, interpretive or conservation facilities not associated with specific heritage assets
- General research projects, unless closely related to a particular heritage asset
- Local authority lending library services.
- Publications, in any medium, not associated with a lottery-funded listing or cataloguing project
- Archaeological excavations, unless a necessary consequence of a lottery funded capital project.
- Regeneration of derelict urban land.

APPLICATIONS

1. The first step is to request the Heritage Lottery Fund: Simple Guide from the fund by contacting the 24-hour enquiry telephone line (see number above). You should then complete the guide's eligibility check.

From March 1996 major museum, library and archive projects (for over £1 million Lottery grant) became subject to a timetabled assessment programme to allow groups of applications to be considered together and a greater regional spread of projects throughout the UK. Additional Guidance Note 2: Major Museum, Library and Archive Projects outlines the key assessment criteria and provides a checklist of the required information. It should be read long with the standard Guidelines.

2. If you are able to answer 'yes' to all of the eligibility questions, request the Guidelines and Applications Pack from the National Heritage Memorial Fund. If you are not sure about the eligibility of your project it is also worth consulting this pack as the criteria are explained in greater detail. There is a request form for the Guidelines and Applications Pack on the back of the Simple Guide, which also asks you to complete a few simple questions about your organisation and, if possible, the project for which you are likely to make an application.

3. Once you have received the Guidelines and Application Pack you must read the guidelines carefully to check the eligibility of your project. If you have any queries about eligibility you should contact the fund on 0171-747 2088.

4. Before filling in the application form you must check there is an application number in the relevant box on the first page (without this the application form is not valid). The application form is fairly short, but requires extensive supporting documentation. *If you have a particularly urgent deadline to meet, for example*

for the purchase of an item which will be put up for sale on a specified date, the Heritage Lottery Fund has a 'fast track' system for urgent cases. In this situation you should notify them as soon as possible, initially by telephone if necessary, followed as soon as possible with your application form.

The application form consists of the following sections:

Details about your organisation

The form starts with a few simple questions about the application, and asks for information about your organisation, such as its address, the date it was established, and your charity, company or VAT number (where appropriate), and asks for the contact name and address for all correspondence concerning the application.

Project details

The form then requests information on the name and location of the project, along with a brief 150 word description of what is involved. This section requires substantial supporting documentation as specified below.

Project timetable and planning permissions

You also need to provide details of when the project is expected to start and finish, and information about planning permissions or statutory consents applied for, granted or expected.

Project costs and funding sources

The next section asks for details of the total estimated project cost, along with the estimated value of any non-cash contributions (such as land, materials or voluntary labour) included in this total figure. You have to specify the amount you wish to receive from the Heritage Lottery Fund and provide evidence of partnership funding from your own organisation and from other sources. Acquisition projects have to provide two independent valuations of the item concerned.

There are two types of project for which additional information is required:

Projects with total cost over £500,000

Apart from projects involving the straightforward acquisition of objects, all projects with a total cost of £500,000 or more are required to submit a business plan along with their application. The standard application pack supplied by the NHMF includes the 10-page booklet: Heritage Lottery Fund: Guide to Preparing a Business Plan. This provides a useful starting-point if your organisation needs to draw up a business plan for its lottery application.

Projects involving new buildings, extensions, conversions and refurbishment

Heritage construction projects should provide a design report which considers the points such as: why the new building is necessary; what sources of advice were used and how these were chosen; methods of procurement employed; how the project will be managed; how much it will cost to run; how the public was consulted; and how access will be provided for people with disabilities.

5. Two copies of the application form, two copies of all supporting documentation and two copies of a covering sheet listing all supporting documents should be sent to the Heritage Lottery Fund (the second copies will be passed to one of the Heritage Lottery Fund's advisers).

Main supporting documentation required

- Copy of audited accounts for the last two complete financial years.
- First-time applicants should supply a copy of Rules, Trust Deed, or Memorandum and Articles of Association as appropriate.
- First-time applicants should also include a brief description of the organisation, its management structure, and the number of trustees or board members.
- The collecting policy of any institution applying for funding for acquiring a collection or archive.
- Evidence that the named contact is authorised to act on behalf of the applying body, such as a copy of committee minutes.
- Detailed project description, including an assessment of its importance to the national heritage (such as whether it is officially designated, for example as a listed building), and whether the application is in any way urgent as the asset concerned is under threat. This should be accompanied by plans, illustrations, maps, diagrams, and photographs as appropriate. At this stage do not send any video material or three-dimensional items (such as models) but indicate if these are available.
- A description of the short, medium and long-term benefits which should accrue from the project when it is completed.
- A description of how public accessibility will be maximised, including access for people with disabilities. Where possible this should include an estimate of the additional number of individuals, and types of user, who will benefit from the project.
- Copies of any feasibility study, design brief, technical or conservation report, restoration or management plan relevant to the project.
- Details of any local, regional or national strategies which would support the project.
- Details of the key professionals/companies who will be involved in the project, such as architects, surveyors, conservators, ecologists.
- Where and when the project or item can be inspected by the National Heritage Memorial Fund or its advisers.
- A detailed timetable for the project, if available, which should include information about phases of work.
- A clear indication if the project for which you are applying is just one phase of a larger programme of work.
- Details of any projects your organisation will be running at the same time.
- Details of how project running costs will be met once lottery funding has ceased.

ONCE YOU HAVE APPLIED

1. Confirmation of your application

You should receive confirmation of your application within 14 days of its receipt by the NHMF. This acknowledgement will: confirm whether your application is eligible, include your application's unique reference number, indicate the date of the trustees' meeting at which the application is likely to be considered, and give you the name of your Lottery Case Officer. This is the person you should contact if you have any enquiries about the decision-making process, quoting your application reference number.

2. Consultation process

The Heritage Lottery Fund will then seek expert advice on your application on which the trustees of the National Heritage Memorial Fund can base their decision. This advice will normally come in the first instance from the relevant public advisory body. In the case of applications concerning historic buildings, for example, they may consult with English Heritage, Historic Scotland, Cadw: Historic Buildings and Monuments in Wales, or Department of the Environment, Northern Ireland. Advice may also be obtained from other specialist bodies and independent experts where appropriate. This process may involve a visit by a Heritage Lottery Fund adviser to discuss and/or visit the project involved.

3. The decision

If your application is eligible, a decision on whether it will receive assistance should be made by the NHMF trustees within 5 months of its receipt. The full board of trustees meet monthly. Grants involving projects below £100,000 are considered by the Small Grants Committee, which has three NHMF trustees as permanent members with the remainder invited on a regular basis. Two expert panels, one for museums, new buildings and refurbishment and one covering historic buildings and land, have also been set up to offer independent advice to the NHMF trustees on applications where there might otherwise be a potential conflict of interests (for example where organisations usually consulted by the NHMF during the assessment phase are involved in applying for funds). These expert panels also consider applications involving major construction work. In addition advisory panels for churches and parks have been established.

You will then be notified of their decision within 7 working days of the meeting of the NHMF trustees at which your application was considered. This decision will fall into one of the following categories:

◆ Approved: a formal offer of a grant will be made and sent to you along with a copy of the associated terms and conditions.

◆ Conditionally approved: approval may only be granted conditionally, for example subject to you raising other elements of partnership funding, or if there is a requirement for the submission of detailed plans, or if there are adjustments to proposals. In such cases you will normally have 12 months in which to meet your specified conditions, after which you will have to submit a new application. Applicants can make 'outline' applications, on which decisions will be made 'in principle'.

◆ Not approved, but reapply: in other cases your application may not be approved for support because the trustees are temporarily unable to make further future commitments of lottery funds. If this is the case they will advise you to try again within a certain period.

◆ Rejected: some applications will inevitably be considered unsuitable for funding and be rejected. The NHMF's reasons for rejection will be given, and an appeal process is in place. If you are unsuccessful and want returned any photographs, plans, drawings or other supporting documentation submitted with your application, you should contact the NHMF within 6 months.

National Heritage Memorial Fund Trustees
Lord Rothschild (chair); Sir Richard Carew Pole; Lindsay Evans; Sir Nicholas Goodison; Sir Martin Holdgate; Caryl Hubbard; Sir Martin Jacomb; John Keegan; Lord Macfarlane of Bearsden; Professor Palmer Newbould; Diane Nutting; Catherine Porteous; Dame Sue Tinson

Small Grants Committee
Sir Richard Carew Pole (chair); Catherine Porteous; Lindsay Evans

Museums, New Buildings and Refurbishment Expert Panel
Sir David Wilson (chair); Lady Anglesea; Professor Edward Hall; Colin Thompson

Historic buildings and land expert panel
Dame Jennifer Jenkins (chair); Sir John Burnett; Peter Inskip; Adrian Phillips; David Walker

Churches Advisory Panel
Catherine Porteous (Chair); Diane Nutting; Richard Haisey

Parks Advisory Panel
Professor Ron Brunskill; Judy Hillman; Dr Hazel Conway; David Lambert

THE MILLENNIUM COMMISSION

2 Little Smith Street, London SW1P 3DH
Tel: 0171-340 2030
Jennifer Page, Director

Grant total: £328 million (1995)

In 1995, £328 million was given to 57 projects. Over half the money went to the four largest grants:

Tate Gallery of Modern Art, to convert Bankside power station (£50,000,000);
The Earth Centre, South Yorkshire, environmental research centre (£50,000,000);
SUSTRANS, nationwide cycle routes (£42,500,000);
Portsmouth Harbour, renaissance leisure development (£40,000,000).

Apart from one of the very largest grants, few other grants in 1995 were for identifiably arts-based projects. Only two other grants were made which are relevant to this guide:

National Museums of Scotland, for SCRAN multi-media project (£7,400,000);
Visions Community Design, Manchester, for resource and visitor centre (£435,000).

It is almost impossible to describe what grants from the Millennium Commission may be for, apart from to say that in principle almost anything is considered if it will form a lasting celebration of the year 2000 and be regarded by future generations as having "made a significant contribution to our national or local history".

More broadly if a project is "exemplary" in its field, it stands a good chance. The Council of Voluntary Service in Goole, though also eligible to apply to the Charities Board, got a grant for a new community centre on this basis, as presumably did the Tate Gallery for its new gallery, despite being an Arts project.

New for 1996 are the Millennium Awards, which will provide grants to realise the aspirations of individual people, and further details of the major Millennium Exhibition and Festival.

CHECK LIST FOR MILLENNIUM COMMISSION FUNDING

✔ Funding for projects which assist communities in marking the year 2000 and the beginning of the third millennium
✔ Millennium Awards Full details of the programme awaited
✔ Capital projects °
   Open to registered charities, non-profit distributing bodies, local authorities and other public bodies, consortia of eligible bodies, and commercial companies (if they receive no commercial gain)
✔ Minimum grant size normally considered: £100,000

✔ Maximum grant size normally considered: £50m

✔ Minimum partnership funding required: at least 50% in most cases

KEY CRITERIA

- Public support and public good
- Contribution to the community
- Marking the millennium (with appropriate completion date)
- Capital projects
- Long-term viability and effective management
- Project quality
- Other primary sources of funding not available (including outside scope of other lottery distributors)

GENERAL PRIORITIES

The Millennium Commission is using its share of the lottery proceeds to support three main types of project, the first two of which are being administered separately:

Millennium Exhibition and Festival

The commission will support a Millennium Exhibition to act as a focus for celebrations in the year 2000. It shortlisted four potential sites for this exhibition: Greenwich, Stratford (both in London), Birmingham and Derby from which it chose Greenwich.

Apart from the Millennium Exhibition, the commission will decide in 1996 the form of any support for a wider programme of smaller festival events across the country. If you have a suitable festival event you should register your interest with the commission and they will send further information when it becomes available.

Millennium Awards

The interest from a £100 million endowment in the year 2000 will provide an estimated £10 million a year for individuals with projects and ideas to benefit their communities. The commission is currently developing a Millennium Awards programme which will provide bursaries to enable individuals to "achieve their personal aspirations and release their potential, enriching their lives and their communities in the new millennium". Millennium Awards will be operated in partnership with existing non-profit making bodies with a track record in this form of grant-giving. These "award partners" will run the application and assessment process, although the Millennium Commission will retain the final decision-making responsibility when it comes to making an award.

The awards will focus on a number of themes, the first theme announced in early 1996 was "You and Your Community". The first award schemes were expected to be announced in late July 1996 with the first applications from individuals announced in September 1996.

Closer to the year 2000 schemes may have a more celebratory emphasis, perhaps including arts, history and projects to record the turn of the millennium. There are expected to be a variety of schemes, each with differing emphases, some open to individuals and others also to small groups. The minimum grant size is expected to be at least £2,000, and matching funding will normally be required only from 'award partners' and not the individual recipients.

CAPITAL PROJECTS

The Millennium Commission intends to fund around a dozen major capital projects of national importance spread across the UK, which are expected to become landmarks for the 21st century. They will each receive up to £50 million. Five landmark schemes were announced during 1995 and include the four largest grants listed at the head of this entry.

The commission will also fund hundreds of smaller one-off capital projects of regional or local significance with grants from £100,000 upwards. Applications will also be considered relating to joint proposals for schemes with a common theme that might otherwise be too small to apply - 'umbrella' projects have already been successful, such as Groundwork's "Changing Places". The remainder of this section deals solely with applying for funding for a capital project of local, regional or national significance.

The Millennium Commission is running regular time-limited competitions for grants. Applications received after the closing date for any particular grants round will be returned, although they can be re-submitted for consideration in the next round.

The third application round was expected to take place towards the latter part of 1996. There may be subsequent funding rounds, but the Millennium Commission will make no firm commitment on this before the end of 1996.

WHO CAN APPLY

Millennium Commission funding for capital projects to mark the year 2000 is open to: registered charities; non-profit distributing bodies; local authorities and other public bodies, where there is no substitution for public expenditure; and consortia or partnerships of eligible bodies specifically established for the purpose of submitting an application, with an identified lead organisation. Commercial or for-profit organisations can only apply if projects are for the public good rather than commercial gain. Applicants and their projects must be located in the UK.

WHO CANNOT APPLY?

The main exclusions are that individuals cannot request funds on their own behalf for a capital project, although this restriction does not apply for the Millennium Awards detailed above. Private sector organisations are excluded if their proposals are for commercial gain rather than for the public good.

WHAT WILL BE FUNDED?

The Millennium Commission is much less specific than any other distributing body about the types of projects it will and will not support, mainly because it had no real precedent. Its primary objective is to support capital projects which suitably mark the turn of the millennium, but beyond this it states only that applicants are encouraged to be ambitious, innovative and imaginative about the projects they want to pursue.

When the Millennium Commission is considering applications for capital projects it takes the following criteria into account:

Marking the millennium

Projects should look back over the current millennium or forward into the new one, and have the potential to be viewed by future generations as marking a significant moment in local or national history. In other words, the Commission is looking for projects which are innovative, which make an impact, which have the potential to be held up as an example to other groups.

Completion date

The commission has fairly tight completion dates, because of the very nature of its purpose. Projects funded in the first applications round are expected to be operational in the year 2000, those receiving money in the second round should be in operation by 2001. Deadlines for future application rounds will probably be similar.

Primarily capital projects

Millennium Commission funding is primarily available for capital funding toward projects designed to mark the new millennium. This includes expenditure on the purchase, restoration, construction or creation of an asset, as well as expenditure on improvements designed to extend an asset's life span, capacity, quality or value. Revenue funding will not normally be provided.

Funding thresholds

The commission has stated that it normally expects to keep its contribution toward total project costs within £10 million to £50 million for the dozen landmark capital projects of national significance, and £100,000 to £15 million for projects of local or regional significance. Unless you are part of a consortium, you must ask for at least £100,000 from the Millennium Commission for your project to be considered.

Partnership funding

The Millennium Commission will not provide funding to cover the entire costs of any project, and normally requires at least 50 % of the cost of any proposal to come from other non-lottery sources, although in exceptional circumstances the required level of partnership funding may be reduced. A high proportion of both revenue and capital funding from other sources will be interpreted by the commission as an indication of greater community support for your project.

Public good

One essential requirement is that projects should be for the public good and make a substantial contribution to the life of the community they are designed to serve. They are normally expected to offer "genuinely open access" to the whole community.

Long term viability and effective management

Your project must be a viable concern once Millennium Commission funding has finished, and you should be able to meet running costs for a reasonable period following completion from other sources. Where appropriate you are expected to provide a cash flow forecast, fully worked-up project appraisals, and a business plan. The project should also be managed effectively both before and after completion.

Quality of project

Proposals should demonstrate a high standard of design, architecture and environmental quality. Buildings should be environmentally sound, energy efficient, and fully accessible to people with a disability.

Applications will normally only be considered if they are not eligible for funding from any of the other distributors of lottery funding or statutory sources. Projects should not be possible without the support of the Millennium Commission.

WHAT IS EXCLUDED?

As Millennium Commission funding is primarily available for capital expenditure, projects are excluded if they are mainly asking for revenue funding. The Millennium Commission also expects its usual contribution to be greater than £100,000, even for projects of solely local significance. Unless your organisation is part of a larger consortium, requests for less than £100,000 are likely to be rejected. At the other end of the scale, the commission will not normally make any contribution greater than £50 million towards any project, even if it is of national significance.

HOW TO APPLY FOR FUNDING FOR A CAPITAL PROJECT

1. Obtain Proposal Form and Guidance Notes

If you want a brief summary of the Millennium Commission's activities you should ask for a copy of the Introduction to the Millennium Commission leaflet. In order to initiate the application process, you should ask for a proposal form pack, including Guidance Notes. Four regional programme teams based at its London head office field enquiries:

London and Eastern Region Tel: 0171-340 2016
Greater London, East Anglia, Essex, Cambridgeshire, Berkshire, Bedfordshire, Surrey, West and East Sussex, Hampshire, Isle of Wight, Buckinghamshire, Hertfordshire.

Central Region Tel: 0171-340 2036
Lancashire, Greater Manchester, Merseyside, Yorkshire, Humberside, Derbyshire, Nottinghamshire, Leicestershire, Lincolnshire.

Northern Region Tel: 0171-340 2031
Scotland, Northern Ireland, Cumbria, Durham, Tyne and Wear, Northumberland, Cleveland.

Western Region Tel: 0171-340 2011
Wales, Hereford and Worcester, Staffordshire, West Midlands, Warwickshire, Shropshire, Oxfordshire, Wiltshire, Gloucestershire, the West Country.

2. Submit Proposal Form before the given deadline

If, having read the Guidance Notes, you consider your project suitable for funding, the next stage is to submit a three page Proposal Form before the given deadline. The Proposal Form asks you to summarise the main features of your organisation and your project, including its locations, its estimated costs, and main funding sources. You do not have to state whether you are proposing a landmark project or a more local/regional one, as the commission will make this assessment when it comes to considering any full application. The completed Proposal Form should be sent to the Millennium Commission. You can include a covering letter with this form, but it should be no longer than two pages. If you send any other detailed information it will be returned.

3. Receive acknowledgement of Proposal Form

The Millennium Commission will send you a letter to acknowledge receipt of your Proposal Form including a Unique Project Reference number which should be quoted in all future correspondence. You should receive this acknowledgement within one week of your proposal being received by the commission.

4. Receive results of initial consideration

The commission will then assess your proposal against their criteria. Within three weeks of sending your proposal form you should receive a letter saying whether or your project meets the requirements. If it does so you will be sent an application pack and details of the project team dealing with your full application. You can then apply for funding.

If your proposal does not meet the commission's criteria, they will advise you that they do not think that you would be wise to spend more time and effort in completing a full application. You are not prohibited from doing so, however, and you can still request an application pack and go ahead with a full application if you so wish.

5. Submit Application Form and details of your project before stated deadline

The next stage is to complete and return your Application Form along with a document giving details of your project. You must submit the Application Form before the applications deadline for the grants competition in which you wish to be considered. You will be offered the chance to attend a workshop session with the commission between the time they receive your Application Form and the deadline for full application. If you send it after the closing date the form will be returned to you, although you can re-submit it for the next competition.

The Millennium Commission's application form for capital projects is one of the shortest of any of the distributing bodies, and asks for brief details about your organisation and your project. This is because you also have to submit a document setting out in your own words the main features of your project - this should be no longer than 20 pages of A4 accompanied by any maps, diagrams or drawings to illustrate the text. The main aspects which you should cover in this project document are:

Project Overview

You should give a full description of the proposed project including details about: how the project was conceived and what it involves; the benefit it will provide to the community and the estimated number of users or visitors; its national, regional or local significance; and the degree of public support.

Project implementation

You should show how the project will be implemented, the organisations involved, and the development timetable. You also need to demonstrate how design and environmental issues have been taken into account, and whether European procurement regulations apply.

Project finance

You must give details of the total project cost, and how funding will be provided, including the size of contribution required from the Millennium Commission. An outline project plan should also be given along with a detailed financial appraisal.

Land and assets required

Give information about any land or assets that you might need to purchase, any planning permissions required or gained, and any infrastructure issues which will need to be addressed.

Post implementation stages

You should also give details about the future use and management of the project, including predicted running costs and how these will be met.

The Application Form includes a checklist of points you should include in your project description. You may not be able to provide all of the information requested if you have not yet conducted a full feasibility study or you have experienced delays in the planning process. If this is the case, you should give details of how you expect to proceed. If any information is missing, your application will still be considered but no grant will be made until the commission is satisfied on all points. Supporting documentation required:

- A copy of your audited accounts for the last two years and your two most recent annual reports, if available.
- Evidence that the named contact person is authorised to act on your organisation's behalf.
- A copy of your Trust Deed, Memorandum and Articles of Association, or other appropriate governing material.
- Names and addresses of all sources of partnership funding.
- Names and addresses of all sources of revenue funding.
- Contact names and addresses for planning and other matters in your local authority.

ONCE YOU HAVE APPLIED

1. Receive acknowledgement of application

The Millennium Commission will send you a letter of acknowledgement once it has received your full application.

2. Initial assessment and long-listing

Your application will then go through the Millennium Commission's initial assessment process. First, it will be checked against the commission's criteria for capital projects. If it fulfils these criteria, its financial viability and technical feasibility will be appraised. All of the applications which have satisfactorily passed this initial review will be considered together for long-listing by the commission. The projects believed to have the best potential to be developed as successful millennium projects and delivered to time and on budget, will be long-listed for a more detailed assessment. The remainder will be rejected.

You will be informed of the commission's decision at this stage. You should, however, be aware that just because the Millennium Commission believes your project to be worthy of further consideration it is not guaranteed to receive funding.

3. Site visits and detailed appraisals

If your proposal has been long-listed for further consideration, the commission will arrange a visit to the site, and set up a meeting between your representatives and their staff, possibly even including visits by some of the commissioners themselves. It will also ask for more detailed information about your project, confirm sources of partnership funding, and seek the views of your local authority with regard to the planning and other implications of your proposals. The commission may consult with other public or advisory bodies for their views on individual aspects of the project, and also appoint a consultant to undertake an appraisal of your project. This detailed assessment stage is probably the most important and most demanding part of the assessment process.

The commission will also provide you with a draft copy of the standard grant terms and conditions which will apply as a minimum if you are offered a grant.

4. Final decision by Millennium Commissioners

Once the site visits and meetings have taken place, the Commission will look at all the applications which it thought worthy of further consideration. The Millennium Commissioners (see below) will make the final decision about which projects will be funded. If you are successful, you will receive either an immediate offer of a grant, or your project will be put on a short-list to be given a grant when lottery funds are available. You will be informed of the expected date upon which money will be available, at which point a formal offer of a grant will be made. Some projects may be asked to undertake further preparation, or asked to undertake a feasibility study, raise further partnership funds, provide an investment appraisal or business plan, or undertake other further preparation before a final decision is made. The commission will identify whatever extra work is required, and set a deadline for its completion. Even at this stage, however, you may still find that your proposal is rejected and will not receive support from the Millennium Commission.

If at any stage of the application or assessment process you have any questions you should contact the Millennium Commission on 0171-340 2001. The commission also holds a series of workshops for applicants who have passed through the Proposal Form stage. Everyone who receives an Application Pack from the commission will be informed of workshops in their area, at which they should be able to iron out any difficulties with applications under preparation. The application process and timetable is slightly different for projects which have previously submitted a proposal, but did not reach the long-listing stage for any reason. The Millennium Commission's literature provides fuller details.

Millennium Commissioners

Virginia Bottomley MP (chair); Professor Heather Couper; Earl of Dalkeith; Lord Glentoran; Sir John Hall; Michael Heseltine MP; Simon Jenkins; Michael Montague; Patricia Scotland

REGIONAL ARTS BOARDS

East Midlands Arts

Eastern Arts

London Arts Board

North West Arts

Northern Arts

South East Arts

South West Arts

Southern Arts

West Midlands Arts

Yorkshire & Humberside Arts

THE REGIONAL ARTS BOARDS

The Regional Arts Boards (RABs) are partners with the Arts Council of England (ACE), British Film Institute, Crafts Council, and local authorities in the system for sustaining, promoting and developing the arts in England. RABs are concerned with all the arts and plan jointly with their major funding partners. They work as arts development agencies (in the broadest sense) identifying needs and formulating strategies for arts provision in conjunction with their funding partners, other government departments, non-arts agencies and the private sector.

SUPPORT TO ORGANISATIONS

The RABs provide financial support for professional theatre companies, dance and mime companies, music ensembles, literature, arts centres, galleries, community projects, arts education and training and a wide range of local arts bodies which promote arts events. The greater part of RAB funding is allocated to the professional sector, largely because of the greater expenses of professional arts companies and because amateur activities are more generally seen as the responsibility of local rather than regional authorities. Nevertheless some assistance is provided to support amateur work.

SUPPORT TO INDIVIDUAL ARTISTS

RABs offer a number of opportunities for individual artists; many of these are aimed at helping artists to reach a new and wider audience. A variety of commissions, bursaries, fellowships and residencies are available to writers, artists, craftspeople, composers, photographers. Professional artists, writers, composers etc. seeking financial help should contact their own RAB initially as the ACE has delegated many of its awards and schemes for individuals to the RABs.

PRIORITIES

Each RAB establishes its own priorities from year to year, in line with a strategy agreed with the Arts Council. Generally, RABs are concerned to develop ventures in areas where provision is poor. Obviously chances of receiving a grant increase if activities/projects coincide with current RAB priorities in content and/or geographically. As with the Arts Council the relevant RAB department will want to see your work before they decide whether or not to make a grant.

SERVICES PROVIDED

RABs employ specialist officers to deal with particular art forms or combinations of these. Other officers provide financial, marketing, PR, publications and administration services. RABs offer a range of marketing services to regional and touring arts organisations and many co-ordinate with the Association of Business Sponsorship of the Arts (ABSA) (see separate entry) on advice sessions about how to raise sponsorship. Via these staff and reference facilities, the RABs provide funding, information, publicity, planning and guidance to arts organisations and individual artists in their regions.

Contact the RABs to obtain further information on policies and grant guidelines. Their annual reports list grant recipients during that year providing helpful background information for new applicants.

THE LOTTERY

With the advent of the National Lottery, the RABs act as agents for the ACE in the assessment of applications for awards. Whilst the initial focus has been almost exclusively on capital funding – equally available to professional and amateur/ voluntary arts organisations – changes in the Department of National Heritage's Lottery Directions are likely to increase the range of projects which may qualify for assistance. RABs will be able to advise as to the possibilities. Advice and discussion of Lottery bids is given prior to applications being formally made.

LOCAL AUTHORITIES

RABs can be very useful to help locate the relevant arts officer for funding from local authorities and the local arts councils/associations which are usually funded by local authorities and often help support amateur activities.

FILM AND VIDEO

Not all RABs fund film, video and broadcasting. At the time of writing, Spring 1996, there were separate organisations in London (the London Film and Video Agency) and another emerging in the South West (the South West Film and Video Agency). It is possible that more such organisations may be formed during the next few years.

The entries on the individual RABs which follow indicate the scale of their annual funding and give details of the grant schemes available in addition to the funding provided to its "revenue clients". These organisations are funded over a number of years or on an annual basis. This funding absorbs the lion's share of RAB grant-aid. Readers need to appreciate that the funds available for projects are small and in total would usually be between only 10-20% of total grant-aid. Funds are often heavily over-subscribed.

The co-ordinatory body for the boards is:
English Regional Arts Board
5 City Road, Winchester, Hampshire SO23 8SD
Tel: 01962-851063; Fax: 01962-842033
Chief Executive: Christopher Gordon

EAST MIDLANDS ARTS

Mountfields House, Epinal Way,
Loughborough LE11 OQE
Tel: 01509-218292; **Fax:** 01509-262214
John Buston, Chief Executive
Area covered: Northamptonshire,
Leicestershire, Derbyshire (excluding the
High Peak district) and Nottinghamshire.

Grant total: £3,771,000 (1994/95)

Breakdown of grants by Artform and type 1994/95

Artform/type	Regularly funded organisations	Project grants £	Total £
Performing Arts			
Drama	2,086,000	24,000	2,110,000
Dance	76,000	77,000	153,000
Music	82,000	87,000	169,000
Cross-form	–	30,000	30,000
Totals	2,244,000	218,000	2,462,000
Media, Publishing & Visual Arts			
Film	129,000	89,000	218,000
Literature	26,000	85,000	111,000
Visual Arts	215,000	88,000	303,000
Totals	370,000	262,000	632,000
Combined Arts & Planning			
Local Arts	430,000	116,000	546,000
Education	–	45,000	45,000
Training	33,000	22,000	55,000
Disability	–	11,000	11,000
Totals	463,000	194,000	657,000
Marketing/Innovation	–	21,000	21,000

As with all Regional Arts Board the following grants for projects and schemes comprise only a small proportion of the total annual spend to support the arts. The vast majority is allocated to revenue and fixed term clients.

GRANTS AND SCHEMES 1996/97

Applicants are advised to contact the relevant department to check that funds are available and whether the proposal is eligible for grant-aid. Applications are required at least eight weeks in advance of the event or project, unless otherwise stated.

◆ COMBINED ARTS AND PLANNING

Combined arts projects and policy development in areas such as disability arts, education, training, African/Caribbean and South Asian arts.
Contacts: See below also Susan Wyatt, Head of Local Arts Strategy & Development; Debbie Read, Local Arts Development and Education

African, Caribbean and South Asian Arts

Combined Black arts projects that illustrate a holistic approach.

Artists at your Service

Easy access workshop scheme to encourage education and community participation in the arts. 50% of artists' fees up to a maximum grant of £350. Directory of artists offering workshops available upon request.

BT/EMA Innovation Awards

Supports the creation of an original, imaginative art or media work including elements of experimentation. Contact EMA for closing date.

Cluster Fund

Encourages groups of educational institutions to work collaboratively in the arts and media.

Combined Arts Festivals

Supports festivals with a clear strategic role in the relevant local authority arts plan. Applications with less than three art forms should be directed to the appropriate artform department.

Disability Arts

For new work and development of artistic skills within Disability Arts. Grants for the creation of innovative new and challenging work and training individuals who seek to advance their knowledge and skills which will progress the work of disabled people.

Training Bursaries

Individual artists, arts and media professionals eligible for small bursaries towards short courses, work placements, job swaps and shadowing, "Go and See" grants seminar or conference attendance. Venue Development Training Bursaries and Touring Development funding also available. Enquiries to the department dealing with the particular artform.

Youth Projects Awards

For exciting, cross-artform projects involving professional artists working alongside young people. Awards also aim to highlight good practice.

◆ MEDIA, PUBLISHING AND VISUAL ARTS

Responsible for developing literature, film and video, visual arts, crafts, photography and broadcasting.
Contacts: Debbie Hicks, Head of Media, Publishing and Visual Arts (with responsibility for Literature); Caroline Pick/ Rosalind Attile, Film, Video, Broadcasting; Fennah Davies, Visual Arts; Janet Currie, Fine Art and Print

Bursary Scheme

Four awards of £2,000 to support the production of new work by established visual arts.
Deadline: April.

Commissions Scheme

Funding for exhibitions, events and initiatives which result in the development or presentation of innovative work. Includes touring, first-stage public arts, residencies and artist-led initiatives.
Deadlines: March, then on-going.

Critically Write

Appraisal scheme for writers. A further attachment scheme provides the chance to meet and work with writers within a long-term relationship.

Development Scheme

Awards up to £600 to individual artists developing professional practice such as trade fairs, print, research, conferences, training, exhibitions and equipment. On-going scheme.

First Cut

Production scheme for new film and video directors. Funding accessible for a series of short films or videos which are intended for broadcast.

New Curators Bursaries

Practising visual artists and new curators wishing to develop and present quality, innovative exhibitions are now supported.

Publications Grants

Annual publishing programme for funding magazines and small presses. Small publication grants also offered to workshops within the region on a one-off basis. Literary excellence the over-riding consideration.
Deadline: February.

Schools Studio Project

Young artists needing studio space are matched with schools requiring an arts residency over a year. Emphasis on creating a partnership in which the work of both the school and the artist are enriched. On-going scheme.

Start-Up

Award of £400 for artists at an early stage in their career. Includes information and advice package, and training opportunities.
Deadlines: May and November.

Writer's Bursary

Three bursaries of £2,000 awarded annually to writers wishing to devote time to further development of their writing talents.
Deadline: April.

Writers Live

To help promote writers' talks, reading and performances across the region. On-going scheme.

◆ PERFORMING ARTS

Responsible for the performing arts including music, dance, mime and drama. When assessing applications, the emphasis is placed on quality, creativity and access.
Contacts: Helen Flach, Head of Performing Arts (with responsibility for Drama; Debbie Williams, Dance; Penny Hefferan, Music)

African, Caribbean & Asian Drama, Dance & Music

Development projects (up to £500 for individuals and £1,000 for organisations).

Amateur Orchestral & Choral Societies

Professional soloists, leaders and conductors enabled to work with amateur organisations in their annual concert series. Funds usually allocated early in the financial year.
Deadline: March.

Bursaries for Training Skills & Development

In areas such as arts skills, finance and human resource management, marketing and administration, for arts and media professionals living and working in the region. Applications for up to 50% to a maximum of £200 training costs.

Contemporary Popular Music

Recording and performing now funded by a number of schemes. Enquiries must be directed through The Network.
Contact: Alison Brown, Northamptonshire 01536-460555; Mark Spivey, Nottinghamshire 01623-422962; Norman Wright, South Derbyshire 01283-552 962.

Dance Promoter Development Scheme

For small and middle-scale dance promoters.
Deadline: May.

Drama

For new and exciting initiatives, up to 50% of the cost or 50% the loss of the project whichever is the smaller.

Jazz & World Music

Bands and promoters receive support for various forms, including annual programming, regional touring and educational projects. Collaborative and innovative projects are of particular interest.

Jazz, Folk & Non-Western Music

Recording grants for bands and individuals wishing to release their own self-financing recordings. Not applicable to demo tapes.

Musical Instrument Purchase Challenge Scheme

Performing groups, arts organisations and local authorities assisted in the purchase of non-western musical instruments.

New Circus Development

Priority given to research and development projects which progress the applicant's work as well as the form.

New Music Commission Support Scheme

For organisations commissioning a composer to write a new work or artists engaging in improvisational or experimental projects. Funds usually allocated early in the financial year.

Opera

Priority to small-scale opera companies performing in places where opera is not usually heard. The number of projects is limited and one-off visits by touring companies cannot be supported.

Performing Arts & Disability

Applications up to £500 for individuals and £1,000 for organisations.

Small Scale Promoter and Venue Development

Dance, drama and music promoters supported for a programme of no less than four professional events. Minimum subsidy for music £500. For dance, drama and mime programmes the maximum awards averages no more than £350 per performance.
Deadline: March.

Visiting Drama, Dance, Mime Companies

Direct grants to promoters or companies undertaking work with specialist audiences outside their regular setting (up to £350 per performance or 50% of the loss, whichever is the lower).

Dance and Mime Projects

Targeted at the creation of new and exciting initiatives in the region. Projects by, or in collaboration with artists, dance and mime development workers, a large arts centre or a small community group, located in the inner city or rural part of the region Up to 50% of the cost and evidence of other sources of income required.

Write In

Playwrights resident in the region may join a scheme to ensure scripts are read and writers receive feedback. Scripts which may benefit are given a workshop with experienced directors or writers.

EASTERN ARTS

Cherry Hinton Hall, Cambridge CB1 4DW
Tel: 01223-215355; Fax: 01223-248075
Lou Stein, Chief Executive
Area covered: Bedfordshire, Essex, Hertfordshire, Cambridgeshire, Norfolk, Suffolk, and Lincolnshire.

Grant total: £4,723,500 (1994/95)

As with all Regional Arts Board the following grants for projects and schemes comprise only a small proportion of the total annual spend to support the arts, most of which is allocated to revenue and fixed term clients.

Expenditure on Grants, Projects and Schemes 1994/95

	Projects/schemes £	Total £
Performing Arts	502,000	3,063,000
Visual and Media Arts	364,000	941,000
Planning & Development	394,000	486,000
Resources	–	235,000

PROJECTS AND SCHEMES - 1996/97

◆ PERFORMING ARTS DEPARTMENT
Contact: Alan Orme, Head of Performing Arts

Commissioning Scheme
Full details to be announced at time of writing.

Training and Project Research Scheme
To enable individual artists to improve their skills. To provide support to enable individuals or organisations to research and develop future national or international arts projects which encourage the exchange of ideas, information, skills and expertise. Full costs not normally covered. Maximum award usually £400.

Visual Arts and Media Department
One application form covers all schemes except the Film and Video Production Scheme. Deadlines are given for the month/s only to indicate the frequency of consideration. Be sure to check for the exact date and remember that these schemes may vary from year to year.

Art in Public Places
To encourage and facilitate the commissioning of works by visual and media artists and to encourage innovative work in new areas of public art. Commission East will provide an initial free advisory service to organisations wishing to commission works (contact David Wright 01223-356882). Funding available: 50% of project costs up to a maximum of £5,000.
Contact: Alison McFarlane
Deadline: March for projects taking place between 1996/97.

Artists Development Fund

The department offers support across contemporary visual arts, crafts, photography, multimedia, live art, cinema, television and radio. This scheme aims to support artists in their professional development with grants up to £2,000.
Contact: Alison McFarlane
Deadlines: March, September and January.

Community Broadcasting Scheme

This scheme aims to encourage partnerships by broadcasters for the establishment of arts activity in local radio and television trusts. Priorities for assistance are the showcasing of new work and reaching new audiences and to assist regional arts organisations achieve maximum visibility for their activities through broadcasting and other forms of media distribution. Funding up to 50% of project costs.
Contact: Martin Ayres
Deadline: March.

Festival Scheme

To develop festivals to reach new audiences, showcase and introduce new work, review past practice and to celebrate and debate. Funding for up to 50% of the costs.
Contact: Rosy Greenlees
Deadline: March.

Film and Video Production Scheme

To provide financial support and professional guidance for development of short, low-budget film and video productions, which explore innovative and challenging uses of these media with a specific audience in mind. Projects can be drama, documentary or experimental animation, or combinations of these, aimed at broadcast or non-broadcast, educational, festival, cinema or gallery audiences.
Contact: Martin Ayres
Development Bursaries, up to £500 to develop proposals to production stage (but not a guarantee of receiving a full production award).
Production Awards, up to £5,000, for production or post-production.

New Work Scheme

To encourage the development of new and innovative work; collaborations between the visual and media arts and other artforms; extending the range of work produced in the region and the exchange of ideas, skills and expertise. Funding for up to 50% of costs.
Contact: Alastair Haines
Deadline: March.

◆ OTHER SUPPORT

Write Lines

Writers living in the region can send their work for free professional appraisal. It must fall within one or more of the following categories: stage plays; novels (a minimum of 5,000 consecutive words with a summary if sending the entire manuscript); short stories (not exceeding 15,000 words); between 25 and 100 poems; television, film or video scripts (shooting script, or treatment with at least 2 dialogue scenes); radio (complete script).
Contact: John Hampson

LONDON ARTS BOARD

Elme House, 133 Long Acre,
Covent Garden, London WC2E 9AF
Tel: 0171-240 1313; **Fax:** 0171-240 4580;
Helpline: 0171-240 4578
Sue Robertson, Chief Executive
Area covered: The 32 London boroughs
and the Corporation of the City of London.

Grant total: £12,336,000 (1994/95)

Grant Breakdown 1994/95

Artform	£	%	Strategic Development	£	%
Combined Arts	1,766,000	14	Arts Services	45,000	
Cross-Artform	95,000	1	Broadcasting	55,000	
Dance	966,000	8	Education	377,000	
Drama	5,188,000	42	Public Affairs	51,000	
Literature	398,0003		Regional Development	161,000	
Music	1,177,000	9	Research/Conferences	103,000	
Visual Arts & Crafts	1,767,000	14	Tourism	36,000	
Total	11,357,000	91	Training	91,000	
			Other	60,000	
			Total	979,000	9

FUNDING PROGRAMMES 1996/97

Deadline/s are indicated by the month/s only. Be sure to check for exact date/s.

NB. These programmes only use a small proportion of the board's annual total grant-aid which goes primarily to revenue and fixed-term clients. The annual programmes may change may change depending on the funding available.

* A fund not open to organisations receiving LAB revenue or fixed term funding.

◆ CROSS ARTFORM

London Calling
Major "landmark" productions and events in London only.
Deadline: April.

Go & Watch
For promoters, programmers and curators to assess touring product, plan collaborative work and view work in progress. Overseas visits must be directly related to the organisation's programming strategy.
Deadline: At any time, leaving 10 working days for application processing (15 for overseas visits).

International Go & See
Towards costs of short overseas visits by London-based arts workers.
Deadline: At any time, but no sooner than six weeks ahead.

Programming Development for Small Venues (Touring)

Towards programming professional touring product in small scale venues. Priority to outer London boroughs.
Deadline: September for work in the following Spring or Autumn. Summer programmes not supported unless directly related to established regional festivals.

◆ COMBINED ARTS

Contact: Paula Brown, Principal Combined Arts Officer

London Collaborations

To encourage new forms of collaboration between artists from different artforms in equal partnership. Funds will be given for research & development and for production.
Deadline: May.

Venue Development for Live Art

To enable a variety of London venues to promote new programmes of Live Art events and develop new audiences.
Deadline: April.

Carnival Development Pilot Scheme 1996/97

To extend the development of carnival and encourage partnerships by offering opportunities for individual artist to collaborate with carnival arts organisations.
Deadline: March for summary applications, April for full applications.

◆ DANCE

Contact: Rachel Gibson, Principal Dance Officer

New Choreographers' Awards*

Small encouragement grants to individuals and companies who have not previously received significant public investment.
Deadline: April.

Creative Developments in Dance*

To support through choreographic research and production grants, the creation and development of work by London-based choreographers and companies with a record of achievement in producing original dance.
Deadlines: April, September.

New Bases for Dance

To encourage the development of London-wide dance infrastructure by supporting venues and organisations that show potential to develop as focal points for dance activity in their area through a programme of dance performance and/or participation.

Not open to LAB dance revenue/fixed term clients, but open to all other LAB revenue/fixed term clients.
Deadline: June.

Promoters' Commissioning Fund

Support to promoters (building and non-building based) wishing to commission a new dance work from a choreographer or company.
Deadline: June.

Dance Administration Development Fund

Support to administrators seeking to provide services for emerging companies and to encourage good administrative practice.
Deadline: November.

◆ DRAMA

Contact: Sue Timothy, Principal Drama Officer

Theatre Production Fund*

For the production of challenging new work throughout London in a variety of venues, taking into consideration the cultural diversity of the region.
Deadlines: May, November.

Theatre for Young People Fund

To support Theatre for Young People companies to produce innovative work across London.
Deadline: October.

◆ EDUCATION

Contact: Adrian Chappell, Senior Education Officer

Arts Education Networks

To support and encourage the development of local and regional arts and education networks.
Deadline: At any time, but at least six weeks before the grant is required.

Arts Education Projects*

To support individual artists and arts organisations undertaking activities with the state-funded education sectors (5-18 years). Workshops, residencies and performances taking place in schools, colleges and arts venues.
Deadline: April for work beginning in September.

Local Authority Arts Education Programme

An annual programme to encourage the strategic development of arts education activity in the statutory sector (5-18 years) on a borough-wide level. Applications will be planned and co-ordinated by borough arts education fora, LEA advisers, local authority arts officers or by local arts councils.
Deadline: June for work commencing in September.

London Education Arts Partnership

A three year funding programme to support long-term development of arts education programmes and networks for young people (5-25 years) in and outside schools. Open to applications from borough based networks/fora.
Deadline: Advance notice by March for full application by May.

Developing Youth Arts*

For the development of arts activities by young people (up to the age of 25) outside the formal education sector. Open to arts organisations and youth services.
Deadline: January.

◆ FILM AND VIDEO

See entry for the London Film and Video Development Agency which also administers the Carlton Television and Channel Four funded London Production Fund.

Disability Arts Video Project

Contact the Arts Council of England (see separate entry).

◆ LITERATURE

Contact: John Hampson, Principal Literature Officer

Literature Live

For a range of literature events such as storytelling and fiction or poetry readings, and to promote new ways for audiences of all ages to experience literature in live performance.
Deadline: May.

Publishing New Writing

To support and develop new presses and literary magazines in the publishing of new or under-represented fiction and poetry. This fund is only open to groups for whom publishing is a central activity.
Deadline: August.

New London writers' Awards

Four bursaries of £3,500 for London writers who have published one book of poetry/fiction, and need to "buy time" to work on a second.
Deadline: January.

◆ Music
Contact: Andrew McKenzie, Principal
Music Officer

Creative Music
(This fund consolidates music programmes
which the board has operated over the past
four years: New Music, Small to Medium
Scale Opera/Music Theatre; Jazz and
Improvised Music Development; and New
Approaches to Musical Traditions.) To
provide funds for live music projects which
aim to engage audiences creatively in areas
of music which have little commercial or
subsidised infrastructure or support. The
fund will offer grants in the following areas;
contemporary classical music; jazz;
electronic music; small to medium scale
music theatre; music from African, Asian or
Caribbean origins; the musical element of
cross artform work (dance, visual arts,
multimedia etc).
Deadlines: April, October.

Music Commissions & New Work
For commissioning of new work in the
areas of contemporary, African, Caribbean
and Asian music, opera/music theatre,
dance and combined arts.
Deadlines: April, October.

◆ Training
Contact: Kathy O'Brien, Development
Officer

Training Development for Arts Organisations
For a programme of organisational and
individual training for arts organisations
over one year. A training analysis will be
required with each application.
Deadline: July.

Arts Training: New Developments
For training research projects for groups of
artists or arts organisations. These could
include research and investigation into new
skills and developments in the arts, not
necessarily linked to an end product.
Deadline: September.

Training Opportunities
Support is given by the board to a number
of short course training opportunities in
London. This includes direct subsidy for
courses held by Interchange, the
Independent Theatre Council and the
Management Centre. Other support may
occur throughout the year. Small grants are
also available for attendance at seminars
and conferences. Information available
throughout the year.

◆ Visual Arts and Crafts
Contact: Holly Tebbutt, Principal Visual Arts
and Crafts

London Exhibitions and E vents Fund*
To create new and increased opportunities
for the public to engage with contemporary
visual arts and crafts through exhibitions
and events. Funds will be given for research
& development and production.
Deadline: June.

Awards for Individual Artists, Photographers & Craftspeople
To assist the development of the visual
artist's creative process. Grants will be
available for research & development and
production costs.
Deadline: November.

◆ Arts Challenge
Guidelines not available for 1996/97 at time
of editing, but will remain linked to artist
involvement in major regeneration schemes.
Deadline: October.

NORTH WEST ARTS

Manchester House, 22 Bridge Street,
Manchester M3 3AB
Tel: 0161-834 6644; Fax: 0161-834 6969
Sue Harrison, Chief Executive
Area covered: Greater Manchester,
Lancashire, Merseyside, Cheshire and
the High Peak of Derbyshire.

Grant total: £7,985,000 (1994/95)

Grants by Artform 1994/95

Performing Arts		
Performing Art	£277,000
Dance, Mime, Circus	£308,000
Music	£273,000
Theatre	£3,526,000
Total	£4,384,000

Visual Arts	
Visual Arts	£571,000
Crafts	£174,000
Photography	£116,000
Total	£861,000

Film, Video, Broadcasting	£370,000
Literature	£196,000
Touring	£162,000
Business Services, Information, Research	£231,000
Combined & Community Arts	£876,000
Local Authority Funding, Partnerships, Strategic Initiatives	£682,000
Channelled Grants	£211,000
NW Arts Board, AGMA Joint Funding	£11,000

GRANT SCHEMES 1996/97

The following schemes (in addition to its direct support to arts organisations which absorbs the major part of its grant-aid) are available for groups and/or individuals.

The deadlines are only indicated by month, not the exact day. This was the month given as a deadline for applications in 1996/97 which may change in following years. Be sure to check for up-to-date deadlines.

◆ PERFORMING & COMBINED ARTS DEPARTMENT

COMBINED ARTS
Contact: Jane Beardsworth, Combined Arts Officer

General Development Fund
For one-off projects combining two or more artforms: performing arts, visual arts, literature, film and video. This may be a festival or celebration, a community arts initiative or a programme targeted at a specific community.
Deadlines: During February, June, September.

Live Arts & Collaborations Fund
For one-off projects which develop activities/events/programmes between artists of different disciplines., Two or more artforms (see list above) must be involved.
Deadlines: During February, June.

Individual Development Fund

To enable individuals to attend courses and conferences which contribute to their development in combined arts.
Deadlines: None, but not less than six weeks before the start.

PERFORMING ARTS

Contacts: Richard Cragg, Head of Performing Arts; Post vacant at time of writing, Dance Officer; Debra King, Music Officer

Professional Artists Seeking Further Training

Applications from individuals seeking artform related training and from organisations offering performing arts training in the region.
Deadlines: None, open all year round.

Creation and Presentation of Work; Education, Training, Youth & Community Projects

To support and develop live performance activity throughout the region (either for a single event or as part of an ongoing programme).
Deadlines; February, June.

Music commissions

To support commissioning of new music.
Deadlines: February, June.

◆ VISUAL ARTS AND MEDIA DEPARTMENT

VISUAL ARTS

Contacts: Aileen McEvoy, Head of Visual Arts; Tony Woof, Visual Arts Officer; Barney Hare-Duke, Crafts Officer

Grants for Artists in Crafts, Photography and Visual Arts

To support professional practice and creative development of work eg. marketing and promotional material, training, attendance at craft and trade fairs, travel and production awards.
Deadlines: June, January.

General Projects in Crafts, Photography and Visual Arts

For individuals and organisations planning activities in the region such as conferences, touring exhibitions, practical workshops, residencies, public art commissions.
Deadline: March.

FILM AND VIDEO

Contact: Howard Rifkin, Senior Film and Video Officer

Development, Production and Completion Awards

Deadline: June only.

Exhibition and Distribution Projects

Deadlines: March, September.

◆ LITERATURE

Contacts: Christine Bridgwood, and Marc Collett, Literature Officers (jobshare)

Live Writing

To support and develop writing in performance, assisting promoters in establishing regular programmes and venues.
Deadlines: March, September.

Mushairas

To support Mushairas and Kave Samellan in the region
Deadines: March, September.

Residencies and Placements

To support and develop writers' placements in a wide range of settings, assisting groups and organisations with the costs of employing professional writers.
Deadlines: March, September.

Publishing

To support and develop the publication, distribution and marketing of new writing.
Deadlines: March, September.

Writers' Bursaries

Three awards to enable writers at a critical stage in their careers to concentrate on specific writing projects.

♦ **RESOURCE DEVELOPMENT DEPARTMENT**

Business Development

Awards of up to 50% of total coasts (£3,000 maximum), eg. development,

implementation of a marketing strategy, start-up of a fundraising campaign, training needs analysis, creation of a designer/ maker's portfolio.

Deadlines: None, open all year round.

Business Training

Grants for up to 50% of the costs of training courses in business skills.

Deadlines: None, open all year round.

NORTHERN ARTS

10 Osborne Terrace,
Newcastle upon Tyne NE2 1NZ
Tel: 0191-281 6334; Fax: 0191-281 3276
Peter Hewitt, Chief Executive
Area covered: Cleveland, Cumbria, Durham, Northumberland and Tyne & Wear.

Grant total: £5,491,000 (1995/96)

Breakdown of Arts Expenditure 1995/96

Performing Arts

Revenue Clients	£1,256,000
Projects Fund	£331,000
Agencies/Development Funds	£274,000
Touring/Venue Support	£239,000
Symphony Concert Series, Festivals, Artists Support	£117,000
Total	£2,217,000

Published & Broadcast Arts

Film, Video, Broadcasting	£499,000
Literature	£185,000
Photography	£215,000
Total	£899,000

Visual Arts

Client, Gallery and Organisation Developments	£521,000
Artists' Support	£118,000
Flexible Funds	£378,000
Total	£1,017,000

Regional Development

Local Arts Development Agency commitments	£1,095,000
Regional Agencies, Development & Education, Priority Areas, Special Initiatives	£263,000
Total	£1,358,000

PROJECT AND SCHEME GUIDELINES 1996/97

Deadline/s are indicated by the month/s only. These programmes use only a small proportion of the board's total annual grant-aid which goes primarily to revenue and fixed-term clients. The following annual programme for projects and schemes may change depending on the funding available. Be sure to check for up-to-date details and exact dates.

◆ PERFORMING ARTS

Regional Drama Development Fund

To encourage and support the commissioning of quality professional drama production by Local Arts Development Agencies, promoters, venue managers, and other appropriate agencies in partnership with theatre producers.
Lead Officer: Mark Mulqueen
Deadlines: May and November.

Drama Projects Fund

To support small companies producing quality innovative drama within the region. To enable a selected number of small companies to produce independent creative work that is developmental in nature.
Lead Officer: Mark Mulqueen
Deadlines: May and November.

Drama New Opportunities Fund

To encourage new talent, innovation and initial project development in drama production.
Lead Officer: Mark Mulqueen
Deadlines: December and October.

Dance Projects Fund

To support professional dance development initiatvies through commissions, residencies and other dance dance production projects. To support the development of Dance Action Centres. To enable commissioning organisations to hire professional choreographers.
Lead Officer: Mark Mulqueen
Deadlines: None, open throughout the year.

Mime and Circus Production Fund

To support the creation of new work in Mime (including work known as Physical Theatre) and in New Circus.
Lead Officer: Mark Mulqueen
Deadlines: None, open throughout the year.

Music Agency Development Fund

A strategic fund to assist with the development of Music Agency functions in jazz, contemporary popular and rock music.
Lead Officer: Mark Monument
Deadlines: Applications welcomed throughout the year after discussion with the lead officer at least four months prior to the intended project.

Music Production Fund

To support the production of high quality music in the region with funding for the development and rehearsal of new, enterprising and innovative musical events and tours in partnership with LADAs and promoters.
Lead Officer: Mark Mulqueen
Deadlines: None, but the application should be discussed with the lead officer at least three months prior to the intended project.

Innovative Music Performances Fund

To support promotion to commission and present new musical compositions and to stage and present musical performances in new and innovative ways. Also to support the presentation of musical events in new or special venues that have a particular relevance to new audience development.
Lead Officer: Mark Monument
Deadlines: None but the application should be discussed with the lead officer at least four months prior to the project.

Music Commissions and Awards

To support the Northern Arts Composer Fellowships and residencies in partnership with host universities and colleges. To assist with the commissioning of new work principally for concert performance in any form of music.
Lead Officer: Mark Mulqueen
Deadlines: None.

Large Scale Touring Initiatives

To assist with the promotion of high quality national and international performing arts work in the region's large scale theatre and /or concert venues, particularly where partnerships between the venues and the Arts Council of England Touring Department are proposed.
Lead Officer: Brian Denham
Deadlines: None, but discussions must be held with the lead officer at least three months prior to the intended event.

Small Scale Touring Fund

To support high quality small scale professional performing arts touring of innovative work, promoted and co-ordinated by a number of LADAs, venues and promoters in the region.
Lead Officer: Mark Monument
Deadlines: None, but discussions must be held with the lead officer at least three months prior to the intended tour.

Music Touring Development Fund

To support high quality music touring of all kinds in the region, through direct support to promoters of concert series or music events.
Deadlines: None, but discussions should be held with the lead officer at least three months prior to the intended project.

Festival Development Fund

To encourage: 1) International Work; 2) Major Regional Festivals; 3) Small Festivals.
Lead Officer: Mark Monument
Deadlines: None, but discussions should be held with the lead officer at least six months before the intended event.

Venue Development Fund

To assist LADA officers and venue managers to improve the quality of their programming, marketing and audience development through: 1) Go and See grants; 2) Marketing and research enhancement; 3) Local partnerships.
Lead Officer: Mark Monument
Deadlines: None, but discussions should be held with the lead officer at least three months prior to the intended project.

Venue Guarantee Fund

To encourage the use of non-established venues, new venues and outdoor spaces for professional performing arts events.
Lead Officer: Mark Monument
Deadlines: None, but discussions should held with the lead officer at least three months prior to the intended events.

Middle Scale Touring Fund

To encourage greater collaboration with the Arts Council of England Touring Department to support high quality professional middle scale music, drama and dance touring for venues working collaboratively across the Greater North region.
Lead Officer: Mark Monument
Deadlines: None, but at least six months in advance of the project.

Bursaries and Residencies

Lead Officer: Brian Denham
Deadlines: None.

Project Fund

To encourage and support collaboration and exchange of skills and knowledge between professional performers and writers and to support networking initiatives between performing artists and arts organisations.
Lead Officer: Brian Denham
Deadlines: None.

Travel and Training (International)

For individual arts practitioner to travel/train outside mainland Britain.
Lead Officer: Brian Denham
Deadlines: January, March, June, October.

International Initiatives Fund

To fund senior managers and other practitioners to travel abroad to further and develop international projects of benefit to the Northern region (50% Visual Arts).
Lead Officer: Brian Denham
Deadlines: None, but at least six weeks before any proposed foreign travel.

Strategic Disability Fund

To assist the artistic development of Disability Arts Groups aiming to produce quality and innovative performing arts work.
Lead Officer: Mark Mulqueen
Deadlines: May.

◆ VISUAL ARTS

Awards to Visual Arts and Craftspeople

To assist individual visual artists and craftspeople in the production and development of their artistic practise.
Lead Officer: James Bustard
Deadlines: For small awards, at any time; for major awards, November.

Exhibitions, Events and Commissions

Lead Officer: James Bustard
Deadlines: None.

Exhibition Payment Right

To pay visual artists, photographers and craftspeople a fixed rate fee for public exhibition, as of right.
Lead Officer: James Bustard
Deadlines: None.

◆ PUBLISHED AND BROADCAST ARTS

Broadcasting

To develop partnerships between artists and broadcasters.
Lead Officer: Jenny Attala.
Deadlines: None.

Digital Strategy

To nurture the development of digitally based work, particularly of those artists working in published and broadcast arts.
Lead Officer: Margaret O'Connor
Deadlines: None.

Literature Audience Development

To support literature development, residencies, courses and promotion of literature.
Lead Officer: Jenny Attala
Deadlines: April/May.

Literature Festivals, New Writing and Touring

Lead Officer: Jenny Attala
Deadline: April.

Media Education and Training

Support for script writing courses, archives, development of media education networks and conferences, and radio training.
Lead Officer: Margaret O'Connor
Deadlines: None.

Media Promotions and Services

To support marketing and other projects which improve media exhibition, production and distribution.
Lead Officer: Margaret O'Connor
Deadlines: None.

Northern Production Fund

Support for script development or project research, production and company support. Includes provision for New Voices partnership with Tyne Tees – a collaboration with Yorkshire and Humberside Arts, North West Arts and with Yorkshire and Granada Television. Radio is included.
Lead Officer: Margaret O'Connor
Deadlines: Three per year: February; August; third not known.

Photography Production Awards

To support the production of new work by the region's photographers.
Lead Officer: Jenny Attala
Deadline: February/March.

Publishing Initiatives

To support the range of literary publications and publishing projects, including photographic work. Publishers in the region producing regular programmes of work of literary or photographic quality may apply. Publishing marketing and promotional initiatives.
Lead Officer: Jenny Attala
Deadlines: None.

Writers' Awards and Bursaries

Lead Officer: Jenny Attala
Deadline: July.

◆ REGIONAL DEVELOPMENT

Education and Artists in Schools

To create partnership arrangements with local authorities which support projects employing professional artists in schools.
Lead Officer: Shirley Campbell
Deadlines: Enquire, 1996/97 disbursed.

Education Project Fund

To support conferences, services and model projects in arts education.
Lead Officer: Shirley Campbell
Deadlines: None.

Strategic Disability Fund

To support short to medium projects which facilitate the strategic development of arts practice by disabled people.
Lead Officer: Shirley Campbell
Deadlines: None.

Cultural Diversity Fund

To support initiatives for the strategic development of culturally diverse programming and employment with specific regard to the arts produced by and for the Black and Asian communities of the region.
Lead Officer: Sarah Maxfield
Deadlines: None.

Arts and Disability Agencies

To establish a network of sub-regional agencies to promote events and activities which facilitate improved access to the arts for disabled people.
Lead Officer: Shirley Campbell

Disability Access Fund

To assist towards the costs of access audits, structural adaptation and capital equipment, to improve access to arts venues for disabled people.
Lead Officer: Shirley Campbell
Deadlines: None.

Capital Research Projects

To fund research and development of capital projects and regional strategies for the Lottery.
Lead Officer: Andrew Dixon
Deadlines: None.

Audience Development Fund

To fund a series of demonstration projects aimed at building new audiences by introducing new people to the arts or extending the range of arts experienced by a given audience. To identify effective audience development strategies and develop appropriate ways of measuring and evaluating success in this field.
Lead Officer: Sarah Maxfield
Deadline: August.

◆ FINANCE AND RESOURCES

Recruitment Fund

To provide assistance towards the recruitment cost for senior personnel in the region.
Lead Officer: Pete O'Hara
Deadlines: None.

Training (In-Country)

To fund training by individuals or organisations, both training courses/programmes and conference and seminar attendance.
Lead Officer: Pete O'Hara
Deadlines: None, but applications at least six weeks before the start of a course or programme.

SOUTH EAST ARTS

10 Mount Ephraim, Tunbridge Wells, Kent TN4 8AS
Tel: 01892-515210; Fax: 01892-549383
Christopher Cooper, Chief Executive
Area covered: Kent, Surrey, East and West Sussex

Grant total: £2,504,000 (1994/95)

Grants by Artform 1994/95

Drama	£571,000	23%	Combined Arts	£163,000	6%
Local Authority			Dance	£142,000	6%
Developments			Literature	£128,000	5%
& Agencies	£336,000	13%	Film/Television	£105,000	4%
Music	£267,000	11%	Crafts	£98,000	4%
Art	£197,000	8%	Photography	£68,000	3%
Festivals	£196,000	8%	Lateral Issues	£44,000	2%
Marketing, Press,					
Information	£188,000	7%			

As with all Regional Arts Boards the following grants for projects and schemes comprise only a small proportion of the total annual spend to support the arts. The vast majority is allocated to revenue and fixed term clients.

GRANT SCHEMES 1996/97

The deadlines give the month only to indicate frequency of consideration. Be sure to check for exact deadlines.

◆ GENERAL

"Go and See"
For artists to travel abroad
Deadline: Five weeks before intended visit.
Contact: Performing Arts Manager x 225

Mixed Arts Festivals
Deadline: March.
Contact: Planning and Arts Development x221 or 220

◆ PERFORMING ARTS

DANCE AND MIME
Contact: Performing Arts Officer (Dance) x230 or 229
NB Most of the funds are spent after the first closing date

Production Grants
Deadlines: March, September.

Tour of Existing Work
Deadlines: March, September.

Programming and/or Commissioning
For professional artists and companies to present, create and premiere work within the region
Deadlines: March, September.

Dance and Mime in Schools
Deadlines: March, September.

Bursaries

For training and development of youth dance leaders
Deadlines: At any time, at least six weeks before the start of the project.

Youth Dance Choreographic Development Fund

Deadlines: March, September.

Dance and Mime Networks/ Activities

Deadlines: March, September.

DRAMA

Contact: Performing Arts Officer (Drama) x224 or 228

Small Scale Drama Production Awards

For creation and presentation of new and innovative work.
Deadline: April.

Start Up Scheme

For new theatre companies based in the region
Deadline: April.

Theatre in Education/Theatre

For Young People
Deadline: May.

Bursaries

Deadline: April.

MUSIC

Contact: Performing Arts Manager x225 or 228 (unless otherwise indicated)

New Music and Commissions

Deadline: March.

Education and Community Projects

Deadline: June.

Music Diversity - Festival Showcases

Deadlines: Monthly from April to September.

Diversity Performing

For groups of no less than three players. 80% of the group must be resident in the region
Deadline: October.

Promoters, Venues and Organisations

For those wishing to engage bands and qualify for 50% subsidy on fees
Deadlines: Individual to each tour but normally January, April and September.

Support for Folk

For promoters engaging professional musicians with priority to innovative and unusual programmes, development of new audiences etc
Deadline: May.

Support for Jazz

For promoters putting on high quality professional events
Deadline: July.

Support for Voluntary Societies

Deadline: April.

Support for Festivals

Deadline: March.

Support for Orchestral Concerts

Deadline: June.

Support for Special Needs Projects

Deadline: April.

Young Musicians Platform Scheme

To promote musicians under 30 years by offering a series of concerts to promoters.
Deadlines: For musicians - May, assessments at July auditions; for concert bookings - March.
Contact: Miriam Juviler, South East Music Schemes 0181-566 8559

Award for Advanced Study Scheme

For postgraduate students under 30 living in the region for study abroad or with individual teachers in the UK.
Deadline: May, for assessment in July.
Contact: Miriam Juviler, South East Music Schemes 0181-566 8559

Ensemble in Residence Programme

To encourage promoters and venues to engage larger ensembles.
Deadlines: May for assessment July.
Contact: Miriam Juviler, South East Music Schemes 0181-566 8559

◆ MEDIA AND PUBLISHED ARTS

Contact: Media and Published Arts Manager x 212 or 211 (unless indicated otherwise)

PHOTOGRAPHY

Exhibition support for Photographers
Deadlines: April, September.

FILM

Production Grants for Beginners
Deadlines: Throughout the year.

Other Production Grants

These are advertised. Applicants should ask to be put on the mailing list.

Film Exhibition Subsidy
Deadline: February.

LITERATURE

Live Literature
Deadlines: Six weeks prior to event.
Contact: Literature Officer x210, or 211

Writers in Education
Deadlines: for events from April to July - March; for events from August to December - July.

◆ VISUAL ARTS AND CRAFTS

Contact: Visual Arts and Crafts Assistant x 216

Artists and Craftspeople Major Awards

Two awards, one for an artists and one for a craftsperson
Deadline: September.

Travel Bursaries

Two bursaries
Deadline: September.

Direct Support Grants
Deadline: February.

Exhibitions and Events: Touring Plan Fund
Deadline: February.

Exhibitions and Events: Project and Programming Grants
Deadline: February.

Exhibitions and Events: Development Grants
Deadlines: February and September.

Artists and Craftspeople in Education
Contact: Deborah Rawson, Education and Training Project Co-ordinator 01424-461 232

Gallery Education and Training

For Artists and Craftspeople
Contact: Deborah Rawson (see above)

SOUTH WEST ARTS

Bradninch Place, Gandy Street,
Exeter EX4 3LS
Tel: 01392-218188; **Fax:** 01392-413554
Graham Long, Chief Executive
Area covered: Avon, Cornwall, Devon,
Dorset (except Bournemouth, Christchurch
& Poole districts), Somerset, Gloucestershire.

Grant total: £3,886,000 (1994/95)

Grant Aid Breakdown 1994/95

Key Strategic Organisations	£2,564,000
Other Funded Organisations	£519,500
Projects & Schemes	£802,600

Grant Aid by Artform 1994/95

Theatre/Puppetry	55%
Cross Art Form	18%
Visual Arts/Photography	7%
Music	7%
Literature	4%
Dance	4%
Film/TV	3%
Crafts	2%

ARTFORM CONTACTS

Nick Capaldi, Director of Performing Arts; David Drake, Director of Media and Published Arts; Val Millington, Director of Visual Arts and Crafts

The major part of South West Arts' funding is its long-term grant-aid to key arts organisations in the region. Other project and development funds are not open to competitive application but agreed as part of an annual plan.

OPEN FUNDS 1996/97

"Art Electric" Exhibition Payment Right

A fee to professional artists, craftspeople and photographers endorsed by the National Artists Association. Grants of £140 to EPR payments, sponsored by SWEB in 1996/97.
Deadline: None, open throughout the year.

Literature Live

To support and professionalise the promotion of live performance by poets and prose writers. Grants for no more than 50% of costs and no less than £125 or more than £2,000.
Deadline: May.

Writers at Large

For educational projects with a high level of interaction between writers and participants enhancing the appreciation and practice of contemporary literature. (No single residencies.)
Deadlines: April and September.

Music Commissions, by promoters, performers and other music makers

For commissions to be premiered in the South West Region.
Deadlines: August and February.

Music Promotion

For music of all types and cultural traditions.
Deadlines: May, November.

Support for Independent Publishers

For small presses, publishers and magazines based in the region and registered with South West Arts. Grants may cover publishing franchise, development, marketing and training, business consultancy, distribution.
Deadlines: April, September.

Theatre and Dance Production

For the development and production of newly created work to be premiered and toured with the region. The definition of theatre and dance is broad and inclusive including performance work, puppetry, mime, physical theatre, new circus and live art.
Deadline: March.

Training and Marketing Bursaries

For individual artists in any artform. Only half the costs are eligible for subsidy and maximum grants are £250.
Deadlines: At least six weeks before the event.
Contact: Advice on training and information about further training bursaries available from Katie Venner, Arts Training South West (01823-334767).

Visual Arts Exhibitions and Events

For contemporary visual arts and crafts, for organisations, galleries, promoters, curators and local authorities (minimum £400, maximum £4,000).
Deadlines: March, September.

Visual Arts, Crafts and Photography Annual Awards

For individual professional artists resident in the region. Major awards up to £3,000; project awards up to £1,000.
Deadline: November.

From April 1996 the **South West Media Development Agency** (see separate entry) took over all the film and television work formerly undertaken by South West Arts. At the time of writing this, the agency still shared its address with South West Arts.

SOUTHERN ARTS

13 St Clement Street, Winchester,
Hampshire SO23 9DQ
Tel: 01962-855099; Fax: 01962-861186
Robert Hutchison, Executive Director
Area covered: Berkshire, Buckinghamshire,
south east Dorset (Bournemouth, Poole and
Christchurch districts), Hampshire, Isle of
Wight, Oxfordshire, Wiltshire.

Grant total: £3,161,000 (1994/95)

Breakdown by Artform 1994/95

Theatre	£1,029,000	36%	Multidisciplinary	£148,000	5%
Local Arts			Crafts	£123,000	4%
Development	£532,000	18%	Literature	£97,000	3%
Music	£355,000	12%			
Visual Arts	£234,000	8%	**Grants breakdown 1994/95**		
Dance	£192,000	7%	Arts Unit		£2,877,000
Film/Video/			Planning Unit		£232,000
Broadcasting	£165,000	6%	Resources Unit		£53,000

Southern Arts gives two kinds of financial support: Core funding to established organisations including salaries and overhead costs; Development funding for a set period of time to enable and encourage specific developments in the arts. It is available to individuals and organisations for specific initiatives which are not covered within core funding. As with all RABs it is a small proportion of its total funding.

DEVELOPMENT FUNDS

The following funds are also categorised under the following aims: arts and disability, cultural diversity, education, international, new work, participation and audience development, training, venue/programme support. Detailed fund guidelines with deadlines are available. Also consult the lead officer.

◆ CRAFTS
David Kay, Crafts Officer
Crafts development fund for organisations
Crafts development fund for individuals
Crafts training awards for individuals
Craft education development fund

◆ DANCE
Sally Abbott, Dance Officer
Dance development network fund: Support-
ing specialist dance agencies and posts
Dance commissions fund: Commissioning
and presentation of new work.
South Asian dance development fund
Dance training awards for individuals

Dance programme development fund, for
  small and middle scale venues
Dance education development fund
Dance and disability fund

◆ EDUCATION & PLANNING
**Jane Bryant, Education & Planning
Officer**
Arts education partnership fund
Arts and tourism projects fund

◆ FILM, VIDEO & BROADCASTING
**Jane Gerson, Film, Video &
Broadcasting Officer**
Film & video network development fund
Film & video exhibition development fund
Film & video production fund
Film & video production training fund (Black
  & Asian)
Film & video production training fund
  (disabled people)
Film & video education development fund
David Altshul Award, competitive award for
  young film and video makers

◆ LITERATURE
Keiren Phelan, Literature Officer
Literature commissions fund, poetry
  commissions for public sites
Writer's award
Literature Prize, celebratory competitive
  award for the year's best book
Black & Asian writers programming fund
Overseas writer's placement
Writers Live
Literature education development fund
Writer and storytelling placements
Literature and new technology
New writing development

◆ LOCAL AUTHORITY LIAISON
**Richard Russell, Local Authorities
Liaison Officer**
Programme funding
Research, audits and plans
Arts development posts

◆ LOCAL ARTS DEVELOPMENT
**Joanna Day, Local Arts Development
Officer**
Multi-artform development fund
Arts & disability network fund
Venue development fund

◆ MARKETING
**Paul Clough, Information & Marketing
Officer**
Arts marketing training fund
Arts marketing research fund

◆ MULTI-DISCIPLINARY
**Director of Arts, (position vacant at
time of editing)**
International initiatives fund
Southern collaborations
Festival development fund

◆ MUSIC
Michael Marx, Music Officer
Music theatre promoters development
  fund, for 20th century and contemporary
  music theatre
New music development fund, encouraging
  residencies in the region for composers
  and groups specialising in new music
Music commissions fund
Music training awards for individuals
Music programme development fund
Music education development fund
Music societies scheme

◆ THEATRE
Sheena Wrigley, Theatre Officer
Physical theatre new work fund
Theatre training awards for individuals
Theatre programme development fund
Theatre education development fund
Amateur theatre development fund

◆ VISUAL ARTS
**Visual Arts Officer (position vacant at
time of editing)**
Visual arts development fund for organisa-
  tions
Visual arts new work fund
Visual arts training awards for individuals
Visual arts education development fund

West Midlands Arts

82 Granville Street, Birmingham B1 2LH
Tel: 0121-631 3121; **Fax:** 0121-643 7239
Michael Elliott, Chief Executive
Area covered: West Midlands, Shropshire,
Staffordshire, Warwickshire, Hereford &
Worcester.

Grant total: £5,000,000 (1994/95)

Grants Breakdown

Cultural Investment		Strategic Developments	£101,000
Centres & Services	£2,825,000	Education	£70,000
Promoters, Venues		Audit & Feasibility	
& Touring	£482,000	Studies	£26,000
Local Arts & Community		Documentation	£12,000
Projects	£253,000	Total	£409,000
New Work & Productions	£904,000		
Total	£4,464,000	**Business Development**	
		Training	£19,000
Planning		Business Support	£109,000
Local Agreements	£200,000	Total	£128,000

Deputy Chief Executive: Sally Luton
Director of Performing and Combined Arts: Alun Bond
Director of Visual Arts, Crafts & Media: Caroline Foxhall
Director of Planning: Felicity Harvest

Development Funding Schemes 1996/97

Further information is available from **Information Services** on 0121-631 3121/
624 3200; or book a surgery with your artform or lead officer.

The information below lists the months when deadlines occurred in 1996/97
to indicate the frequency of application openings. Be sure to check the specific
date and remember that changes occur from year to year. Details of Development
Funding Schemes for 1997/98 will be available in early 1997.

Schemes marked * cannot accept new applications in 1996/97 because they
are heavily oversubscribed.

◆ Open to all artforms

**Arts Education
Development Fund***
Support for schools consortia. LEAs and
colleges to fund programmes of arts activity
in educational settings. Only available to
school clusters/consortia in areas where
there is no funding agreement with the
LEA.
Deadlines: March, June, November,
January.

Arts in Healthcare

Funds hospitals and other health sector organisations to produce arts plans or carry out action research into arts in health opportunities.
Deadlines: At any time, but at least six weeks before the project takes place.

Community Partnerships

Support medium to large scale community art projects developed and run by two partners, including professional and amateur arts groups, voluntary groups, agencies or venues..
Deadlines: March, September.

Participate

Fund career and skills development for those involved in participatory arts. Available for placements, secondments, attending conferences and major events, and other development activities. Open to community arts practitioners, those organising amateur arts activities and professional artists who wish to work in participatory arts.
Deadline: January.

International Training Awards

For individuals artists to develop their artistic and creative skills, by supporting international study trips over a month in duration.
Deadline: June.

Regional Training Awards*

Funding for those putting on courses and bursaries in arts and management skills in the region.
Deadlines: March, September.

Senior Arts Manager Bursaries

Three bursaries funding attendance at short management courses at Cranfield Business School.
Deadline: November.

Village Arts Fund

Funds for local groups in rural settlements with a population of less than 10,000, who want to run arts activities.

Deadlines: Applications can be made at any time but must arrive at least six weeks before a project takes place.

◆ PERFORMING & COMBINED ARTS

New Work & Production Awards

Support the devising and creation of new work in the region, available for dance and mime, new circus, puppetry, drama, music and mixed artform applications.
Deadlines: March, September.

Promoters, Venues and Touring*

Support for key regional promoters, including dance and mime, drama, music, and mixed artform.
Deadlines: January, March, June, January.

Performing Miracles

Bursaries for creative/artistic directors working in the performing arts in the region.
Deadline: September.

◆ MUSIC

Breakthrough Awards

Fund recording, touring and work with professional artists in informal music, such as improvised music, folk and roots, jazz, Black music, contemporary Asian music, and other popular contemporary music styles.
Deadline: September.

Key Change Awards

Reward excellence in programming and commissioning by voluntary music societies and concert clubs, choirs, orchestras and ensembles.
Deadline: March.

◆ DRAMA

Stagewrite

Encourages the commission and production of new theatre writing and the development of new audiences for that writing.
Deadline: September.

◆ VISUAL ARTS, CRAFTS & MEDIA

New Work & Production Awards

Support the devising and creation of new work in the region. Available for work in visual arts, crafts, photography, literature, film & video, and new technology applications.
Deadlines: March, September.

Promoters, Venues and Touring*

Support for presenting new work in the region in the visual arts, crafts, photography, literature, film & video.
Deadlines: January, March, June, January.

Artists Bursaries

Fund research projects and career breaks that stimulate the production of new and innovative work which experiments with ideas, issues, materials and technology. Open to visual artists, crafts makers, photographers, film and video makers.
Deadline: January.

Go & See Awards

Assist attendance at conferences and seminars which extend awareness and critical debate around a range of key issues. Open to exhibition organisers, freelance curators, visual artists, crafts makers, photographers and curators.
Deadlines: Applications are welcome at any time but should be received at least four weeks before the event.

Visual Arts, Crafts and Photography Placements

Enable individual visual artists, crafts practitioners, photographers, exhibition organisers and freelance curators to train in exhibition organising within established venues or to develop specific curatorial skills.
Deadline: September.

◆ CRAFTS

Chelsea Crafts Fair Bursaries

Support for regional crafts makers selected by the Crafts Council to attend the fair for the first time.
Deadline: To be received at least four weeks before the fair.

◆ FILM & VIDEO

Film & Video Research and Development Awards

Fund the development of proposals for future production funding, whether from West Midlands Arts, or national schemes supported by funding agencies and broadcasters.
Dealines: March, September.

◆ PHOTOGRAPHY

Photography Portfolio Awards

Enable practitioners to attain the highest possible standards of quality and innovation in the presentation of their portfolios.
Deadlines: March, September.

◆ LITERATURE

Literature Reading Service

Expert feedback from a professional writer. Open to unpublished poetry, prose fiction, memories and writing from the oral tradition. Fee of £15 for each appraisal.
Deadline: Application can be made at any time.

Yorkshire & Humberside Arts

21 Bond Street, Dewsbury,
West Yorkshire WF13 1AX
Tel: 01924-455555; 01924-466522
Roger Lancaster, Chief Executive
Area covered: North, South and West
Yorkshire and Humberside

Total grants & guarantees: £6,199,500 (1994/95)

Total Grants & Guarantees Breakdown 1994/95

Arts Development		Projects & Schemes	£937,200
Franchise Funded	£3,928,400	Planning, Communications,	
Annual Programme	£743,700	& Business Services	£590,200

Franchise agreements are offered to organisations of strategic importance to arts provision in the region. Initially organisations submit in autumn business and artistic plans for a three year period. An update is submitted each year. These organisations are not usually eligible for project or scheme grants.

Annual programme grants are offered to organisations which operate a year long programme, to activities such as festivals which recur annually and to animateurs whose work extends beyond one year. Applications are made in late autumn for the following year.

Scheme grants operate to agreed policies each with different conditions, deadlines etc. See outlines below.

Key Artform Staff

Director of Performing Arts: Jim Beirne
Drama Officer: Shea Connolly
Music Officer: Glyn Foley
Dance Officer: Mileva Drljaca

Director of Visual & Media Arts: Caroline Taylor
Visual Arts & Crafts Officer: Jennifer Hallam
Film & Broadcasting Officer: Terry Morden

Photography & Multi-Media Officer: Adrian Friedli
Literature Officer: Steve Dearden

Director of Planning: Andy Carver
Planning Officer (Arts & Education): Julia Calver
Planning Officer (Access): Karen Smith
Planning Officer (Resources): Toby Hyam
Arts Business Services Officer: Miles Harrison

GRANTS 1996/97

The exact deadlines are not given below. Many are for the first day of April, July, October, January. Decisions are made within six weeks of the deadlines. Readers need to check the exact dates and to get the most up-to-date grant guidelines. Contact the Administrator within the particular artform department.

◆ COMBINED ARTS

Funding to support projects that cross boundaries between visual arts, performing arts, broadcast and published arts. This includes community and school-based festivals, carnivals and galas as well as collaborations between artists and arts organisations from a range of disciplines.

Key Participatory Projects

For participatory projects which often recur annually.
Deadlines: April, July, October, January.

Local Community Festivals

For the arts element in local festivals and galas.
Deadlines: April, July, October, January.

Access

Support for small-scale participatory arts projects.
Deadlines: April, July, October, January.

Innovative Work

Support for the creation of cross artform work.
Deadlines: April, July, October, January.

Live Art

Support for new work and related projects in the area of performance art, certain kinds of installation and time-based work, most recently including new technologies allied to the delivery and development of such work.
Deadlines: April, July, October, January.

New Beginnings

Support for new work in radio, dance and literature – see under individual artforms.

International

Support for international projects including conferences, seminars, presentations, networking.
Deadlines: April, July, October, January.

◆ PERFORMING ARTS

Performing Arts Projects

To encourage participatory activity particularly in cross-artform work involving some or all of the performing arts. In addition this funding can be used to support seminars and conferences which encourage debate about the performing arts and to promote the work of companies involved in New Circus and Cabaret.
Deadlines: April, July, October, January.

Drama and Dance Touring

Funding to enable artists/companies to tour their work into the region. Support is usually directed via the venue or promoter.
Deadlines: April, July, October, January.

Touring & Venue Development

To develop the producing role of venues, promoters and companies in the region. Funding is available for collective commissioning by venues and training companies, to help create networks and for research and development of project ideas.

◆ DANCE

Dance and Mime Projects

To support dance and mime projects across a wide spectrum of styles and contexts.
Deadlines:
April, July, October, January.

New Beginnings

"New Beginnings" awards or £1,500 each to enable dancers/mime artists in the region, at a critical stage in their development, to concentrate on exploring new approaches to their work either as choreographers or teachers.

◆ DRAMA

Drama Projects and Schemes

Funding to support work and training in the fields of drama and puppetry, with a maximum award of between £1,500 and £2,000.

◆ MUSIC

Music Projects and Schemes

To support a wide variety of work – such as concert promotions, educational schemes, workshops, training, the use of animateurs, musicians in residence, festivals, community projects, publicity and marketing and consultancy studies. This funding cannot be used to support individual instrument tuition or for course fees in higher education.
Deadlines: April, July, October, January.

Commissioning of New Work

Grants may vary between £300 and £2,000 and applications should normally be received at least six months before the date of the first performance.
Deadlines: April, July, October, January.

Large Scale Music Touring

To facilitate orchestral touring and other types of large scale music touring in the region.
Deadlines: April, July, October, January.

Musicians in residence

To help promoters book established musicians, resident in the region, at subsidised fees. The scheme includes folk, jazz, classical, non-western and electronic music.
Deadlines: Check these dates.

Studio Time Scheme

To enable young musicians to have access to time in a recording studio. At least one member of the band or group must be unwaged. Subject to funding being available, the aim is to provide 50% of the recording fees up to a maximum of £100 per individual or group, and one of the specified studios on the scheme must be used.
Deadline: Not applicable.

◆ FILM AND BROADCASTING

Film Development Awards 1996

Support to individual film and video makers in the region for the development of short films. Awards of £500 for writers or directors to enable them to develop their project to the stage where a Production Funding Application can be made.
Deadline: November, 1996.

Short Film Production Scheme 1997

Production Awards of up to £10,000 for film or video productions of up to 10 minutes. Original creative work in a variety of forms can qualify: fiction, documentary, animation or experimental. Productions can be intended for theatrical distribution, broadcast television, or installation display in galleries etc.

Course in Scriptwriting for Short Film

This course covers basic scriptwriting techniques. Applicants must submit the first draft of a script to be developed while on the course. The course is taught by the Northern School of Film and Television in Leeds and is one evening per week for twelve weeks from October to March.
Deadline: September 1996.

One Minute Radio Scheme – New Beginnings

To commission five one minute pieces of audio work for possible transmission on radio. Each commission: £500.
Deadline: October 1996.

Community Radio Training Scheme

To support training in basic radio skills for community radio groups planning to broadcast with a restricted licence. Maximum available to each group: £300.
Deadline: October 1996.

Community Video Awards

To provide grants up to £500 to groups requiring training in video for community projects. Groups wishing to apply under this scheme should approach Vera Productions (30/38 Dock Street, Leeds LS10 IJF Tel: 0113-242 8646) if they live in West Yorkshire, or Yorkshire & Humberside Arts directly if they live in other parts of the region.
Deadline: Please check this.

◆ PHOTOGRAPHY AND MULTI-MEDIA

Photography Production Awards

To enable photographers to undertake original creative work in traditional and electronic media. There is normally one major award of £5,000, three standard awards of £2,000 and five development awards of £500.
Deadline: September 1996.

New Shoots

Five awards of £300 are offered to photographers who have never applied to YHA before.
Deadline: August 1996.

◆ LITERATURE

Black Literature Development Scheme

Support of black writers and readers' groups, promoters, publishers and translators.
Deadlines: Please check.

Live Writing

To promote public readings and performances by writers of all genres,
including international writers.
Deadlines: Applications for funding must be made at least eight weeks before the event.

Literature Publication Awards

To support a wide range of publications, with preference for imaginative writing.
Deadline: April 1997.

New Beginnings - Writers Awards

Awards up to £1,500 each to enable writers to concentrate on specific writing projects. Available only to writers living in the region.
Deadline: October 1996.

Writer Development Scheme

To allow groups committed to developing craft skills to work over an extended period with a writer or writers.
Deadlines: July 1996, January 1997.

Young People Writing

To enable young people and agencies working with them to employ writers. Schools are eligible to apply but priority will be given to projects with community links and those occurring outside the curriculum.

Literature Projects

Support to literature projects not covered by any of the above.

Arvon Foundation

Bursaries for writing courses from applicants living in the YHA region at the Arvon Foundation. Applications should be made through Arvon by telephoning Ann Anderton on 01422-843714.

◆ VISUAL ARTS AND CRAFTS

Applications which develop the visual arts in any area are encouraged (minimum £200, maximum £5,000). However the following areas were highlighted in 1996/97.

Exhibitions/Presentations

Freelance curators and organisations within the region may apply for funding towards

the exhibition and presentation of contemporary work eg. exhibition production, research, administration, documentation, education, publicity and touring.
Deadlines: April, July, October, January.

Partnership

Supports work which makes new partnerships with other sectors eg. education, tourism, health, environment, international partnerships and retailing. Priority will be given to projects that establish major ongoing initiatives. Groups of schools may be eligible for support.
Deadlines: April, July, October, January.

Individual Awards for Visual Artists, Craftspeople and Live Art Practitioners

To support individual artists in the production of new work and the exhibition, sale or marketing of existing work. Only artists and craftspeople living in the region are eligible to apply and the maximum award is £2,000.
Deadlines: May, November 1996.

◆ TRAINING

Artform Training

Small grants are available towards the costs of training courses in all artforms.

Arts Business Services

Individuals and organisations within the region can apply for a contribution towards the cost of management training up to a maximum of £500. Applicants will normally not receive more than half their training fees and the YHA will not normally subsidise fees for training courses run by Yorkshire and Humberside Business in the Arts. Please note that training grants are not normally given to YHA Franchise and Annual clients.

Community Development and Participatory Arts Training

Support for individuals and organisations to assist with the costs of taking up appropriate training opportunities aimed at the development of participatory arts and arts in the community. Assistance with the costs of attending courses and conferences or undertaking project attachments, project exchanges and visits will be considered.

Education

Grants for practising artists to attend courses and conferences to develop or improve the use of their artform skill in educational settings. Grants are normally up to 50% of the course fee and travel expenses.

METROPOLITAN AREA GRANT SCHEMES

Associations of Metropolitan Boroughs

The London Borough Grants Scheme

Greater Manchester Grants Scheme

West Yorkshire Grants Scheme

Associations of Metropolitan Boroughs

In the late 1980s the metropolitan counties were abolished. There were provisions which allowed all the constituent metropolitan boroughs of a former metropolitan county to set themselves up as an association with the capacity to levy a contribution from all of them for the purposes of providing common services, including the arts. The arts funding arrangements of all three borough associations which developed from this capability are given below. They provide significant support for arts organisations which cover more than one of the constituent boroughs.

The London Borough Grants Committee

London Borough Grants Unit (Arts),
5th Floor Regal House, London Road,
Twickenham TW1 3QS
Tel: 0181-744 9864 ext 224/5/6/7/8;
Fax: 0181-891 5874
Contact: Andy Ganf, Principal Arts Officer

The committee which arose after the demise of the Greater London Council is the largest funder of the voluntary sector in London with over 650 organisations receiving grants in any one year (£27 million in 1993/94). Each of the 33 London boroughs contributes to the budget of the scheme on the basis of its population. Its work covers a wide range of voluntary initiatives – housing, social services, community work, legal and other advice centres, employment, arts, recreation and the environment.

   Grants are made to non profit-making organisations which provide a service of benefit to London as a whole or an area covering more than one borough. The committee's highest priority is tacking poverty and combating disadvantage, discrimination and deprivation. Arts grant total: £3,979,000 (1995/96)

The Arts Funding Policy aims to:
+ increase popular participation, involvement and access
+ develop support for grass roots, special communities of interest and minority arts
+ foster greater dynamism in the arts

◆ improve the geographical spread of arts provision.

The committee is interested in funding strategic initiatives, rather than small highly localised activities, whatever their worth.

The major part of the unit arts grant is for recurrent funding for building-based (£1,890,000), touring (£339,000), or co-ordinatory (£129,000) organisations, museums (£95,000), festivals (£189,000) and community radio (£28,000).

SPECIAL SCHEMES

All these funds are for not more than 75% of cost, exclusive of VAT

Arts Festivals Fund
Grant total: £77,000 (1995/96)
A wide range of festivals are eligible – large international and national festivals, London wide festivals, smaller regional carnivals and galas. Grants are unlikely to exceed £7,500. Applications should be made by mid/late January.

Arts Projects Fund
Grant total: £57,000 (1995/96)
This fund, aimed at up and coming groups, is not open to revenue clients of the LBGU, the Arts Council and the London Arts Board. Groups are either completely new clients or have only received one-off project grants. Grants are unlikely to exceed £5,000. Applications have to be made by mid/late January.

Museum Development Fund
Grant total: £22,000 (1995/96)
Grants are for independent, not for profit organisations (not public or local authority museums). They are unlikely to exceed £5,000. Applications should be made by mid/late February.

Outer London Arts Development Fund
Grant total: £200,000 (1995/96)
This scheme, administered in association with individual outer London boroughs, provides one-off, non-recurrent grants for projects which improve the accessibility and availability of the arts in outer London and contribute to their development. Applications are available both from borough arts officers and the LBGU. Grants are unlikely to exceed £15,000. Applications have to be submitted around mid/late February.

Applications: Full guidelines and application forms are available for the above funds which open in October/November each year for the following financial year. Grant surgeries are run a few weeks before the closing date for each of these schemes to assist applicants with draft applications before making a formal submission.

The main recurrent grant applications are sought between July and September each year.

Applicants should expect to know the decisions of the committee by late April.

GREATER MANCHESTER GRANTS SCHEME

AGMA Grants Unit, Chief Executive's
Department, PO Box 532, Town Hall,
Manchester M60 2LA
Tel: 0161-234 3364; Fax: 0161-236 5909/5405
Contact: Grants Officer

Grant total: £2,358,000 (1994/95)

This scheme was established following the abolition of the Greater Manchester Council in 1986. The Association of Greater Manchester Authorities (AGMA) comprises the 10 local councils (Bolton, Bury, Manchester, Oldham, Rochdale, Salford, Stockport, Tameside, Trafford, Wigan). Funding is sharply focused on strategic countywide services. The grants committee now has two major priorities, either or both of which an organisation must meet:

◆ to contribute to the recognition of Greater Manchester locally, nationally and internationally as a creative and vibrant county helping to create the conditions necessary to attract potential investment,

◆ to contribute to an improved quality of life for all its residents through its first priority above and by supporting agencies which assist those who are vulnerable or disadvantaged.

In addition emphasis is placed on organisations which:

◆ attract significant revenue from other sources

◆ provide a countywide service or form part of a countywide service or which contribute to an issue of countywide concern.

◆ provide coverage over at least the majority of the 10 districts.

In 1994/95 most of the funding (£2.27 million) was distributed in revenue grant aid to 38 organisations. The major part of this funding (73%) was disbursed to 18 arts organisations.

The largest grants were made to:
North West Arts Board (£324,000);
Hallé Concerts Society (£315,000);
National Museum of Labour History (£298,000);
Royal Exchange Theatre Company (£199,000);
Contact Theatre Company (£126,000);

Other revenue grants included:
Nia Centre (£50,000);
Dance Initiative Greater Manchester (£45,000);
North West Sound Archive (£17,000);
North West Playwrights (£13,000);
North West Film Archive (£7,700).

In 1994/95 a further £95,000 was distributed in one-off grant aid to support time limited events, projects and activities. Grants ranged between £750 and £10,000. Eighteen arts organisations received £41,000, 43% of the total one-off funding. Recipients included: Live Music Now! North West (£5,000); Peshkar Theatre Company, Skylight Circus, Manchester Youth Theatre, (£2,000 each).

It is understood that AGMA has had to cut its expenditure and less funding will be available in 1996/97 for one-off grants.

Exclusions: Individuals.

Applications: Full guidelines and an application form should be obtained for the one-off funding. In 1996/97 there were three deadlines: January for consideration in May, May for consideration in September; September for consideration in January.

WEST YORKSHIRE GRANTS

County Hall, Wakefield WF1 2QW
Tel: 01924-305065/7; **Fax:** 01924-305214
Contact: Grants Officer

Grant total: £1,308,000 (1995/96)

West Yorkshire Grants supports voluntary activity of a strategic nature operating on a county-side basis. Preference is given to organisations which operate in three or more districts. The minimum amount for revenue grants is £5,000, and for one-off events or projects, £1,000.

Most of the funds, £1,006,500, in 1995/96 were disbursed to arts organisations and a museum. Practically all of this was allocated in revenue funding with only £20,000 given for one-off arts activities.

Major revenue grants went to:
Opera North (£295,000);
Northern Ballet Theatre (£200,000);
West Yorkshire Playhouse (£99,500);
Yorkshire Mining Museum (£95,000).

One-off grants included:
Bradford Festival (£2,500);
Skinning the Cat (£1,000).

Exclusions: Individuals.

Applications: Revenue clients apply annually by the end of October each year for funding during the following financial year. Proposals for one-off grants have to be submitted by 15 January each year for the following financial year.

LOCAL AUTHORITY FUNDING

LOCAL AUTHORITY FUNDING

Most arts groups – whether large, medium, or small; conventional or experimental; new or long-established; professional or amateur; performance, visual, literary – find that the local authority/authorities in which they work are very important to them for the assistance they can offer. This is most obvious in financial terms. Overall local authorities provide more money for the arts as central government.

Increasingly local authorities have been employing arts officers to develop local arts strategies. The relationships that arts organisations build up with their local authorities (both officers and elected representatives) are extremely important and cannot only be measured in financial terms.

LOCAL GOVERNMENT REORGANISATION

The pattern of local authority support for the arts is undergoing a period of upheaval because of the changes arising from local government reorganisation. At this point in time (Spring 1996) it is not possible to describe the likely effects of this reorganisation except in the broadest terms. The situation is extremely complex with the reorganisation effecting different parts of the UK differently. It is important for arts organisations to be fully aware of any changes in their area, which will lead to inevitable changes in the budgets and the officers relevant to arts organisations.

In the early 1990s the government embarked upon a review of local government and its two-tier structure of county and district councils. It believed that it would be preferable to introduce a new form of local authority, the *unitary authority*. This new structure would be responsible within its area for *all* local authority functions, both those carried out by a county council and those carried out by a district council. It was thought a single (unitary) authority could improve the cost-effectiveness, quality and co-ordination of local services.

However unitary authorities are not being introduced throughout the UK. The pattern of change is not consistent except in Scotland and Wales where from April 1996 the former regional and district/highland and island councils in Scotland have been replaced by 29 unitary authorities and in Wales 22 unitary authorities have replaced the county and district councils. The population size of unitary authorities varies considerably as does their geographical area.

No changes are to be made in Northern Ireland whilst the metropolitan areas of England and the London boroughs also remain unchanged since these authorities carry out the full range of local authority duties already (and are in effect unitary authorities).

The reorganisation in England mainly takes effect from April 1997. (A handful of unitary authorities started in 1996 – Isle of Wight, York and four new unitary authorities taking over in both Avon and Cleveland.)

In England, unlike Scotland and Wales, there is to be no consistent pattern for the introduction of unitary authorities. Some counties and districts are to be abolished and replaced entirely by unitary authorities (Berkshire) whilst other counties will remain (Surrey). In many counties new unitary authorities will co-exist alongside the counties of which they had formerly been a part. For instance two new unitary authorities have been created from within Leicestershire – Leicester City and Rutland – leaving a smaller Leicestershire County Council with seven district councils.

So the local authority system in England will become extremely varied and will create extraordinary administrative and financial problems during the period of readjustment. This will inevitably lead to a period of great uncertainty for arts and art-related organisations and ventures which have a history of receiving local authority support.

The anxieties about the implications of local government reorganisation include:

◆ Doubts about the willingness of smaller authorities to contribute to cultural activity outside their own boundaries.

◆ Lower commitment to cultural investment from authorities with a smaller revenue base.

◆ Disruption to long-standing funding arrangements and a reduced range of funding sources.

◆ Downgrading of arts and museums within larger departments and service committees.

THE TWO-TIER STRUCTURE

Since the two-tier structure of county and district councils will remain in many areas it is important to distinguish their different responsibilities. The following table shows which level of council to approach, the overlapping interests and also those areas that are not specifically arts-related but which can be important sources of support, for instance:

◆ Education departments (buildings, artists in schools programmes, discretionary grants to young people for advanced study in the arts, etc);

◆ Libraries and museums services (organisation of events as part of educational and outreach work);

◆ Economic development and tourism departments (strategies to attract visitors and inward investment particularly the Single Regeneration Budget and European funding);

◆ Planning departments (urban and rural development);

◆ Social services (arts activities for client groups).

Many authorities, both county and district have European Officers. (enquire of the Chief Executive's Department.)

COUNTY AND DISTRICT COUNCILS

County councils, in many areas of the country, have a long history of working in close co-operation with district councils to develop the arts. Districts tend to provide facilities and support for community arts and the amateur arts sector, while county councils concentrate on support for strategic arts organisations, links with library and education services, and the development of innovative arts projects. Despite the varied provision in a non-statutory service, there are numerous examples of good practice across the country where the partnership of county and district has worked to the benefit of the arts.

Main Functions of County and District Councils

County Councils	District Councils
EDUCATION	ELECTORAL REGISTRATION
• Most schools	
• Special education	
• Nursery, adult and community	COUNCIL TAX AND
• Planning and quality assurance	UNIFORM BUSINESS RATE
• Resource management	
PERSONAL SOCIAL SERVICES	HOUSING
• Provision for the elderly, children, those with disabilities (including care in the community)	
• Policy planning and quality assurance	
PLANNING	PLANNING
• Strategic planning	• Local plans
• Mineral and waste planning	• Planning applications
• Highway development control	
• Historic buildings	
TRANSPORT	TRANSPORT
• Public transport	• Unclassified roads
• Highways & parking	• Off-street car parking
• Traffic management	• Footpaths & bridleways
• Footpaths & bridleways	• Street lighting
• Transport planning	
EMERGENCY PLANNING	EMERGENCY PLANNING
ENVIRONMENTAL SERVICES	ENVIRONMENTAL SERVICES
• Refuse disposal	• Refuse collection
	• Building regulations
	• General environmental services
	• Street cleaning
RECREATION & ART	RECREATION & ART
• Parks & open spaces	• Parks & open spaces
• Support for the arts	• Leisure centres and swimming pools
• Museums	• Museums and art galleries
• Encouraging tourism	• Support for the arts
	• Encouraging tourism
ECONOMIC DEVELOPMENT	ECONOMIC DEVELOPMENT
LIBRARIES	
POLICE	
FIRE	

Source: Local Government Commission for England (a few functions such as allotments, smallholdings and cemeteries have been omitted)

Total Net Revenue Expenditure by Main Budgetary Heading and Authority Type 1993/94

£ millions

	Counties	Districts	Met	London	Section 48	Total (a)
Net spending on venues	4.1	42.2	15.6	31.8	–	93.9
Arts officers/development	2.3	5.4	2.4	1.9	–	12.0
Net spending on promotions	0.5	2.1	1.3	0.5	–	4.3
RAB subscriptions	1.2	0.6	0.6	–	0.3	2.8
Grants to artists/arts organisations	6.2	7.6	11.8	5.0	4.5	35.1
Total net revenue spend (b)	14.3	58.0	31.7	39.3	4.8	148.1

(a)   includes City of London
(b)   totals may not sum due to rounding

Source: "Local Authority Expenditure on the Arts in England, 1993/94" Arts Council of England, October 1995

The figures above do not include the expenditure on local museums (739 local authority run museums and 676 independent museums most of which receive funding) and the network of over 3,000 public libraries.

Although the counties are responsible for most of *total* local government expenditure (85%), the districts contribute most to arts spending. The districts spend most of their money on facilities such as theatres, halls and art galleries giving only 14% of their money to independent art organisations (including RABs). In contrast the county councils have given over half of their arts budget in grant aid to independent arts organisations (including RABs).

WHO TO CONTACT AND WHERE

Shadow Unitary Authorities are appointed for the year before the take-over during which time they have to produce Draft Service Delivery Plans. Arts organisations are advised to consult the draft plans themselves and make a comment to the shadow authorities if they wish.

POWERS TO SUPPORT THE ARTS

In Scotland the previous *statutory duty* for district authorities "to ensure adequate provision of cultural activities and library services in their areas" has been maintained. The new councils are also permitted to contribute to regional or national cultural bodies or to promote cultural facilities and activities.

In Wales the unitary authorities have retained *discretionary* powers to support the arts.

In England the current powers of county and district councils to foster the arts are *discretionary or permissive*. The powers of the new unitary authorities are the same. There are arguments that a statutory duty without sufficient funding support would lead to greater problems for local authorities.

REGIONAL CONTACTS

Arts organisations are advised to keep in touch with their relevant Regional Arts Boards and Area Museums Councils about the plans and the changes that are taking place. They are also invaluable sources of information about which officers to contact in the local authorities.

In those areas where significant changes are being made to the two-tier structure, the loss of a strategic overview (from the former counties) will necessitate even closer liaison between the remaining authorities and the RABs and the Area Museums Councils.

LOCAL CONTACTS

Readers seeking grants and other forms of advice and support should be in touch with the officers responsible for the arts who service these committees and also find out the names of the councillors serving on committees, particularly the chairperson.

There are very few committees dealing solely with the arts. Responsibility for the arts may be shared with leisure, sport, tourism, community development, environment and amenities, and so on.

The most common form of decision-making body for making grants to arts organisations and individual artists is the Leisure Services Committee (or similar bodies such as Leisure and Amenities, Leisure and Tourism, Community and Leisure, Recreation and Tourism, and occasionally Tourism and Economic Development). Often more than one committee may be involved and the full leisure committee may work in tandem with a financial committee – Policy and Resources, or General Purposes.

Whilst there are a few authorities with specialist arts committees or committees with arts in their title, the general pattern is for a sub-committee, answerable to a policy and resources or leisure committee, to have delegated responsibility for arts grants and/or grants generally.

The following list illustrates the names of the committees etc. dealing with arts provision in West Sussex and Cornwall, two counties which will remain unchanged by reorganisation. It also shows where a specialist arts officer has been employed

West Sussex County
Policy and Resources Committee
   Arts Working Party (meets quarterly)
Adur District Council
   Leisure & Amenities Committee (meets 5 times a year)
Arun District Council
   Environment, Tourism and Leisure Committee (meets 6 times a year)
Chichester District Council
   Leisure and Tourism Committee (meets 6 times a year)
Crawley Borough Council
   Leisure Services (meets monthly)
Horsham District Council
   Leisure Department (Arts Development Officer)

Mid Sussex District Council
  Leisure Services Committee (meets five times a year)
  Arts Panel with Arts Development Officer
  Capital Projects (Leisure Planning)
Worthing Borough Council
  Community Services
  Entertainments and Tourism Committee
  Tourism and Entertainments Manager with responsibility for the arts
  Policy & Resources Committees for grants to voluntary bodies

Cornwall County Council
Environment and Community Services Committee (meets three times a year)
Libraries and Arts Department with Arts Officer who also services the Cornwall
Arts Forum
Caradon District Council
  Direct Services
Carrick District Council
  Environmental & Community Services (meets five times a year)
  Arts Working Party
  Grants Sub-Committee
Kerrier District Council
  Amenities Committee
  Grant Scheme
North Cornwall District Council
  Policy Committee (meets every six weeks)
  Finance Committee re grants and donations
Penwith District Council
  Clerk to the Council
Restormel District Council
  Tourism and Leisure Services
  Arts Development Working Party

                              (details correct at Summer 1996)

DEVELOPING RELATIONSHIPS WITH LOCAL AUTHORITIES

The level of support given to the arts will vary considerably from one council to another, with some being generous, and others giving practically nothing. Where a group is based (or, if itinerant, where it performs or mounts its exhibitions) can make an enormous difference to its chances of getting support and to the number of levels of council officialdom it has to contact and the degree of advice and support it obtains.

FIND OUT ABOUT THEIR ARTS INTERESTS

Before approaching councillors and council officers, it is wise to find out how much your local council gives to the arts and the particular projects it supports.

This information is readily available in the minutes of local meetings. It is also interesting to find out what comparable councils give. If yours is one of the councils which is spending little on the arts, it may be useful long-term ammunition to be able to underline this point to your council by making suitable comparisons, though this will probably not help you much in the short term where changes in council budgets are unlikely.

VITAL RESEARCH

Acquaint yourself with the working procedures of your local councils. Find out:

- What principal responsibilities each tier or type in your area has, particularly with regard to the arts;
- What each relevant council's stated policies are, so that if, for example, a council lays strong emphasis on providing educational facilities and services you may be able to take advantage of this when applying for a grant for any part of your operation which fits into the education category;
- How and when decisions on grant-making are taken;
- What organisations they have funded in the past and the amounts they have given in individual grants. This more than anything else will give you a picture of their general approach and preferences for arts support.
- Which councillors and council officers will be involved in the decisions to fund you and which are likely to be sympathetic to your organisation. Some councils have specially appointed arts officers and if there is one in your area he/she should obviously be your first contact.

A good source of information on your council's attitude to the arts should be, once again, your Regional Arts Board. Its staff will be experienced in dealing with all the different local authorities in their region and will know many of the problems you are likely to come up against as well as, hopefully, some factors which might operate in your favour. There are many funding partnerships between local authorities and RABs, and certainly much mutual consultation between these bodies.

MAKING YOUR CASE

Once you have discovered the councillors and council officers whose support you need, you need to spend time interesting and involving them in your organisation. Invite them to events, which will also be a good opportunity for them to meet your colleagues. If there are people with local influence on your board or who support you in some way, persuade them to talk to some of the key councillors and officials about the value of your organisation. (It is advisable to check these local VIPs' political persuasions first, and 'match' them with councillors with similar political views) It is a good idea to prepare the ground in this way before a formal application is made for grant, so that you have a fair idea of what will be acceptable and what will not. Make sure that all those responsible for contacting and lobbying councillors are properly briefed: first, on the local importance of the organisation (backed up by audience figures, analysis etc.), and, second, on what is needed from the council. If councillors receive conflicting or muddled statements from a variety of sources this could damage your case considerably.

PARTICULAR CONSIDERATIONS

Apart from information particular to your council, there are criteria which all councils are likely to use when considering your proposal which you should take into account at an early stage.

- How well does the work and objectives of your organisation fit in with your council's stated policies and priorities?
- Are there any organisations in the area doing similar work? If there are, do these organisations receive local authority funding? Are there sound reasons why the authority should fund your organisation as well as, or instead of, those it is already funding?
- How successful are you? Is your work of a high calibre? And what outside evidence can you obtain to support this? How many people attend your events? And how many of them come from the local authority area? Are there other ways in which you can demonstrate local community support, such as membership or local fund-raising?
- How well organised are you in terms of financial and administrative control? Are you reliable? Is your work endorsed by way of grants from the Arts Council, your RAB or one or other of the leading trusts with an interest in the arts?
- How strongly do the local people feel about you as a valuable amenity? Would local opposition be strong if you were forced to disband from lack of funds?

MEDIA COVERAGE

While you are talking privately to council officers and councillors you should also be directing your efforts at your local media to reinforce your message. Items on local radio and in the local paper about the importance and quality of your work, reviews and interviews in which you outline future plans of benefit to the community should also have an effect on councillors' opinions.

RATE RELIEF

In addition to giving you a grant, or as an alternative, the District Council can also give you relief on your Business Rates. If you organisation is a registered charity you are *entitled to 80% rate relief on any premises you occupy.* Your local authority can also at its own discretion give you relief on all or part of the remaining 20%. Rate relief is given only if you apply for it and only for the current and following rate years (1st April to 31st March). It cannot be granted retrospectively. You can still apply for rate relief, however, even if your charitable status has not yet been officially approved by the Charity Commission (the Inland Revenue in Scotland and Northern Ireland).

Once you have been granted rate relief, you should continue to obtain it automatically, but check your annual rates bill to make sure this is happening. Because of pressure on financial resources, many councils are now less willing to give discretionary relief. But it is certainly worth applying for it, and continuing to apply for it each year, if you are unsuccessful at the first attempt.

Local councils may be able to offer you gifts in kind as well as cash grants: second-hand office equipment and furniture; premises for your use either free or at a low rent; help with transport maintenance; staff secondments (though these are rarely made in the arts field); access to the council bulk purchasing scheme which may offer lower prices than elsewhere. But you will only be able to find out if such support is available if your contacts with councillors and council officials are good.

REGULAR CONTACT

Whatever support you are looking for, you should be talking regularly to councillors and council officials, especially those who are of particular importance to you. Keep them informed of your activities throughout the year, not just when grant application time looms again. Many arts organisations have a representative from their local authority on their board of trustees or management. This can be an excellent way of ensuring the continuing interest and commitment of your local authority. Don't forget to maintain the interest and support of all the political parties represented on your council so that, whichever party has the majority at a particular time, those in power will always be aware of and sympathetic to your organisation.

ACKNOWLEDGEMENTS AND PERSONAL THANKS

And, as always, you must say thank you for any assistance you receive from them. Remember too, to credit the council in publicity material, in media interviews and in formal speeches. The council (as well as councillors who will always have one eye on the next election) needs a good press as much as you do.

Thanks are owing particularly to the Arts Council of England and the National Campaign for the Arts for the information they have provided about local authority funding and government reorganisation.

THE CRAFTS COUNCIL

THE CRAFTS COUNCIL

44a Pentonville Road, London N1 9BY
Tel: 0171-278 7700; **Fax:** 0171-837 6891
Tony Ford, Director;
Wendy Shales, Grants Officer

Grant total: £1,066,865

Breakdown of Grants

Ten Regional Arts Boards:	£642,300	Setting-up Grants:	£166,415
Arts Council for Wales:	£101,400	Project and Exhibition	
Other Grant:	£59,000	Grants:	£98,050

The Crafts Council, a registered charity incorporated under Royal Charter, receives an annual grant from the Department of National Heritage.

The council offers business advice and finance to artist craftsmen and women, as well as subsidy for craft projects. Quality of work is the principal criterion for offering financial assistance, but other factors are taken into account according to the guidelines of the different schemes. Craftspeople applying for support should show a high level of design and technical ability.

The council's funding schemes are open to craftspeople in both England and Wales.

Setting-up Scheme
Grant total: £166,000 (1994/95)
Grants are offered to help with the costs of setting up a first workshop. Applications can be made either before the workshop is established, or at any time during the first two years of operation. Applicants must plan to spend the majority of their time in the workshop (a maximum of 16 hours employment outside the workshop each week is allowed). Makers working from home are eligible provided that the space is considered suitable.

This scheme consists of two parts, maintenance and equipment. Makers can apply for both or one of these types of grant, but it is not possible to apply separately at different times. The level of grant may also depend on the other grants given towards the costs setting up and running the business.

- Equipment grants are for 50% of the total cost of essential equipment up to a maximum of £5,000 (eg. 50% of £10,000). Second-hand equipment is eligible. For certain expensive items not constantly in use, 50% of the hiring costs during the first year will be considered.
- Maintenance grants are for £2,500 for one year. The grant is paid in quarterly instalments with the first instalment released when the workshop is in production.

A total of 37 grants were given in 1994/95. A two-day business and marketing course was also provided for all grant recipients.

Applications: Obtain the current guidelines. Application forms, accompanied by a curriculum vitae and six slides of recent work. Applications are considered four times a year the closing dates are 1st March, 1st June, 1st September and 1st December.

Project and Exhibition Grants

Grant total: £98,000 (1994/95)

These grants are available for contemporary craft projects and exhibitions taking place in England and Wales. All organisations including commercial ones, are eligible to apply.

In 1994/95 20 projects and exhibitions were supported with grant ranging between £15,000 and £1,000. Grants made in 1994/95 included:

Shipley Art Gallery, for Henry Rothschild and "Primavera" exhibition (£15,000);

Derby University, for Joanna Constantinidis exhibition (£7,300); Ceramic Review, for conference (£1,400).

Applications: Applicants are advised to discuss their proposal first with the Grant Officer before completing the application form. The four closing dates are the same as for the Set-up Scheme and decisions are normally given within one month of the closing date. In the case of exhibitions and large scale projects an application must be made at least one year in advance of the event.

Exhibitions Bursary Scheme

Three awards of £3,000 are made to encourage new curators in the crafts, particularly those with some exhibition experience but not currently engaged in the crafts and those people not currently engaged in work on major exhibitions but who can put forward development proposals for touring shows. Open to both postholders and freelance people.

Applications: June but be sure to check.

FILM & TELEVISION

National

The British Film Institute
British Screen, including European
    Co-Production Fund
The Scottish Film Council
The Scottish Film Production Fund
The Gaelic Television Committee
The Wales Film Council
The Northern Ireland Film Council

Regional

East Midlands Media Initiative
London Film and Video Agency
South West Media Development Agency
See also the Regional Arts Boards

Local

The Edinburgh and Lothian Screen
    Industries Office Ltd
The Glasgow Film Fund
The Merseyside Film Production Fund
The Sheffield Media Development Fund

Others

BBC New Film Makers Fund
The Lloyds Bank/Channel 4 Film Challenge

See under "Europe"

Eurimages
European Guarantee Fund
The MEDIA Programme

NATIONAL

THE BRITISH FILM INSTITUTE

21 Stephen Street, London W1P 2LN
Tel: 0171-255 1444; Fax: 0171-436 7950
Wilf Stevenson, Director

The British Film Institute (BFI) aims to encourage the development of the art of film and television. About half its funding comes from the Department of National Heritage with the rest raised from membership subscriptions, sponsorship, donations, and provision of services. It makes grants in the following areas.

Cinema Services and Development Division
Contact: Irene Whitehead, Head
The division works to maintain and increase the range of films and work on video available to audiences throughout the UK and has three sections: the Exhibition Department, the Distribution Department, and the Funding Unit and also houses the UK MEDIA Desk (see separate entry).

The Funding Unit (0171-255 1444 x251)
Contact: Carole Comely, Head
The unit makes annual grants to the English Regional Arts Boards, the Wales Film Council and the London Film and Video Development Agency and the South West Media Development Agency. Grants are also made to support an existing network of regional film theatres. In addition the unit administers the following schemes:

- *The Planning and Development Fund* operates in association with other partnership funds to facilitate medium and large-scale capital projects. Applications are considered in January of the year preceding their allocation.
- *The Regional Exhibition Projects Fund* is a strategic fund for the development of cultural film and video exhibition. It provides one-off or seed funding in the areas of marketing/publicity enhancement; and education. Applications are considered in February of the year preceding their allocation. In 1996/97 a total of 21 projects were supported with grants ranging between £222 and £2,500.
- *Federation of Film Societies Group Grants.* Grants are awarded to national, Wales, Scottish and regional groups.

BFI Production Board

29 Rathbone Street, London WIP 1AG (0171-636 5587)
Contact: Ben Gibson, Head of Production
Total funding: £1,000,000 annually
This fund is financed in equal proportions by the Department of National Heritage and Channel Four Television. The board earmarks £700,000 every year to develop and invest in feature films.

Feature Film Development & Production

Grant total: £700,000 (1996/97)
Script development and production money is allocated to British-based writers and filmmakers with innovative treatments or ideas. This fund is limited and goes to filmmakers with a proven cinematic style. Currently the board is prioritising feature films to maximum budgets of £500,000.

Around 300 feature scripts are received each year, some eight of these are developed further, whilst about two of these projects go through to the production each year. Successful projects receive professional production and distribution support, including reduced office overheads, editing rooms and a preview theatre.
Exclusions: 60 minute documentaries and television drama scripts are not considered.
Applications: All applications should be made with the BFI Features cover application form and must be accompanied by a treatment or script, the proposed director's show reel (if any) and CVs of other key personnel. Scripts which have potential for cinema exhibition should be between 70-90 pages long. Film treatments should include a story outline and an indication of visual style. Feature length documentaries for the cinema are welcomed. Applications are received, logged and acknowledged by the Script Co-ordinator. Decisions on scripts take 6-8 weeks.

Projects Fund

Contact: Steve Brookes, Executive Producer
This fund supports development, co-production and completion. Fifteen films were financed or co-financed in 1994/95. Applications are judged on the basis of the unique requirements of each project and so a realistic indication of desired funding is required. The BFI is committed to innovative work within a low-budget framework. The following figures give guidance:
Development - from £500 to £5,000
Production - sums up to a ceiling of £25,000
Completion - sums up to a ceiling of around £15,000.
Exclusions: Directors who are students in full-time education. The following proposals are not normally considered: feature length drama; literary adaptation; documentation of events or performances within other art forms; educational films or videos.
Applications: Proposals are accepted from 1 April. There is no deadline. An application form needs to be completed and accompanied by the script or storyboard, with full notes, budget, details of key personnel, as appropriate. Applications will not be considered unless supported by show reel material.

New Directors

This scheme supports short cinema films by new writers and directors. (Potential applicants need to be alert to its changing annual arrangements and keep in touch with the BFI so that any deadlines are not missed.) The 1996/97 scheme was described as follows: "We are looking for one page proposals which respond to the theme 'Another Saturday Night'. The BFI and Channel 4 want to encourage cinematic short films which show a strong sense of personal vision as well as a distinctive approach to storytelling. Innovative filmmaking which breaks genre boundaries will be welcomed."

Film proposals were expected to be between 4 and 20 minutes in length, and capable of being shot within 6 days with a maximum budget of £35,000. 19 scripts have been commissioned for development to first draft; 6-10 of these will be chosen for productions The completed films will hopefully be distributed both individually and in a feature length programme broadcast by Channel 4 under the title, 'Another Saturday Night'.

Exclusions: "It is unlikely that straightforward documentaries and work that is regularly covered by television will be funded."

Applications: The deadline was 24 November 1995, for New Directors 1996/97. Details of the scheme for 1997/98 will be known at the end of September 1996.

BRITISH SCREEN, INCLUDING EUROPEAN CO-PRODUCTION FUND

14/17 Wells Mews, London W1P 3FL

Tel: 0171-323 9080; Fax: 0171-323 0092

Simon Perry, Chief Executive; Stephen Cleary, Head of Development

Total Funds: Between £5 million and £7 million annually for British Screen and the European Co-Production Fund; £5 million Greenlight Fund from the Lottery (1995)

British Screen Finance Limited, the successor to the National Film Finance Corporation, supports feature film development and production in the UK. It is mainly funded by returns on loans made by the company and by an annual grant from the Department of National Heritage.

It has helped finance up to 20 feature films productions each year, typically providing about 20% of the film's production budget. Its financing of development has comprised support for the writing and practical development of 30-40 new feature film projects each year and for an annual programme of short film production. Its policy has favoured new directors, writers and producers. Among the most successful films supported are "The Crying Game", "Orlando", "Scandal", and "Jack and Sarah".

In October 1995 a new resource, the Greenlight Fund (£5 million), was made available from the National Lottery via the Arts Council of England. Its purpose described as "to stem the talent-drain and to reinforce the infrastructure of the industry". British Screen expects to invest the new money in up to four new, high-profile, British films during the first "pilot" year. Investments will be minority participations (limited to 30% of a film's budget, to a maximum of £2 million). Finance will be in the form of commercial loans. Projects will be selected and investment terms negotiated by British Screen working closely with the Arts Council of England. (The Lottery Act requires final approval to rest with the council.) British Screen hopes to secure approval for retention by the fund of earning on its investments and for further annual injections of Lottery money.

British Screen selects films to be offered production finance from amongst those projects which have received development support.

Three types of development funding are available:

- Screenplay Loans, to stimulate the writing of first draft screenplays, particularly by new writers and writers new to the cinema;
- Development Loans, to support producers throughout the process of developing a commercial feature film project, whether the writer is new or experienced;
- Preparation Loans, to enable producers to finance further or final development of feature film projects where British Screen is intending to provide finance for their production.

British Screen will not consider applications for development of television films.

Screenplay Loans

Application for an interest-free Screenplay Loan should be made by the writer/s, who should submit to the Head of Development only an outline or short treatment of the proposed screenplay. There is no application form for this type of funding, but where the screenplay is to be based on another work, the availability of rights in that work should be indicated in an accompanying letter.

While there can be no absolute criteria by which applications will be assessed, the Head of Development and consultants will seek to be convinced that:

- the eventual film, as envisaged by the writer, is likely to appeal to a wide, paying audience in cinemas throughout the world, both in its original language and in other language versions;
- the story of the film is inherently dramatic and cinematic by virtue of its potential to stimulate powerfully the emotions and visual senses of an audience, and that the writer is capable of realising that potential;
- either the concept of the film, or the intention of the writer/s in developing the concept into a screenplay, is in some identifiable way original.

Preference is given to writer/s yet to achieve feature film credits; contemporary stories; stories which in character, setting or perspective are identifiably European.

Screenplay Loans will not be given as retrospective support for work already done, and are not available for the writing of second or further drafts.

Development Loans

Application for an interest-free Development Loan should be made by the producer/s, who should initially submit to the Head of Development only an outline or short treatment of the proposed screenplay together with the name of the writer, with credits (if any); the name(s) of other personnel attached to the project; where the screenplay is to be based on another work, an indication as to availability of rights in that work.

The producer may be asked at a later stage to complete an application form: this will depend upon the Head of Development's response to the outline/treatment and is not necessary initially.

The criteria by which applications are assessed are the same as those for screenplay loans with the additional proviso that the producer (in the case of a team, at least one member of the team) either has a track record as a feature film producer or is dedicated to becoming a feature film producer.

As with screenplay loans, preference is given to contemporary stories and stories which in character, setting or perspective are identifiably European. The only screenplays which will automatically be accepted as submissions for development loans will be those written as a result of screenplay loans.

Preparation Loans

A Preparation Loan is available to a Producer only when (a) a project has been submitted to British Screen for production funding (i.e. when development is at an advanced stage) and (b) British Screen's response to the project has been positive to the extent that it has identified the project as a 'prospect' for production funding. There is no formal method of application: an offer of a Preparation Loan will be follow discussion of the project by British Screen with the producer and, where appropriate, the writer and the director. A request for a Preparation Loan cannot be considered until the director is in place.

European Co-Production Fund

This fund promotes collaboration between British film producers and other film producers in the European Union by providing commercial loans. Films should have a demonstrable commercial market in Europe but be unable to cover their production costs out of the European market alone. They must be full-length feature films. Preference is given to companies which are independently owned or controlled by the applicants. Preference will generally be given to film projects originated by British talents and initiated by British producers. The ECF is unlikely to invest in a film with a non-European director.

The EFC is a purely British initiative and it is not part of the European Union's MEDIA programme and has no connection to the Council of Europe's support fund, "Eurimages" (see separate entries).

Criteria are different from British Screen's production loans criteria. An ECF loan is up to a maximum of £500,000 and may not be higher than 30% of the film's budget.

Films must be co-productions involving at least two production companies, with no link of common ownership, one registered in the UK and at least one other registered in another EU member state. The National Film Trustee Company (c/o British Screen) collects and disburses net revenues accruing from productions made with British Screen and ECF investment.

THE SCOTTISH FILM COUNCIL

74 Victoria Crescent Road, Glasgow G12 9JN
Tel: 0141-334 4445; Fax: 0141-334 8132
Jamie Hall, Information Officer

The Scottish Film Council (SFC) is the national body for the promotion of moving image culture in Scotland. It is set up as an independent company with charitable status and receives the bulk of its funding as grant-in-aid from the Scottish Office Education Department. In 1994/95 this amounted to £1,019,000. SFC's main areas of activity are:

Exhibition
Grant Total: £451,000 (1994/95)
Funding the work of a network of regional film theatres, community cinemas, film festivals and mobile cinemas. The major funding is in annual revenue grants. Nine organisations received a total of £302,500 in 1994/95 with the largest grants to the Glasgow Film Theatre (£105,000), Filmhouse, Edinburgh (£92,000) and the Edinburgh International Film Festival (£60,000). Other grants for exhibition totalled £149,000.

Production & Training
Grant Total: £92,500 (1994/95)
Including financial support to Scottish Screen Locations (£8,000), and to Scottish Broadcast and Film Training (£14,000) 'First Reels', a production support fund run in association with Scottish Television which encourages young and first-time film makers. Other grants totalling £70,000 were given to 17 organisations with the largest grants to film and video workshops.

Publications and Information Services
Including managing 'MEDIA Antenna' which assists Scotland's film and television producers to make the most of funding opportunities in Europe.

Scottish Film Archive
Managing the Scottish Film Archive and developing a Scottish film museum at Coatbridge to house the SFC collections.

Education

Furthering media education throughout the community by providing teaching materials, teacher training and advocacy.

The Scottish Film Council will consider applications for financial help under the above headings, although production assistance is primarily the responsibility of the Scottish Film Production Fund (see separate entry below) and there is no duplication of their work. Specific funding schemes are:

Strategic Interventions Fund

Grant Total: £33,000 (1994/95)
Contact: Erika E King

For special projects and one-off grants to augment funds already available from the SFC and the Scottish Film Production Fund and other agencies. Awards mainly between £2,000 and £10,000 and applicants are encouraged to seek funds from other sources.

Exhibition Development Fund

Grant Total: £10,000 (1995/96)
Contact: Alan Knowles

Grants normally up to 50% of the project costs or £3,000.

Go and See Fund

Grant Total: £5,000 (1994/95)
Contact: Erika King

To encourage contact between organisations and groups in Scotland in the not-for-profit sector with their counterparts in other parts of the world. Individual awards usually up to a maximum of £300.

Centenary Reels Scheme

Grant Total: £40,000 (1995/96)
Contact: Dan MacRae

(Running in conjunction with Scottish Television for a three year period from 1995 as a successor to "First Reels") for new film and video makers to produce work which will celebrate the spirit of the early pioneers of the moving image form. Awards up to £4,000 for projects with completion/post production awards of up to £1,000. Animation is not included but a new scheme supporting animation projects is planned (winter 1996).

Further details are available about all these schemes and applicants are strongly advised to make informal contact prior to drafting an approach.

THE SCOTTISH FILM PRODUCTION FUND

74 Victoria Crescent Road, Glasgow G12 9JN
Tel: 0141-337 2526; Fax: 0141-337 2562
Eddie Dick, Director

Grant total: about £550,000 a year

The fund has been established as an independent body by the Scottish Film Council and the Scottish Art Council. Its income derives mainly from the Scottish Education Department, the Scottish Arts Council and BBC Scotland. The fund works with both new and established Scottish film-makers who will make a continuing contribution to the film culture and industry in Scotland. (Scotland as a location for filming does not necessarily make the project eligible.)

The fund supports and finances narrative fiction films with priority given to short film production and feature film development. The modest resources of the fund mean that contributions to feature film production are rare. As a general guide the maximum levels of support are £15,000 for feature film script development and £50,000 for feature film production finance. A number of short film schemes were operating in early 1996:

Tartan Shorts - funded jointly with BBC Scotland, awards up to £45,000 for three short films of approximately 10 minutes (16mm or 35mm film). The films will be treated as independent commissions from BBC Scotland whose usual contractual procedures apply. In 1995 the deadline was 2nd October.
Prime Cuts - funded jointly with British Screen and Scottish Television, awards up to a maximum of £23,000 to six short drama films around five minutes and shot on 16 mm.
Geur Ghearr -this scheme for Gaelic film makers, supported jointly with CTG and BBC Scotland, awards £45,000 to two 10 minute films. In 1996 the submission deadline was 16th February.
New Voices - a competition, sponsored by the Bank of Scotland, for new Scottish screenwriters. awards of £500 each. The closing date in 1995 was 17th November.

The Scottish Film Production Fund administers the *Glasgow Film Fund* (see separate entry).
Contact: Catherine Aitken
Exclusions: Television series, serials or mini-series and educational films. The following are also excluded as a general rule: completion of films, community video and amateur film-making.
Applications: Potential applicants should first approach the fund offices for an initial discussion. Full published guidelines and application forms are available.

THE GAELIC TELEVISION COMMITTEE

4 Harbour View, Cromwell Street Quay,
Stornoway, Isle of Lewis HS1 2DF
Tel: 01851-705550; Fax: 01851-706432
John Angus Mackay, Director

Gaelic Television Fund
Grant total: £8,738,000 (1994/95)
The fund finances a wide variety of programmes and series for the Gaelic speaking community. In 1994/95 40 projects were funded. The majority of the funds went to ITV (46%) and the BBC (35%) The independent production sector was well represented and received some 20% of the fund's total support.

The Gaelic Television Training Trust
Grant total: £226,000 (1994/95)
Funding is provided for full-time training through this trust. The committee also funds placements and short courses (23 individuals benefited in 1994/95) to enhance skills already developed within the industry.

THE WALES FILM COUNCIL

Screen Centre, Llantrisant Road,
Llandaff, Cardiff CF5 2PU
Tel: 01222-578633; Fax: 01222-578654
Luned Meredith, Grants and Projects
Manager

Grant total: £157,000 (1996/97)

The council was established in 1992. About half its funding comes from the Arts Council of Wales with the remainder from the British Film Institute, S4C and BBC Wales. It aims to help provide Wales with a cultural infrastructure for the development of film and the moving image. Its concerns range across most aspects of film: production; exhibition; preservation/conservation; education; publishing and research. In particular it provides funding support as follows:

Revenue Funding

Grant total: (£71,500 (1996/97)

Six clients were supported with the largest grant to Media Education Wales (£26,000) and the smallest to Film Societies Welsh Group (£2,000).

The Welsh Production Fund

Grant total: £61,000 (1996/97)

The fund, launched in 1994, seeks to encourage new talent and new ideas and particularly wishes to support the development of films which explore alternatives to mainstream production. Grants are offered for:

- Development Awards, with support up to £5,000;
- Production Awards, with support of up to £10,000 each for production or part-production costs:
- Completion Awards, with support up to £1,500. Retrospective production costs are not covered.

Detailed guidance notes and application forms are available, Applicants should be Welsh-born, or resident in Wales for two years prior to application, or Welsh-speakers. Students in full-time higher or further education are only eligible for awards in the "Completion" category.

Cinema Programme Support Fund

Grant total: £23,000 (199697)

Applications are invited from cinema exhibition venues to help develop their cultural programming policy. In particular the fund is interested in

- film education projects
- special programmes and joint touring packages
- staff training

In 1995/96 six grants were made with the largest to Valley Arts Marketing £3,000).

International Travel Bursaries

Grant total: £1,500 (1996/97)

These awards aim to broaden and enrich professional experience in an international context (outside Wales and the UK). Awards may be given towards the expenses of attending recognised film academies and institutions, professional placements, and other centres for career development. In 1995/96 six awards ranging between £300 and £600 were made.

European Film College Scholarship

The award (£6,000 in 1995/96) enables a Welsh student to attend the eight month film and television course in Ebeltoft, Denmark.

Applications: There are generally two deadlines for each scheme in Spring and Autumn each year. Enquire for exact dates which change from year to year.

THE NORTHERN IRELAND FILM COUNCIL

7 Lower Crescent, Belfast BT7 1NR
Tel: 01232-232444
Richard Taylor, Director

Like the other national film councils, the Northern Ireland Film Council promotes film and television and encourages the integration of commercial and cultural concerns in four key areas: education; training; production; exhibition.

Training
The council works with Skillset, the Industry Training Organisation, with UTV, the BBC and Channel 4 to provide professional short courses and to assist individuals to attend specialist courses elsewhere.

Production
In 1993/94 a Production Fund of some £80,000 supported the development and production of 22 projects. At the time of editing this guide (Winter 1996) such funds were not available but interested readers should check with the council.

Northern Lights, is a NIFC/BBC NI scheme for first short films by new directors. *The Bill Miskelly Award* of £1,000 is given annually to a postgraduate student undertaking a film and television study course.

REGIONAL

EAST MIDLANDS MEDIA INITIATIVE (EMMI)

c/o Intermedia Film & Video (Nottingham)
Limited, 19 Heathcoat Street, Nottingham NG1 3AF
Tel: 0115-952 0568; Fax: 0115-955 9956
Peter Carlton, Head of Production Development

EMMI is a development fund for the promotion audio-visual media in the East Midlands. It is being jointly funded by the city council, county council, East Midlands Arts and the European Regional Development Fund. Funding arrangements were being finalised at the time of editing this guide so the total funds available are not known. It is administered by "Fast Track", intermedia's production development service. The fund mainly assists the development of broadcast programmes of any format or genre but applications are welcome from all areas of film, television and the related media such as CD-ROM. Awards mainly range between £1,000 and £5,000.
Applications: Producers, directors and writers living and working in the East Midlands are targeted. Applications may also be considered from producers outside the region seeking the produce projects in partnership with regional groups or individuals. Closing dates are March, June and October.

THE LONDON FILM AND VIDEO DEVELOPMENT AGENCY

114 Whitfield Street, London WIP 5RW
Tel: 0171-383 7755; Fax: 0171-383 7745
Steve McIntyre, Chief Executive

Grant total: approx £300,000, not including
the London Production Fund (1994/95)

The LFVDA, which is mainly funded by the British Film Institute, aims to support, strengthen and promote all aspects of independent film, video and television in London. This includes production, training, exhibition, distribution and education.

It provides funding, information, advice and professional support. Its concern is with new and innovative work and with activities and operations that "interrogate and challenge established and traditional forms and practices".

While there is no set upper limit on awards, it is rare that project grants to organisations or individuals exceed £5,000.

The LVDA also advises the National Lottery: it assesses film/video capital bids from London-based projects as well as convening the Independent Film Advisory Panel which advises on low-budget production applications.

Funding schedule 1995/96

Core revenue clients	£118,875	Project	£66,944
Exhibition/distribution		Capital/new initiatives	£11,995
Revenue	£28,000	**Cultural spaces**	
Project	£35,376	Revenue	£14,606
Training/education		Project	£1,000
Revenue	£32,826		

London Production Fund

Grant total: about £200,000 (1995/96)
Contact: Maggie Ellis, Co-ordinator (0171-383 7766)
The LPF is supported by Carlton Television and Channel 4. It offers Development Awards of up to £3,000 each and Production and Completion Awards of up to £15,000. Selection is made on the basis of written proposals and usually, a consideration of the applicant's previous work. The fund is prepared to support first-time film and video makers. The fund is open to film and video makers living and/or working in the London region. Full-time students are not eligible.

Whilst funded by broadcasters the scheme does not tie up any rights with them. Producers can also get money from elsewhere.

SOUTH WEST MEDIA DEVELOPMENT AGENCY

Mariner House, 62 Prince Street, Bristol BS1 4QD
Tel: 0117-930618; **Fax:** 0117-930658
Judith Higginbottom, Director;
Sarah-Jane Meredith, Administrator

The agency was set up in April 1996 and covers the work previously undertaken by South West Arts with an additional remit to raise new funds for production and other areas of work. It provides financial support and advice and development work for a wide range of media activities. The agency supports a network of film and video resource centres and workshops which provide access to film and video equipment. Many have their own production programmes as well as undertaking skills training. It also supports film and video organisations with a specialist area of work or a particular community of interest. Film, television and video production is supported through a series of financial awards and funding schemes:

Western Lights
A joint scheme of HTV and the South West Film and Video Agency
Total fund: £150,000 (1996)
Four half-hour television dramas were commissioned from writers, directors and producers with a track record of low budget productions but without substantial experience of drama projects for television. Applications may be forwarded to the National Lottery (Arts Council of England) for additional funding. This scheme follows a previous joint initiative between HTV and South West Arts and may well continue in future years.
Closing date: May 1996.

Full announcements of the agency's awards and funding schemes will be made in Autumn 1996.

LOCAL

THE EDINBURGH AND LOTHIAN SCREEN INDUSTRIES OFFICE LTD

Filmhouse, 88 Lothian Road, Edinburgh EH3 9BZ
Tel: 0131-228 5960; Fax: 0131-228 5967
Contact: George Carlaw

This is an independent company set up by the City of Edinburgh and Lothian Regional Council which aims to support film and television production in the region.

Edinburgh Development Fund
Finance: £40,000 a year
The fund, supported by the City of Edinburgh District Council and Lothian and Edinburgh Enterprise Ltd, aims to assist the development of film and television projects in the Edinburgh area. It was set up in 1994 initially with a three year life. It aims to help producers develop scripts or business plans. Applications are invited from commercially oriented projects across the range of feature and short film, non-broadcast video and television programme formats and genres. Loans are provided for the production of original screenplays, the costs of project development, the production of business plans or sales and distribution packaging. The awards panel will look for projects with a high chance of commercial success and for which a high proportion of the location and/or post-production work is likely to be done in Lothian. Full details and an application form are available from the above address.

Edinburgh Producers Development Initiative
Finance: £20,000 a year
This scheme is funded by Lothian and Edinburgh Enterprise Limited to help develop the managing and marketing skills of independent producers in Edinburgh and the Lothians so that they can compete successfully in Scottish, UK and international markets. Assistance is available to individuals, producers and companies who can demonstrate a commitment to the region's economy. It is in the form of bursaries which cover up to 50% of eligible costs. These may include training courses whether in production or business management, activities which help develop international markets, EC funded media programmes, attendance at trade fairs and events. Full details and an application form are available from the above address.

THE GLASGOW FILM FUND

c/o Scottish Film Production Fund,
74 Victoria Crescent Road, Glasgow G12 9JN
Tel: 0141-337 2526; **Fax:** 0141-337 2562
Contact: Eddie Dick
Finance: £300,000

This scheme, administered by the Scottish Film Production Fund (see separate entry), is financed by the Glasgow Development Agency, City of Glasgow District Council, Strathclyde Regional Council and the European Regional Development Fund through the Strathclyde Integrated Development Operation. Any theatrical feature film, of at least 70 minutes duration, shooting in the Glasgow area or produced by, or with, a Glasgow-based company may apply for production finance only. (Projects must be fully developed prior to application.)

The budget for the film should be at least £500,000, and the maximum investment in any one project will be £150,000 or 20% of the production budget, whichever is less. "Shallow Grave" was the first film backed by the fund.

Applications: Potential applicants are advised to obtain full details and then arrange an exploratory meeting to discuss the project. The board meets quarterly to make decisions.

THE MERSEYSIDE FILM PRODUCTION FUND

109 Mount Pleasant, Liverpool L3 5TF
Tel: 0151-708 9858; **Fax:** 0151-708 8959
Contact: Roger Shannon

Grant total: £240,000 (1994/95)

This fund is an initiative of the Moving Image Development Agency (MIDA) supported by the European Regional Development Fund, Liverpool City Council and Merseyside Development Corporation. Top-up finance if offered to producers intending to produce feature films, and dramas of over 60 minutes, in the Merseyside area. "Butterfly Kiss" is one of the productions which has received support.

Applications: Application forms are available.

SHEFFIELD MEDIA DEVELOPMENT FUND

Department of Employment & Economic
Development, Sheffield City Council,
2nd Floor New Town Hall, Sheffield S1 2HH
Tel: 0114-273 6942; Fax: 0114-273 6972
Contact: Ann Tobin, Media Industries Co-ordinator

In October 1995 three new sources of production funding and support were launched with money awarded by the European Regional Development Fund (total value £420,000). In all cases either the production or the producer company must be based in Sheffield or South Yorkshire.

Media Development Fund
Run by Sheffield City Council provides loan finance to develop ideas and scripts so that they can be considered for commercial production. The awards vary in size but generally range between £600 to £5,000.
Applications are called for about three times a year.
Contact: Ann Tobin (see above).

Sheffield and South Yorkshire Production Fund
Run by Sheffield Independent Film helps existing productions which have already attracted some financial backing. The fund will only provide 20% of the total production cost. The investments are repayable out of net profit from the project over a three year period. The fund also helps independent productions to attract funding from other sources.
Contact: Colin Pons, Sheffield Independent Film, 5 Brown Street, Sheffield S1 2BS (0114-249 2204).

Producer Development Fund
Run by the Northern Media School, a branch of Sheffield Hallam University. The fund provides independent projects with help and advice on the business side of film and television production through the offering of consultancy services.
Contact: Jeff Baggot, Business Manager, Northern Media School, The Workstation, 15 Paternoster Row, Sheffield S1 2BX (0114-275-3511).

OTHERS

BBC NEW FILM MAKERS FUND

Room D333, BBC Centre House,
56 Wood Lane, London W12 7SB
Tel: 0181-743 8000
Contact: Jenny Killick, Independents
Development Executive

Two activities are covered by the New Film Makers Fund:

Screen Firsts
Acquires for transmission four to six completed films of between five and twenty minutes long from new film making talent. Apply to the above department.

Brief Encounters
A series of eight short films, each 11 minutes long, jointly commissioned and co-produced by the BBC and Channel Four. All are shot on 35mm with budgets fixed at £80,000 each. The scheme is for new feature writers, directors and producers. It is not open to people who have made a "Brief Encounter" film or a "Short & Curlies" for Channel Four or a feature, although submissions are welcomed from people with experience in television.

Exclusions: No development finance is given, so treatments or outlines are not considered. Completion finance is not given; only the two broadcasters are involved in financing the production.
Applications: No applications forms. Submissions are accepted each year from 1st January to 1st September (no later). Films are commissioned annually in Autumn/Winter. Scripts of 10-15 pages long should be submitted. Only one by a writer.

Submissions can be made to both the BBC and Channel Four as material is exchanged between them. Drama Department, Channel Four TV, 124 Horseferry Road, London SW1P 2TX.

THE LLOYDS BANK CHANNEL 4 FILM CHALLENGE

see entry under "Companies"
Contact: Compulsive Viewing Ltd (0171-284 0060)

These awards for new young scriptwriting talent were in their third year in 1995. A 10 minute script in either drama, documentary, animation or entertainment can be submitted by people between the ages of 11 and 25. The six winning scripts will be made and transmitted nationally on Channel 4. In 1995 the bank added another strand. Once the six winning films have been completed the panel of judges will select the overall winner who will receive a bursary to further their writing/programme making.
Deadline: Mid December.

HERITAGE, LIBRARIES, GALLERIES & MUSEUMS

The British Library
The National Heritage Memorial Fund
The Heritage Grant Fund
The Museums & Galleries Commission
The National Fund for Acquisitions (Scotland)
The Scottish Museums Council
The Council of Museums in Wales
The Northern Ireland Museums Council
Area Museums Councils

See under "The National Lottery"
The Heritage Lottery Fund

See also under "Europe"
Kaleidoscope
RAPHAEL

THE BRITISH LIBRARY

Research and Development Department,
2 Sheraton Street, London W1V 4BH
Tel: 0171-412 7058/7041

Research Grants
Grant total: £1,640,000 (1995/96)
The British Library Research and Development Department is the major funding agency for research and development work in the field of library and information science in the UK. The department has wide-ranging interests which encompass most aspects of the generation, storage, transfer and use of information. The overall aim of the department is to assist in the improvement of the provision of information for the benefit of library and information users of all kinds.

Most of the work supported takes the form of individual, fixed-length projects based either at academic institutions or in working libraries and information services. This does not, however, rule out awards to other types of institution. Most grants fall within the range £5,000-£150,000.

Applications: These are welcome at any time. Applicants should submit outline proposals for discussion, after which full proposals may be invited. Proposals are normally referred externally before a decision is made. Guides available include: *Introducing The Research and Development Department*; *Research Plan 1993-98*; *Guide to the Preparation of a Research Proposal*.

Other special activities of the department:

Study Visits Overseas
Awards are made to enable researchers working on British Library-funded projects to attend meetings or projects related to their research.

The British National Bibliography Research Fund
Grant total: £35,000 each year
For further information – Tel: 0171-412 7044; Fax: 0171-412 7251.

Grants for Cataloguing and Preservation
Grant total: £179,500 (1993/94)
For further information – Tel: 0171-412 7048; Fax: 0171-412 7251.

Special Initiatives of the Department of National Heritage
For further information – 0171-7051/7130; Fax: 0171-412 7251.

Public Library Development Incentive Scheme
This scheme, which was administered for the Department of National Heritage by the British Library for six years from 1988, was discontinued but a successor scheme will start during 1996/97. At this stage (Winter 1996) it is not certain whether the

British Library as the scheme's administrator (though it seems likely). For further information contact: Department of National Heritage Libraries Division Tel: 0171-211 6129.

THE NATIONAL HERITAGE MEMORIAL FUND

10 St James's Street, London SW1A 1EF
Tel: 0171-930 0963; Fax: 0171-930 0968
Mrs Anthea Case, Director

Grants: £9,689,000 (1994/95)
Loans: £759,000 (1994/95)
Number of projects supported: 74

The National Heritage Memorial Fund (NHMF) was set up in 1980 in memory of the people who have given their lives for the United Kingdom. It is now funded annually by the Department of National Heritage but was initially funded by the sale of land compulsorily purchased for military reasons in wartime. The fund's role is to protect land, buildings, objects and collections which are of outstanding interest and are important to the national heritage.

The NHMF has become the national distributor of the Heritage Lottery Fund (see separate entry in the National Lottery section) which has transformed this small organisation greatly increasing it size, powers and responsibilities. However Heritage Memorial Fund still carries out its original functions with which it enjoys wider grant making powers than the Heritage Lottery Fund, and it is able in an emergency to move with great rapidity. Grants and loans are provided for buying items which:

◆ are at risk of being sold abroad, developed, damaged or lost;
◆ have a clear memorial link.

Funding has been provided for land, buildings, works of art, museum collections, manuscripts and items of transport and industrial history. It also provides grants and loans to maintain and preserve most of these items.

Applications should only be made as a last resort, after all other possible sources of funding have been tried. The fund will only pay for the total cost of a project in exceptional cases.

Projects, whether large or small, will only be considered if all the following points apply.

◆ Projects to buy, maintain or preserve land, buildings, objects or collections of outstanding interest and importance to the national heritage.
◆ Projects based in the UK.

- Projects which have already received financial help from other sources of funding but which need more money to be finished off or projects for which no other funding is available.
- Projects to which the public will have access, unless public access might reduce the value of the item.
- Projects which will be financially secure in the long-term.
- Projects where there is a genuine worry that the item is otherwise going to be lost or damaged.

Examples of projects supported in 1994/95

The largest support was given to the National Galleries of Scotland and the Victoria and Albert Museum to retain Canova's "The Three Graces" (£3 million grant plus a loan of £600,000). In addition a challenge grant of £3 million was offered to Dulwich Picture Gallery as part of an endowment to assure its future.

Smaller grants included:

Norfolk Museums Service for John Crome's "Norwich River: Afternoon" (£330,000); North West Film Archive for film preservation (£19,232);

PCC of St Michael and All Angels, Great Witley, conservation of ceiling paintings (£17,447).

Exclusions: Private individuals and businesses. Grants to repair or restore buildings. For such assistance contact: English Heritage, Cadw or Historic Scotland, the Department of the Environment Northern Ireland, or the relevant local authority.

Applications: These should be made in writing and sent to the head of the fund, signed by the chairman, director or chief executive, and with a full justification of the need for help from the fund including:

- The reason for the grant.
- A full description of the project.
- Photographs of the item, and for land and buildings, a map showing exactly where the property is and a site plan.
- Full financial details, including an account of the money already raised or promised from other sources.
- Where appropriate, a formal valuation of the item.
- A description of the body applying for assistance, its finances, and plans to care for/manage the project in the future.

Applications are usually acknowledged within three working days. If the proposal meets all the conditions for applying for grants or loans, the applicant will be informed of the date when the trustees meet.

THE HERITAGE GRANT FUND

Heritage 4, Department of National
Heritage, 3rd Floor, 2-4 Cockspur Street,
London SW1Y 5DH
Tel: 0171-211 6368; **Fax:** 0171-211 6382
Contact: Luella Barker

Grant total: £546,000 (1996/97)

The Heritage Grant Fund (HGF) of the Department of National Heritage assists voluntary organisations in England for activities which further its policy objectives in relation to the historic environment. Normally only organisations providing national coverage are considered for grant although "local projects providing an exemplar of good practice with potential for wider application" are also considered. The two main types of grant are:

- project grants for innovative or experimental projects
- time limited management grants, usually of 3 years, to help meet the administrative or start up costs.

The HGF applies to England only and is not available to support activities covered by other DNH funding, including grants for capital projects such as repairs to historic buildings and monuments available from English Heritage and museums and galleries funding available from the Museum and Galleries Commission and the Museums and Galleries Improvement Fund.

Priorities for 1996/97

- Identifying and recording neglected aspects of the historic environment;
- Promoting high standards in conservation practice;
- Promoting understanding and enjoyment of the historic environment and widening access for all.

Grants have ranged between £2,000 and £60,000 and in 1995/96 a total of 28 grants were made.

Applications: Application forms and grant guidelines are available. Grants are normally limited to 50% of costs, but may be tapered to reduce the percentage of the costs met by grant in later years. Matching income must come from non-public sources.

THE MUSEUMS & GALLERIES COMMISSION

16 Queen Anne's Gate, London SW1H 9AA
Tel: 0171-233 4200; **Fax:** 0171-233 3686
Contact: Ruth Selman, Grants and Lottery Officer

The Museums & Galleries Commission supports the development of museums and galleries in the UK. It promotes their establishment, activities, good management, mutual co-operation and the public's interest in them. It advises on general and specific matters and assists potential benefactors. It is active in advising on and developing conservation skills.

The commission is a registered charity, and incorporated under Royal Charter. It is funded by the Department of National Heritage and in 1994/95 received grant-in-aid of £9 million from the DNH.

MGC grants are a vital source of funding for many non-national museums. Some grants are administered directly, others at 'arm's length' through the English Area Museum Councils, the Science Museum and the Victoria & Albert Museum. The commission provides revenue funding for the seven Area Museum Councils in England. (Those in Scotland, Northern Ireland and Wales receive money from the Scottish, Northern Ireland and Welsh Offices respectively). All grants to museums are given towards specific projects.

MGC/V & A Purchase Grant Fund
Grant total: £1,711,000 (1994/95)
Contact: Purchase Grant Fund Officer, V & A Museum, London SW7 2RL (Tel: 0171-938 9641
This fund, administered by the Victoria and Albert Museum on behalf of the MGC, helps with the purchase of objects relating to the arts, literature and history by non-national museums, art galleries, libraries and record offices in England and Wales. In Scotland a similar scheme is administered by the National Museums of Scotland (see separate entry).

Museums and galleries, record offices and specialist libraries which exist for the benefit of the public and meet professional standards are eligible to apply. They should maintain a permanent collection housed in acceptable conditions, be staffed by suitably qualified personnel, have an acceptable constitution and financial base. Museums and galleries should be fully registered under the MGC scheme. Nationally funded institutions and Friends organisations are not eligible to apply.
Eligible items: Any museum item or collection priced at £500 and over. Manuscripts priced at £350 and over.
Grant-aid available: 50% of the purchase price (exclusive of VAT). Grant aid is calculated at the rate of £2 for each £1 raised from local sources. The balance can be sought from other nationally administered grant-aid schemes (contact the office if advice required on this matter).

In 1994/95 a total of 266 grants were offered (out of 404 applications) ranging from £228 to £80,000. Examples were:

Birmingham Public Libraries, family and personal papers of James Watt (£80,000);

Ipswich Museums and Art Gallery, Anglo-Saxon grave goods from Boss Hall (£46,666);

Harris Museum & Art Gallery, Preston, L S Lowry painting, 1948 (£24,500);

Luton Museum and Art Gallery, straw-hat 1750-60 (£1,955);

Carlisle Museum and Art Gallery, felt hanging by Sally Thompson, 1993 (£600).

Exclusions: Grants are not available for artificial groupings of items priced at less than £500 (£350 for archival material), circulating exhibition services or loan schemes, reproductions, facsimiles, current publications, museum or library equipment, conservation costs, delivery charges, framing charges, valuation charges or for VAT.

Applications: Guidelines and application forms are available from the above address. There is no deadline for applications.

Preservation of Industrial and Scientific Material (PRISM)

Total grants: £254,000 (1994/95)

Contact: The Administrator, PRISM Grant Fund, The Science Museum, South Kensington, London SW7 2DD (Tel: 0171-938 8005; Fax: 0171-938 9736)

The Preservation of Industrial and Scientific Material (PRISM) Fund, administered by the Science Museum on behalf of the MGC, aims to further the preservation in the public domain of items or collections important for the history and development of technology and science in all their branches.

Fully or provisionally registered English and Welsh non-national museums and galleries are eligible to apply. In Scotland a similar scheme is administered by the National Museums of Scotland (see separate entry). Applications may be considered from non MGC registered museums, and charitable organisations at the fund manager's discretion.

Eligible material:
- maximum grant of £20,000 on any individual object or institution in one financial year;
- any moveable object or group of objects illustrating the history of any branch of technology or science (including natural history).
- archives and manuscript material with a significant technological, scientific or industrial content, but excluding books acquired for library or reference purposes.
- applicants must be able to demonstrate that the proposed acquisition or conservation projects agrees with a collecting policy discussed/agreed with other museums which collect in a similar subject/geographical area.

Eligible costs:
- purchase price
- dismantling, transport, re-erection costs
- conservation of material, either on acquisition or from existing collections. Priority will be given to items of more than local significance already in museum collections.

♦ gross costs of less than £500 are not normally considered.

A total of 77 grants were awarded in 1994/95 ranging between £182 and £20,000 43 for acquisition totalling £152,000 and 34 for conservation totalling £103,000). Examples of grants:

Windermere Steamboat Museum, purchase of steam launch "Otto" by Forrest & Sons, Wivenhoe, 1896 (£20,000);

Thackray Medical Museum, orthopaedic correction frame, 17th century (£10,000);

Russell-Cotes Art Gallery & Museum, celestial globe by Cruchley, 1869 (£1,550);

Exclusions: Capital items such as showcases, display material, lighting or environmental control equipment, apparatus for providing motive power for working exhibits; direct labour costs; maintenance and repair; retrospective applications.

Applications: Guidelines and application forms are available from the above address. There are no deadlines for applications.

Conservation Unit Grants

Grant total: approximately £105,000 (1995/96)

Additional funds are raised through sponsorship, eg. Conservation Awards Scheme funded by the Jerwood Foundation

Contact: Grants and Lottery Unit. Tel: 0171-233 4200

The aim of the Conservation Unit's grant programme is to promote and encourage high standards of conservation practice within England, Wales and Northern Ireland. In Scotland grants are available from Historic Scotland: Scottish Conservation Bureau.

Grant proposals should demonstrate that they lead to an identifiable improvement in the expertise or facilities available or the public appreciation of conservation. The Unit therefore supports individual practising conservators in both the institutional and private sectors, conservation workshops, and training and research establishments.

Following a re-evaluation, grants are available under the following headings:

♦ Ongoing professional development (closing dates 1 March, 1 June, 1 September, 1 December)
♦ Development of strategic services (closing date 1 June)
♦ Publications and exhibitions grants (closing date 1 June)
♦ Student placements (support up to £20,000 used amongst the major training courses; no individual support)
♦ Internships (details circulated direct to relevant training courses)
♦ Conservation research, contribution to SERC/CASE studentships
♦ Jerwood Conservation Awards, 4 winners in 1995/96
♦ Gabo Trust for Sculpture Conservation, travelling scholarships

Grants are not given for conservation or research work, consumables, primary training courses or attendances at IAP Summer Schools (which are funded directly). Normally, not more than 50% of the total project costs can be covered. Grants range from £100 to £10,000.

Applications: Full details, guidelines and application forms are available from the Grants and Lottery Unit.

Travel Grants
Grant total: £10,000 (1995/96)
Contact: Grants and Lottery Officer, MGC
Grants are available to assist with the cost of study tours to museums and other appropriate sites and towards the cost of attending museum-related conferences outside the UK.
Eligible costs: Travel, conference fees, accommodation and subsistence. The grants are only available to permanent UK residents working in museums or museum-related bodies. Priority is given to applicants who would not normally have direct access to funds for overseas travel, and to those working in registered museums. Preference is given to applicants with additional sources of support, and to tour proposals which clearly serve to develop longer-term museum links. The maximum grant available will be £300 within Europe and £500 for the rest of the world, or 50% of total cost, which ever is the lower figure.
In 1994/95 30 grants were awarded ranging between £60 and £800.
Applications: Guidelines and application forms are available. Closing dates for 1996/97: 22nd March, 1st June, 1st September, 1st December 1996

THE NATIONAL FUND FOR ACQUISITIONS (SCOTLAND)

Royal Museum of Scotland, Chambers Street,
Edinburgh EH1 1JF
Tel: 0131-225 7534; **Fax:** 0131-247 4308
Contact: Hazel Williamson, Fund Administrator

Grant total: £285,000 (1995/96)

The fund is provided annually by the Scottish Office to the trustees of the National Museums of Scotland and is administered by the NMS. The fund is divided into two parts:

The Art Fund
Grant total: £188,000 in 153 grants, 1994/95
This fund assists in the acquisition of objects relating to the arts, literature and history. Only exceptionally can this fund be used to assist with the dismantling and removal of objects. Grants for the conservation of objects will not normally be made, although potential conservation needs should be covered in all applications.

The Science Fund

Grant total: £82,000 in 19 grants, 1994/95

This fund assists with the acquisition of objects and manuscripts relating to the history of science, natural sciences, technology, industry and medicine. Grants may be made towards dismantling, emergency restoration, transport and re-assembly, where these are closely connected to the acquisition process.

Not for profit museums, art galleries, libraries, record offices and other similar institutions in Scotland can apply. The collection must be permanent, housed in suitable conditions, normally open to the public, and staffed or supervised by qualified personnel.

For museums and galleries, grants may be made to assist in the purchase of any appropriate object, or group of objects. For libraries and record offices, grants may be made to assist in the purchase of works of art, printed items in rare or limited editions or of local or specialist interest (other than reproductions or current publications), manuscripts, manuscript maps or plans, documents and archival photographs.

From time to time the NMS director may vary the balance between the Art Fund and the Science Fund, in order to encourage acquisition from one or other sector. The total amount of grant payable in any particular case will be at the discretion of the NMS director subject to the following conditions:

- The maximum level of grant will normally be 50% of total eligible costs;
- In assessing the level of assistance, account will be taken of any other sources of funding of a national character (for example, the National Heritage Memorial Fund or the National Art-Collections Fund);
- At least 25% of the total costs must be forthcoming from local sources, whether from the applicant's own resources, or from contributions made by private individuals, locally-administered charitable trusts etc.

The director may specify a maximum figure for assistance towards the purchase of any single object; he may also set a limit on the amount of assistance receivable by any one institution within a financial year.

Examples of grants offered in 1994/95:

Aberdeen University Library, Letter signed by James 1, 1615 (£450);

Tweeddale Museum, treasure trove – hoard of 282 denarii dug up by a forestry worker in 1994 (£3,612).

Exclusions: Normally the museums and galleries of private societies or commercial companies are excluded from this scheme, as are the nationally funded museums and galleries. Grants are not made for the purchase or restoration of museum, gallery or library equipment, for framing, or for display materials. Friends organisations are not eligible to apply. Grants will not be made towards the acquisition of objects (or coherent groups of objects) whose value is less than £100.

Applications: A booklet of guidance to applicants should be obtained first. This section only covers some key points.

An application form must be completed and signed by the chairman of the governing body of the applying institution, or the curator or other head. A photograph of the object should be enclosed wherever possible. In the case of books and manuscripts this may be a photocopy of as much of the material as is required to show its nature and quality.

Bids at auction sales can cause problems and at least five working days are normally required prior to the sale for proper assessment.

No application can be considered where the object is the subject of a binding agreement to purchase or has already been acquired and paid for.

Decisions on grant applications are made after consultation, as appropriate, with staff of the three Scottish National Institutions (NMS, the National Galleries of Scotland and the National Library of Scotland). The decision reached by the Director of the NMS is final.

THE SCOTTISH MUSEUMS COUNCIL

County House, 20-22 Torphichen Street,
Edinburgh ED3 8JB
Tel: 0131-229 7465; **Fax:** 0131-229 2728
Jane Ryder, Director

Grant Total: £287,000 (1996/97)

The Scottish Museums Council is an independent body with charitable status funded principally by the Secretary of State for Scotland via the Scottish Office Education Department. The council's main aim is to improve the quality of local museum provision in Scotland.

Membership is open to local authorities, independent museums and galleries, historic houses – in fact to any museum, gallery or similar body in Scotland. Full membership of the Council is open to all local authorities and to the governing bodies of museums registered under the Museums & Galleries Commission's registration scheme. (Associate membership, open to museum projects in their early stages, and to similar collections-based organisations, entitles a museum to all council membership benefits except grant-aid.)

The council represents the interests of local museums in Scotland, and all members can benefit from the council's advisory, training and information services. Members eligible for grant-aid have access to a wide range of financial assistance schemes (revenue funding is not provided). To qualify for financial assistance, a museum's constitution or trust deed must be approved by the Scottish Museums Council. There are further detailed provisions about what is expected from trustees and staff.

Grants are available for the following:

- Management, Marketing and Fundraising;
- Collections Management and Conservation - including Conservation Management & Planning, Documentation, Environmental Monitoring & Control, Security, Remedial Conservation, Storage;
- Training;
- Interpretation - including interpretive Planning, Premises and Equipment, Touring Exhibitions, Publications, Environmental Initiative Projects;
- Education;
- New Posts.

In addition the council runs:

- The Small Museums Fund for limited but immediate response to the needs of small independent museums;
- The Conservation Fund for immediate response to remedial conservation costs or projects which cannot be incorporated in grant-aid applications;
- endorsement

The Environmental Initiative 1994/1997 (jointly managed by the Scottish Museums Council, Scottish Natural Heritage and the Crown Estate) promotes appreciation of the environment through Scotland's museums. Projects may be eligible for funding from the council and a range of other bodies. For further information contact the Environmental Initiative Co-ordinator based at the council.

Exclusions: Revenue funding; purchase of objects for collections; work funded through insurance claims.

Applications: Grant applications should be discussed with council staff at an early stage. Further details on criteria for grant-making under each of the headings listed above is available from the Finance Manager. (NB Minimum application value: £200 from any member with an annual budget over £18,000.)

THE COUNCIL OF MUSEUMS IN WALES

The Courtyard, Letty Street, Cathays, Cardiff CF2 4EL
Tel: 01222-225432/228238; Fax: 01222-668516
D Gareth Davies, Director

Grant Total: £193,000 (1994/95)

The Council of Museums in Wales is a membership body composed of local authorities and non-nationally funded museums registered with the Museums and Galleries Commission within the Principality. The spectrum ranges from small society museums through to large municipal institutions and includes regimental, university and country house museums besides industrial complexes. It is established as a charitable, limited company mainly funded by Welsh Office grant-in-aid and based in Cardiff with a second office in North Wales. It fosters the preservation of the Welsh heritage through support of local museums as both a provider and enabler. In the former role it offers professional, management, curatorial, conservation and training advice; training packages; display services including travelling exhibitions. It also represents its members at local and national level. As an enabler the council administers governmental, subscription and earned income as grant aid for project and challenge-funding to eligible museums (MGC registered).

Priority areas in 1996/97, which feature in CMW's forward plan are:

- Subsidised Post Scheme
- Care of Collections
- Training
- Education

- Marketing
- MGC Registration
- Display and Interpretation

In 1994/95 a total of £193,00 was awarded in 154 grants. Its annual report showed these listed in the following categories:

- Subsidised Curator Scheme: £77,000 (11 grants);
- Conservation: £34,300 (61 grants) covering Arts, Antiquities, Furniture, Natural History;
- Collection/Museum Management: £34,200 (53 grants) covering Environmental Control/Equipment, Storage/Equipment, Documentation, Security, Training, Marketing, Education;
- Feasibility Studies: £459 (1 grant);
- Capital Projects: £10,303 (6 grants);
- Display/Exhibitions: £36,608 (22 grants).

Applications: The bulk of grant applications are processed together in February/March for availability early in the incoming financial year, though depending on resources awards continue to be made throughout the period. Projects should be discussed with council officers well in advance of submission.

NORTHERN IRELAND MUSEUMS COUNCIL

185 Stranmillis Road, Belfast BT9 5DU
Tel: 01232-661023; Fax: 01232-683513
Aidan Walsh, Director

Grant total: £31,000 (1994/95)

The council is a non-departmental public body set up as an independent charity. Its core funding is provided by the Department of Education Northern Ireland. It provides advisory, information and training services as well as grant-aid.

Grants for improvement and new development are mainly available to council members. Up to 50% of the total cost of the project or purchase is provided. 21 projects and purchases were supported in 1994/95. These grants ranged from under £100 to £3,800.

Grants can cover:

* Collections care including preventive and remedial conservation, documentation, security and storage;
* Education services;
* Marketing and promotion;
* Interpretation, design and display;
* Feasibility studies;
* Travel and training;
* Specimen purchase fund; a new fund to help by arts, literature, archaeology, history and science artefacts. This fund was expected to exceed £20,000 in 1995/96.

AREA MUSEUMS COUNCILS

Grant total: £5.8 million for all ten councils (1996/97); £4.37 million for the seven councils in England (1996/97)

The Area Museum Councils (AMCs) are the regional development agencies charged with the support of charitable trust, university and local authority museums. They are independent charitable companies run by their members; these include virtually all the 1,650 registered museums in the UK. They offer their members a range of advisory services and training, as well as (in some cases) technical services like design and conservation.

They work very closely with other regional agencies (eg. Regional Arts Boards) and government departments, and can provide a strategic overview and information on the museum scene in their regions. AMCs advise the Heritage Lottery Fund and the Regional Government Offices on grant applications from museums. They are particularly well placed to advise on proposals to set up new museums or redevelop existing ones. They can also recommend consultants for more detailed studies.

The AMCs receive grant from the government channelled through the Museums & Galleries Commission. They offer grants to their members in support of improvements. These are normally 50% of the project cost, (occasionally higher) and are one-off grants for specific short-term projects. *AMCs do not offer revenue funding.*

Each AMC determines its grant priorities according to its particular development strategy, and potential applicants normally discuss their plans well in advance with AMC staff. Grants are equally available to the very smallest and the very largest museums.

Types of project eligible for AMC grant include:

◆ Improvements to display and other developments;
◆ Marketing initiatives;
◆ Development of new educational activities;
◆ Improvements to access for people with disabilities;
◆ Training for staff and volunteers;
◆ Improvements to the environmental conditions, storage, documentation or security of collections;
◆ Conservation of objects;
◆ Networking between museums.

Committee of Area Museum Councils (the co-ordinatory body for all 10 councils including those for Scotland, Wales and Northern Ireland)
141 Cheltenham Road, Cirencester, Gloucestershire GL7 2JF
Tel & Fax: 01285-640428; Crispin Paine, Secretary

West Midlands Area Museums Service
Hanbury Road Stoke Prior, Bromsgrove B60 4AD
Tel: 01527-872258; Fax: 01527-576960; Kathy Gee, Director

North of England Museums Service
House of Recovery, Bath Lane, Newcastle upon Tyne NE4 5SQ
Tel: 0191-222 1661; Fax: 0191-261 4725; Sue Underwood, Director

East Midlands Museums Service
Courtyard Buildings, Wollaton Park, Nottingham NG8 2AE
Tel: 01602-854534; Fax: 01602-280038; Adrian Babbidge, Director

North West Museums Service
Griffin Lodge, Cavendish Place, Blackburn BB2 2PH
Tel: 01254-670211; Fax: 01254-2681995; Ian Taylor, Director

Area Museums Council for the South West
Hestercombe House, Cheddon Fitzpaine, Taunton TA2 8LQ
Tel: 01823-259696; Fax: 01823-413114; Sam Hunt, Director

Yorkshire & Humberside Museums Council
Farnley Hall, Hall Lane, Leeds LS12 5HA
Tel: 0133-263 8909; Fax: 0113-279 1479; Barbara Woroncow, Director

South Eastern Museums Service
Ferroners House, Barbican, London EC2Y 8AA
Tel: 0171-600 0219; Fax: 0171-600 2581; Dan Chadwick, Director

See separate entries for the museums councils in Scotland, Wales and Northern Ireland.

THE NORTHERN IRELAND COMMUNITY RELATIONS COUNCIL, CULTURAL TRADITIONS GROUP

6 Murray Street, Belfast BT1 6DN
Tel: 01232-439953; Fax: 01232-235208
Contact: Dr Maura Crozier, Development Officer

Grant total: £280,000 (1994/95)

The council was established in 1990 as a registered charity and limited company with the aim to increase understanding and co-operation between political, cultural and religious communities in Northern Ireland. The Cultural Traditions Group is a committee of the NI Community Relations Council (Dr Jonathan Bardon, Chairman, Sean Nolan, Vice-chairman). It operates a number of grant schemes to support community relations work including:

Local Cultural Traditions Grant Scheme
(approx. £100,000 in 1995/96)
Aimed at community and voluntary groups developing projects to encourage cultural confidence and acceptance of cultural diversity. Projects may involve groups

in single-identity work as well as work exploring local traditions other than their own. Many cultural traditions projects also have across-community base. Grants up to £1,500. Most grants do not exceed £500. One hundred and ten groups were supported in 1994/95 and included:

Centre Stage, towards costs of a play about Louis McNeice and W R Rodgers;
Making Links, intergenerational community art project in L'Derry;
Ardoyne Fleadh Project, arts, craft and cultural workshops;
Gown Literary Supplement, towards a new magazine on new writing and arts;
Holywell Trust, training course for beginners in musical and cultural traditions.

Cultural Traditions Publications Grant Scheme
(£100,000 in 1995/96)

Helps to subsidise publications, which have found a publisher and which promote the cultural traditions objectives of the council, to reach a wider audience. Seventeen publishers received support in 1994/95 for a larger number of publications. Applications from Northern Ireland publishers only.

Media Grants
(£80,000 in 1995/96)

Supports professional, independent television/film projects which contribute to a better understanding of cultural diversity and community issues within Northern Ireland. Since 1992 this scheme has taken the form of an annual competition, advertised in the local press. There were eight winners in 1994/95.

Cultural Traditions Fellowships

Available for one year, are advertised annually. Six fellowships of about £6,000 each were awarded in 1993.

The Community Relations Council also provides core funding grants to a number of reconciliation, community and cultural traditions groups. These have included: Belfast Youth & Community Theatre, the Federation of Ulster Local Studies and Pointfields Theatre Company.

Exclusions: No grants available for capital costs.
Applications: Contact the office for the grant booklet and application forms.

EDUCATION & YOUTH

Department of Education and
    Employment, Youth Service Unit
Youth Work Development Grants
Scottish Office Education & Industry
    Department
Welsh Office Education Department
Welsh Language Board

See also under "International"
The Commonwealth Youth Exchange
    Council
The Youth Exchange Centre
Youth for Europe

DEPARTMENT FOR EDUCATION AND EMPLOYMENT

Youth Service Unit
Sanctuary Buildings, Great Smith Street,
London SW1P 3BT
Tel: 0171-925 5270; Fax: 0171925 6954
Contact: Geoff Murray

Grants to National Voluntary Youth Organisations (NVYOs)
Grant total: £9.1 million (for the three years 1996/99)
Through its schemes of grants to NVYOs, the department seeks to promote the personal and social education of young people through programmes of work which offer them opportunities that are participative, educative and enabling. A fresh three-year scheme effective from April 1996 to March 1999, is aimed at 13-19 year olds in particular and gives priority to work involving the disadvantaged, the disabled, those from rural areas and from minority ethnic communities, especially where this may contribute to crime prevention, health education, the encouragement of volunteering and the participation of young people themselves.

Over the three years of the scheme over 60 organisations will share some £9.1 million of grant. Among these are arts -based organisations, including the National Association of Youth Theatres, the National Youth Orchestra of Great Britain, the National Youth and Music Theatre and the National Youth Theatre of Great Britain.

YOUTH WORK DEVELOPMENT GRANTS

National Youth Agency,
17-23 Albion Street, Leicester LE1 6GD
Tel: 0116-285 6789
Contact: Terry Cane

Grant total: £400,000 every 3 years

The three-year scheme is supported through local authority funding and is administered on behalf of the local authorities by the National Youth Agency (NYA). Under the scheme grants of up to three years' duration may be made to local or regional voluntary organisations for projects involving significantly new pieces of work in priority areas which could provide examples of good practice for dissemination to the field. The next tranche of funding will be considered in December 1999.

SCOTTISH OFFICE EDUCATION & INDUSTRY DEPARTMENT

Arts & Cultural Heritage Division
1st Floor West, Victoria Quay,
Edinburgh EH6 6QQ
Tel: 0131-244 0337; **Fax:** 0131-244 0353
Contact: David M Tulloch

The Scottish Office Education and Industry Department is responsible for the administration of public education in Scotland; youth and community services; the arts; libraries; museums and galleries; sport; investment and expansion of Scottish industry at home and abroad; tourism and energy related matters.

Grants for Cultural Organisations
Grant total: £738,000 (1995/96)
Under the provisions of Section 23 of the National Heritage (Scotland) Act 1985, the department can make grants to cultural organisations. To be considered for a grant an organisation must show the ability to promote the practice or understanding of the arts or cultural topics. Some of its activities must be broadly educational. It must demonstrate that its membership or support is drawn from the whole of Scotland or that its activities are of benefit nationally. An organisation must also show that it is financially sound and is actively seeking funds from relevant sources, including sponsorship. In 1995/96 grants ranged in size from £1,170 to £243,000.

Grants relevant to this guide were given in 1995/96 to:

Sabhal Mor Ostaig (£135,450);

Scottish Youth Theatre (£62,920);

National Youth Orchestra of Scotland (£42,000);

An Comunn Gaidhealach (£40,750);

Scottish Community Drama Association (£25,175).

Applications: Grant guidelines and application forms are available from the above address. All applications received by 30 September will considered for funding in the following financial year.

WELSH OFFICE EDUCATION DEPARTMENT

Cathays Parc, Cardiff CF1 3NQ
Tel: 01222-825111
Contact: Russell Dobbins (01222-825854)

Grants to National Voluntary Youth Organisations in Wales
Grant total: £371,000 in 19 grants (1995/96)
Under the provisions of the Education (Grant) Regulations 1990 the Welsh Office is empowered to make grants to national voluntary youth organisations (NVYOs) in Wales.

The scheme aims to assist youth work organisations to increase the extent and quality of programmes of informal and social education for young people in Wales. Grant is available for central costs and project-based work over a period of up to three years.
Applications: Detailed guidance notes and application forms can be obtained from Further and Higher Education Division 2 of the Welsh Office Education Department. Information and advice on the scheme and youth work in Wales generally can be obtained from the Wales Youth Agency, Llys Leslie, Lon y Lon, Caerphilly, Mid Glamorgan CF8 1BQ (Tel/Fax: 01222-880088/824)
Contact: Gareth Ioan.

WELSH LANGUAGE BOARD

Market Chambers, 5-7 St Mary Street,
Cardiff CF1 2AT
Tel: 01222-224744; Fax: 01222-224577
Contact: Efa Geuffudd, Grants Officer

Grant total: £680,000 (1996/97)

The board, established under the Welsh Language Act and funded by the Welsh Office, aims to increase and facilitate the use of Welsh. Grants are given for both core funding and for projects. In 1996/97 a total of 56 organisations received firm offers of grant support ranging from £87,261 to Menter Cwm Gwendraeth to £127 to the British Association of Art Therapists.

The board is seeking to develop a Small Grants Scheme in 1996 to encourage more use of Welsh in the private and voluntary sector whereby grants to 50% of the total cost up to a maximum £500 contribution may be made towards the cost of translating, designing and publishing materials in Welsh. Make enquiries of the grants officer about this progress of this scheme.

Applications: Full guidelines are available. Application forms are available from July. Deadline for applications 1 November, for support in the following financial year.

Contact the grants officer for advice.

ECONOMIC & SOCIAL DEVELOPMENT

Single Regeneration Budget
Urban Development Corporations
Training & Enterprise Council/TEC National
    Council
Scottish Enterprise
Highlands and Islands Enterprise Network
The Rural Development Commission
The Rural Development Council for
    Northern Ireland

See also under "Europe"
Structural Funds
    European Social Fund
    Regional Development Fund

SINGLE REGENERATION BUDGET

The Single Regeneration Budget (SRB) which started in 1994, combines 20 separate programmes under one banner. These had previously been operated by four different government departments: the Department of the Environment, Home Office, the Department for Education and Employment and the Department of Trade and Industry. The aim of SRB is to provide a more flexible fund for local regeneration in a way which meets local needs and priorities. Programmes that now form part of the wider SRB include:

◆ Urban Development Corporations (see separate entry)
◆ City Challenge (the forerunner to the Challenge Fund and based on the same principles of partnership and competition and now paid via the Challenge Fund) 31 City Challenge winners each receive £7.5 million a year over a 5 year period for the social, economic and environmental regeneration of their areas.

Most of the budget for SRB is administered by the new Government Offices for the Regions which co-ordinate the main programmes and policies at local level and ensure that businesses and local government have just one port of call.

Challenge Fund

From 1995/96 a proportion of SRB has been devoted to its Challenge Fund which encourages local communities to come up with comprehensive packages to improve the quality of life in their area.

Challenge Fund partnerships are expected to involve a diverse range of organisations in their management and should harness the talent, resources and experience of local business people, the voluntary sector and the local community.

Challenge Fund bids are expected to include some or all of the following objectives:

◆ enhance the employment prospects, education and skills of local peality of opportunity;
◆ encourage sustainable economic growth and wealth creation by improving the competitiveness of the local economy, including support for new and existing businesses;
◆ promote and improve the environment and infrastructure and promote good design;
◆ improve housing and housing conditions for local people through physical improvements, better maintenance, improved management and greater choice and diversity;
◆ promote initiatives of benefit to ethnic minorities;
◆ tackle crime and improve community safety;
◆ enhance the quality of life of local people, including their health and cultural and sports opportunities.

Funding is made available in response to "bids" submitted to the relevant regional offices. Bids are expected to maximise both the leverage of private sector investment and co-ordination with European Structural Funds. Bids are expected to "harness the talents and resources of the voluntary sector and volunteers and involve local communities". Funding will be available for bids lasting from one to seven years, if resources permit. A strong emphasis is placed on the need for local partnerships between relevant bodies in submitting bids. Likely partners are local authorities, TECs, the private sector, other public bodies, the voluntary sector and the local community.

Small free-standing schemes, especially those which do not link into a local regeneration strategy, are unlikely to achieve, either locally or collectively, the comprehensive impact which the Challenge Fund is intended to encourage. However fund resources can contribute to a comprehensive strategy concentrated on a relatively small area eg. a rundown town centre, one or more housing estates or a large, multi-faceted development site.

Some examples of SRB Challenge Fund partnerships with arts projects:

Brighton Regeneration Partnership
The Print (£675,000 over 2 years; total budget £1.619 million, plus a lottery bid)
The plan is to secure a redundant office block and convert it for use by people connected with the cultural industries sector and other local arts and community groups. Public access workspace is a key feature within this project.
Fabrica (£80,000 over 3 years; total budget approx £440,000, not including Lottery bid)
Fabrica, the company set up Red Herring and other arts groups, are converting the former Holy Trinity church in Brighton Centre into an arts centre. Work has started on the building in conjunction with Southern Arts and the local community. The building will form a focal point for networking between local artists and will enable direct exchange with the public through workshops, discussions and conferences.
Brighton Media Centre (£360,000 over 3 years; total budget over £1 million)
The Media Centre has been a successful initiative to co-locate small companies and agencies working across the spectrum of media disciplines and is moving ahead with a second phase which will allow expansion and a greater degree of public contact and access.

Reading Borough Council - Oxford Road Partnership
The keep building at Brock Barracks houses two artists' groups who run a complex of studios for individual artists. One of the groups, Open Hand Studios, has also programmed and managed a small public gallery with exhibitions, workshops and lectures. This area of work is currently being expanded, and in 1997 a new gallery and workshop space will be opening. This will be a regional cultural facility focusing on contemporary art, and has already attracted £100,000 of capital funding from Southern Arts, the Foundation for Sport and the Arts and Reading Borough Council. The Challenge Fund is supporting the following programmes at this base:

+ educational and community workshops relating to the exhibitions programme at the new gallery;

- outreach projects with schools and community groups in the Oxford Road area involving artists.

In addition the Challenge Fund will support:

- the employment of artists to be part of the design team undertaking environmental improvements in the area. Their brief will be to create opportunities for community involvement in the design and implementation of the improvements so they are responsive to the needs of people living and working in the area, reflecting the local identity;
- a programme of community-based arts projects under two headings: "Through Our Eyes" and "Home from Home". These projects have already been run successfully with groups throughout Reading and aim to enable people in the area to explore and communicate their concerns and aspirations in an effective and imaginative way. The "Home from Home" projects is specifically for ethnic communities.

Other arts related initiatives supported:

Luton Media Centre;

Octavia Hill Museum, Wisbech and Angles Theatre, Wisbech;

Middlesborough Multi-Media Centre;

Palace Theatre, Plymouth.

Funding: A second bidding round was launched in April 1995 which will build up to £200 million spend in 1997/98, with £40 million available in 1996/97 for early funding of approved projects.

Applications: A guide to funding from the SRB is available from the regional offices. The bidding round opens in April for funding in the following year, and bids should be submitted at the beginning of September.

Information: Invaluable information and advice for voluntary organisations is contained in *"The Single Regeneration Budget Handbook, A Guide to Making Bids to the Challenge Fund"* by Greg Clark, published by the National Council for Voluntary Organisations, Regent's Wharf, 8 All Saints Street, London N1 9RL Tel: 0171-713 6161; Fax: 0171-713 6300 £8.25 including p&p.

SRB Regional Contacts

Government Office for the Eastern Region
Heron House, 40-50 Goldington Road, Bedford MK20 3LL;
Tel: 01234-276106; Fax: 01234-276252

Government Office for the East Midlands
The Belgrave Centre, Stanley Place, Talbot Street, Nottingham NG1 5GG;
Tel: 0115-971 9971; Fax: 0115-971 2558

Government Office for London
Room 2606 Millbank Tower, 21-24 Millbank, London SW1P 4QU;
Tel: 0171-217 4657; Fax: 0171-217 4509

Government Office for Merseyside
Room 424, Graeme House, Derby Square, Liverpool L2 7SU;
Tel: 0151-224 6467; Fax: 0151-224 6470

Government Office for the North East
Stanegate House, Groat Market, Newcastle Upon Tyne NE1 1YN;
Tel: 0191-201 3300; Fax: 0191-202 3830

Government Office for the
North West
Room 1317, Sunley Tower, Piccadilly
Plaza, Manchester M1 4BE;
Tel: 0161-952 4303; Fax: 0161-952 4365

Government Office for the South East
Bridge House, 1 Walnut Tree Close,
Guildford, Surrey GU1 4GA;
Tel: 01483-882322; Fax: 01483-882309

Government Office for the
South West
Room 220 Tollgate House,
Houlton Street, Bristol BS2 9DJ;
Tel: 0117-987 8122; Fax: 0117-987 8269

Government Office for the
West Midlands
Room 818 Fiveways Tower,
Frederick Road, Edgbaston,
Birmingham B15 1SJ;
Tel: 0121-626 2733; Fax: 0121-626 3699

Government Office for the
Yorkshire and Humberside
Room 1213 City House,
New Station Road, Leeds LS1 4JD;
Tel: 0113-283 6402; Fax: 0113-283 6653

Scotland
Until 1996 the Urban Programme co-ordinated at the Scottish Office provided competitive funding for regeneration schemes in the most deprived areas of Scotland. Applications were made via the relevant local authority and arts groups have been funded in this way. The Urban Programme was under review in Spring 1996 and in future local authorities themselves may be in charge of their own budgets for more wide-ranging regeneration strategies.

Contact the Scottish Office or the Economic Development Department or equivalent section of your local authority to find out up-to-date information.

Scottish Office, New St Andrew's House, St James Centre, Edinburgh EH1 3TG
Tel: 0131-244 5285; Contact: David Hart, Assistant Secretary

Wales
Welsh Office, Cathays Park, Cardiff CF1 3NQ; Tel: 01222-823770
Contact: Dr Ian Thomas

Northern Ireland
Northern Ireland Office, Brookmount Building, 42 Fountain Street, Belfast BT1 5EE; Tel: 01232-251455; Fax: 01232-251951; Contact: Tony McCusker

URBAN DEVELOPMENT CORPORATIONS

Grant total: over £11 million, for voluntary
organisations and the provision of social
facilities (1993/94)

Urban Development Corporations (UDCs) are public bodies established to secure
the regeneration of inner-city areas by "bringing land and buildings into effective
use, encouraging the development of existing and new industry and commerce,
creating an attractive environment and ensuring that housing and social facilities
are available to encourage people to live and work in the area". UDCs have general
powers to hold land, carry out building, provide services and generally "do anything
necessary or expedient" to regenerate their areas.

An UDC has the powers to provide grants to encourage firms to develop and
expand in inner areas. It may also make loans (at rates of interest agreed by the
Treasury) for building on land it has sold or let. Commercially viable projects are
normally financed by loan. However, there are few such projects because the type
of work carried out by the UDCs (with emphasis on preparing difficult sites for
disposal to the private sector, rather than carrying through the development itself)
is not inherently profitable. Grant-eligible activities include the acquisition,
reclamation and preparation of land; the provision of roads and services;
environmental works and works for the restoration of historic buildings; support
for the provision of health, education, training and community facilities, and for
the voluntary sector.

Applications: The applications procedure varies according to the type of assistance
being sought. Details are available direct from each UDC.

Further information: *Urban Development Corporations Division*, Room N19/06,
Department of the Environment, 2 Marsham Street, London SW1P 3EB
Tel: 0171-276 4498/4603; Fax: 0171276 0732.

All the English UDCs except Sheffield are scheduled to wind-up on 31 March 1998.

Birmingham Heartlands: Tel: 0121-333 3060; Fax: 0121-333 3246;
Black Country: Tel: 0121-511 2000; Fax: 0121-552 0490;
London Docklands: Tel: 0171-512 3000; Fax: 0171-512 0777;
Central Manchester: Tel: 0161-236 1166; Fax: 0161-236 7615;
Merseyside: Tel: 0151-236 6090; Fax: 0151-227 3174;
Plymouth: 0175-225 6132; Fax: 0175-225 6133;
Sheffield: Tel: 0114-272 0100; Fax: 0114 272 6359 (wind-up date March 31 1997);
Teesside Tel: 0164-267 7123; Fax: 0164-267 6123;
Trafford Park: Tel: 0161-848 8000; Fax: 0161-848 8638;
Tyne and Wear: Tel: 0191-226 1234; Fax: 0191-226 1388;
Cardiff Bay: Welsh Office 01222-823733;
Laganside: Northern Ireland Office 01232-328507.

TRAINING AND ENTERPRISE COUNCILS/ TEC NATIONAL COUNCIL

Westminster Tower, 3 Albert Embankment,
London SE1 7SX
Tel: 0171-735 0010; **Fax:** 0171-735 0090
Contact: Godfrey Blakeley, Press Officer

Training and Enterprise Councils (TECs) have responsibility for the delivery of youth and adult training, together with a number of other government programmes.

There are 82 TECs, covering England and Wales. In Scotland, similar work is the responsibility of the network of local enterprise companies (LECS, see separate entry).

Each TEC is an independent company operating under a contract with the Secretary of State for Employment. Each TEC has a Board of Directors of between 9 and 15 members, two thirds of whom have to be appointed from the private sector with the remaining places open to local authorities, the voluntary sector, trade unions, education authorities and other in the community. Each TEC has its own priorities and methods of operating and links with arts (and entertainment) are made in a variety of ways. The main programmes through which they could work are:

- Training for work
- Youth training for those aged between 16-24
- Investors in People, the staff development programme
- New business start-up schemes providing business skills training and support
- Business training schemes – specialist and high quality training

Training for Work Scheme
The Training for Work Scheme was introduced in April 1993, replacing the Employment Training Scheme (ET), the Youth Training Scheme (YT) and High Technology National Training (HTNT). The objective of Training for Work is to help unemployed people aged from 18 to 59 to find jobs and improve their work-related skills, through the provision of appropriate training and structured work activity in line with assessed needs. Priority is given to unemployed people with disabilities, and people who have been unemployed for 12 months and who have been referred from an Employment Service Jobplan workshop. TECS are free to deliver the mix of skills training, work preparation and temporary work they judge appropriate to the local labour market. Arts organisations providing services under the Training for Work scheme and other Employment Service schemes compete with other providers for TEC contracts. Decisions about the value of contracts and the structure and staging of payments is a matter for individual TECs to decide at the local level. This is complicated by a move to funding in arrears and performance-

based contracts which allow a proportion of the funding to be paid on delivery of certain defined positive outcomes.

Training providers awarded contracts are paid a unit price per trainee week. Travel and childcare costs are in some cases included in the unit cost.

The changes to the funding system coupled with the uncertainty about the securing of contracts has resulted in problems for many voluntary organisations. Nevertheless many continue to provide training through contracts with TECs. In many cases, TECs are rationalising the numbers of training providers with which they contract directly. Many training organisations may therefore have to rely on sub-contracts with the main contractors.

Training providers contracting with the TEC to provide services may apply for a loan through the TEC from the Working Capital Loan Fund to help overcome the difficulties which are likely to be encountered for voluntary organisations dealing with a system of payment in arrears.

Local Initiatives Fund

Each operational TEC has a Local Initiatives Fund which is used to support innovative projects in training and enterprise. This funding has to be matched from other sources and contributions from other public sources are not eligible. The size of this fund varies from TEC to TEC. For further information about this contact your local TEC.

Small businesses start-up schemes

In the past, groups of artists, particularly those in the visual arts and crafts fields, have benefited from the former Enterprise Allowance Scheme which offered help to unemployed people who wished to set up their own businesses. Nowadays TECS each have a range of schemes to support new small businesses. The schemes vary from TEC to TEC, and you should apply to your local TEC for details of the schemes operating in your area.

Ethnic Minority Grant

Section 11 Ethnic Minority Grant (EMG) is a Home Office grant scheme administered through TECs whereby voluntary organisations provide services in the field of training, employment and enterprise for people from ethnic minority communities. Projects have to fall within the general remit of TECs, and they must meet an identifiable need to overcome disadvantage. The key requirement is to demonstrate a special need in the target group that cannot be properly addressed without the additional help of a specific grant. The normal rate of grant will be 75% but there is a possibility that a higher rate may be payable in exceptional circumstances.

Voluntary organisations can apply direct for EMG to a TEC which will consider applications and decide whether to pass them onto the Home Office for approval. TECs are not obliged to pass on applications to the Home Office. A TEC is required to consult with voluntary groups, ethnic minority communities and other agencies such as the local authority.

Further information and application forms may be obtained from the relevant TEC.

Scottish Enterprise

120 Bothwell Street, Glasgow G2 7JP
Tel: 0141-248 2700; Fax: 0141-228 2511

The Scottish Enterprise Network comprises 13 local enterprise companies (LECs) established to help build the economy and improve the quality of life in the areas they cover. It has also taken over responsibility in the southern half of Scotland for the delivery of youth and adult training. A range of grants, business loans, financial and marketing advice is available for business and small or new firms. Each LEC operates its own schemes and the relevant regional offices (see contact points below) should be able to assist with details.

It is worth quoting from the 1994/95 Scottish Arts Council Annual Report. "The LECs are increasingly recognising that the arts have an economic as well as social role to play in the development of a community. This was very much the case when Scottish Borders Enterprise led the development of the River Tweed Festival."

The following scheme is common to all LECs operating in urban areas:

Local Enterprise Grants for Urban Projects (LEG-UP)
This scheme aims to promote economic developments and environmental improvements in urban areas of particular social, economic and environmental need by encouraging private-sector investment in appropriate projects.

Priority is reserved for project in areas of high unemployment or extreme urban dereliction. LEG-UP places no restriction on the type of project eligible provided it fits the schemes main objectives.

Network Members
Dumfries & Galloway Enterprise Co, Dumfries; Tel: 01387-245000;
Fax: 01387-246224;
Fife Enterprise Ltd, Glenrothes; Tel: 01592-621000; Fax: 01592-742609;
Grampian Enterprise Co, Aberdeen; Tel: 01224-211500; Fax: 01224-213417;
Dunbartonshire Enterprise, Glasgow; Tel: 0141-951 2121; Fax: 0141-951 1907;
Forth Valley Enterprise, Stirling; Tel: 01786-451919; Fax: 01786-478123;
Lanarkshire Development Agency, Bellshill; Tel: 01698-745454;
Fax: 01698-842211;
Renfrewshire Enterprise, Paisley; Tel: 0141-8480101; Fax: 0141-848 6930;
Scottish Enterprise Tayside, Dundee; Tel: 01382-223100; Fax: 01382-201319;
Enterprise Ayrshire, Kilmarnock; Tel: 01563-526623; Fax: 01563-543636;
Glasgow Development Agency, Glasgow; Tel: 0141-204 111; Fax: 0141-248 1600;
Lothian and Edinburgh Enterprise Ltd, Edinburgh; Tel: 0131-313 4000;
Fax: 0131-313 4231;
Scottish Borders Enterprise, Galashiels; Tel: 01896-758991; 01896-758625

HIGHLANDS AND ISLANDS ENTERPRISE NETWORK

Bridge House, 20 Bridge Street, Inverness IVI IQR
Tel: 01463-244271; **Fax:** 01463-244331
Contact: Robert Livingstone, HI Arts Ltd,
Arts Development Officer

The Highlands and Islands Enterprise Network, launched in April 1991, comprises Highlands and Islands Enterprise (HIE) at the core, and ten Local Enterprise Companies (LECs) established to help the people and the communities of the northern half of Scotland improve their economic and social conditions. The HIE core provides a strategic overview for the network of LECs. Each LEC is run by a board of directors drawn from local businesses and other key sectors of the local community. The LECs provide most of HIE's services to the areas in which they operate. HIE's central office provides technical and financial back-up for those projects which cross LEC boundaries, are of strategic benefit to the Highlands and Islands as a whole and which, even within a single LEC's area, are beyond its individual resources.

One of HIE's stated objectives is "to maintain and develop the social community and cultural values of the different parts of the area", and has made the following statement about how it will support the arts: "Highlands and Islands Enterprise wishes to support and assist projects or events which use the arts in the broadest sense to stimulate social and economic development and thus enhance and strengthen the sense of cultural identity in the area. It hopes to enhance and build on present arts activity and also to encourage new initiatives".

HI Arts (Highlands & Islands Arts Ltd) has been set up as an independent body funded by HIE and the Scottish Arts Council to further the proactive role of HIE in arts development, a unique initiative in the context of UK development agencies. It can provide information and advice on approaching either HIE centrally, or any of the 10 LECs.

Criteria for Assistance
Proposals should come from properly constituted voluntary organisations or groups whose membership is open to the whole community. Funding will be for new or enhanced projects, rather than towards normal running costs. Highlands and Islands Enterprise will not normally be the sole funders and groups will be expected to look for funds from other public and private sources. Proposals should satisfy as many of the criteria listed as possible. Projects or events should:

• Recognise or reflect the culture of the Highlands and Islands, enhancing and developing the local community's sense of place and identity;

• Have the potential to act as the starting point for further arts activity in the future. The project or event itself need not necessarily continue, but the effect should;

- Be participatory and try to involve as wide a range of people as possible, with particular emphasis on the young;
- Foster links between different groups, organisations and schools in a community;
- Motivate and inspire people to use arts activity as a means of expression;
- Establish, create and develop links between traditional skills and new arts activity and experiences;
- Develop links between communities in the Highlands and Islands;
- Help generate income and jobs;
- Include scope for evaluation with a view to potential future arts activity in the community;
- Appeal to visitors and enrich their experiences of the Highlands and Islands.

Examples of recent recipients from HIE central funds:

Highland Festival, towards start-up costs of this new festival (£40,000);

Invisible Bouncers Theatre Company, to assist restructuring and development of a new tour (£5,000);

Examples of recent grants from LECs

Nairn Performing Arts Guild, for mounting performances (£1,967);

Orkney Camerata, for purchase of equipment (£400);

Ballet West for tour of "Cinderella" in Argyll and the Islands (£8,500).

Network Members

Argyll & The Islands Enterprise,
Lochgilphead;
Tel: 01546-602281/602563;
Fax: 01546-603964

Caithness & Sutherland Enterprise,
Thurso;
Tel: 01847-66115; Fax: 01847-63383

Inverness & Nairn Enterprise,
Inverness;
Tel: 01463-713504; Fax: 01463-712002

Lochaber Limited,
Fort William;
Tel: 01397-702160; Fax: 01397-705309

Moray, Badenoch, & Strathspey Enterprise Company, Elgin;
Tel: 01343-550567; Fax: 01343-550678;

Orkney Enterprise, Kirkwall;
Tel: 01856-874638; Fax: 01856-872915

Ross & Cromarty Enterprise,
Invergordon;
Tel: 01349-853666; Fax: 01349-853833

Shetland Enterprise, Lerwick;
Tel: 01595-3177; Fax: 01595-3208

Skye & Lochalsh Enterprise, Portree;
Tel: 01478-612841; Fax: 01478-612164

Western Isles Enterprise, Stornoway;
Tel: 01851-703625; Fax: 01851-704130

THE RURAL DEVELOPMENT COMMISSION

Dacre House, 19 Dacre Street,
London SWiH ODH
Tel: 0171-340 2900

The Rural Development Commission is the government's agency for economic and social development in rural England. As such one of its key aims is to stimulate job creation and the provision of essential services in the countryside.

In its *Rural Development Areas*, it can provide advice and funding for a wide range of arts and arts related projects. The majority are focused on the needs of the local community and include: video projects with socially disadvantaged youngsters, resource materials for remote communities, rural arts workers (such as animateurs and writers in residence), as well as improvements to theatres and other arts centres. Many, however, are linked to the improvement of the local economy and it tourist attractions. These would include heritage and exhibition centres, museums, festivals and arts education for residents and visitors.

The Commission can also assist established businesses in the arts and crafts, so long as they are eligible, and provides training courses in seven craft trades, such as forgework, furniture restoration and saddlery. Across rural England the Commission has a grant scheme for village halls and community centres, particularly to assist in extending the use of these buildings.

The Commission also provides funding to and works closely with the 38 Rural Community Councils. Through the RCCs many local arts projects are developed and supported.

Arts projects supported during 1995/96 included:

The Almonry, Somerset, workshop, gallery and courses (£18,000);
Decorative Arts Exhibition Centre, West Midlands (£15,000);
Farm based Art Centre, East Anglia, includes workshop and sales area (£15,000);
Disability Arts, Yorkshire (£10,000 over 2 years);
Village Activities Projects, Isle of Wight (£9,600);
Play/Art Development Worker, North West (£4,500);
Video Box Project, East Durham (£2,900);
North Pennine Concert Hall (£2,500);
Dance Animateur, East Lindsay, Lincolnshire (£2,500);
Hebden Bridge Arts Festival, Yorkshire (£2,000);
Seahouse Museum, North West (£1,000).

A total of £127,000 was disbursed to 20 projects by potters, picture framers, textiles and a glassblower.

For general information contact:

Information Section,
Rural Development Commission,
141 Castle Street, Salisbury,
Wilts SP1 3TP
Tel: 01722-336255; Fax: 01722-432773

For individual projects contact the
relevant Commission Area Office:

**Durham, Cleveland, Northumberland,
Tyne & Wear**
Morton Road, Yarm Road Industrial
Estate, Darlington, Co Durham DL1 4PT
Tel: 01325-487123; Fax: 01325-488108

Humberside & Yorkshire
Spitfire House, Aviator Court,
Clifton Moor, York YO3 4UZ
Tel: 01904-693335; Fax: 01904-693288

Cheshire, Cumbria, Lancashire
Hawesworth Road, Penrith,
Cumbria CA11 7EH
Tel: 01768-865752; Fax: 01768-890414

**Derbyshire, Leicestershire,
Lincolnshire, Nottinghamshire**
18 Market Place, Bingham,
Nottingham NG1 8AP
Tel: 01949-876200; Fax: 01949-876222

**Gloucestershire, Hereford & Worcester,
Shropshire, Staffordshire, Warwickshire**
Strickland House, The Lawns,
Park Street, Wellington, Telford,
Shropshire TF1 3BX
Tel: 01952-247161; Fax: 01952-248700

**Bedfordshire, Cambridgeshire, Essex,
Hertfordshire, Norfolk,
Northamptonshire, Suffolk**
Lees Smith House, 12 Looms Lane,
Bury St Edmunds, Suffolk IP33 1HE
Tel: 01284-701743; Fax: 01284-704640

**Oxfordshire, Buckinghamshire,
Berkshire, Kent, Surrey, E & W Sussex,
Hampshire, Isle of Wight**
Sterling House, 7 Ashford Road,
Maidstone, Kent ME14 5BJ
Tel: 01622-765222; Fax: 01622-662102

Avon, Dorset, Somerset, Wiltshire
3 Chartfield House, Castle, Street,
Taunton, Somerset TA1 4AS
Tel: 01823-276905; Fax: 01823-338673

Cornwall, Isles of Scilly, Devon
27 Victoria Park Road, Exeter,
Devon EX2 4NT
Tel: 01392-421245; Fax: 01392-421244

THE RURAL DEVELOPMENT COUNCIL FOR NORTHERN IRELAND

Loughry College, Cookstown, Co Tyrone,
Northern Ireland BT80 9AA
Tel: 016487-66980; **Fax:** 016487-66922

Grant total: £280,000 annually

The RDC can grant aid disadvantaged rural communities who want to become involved in the economic and social development of their area. It is particularly interested in assisting with the costs of identifying, appraising, planning and running projects which will create employment. Training in technical and managerial skills are also eligible. Small grants are also available to help communities include a wider range of people in their activities and get them working effectively as a group.

Most of the grant budget is paid in the communities targeted for assistance on the recommendation of the three Project Managers following local consultation. Groups in communities not so targeted may also receive support if they are: established as a community group; located in a disadvantaged rural area; representative of their community; a not-for-profit organisation.

Grants offered in 1994/95 included:

Community Radio 1994, business plan and evaluation (£2,000);
Dungiven Community Hall, to establish and develop arts activities (£400);
Glens of Antrim Historical Society, renting and furnishing office space (£2,000).

Exclusions: Capital costs involved in project start-up.
Applications: Obtain guidelines on grant-aid for full details. Advice and guidance will initially be given by the Project Managers (see names below). Applications are sent to the main office in Cookstown. Decisions of grants of less than £5,000 will be made by staff. Larger grants are decided at a full council meeting.

West Region (Fermanagh, Omagh, and Strabane District Council areas)
Contact: Ms Moninne Dargan

North Region (Derry, Limavady, Coleraine, Moyle, Ballymena, Ballymoney, Larne, Magherafelt and Cookstown District Council areas)
Contact: Albert Hunter

South Region (Dungannon, Armagh, Newry & Mourne, Down, Ards, Craigavon and Banbridge District Council areas)
Contact: Shaun Henry

PART TWO

INTERNATIONAL PROGRAMMES

General introduction

British support for visits/exchanges

European programmes

Funding from the USA

INTRODUCTION

This section falls into three areas of information:
1. British programmes facilitating visits/exchanges to and from the UK;
2. Funding from Europe;
3. Funding from the USA.

All organisations developing a project to take place overseas or wanting to arrange visits from other countries should be sure to be in early contact with the ministries of culture and the arts councils in those countries. Most embassies have cultural branches which can be an invaluable source of advice and contacts. Many developed countries have specific budgets for international activities. Sometimes there are associated organisations eg. the Japan Foundation in London, the Japanese equivalent of the British Council, which can provide support for exhibitions, film production and publications.

   All readers are urged to make early approaches to the advice and information provided by the International Arts Bureau in London, the International Cultural Desk in Edinburgh and the British American Arts Association (see information which follows).

INTERNATIONAL ARTS BUREAU LTD

4 Baden Place, Crosby Row, London SE1 1YW
Tel: 0171-403 7001; Fax: 0171-403 2009
Contact: Rod Fisher; Fiona Gallagher

This independent bureau was set up in 1994 and undertakes the services previously covered by the International Affairs Unit of the Arts Council of England. These include:

An information service for all arts related bodies, individual artists, researchers etc, covering:
- the organisation and cultural policies of the European Union, Council of Europe, UNESCO etc;
- Funding opportunities available from overseas institutions, foundations, schemes and funding from the UK for overseas visits, exchanges and projects;
- contact addresses of ministries of culture, arts councils and arts organisations overseas, international cultural networks, arts management training overseas;
- Structures, policies, research and good practice in different countries;

◆ sources of information on the arts overseas.

The service is free, but a fee may be charged for enquiries needing extensive research. Telephone or fax the above number *Tuesdays to Thursdays 19.00-13.00 and 14.00-17.00.*

Monthly advice surgeries, also free, are held usually on a Friday. Ring of fax to book an appointment for a one-to-one discussion.

Publications include:
More Bread and Circuses: Who does what for the Arts in Europe (previous title *European Funding Guide for the Arts*) by Louise Scott.
A comprehensive guide to the policies and funding potential of the supra-national and intergovernmental agencies and pan-European foundations including the European Commission, Council of Europe and UNESCO. It describes measures in the cultural, audiovisual, educational and training, young people and cultural co-operation fields etc relevant to those working in the performing arts, music, visual arts, film, video, architectural heritage and museums. Case studies of grant recipients of each of the schemes brings the often daunting and impersonal guidelines to life. They are all the more valuable because the greater part of European Community funds for culture originate from programmes and schemes designed to fulfil other objectives. A vital tool to help negotiate Brussels funding mechanisms. Published 1995; 488 pages; £27.00 including postage.

International Update; published 10 x pa; rates between £130 and £250 according to status.

International Arts Digest; quarterly; produced for the Arts Council of England and available with the *Arts Council News*.

THE INTERNATIONAL CULTURAL DESK

6 Belmont Crescent, Glasgow G12 8ES
Tel: 0141-339 0090; **Fax:** 0141-337 2271
Contact: Hilde Bollen, Development Manager

The International Cultural Desk is an independent organisation, jointly established in 1994 by the British Council, the Scottish Arts Council and the Scottish Museums Council with additional funding from Scottish Enterprise and Highlands and Islands Enterprise.

It is the first central clearing house in Scotland for enquiries about international opportunities in the arts and culture. It aims to assist Scottish arts and cultural community to operate more effectively in an international context. It deals with all art forms and practices except film where the Scottish Film Council (see separate entry) provides its own information service. It is concentrating initially on Europe and North America, but plans to extend its work to cover countries in Australasia, Central/South America, Asia and Africa.

The desk produces Fact Sheets and "Communication", a bi-monthly information update; £8.00 (individuals); £20.00 (non-profit organisations); £40.00 (other).

British Support for Visits & Exchanges

The British Council Arts Division

The Visiting Arts Office of Great Britain and
  Northern Ireland

Youth Exchange Centre (and Youth for Europe)

Commonwealth Youth Exchange

THE BRITISH COUNCIL ARTS DIVISION

11 Portland Place, London W1N 4EJ
Tel: 0171-930 8466; **Fax:** 0171-389 3199
Contact: John Tod, Arts Division Director

The aim of the British Council is to promote cultural, educational and technical co-operation between Britain and other countries. Its work is designed to develop worldwide partnerships and improve international understanding. It promotes British ideas, talent and experience primarily through the provision of education and training services, books and periodicals, English language teaching and the management of arts events.

The council is represented in 224 towns and cities in 109 countries. It provides an impressive network of contacts with government departments, universities, embassies, professional bodies, arts organisations and businesses in Britain and overseas.

The council's 1994/95 turnover was £426 million, made up of government grants, expenditure on behalf of Britain's overseas aid programme and revenue from contract work, English teaching and other services. It also seeks commercial sponsorship for many of its arts events.

In developing countries the council covers most of the costs of its arts events, though elsewhere its financial contribution can drop to very modest grants. It works in close partnership with overseas venues and festivals, and most requests for financial support come from overseas partners.

In 1994/95 about 5 per cent of its total budget went on arts expenditure and only a small part of this sum was given in direct subsidies. Each year the council assists about 2,000 British drama, dance, music, literature and arts events, tours or exhibitions to take place in a variety of countries. It does not usually make 100% grants but contributes only to certain expenses involved in the presentation of arts events abroad.

The council's Arts Division consists of five departments: Visual Arts; Drama and Dance; Music; Literature; Film, Television and Video. Each department is supported by an advisory committee of specialists in the relevant fields Expenditure figures for each department vary widely from year to year, depending on whether major exhibitions, tours etc are being mounted by a department in any one year. It also has an Exhibitions and Audio Visual Unit which produces exhibitions and displays and gives advice on design promotion.

The British Council also administers the Visiting Arts Office of Great Britain and Northern Ireland (see separate entry) on behalf of the Foreign and Commonwealth Office and the Arts Councils.

Visual Arts
Contact: Andrea Rose (0171-389 3055)
The Visual Arts Department operates a Grants to Artists Scheme which assists British Artists to exhibit overseas in public and commercial galleries etc. The scheme is open to all working in the visual arts and crafts who:

♦ Live and work in the UK and have exhibited their work professionally;

◆ Have a firm offer in writing on an exhibition or other project. This offer must state clearly the financial contributions being made by the gallery or organisers.

Grants are given only as contributions towards the transport, packing and insurance of their work and for artist's travel expenses if necessary. The council's Grants to the Artists Committee requires slides of the applicant's recent work to be submitted, and decisions on grants are made on the basis of these slides.

The Subsidies Scheme is intended to complement the department's exhibition activities by providing assistance to public museums or galleries abroad for exhibitions of British art organised without the department's administrative involvement. These are generally solo exhibitions of well-established artists and the subsidies are seen as contributions to the costs borne by the receiving institution, such as international freight or catalogue. They are sometimes supplemented by funding from the overseas offices.

Most initial applications are received by British Council representatives from the host galleries in the countries concerned, but some applications are considered from artists based in Britain who have been invited to show in a gallery overseas. The average subsidy ranges between £2,000 and £3,000.

Applications: For further details of these schemes write to Visual Arts Department. Applications can be submitted up to nine months in advance of the exhibition date concerned.

Examples of support: In 1995 the British Council selected Leon Kossof to represent Britain at the Centenary Venice Biennale and also organised an exhibition of young British artists for the Biennale entitled "General Release". Both exhibitions subsequently travelled to other venues in Europe. In Japan British sculpture was given prominence where the newly opened Metropolitan Museum of Art presented a major retrospective of the work of Sir Anthony Caro. Other exhibitions included "From London" focusing on the six painters at the heart of the "School of London": Francis Bacon, Lucien Freud, Leon Kossof, Frank Auerbach, Michael Andrews and R B Kitaj. Drawing on the council's own extensive collection of twentieth century British art was "Out of the Wood", an exhibition of woodcuts and engravings which had a very successful tour of India.

Drama and Dance
Contact: Simon Gammell (0171-389 3074)

The Drama and Dance Department supports overseas tours by British companies and other forms of joint activity abroad, such as co-productions, professional exchanges, and educational programmes. The department sometimes manages tours in consultation with the council's overseas network and receiving venues. More often it contributes to a company or individual's touring costs, eg towards fees and/or travel expenses. The department will seldom support a tour without having seen the production/s, and it will only support companies with a reputation for artistic excellence. The selection process is monitored by an advisory committee and advice is regularly sought from the Arts Councils and Regional Arts Boards. Works by British playwrights and choreographers are preferred for overseas touring, but this is by no means an exclusive condition. Proposals must fit in with the council's art policy in each of the countries in its network.

Applications: Applicants should approach the council as early as possible. Applicants who have already secured funding from other sources, such as an overseas venue, are more likely to succeed. Further information can be obtained from the department's information officer (0171-389 3097).

Examples of support: A wide range of British dance and theatre toured throughout the world in 1995 and included Cheek by Jowl's production of the "Duchess of Malfi" seen by over 35,000 people in 14 countries across five continents. St Petersburg had its first ever taste of British contemporary dance when the Sioban Davies Company performed "Wild Translations" and "The Art of Touch". Theatre contributed to development issues in a joint British Ugandan production of Bertolt Brecht's "Mother Courage".

Music

Contact: Glynne Stackhouse (0171-389 3069)

The Music Department supports tours that accord with the council's objectives in overseas countries, usually through subsidy towards a proportion of the costs. All forms of music are in principle eligible for support, including opera, early music, classical and contemporary music, jazz, folk and rock music. There must be a substantial amount of British music in the tour repertoire, and there is a growing preference for projects that integrate performance with collaborative, developmental, educational or cross-cultural activity to make a longer-term contribution to the musical life of the country concerned. Musicians must be of high artistic standard with a national reputation in their field. The department seeks opinions on these points from its advisory committee and from the Arts Councils and Regional Arts Boards.

Applications: Proposals, which should show a firm commitment on the part of the overseas promoter to meet a good proportion of the costs involved, should reach the department at least three, and preferably six months before the start of an overseas tour. Preliminary approaches are welcome at any time. Further details may be obtained from the department's information officer (0171-389 3085).

Examples of support: In 1995, the tercentenary of Henry Purcell's death the council supported over 50 events featuring his music and created an exhibition of his life and times that toured 60 countries. A highlight was a joint Syrian British Production of "Dido and Aeneas", whose total audience exceeded 30,000.

Films, Television and Video

Contact: Sean Lewis (0171-389 3061)

The Films, Television and Video Department offers facilities and advice for submitting films to international film festivals, aimed at young film makers and small independent companies. On average about 200 films are entered for 50-60 festivals each year. However, the department does not offer grants towards film production.

Examples of support: In 1995 the council provided feature films and shorts for international festivals ranging from Brussels to Istanbul, from Singapore to Wellintron. With the BFI it co-ordinated the British Stand at the Berlin Film Festival. It's exhibition "Birth of the Movies: was shown in 28 countries.

Literature

Contact: Dr Neil Gilroy-Scott (0171-389 3169)

The Literature Department organises overseas reading tours by British writers and participation in literary festivals and events in response to invitations from other countries. The costs of these visits are met by the council's office in the country concerned and local sponsors, not by Literature Department. The department also promotes British literature through a programme of exhibitions, publications and seminars.

Examples of support: Led by A S Byatt, Alan Hollingshurst and Malcolm Bradbury, three teams of writers who had contributed to the council's annual anthology "New Writing", published by Vantage, toured Germany reading to large audiences in Berlin, Leipzig and Cologne. As a direct result a number of universities will be using "New Writing" for courses on contemporary British writing. A number of library seminars were also held to encourage the development of closer ties between writers, academics, publishers and editors.

Exhibitions Audio-Visual Unit: Christopher Wade (0171-389 3161)

THE VISITING ARTS OFFICE OF GREAT BRITAIN AND NORTHERN IRELAND

11 Portland Place, London WIN 4EJ
Tel: 0171-389 3019; **Fax:** 0171-389 3016
Contact: Terry Sandell, Director

Visiting Arts is a joint venture of the national Arts Councils (England, Scotland, Wales and Northern Ireland), the Crafts Council, the Foreign & Commonwealth Office and the British Council.

It provides consultancy, advisory services, information, training (eg. seminars for UK promoters and arts administrators on the practical aspects of foreign arts visits), and publications (Visiting Arts magazine and Asia Pacific Arts Directory).

It funds specific research in current Visiting Arts priority areas and the following project development grants.

Country Project Awards
Grant total: about £420,000 annually

Most grants are between £2,000 and 35,000 but the situation is flexible. These awards cover the performing arts, visual arts, crafts, design, literature, architecture and applied arts with particular emphasis on contemporary work. However in those cases where the culture of a particular country is best represented by its traditional or folkloric art, the presentation of this is encouraged.

Successful applications under the scheme would normally have been either initiated or encouraged by VA from the outset, or have involved VA during the development of the project. For this reason, although there are no specific deadlines, late applications are normally not able to be considered. Guidelines, criteria and priorities, which vary according to overseas regions, are frequently updated which is an additional reason for close and early involvement of VA in any project.

Eligibility: British promoters and venues promoting quality foreign work which has a clear country specific dimension, which can demonstrate its contribution to the development of cultural awareness and cultural relations and which will produce some kind of continuing impact, influence or follow-up.

In the case of touring events (which are very much encouraged) grants are given to the promoter, organisation or venue which has primary responsibility for the project within the UK.

The degree and quality of direct collaboration with artists and arts organisations in the foreign country are considered important.

Grants are normally given only for foreign companies or artists who have not previously been presented in the UK. In certain cases however, where all other criteria are being met, consideration might possibly be given to the presentation of a company or artists in one region even though previously shown in another.

The degree to which a project is supported either financially or administratively by the cultural authorities and institutions of the country concerned is another factor which is taken into account.

Awards can be made for project-related research and development including necessary travel abroad especially where the UK promoter has been invited by an institution of the overseas country concerned.

Applications: There are no deadlines. Applicants should contact VA for full information about criteria and geographical priorities and/or write giving an outline of the project proposal. Application forms will be sent to those satisfying the essential criteria.

THE COMMONWEALTH YOUTH EXCHANGE COUNCIL

7 Lion Yard, Tremadoc Road, London SW4 7NQ
Tel: 0171-498 6151; **Fax:** 0171-720 5403
Contact: Vic Craggs, Director
Grants allocated: £173,000 (1994/95)

The Commonwealth Youth Exchange Council (CYEC) promotes educational exchange visits between groups of young people in the UK and their contemporaries in all other Commonwealth countries (by means of two-way youth exchange visits. It is established as a national charity which is financed largely by the government through the Youth Exchange Centre (see previous entry) and the Education Department via its National Voluntary Youth Organisations Scheme (see separate entry). CYEC's role includes the provision of advice, information, training and grant aid. CYEC also initiates special projects and organises conferences for young people.

CYEC's funding priorities are: young people who would not normally have the opportunity to take part in an international project; exchanges with Commonwealth countries in Africa, Asia and the Caribbean; local British groups rather than national ones.

Groups should normally number between five and 13 participants, excluding leaders. At least two-thirds of the group must be within the age-range 16-25. UK groups must host as well as visit. One-way visits are not eligible for funding. Return visits should take place within two years. Visits must last at least 21 days for exchanges outside Europe, and at least 14 days for Cyprus, Malta and Gibraltar.

Young hosts must participate together as a fully integrated group. The joint programme should include sustained activity which may, for example, focus on a particular theme, interest or activity, be about the local community or be broadly based on youth issues. Performance tours are not fundable. The programme should include joint social/cultural activities and, if possible, family home-stay experiences. Arts-based cross-cultural youth exchange programmes have proved very successful with examples ranging from youth theatre exchanges to the use of art forms (drama, music, dance, murals, writing, mime, puppetry, photography, video) as key joint activities at the heart of a programme.

Grants are given on a per head basis and represent up to 35% of international travel or hosting costs.

In 1994/95 grants ranged from £170 to £4,500 with a total of 78 group visits supported (43 outgoing from Britain and 35 incoming). Over a thousand young people took part. The average grant covers 20% of the costs of an exchange visit.

Applications: Detailed guidelines and application forms are available on request (SAE required). Potential applicants should make contact with CYEC as early as possible to discuss their proposals. Applications must be submitted during the autumn and at least nine months prior to a visit.

THE YOUTH EXCHANGE CENTRE

The British Council, 10 Spring Gardens,
London SW1A 2BN
Tel: 0171-389 4030; **Fax:** 0171-389 4030
Contact: Ian Pawlby, Head; Gordon Blakely,
Head of Programmes; Joan Anthony,
Information Officer
Grant total: £1,712,000 (1994/95)
Total number of exchange visits: 1,560

The Youth Exchange Centre (YEC), a department of the British Council, promotes international youth exchanges through the provision of advice, information, training and grants. It is funded by the Foreign and Commonwealth Office, through the British Council's grant in aid (£1,918,000 in 1993/94) and by the Department for Education (£245,000 in 1993/94). The Department of Employment also funds YEC for the management of UK Youth Initiative Projects of the European Union PETRA Programme (£16,000 in 1993/94). In addition the YEC is the UK national agency for the European Union funded programme, *Youth for Europe*, which promotes youth exchanges between the EU member states. Priority is given to exchanges involving disadvantaged young people.

The YEC gives grants to British youth groups towards the costs of travelling abroad and hosting visits to the UK by youth groups from other countries. Grants are available for youth exchanges in West and East Europe, the USA and Japan. For Commonwealth countries, separate application should be made to the Commonwealth Youth Exchange Council (see following entry).

Most exchanges supported by the YEC are based around a theme or project, organised by young people themselves, as a free-time activity. These may include arts or cultural projects, environmental or young people's issues.

The YEC has established a series of 12 UK regional committees, comprising youth officers from the statutory and voluntary sectors, and young people. They provide information and training to their local constituencies and also make decisions on grant applications from youth groups within their region.

Grant aid is available to groups of young people aged between 15-25 years. Groups should normally number jointly between 8 and 40 participants.

A minimum duration is recommended, dependent on the country concerned, both for visiting and for hosting. The usual duration, excluding travel, is as follows:

West & East Europe 7 days

USA and elsewhere 21 days

A reciprocal visit must be planned to take place within two calendar years of any initial visit.

The YEC is not able to support the full cost of an exchange programme. Support is given to the round-trip travel costs to the UK group and to their hosting costs in Britain. Normally a grant is calculated and given on a per head basis. Grants are given for a particular financial year. If the project is postponed to another financial year the grant must be returned.

Recurrent funding on an annual basis is not guaranteed and after three years the exchange will be reviewed. Each application is assessed individually, but an average grant would be approximately 30-40% of the travel or hosting costs.

Advance Planning Visit bursaries are available for youth exchange organisers wishing to plan the detail of the exchange with their partner organiser.

Exclusions: Grants are not given retrospectively. The YEC is unable to support: exchanges involving the youth wings of single political parties; tours by performances groups to several countries, or several cities in one country; tours by sporting groups where the purpose is purely competition; one-way visits with no prospect of a return visit (apart from trinational or multinational exchanges funded under Youth for Europe); visits of a purely touristic nature; exchanges which are part of the stated curriculum of an educational establishment.

Applications: Full guidelines and an application form are available. Applications should be submitted at least 12 weeks before the exchange takes place.

YOUTH FOR EUROPE

The British Council, 10 Spring Gardens,
London SW1A 2BN
Tel: 0171-389 4030; Fax: 0171-389 4030
Contact: Ian Pawlby, Head; Gordon Blakely,
Head of Programmes; Joan Anthony,
Information Officer

Exchanges lasting at least one week for young people between the ages of 15 and 25 from two or more Member States may be supported up to 50% of the total expenditure of both the travel and the programme.

Exclusions: Projects taking place within the context of formal education or vocational training are not eligible.

Applications: This programme is administered in the UK by the Youth Exchange Centre (see separate entry).

EUROPEAN PROGRAMMES

FUNDING FROM EUROPE

This section highlights some key avenues of funding in Europe. It should be regarded as an introduction to potential sources of funds, rather than an exhaustive survey of all possible schemes of assistance available. For more detailed information on the cultural role and policies of the supra-national and inter-governmental organisations, and the opportunities they may provide as sources of finance and documentation, readers are advised to contact the International Arts Bureau in London or the International Cultural Desk in Glasgow (see separate entries) and to obtain a copy of *"More Bread and Circuses. Who does what for the arts in Europe?"* available from the International Arts Bureau (see information below for details) and the Arts Council of England.

THE EUROPEAN UNION

Funding for cultural projects from the European Union (EU) originates principally from three departments of the European Commission: Audiovisual Information, Communication and Culture (DGX); Employment, Industrial Relations, Social Affairs (DGV); and Regional Policy (DGXVI). Of these, only the funds from DGX are provided specifically for cultural aims. When aid has been obtained for arts projects through the European Social Fund (DGV) or the European Regional Development Fund (DGXVI), for example, almost invariably it has been in fulfilment of non-arts objectives such as the training of young unemployed people, or tourism infra-structure projects which have created jobs in areas of high unemployment. Thus ingenuity is often a pre-requisite for prospective applicants to enable them to devise projects which meet different sets of criteria without losing their cultural value in the process. Normally the EU's grants are given for limited periods, usually one year. Once a grant has been agreed, the sum cannot usually be increased.

You should also consider whether there is scope for involving organisations involved in similar work in other EU countries or for making a project more relevant to an EU policy. A European dimension to your work will increase the chances of receiving EU financial aid, and is essential in the case of aid from DGX's Cultural Action Office.

Below are some brief descriptions of some of the EU Schemes and programmes of particular interest to the arts world.

Applications: It is understood that the European offices prefer application forms to be obtained from the offices in the member country. When writing for application forms for any of these schemes, ask for an indication of how long applications take to be processed and what the average size of grant is so you can pitch your application accordingly.

Decisions on allocation of funds are often made in January when the EU financial year starts so in those cases where no closing date is specified, it is important to submit applications by November at the latest for schemes requiring funding in the following year. However, pockets of money occasionally become available at other times during the year and, as with government departments here, sometimes unspent money needs to be allocated quickly by the end of the financial year. The Arts Councils and International Arts Bureau may be able to advise you of such short-notice funding opportunities.

UK Offices of the European Union
Representation for the UK
Jean Monnet House, 8 Storey's Gate, London SW1P 3AT; Tel: 0171-973 1992; Fax: 0171-973 1900

Office for Wales
4 Cathedral Close, Cardiff CF1 9SG; Tel: 01222-371 631; Fax: 01222-395 489

Office for Scotland
9 Alva Street, Edinburgh EH2 4PH; Tel: 0131-225 2058; Fax: 0131-226 4105

Office for Northern Ireland
Windsor House, 9/15 Bedford Street, Belfast BT2 7EG; Tel: 01232-240 708; Fax: 01232- 248 241

STRUCTURAL FUNDS

THE EUROPEAN SOCIAL FUND

The European Social Fund (ESF) is one of the three structural funds established under the Treaty of Rome to strengthen social cohesion within the Community. ESF aims to help improve employment opportunities in the European Union by contributing towards the running costs of vocational training, guidance, job creation schemes and employment measures run by a variety of organisations.

Great Britain is a significant beneficiary of ESF (some 20% of the total available). In England and Wales the Department for Education and Employment (DFEE) is responsible for the administration, through its ESF Unit. In Scotland and Northern Ireland, the Scottish Office and Northern Ireland Offices are responsible. The Department of Trade and Industry has overall responsibility for the European Regional Development Fund, another of the Structural Funds.

There are five priority directives, called Objectives:
Objective 1: to improve the development of regions which are currently underdeveloped. Only organisations within these designated areas may apply for Objective 1 money. At present there are three Objective 1 areas in the UK – Northern Ireland, Merseyside and the Highlands and Islands of Scotland.
Objective 2: to regenerate designated areas affected by industrial decline. Only organisations within these designated areas may apply for Objective 2 money. Priorities for Objective 2 include assistance for the development of small and medium-sized

enterprises (SMEs), improving the image and attractiveness of a region, tourism and research and development. At present there are a number of Objective 2 areas in the UK. Some of these will change their status for the period 1997-1999. These changes were still being negotiated at the time of writing. The present Objective 2 areas are: West Midlands (including Birmingham); East England (Yorkshire and Humberside and the East Midlands); North West England; West Cumbria; North East England; Industrial South Wales, East Scotland; West Scotland; East London Lee Valley Corridor; Thanet; Stoke on Trent; Burton on Trent; Plymouth; Barrow and Gibraltar.

Objective 3: to combat long-term unemployment and facilitate the re-entry of young people and those facing exclusion from the labour market and the promotion of equal opportunities of men and women. This is a national programme with no regional restrictions, organisations from anywhere except those in Objective 1 areas may apply.

Objective 4: to provide support for workers having to adapt to industrial change (at least half of Objective 4 money must benefit small and medium-sized enterprises). This is a national programme with no regional restrictions. Organisations from anywhere except those in Objective 1 areas may apply. At present Objective 4 is not being implemented in the UK, at the discretion of the government, but this situation might change for the period 1997-1999.

Objective 5b: to promote the development of rural areas. This is the rural equivalent of Objective 2. At present there are a number of Objective 5b areas in the UK but some of these will change their status for the period 1997-1999. These changes were still being negotiated at the time of writing. The present Objective 5b areas are: Devon, Cornwall and Somerset; Dumfries and Galloway; Rural Wales; the Northern Uplands; East Anglia; English Marches; Lincolnshire; Derbyshire/Staffordshire; Boarders; Rural Stirling; Grampian and Tayside.

No applicant organisation can be in receipt of more than one ESF Objective Fund at the same time. Match funding cannot contain any element of European money.

ESF is a partnership between the European Commission, the DFEE and the applicant organisation. For Objective 3 at present a system of Sector Managers administer the selection process, monitoring and evaluation of projects and representation of applicants on committees etc., with allocations being made on a sectorial basis. This will change for the period 1998-1999, but full details of how to apply were not available at the time of writing. Interested parties should contact the main voluntary sector manager, National Council for Voluntary Organisations (NCVO) for details.

Finance from ESF has to be matched by funds from a match funder, usually a public authority – see the guidance for the individual Objectives for separate match funding requirements. The level of assistance varies according to each Objective, generally between 25%-50% of the running costs of a project (except in Objective 1 areas which can claim up to 75%). Length of funding also varies with different Objectives. For example Objective 3 funding is for a calendar year at a time with no guarantee of future funding. Funding can contribute towards expenditure such as training allowances, scheme preparation, administrative management costs, subsistence and travel, wage subsidies and vocational guidance and counselling.

Examples of Arts Projects:

- Second Wave have been funded to provide a Youth Arts Leadership course for 21 unemployed youths in the London area. This project is match funded by the London Borough of Lewisham;
- Newham Training Network has been funded for a Fashion Design course of 10 women organised in conjunction with a local college;
- The Quicksilver Theatre have obtained funding to train unemployed beneficiaries in Arts Administration, through a wage subsidy scheme. The course is also being supported by the London Arts Board;
- The Half Moon Young People's Theatre have secured ESF funding for their Technical Training Course, which is targeting 14 unemployed young people in the London Docklands.

Information sources

The National Council of Voluntary Organisations (NCVO) is the main sector manager for the voluntary sector in England, with the Scottish Council for Voluntary Organisations (SCVO) and the Wales Council for Voluntary Action (WCVA) running the programme in Scotland and Wales respectively.

The NCVO produces Guidance Notes and information on how to apply for Objective 3 and keeps a database of interested voluntary organisations. This is the channel most likely to be useful for arts projects. Details of Objective 2 funding can be obtained through the six regional offices.

England

Eleanor M Jackson, European Funding
and Employment Team, National Council
for Voluntary Organisations,
Regent's Wharf, 8 All Saints Street,
London N1 9RL;
Tel: 0171-713 6161; Fax: 0171-713 6300

Scotland

Julia Palmer, Scottish Council for
Voluntary Organisations,
18/19 Claremont Crescent,
Edinburgh EH7 4QD;
Tel: 0131-556 3882; Fax: 0131-556 0279

Wales

Dewi Evans, Wales Council for Voluntary
Action – European Office,
Park Lane House, 7 High Street,
Welshpool Powys SY21 7JP;
Tel: 01938-552 379; Fax: 01938-442 092

Regional Offices

Central
Caroline Salzedo, CEFET, 2nd Floor,
7b Broad Street, Nottingham NG1 3AJ;
Tel: 0115-924 0778; Fax: 0115-924 0796

London
Diane Burridge, LVSTC, 1st Floor,
18 Ashwin Street, London E8 3DL;
Tel: 0171-249 4441; Fax: 0171-923 4280

Northern
Donald Dempsey, ESFVON,
The Star Centre, Tyne House,
Jubilee Road, Coxlodge,
Newcastle upon Tyne NE3 3PN;
Tel: 0191-213 1694; Fax: 0191-284 0791

North West
Brenda Wilkinson, North West Network,
Suite 1, 4th Floor, Macintosh House,
Shambles Square, Manchester M3 3AF;
Tel: 0161-832 0404; Fax: 0161-834 2116

South
Eleanor van der Hoest, SAVAGE,
111 Winchester Road, Chandlers
Ford, Hants SO5 2GH;
Tel: 01703-262 655; Fax: 01703-271 811

Yorkshire & Humberside
Nick Scott, VONEF, Mercury House,
4 Manchester Road, Bradford,
West Yorkshire BD5 OQL;
Tel: 01274-742 065; Fax: 01274-742 066

The ESF Units within the government
departments can provide general
information and details of other Sector
Managers:

England and Wales
ESF Unit, Department for Education
and Employment, Level 1,
236 Grays Inn Road, London WC1X 8HI;
Tel: 0171-211 3000; Fax: 0171-211 4749

Scotland
ESF Division, Scottish Office
Development Department,
Floor 2E (2H) Victoria Quay,
Edinburgh EH6 6QQ;
Tel: 0131-244 0732; Fax: 0131-244 0738

Northern Ireland
European Community Branch,
Department of Economic Development,
Netherleigh, Massey Avenue,
Belfast BT4 2JP;
Tel: 01232-529900; Fax: 01232-529485

THE EUROPEAN REGIONAL DEVELOPMENT FUND

The European Regional Development Fund (ERDF) is one of the European Union's Structural Funds (along with the European Social Fund – ESF – and the European Agricultural Guidance and Guarantee Fund – EAGGF. Its aim is to stimulate economic development in the least prosperous areas of the community. Money is only available within designated geographical areas, those with Objective 1, 2 or 5b status (see entry for ESF for current areas).

The fund is primarily a capital fund and is highly flexible. It works on match funding principles, with priorities for the fund and levels of intervention (proportion of costs which can be applied for) decided and monitored by a national representative committee.

In general terms ERDF supports measures to improve the competitiveness of businesses and localities. Some examples of the types of activity that could be funded under ERDF are:

◆ New premises for businesses
◆ New transport and communication infrastructure
◆ New marketing and inward investment initiatives
◆ Technology transfer and innovation activities
◆ Strategic research and development activities
◆ Training and support for small and medium-sized enterprises (SMEs)
◆ Export and trade expansion activities
◆ Improved co-ordination of economic regeneration activities

- Reclaiming derelict sites and land
- Environmental improvements

The UK has been a major beneficiary of the European Development Fund. Projects from the cultural sector have benefited when finance has been made available for tourism infrastructure projects (such as the ERDF funded beautification of Birmingham's Chamberlain Square, the development of the Tate Gallery at St Ives and the restoration of Beamish Museum).

Government Offices – Regional Contacts

Government Office for the Eastern Region
Heron House, 49/53 Goldington Road,
Bedford MK40 3LL;
Tel: 0123-479 6129; Fax: 0123-479 6081

Government Office for the East Midlands
The Belgrave Centre, Stanley Place,
Talbot Street, Nottingham NG1 5GG;
Tel: 0115-971 9971; Fax: 0115-971 2404

Government Office for London
Room 7.2, 7th Floor, Riverwalk House,
157/161 Millbank, London SW1P 4RR;
Tel: 0171-217 3000; Fax: 0171-217 3463

Government Office for Merseyside
Room 325, Graeme House,
Derby Square, Liverpool L2 7SU;
Tel: 0151-224 6444; Fax: 0151-224 6470

Government Office for the North East
Stanegate House, Groat Market,
Newcastle Upon Tyne NE1 1YN;
Tel: 0191-201 3928; Fax: 0191-202 3825

Government Office for the North West
Room 2004, Sunley Tower,
Piccadilly Plaza, Manchester M1 4BE;
Tel: 0161-952 4384; Fax: 0161-952 4199

Government Office for the South East
Bridge House, 1 Walnut Tree Close,
Guildford, Surrey GU1 4GA;
Tel: 01483-882255; Fax: 01483-882529

Government Office for the South West
Phoenix House, Notte Street,
Plymouth PL1 2HF;
Tel: 01752-221 691; Fax: 01752-635 093

Government Office for the West Midlands
77 Paradise Circus, Queensway,
Birmingham B15 1SJ;
Tel: 0121-212 5000; Fax: 0121-212 5185

Government Office for the Yorkshire and Humberside
Room 2 East, 25 Queen Street,
Leeds LS1 2TW;
Tel: 0113- 233 8369; Fax: 0113-233 8301

Scotland

Western Scotland
Strathclyde European Partnership,
94 Elmbank Street, Glasgow G2 4DL;
Tel: 0141-248 9900; Fax: 0141-248 1656

Eastern Scotland
Eastern Scotland Programme Executive,
The Dunfermline Conference Centre,
Halbeath, Dunfermline KY11 5DY;
Tel: 01383- 622 537; Fax: 01383-622 624

Highlands and Islands
Highlands and Islands Programme
Executive, Bridge House, Bridge Street,
Inverness IVI IQR;
Tel: 01463-244 478; Fax: 01463-244 324

Dumfries & Galloway
Dumfries & Galloway European
Partnership, 24 Ninth Place,
Dumfries DG1 2PN;
Tel: 01387-251 360; Fax: 01387-252 733

**Objective 5b North & North West
Grampian, Rural Stirling/upland
Tayside & Borders**
European Fund Division, Victoria Quay,
Edinburgh EH6 6QQ;
Tel: 0131-244 0691; Fax: 0131-244 0738

Wales
Welsh Office
European Regional Development Fund,
European Affairs Division,
Cathays Park, Cardiff CF1 3NQ;
Tel: 01222-823 952;
Fax: 01222-823 257

Northern Ireland
Northern Ireland Office
European Community Division,
Department of Economic
Development, Netherleigh,
Massey Avenue, Belfast BT4 2JP;
Tel: 01232-529 900;
Fax: 01232-529 485

ARIANE PROGRAMME

Cultural Action Unit, Directorate General for
Audiovsiual Media, Information, Communication
and Culture – DG X/D1, European Commission,
102 rue de la Loi, 1049 Brussels, Belgium
Tel: 0032 2 299 92 51; 0032 2 299 9283
Contact: Antonio Zapatero

This programme brings all the literature schemes under one, new umbrella. Its key aspects are:

◆ Promotion and wider dissemination through grants for translation of works of contemporary literature, dramatic works and reference works and also translation and literary prizes;
◆ support measures for networks and partnership, promoting access to literature, and supporting further training and research;
◆ Co-operation with non-member countries.

The programme had not been finalised by February 1996.

THE ARTS EDUCATION AND TRAINING INITIATIVE

Task Force for Human Resources Education Training
and Youth, European Commission, 7 rue Belliard,
1049 Brussels, Belgium
Tel: 0032 2 296 19 14; **Fax:** 0032 2 295 56 99

This scheme aims to promote European co-operation in arts education and training, enhance its quality and introduce innovative elements. Projects should be in the fields of theatre, music, fine arts, dance, design, audiovisual and socio-economic aspects of arts and education training. They should involve at least three member states of the European Union and take place within one, although non-EU countries may participate. An emphasis is placed on the innovative features of the projects which can include demonstration projects such as conferences and seminars with workshops, masterclasses, exchange of experts, student and staff exchanges, publication of materials for innovative courses, etc.
Grants up to a maximum of ECU 10,000.

EUCREA

EUCREA UK, National Disability Arts Forum,
Mea House, Ellison Place,
Newcastle upon Tyne NE1 8XS
Tel: 0191-261 1628; **Fax:** 0191-222 0573
Contact: Geof Armstrong

Grant total: about £150,000 annually

EUCREA stands for European Creativity by Disabled People. It is a non-governmental organisation funded by the EC, and consists of one representative from each EC member state. The National Disability Arts Forum (NDAF) aka EUCREA UK acts as agent for EUCREA by making recommendations for small one-off arts and disability project grants.

The amount of money available for any one project has to form a clearly stated percentage (maximum 50%) of a total budget. Project applications should:

♦ originate from within the European Community and involve at least four member states, including the proposing state;
♦ indicate why the project is important and worthy of support. Evidence of the need should be identified;
♦ show links within the EC with other organisations willing to collaborate and offer assistance;
♦ state aims and objectives, outlining the particular benefits for disabled people;

- include a timescale for implementation for the purposes of monitoring and evaluation;
- detail all funding sources and include an itemised costing;
- include full details (with names and addresses) of the project team.

NDAF encourages applications from outside London. It also requires that the projects reflect a high degree of control by disabled people and are publicised nationally through appropriate media.

Projects supported for 1996 include:

The setting up of an International Disability Arts Worldwide Web Site;

The creation of an animated video on access;

"European Giants Who Care", a performance piece;

A conference for disabled actors working in the European Community.

Applications: Guidelines and application forms are available from the above address in early summer.

EURIMAGES

Council of Europe, 67075 Strasbourg Cedex, France
Tel: 0033 88 41 26 40; Fax: 0033 88 41 27 60

The UK government withdrew its funding from this programme in late 1995 making the position of co-productions headed from the UK difficult.

The Eurimages fund provides soft loans for the co-production of feature films and documentaries, as well as subsidies for distribution. Co-producers must be wholly independent of public or private broadcasting organisations. The director and other key personnel must be European.

Feature films must originate in a member state with at least three co-producers from different member states. Principal photography must not have begun before a funding decision is made. Advances upon receipts up to 20% of the total costs of the co-production up to a maximum of FF 5 million.

Documentaries should be produced by at least two independent co-producers from different member states. The film should already be sold to at least three distributors or broadcasters in different member states. Advances upon receipts not exceeding 15% of the total costs of the co-production up to a maximum of FF 1 million.

Support is also available for European distributors towards the costs of prints and subtitling or dubbing.

Applications: Full guidelines, information on deadlines and application forms are available from the above address and from the UK MEDIA desk (see the MEDIA Programme entry)

EUROPEAN GUARANTEE FUND

The European Commission proposes to set up a European Guarantee Fund to promote cinema and television production, for a four year period 1997-2000. It would aim to strengthen existing support measures especially under the MEDIA 11 programme and introduce additional market-based mechanisms to mobilise new resources.

The fund, of some 90 million ECU, is expected to be administered by the European Investment Fund.

Contact the MEDIA programme for further information.

THE KALEIDOSCOPE PROGRAMME

Cultural Action Unit, Directorate General for
Audiovisual Media, Information, Communication
and Culture – DG X/D.1, European Commission,
102 rue de la Loi, 1049 Brussels, Belgium
Tel: +32 2 299 94 17; **Fax:** +32 2 299 92 83

Grant total: 2,936,200 ECU (1993)

Kaleidoscope aims to promote greater public access to and familiarity with the culture and history of the European peoples, as well as to promote artistic and cultural co-operation between professionals.

A pilot programme was set up in 1990 and the new programme, to run from 1996-98, aims to follow that scheme. Unanimous agreement of all fifteen Member States as well as approval of the European Parliament is required and discussion was still continuing at the time of writing though agreement was expected by early 1996. However, a broad outline can be given about its general aims and timetable. The following is a taken from an information note circulated on 9th January 1996.

"The objective of the Kaleidoscope programme will be to encourage, by means of co-operation, artistic and cultural creation in Europe, and to promote knowledge and dissemination of the culture and cultural life of the European people. This will be done by means of promoting cultural exchanges, and providing financial support to projects of cultural co-operation with a European dimension."

Subject to final approval the programme should incorporate the following main elements:

◆ "projects and events should demonstrate a European dimension by involving partners from at least three Member States, in terms of both organisation of and participation in the project.

◆ Projects submitted must be of European interest, of high quality, innovative or exemplary in nature, and have the potential for lasting co-operation."

All fifteen Member Sates will participate on an equal basis and the programme will also be open to third countries, "including the associated countries of Central and Eastern Europe, as well as to partners from Cyprus and Malta and other countries which have concluded association or co-operation agreements containing cultural clauses".

Timetable in 1996 (subject to the formal adoption of the programme)

March Official announcement of the 1996 Kaleidoscope programme;

Mid May	Deadline for receipt of applications;
May-June	Collation, analysis and preselection;
July-September	Assessment by independent experts, management committee, Commissioner;
October	Announcement of successful projects.

Further details regarding applications forms, procedure, closing dates and the documents to accompany applications will be made available as soon as possible after the formal adoption of the programme.

Applications: Guidelines and entry forms available from the Offices of the Commission of European Communities in England, Northern Ireland, Scotland and Wales (see addresses).

Symbolic and recurrent activities

Besides the projects supported under the Kaleidoscope Programme, aid has also been given for various prestige activities such as the European Community Baroque Orchestra, and the British Centre for Literary Translation in Norwich.

THE MEDIA PROGRAMME

Directorate General for Audiovisual Media
Information, Communication, Culture – DG X,
European Commission, rue de la Loi 200,
1049 Brussels, Belgium
Tel: 0032 2 299 94 36; **Fax:** 0032 2 299 92 14

The aim of MEDIA 11 (Measures pour Encourager Le Development de l'Industrie de Production Audio Visuelle) is to strengthen the audio-visual industries in the member states of the European Union by encouraging greater collaboration between them and the wider distribution of their products. It does this by offering loans and seed money for the development of film and television productions and for training of professionals in the audiovisual sector. The MEDIA Programme absorbs a major part of the cultural budget available from DGX, and the Commission is committed to spending 310 million ECUs over a five-year period between 1996 and 2000. The UK MEDIA Desk and MEDIA Antenna Offices were established in

1992 to provide information and guidance about the MEDIA Programme projects. Guidelines and application forms as appropriate for all support initiatives are available from these offices.

UK MEDIA Desk
c/o British Film Institute, 21 Stephen Street, London WlP lPL (Tel: 0171-255 1444; Fax: 0171-636 6568))
Contact: Susanne Knepscher

Media Antenna Cardiff
c/o Wales Film Council, Screen Centre, Llantrisant Road, Llandaff, Cardiff CF5 2PU (Tel: 01222-578 370; Fax: 01222-578 654)
Contact: Mari Beynon Owen, Chief Executive, until position filled

Media Antenna Glasgow
c/o Scottish Film Council, 74 Victoria Crescent Road, Glasgow G12 9JN (Tel: 0141-334 4445; Fax: 0141-334 8132)
Contact: Louise Scott

At the time of compiling this entry (Spring 1996) the new programme had not been set up, so this entry is necessarily brief and potential applicants should contact the Desk or the Antennae.

Former programmes included: European Film Distribution Office (EFDO); SOURCES – Stimulating Outstanding Resources for Creative European Screenwriting; DOCUMENTARY; European Association of Animated Film (Cartoon); European Audiovisual Entrepreneurs (EAVE); European Script Fund (SCRIPT); Espace Video Europeen (EVE); Media Investment Club (MIC).

Commission support for film and audiovisual programme festivals and for the meetings of professionals in the audiovisual industry
Contact: Philip Cova (at DGX address; Tel: 0032 2 299 9130; Fax: 0032 2 299 91 30)

RAPHAEL

European Commission DG/1.2, 102 rue de la Loi,
1049 Brussels, Belgium
Tel: 0032 2 296 49 17; **Fax:** 0032 2 296 69 74
Contact: A Bouratsis

The RAPHAEL programme is designed to encourage the preservation and extension of Europe's cultural heritage. It is intended to run from 1996-2000 and be allocated 67 million ECU (around £56 million) for that period. It aims to support:

♦ development and promotion of the cultural heritage

- networks and partnerships
- improving access to cultural heritage
- innovation, further training and professional mobility
- co-operation with non-EU countries and international organisations

This programme has been delayed because of lack of agreement by some member countries. If approved the programme will not commence before 1997. Prospective applicants should make further enquiries to the office above.

Pending the adoption of Raphael, the Commission launched a series of pilot actions all of which required submission by May or June 1996, so full details have not been included in this guide.

- Proposals for co-operation in developing and making accessible the cultural heritage of European museums.
- Proposals for activities/events for the preservation and increased awareness of European cultural heritage. These could take place in a range of sectors such as archives, museums, ethnography, stained-glass conservation techniques.
- Proposals to protect and advantage European baroque and archaeological heritage.
- Proposals for the further training and mobility of professionals working in European cultural heritage conservation.

THE EUROPEAN CULTURAL FOUNDATION

Jan Van Goyenkade 5, 1075 HN Amsterdam, Netherlands
Tel: 00-3120 676 02 22; **Fax:** 00-3120 675 22 31
Contact: Dr R Stephan, Secretary General

Grant total: ECU 1,500,000 annually

The European Cultural Foundation is an independent, non-profit organisation which promotes cultural co-operation in Europe. It develops new projects and programmes, acts as a centre for a network of independent associated research institutes and runs a grant programme related to its priorities. In 1995 the foundation agreed the following priorities for the coming years:

- Central and Eastern Europe
- Mediterranean Region
- Cultural Pluralism: Policies and Practices

The foundation will also focus its priorities on the educational and informative dimensions of culture.

The foundation particularly welcomes grant requests in the following fields:

- debates on European cultural issues and policies;

- cultural co-operation: mobility, training and information programmes
- democracy and social integration: cultural and educational initiatives;
- literary culture: cross-border and cross-cultural co-operation in translating, editing and publishing;
- language policies in Europe: cross-border and cross-cultural communication;
- information and media: instruments towards cultural education and co-operation;
- the role of the media in European society and intercultural information.

To qualify for a grant, a project must be distinctively European in character, and must involve the participation of at least three, preferably more, European countries. Grants range between 2,500 ECU and 25,000 ECU. Normally, a foundation grant will cover no more than half the total sum required for a project and the recipient body must demonstrate that it is able to obtain the remaining sum from other sources.

Examples of recent arts grants in the UK:
Central and East European Publishing Project, Oxford;
University of Warwick, Joint School of Theatre Studies;
Hope Street Theatre, Liverpool.

Exclusions: Projects by individuals; performances, exhibitions, tours, audio-visual productions and commercial publications; institutional running or capital costs; exchange programmes.

Applications: Applicants should write direct to the Grants Department of the European Cultural Foundation for guidelines. Project proposals are first submitted in writing. Suitable proposals are then sent an application form. Applications are considered three times a year.

Contact: Veronie Willemars, Grants Officer, for further information after receiving the guidelines.

Advice is also available from Geoffrey Denton, Director of the UK Committee, 7 Oakhill Avenue, London NW3 7RD (0171-794 5955)

FUNDING FROM THE USA

INTRODUCTION

The following section includes basic information about foundations known to have given support to arts organisations in recent years. All prospective applicants need to examine carefully a foundation's up-to-date policy guidelines and advice for applicants plus its most recent annual report before making any approach. Few grants are made to organisations in the UK. Where these may have been made in the past new policies can change the situation eg. the L J Skaggs and Mary C Skaggs Foundation had a history of support for conservation projects with an interest shown in Wiltshire. These policies have changed and the foundation says that it has suspended its active grant making programme and that applications are now by invitation only.

"Blind" applications are most unlikely to be successful. An organisation needs to have built up links with a foundation either through the BAAA or through other contacts in the USA.

THE BRITISH AMERICAN ARTS ASSOCIATION

116 Commercial Street, London E1 6NF
Tel: 0171-247 5385; Fax: 0171-247 5256
Jennifer Williams, Director

The British American Arts Association (BAAA) promotes cultural activity and exchange between Britain and the USA. It provides information, advice and technical assistance to professional artists, administrators and sponsors working in all disciplines throughout both countries. It consists of two complementary organisations: BAAA (UK) Ltd, a registered charity and BAAA (US) Inc, a tax-exempt organisation under US law.

BAAA (US) Inc has a grant programme which aids British arts organisations in raising funds in America and encourages British-American collaboration in cultural activities. As BAAA (US) is a tax-exempt organisation, contributors may make tax-deductible donations to BAAA for its support of specific British-American cultural projects. This programme enables British arts organisations to fundraise in the USA for British-American cultural projects with the advantage of an umbrella tax-exempt status. BAAA (UK) offers a similar service for American cultural organisations.

In order for British cultural organisations to take advantage of the grant-making programme the organisation must apply to become a client of the programme. The following criteria will be taken into account by the BAAA (US) Board in reviewing applications:

- The project involved must be good and worthy of support.
- The project should benefit living American and British culture. Heritage or historical projects are not normally supported by the programme.
- The project, timetable and budget must be reasonable and realistic.
- The applicant should be willing to assume a sufficient degree of responsibility for working with the donor and with BAAA.
- BAAA should benefit now or in the future by establishing a relationship with the project, organisation or donor; there must be no objection to such an association; and the project should not interfere with BAAA's activities and plans.

No single criterion is controlling and some are more important than others. Board members will weigh and balance each criterion in making their decision.

A British cultural organisation wishing to take advantage of the grant programme should contact the grant programme administrator at the BAAA from whom details may be obtained of the application procedure. An administrative fee to compensate BAAA for servicing the grant programme is made. The amount of the administrative fee will be:

- 10 % of grants up to $50,000 in any one year;
- 7.5 % of grants between $50,000 and $150,000 in any one year;
- 5 % of grants between $150,000 and $250,000 in any one year; negotiable for grants over $250,000 in any one year.

There is a minimum limit on grants of $500. Gifts of property (art objects etc.) are accepted only rarely, after negotiation.

US Foundations

The American Express Foundation

The Amoco Foundation Inc

The Annenberg Foundation

The Dayton-Hudson Foundation

Ann and Gordon Getty Foundation

The J Paul Getty Trust

The Glencoe Foundation Inc

The Horace W Goldsmith Foundation

The W Averell and Pamela C Harriman
   Foundation

The Francena T Harrison Foundation

The H J & Drue Heinz Foundation

The Kresge Foundation

The Samuel H Kress Foundation

The Margaret T Morris Foundation

The Pew Charitable Trusts

The Pollock-Krasner Foundation Inc

The Rockefeller Foundation

The Timken International Fund

The Andy Warhol Foundation for the
   Visual Arts Inc

The American Express Foundation

American Express Tower, World Financial
Center, New York 10285-4710, USA

Tel: 212-640-5661
Contact: Cornelia W Higginson, Vice-
President, International Philanthropic
Programme
General: Grants given for education,
cultural programs, employment programs
and community service. In the field of
cultural programs the foundation focuses
on bringing visual and performing arts
projects to large audiences; increasing
accessibility to the arts and helping
organisations develop new audiences;
providing arts education for young people;
preserving historic and cultural assets,
natural sites and parks; encouraging
innovative collaborations. The grants are
mainly within the $10,000 to $20,000
range. A recent example in Britain:
*National Gallery Trust, towards the creation
of the Micro Gallery, an interactive,
computerised system for visitors.*

The Amoco Foundation Inc

200 East Randolph Drive, Chicago, Illinois
60601, USA

Tel: 312-856-6306
Contact: Patricia D Wright, Executive
Director
Grant total: $19,800,000 (1994)
General: In general the foundation focuses
its work in communities where it has
operations. Grants are given for the arts,
education and urban renewal. International
grants are made in countries where the
Amoco company has a presence. In 1994 at
least 4 four grants were made in the UK
mainly to universities.

The Annenberg Foundation

St Davids Center, 150 Radnor Chester Road, Suite A-200, St Davids, Pennsylvania 19087-5293, USA

Tel: 215-341-9270
Contact: Alice C Cory, Secretary-Treasurer
General: Grants given for pre-collegiate education, higher education, medical research, cultural programmes and community service. Grants range between £250 to $5 million.

The Dayton-Hudson Foundation

777 Nicollet Mall, Minneapolis, Minnesota 55402-2055

Tel: 612- 370-6555
Contact: Cynthia Mayeda, Chair
General: Support for social action programmes and 'arts programmes that result in artistic excellence, community leadership in the arts, and increased access to and use of the arts as a means of community expression'. Grants range between £5,000 and $100,000.

Ann and Gordon Getty Foundation

50 California Street, Suite 3315, San Francisco, California 94111

Tel: 415-788-5844
Contact: Lawrence Chazen, Director
General: The foundation gives grants in the fields of music, performing arts (especially opera), education, libraries, anthropology. Unsolicited applications are not welcome. Examples of recent grants in the UK

The J Paul Getty Trust

401 Wilshire Boulevard, Suite 1000, Santa Monica, California 90401-1455, USA

Tel: 310-393-4244; Fax: 310-395-8642
Contact: Deborah Marrow, Director, The Getty Grant Program
General: Support for the visual arts and architecture. Grants are awarded to institutions and individuals throughout the world.

The categories of support include: Research (postdoctoral fellowships, senior research grants and Central and Eastern European Fellowships); Publications; Resources (research centers, archival projects, reference works); Conservation of Works of Art (surveys, treatment, training); Architectural Conservations; Conservation Publications.

The Glencoe Foundation Inc

Building C, Suite 300, Greenville Center, 3801 Kennett Pike, Greenville, Delaware 19807, USA

Tel: 302-654-9933
Contact: Ellice McDonald, President
General: Support for publicly oriented charitable organisations in Scotland or the US which promote Scottish-American traditions and cultures. Grants range from $2,000 to $50,000.

The Horace W Goldsmith Foundation

375 Park Avenue, New York, New York 10152, USA

Tel: 212-319-8700
Contact: Robert R Slaughter, Chief Executive
General: Support for cultural programmes, including performing arts and museums, Jewish welfare, hospitals and higher education. Grants range between $25,000 and $100,000.

The W Averell and Pamela C Harriman Foundation

63 Wall Street, 23rd Floor, New York, NY 10005, USA

Contact: William F Hibberd, Secretary
General: Grants are made for higher education, cultural programmes, foreign policy.

The Francena T Harrison Foundation

PO Box 297, Church Street Station, New York 10008, USA

Contact: M Graff, Vice President, Bankers Trust

General: The foundation gives grants to the performing arts, primarily in New York, but a few international grants are also made.

The H J & Drue Heinz Foundation

606 Oliver Building, 535 Smithfield Street, Pittsburgh PA 15222, USA

Tel: 412-281-5737
Contact: Harry A Thompson II, Manager
Grant total: £4.3 million (1990)
General: Support for fine arts organisations is one of the foundation's six focus areas. Unsolicited applications are not welcome.
Applications: Applications are not accepted.

The Kresge Foundation

3215 West Big Beaver Road, PO Box 3151, Troy, Michigan 48007-0588, USA

Tel: 810-643-9630
Contact: John E Marshall, President
General: The foundation makes challenge grants for building construction and renovation to institutions in the fields of health, welfare, education, science, arts, humanities and public affairs. About one seventh of the total goes to arts organisations.

In 1991 the Royal Academy of Arts received $450,000 for renovation of its diploma galleries. No more up-to-date information on its grants has been made available.
Applications: A policies and procedure booklet outlines the Foundation's requirements. Proposals must be postmarked by 15th of January, February, May, July, August, November for decisions announced four months later.

The Samuel H Kress Foundation

174 East 80th Street, New York, New York 10021, USA

Tel: 212-861-4993
Contact: Dr Marilyn Perry, President
General: Funding is concentrated on the history and preservation of European art, from antiquity to the early 19th century. Programmes include: Kress Fellowships for pre-doctoral research; development of essential resources; sharing of expertise; art conservation research; conservation and restoration projects; special initiatives.
Exclusions: No support for art history programmes below the pre-doctoral level or the purchase of works of art. No grants for living artists, operating budgets, continuing support, annual campaigns, endowments, deficit financing, capital funds or films. No loans.
Applications: Application forms are required for fellowships in art history and art conservation and there are a series of different deadlines. The initial approach for other proposals should be by letter (no faxes), describing the project, its budget and the funds requested.

The Margaret T Morris Foundation

PO Box 592, Prescott 86302, Arizona, USA

Tel: 602-445-4010
Contact: Eugene P Polk, Trustee
General: Support for the arts and other cultural programmes is one of the foundation's priorities.
Exclusions: No grants to individuals. No loans.
Applications: In writing to the correspondent.

The Pew Charitable Trusts

One Commerce Square, 2005 Market Street, Suite 1700, Philadelphia, Pennsylvania 19103-7017, USA

Tel: 215-575-9050; Fax: 215-575-4939
Contact: Rebecca W Rimel, Executive Director
General: Support for culture, education, health and human services, conservation and the environment, public policy, religion. Grants range from $1,500 to $2.25 million. Support is given by invitation only to "international festivals and cultural exchange programs that promote cross-cultural understanding among American artists and audiences about diverse global cultures".
Exclusions: No grants to individuals. No support for endowment funds or deficit financing.
Applications: Initial approach may be made by telephone, letter or proposal. It is recommended that applicants establish initial contact before submitting the required formal proposal. The foundation's annual report includes full details of application guidelines within each funding area. There are deadlines in the culture and education grant areas;. The board meets in March, June, September and December.

The Pollock-Krasner Foundation Inc

725 Park Avenue, New York, New York 10021, USA

Tel: 212-2517-5400
Contact: Linda Selvin, Grants Manager
General: The foundation's aim is to help, internationally, working artists who have embarked on professional careers. The foundation's dual criteria for grants are: recognisable artistic merit and financial need, whether professional, personal, or both. Grants are made to painters, sculptors, and artists who work on paper, including printmakers. Grants are made for one year only. Grants range between $1,000 and $30,000.

Exclusions: No grants to organisations, commercial artists, photographers, video artists, filmmakers, craftsmakers, students. No grants for commissions or projects ordered by others. The foundation does not make grants to cover past debts, legal fees, purchase of land or property, moves to other cities, or to pay for the cost of installations. With very few exceptions, the foundation will not fund travel expenses.
Applications: Application forms and guidelines available from the above address. Applications are considered throughout the year.

The Rockefeller Foundation

1133 Avenue of the Americas, New York, New York 10036, USA

Tel: 212-869-8500
Contact: Lynda Mullen, Secretary
General: Support for science-based international development in agricultural, health and population sciences, arts and the humanities, and equal opportunities. The arts and humanities division encourages creative artists whose work can advance international and intercultural understanding in the USA. Activities supported extend international and intercultural scholarship, and increase artistic experimentation across cultures.

The Timken International Fund

236 Third Street SW, Canton, Ohio 44702, USA

Tel: 216-455-5281
Contact: Don D Dickes, Secretary/Treasurer
General: Grants to educational and charitable institutions outside the USA.

The Andy Warhol Foundation for the Visual Arts Inc

22 East 33rd Street, New York, New York 10016, USA

Tel: 212-683-6456
Contact: Pamela Clapp, Program Director
General: The foundation makes grants in the fields of visual arts and historic

preservation. Very few grants are made outside the USA. The foundation does not fund exhibitions or other activities directly related to the art of Andy Warhol.

PART THREE

SUPPORT FROM COMPANIES

Introduction

Donations

Whilst sponsorship is the support most often connected with business, other kinds of assistance that may be preferable or more convenient. A sponsorship deal inevitably involves a considerable amount of time and energy. A request for a donation may be a simpler and more successful, especially if you're looking for a relatively small sum of money under £1,000. Gifts in kind may also be easier to obtain.

Most major companies have *corporate community affairs departments* responsible for charitable donations. Medium-size companies may have a *donations manager* located in any one of a number of departments, most usually the managing director's office or the company secretary's department, but possibly in the personnel, PR, or marketing department. A few large and medium-sized firms have clearly defined donations policies and budgets, although most give to a wide range of good cause organisations or even claim to consider each appeal on its merits.

In smaller and local companies clearly defined structures or policies for giving are unlikely. Some give according to the special interest of the chairman or even the chairman's spouse; some give in response to requests from clients who support particular causes; some give only the local charities; some give nothing at all.

Local subsidiaries or local plants and branches of large national companies (particularly supermarkets and banks) may have the authority to make local donations, although sometimes requests have to be routed through head office.

The *independent television companies* (see separate list) have a tradition of giving to the 'arts and sciences' with most of their donations go to arts groups operating within each company's transmission area.

Targeting Companies

Your application for a donation will be up against strong competition, whichever company you decide to apply to. So think very carefully why a company might be interested in helping you. Start by investigating local firms – those in your immediate neighbourhood, in your city, county, region, depending on the size of your catchment area. The local authority may keep a list of the larger employers or the larger ratepayers in the area; the local chamber of commerce in your area may be active and, if so, should be able to supply lists of local firms; in your library you should find the appropriate regional section of the *Kompass Register of British Industry and Commerce*, or you can use a *Yellow Pages* directory. From these sources you can begin to build up a list of likely firms. The *Who owns Whom* directory will tell you if the company is part of a much larger group. Companies all produce annual reports.

Check how many local employees the company has and whether a significant number of them form part of your existing audience. Scan the local papers for information on interesting development plans involving your target companies. Do they have a record of community involvement? What kinds of equipment/materials are part of their stock in trade? Are they likely to have a high turnover in office equipment which you could use? Remember that gifts in kind are often easier to obtain than cash and may be worth substantially more to you than a small donation.

Consider, too, the companies with which you have business links: suppliers of art materials, printers, fabric and lighting manufacturers etc. Include in this list your bank, firm of solicitors, accountants, letting agent and so on. Provided you are a good client of theirs, then they might be persuaded to help you develop your work.

Investigate larger national or international firms where there is a product link or where the company has a stated donations policy which includes the arts and/or, as appropriate, employment initiatives, education, youth aid, inner city rejuvenation, ethnic minority support. To help you identify such companies, consult *A Guide to Company Giving* and *The Major Companies Guide* published by the Directory of Social Change (see bibliography at the end of this book).

USE YOUR CONTACTS

Whatever size or variety of company you apply to, personal contacts with senior staff are likely to be of the greatest importance. If one of your trustees or supporters is personally acquainted with a high-ranking member of the company, be it socially or through business, then a direct approach can be worth a great deal more than the carefully calculated 'cold' approach by letter. People like to give to people, particularly people they wish to please or impress.

Many companies are particularly interested in supporting organisations with which their employees are involved. If you have members or volunteers who work with a particular company be sure to make the most of this involvement in your approach. Many companies set aside small sums of £100 to £500 to be used where there is such employee involvement. They also may have funds to match money raised on behalf of an organisation by employees.

OTHER FORMS OF ASSISTANCE

Besides straight cash donations and gifts in kind there are several other possibilities you should consider when approaching industry for support: advertising in programmes, posters etc, staff secondment, business advice, staff participation in fundraising activity.

ADVERTISING

You can ask a company to buy advertising space in your mailing brochure, programme, magazine, annual report, catalogue, etc. This is obviously more of a commercial deal with a flavour of goodwill attached. You will be offering access to a select audience through the medium of your printed materials. You will need to provide the company with accurate data on the number, age and social status of the people the programme (or whatever) will reach so that it can decide whether this is a market it wishes to target. Be prepared to offer a range of advertising options: half page, full page, back page, etc. with discounts for regular advertisements and prices for each advertisement, size and position, based on research into the cost of advertising in comparable publications. Normally, if you are looking for advertising revenue, you should expect to deal with advertising or marketing managers rather than going straight to directors or donations officers.

STAFF SECONDMENT AND BUSINESS ADVICE

Some of the large companies operate staff secondment schemes whereby staff with relevant skills can be 'lent' free of charge for a fixed period – say six months or even as long as one year – to a voluntary organisation. It may be that the company views this operation as part of its community relations programme or, with more self-interest at heart, that it sees secondment as an opportunity for younger staff to gain practical experience in new areas (eg. man-management), or as a way of preparing middle-aged executives to transfer to a different career outside their company or make way for younger colleagues.

The source of free 'person power' could prove useful to arts organisations, though most secondments seem to be made to organisations dealing with enterprise training and environmental issues. However, it is worth exploring the secondment option if you have links with a company that operates such a system, perhaps as an additional form of aid.

Of course secondment need not be only a one-way traffic. Increasingly there are examples of artists and crafts people working for a period in industrial premises and involving employees in their creative work. Equally lunchtime concerts and plays in factories and offices could also provide some reciprocal benefit.

Approach *Business in the Community (BITC)*, 44 Baker Street, London W1M 1DH (0171-224 1600) for help in finding a secondee.

BUSINESS ADVICE/CONSULTANCY

It should be much easier to obtain advice and consultancy services from a wider range of companies. It can be given during company time, or after office hours on a voluntary basis. Finance and marketing are the most common areas where arts organisations can benefit from the expertise of commercial companies. Approach *Business in the Arts* which has regional offices for help (see entry on the Association of Business Sponsorship of the Arts – ABSA which precedes the listing of companies). It has recently launched a scheme whereby business managers serve on the boards of arts organisations – The Business in the Arts/NatWest Board Bank.

STAFF FUNDRAISING

Many companies now encourage their staff to raise money for charity, and sometimes the money raised by staff is matched by a donation from the company.

If a company has a lot of employees in the area where your group operates, and especially if any of them are known to your fundraising team, then you could think of trying to mobilise them to raise funds for you, particularly if your work is likely to be of interest or benefit to them and their families. With this approach you need not seek direct access to a senior executive initially. It may be best to ask those employees known to you if *they* would be interested in organising internal support for your organisation. If they agree, they can then approach the director or manager for permission to do so. The form of this support will depend on how much your ideas appeal to and involve the workforce. Think of ways of giving each donor something in return that acknowledges their help and reinforces their connection to you.

CORPORATE MEMBERSHIP

You might devise some form of corporate membership scheme. In return for a cash contribution, the company gets its name prominently displayed in the programme and has access to a range of other benefits, possibly including free or discounted tickets, which they can make available to employees or customers. This would not only be good for staff relations, but would also help you get bottoms onto empty seats, which in turn would help improve your attendance statistics which in turn would help in your grant applications.

MEETINGS AND PARTIES

If you have attractive premises you might offer these for meetings or for staff Christmas parties, when an added attraction would be your ability to devise an entertainment to suit the event. Training and staff welfare budgets may be very much larger than charitable donations budgets, and your line of contact might well be via the personnel director or manager.

SPONSORSHIP

Many people involved in arts sponsorship, including the influential Association for Business Sponsorship of the Arts (ABSA) emphasise that industrial sponsorship is a commercial transaction between two or more partners. It is not akin to patronage or a charitable donation. The company buys the benefits the arts organisation can provide. Usually the payment is in the form of money, but sometimes the company will also provide the services of its staff, technical help, workspace or other 'gifts in kind'.

It is also important to remember that sponsorship is distinct from advertising. The company which places advertisements in magazines or on television has control over what each advertisement consists of and when and where it appears. The company which sponsors an event or an organisation has no control over the publicity given by the media, though very often it will reach an agreement with the sponsored organisation about where and how often its name will appear in publicity material (programmes, catalogues, posters, etc.).

WHY DO COMPANIES SPONSOR?

There are several good reasons why companies choose to become sponsors. The main reasons are:

◆ To advertise a brand name. If the event being sponsored is assured of major media coverage and, in particular, television coverage, sponsorship may actually be a cheaper way of advertising than using television commercials.

- To improve their general image. Association with a particular organisation may raise its status with the local community, general public or others in the business world. This 'image-polishing' can be particularly useful if the company has been the subject of bad publicity for whatever reason.
- To attract and keep high-quality staff and encourage good PR within the company. They may be offered perks in the form of free tickets to events, a chance to meet celebrities. It may give them the feeling that the company they work for is exciting, adventurous, caring. Sponsorship may offer the company the chance to involve their staff in a worthwhile project or help promote a community spirit.
- To nurture ties with valuable clients and other influential people. Some sponsoring companies are looking principally for opportunities to offer special clients some kind of privileged or exclusive entertainment. A private view of an art exhibition, a concert performance for an invited audience, complimentary tickets for a prestigious production with a chance to meet the stars afterwards – these are some of the ways in which a company may be able to thank established good clients or foster new relationships. Such events may also give the sponsor a chance to invite influential people not immediately connected with their business who can be important to the company – for example, people from the media, politics or finance.
- To create goodwill within a local community. This aim can apply equally to a nationally known company with branches in various parts of the country and to a smaller company with only one or two offices/factories/retail outlets in a particular region. The company will see the organisation it chooses to sponsor as providing a popular, high-profile service to the community where it operates. A good relationship with the community from which it draws its workforce may be significant for its development as a happy and successful enterprise.

WHAT KIND OF COMPANIES SPONSOR?

All kinds and sizes of companies now get involved in sponsorship. Companies producing goods or providing services to the general public are the most likely to sponsor because they are the most likely to gain on several fronts. Sometimes this sponsorship will be undertaken by the company itself, but often it will be in the name of one of its brands or products. Until recently, large holding companies and those which were not engaged in selling directly to the public, generally did not feel the need to sponsor. Some of these companies have changed their policy and incorporated sponsorship into their marketing strategies. Image-building campaigns aimed at shareholders, the media and the politicians have greatly increased recently. In such campaigns, sponsorship can play a significant part.

IS SPONSORSHIP GOOD FOR YOU?

Obtaining sponsorship is rarely easy. Many organisations will spend expensive hours researching, applying and attempting to persuade a company to part with quite a small sum of money. It could be that this expenditure of time, effort and money would be more fruitfully used in improving your sales and marketing. Concentrating on marketing may paradoxically help turn you into a much more attractive sponsorship proposition. It will make you more professional, better organised and more aware of your commercial potential. Most of all it will make you think very carefully about what you have to offer your audience, who that audience is, how you and they can make the most of each other.

ETHICAL CONSIDERATIONS

Each arts organisation has to decide whether it has any moral objections to being associated with a particular company. It may not just be a matter of your own ethics. There may be other practical reasons – the actors or performers may refuse to play, your loyal audience might decide to stay away, your funding bodies may decide to withdraw their support or there might be bad publicity for both parties. This issue applies equally but less visibly to charitable donations. Only you and your management board can decide where to draw the line. You need to do this first before embarking on sponsorship approaches.

WHAT HAVE YOU GOT TO OFFER?

Some organisations find it far easier to attract sponsorship than others. They have the status, the facilities and the product which make them desirable partners for companies. They can inspire confidence that they will be able to deliver the benefits that business is seeking. This does not rule out the possibility of sponsorship for radical theatre groups or small presses. More 'difficult' projects or organisations will have to think more carefully about why sponsors might be interested in them and which companies are likely to want to do so.

If you're not genuinely convinced of your worth to potential sponsors, far better to look for donations, as it is almost impossible to persuade a company to enter into sponsorship without an informed conviction that you have something they need. This question does not have a once and for all answer. The situation can always be re-examined as your organisation develops.

Many of the initial stages in planning a sponsorship campaign are the same as those required for any kind of major fundraising effort. You need to look hard at your organisation, what you have and what you require, you need to discover who your audience/users are, you need to do research into the kind of companies likely to sponsor, and likely to sponsor you.

Some key points to bear in mind in the early stages of developing a sponsorship campaign:

◆ Don't seek sponsorship for your normal administration costs. This isn't attractive or exciting for a would-be sponsor. Think in terms of something identifiable which will bring kudos to the company – a new production, a special event, a festival, a competition, your education programme.

◆ Don't think of sponsorship as a long-term solution to your financial problems. Many sponsorships are one-offs, some are repeated from year to year (and the sums involved may go down as well as up) but none last forever. The decision to sponsor may be dictated by many factors completely outside your control, such as how well the sponsoring company is doing financially, changes in company personnel, rival sponsorship opportunities, and so on.

◆ Make sure you have the expertise, time and money (for salaries, unless using volunteers, and overheads) to make a success of the venture and provide all the promised benefits to the sponsor.

- Plan ahead as far as you can. Sponsoring companies, even if interested in your organisation, may not be able to allocate any money to you for up to two years from your initial approach, though some companies may be able to respond more quickly, particularly smaller companies or where lesser amounts of money are involved.

Armed with clear ideas about what your organisation has done, is doing and wishes to do in the future, together with properly researched information on your audience you can now devise some initial ideas for 'sponsorship packages'. A 'package' will comprise project/s you wish to undertake, a list of the features of which should appeal to your audience and to a sponsor and what you would be able to offer in terms of publicity, client/employee entertainment and other benefits. In compiling this list you will probably be able to identify some which should have special appeal to certain kinds of companies.

- Publicity. You can offer acknowledgement of the sponsorship with varying degrees of prominence on any printed material you produce in connection with the project. Be precise about what publicity you will organise. It may be as well to offer to collaborate on publicity, with the sponsor having a say in design, print quantity etc. Some of the printed material, such as catalogues, can be used by the audience or on display at a gallery or theatre for a much longer period than the project itself. Make sure you point out such longer-lasting benefits to the potential sponsor. If you are confident of television, radio or newspaper coverage of your work, this will be an important selling point, even though you may never be sure that sponsor will be acknowledged verbally, or even that any banners or other material displaying the sponsor's name at the event will be in view of the television cameras. If you give the project a title which incorporates the sponsor company's name, such as 'the Guinness Poetry Marathon', there is a better chance of ensuring that the sponsor will be acknowledged by the media. In any case offer all the help you can in persuading the media to acknowledge the sponsor.
- Entertainment. You might offer some complimentary or reduced-rate tickets, and/or a priority booking facility. Special performances or private views for audiences invited by the sponsor, a press launch or first night party can all be good 'payments' to a sponsor. Special membership schemes have proved attractive to companies.

The sponsor's payment to you, ie. the amount of money/services which you seek from the company, must be very carefully worked out. Don't either over- or under-estimate the amount you need to finance your project. Either mistake will lose you credibility. Make known to the sponsor in the early stages of a negotiation how much money is required and be ready to back this up with detailed estimates. Remember that the sponsor may be receiving dozens of proposals, and is likely to know the 'going rate' for sponsorship.

WHERE AND HOW TO LOOK FOR SPONSORS

Begin with the companies that have a presence in your locality or those larger companies where there is a very obvious link to be made between your project's theme or your organisation and their products. Use the reference guide listed in the "Donations" section above. Check if any of the companies you've listed are members of the Association for Business Sponsorship of the Arts (ABSA) by obtaining a copy of their annual report. See the entry following this section about ABSA and the Pairing Scheme which encourages new sponsorships with a matching grant. However, if a company is not on ABSA's membership list do not infer that this company has not sponsored or will not sponsor the arts. There are several prominent arts sponsors who prefer to remain independent and do things their way.

Look to see if it is concerned with its corporate image as well as with selling its products – you can get clues about this from the company's track record in community affairs, the presentation and content of its annual report and advertisements. Look at what companies are advertising in the local or national press, and think about whether sponsorship of your organisation could offer them better value for money in selling their products. A most important area to investigate is who are clients/customers, employees and business partners of each potential sponsor. Then ask yourself to what degree does their 'audience' and yours match. Most companies will see the importance of promoting the well-being and commitment of their employees by other means as well as financial ones.

TACKLING YOUR TARGET SPONSORS

The right person to contact initially depends very much on the size and structure of the company, whether anyone in your organisation has personal links with managers or directors of the company, how much you know about the company's policy and the private interests of its top personnel. The very large companies have *sponsorship managers* or channel all sponsorship proposals through the *community affairs department*. Otherwise, it is best to start with the *public relations department* of the company or the manager of the particular branch that you would like to tie in to the sponsorship, unless you have special reasons for going to the managing director or chairman.

If the company has had no previous experience of sponsorship, the first telephone conversation may well be difficult. Unless the person shows marked interest, keep this first conversation brief. Suggest that you would be interested in hearing their views on arts sponsorship, and say that you will be writing to them about the possibility of working together on a project which you think holds considerable potential for them. If you have been recommended to approach the company for a particular reason by a 'person of influence' whose name or position the PR manager is likely to recognise, then mention this immediately to establish your credibility.

Even if you are speaking to a branch office with no power to authorise sponsorship, foster the local link by writing to the branch PR manager as well as to head office. Try to arrange a meeting with the local person to discuss the local benefits of a sponsored project, perhaps even before you write to head office.

A meeting with the local executive should at the very least provide you with useful information about the company's priorities, the status of the branch and, if you're lucky, some additional reasons why your sponsorship project might suit them. Equally, if the head office manager considers your project seriously, s/he is virtually certain to consult the branch. If the branch manger is already informed and enthused by your project and your organisation this is obviously a great advantage.

At your first meeting with the company, at whatever level, begin by asking for advice and about how your project would be viewed from a businessman's point of view. Also ask him/her general questions about the company's PR and marketing activities: what business entertainment do they undertake, have they plans to find a new market, launch a new product? The answers to these and similar questions may be the key to developing your discussions to a point where sponsoring your project becomes a serious proposition. You need early on to give an outline of your organisation, its size, achievements and general aims. Be prepared to answer these points but at this stage give only brief general answers and offer to put more detail on paper for the company. You might consider taking along some well presented, typed sheets, covering the salient facts. If you have produced a promotional brochure include this as well. Or you can simply send these immediately after the meeting. In either case, say that you will ring again in about two weeks' time to hear their reactions. This will give them an added incentive not to put the papers to one side.

If it proves difficult to arrange an exploratory meeting with the PR manager, then you will have to begin with a letter and accompanying documents. This is obviously much less desirable because you have no way of finding out directly about any new developments in the company's PR policy, to discover things that your previous research into the company has not brought to light, to pick up on any interesting comments from your contact, to establish a personal rapport. So your written presentation will be vitally important. It will have to capture the imagination of someone who is probably deluged every day with mail, often of a 'selling' nature. You must ensure that what you propose makes good commercial sense and that you spell out the likely benefits of the arrangement.

Offer the company the chance to be forward-looking, imaginative, to steal a PR march on competitors. At this stage all you have to do is 'catch their eye': make the person who reads your letter interested in you and your project and aware that there may be something in it for his/her company. So keep your written presentation brief – no more than two A4 sheets plus a short covering letter.

What to Include in Your Presentation

- Say briefly what your organisation is, what it has recently achieved (including any outstanding marks of recognition of achievement which it has received), what it aims to do in the next few years.
- List other sources of financial support as this will encourage the reader to accept you as bona fide and worthwhile.
- Describe your audience (its age, social composition, etc) and give average sales/ attendance figures for events.
- Outline the project for which you are seeking sponsorship. Don't forget to mention when and where it is meant to happen.
- Say how much sponsorship money you need. Leave a detailed breakdown of figures till later – the total required will suffice here.

- Outline the particular attractions of your project – the benefits it offers to this particular company in terms of publicity, hospitality etc.
- The covering letter should simply say why you are writing, what you are enclosing and that you will be phoning in two weeks' time to arrange a meeting unless you hear from them first.

At each stage of your sponsorship campaign remember to keep a record of what has taken place. Be willing to modify your ideas within reason to meet the company's requirements.

If a company seems generally well disposed towards you, but turns down a particular sponsorship proposal, don't write them off completely. Invite them to events, to see your work, keep them informed of notable successes/achievements. Keep tabs on significant personnel changes. The day may come when they may change their minds about you. Don't forget to write and say thank you for any meeting or any trouble they have taken on your behalf.

WORKING WITH YOUR SPONSOR

Once a company has accepted a sponsorship proposal in principle it is necessary to contract a written agreement as soon as possible. Some companies will want a formal contract. Others will be content with a letter setting out the terms of sponsorship, signed by both parties. In the Association for Business Sponsorship of the Arts' *Sponsorship Manual* there are several sample letters of agreement and sponsorship contracts which show you what such documents should contain. The manual also contains useful advice on working with sponsors on the timetable for your project and the areas where you need to co-ordinate activities with them.

ARTS SPONSORSHIP DATABASE

A company called European Marketing Consultants (EMC) operate a computerised 'match-making' service which can pair potential arts sponsors with sponsorship opportunities anywhere in the UK. The service is called Arts Connect and its database contains details of about 1000 arts projects seeking sponsorship. The system first identifies marketing objectives of the potential sponsor before conducting a database search for appropriate opportunities up to three years ahead. Once a short list has been drawn up EMC present a report including recommendations on timescales, budgets and logistics with an assessment of the promotional opportunities available with each short-listed project. Arts organisations can be included in the database free of charge.

If you want to register your sponsorship projects with Arts Connect write for details to: *European Marketing Consultants Ltd*, Spa House, 11/17 Worple Road, London SW19 4JS, Tel: 0181-879 3033; Fax: 0181-947 9042, Contact: Cheryl Lawrence.

Readers should also consult the bibliography at the end of this book for details of further useful reading.

This article has largely been reproduced from the previous edition of this guide and thanks are due to Anne-Marie Doulton.

THE ASSOCIATION FOR BUSINESS SPONSORSHIP OF THE ARTS (ABSA)

Nutmeg House, 60 Gainsford Street, Butlers Wharf,
London SE1 2NY
Tel: 0171-378 8143; Fax: 0171-407 7527
Contact: Colin Tweedy, Director General

ABSA is an independent organisation set up and funded by companies already involved in arts sponsorship. Membership is solely for companies, not arts organisations. It exists to promote arts sponsorship and advises both businesses and arts organisations on good practice in sponsorship and how to go about it. It also promotes the aims and advantages of sponsorship among politicians and the media. It presents a number of prestigious annual awards to companies and individuals which it records in its annual report along with lists of organisations sponsored by its members.

ABSA organises special events, particularly via its regional offices, which enable companies and arts groups to make contact and learn more about each other. It publishes detailed advice to arts organisations on achieving and maintaining sponsorship (see bibliography).

ABSA Midlands
(office also in Nottingham)
Central House, Broad Street,
Birmingham BI 2JP;
Tel: 0121-634 4101;
Fax: 0121-634 4105;
Director: Marian Ruston

ABSA North
(offices also in Manchester and
Newcastle)
Dean Clough, Halifax,
West Yorkshire HX3 5AX;
Tel: 01422-367 860;
Fax: 01422-363 254;
Director: Chris Pulleine

ABSA Northern Ireland
185 Stranmillis Road,
Belfast BT9 5DU;
Tel: 01232-664 736;
Fax: 01232-664 500;
Director: John McCaffrey

ABSA Scotland
100 Wellington Street,
Glasgow G2 6PB;
Tel: 0141-204 3864;
Director: Peggy Macleod

ABSA Wales
9 Museum Place,
Cardiff CF1 3NX;
Tel: 01222-221 382;
Fax: 01222-221 447;
Director: Guy Silk

The Pairing Scheme (National Heritage Arts Sponsorship Scheme)
Grant total: £4,575,000 in 635 awards (1994/95)
Contact: Sarah Weir, Head of Pairing Scheme

Breakdown by Regions 1994/95

Eastern	£165,000	South East	£384,600
East Midlands	£170,000	South West	£160,000
Greater London	£1,393,000	West Midlands	£220,700
Northern	£70,500	Yorkshire & Humberside	£211,000
North West	£606,000	Scotland	£421,500
Southern	£301,600	Wales	£272,700
		Northern Ireland	£197,700

ABSA administers the government's arts sponsorship initiative (formerly called the Business Sponsorship Incentive Scheme) funded by the Department of National Heritage. The scheme started in 1984. Modified rules were introduced in 1996. The scheme has four main objects:

- to encourage businesses to sponsor the arts for the first time
- to encourage existing sponsors to increase their support
- to develop strong, lasting partnerships between business and the arts
- to develop wider access to the arts through business sponsorship

The scheme has always been an incentive for new sponsors to enter the market and for existing sponsors to increase their commitment. In addition to these objectives, the new rules are specifically designed to encourage arts organisations and sponsors to develop strong, lasting partnerships. In the main it does this by offering "new sponsors" the opportunity to have all their sponsorships matched on a 50% basis over the first three years of their sponsorship programme.

The new scheme works on two levels:

1. New Sponsors
A business in its first three years of arts sponsorship, may have all arts sponsorships matched on a 50% basis, providing that:

- the business' overall financial commitment to arts sponsorship does not decrease.
- the financial commitment to the arts organisation the business is in partnership with does not decrease.
- each sponsorship is at least £1,000.

Two additional incentives were offered from 1996 for first time sponsors.

- if the business decides to support the same arts organisation for a three-year period, completing an agreed contract, these contributions may be matched by 100% in each one of these three years.
- alternatively, if the Pairing Scheme Committee considers the sponsorship of exceptional value in increasing access to the arts, it may be able to match the contribution on a 100% basis. All subsequent sponsorships undertaken in the three year period may then be matched on a 50% basis.

2. Established Sponsors

For a business which has already sponsored the arts for at least three years and decides to increase its level of support, the increase may be matched on a 25% basis providing that firstly:

◆ the business' overall annual sponsorship budget increases by at least £2,000.

In addition:

◆ the amount of sponsorship being paid to the partner arts organisation must be increased by at least £2,000.

The total amount of Pairing Scheme money available to an arts organisation in one financial year and the maximum award given for an individual sponsorship is £75,000.

The minimum amount of eligible sponsorship money a business can put in is £1,000 and the minimum single award is £500.

Arts organisations can apply to the Pairing Scheme for as many awards as they want up to a maximum value of £75,000.

Businesses may apply to the scheme as many times as they wish.

Applications: Once an arts organisation and a business sponsor have agreed all terms of the sponsorship, both parties complete their respective sections of the application form. This should give as much detail as possible, especially with regard to what additional benefits would result from the award. The arts organisation submits both sections of the application form at least eight weeks before the start of the sponsored project. Details of the application are discussed with both parties by a member of the staff team who oversees its progress to the committee meeting.

Built Heritage Pairing Scheme (a pilot project for the North of England)

ABSA North, Dean Clough, Halifax, West Yorkshire HX3 5AX; Tel: 01422-367860; Fax: 01422-363254

Contact: Ceris Morris, Project Manager

Grant total: £150,000 (1996/97)

This pilot scheme, funded by the Department of National Heritage, was launched in 1995 and has been funded again for 1996/97. It is hoped the scheme will eventually be extended to cover the whole of the country but readers should check its status.

The scheme covers Yorkshire & Humberside, North-West and Northern regions It operates on three tiers matching new money from:

A First Time Sponsor: a business which has never sponsored the built heritage may have its sponsorship matched on a 1:1 ratio (minimum amount of sponsorship is £1,000).

A Second Time Sponsor: A business sponsoring the built heritage for the second time may have the increase on its previous sponsorship matched on a 1:2 ratio (minimum amount of sponsorship is £2,000 of new money).

An Established Sponsor: A business sponsoring the built heritage for its third time or more may have the increase on its previous sponsorship matched on a 1:4 ratio (minimum amount of sponsorship is £4,000 of new money).

Heritage organisations may receive four awards per financial year (April to March) which when added together cannot exceed £50,000.

The minimum amount of matching money available for each sponsorship is £1,000 and the maximum is £35,000. There is no restriction on the number of times a business may apply.

Eligible organisations are listed buildings, scheduled ancient monuments, parks and gardens registered with English Heritage. Eligible activities should contribute towards the repair of the built heritage or widen access to it (these can include repairs, events such as concerts and performances, interpretation centres, literature and marketing activities, educational and community programmes).

Applications: Full details are available with applications forms which must be received one month before the start date of the sponsored activity.

Business In The Arts
Contact: Tim Stockil, Director (see Head Office address above)

Affiliated Offices:

Business in the Arts East Midlands*
4 Russel Place, Talbot Street,
Nottingham NG1 5HJ;
Tel: 0115-941 9949;
Fax: 0115-948 3343;
Manager: Liz Johnson

Business in the Arts London
(see ABSA Head Office address above)
Manager: Ruth Ingledow

Business in the Arts North
c/o Tyne & Wear Foundation, MEA House, Newcastle Upon Tyne NE1 8XS;
Tel: 0191-222 0945;
Fax: 0191-230 0689;
Manager: Ron Parsons

Business in the Arts North West*
59 Rodney Street, Liverpool L1 9ER;
Tel: 0151-709 8780;
Fax: 0151-707 0758;
Manager: Vivienne Tyler

Business in the Arts Northern Ireland
(see ABSA address above)
Manager: Caroline Kieran

Business in the Arts Scotland
(see ABSA address above)
Manager: Alison Weedall

Business in the Arts South*
Room HC104, Herbert Collins Building,
Southampton Institute, East Park Terrace,
Southampton SO14 WW;
Tel: 01703-319650/576;
Fax: 01703-319576;
Manager: John Holden

Business in the Arts West Midlands
(see ABSA Midlands office address above)
Manager: Sally McComb

Yorkshire and Humberside Business in the Arts*
Dean Clough Office Park, Halifax,
West Yorkshire, HX3 5AX;
Tel: 01422-320718; Fax: 01422-363254;
Manager: Liz Whitehouse

Business in the Arts Wales
(see ABSA office address)
Manager: Gillian Wells

* Independent but operating the Business in the Arts programme under license.

Business in the Arts recruits business managers with relevant skills and matches them with arts organisations on a planned, voluntary basis, to tackle management issues. Arts managers are also offered opportunities to benefit from management training courses run by businesses for their own staff or by specialist training providers at little or no cost.

The Business in the Arts/NatWest Board Bank, a register of middle and senior business managers who would like to join the board of non-executive directors of arts organisations, was launched in March 1996. The scheme had been piloted in the North West and Scotland and was operational in London at the time of the launch.

Contact your local office for further information about the development of the scheme in your area.

Arts at Work
Marks & Spencer and Sainsbury's have pioneered schemes which bring the arts directly to employees in their places of work. ABSA is aiming to build on these initiatives and develop a wider scheme to help generate new audiences by encouraging companies to bring the arts into the workplace.

ABSA Consulting
A trading subsidiary providing two main services. Firstly for business, local authorities and others, a research service providing strategic advice on private sector partnerships with the arts and heritage sectors. Secondly for arts and heritage applicants for Lottery funding, it undertakes feasibility studies and business plans and advises on the application process.

Training in Sponsorship for Arts Organisations
Training seminars are arranged regularly by the ABSA regional offices, usually in conjunction with the relevant Regional Arts Board. For instance in London day seminars are held each month (£25.00 per place).

INDEPENDENT TELEVISION COMPANIES

Anglia Television Ltd

Border Television plc

Carlton Broadcasting Ltd

Central Broadcasting Ltd

Channel Four Television Corporation

GMTV Ltd

Grampian Television plc

Granada Television Ltd

HTV (Cymru) Wales

London Weekend Television Ltd

Meridian Broadcasting

S4C

Scottish Television plc

Tyne Tees Television Ltd

Ulster Television plc

Westcountry Television Ltd

Yorkshire - Tyne Tees Television Holdings plc

Anglia Television Ltd

Anglia House, Norwich NR1 3JG

Tel: 01603-615151
Transmission area: East of England
Sponsorship contact: Martin Morrall
Donations contact: Gina Boltwood, Secretary, Grants Committee
Policy: All requests must be relevant to activity within Anglia Television's transmission area. There is apparently no preference for sponsorship as opposed to donations or for a particular artform.

Border Television plc

The Broadcasting Centre, Durranhill, Carlisle CA1 3NT

Tel: 01228-25101
Transmission area: Borders and the Isle of Man
Donations contact: Peter Brownlow, Financial Director

Carlton Broadcasting Ltd

101 St Martin's Lane, London WC2N 4AZ

Tel: 0171-240-4000
Transmission area: London weekday television, subsidiary of Carlton Communications (see separate entry)
Sponsorship contact: Colin Standbridge, Controller of Public Affairs
Policy: See also the Carlton Television Trust in the "Trusts" section.

Central Broadcasting Ltd

Central House, Broad Street, Birmingham B1 2JP

Tel: 0121-643 9898
Transmission area: Television broadcasting in the Birmingham area; a subsidiary of

Carlton Communications plc (see separate entry)
Sponsorship contact: Pauline Woodhead, Community Affairs Co-ordinator

Channel Four Television Corporation

124 Horseferry Road, London SW1P 2TX

Tel: 0171-396 4444
Transmission area: Susan Dunkley, Corporate Marketing & Sponsorship Manager
Donations contact: See above
Policy: Channel 4 tries to concentrate its sponsorship support on projects related to its programmes and its role as a national broadcaster.
Recent arts sponsorships have included:
The Turner Prize;
Serpentine Gallery;
Glyndebourne;
London, Edinburgh, Leeds and Birmingham Film Festivals;
Edinburgh Gilded Balloon;
Cardiff Animation Festival.
Membership: ABSA

GMTV Ltd

The London Television Centre, Upper Ground, London SE1 9TT

Tel: 0171-827 7000
Transmission area: National, breakfast-time
Sponsorship contact: Ray Magnus, Head of Broadcast Sponsorship Sales, Grampian Television plc, Queen's Cross, Aberdeen AB9 2XJ, Tel: 01224-846846
Company activity: North of Scotland
Sponsorship contact: Graham Good, Company Secretary & Financial Director
Donations contact: See above
Policy: The company has a preference for arts sponsorship: *"We consider arts/media/ broadcasting-related applications from individuals or organisations within our transmission area which is the North of Scotland. Applicants outside this area need not apply as their requests will not be considered."* No support to circulars or students. A definite preference for media/

performance related schemes:
Recent arts sponsorships include:
Aberdeen Opera Company;
Scottish Opera;
Scottish Ballet.
Its sponsorship budget in 1996 was £50,000 (proportion to the arts not known).

Grampian Television plc

Queen's Cross, Aberdeen AB9 2XJ

Tel: 01224-846846
Transmission area: North of Scotland
Sponsorship contact: Graham Good, Company Secretary & Financial Director
Donations contact: see above
Policy: The company has a preference for arts sponsorship: "We consider arts/media/ broadcasting-related applications from individuals or organisations within our transmission area which is the *North of Scotland. Applicants outside this area need not apply as their requests will not be considered.* No support to circulars or students. A definite preference for media/ performance related schemes.
Recent arts sponsorships include:
Aberdeen Opera Company;
Scottish Opera;
Scottish Ballet.
Its sponsorship budget in 1996 was £50,000 (proportion to the arts not known).

Granada Television Ltd

Granada Television Centre, Manchester M60 9EA

Tel: 0161-832 7211
Transmission area: North-West England
Sponsorship contact: Rob McLoughlin, Head of Regional Affairs
Donations contact: See above
Policy: The company contributes in excess of £250,000 to charities, artistic and educational institutions in the North West. Support has been given to Salford University's Media Studies Department. It has sponsored art exhibitions, Hallé

concerts and other events in the North West. It is a corporate member of a number of theatres including Chester Gateway and Liverpool Playhouse, as well as the Liverpool Philharmonic.

See also the Granada Foundation under "Trusts".

Membership: ABSA patron

HTV (Cymru) Wales

The Television Centre, Culverhouse Cross, Cardiff CF5 6XJ

Tel: 01222-590590
Transmission area: Wales
Sponsorship contact: Mansel Jones, Head of Public Relations
Donations contact: See above
Policy: The company did not want to be included in this guide as "they do very little arts sponsorship".

HTV Ltd

The Television Centre, Bath Road, Bristol BS4 3HG

Tel: 0117-977 8366
Transmission area: West of England
Sponsorship contact: Richard Lister, Press/PR Manager
Policy: An annual competition for independent experimental film-makers is run with South West Arts with programming of the winners.

The company does not have a specific arts budget either for sponsorship or donations.

London Weekend Television Ltd

Upper Ground, London SE1 9LT

Tel: 0171-620 1620
Transmission area: Television in the London area at the weekend, subsidiary of the Granada Group plc.
Sponsorship contact: Suzy Stoyel, Regional Affairs Manager
Policy: The company supports local arts within its transmission area, including national organisations based in the capital. Recent support has been given to:

British Film Institute;
National Film & Television School;
National Film & Television Archive;
Royal National Theatre;
Royal Television Society;
London Philharmonic Orchestra;
London International Festival of Theatre (LIFT);
Actors' Centre;
Coin Street Festival;
The LWT Plays on Stage.
Membership: ABSA

Meridian Broadcasting

Television Centre, Southampton SO14 4PZ

Tel: 01703-222555
Transmission area: South and South East England
Sponsorship contact: Allan Robertson, Head of Press and Regional Affairs
Donations contact: See above
Policy: The company's policy for both arts sponsorship and arts donations is to support "disability groups or individuals in any artform, based upon set criteria".

S4C

Parc Busnes Ty Glas, Llanisien, Cardiff CF4 5DU

Tel: 01222-741400
Transmission area: Wales, transmitted on the Fourth Channel in Wales, broadcasting on average 32 hours a week in Welsh mainly during peak hours
Sponsorship contact: Catrin Brace, Head of PR and Sponsorship
Policy: Applications which have an all-Wales basis or have a link with the television industry are favoured. It sometimes gives support to local events which help S4C to relate to its audience in that area.

Recent support has included:
Animation Festival;
BAFTA;
Celtic Film Association;
Edinburgh International Television Festival;
LLangollen International Festival;
St David's Hall, Cardiff;

Welsh International Film Festival.
Applications: Its sponsorship budget is allocated twice yearly, usually in the month preceding its financial year (December to January) and around April or May.
Membership: ABSA

Scottish Television plc

Cowcaddens, Glasgow G2 3PR

Tel: 0141-332 9999
Transmission area: Television programme contractor for Central Scotland
Sponsorship contact: David Whitton, Head of Public Affairs
Donations: £224,507 (31/12/95)
Policy: Sponsorship budget: £152,000, percentage to the arts not known (1996)
The company has a policy of providing assistance to professional, community and amateur organisations and individuals concerned with theatrical and musical performances. It is interested in sponsoring projects which give some element of training for newcomers to theatre or television.

It will also consider charitable or social organisations undertaking new or special activities. Local charities in Central Scotland are preferred with grants ranging from £100 to £15,000, the exception being £150,000 to Sabhal Mor Ostaig.

National grants range from £500 to £10,000 with the exception being £18,000 to the National Television Archive. Organisations given recent substantial support include:
Scottish Opera;
Scottish Ballet;
Edinburgh International Television Festival;
Drambuie Edinburgh Film Festival;
Celtic Film & TV Festival;
Museum of Scotland Projects;
Royal Scottish National Orchestra.
In addition community festivals, young trainee film makers and Comunn Na Gaidhlig has been supported.
Applications: The Community Programmes Co-ordinator should be contacted regarding the social action broadcasts.
Membership: % Club, ABSA

Tyne Tees Television Ltd

The Television Centre, City Road, Newcastle upon Tyne NE1 2AL

Tel: 0191-261 0181
Sponsorship contact: Ruth Laing, Press Officer
Policy: See also Yorkshire-Tyne Tees Television Holdings plc.

Ulster Television plc

Havelock House, Ormeau Road, Belfast BT7 1EB

Tel: 01232-328122
Transmission area: Northern Ireland
Sponsorship contact: Mike McCann, Head of Public Affairs

Westcountry Television Ltd

Western Wood Way, Language Science Park, Plymouth PL7 5BG

Tel: 01752-333333
Transmission area: South-West England
Sponsorship contact: Mark Clare, Controller, Public Affairs
Policy: "We consider all applications but very much prefer applications from within our transmission area. We prefer supporting smaller projects which benefit the community as a whole."

Yorkshire - Tyne Tees Television Holdings plc

The Television Centre, Leeds LS3 1JS
Tel: 0113-243 8283
Transmission area: Independent TV programme contractor
Sponsorship contact: Dr G Brownlee, Director, Group Corporate Affairs
Donations: £311,000 (30/9/1993)
Policy: The company "has a long established policy of supporting the arts in the region, giving vitality to new and existing initiatives and raising the quality of cultural life within the community." It has an arts committee, covering both Tyne Tees Television Ltd and Yorkshire Television Ltd,

which meets regularly.

Its recent support includes:

Harrogate International Festival;

Northern Sinfonia;

Opera North;

West Riding Opera.

Prior to the linking of the two companies it is known that Yorkshire Television made grants for theatres, the arts, festivals and events, ranging from Sheffield Crucible, Leeds Playhouse, Jorvik Festival and Yorkshire Sculpture Park to the Ilkley Players, Leeds University Union Debating Society and Dewsbury Arts Group.

Membership: ABSA patron

COMPANIES

Allied Domecq PLC

AMEC plc

Amerada Hess Ltd

Arthur Andersen

Anglia Television Ltd

Associated British Ports Holdings plc

ASW Holdings

BAA plc

Bank of Scotland

Bankers Trust Company

Barclays PLC

BASF plc

Bass plc

BAT Industries plc

Bayer plc

Blue Circle Industries plc

BMW (GB) Ltd

BOC Group plc

Booker plc

Border Television plc

Bristol & West Building Society

British Alcan Aluminium plc

British Gas plc

British Land Company

British Nuclear Fuels plc

The British Petroleum Company plc

British Telecommunications plc

Burmah Castrol plc

Calor Group plc

Carlton Broadcasting Ltd

Carlton Communications plc

Central Broadcasting Ltd

Channel Four Television Corporation

Charter plc

Charterhouse plc

Chevron UK Ltd

Christies International plc

Ciba-Geigy plc

Classic FM

Clydesdale Bank PLC

Coats Viyella plc

Commercial Union plc

Coopers & Lybrand

Courtaulds plc

Digital Equipment Co Ltd

Dixons Group plc

East Midlands Electricity plc

Eastern Group plc

Economist Newspaper Ltd

Elf Enterprise Caledonia Ltd

Ernst & Young

Fenwick Ltd

Ford Motor Company Ltd

Friends' Provident Life Office

Gallaher Ltd

General Accident plc

General Electric Company plc

Girobank plc

GKN plc

Glaxo Wellcome plc

Glynwed International plc

GMTV Ltd

Grampian Television plc

Granada Group plc

Granada Television Ltd

Grand Metropolitan PLC

The Guardian and the Observer

Guinness PLC

Halifax Building Society

Honeywell Ltd

HTV (Cymru) Wales

HTV Ltd

IBM United Kingdom Ltd

Imperial Chemical Industries

Inchcape plc

Jaguar Cars Ltd

Johnson Matthey

Johnson Wax

Kleinwort Benson

Kodak Ltd

KPMG

Laporte plc

LASMO plc

Legal & General plc

John Lewis Partnership plc

Lex Service PLC

Lloyds Bank plc

Lloyds TSB Group (see separate entries under Lloyds and TSB)

London Electricity plc

London Stock Exchange

Manchester Airport

Manweb plc

Marks and Spencer plc

Mars UK Ltd

John Menzies plc

Mercury Communications Ltd

Meridian Broadcasting

Midland Bank plc

Midlands Electricity plc

Miller Group Ltd

Mobil Oil Company Ltd

Morgan Crucible Company plc

Morgan Grenfell Group plc

The National Grid Company plc

National Power plc

National & Provincial Building Society

NatWest Group

Nestlé UK Ltd

News International plc

Northern Electric plc

Northern Foods

Northern Rock Building Society

NORWEB plc

Norwich Union Life Insurance Society

Pannell Kerr Forster

Pearson plc

Pilkington plc

Post Office Group

PowerGen plc

Price Waterhouse - United Kingdom

Private Patients Plan Ltd

Prudential Corporation plc

Reader's Digest Association Ltd

Really Useful Group Ltd

Reed Elsevier

RIBA/BT Community Projects Awards

The Royal Bank of Scotland Group plc

Royal Insurance Holdings plc

RTZ Corporation PLC

S4C

J Sainsbury plc

Christian Salvesen plc

Scapa Group plc

Schroders plc

Scottish Amicable

Scottish Hydro-Electric plc

Scottish & Newcastle Breweries plc

Scottish Power plc

Scottish Television plc

Sears plc

Sedgwick Group plc

SEEBOARD plc

Shell UK Ltd

Slough Estates plc

W H Smith Group plc

SmithKline Beecham plc

Sony United Kingdom Ltd

Sotheby's

South Western Electricity plc

Robert Stephen Holdings Ltd

Tarmac plc

Tate & Lyle plc

Tesco plc

Texaco Ltd

Thames Water Utilities

THORN EMI plc

3i Group plc

TI Group plc

Toyota (GB) Ltd /Lexus (GB) Ltd

TSB Bank plc

Tyne Tees Television Ltd

Ulster Television plc

Unilever

Unisys Ltd

United Biscuits (UK) Ltd

Vauxhall Motors Ltd

Vodafone Group plc

S G Warburg Group plc

Westcountry Television Ltd

Whitbread plc

Willis Corroon Group plc

Woolwich Building Society

Yorkshire Bank plc

Yorkshire Electricity Group plc

Yorkshire - Tyne Tees Television
   Holdings plc

Yorkshire Water plc

Allied Domecq PLC

24 Portland Place, London W1N 4BB

Tel: 0171-323 9000

Company activity: Brewers, vintners, food manufacturers & retailers

Sponsorship contact: Ian Oag, Corporate Affairs Manager

Donations contact: Clive Burns, Secretary, Charitable Trust

Donations: £743,000 (5/3/94)

Policy: Allied Domecq's community activities centre on the three main areas of education, the environment and the arts. These are supplemented by a whole range of activities undertaken by employees worldwide who give their time as well as financial support to a variety of projects.

In 1994/95 the total value of its involvement in the communities in which the company operates - including £646,702 given to charities by the Allied Domecq Trust - was estimated to be worth £10 million, excluding management time and employee volunteering.

Parent company arts sponsorship is focused on the theatre. Allied Domecq is the principal sponsor of the Royal Shakespeare Company. Its contribution over three years of £3.3 million is the largest ever UK arts sponsorship. Specific projects funded by this sponsorship include the Prince of Wales's Summer School for Teachers, a children's magazine, expansion of the in-school drama workshops and a new in depth school project called "Willpower".

Other theatrical organisations supported include: English National Opera; Royal Opera House; Glyndebourne Festival Opera.

The company is landlord and supporter of three of London's top fringe theatres – the Bush, the Gate and the King's Head.

The Allied Domecq Playwright Award. Playwrights whose work has not been produced professionally can apply for the £5,000 award to develop a play and have the chance of it being staged at the Bush. (The closing date was 28 September in 1995.) Entry leaflets and further information available by writing to the Bush Theatre, Shepherds Bush Green, London

W12 8QD and from Scope Sponsorship Tel: 0171-379 3234; Fax: 0171-465 8241.

The Thames Path Public Art project has received £90,000 over three years to finance six artists to research art proposals to enhance the Thames Path and to implement some of their ideas.

Many operating companies sponsor local art groups:

Burton Brewery sponsors the Royal Exchange Theatre, Manchester;

Ind Coope Retail sponsors the London Philharmonic;

Ansells sponsors the Birmingham Jazz Festival;

Carlsberg-Tetley are leading sponsors of rock festivals;

Allied Domecq Spirits & Wine have sponsored the Portway Players from Bristol.

Membership: ABSA, %Club, BITC

AMEC plc

Sandiway House, Hartford, Northwich, Cheshire CW8 2YA

Tel: 01606-883885
Company activity: Civil engineering & building contractors
Sponsorship contact: C L Fidler, Sponsorship and Donations
Donations: £71,000 (31/12/94)
Policy: The company has supported the English National Opera.
Applications: In writing to the correspondent.
Membership: % Club, BITC

Amerada Hess Ltd

33 Grosvenor Place, London SW1X 7HY

Tel: 0171-823 2626
Company activity: Oil industry
Sponsorship contact: Charles Naylor, Head of Public Relations
Donations contact: See above
Donations: £80,000 (31/12/95)
Policy: The company prefers to support appeals relevant to company business and local charities in areas of company presence with head office (London) supporting mainly charities working in London, and the Aberdeen office dealing with appeals relevant to that region.

In 1992, local support of community activities in Aberdeen included the annual painting competition for local school children and the Scottish Ballet education unit's work in the Grampian Region. In London, the company extended its association with the Docklands Sinfonietta to include an education programme for schools on the connection between science and music. This was repeated in 1995/96 with Sinfonia 21 (formerly Docklands Sinfonietta) when Jonathan Harvey was commissioned to write a new piece.

Most arts sponsorships are in the London and Aberdeen regions. In 1991, the company won the ABSA Scottish Award for Sponsorship of New Work, for its sponsorship of "The Vanishing Bridegroom" by the Scottish Opera.

Applications: The Aberdeen office (Scott House, Hareness Road, Altens, Aberdeen AB1 4LE 01224-243000) deals with appeals relevant to that region.
Membership: ABSA

Arthur Andersen

1 Surrey Street, London WC2R 2PS

Tel: 0171-438 3000
Company activity: Chartered accountants
Sponsorship contact: Francis Quinlan, Director of Marketing Services
Donations contact: Charles Bremner, Company Secretary
Donations: £1.2 million (31/12/1994)
Policy: Charitable support is given through the Arthur Andersen Foundation. This makes donations to registered or exempt charities established for educational and medical causes, the arts, disadvantaged groups, organisations working for the community and to institutions that support British heritage. In 1994, the total income of the foundation was £1.15 million. 507 charities received almost £1.2 million. Donations were broken down as follows:
Education £236,100 20%
Health £321,300 28%

Community £304,800 26%
Arts £127,500 11%
Other £178,400 15%
Arts grants included:
Glyndebourne Festival Society (£30,000);
Royal Marines Museum Heritage Appeal
  (£5,000);
Birmingham Hippodrome Theatre (£1,500);
Friends of Hampshire City Youth Orchestra
  (£2,000);
Royal Glasgow Institute of Fine Arts
  (£1,000).
The company is a corporate member of the
Courtauld Institute of Art, the English
National Ballet, the English National Opera,
Glyndebourne Festival Opera, the Royal
Academy of Arts, the Royal Opera House,
the Royal Shakespeare Company.
Membership: ABSA, % Club, BITC

Associated British Ports Holdings plc

150 Holborn, London EC1N 2LR

Tel: 0171-430 1177
Company activity: Port operators &
property developers
Sponsorship contact: Mrs M Collins, Press
and Publicity Manager
Donations contact: See above
Donations: £79,000 (31/12/94)
Policy: Arts sponsorship budget: £137,500
(1995). The arts sponsorship policy of the
company is centred on the support of arts
and arts-related organisations and
companies in the local communities where
it either owns a port or operates a business.
It commends and supports the work of
organisations and companies which
encourage and cultivate enterprise, foster
artistic talent among the youth and the
citizens not only of the communities in
which it operates but also elsewhere. It also
supports companies and initiatives whose
reach, influence and quality of work enable
many people to experience and appreciate
works which would normally not be readily
available to them.
Recent sponsorships:
Welsh National Opera;
Opera North;

Scottish Opera;
English National Ballet;
Bournemouth Orchestras;
National Youth Orchestra of Great Britain;
National Youth Orchestra of Wales;
Humberside Arts;
English National Opera;
Dartington International Summer School;
King's Lynn Festival.
The company's charitable donations policy
concentrates on medical and maritime
charities, with an emphasis on those
operating within the locality of ABP's ports.

ASW Holdings

PO Box 207, St Mellons, Cardiff CF3 0YJ

Tel: 01222-471333
Company activity: Steel-making and re-
rolling
Sponsorship contact: Eira Purves, Public
Relations Manager
Donations contact: See above
Policy: Arts sponsorship policy:

 • Projects involving as many members of
   the community as possible to undertake
   activities which would otherwise not be
   accessible to them.
 • Projects supported for a minimum of two
   years to allow for development.
 • Projects of the very highest quality.
 • Where possible, to concentrate on young
   people specifically.
Recent sponsorship has included:
Diversions Dance Company;
Hijinx Theatre;
Live Music Now;
NoFit State Circus;
Rubicon Community Dance;
Vale of Glamorgan Festival;
Welsh National Opera.
The company has a preference for arts
sponsorship as opposed to donations but
says it has no preference for any particular
artform.
Membership: ABSA; BITC

BAA plc

130 Wilton Road, London SW1V 1LQ

Tel: 0171-834 9449
Company activity: Airport operators
Sponsorship contact: No name given
Donations contact: Rachel Rowson,
Company Secretary
Donations: £553,000 (31/03/95)
Policy: The company has in the past
supported a range of arts activities, centring
on visual art and opera. But now the
greater part of BAA's sponsorship and
charitable giving is done through the
subsidiary companies. Increasingly support
will be focused on charities and community
projects in the vicinity of their airports
through the company's own charity (being
registered in 1996).
Applications: Contacts for local appeals:
Heathrow Airport Ltd: Amanda Poole,
Community Relations Manager, Hounslow,
Middlesex (0181-745 4494);
Gatwick Airport Ltd: Suzanne McCulloch,
Public Affairs, Gatwick, West Sussex RH6
0NP (01293-504192);
Stansted Airport Ltd: John Williams,
External Relations Manager, Stansted, Essex
CM24 8QW (01279-502710);
Scottish Airports Ltd: Sandy Ferrar, Head
of Public Affairs, St Andrew's Drive, Paisley,
Renfrewshire PA3 2ST (0141-848 4293).
Membership: ABSA, BITC

Bank of Scotland

PO Box No.5, The Mound, Edinburgh
EH1 1YZ

Tel: 0131-243 5451
Company activity: Banking
Sponsorship contact: R E Scott,
Sponsorship Manager
Donations contact: D Miller
Donations: £760,000 (28/02/95)
Policy: In 1994, the bank and its sub-
sidiaries in the UK contributed £2.2 million
through financial donations, sponsorships,
secondments to charitable organisations
and other community-related projects.

Sponsorship is only undertaken on a
commercial basis and the bank does NOT
sponsor charities. The events cover the arts,
agriculture, sport and community-based
events, and range from the very small to
the very large. The bank also seconds staff
to work with particular organisations.
Arts sponsorship: The bank sponsors arts
events throughout Scotland and aims to
make these readily accessible. In 1990 it
received the ABSA Scottish Award for
outstanding sponsorship of the arts.
Organisations recently sponsored include:
Edinburgh Festival Fringe;
Edinburgh International Festival;
National Youth Orchestra of Scotland;
Pitlochry Festival Theatre;
Royal Lyceum Theatre;
Royal Scottish National Orchestra;
Scottish Ballet;
Scottish Opera;
Scottish International Children's Festival;
Glasgow Citizens' Theatre;
Traverse Theatre.
Applications: Donations are decided upon
by a donations committee which meets as
required. Local appeals can be addressed
either to head office or to the local branch
manager. Sponsorship applications should
be made to R E Scott, Sponsorship
Manager, Bank of Scotland, 61
Grassmarket, Edinburgh EH1 2JF. Two
subsidiaries, the Bank of Wales plc,
Kingsway, Cardiff CF1 4YB and NWS Bank
plc, NWS House, City Road, Chester CH99
3AN, make grants independently of head
office. Applications should be addressed to
the secretary in each case.
Membership: ABSA, %Club

Bankers Trust Company

1 Appold Street, London EC2A 2HE

Tel: 0171-982 2003
Company activity: Finance
Sponsorship contact: Michael Rose,
Community Affairs Adviser
Donations contact: See above
Policy: Arts sponsorship and donations are
handled together with no stated preference
for either.

The company has a specific interest in
supporting the teaching of arts subjects in

inner London schools."

Support for arts projects forms part of the broader-based London community programme, which helps to meet the fundamental needs of disadvantaged people in the inner London area." Recent sponsorships include:

British Youth Opera;

Royal Opera House, "Centre Stage" programme for London schools;

Royal National Theatre, "Stage Door" programme for London schools.

Pyramid Awards (£5,000 each) are offered to support outstanding artists in their year after leaving either the Guildhall School of Music and Drama or the Royal College of Art. The winners are expected to contribute to some facet of the company's community development programme. Closing date during March in 1996.

Membership: ABSA

Barclays PLC

Community Affairs, 54 Lombard Street, London EC3P 3AH

Tel: 0171-699 5000

Company activity: Financial services

Sponsorship contact: Ros Frost, Sponsorship Manager

Donations contact: Mags Gasson, Donations Manager

Donations: £2,193,000 (UK only) (31/12/95)

Policy: In 1995, total contributions in the UK were £6.4 million and included:

Sponsorship £3.2 million

Donations £2.19 million

Economic regeneration £0.7 million

Barclays national sponsorship programme is entirely proactive. Unsolicited requests are not sought. Requests for arts donations are declined. Current national sponsorship initiatives include:

Barclays Stage Partners: £1.5 million programme to enable regional theatre partnerships to stage and tour high quality mainstream work across the country. The Arts Council of England is contributing an additional £1 million to the initiative over the three year period (1996/98).

Barclays New Stages: annual festival of independent theatre in association with the Royal Court Theatre.

Barclays New Futures: £5 million, five year initiative enabling secondary schools to take positive action in their local communities.

Local appeals should be directed to the bank's network of 13 regional offices, each of which has separate budgets for donations and sponsorship activities within its own region. the following examples illustrate this local support:

Alcester Music Festival Fund;

Art Touring Avon, Bewdley Arts Festival;

Falmouth School of Art and Design;

Haverhill Sinfonia;

Honiton Festival;

King's Lynn Festival;

Louth Theatre;

Midland Independent Dance Arts Association;

Questors' Theatre, Ealing;

Southport Music Festival;

Totnes Museum;

West Bridgford Operatic Society.

Applications: See above. Barclays de Zoete Wedd and Mercantile Credit make grants independently of head office. Appeals to Barclays de Zoete Wedd should be sent to Ms A McGill at Ebbgate House, 2 Swan Lane, London EC4R 3TS. Appeals to Mercantile Credit should be sent to C F Schoolbred, Churchill Plaza, Churchill Way, Basingstoke, Hampshire RG21 1GP. However they have limited funds available and applicants are more likely to succeed if they have some business connections.

No specific application forms are required. However, a copy of the latest annual report and audited accounts (the last two years in the case of an initial approach), full information on the project/appeal, including detailed break-down of costs, and where appropriate, full background information on the charity/voluntary organisation and cashflow projections etc., are normally required.

Membership: ABSA, % Club, BITC

BASF plc

151 Wembley Park Drive, Wembley,
Middlesex HA9 8JG

Tel: 0181-908 3188

Company activity: Chemical & audio video products

Sponsorship contact: H C Pattinson, Manager of External Affairs

Donations: £63,116 (31/12/93)

Policy: Arts sponsorship relates to its business and the areas where it operates, in order to demonstrate the company's concern for the welfare of the arts in the community. Music appears to be a predominant interest.

Recent sponsorships include:

Hallé Concerts Society;
Palace Theatre, Manchester;
Royal Philharmonic Orchestra;
Stockport Symphony Orchestra.

Donations to arts organisations are only made regionally. Local branches have their own budgets for community support.

Membership: BITC

Bass plc

20 North Audley Street, London W1Y 1WE

Tel: 0171-409 1919

Company activity: Brewers, hotels & leisure, pub retailing

Sponsorship contact: Aodh O'Dochartaigh, Director of Communications.

Donations contact: Walter J Barratt, Charities Administrator

Donations: £722,000 (UK) (30/09/95)

Policy: No central record is kept of the group's total community investment expenditure, much of which is undertaken by individual Bass companies. Many run community award schemes intended to benefit community initiatives in their particular geographical areas. Donations are preferred to sponsorship.

Arts donations: The arts absorb 25% of the donations budget along with community, youth and education and the environment. Its policy is to provide "patronage for all visual and performing arts with consideration also for museums.

As a major UK and expanding international company a noticeable arts presence in London is encouraged. The company seeks recognition with key audiences and provides corporate entertaining where appropriate. Development of the talents of young people and encouragement of national initiatives and organisations are prime objectives."

Donations in 1995 included:

Foundation for Young Musicians (£5,000);
Royal Academy of Music, Live Music Now!
  (£3,000 each);
National Art Collections Fund, British
  Federation of Young Choirs, National
  Youth Brass Band (£2,000 each).

Sponsorship: The company was a major sponsor of Glasgow City of Culture and more recently to the East of England Orchestra.

Applications: Grants at head office are decided by a donations committee which meets quarterly. Applications, with up-to-date audited accounts, should be addressed to the Charities Administrator.

All subsidiaries have authority to support charities, while some collect and distribute money for charity. Local appeals should be directed to the appropriate regional office (see below).

Company contacts: See above and in addition:

Bass Taverns Ltd, Cape Hill Brewery, PO Box 27, Birmingham B16 0PQ. R J Cartwright, Director of Communications, Bass Brewers Ltd, PO Box 23, 137 High Street, Burton-on-Trent DE14 1EW. I Morris, Communications Director.

Bass Leisure Ltd, New Castle House, Castle Boulevard, Nottingham NG7 1FT. R W Collins, Human Resources Director.

Membership: BITC

BAT Industries plc

Windsor House, 50 Victoria Street, London SW1H 0NL

Tel: 0171-222 7979

Company activity: Tobacco, financial services

Sponsorship contact: Miss S Fisher

Donations contact: A R Holliman, Secretary to the Appeals
Donations: £3,400,000 (UK only) (31/12/94)
Policy: The company gives support principally through donations and corporate membership. It is a corporate member of Glyndebourne, the Royal Opera House Covent Garden, the Royal Academy, the NACF, and the Philharmonia Orchestra.
Membership: ABSA patron, % Club, BITC

Bayer plc

Bayer House, Strawberry Hill, Newbury, Berkshire RG13 1JA
Tel: 01635-39000
Company activity: Marketing of products of Bayer AG, international chemicals and health care company
Sponsorship contact: Andrew Craven, Public Relations Manager
Donations: £169,020 (31/12/94)
Policy: The company supports charities that have a business link, a staff link or a geographical link. The company's main sites are Selby, Newbury, Marlow, Bridgend, Bromsgrove and Bury St Edmunds.
   Preferred areas of support are children/youth, education, arts, medical, and environment and heritage.
Membership: % Club, ABSA

Blue Circle Industries plc

84 Eccleston Square, London SW1V 1PX
Tel: 0171-828 3456
Company activity: Cement & allied products
Sponsorship contact: Ms Jacqueline Sinclair-Browne, Head of Corporate Affairs
Donations contact: Mrs Margaret Nunn
Donations: £351,424 (UK) (31/12/94)
Policy: In 1994, the environment, the arts and sport received 31% of the total donations of over £351,000. An estimate of 17% to the arts was given in previous years.
   The majority of its grants (80%) were made to national organisations and ranged between £100 to £100,000, with local

grants from £25 to £100. Some preference is given to projects in which a member of staff is involved, charities in areas of company presence and appeals related to company presence. The company undertakes limited sponsorship of opera.
Membership: % Club, BITC

BMW (GB) Ltd

Ellesfield Avenue, Bracknell, Berkshire RG12 8TA
Tel: 01344-426565
Company activity: Distributors of BMW cars
Sponsorship contact: Rosemary Davies, Public Relations
Policy: The company aims to be associated with artistic innovation, quality and excellence in a range of art forms. Its sponsorship strategy is developed in association with Arts and Industry, the sponsorship agency.
Recent support has included:
Aldeburgh Festival;
City of Birmingham Symphony Orchestra;
English Chamber Orchestra (corporate member);
English National Opera (corporate member);
Royal Academy of Arts (corporate member).
Membership: ABSA

BOC Group plc

Chertsey Road, Windlesham, Surrey GU20 6HJ
Tel: 01276-477222
Company activity: Industrial gases, health care, vacuum technology
Sponsorship contact: Barbara Shorter, Group Manager Corporate Relations
Donations contact: Julia Humberstone, Asst Manager, Corporate Relations
Donations: £959,000 (30/09/95)
Policy: The main areas of charitable support are the arts, health, medical research and the environment. It prefers to maintain a small number of long-term commitments.
   The company has said that its on-going sponsorship of the BOC Covent Garden

Festival and the National Youth Orchestra means it cannot consider any arts sponsorship projects at present (1996).

Applications: Appeals to head office and local appeals from the Surrey Heath area should be addressed to the correspondent. Otherwise, they should go to the group's regional offices around the UK. Grant decisions at head office are made by a donations committee in combination with specialist staff members in the community affairs department.

The subsidiary company, BOC Gases, makes its own grants independently of head office. Appeals should be addressed to Bob Pirie, **BOC Gases**, Priestley Centre, 10 Priestley Road, Guildford, Surrey.

Membership: ABSA, % Club, BITC.

Booker plc

Portland House, Stag Place, London SW1E 5AY

Tel: 0171-828 9850

Company activity: Food distribution

Sponsorship contact: S C West, Head of Corporate Affairs

Donations contact: Shirley Johnson, Assistant to the Company Secretary

Donations: £79,000 approx (31/12/95)

Policy: Its main sponsorship is the well-established Booker Prize for Fiction (£20,000), with associated display competitions in UK and British Council libraries and book recordings for the blind. It also sponsors the Russian Prize (£10,000). Other recent sponsorships include:

English National Opera;
Royal National Theatre;
London Mozart Players;
Bodleian Library Appeal.

It prefers to support internationally known organisations.

Subsidiary companies are responsible for their own sponsorship focusing in areas where they operate. For example in 1989, Agatha Christie Ltd sponsored the Welsh National Opera.

Membership: ABSA

Bristol & West Building Society

Bristol & West Building, PO Box 27, Broad Quay, Bristol BS99 7AX

Tel: 0117-979 2222

Company activity: Building society

Sponsorship contact: Sharon Chilcott, Head of Corporate Communications

Donations contact: a) Doreen Hill; b) Michele Webber, a) Charity Committee; b) Community Affairs Manager

Donations: £84,158 (31/12/94)

Policy: In Spring 1996 the society was taken over by the Bank of Ireland, so considerable changes may arise.

Donations: Most of the society's charitable donations are made through the Bristol & West Charitable Trust, whose trustees are Sir John Wills (President of the Society), Christopher Thomas (non-executive director and joint vice-chairman) and Stewart Wright (head of customer administration). In total £84,000 was given in 120 charitable donations. Preferred areas of support are children and youth, education and development of individuals and communities. The society is keen to involve its staff, where this is appropriate, as volunteers for assignments or on secondment. There is a strong emphasis, as expected, on charities in the south west, especially Avon.

Applications: In writing to the correspondent.

Membership: BITC

British Alcan Aluminium plc

Chalfont Park, Gerrards Cross, Buckinghamshire SL9 0QB

Tel: 01753-887373

Company activity: Aluminium and alumena chemicals producer

Sponsorship contact: R J Gaunt, Corporate Affairs Manager

Donations contact: Secretary to the Charitable Trust

Donations: £249,000 (31/12/94)

Policy: The company donates to good causes at a local level. Typical donations range from £100 to £1,000.

Applications: Grant decisions are made by a donations committee which meets half-yearly. All divisions/subsidiaries channel appeals to the trust.
Membership: BITC

British Gas plc

Rivermill House, 152 Grosvenor Road, London SW1V 3JL

Tel: 0171-821 1444
Company activity: Gas suppliers
Sponsorship contact: Kate Wilkins, Head of Community Relations
Donations contact: See above
Donations: £1,300,000 (31/12/94)
Policy: The company is a patron of ABSA, spending approximately £1 million on arts sponsorship. Its support has included:
Cathedral Classics LPO tour;
National Youth Jazz Orchestra;
London Bubble Theatre;
Greater Manchester Museum of Science & Industry;
Central Ballet, a small London-based ballet school with special emphasis on finding and promoting young talent.
A number of awards are sponsored, with the Arts Council of England, including:
"Working for Cities" which rewards people who create and use the arts in rejuvenation of towns and cities;
BBC Wildlife Photographer of the Year;
National Heritage Museum of the Year Awards.
Applications: In writing to the correspondent. British Gas Regions deal with requests for assistance in local projects. The unit at headquarters handles all requests which have national implications.
Membership: ABSA, % Club, BITC

British Land Company

10 Cornwall Terrace, Regent's Park, London NW1 4QP

Tel: 01710486 4466
Company activity: Property Investment
Sponsorship contact: John Ritblat, Chairman

Donations contact: See above
Policy: The company give half a percent of profits in donations, sponsorship and other support.
Arts sponsorship: The company has a preference for sponsorship but not for a particular artform. It sponsorship policy: "British Land is strongly committed to investing in the future by providing facilities for young people and children through arts, sport and education, and by funding and fostering support for improvement of the environment." Sponsorships have included:
Sole sponsor of Wright of Derby Exhibition at the Tate Gallery, 1990;
Sole sponsor of Ben Nicholson Exhibition at the Tate Gallery, 1993;
Royal Opera House;
Birmingham Royal Ballet;
London Philharmonic Orchestra;
English National Opera;
Royal National Theatre;
Serpentine Gallery, London.
Membership: ABSA

British Nuclear Fuels plc

Risley, Warrington, Cheshire WA3 6AS

Tel: 01925-832000
Company activity: Nuclear fuel services
Sponsorship contact: R K Williams, Head of Corporate Affairs
Donations contact: See above
Donations: £1,800,000 (31/03/95)
Policy: The company supports schemes and charities in the North West (including national appeals based in the North West). Within this, there may be a preference for West Cumbria.
Sponsorship: Approaches for arts sponsorship are welcomed. Arts exhibitions, theatre productions and musicals are all sponsored. Support has been given to Chester Gateway Theatre and the Royal Liverpool Philharmonic Orchestra. A typical sponsorship ranges from £100 to £5,000.
Charitable donations: The focus is on youth related charities. Support has also been given to the elderly, sport, health, education, arts and museums. Typical national grants range from £100 to

£15,000. Local grants range from £25 to
£1,000.
Applications: In writing either to the
correspondent above or to the general
manager of the nearest factory. A donations
committee meets monthly.
Membership: % Club, BITC

The British Petroleum Company plc

Britannic House, 1 Finsbury Circus, London
EC2M 7BA

Tel: 0171-496 4000
Company activity: Oil industry
Sponsorship contact: Jeremy Nicholls
Donations contact: Chris Marsden,
Community & Public Affairs
Donations: £5,000,000 (31/12/94)
Policy: BP has reviewed its arts sponsorship
policy. It is believed now to be focusing its
contribution on a small number of major
arts institutions and events. Sponsorships
include:
Barbican Art Gallery;
Natural History Museum;
Royal National Theatre;
Royal Opera House;
Tate Gallery (annual rehang).
Annual awards include:
Cardiff Singer of the World Award;
*BP Portrait Award with National Portrait
   Gallery, for artists between 18 and 40
   years old; First Prize £10,000, plus
   discretionary commission worth £2,000;
   Second Prize: £4,000; Third Prize £2,000;
   plus up to 5 commendations of £500
   each. Plus associated BP Travel Award. The
   closing date was April in 1996. For further
   information contact the National Portrait
   Gallery: 0171-306 0055 x245/232.*
Applications: Contacts in other UK
countries:
Scotland: Anne Harper, The British
Petroleum Company plc, 44 Charlotte
Square, Edinburgh EH2 4HR; Charles
Moncur, BP Exploration, 301 St Vincent
Street, Glasgow G2 5DD
Wales: Joe Edmunds, BP Chemicals Ltd,
Seaway Parade, Port Talbot, West
Glamorgan SA12 7BP Northern Ireland: Roy

MacDougall, BP Oil Ltd, Airport Road West,
Belfast BT3 9EA
Membership: ABSA, BITC

British Telecommunications plc

BT Community Affairs, B3001,
81 Newgate Street, London EC1A 7AJ

Tel: 0171-356 5000
Company activity: Telecommunications
services
Sponsorship contact: Roger Broad, Head
of Sponsorship & Publicity
Donations contact: Linda Dowell,
Community Affairs Co-ordinator
Donations: £2,231,000 (31/03/95)
Policy: In 1994/95, BT gave over £14.8
million in community contributions including
financial donations and other support. The
programme is administered under six main
headings, with expenditure under those
headings in 1994/95 as follows:
Arts £2,150,041
Education £2,760,378
People in need £3,198,237
People with disabilities £3,371,502
Economic regeneration £1,973,810
Environment £1,415,196
The general policy is to give a significant
gift for a specific purpose rather than
scatter smaller sums, and to give fewer but
larger donations. Grants to national
organisations range from £250 to
£100,000, and to local organisations from
£50 to £50,000. The company also has a
programme for the provision of
management support for community and
charitable organisations.
   The arts programme is based on selected
countrywide projects rather than major
events in central London. This includes
sponsorship of major company tours of the
UK, usually to locations which, otherwise,
would not normally receive work of the
calibre presented – for example, Northern
Ballet Theatre, South Bank Centre's National
Touring Exhibitions and the BT New
Contemporaries Art Exhibition and Tour
which features the work of young artists.
   Support is also given to amateur arts
including the BT Biennial for Amateur

Theatre and "Making More of Music", a programme of over 100 events in support of amateur music organised by the National Federation of Music Societies.

Two major additions to the programme in 1994 were: the BT Orchestral Series involving all major British Symphony Orchestras in a series of concerts between September 1994 and June 1997; BT National Connections involving work with the National Theatre and groups of young people throughout the UK in a three year project including profession-ally led workshops, regional festivals and a showcase of their work at the National Theatre.

A wide range of local projects such as the Edinburgh Festival, the Belfast Festival and the Welsh International Eisteddfod make up the programme.

See also separate entry for RIBA/BT Community Projects Awards.

Applications: Decisions on major grants are made at head office by the Board Community and Charities Committee which meets quarterly. Smaller grants can be made by staff of the relevant Community Unit at their discretion. Local appeals should be sent to the appropriate BT local office (Contact head office for information. Because of internal reorganisation a list cannot be provided). Each BT zone has its own community affairs staff operating a programme which reflects the needs of that area.

Contacts:
Arts sponsorship: Roger Broad, Head of Sponsorship & Publicity – 0171-356 5388; Secondment: Michele Weiss, Executive Programme Manager – 0171-356 5473; Manpower: Sharon Dove, Resourcing Specialist – 0171-356 4740; Education, including higher education: Peter Thompson, Head of Education Services – 0171-356 4886.

Membership: ABSA, % Club, BITC

Burmah Castrol plc

Burmah Castrol House, Pipers Way, Swindon SN3 1RE

Tel: 01793-511521
Company activity: Oil industry

Sponsorship contact: Liz Rouse, Community Relations Executive
Donations contact: Secretary to the Appeals Committee
Donations: £195,000 (31/12/94)
Policy: Arts projects can be supported from either the sponsorship or the charity budget. All support is restricted to projects taking place in Thamesdown and Wiltshire.
Arts Sponsorship: £15,000 budget in 1995.

Projects supported from the sponsorship budget are ones which:
* are likely to gain good media coverage
* are likely to provide medium to long-term corporate exposure
* have logical synergy with other parts Burmah Castrol's community relations activities
* encourage excellence in arts practice
* provide corporate hospitality opportunities
* include benefits for Burmah Castrol employees

Recent arts sponsorships include:
Swindon College of Art and Design;
Swindon Art Gallery and Museum;
Swindon Arts Centre;
Swindon Old Town Festival;
Wiltshire Kite Festival;
Wiltshire Youth Orchestra.

Arts donations: Projects supported from the charitable donations budget generally provide little or no corporate exposure, but are likely to meet the objectives of:
* providing greater opportunities for people with disabilities to have access to the arts
* using arts-based projects for therapeutic and/or educational purposes

Examples of arts donations include:
Music classes for hearing impaired children;
Drama therapy classes.
Membership: ABSA, % Club, BITC

Calor Group plc

Appleton Park, Riding Court Road, Datchet, Slough SL3 9JG

Tel: 01753-540000
Company activity: Petroleum gas
Sponsorship contact: James P Wilson, National Sales Manager

Donations contact: See above
Donations: £54,267 (31/12/94)
Policy: "We recognise that the cultural well-being of our society is essential and that the arts and sport are direct generators of jobs and revenue in the community. We are continually seeking to develop initiatives that provide arts and sporting activities particularly for the younger generation and the under privileged."

Support and sponsorship has been given to a range of projects such as arts programmes at Wells Cathedral, ballet and curling in Scotland. Sponsorship and donations are handled together and there is no preference for either.
Membership: BITC

Carlton Communications plc

15 St George Street, Hanover Square, London W1R 9DE

Tel: 0171-499 8050
Company activity: TV & photographic production. Carlton Television broadcasts in the London franchise region and Central Independent Television in the Birmingham area.
Sponsorship contact: Beverley Matthews
Donations: £1,345,000 (30/09/94)
Policy: Support is concentrated in the London and Central television broadcast areas and is given for:

* Education/training: Special interest in media fields. There is a general preference for educational establishments rather than individuals' programmes.
* The community: Disadvantaged young people and homeless people.
* The arts: Both Carlton and Central support the National Film and Television Archive, the National Film and Television School and Ravensbourne College. Both also aim to encourage creative talent. For example Carlton is the principal sponsor of the Donmar Warehouse Theatre and funds courses in screen writing, television acting, directing and producing.
* Health: Medical research, victims of disease, illness and people with physical/mental disabilities.

Carlton and Central donate about £1.3 million between them to charities, community schemes and educational projects in their regions, with a preference for appeals relevant to company business and charities in which a member of company staff is involved. Grants range from £100 to £5,000.

Support is also given through donation of stock or equipment, professional services and the use of in-house facilities either free of charge or at cost price.

In addition, in May 1993, the company launched the Carlton Television Trust, to benefit organisations in the former Thames region (see entry under "Trusts")
Membership: ABSA, % Club

Charter plc

7 Hobart Place, London SW1W 0HH

Tel: 0171-838 7000
Company activity: Group parent of companies engaged in rail track equipment, welding, building products & services
Sponsorship contact: See below
Donations contact: Lynda Treacy, Charity Committee Secretary
Donations: £196,000 (31/12/95)
Policy: Charter undertakes arts sponsorship. These have included:
Royal Opera House;
Bath Festival;
Society of Contemporary Arts.
The company says that half its charitable spending goes to educational causes. It is "careful to select only one charity in each of the areas we consider important and make fairly long-term commitments to them".

Donations and sponsorship are handled together.
Applications: In writing to the correspondent. Many more applications are received than can be supported, and applicants are advised to consider if there is any particular reason why their appeal should be supported by the company.
Membership: %Club, BITC

Charterhouse plc

1 Paternoster Row, St Paul's, London EC4M 7DH

Tel: 0171-248 4000
Company activity: Banking
Donations contact: J P Craze, Secretary Charterhouse Charitable Trust
Donations: £68,1117 (31/12/94)
Policy: Donations are made through the Charterhouse Charitable Trust. The trust makes "positive and meaningful contributions" to registered charities only, particularly national charities or those operating in areas where the company has a presence (Liverpool and London).

In 1994/95, the trust had assets with a market value of £644,000 and an income of £123,959 including £50,000 covenant from Charterhouse plc, £5,000 covenant from Charterhouse Bank Ltd, and £50,625 from investment income. Its income is distributed between:

1. Inner city welfare including homelessness & drug or alcohol dependency
2. Major educational charities
3. Fixed annual donations
4. Miscellaneous donations in response to appeals.

The company has been the principal sponsor of the Orchestra of the Age of Enlightenment for the last seven years.
Applications: All appeals should be in writing, and not by telephone, to the correspondent. The charitable trust meets formally four times a year, but suitable appeals are considered by the trustees on a monthly basis.
Membership: BITC

Chevron UK Ltd

2 Portman Street, London W1H 0AN

Tel: 0171-487 8100
Company activity: Distribution of petroleum products
Sponsorship contact: C W Lavington, Government & Public Affairs Manager
Donations: £106,000 (31/12/92)
Policy: Sponsorship: The company sponsors major arts organisations but also looks to the future by encouraging less established artists and musicians. It has supported:
New London Orchestra;
Scottish National Orchestra;
Scottish Ballet;
Scottish Community Drama;
Polka Children's Theatre;
Contemporary Dance Trust.
Donations: Its support is spread across the arts, education, community and health, environment and social welfare organisations, largely in north-east Scotland, the company's operations base. One example is Art in Nature.
Applications: In writing to the correspondent above. Groups in the Cheltenham area should write to: Guy Wareing, Manager, Public Affairs, Gulf Oil, Rosehill, New Barn Lane, Cheltenham, Glos GL52 3LA.
Membership: ABSA

Christies International plc

8 King Street, St James', London SW1Y 6QT

Tel: 0171-839 9060
Company activity: Auctioneers
Sponsorship contact: Mrs Robin Hambro, Charities & Sponsorship Department
Donations: £283,000 (31/12/94)
Policy: "Christies sponsorship and donations policy is based on the ethos that the arts are of prime importance to the cultural life of the community. Therefore, the major portion of their charitable donations goes to underwriting a broad scope of arts-related causes and projects on all economic levels. These range from the conservation of paintings and the fabric of small country churches to the sponsorship of major exhibitions in national museums, arts centres or on the Christies premises at King Street.

One of the important areas of sponsorship is the underwriting of art exhibition catalogues. Christies believes the recording of research on known and lesser known art works is important for future generations of art historians, students and the interested general public. In addition to underwriting the work of a great many health, community, youth and educational projects Christie's also uses its auctioneering expertise to raise money for both health and arts-related charities. This consistent level of charitable support has made Christie's UK a member of the Percent Club."

Exhibitions sponsored in the UK:

New English Arts Club Annual Exhibition 1989 to 1995;

John Channon & Brass Inlaid Furniture Exhibition at the Victoria & Albert Museum 1994;

20th Century Old Etonian Artist's Exhibition 1990;

Kent County Council – Old Master Drawings 1991.

Exhibitions Mounted by Christie's:

Copplestone Warre Bampfylde 1995;

James Smeatham Exhibition 1995;

Foundations for the Future 1995 – an exhibition looking at the past and future of Cambridge University;

The American Museum in Britain 1994 - Fundraising exhibition for the benefit of the museum.

Catalogue Sponsorship includes catalogues for:

The Victoria & Albert Museum;

The Fitzwilliam Museum, Cambridge;

Series of catalogues of Art in British Embassies abroad.

Charitable exhibitions include those held in aid of:

British Field Sport Society;

Art in Academia;

African Medical & Research Foundation;

Wardour Chapel Appeal;

William Heath Robinson Trust;

Bursaries, Funds, Education:

The National Gallery Furniture Fund;

British Library Manuscript Conservation Fund;

Royal Holloway & Bedford New College Bursary;

Centre for the Study of Victorian Art and Architecture.

European Sponsorship: Includes supporting the International Castles Institute, Europa Nostra, and the World Monument Fund

Awards: The Garden of the Year Award in conjunction with the Historic Houses Association 1985-1995 The Europa Nostra Restoration Award

Applications: In writing to the correspondent. Those with particular reference to the company's charitable programme are submitted to a committee who make grant decisions.

Membership: % Club

Ciba-Geigy plc

Hulley Road, Macclesfield, Cheshire SK10 2NX

Tel: 01625-421933

Company activity: Chemical and biological activities.

Sponsorship contact: K V Turpie, Communications Manager

Donations contact: Mrs D Anderson, Secretary to Charities Committee

Donations: £94,000 (31/12/93)

Policy: Support is concentrated on activities in areas where the company has a presence. Each operating unit makes its own decisions about making links with arts activities which tend to focus on young people and be musical/theatrical.

Organisations which have received support include:

Bitesize Theatre Company;

Cambridge Arts Theatre;

Cambridge Youth Theatre;

Children's Circus Theatre;

Grimsby Philharmonic Society;

Horsham Music Circuit;

King's Music Centre, Macclesfield;

Live Music Now!;

Macclesfield Music Festival.

Membership: ABSA

Classic FM

Academic House, Oval Road, London NW1 7DJ

Tel: 0171-284 3000

Company activity: Broadcaster

Sponsorship contact: Douglas Thackaway, Development Manager

Donations contact: See above

Policy: "Classic FM does not have a sponsorship fund but support events in kind with on-air promotion and editorial benefits. Where possible it tries to develop direct listener and staff benefits such as reduced entrance and special evenings. It aims to support each area of the arts at least once a year and is normally pro-active in its selection.

"Classic FM also raises substantial sponsorship funds for its own events such as the EDS Gallery Concert Series."
Recent support has been given to:
Barbican Cinema;
Mark Morris Dance Group;
Royal Academy of Arts;
Tate on Tour;
Sense & Sensibility;
Visual Arts UK (The Year of Visual Arts);
Adventures in Motion Pictures;
Royal Philharmonic Orchestra;
National Appeal for Music Therapy;various
summer festivals.
Applications: Applications are considered, but less than 1% are accepted.
Membership: ABSA

Clydesdale Bank PLC

30 St Vincent Place, Glasgow G1 2HL
Tel: 0141-248 7070
Company activity: Banking
Sponsorship contact: George Edwards, Head of Corporate Affairs
Donations contact: See above
Donations: £85,000 (30/09/95)
Policy: The bank sponsors the arts, sport, and environment and business related organisations/events. The typical sponsorship range is from £100 to £25,000. Arts bodies sponsored tend to be nationally recognised and have included:
Art is Magic;
City of Glasgow Chorus;
Haddo Arts Trust;
National Museums of Scotland;
National Galleries of Scotland;
Scottish Ballet;
Scottish Opera;
Royal Scottish Academy; Traverse Theatre.
Membership: ABSA

Coats Viyella plc

28 Savile Row, London W1X 2DD
Tel: 0171-734 5321
Company activity: Textiles
Sponsorship contact: see below
Donations contact: Sam Dow, Company Secretary
Donations: £175,000 (31/12/95)
Policy: Charitable donations: These are usually given under the following headings: education, the community, the arts, medical research and healthcare, and the environment. Beneficiaries are almost invariably closely associated with the company and its associates. Typical grants to national organisations range from £2,000 to £10,000 and to local organisations from £1,000 to £10,000.

About 25% of it donations budget is given to the arts.

Donations and sponsorship are handled together but sponsorship is very limited and there is a far greater chance of being given a donation.

No particular artform is preferred.
Applications: In writing to the correspondent.
Membership: ABSA, % Club, BITC

Commercial Union plc

St Helen's, 1 Undershaft, London EC3P 3DQ
Tel: 0171-283 7500
Company activity: Insurance & life assurance
Sponsorship contact: Moira Buck, Corporate Hospitality Officer
Donations contact: Jane Miller, Appeals Officer
Donations: £265,267 (31/12/95)
Policy: Sponsorship: The company has sponsored a range of national arts organisations including:
English Chamber Orchestra;
London Philharmonic Orchestra;
Monteverdi Trust;
Royal Opera House;
National Festival of Music for Youth;
School Prom concerts in London and
Cardiff.

Charitable donations: The main areas of charitable support are community welfare, medicine, conservation and the arts, with a particular emphasis on young people. Its giving is concentrated on a small group of national charities which receive long-term support.

Applications: Most of the company's charitable budget is committed leaving little funding available for single donations.

Membership: ABSA, BITC

Coopers & Lybrand

1 Embankment Place, London WC2N 6NN

Tel: 0171-583 5000
Company activity: Accountants
Sponsorship contact: Suzanne Harris
Donations contact: Clare Gardner
Policy: Community support, including staff time exceeded £1.5 million. (No separate figure is available for charitable donations.)

In addition to charitable donations, business advisory services are provided on an honorary basis to many charities and community causes, and office facilities are provided for meetings. The firm focuses on education (mainly higher education), job creation and urban regeneration as well as charities with which partners and staff are involved.

Sponsorship: The firm prefers to sponsor arts organisations which are also registered charities and event which provide client entertainment opportunities. Music, theatre and the visual arts are preferred. Some arts sponsorship occurs through head office but most takes place at regional level. Recent recipients of support include:
Scottish Ballet;
City of Birmingham Symphony Orchestra;
North West Business in the Arts – Business Adviser of the Year Award;
Hallé Orchestra;
Just Jazz Concert in Scotland;
Opera North.
Charitable donations: Donations are only made in exceptional circumstances to arts organisations. It supports young British artists directly by purchasing their paintings and sculptures. Recent donations have been made to:
Scarborough Theatre;
Young Musicians Trust.
Membership: ABSA patron, % Club, BITC

Courtaulds plc

50 George Street, London W1A 2BB

Tel: 0171-612 1000
Company activity: Coatings, performance materials, chemicals
Sponsorship contact: Donald Anderson, Corporate Communications
Donations contact: D A Stevens, Deputy Company Secretary
Donations: £203,433 (31/03/95)
Policy: The company channels its sponsorship and charitable donations principally to causes which publicise its products in relevant markets, which foster an understanding of the chemical industry (particularly in schools and universities), which benefit local communities in which Courtaulds is a significant employer, or which otherwise benefit the company.

In the educational and cultural fields Courtaulds has supported:
Design Museum (founding sponsor);
Courtauld Institute of Art;
Friends of the Royal Botanic Gardens, Kew, the theme being man's use of cellulose, a major raw material for Courtaulds;
National Museum of Science & Industry (corporate member);

Digital Equipment Co Ltd

Worton Grange, Imperial Way, Reading, Berkshire RG2 0TR

Tel: 01734-868711
Company activity: Distributors of digital computers
Sponsorship contact: Jane Mocock
Donations contact: See above
Donations: £1,400,000 (30/06/93)
Policy: Charitable donations: Digital makes donations in three ways:
♦ Computer equipment donations. Ranging from a PC and printer to large networked systems.

♦ A cash budget used in conjunction with employee fundraising activities and to add leverage to equipment donations where necessary.

♦ Contributions via the Digital Charitable Society (see below).

In kind support: The company has provided many of its arts partners with computer equipment. Sadler's Wells, the Royal National Theatre, the Young Vic, Tate Gallery and Royal Academy of Arts are among the recipients. The British Library and Royal Academy of Music are the most recent beneficiaries. Recipient charities should be able to show the need for, and ability to use, the relevant product or service.

Sponsorship: The company spent about £500,000 on its "Partners in Arts" sponsorship programme in 1992/93, mainly on dance and theatre. In dance, the company supports English National Ballet and Northern Ballet Theatre and launched in 1993/94 a new scheme to support dance development, from professional training to new choreography. In theatre, Digital supports productions at the Royal National Theatre.

Digital has won four ABSA Awards since 1987 for its "Partners in Arts" programme.

Membership: ABSA, % club, BITC

Dixons Group plc

29 Farm Street, London W1X 7RD

Tel: 0171-499 3494
Company activity: Retail of electrical goods
Sponsorship contact: Director of Corporate Affairs
Donations contact: Corporate Affairs Department
Donations: £280,000 (30/04/94)
Policy: The company gives assistance through financial support, staff time and contributions in kind.

The company supports all types of charities concentrating on education, medical research, welfare, youth and the arts, enterprise/training and environment/ heritage. All giving for the group is centralised. Requests from national charities are administered by the Dixons Charitable Trust Committee. Grants range from £100 to £10,000.

The company has sponsored museums, music and the visual arts.

Applications: All charity requests are put before a committee on a regular basis and should be made in writing to the correspondent.

Membership: ABSA, % Club, BITC

East Midlands Electricity plc

398 Coppice Road, Arnold, Nottingham NG5 7HX

Tel: 0115-926 9711
Company activity: Electricity supply
Sponsorship contact: Sue Laver, Community Manager
Donations contact: See above
Donations: £80,000 (31/03/95)
Policy: The company seeks to form partnerships with organisations rather than just give cash donations. Support is given to organisations and projects within the areas in which the company operates.

The company has a joint initiative with East Midlands Arts Marketing, the East Midlands Electricity Arts Marketing Fund, which gives grants of up to £500 to arts organisations within the EME region (special leaflet available from EMA).

Arts organisations which have also received support include:
Nottingham Philharmonic Choir;
Nottingham Playhouse;
Royal Philharmonic Orchestra.
Applications: In writing to the Community Affairs Manager.

Membership: ABSA, East Midlands Arts, BITC

Eastern Group plc

PO Box 40, Wherstead, Ipswich IP9 2AQ
Tel: 01473-688688
Company activity: Electricity supply
Sponsorship contact: Peter Gray, Public Relations Manager
Donations contact: Philip Ellis, Company Secretary
Donations: £260,360 (31/03/95)
Policy: Sponsorship: In 1994/95, community sponsorships were around £1 million (excluding donations). The company gives preference to charities in the company's region or national charities which will direct money to the region. Preference for children and youth, the disadvantaged, older people and the environment.

The company undertakes arts sponsorship as part of its commitment to its region. Examples are:
Aldeburgh Foundation (corporate member);
City of London Sinfonia (corporate member);
Royal Opera House (corporate member);
Britten Sinfonia.
Membership: ABSA, %Club, BITC

Economist Newspaper Ltd

25 St James's Street, London SW1A 1HG
Tel: 0171-830 7000
Company activity: Newspaper publishers
Sponsorship contact: Helen Mann
Donations contact: Jean Simkins, Chairman, Group Charities Committee
Donations: £83,000 (worldwide) (31/03/95)
Policy: Charitable donations: Its policy is as follows: "Limited donations are given (typical grants range from £50 to £300) usually to small organisations or projects where sums of this order will have real effect.

"Overall policy directs most donations a) to welfare and (usually medical) research including self-help groups for specific medical conditions or social problems and b) to education very broadly defined, from personal development through community service to public education...

"Contributions to charities which have claims on the company because of business, staff or local connections also take a (carefully controlled) part of the budget. Giving to the arts is a small proportion of the total and always carefully directed to grass-roots projects, or those overlapping with areas of disability or educational disadvantage.

"Within these limitations, visual and performing arts and community arts projects have at various times received modest help."
Arts sponsorship: ONLY supports an annual student exhibition and purchases inexpensive contemporary prints for its offices. NO FURTHER SUPPORT.
Applications: The Group Charities Committee administers the Economist Charitable Trust and consists of volunteers from staff and retirees and meets about 10 times a year. This committee does not involve itself in commercial sponsorship. Please make no sponsorship approaches.
Membership: % Club

Elf Enterprise Caledonia Ltd

1 Claymore Drive, Bridge of Don, Aberdeen AB23 8GB
Tel: 01224-233000
Company activity: Oil & gas exploration and production
Sponsorship contact: Adrienne Gowdy, Public Relations Department
Donations: £667,260 (31/12/93)
Policy: The company is committed to supporting the arts, the environment, education and social welfare groups within the communities in which it operates, principally Aberdeen and Orkney. Preference is given to charities in which a member of company staff is involved. Grants to national organisations range from £1,000 to £20,000. Grants to local organisations range from £50 to £500. Arts organisations which have received support include:
Aberdeen Alternative Festival;
Aberdeen Art Gallery;
Kaleidoscope;

The National Gallery, Edinburgh;
Theatre Cryptic;
Scottish Opera;
St Magnus Festival Concert.
Applications: The company did not wish to have an entry in this guide.
Membership: ABSA

Ernst & Young

Becket House, Lambeth Palace Road, London SE1 7EU

Tel: 0171-928 2000
Company activity: Accountants
Sponsorship contact: Ms Catherine McCormack, Marketing Co-ordinator
Donations: n/a
Policy: The firm supports charitable organisations on a national basis and through its network of regional offices.
Sponsorship: National arts projects, such as sponsorship of the major Picasso (1994) and Cézanne (1996) exhibitions at the Tate, are supported through head office. Other sponsorships include:
English National Opera;
Monteverdi Choir and Orchestra;
Royal Philharmonic Orchestra;
Royal Opera House.

Other UK offices support local initiatives which in 1994/95 included:
The Importance of Being Earnest at the Royal Exchange, Manchester;
The Mayflower Theatre, Southampton;
City of Birmingham Orchestra;
Scottish Opera as well as numerous smaller sponsorships.
Membership: ABSA, % Club, BITC

Fenwick Ltd

39 Northumberland Street, Newcastle-upon-Tyne NE99 1AR

Tel: 0191-232 5100
Company activity: Departmental stores
Sponsorship contact: I J Dixon, Company Secretary
Donations: £91,042 (27/01/1995)
Policy: Sponsorship: has included:
Northern Symphonia Orchestra;
Royal Opera House Trust ;

Royal Shakespeare Theatre Trust.
Charitable donations: Preference is given to projects in areas where the company has a presence (mainly the North East, North Yorkshire, East Midlands and South East).
Applications: In writing to the correspondent. Local stores have an independent budget for appeals.

Ford Motor Company Ltd

Eagle Way, Brentwood, Essex CM13 3BW

Tel: 01277-253000
Company activity: Motor vehicle manufacturers
Sponsorship contact: Don Hume, Public Affairs Manager x2029
Donations contact: R M Metcalf, Administrator, Ford of Britain Trust
Donations: £307,000 (31/12/94)
Policy: Ford makes contributions to the arts. Recent examples have been:
Globe Theatre;
Glyndebourne Opera;
Royal Philharmonic.
(The charitable donations disbursed by the Ford of Britain Trust cover a wide range of activities but the arts hardly feature except for a few local activities. Organisations without a strong employee involvement are advised against making any approaches.)
Membership: BITC

Friends' Provident Life Office

United Kingdom House, Castle Street, Salisbury SP1 3SH

Tel: 01722-413366
Company activity: Long-term insurance
Sponsorship contact: Miss M Ward, Corporate Advertising & Promotions Executive
Donations: £82,232 (31/12/94)
Policy: Criteria includes possible TV coverage, national press coverage, opportunities for corporate hospitality, and an ethical, clean image. Examples of support:
Salisbury Arts Festival;
Mole Valley Arts Festival;
Taverner concerts.

Applications: Unsolicited requests are not considered.
Membership: ABSA

Gallaher Ltd

Members Hill, Brooklands Road, Weybridge KT13 0QU

Tel: 01932-859777
Company activity: Tobacco, optics, housewares, distilled spirits
Sponsorship contact: see below
Donations contact: Miss H J Day, Secretary, Charities Committee
Donations: £481,249 (31/12/94)
Policy: Sponsorship: This is undertaken to support awareness of its main brands, Benson & Hedges and Silk Cut , eg. Silk Cut City Jazz. Gallaher NI sponsors the Ulster Orchestra and its recordings. Requests for sponsorship will not be considered.

Subsidiary companies have their own budgets for charities, and their charitable giving is autonomous, although budget levels are agreed with the parent company.
Applications: Regional contacts for local appeals only:

Mrs J Parker, Virginia House, Gregory Street, Newton, Hyde, Cheshire SK14 4RL

Ms J Kennedy, J R Freeman & Son, PO Box 54, Freeman House, 236 Penarth Road, Cardiff CF1 1RF.

R D Clarke, Virginia House, Weston Road, Crewe, Cheshire CW1 1GH.

C Cunningham, 201 Galgorm Road, Lisnafillan, Gracehill, Ballymena, Co Antrim, N Ireland BT24 1HS.
Membership: ABSA

General Accident plc

Pitheavlis, Perth PH2 0NH

Tel: 01738-621202
Company activity: Insurance
Sponsorship contact: Christeen Payne, Events Manager
Donations contact: P M White, Assistant Secretary
Donations: £395,800 (31/12/94)
Policy: Sponsorship: Arts sponsorship is focused near the Perth main offices or in

Scotland and includes in recent years:
Perth Festival of the Arts;
Perth Theatre;
Royal Scottish National Opera;
Scottish Ballet;
Scottish Chamber Orchestra;
Scottish Opera.
Charitable donations: The company head office only supports national charities covering the fields of education, the arts, historic buildings, medical research and health care, children and elderly people, and social welfare. Local charities are supported by local branches and are made from a budget allocated to each branch.
Applications: In writing to the correspondent, including full details of the work of the organisation concerned, its charitable status and a copy of its most recent audited accounts.
Membership: ABSA

General Electric Company plc

1 Stanhope Gate, London W1A 1EH

Tel: 0171-493 8484
Company activity: Manufacturers of electronic, electrical and power generation apparatus and systems
Sponsorship contact: The Hon Mrs Sara Morrison, Director
Donations: £815,000 (31/03/95)
Policy: The company has formed the GEC Community Service, which in addition to making charitable donations and supporting voluntary agencies, is "intended to respond to national needs and to stimulate community activities wherever GEC has operating units".

The main areas of charitable support are social welfare, education and training. Preference is given to local charities in areas of company presence, appeals relevant to company business and charities in which a member of staff is involved. Direct support is preferred. Grants to national organisations range from £1,000 to 30,000 and to local organisations from £500 to £2,000.

Most support for the arts is for 'educational' activities mainly at a local, rather than national level.

The company is a corporate member of the Royal Academy of Arts and various other arts organisations in the localities of its operating units.

Applications: Appeals (other than local appeals) should be made in writing to the correspondent, who also considers sponsorship proposals.

Applications for local support should be made in writing to the local GEC operating units of which there are 220 in the UK. These subsidiaries and operating units have their own grant budgets. Some of the units also operate a staff charity fund, where the staff collect and distribute money to charity on their own initiative.

Membership: ABSA, BITC

Girobank plc

Bridle Road, Bootle, Merseyside GIR 0AA

Tel: 0151-928 8181

Company activity: Banking

Sponsorship contact: Philip Lloyd, Head of Marketing and Planning

Donations contact: Bob Sayer

Donations: £147,883 (31/12/94)

Policy: Charitable donations: The bank's policy is to support registered charities in the North West of England. It aims to support a wide range of charities with preference for children and youth, community, medical, schools, and enterprise/training. Typically, donations range from £50 to £200 although larger grants have been given (see below).

The bank does not normally support circular appeals, fund-raising events, advertising in charity brochures.

In 1994, major grant recipients included:
Royal Liverpool Philharmonic Society
    Development Trust (£13,333);
Royal Opera House Trust (£6,000);
Liverpool Playhouse (£2,350).

Sponsorship: This includes the Royal Liverpool Philharmonic Orchestra.

Applications: Appeals, in writing, should be addressed to Manager Cashiers.

Membership: % Club, BITC

GKN plc

PO Box 55, Ipsley House, Ipsley Church Lane, Redditch, Hereford & Worcester B98 0TL

Tel: 01527-517715

Company activity: Automotive, defence & industrial services

Sponsorship contact: Nicholas de Jongh, Corporate Director of Public Affairs

Donations contact: Grey Denham, Company Secretary

Donations: £148,000 (31/12/94)

Policy: The company has a limited budget for arts sponsorship (£30,000 in 1994) with which it sponsored an annual concert by the London Philharmonic Orchestra. It has also supported the Ironbridge Gorge Museum.

Applications: Grant decisions at head office are made by a donations committee which meets quarterly. Appeals, in writing, should be addressed to the Company Secretary. Local appeals should be sent to local branches. Subsidiary companies make small grants independently of head office.

Membership: % Club, BITC

Glaxo Wellcome plc

Lansdowne House, Berkeley Square, London W1X 6BQ

Tel: 0171-493 4060

Company activity: Pharmaceuticals

Sponsorship contact: Claire Jowett, Corporate Events Manager (see address below)

Donations contact: Ruth Seabrook, Manager - Charitable Contributions

Donations: £6,500,000 (30/06/94)

Policy: On 1 May 1995 Glaxo plc became Glaxo Wellcome plc, following its merger with Wellcome plc. Prior to the merger of the two companies, both Glaxo and Wellcome had long established programmes of charitable and community support. "Glaxo Wellcome will build upon these traditions and take forward the company's commitment to being a socially responsible and caring organisation".

Charitable donations: All charitable

donations made in the UK are agreed by the Group Appeals Committee, which is a Committee of the Board of Glaxo Wellcome plc. The company considers appeals that fall within the following categories, with particular emphasis on the first two:

• Healthcare in the UK
• Scientific & Medical Education
• International Healthcare
• Environment
• Arts Support - to enable or facilitate the performance, display or establishment of worthy arts projects.

Sponsorship: The company seeks "to encourage the creation, performance and display of diverse and enlightening works as well as supporting innovative educational opportunities for young people". It aims to promote the new Glaxo Wellcome corporate identity to key opinion-formers, to enhance its reputation and create goodwill.

In the arts, the company has sponsored the National Gallery's international exhibition 'Spanish Still Life: From Velazquez to Goya' - seen in London in 1995 by 126,000 people.

Other arts sponsorships have included:
Courtauld Institute of Art;
City of London Festival;
Edinburgh International Festival;
Hertfordshire Chorus;
Music for Youth;
London Musici;
Pavilion Opera Educational Trust;
Royal Opera House overtures programme.
The company is also a corporate member of a number of arts organisations, including the British Museum, City of London Sinfonia, Glyndebourne Festival Opera, the National Gallery, National Art Collections Fund, the Royal Academy of Arts, the Science Museum, Sadlers Wells Theatre, the Royal Philharmonic Orchestra and the Tate Gallery.

Applications: Sponsorship approaches should be made to Claire Jowett, Corporate Events Manager, Glaxo Wellcome plc, Glaxo Wellcome House, Berkeley Avenue, Greenford, Middx UB6 ONN
0171-493 4060.

Organisations seeking support for community projects within the locality or region of company sites should contact the relevant site to request the correct contact.

Applicants are asked to supply a concise summary of their aims, objectives and funding requirements together with a copy of their most up to date audited accounts.
Membership: ABSA, % Club, BITC

Glynwed International plc

Headland House, New Coventry Road, Sheldon, Birmingham B26 3AZ

Tel: 0121-742 2366
Company activity: Engineering & building products, steel
Sponsorship contact: Barry Green, Group Public Relations Manager
Donations contact: Mrs Spurrier, Secretary to the Corporate Services Director
Donations: £120,356 (31/12/94)
Policy: The company supports classical, orchestral concerts. It prefers to support organisations local to the company, to encourage local talent and youth and cultural activities. It is also interested in opportunities for customer entertainment. Organisations known to have received support include:
City of Birmingham Symphony Orchestra; Lichfield Festival.
Membership: % Club

Granada Group plc

36 Golden Square, London W1R 4AH
Tel: 0171-734 8080
Company activity: Entertainments. Subsidiaries include Granada Television Ltd and London Weekend Television.
Sponsorship contact: Monica Deakin
Donations contact: G J Parrott, Commercial Director
Donations: £300,000 (01/10/94)
Policy: Operating companies within the group are encouraged to budget for contributions to charities relevant either to their own operations or the geographical areas in which they operate. Preferred areas of support are children and youth, medical,

education, and the arts. In 1994, five of the main grants awarded were to:
Royal Court Theatre;
Royal Opera House;
Media Trust;
National Film & Television School;
Cinema and Television Benevolent Fund.(See also the Granada Foundation in the "Trusts" section.)
Membership: ABSA, BITC

Grand Metropolitan PLC

20 St James's Square, London SW1Y 4RR
Tel: 0171-321 6000
Company activity: Food, drink, retailing
Sponsorship contact: Fiona Finch, Resourcing & Development Manager
Donations contact: T J Coleman, Trustee & Secretary, GrandMet Charitable Trust (address below)
Donations: £4,755,000 (30/09/94)
Policy: "GrandMet's vision is to contribute actively to the communities in which it operates, seeking to demonstrate a leadership role in helping others to help themselves; empowerment." Most of the group's community work is done through education, training and enterprise programmes which offer opportunities, particularly to young people, to achieve self-sufficiency. These programmes are supported by the Community Relations Team in Brighton (see GrandMet Charitable Trust address see "Applications" below). Arts organisations supported/sponsored include;
Royal Albert Hall;
Royal Academy of Music.
A number of regional projects are supported through subsidiary companies.
Applications: Grants from the GrandMet Charitable Trust are decided by trustees who meet monthly. Applications should be made to T J Coleman, Trustee, GrandMet Charitable Trust at 64/65 North Road, Brighton, East Sussex BN1 1YD 01273-570170.
Membership: ABSA patron, % Club, BITC

The Guardian and the Observer

119 Farringdon Road, London EC1R 3ER
Tel: 0171-278 2332
Sponsorship contact: Camilla Nicholls, Head of Press and PR
Donations contact: n/a
Policy: Both papers benefit from arts sponsorship by:
* associating an existing strength within the paper with a quality event;
* raising the profile of the paper and its arts coverage amongst existing readers and reaching non-readers;
* enabling direct sampling or promotional opportunities.
The sponsorships reflect the papers' readership: educated with a healthy interest in contemporary culture, particularly theatre, music, modern arts, film and dance. It targets its sponsorships to reach a young dynamic audience and prefers national events. For this reason, the most attractive are those that are cutting edge, fresh and progressive ".
Recent sponsorships include:
Observer, John Baldessari Exhibition, Serpentine Gallery;
Guardian, Rites of Passage Exhibition , the Tate Gallery;
Observer, Emil Nolde Exhibition, Whitechapel Art Gallery.
Membership: ABSA

Guinness PLC

39 Portman Square, London W1H 0EE
Tel: 0171-486 0288
Company activity: Brewers & distillers
Sponsorship contact: Ms Lynn Shepherd, Community Affairs Manager
Donations: £1,800,000 (31/12/94)
Policy: Sponsorship: A wide variety of art forms are supported concentrating on London and other regional centres throughout the UK where is has operational sites. The company also supports overseas tours by British art groups to countries where it has a presence.
In 1995 the company launched a major

new project the Guinness "Ingenuity" Awards for Pub Theatre, in association with the Royal National Theatre. This will sponsor around 30 new productions in London in 1996, and will be extended nationwide in 1997. In 1995 the company also sponsored the Royal Academy Summer Exhibition for the fifth consecutive year.

Sponsorship was also given to local groups where the company operates including:
Lyric Theatre, Hammersmith;
Edinburgh Festival Theatre;
Wexford Opera Festival in Ireland.
Charitable donations: Organisations must be registered charities. Specific target areas are the environment, education, the arts and medical (focusing on palliative care).
United Distillers - Sponsorship contact: Janice Mack, United Distillers plc, Distillers House, 33 Ellersly Road, Edinburgh EH12 6JW (0131-337 7373)

Support is concentrated on arts organisa-tions which are based in or have links with the communities in which it has commercial operations. Support is also given to national or regional arts projects which tour the more remote areas of the UK. It particularly looks at the potential for enhanced participation through workshops and masterclasses for the community, including employees. Recent support has included:
Edinburgh Festival Theatre;
EssexDance;
Hammersmith Lyric Theatre;
Scottish Ballet;
Scottish Fisheries Museum.
Applications: The company is taking an increasingly pro-active approach to its community programme, and therefore the number of successful on-spec applications is extremely small.
Membership: ABSA, % Club, BITC

Halifax Building Society

Trinity Road, Halifax, West Yorkshire HX1 2RG
Tel: 01422-333333
Sponsorship contact: Charlotte Weightman, Manager of Sponsorship & Media

Donations contact: Manager, Group Community Affairs
Donations: £1,073,918 (31/1/95)
Policy: The community affairs department is particularly interested in support towards: homelessness, job creation, education/ special schools, elderly and disabled people, medical research, the environment. Arts support is given to projects linked in some way to these interests.

The society is a corporate member of the English National Opera, Northern Ballet, and Royal Philharmonic Orchestra.
Recent support has also been given to:
Huddersfield Contemporary Music Festival;
Opera North.
Membership: ABSA

Honeywell Ltd

Honeywell House, Arlington Business Park, Bracknell RG12 1EB

Tel: 01344-826000
Company activity: Control systems
Sponsorship contact: M Barker, Marketing Promotions Officer
Donations contact: Mrs J A Griffiths, Community Relations Officer
Donations: £25,870 (31/12/93)
Policy: The company aims to support the communities in which it operates and "associate Honeywell with arts organisations producing work of the highest standard. To entertain customers in different parts of the UK. To provide an opportunity for employee participation in the arts".
Organisations supported include:
Hallé Orchestra;
Oxford Playhouse; Royal National Theatre;
Royal Shakespeare Theatre;
Glyndebourne Festival Opera (corporate member);
South Hill Park Trust (corporate member);
Windsor Theatre Royal (corporate member).

IBM United Kingdom Ltd

PO Box 9108, London SW14 8ZN

Company activity: Computers and information technology equipment, systems and services: research, development, manufacturing and marketing

Sponsorship contact: Peter Wilkinson, Peter Wilkinson Associates

Policy: Sponsorship: Support is focused on a small number of sponsorships, including concerts in locations across the UK in cities where it has a business presence. The sponsorships are selected proactively by developing and maintaining relationships with a range of arts organisations. *IBM does not undertake sponsorships proposed through unsolicited requests*. Support has included:
IBM Community Connections Awards;
Concerts at Edinburgh International Festival;
1995 UK tours of the European Community
  Chamber Orchestra;
Opening concert at Belfast Festival at
  Queen's;
Celtic Connections Festival, Glasgow;
Royal Academy of Arts corporate brochure;
National Heritage IBM Museum of the Year
  Awards.

Applications: The majority of community support is given through specific programmes with their own application procedures and criteria. For further information contact the London offices: 76 Upper Ground, London SE1 9PZ (0171-202 3000).

Enquiries from local organisations close to IBM offices and plants should be directed to the Location Manager.

Membership: ABSA founder patron

Imperial Chemical Industries

9 Millbank, London SW1P 3JF

Tel: 0171-834 4444
Company activity: Chemicals
Sponsorship contact: Mrs C L Bean, Group Public Affairs Department
Donations contact: K J Rushton, Appeals Secretary
Donations: £900,000 (31/12/94)

Policy: The company considers approaches from arts organisations/projects in areas where it has a strong presence, organisations of national importance and approaches from groups/projects which involve young or disabled people.

ICI is committed to the communities of which it is a part. Much of its support is therefore at a local level with responsibility for putting this commitment into practice belonging to the local managers. Main UK locations are Billingham, Dumfries, London , Runcorn, Slough, Thorton Cleveleys and Wilton.

It is a corporate member of many major organisations including:
British Museum;
Glyndebourne Festival Opera;
National Art Collections Fund;
National Youth Theatre;
Orchestra of St John's Smith Square;
Royal Academy of Arts;
Royal Choral Society;
Royal Opera House;
Victoria & Albert Museum.

In kind support is given by the *Dulux Community Projects Scheme*, whereby community groups receive free paint. The scheme is designed to "provide help and encouragement to recognised voluntary groups who wish to carry out painting projects for the benefit of the community". In addition cash awards are made to selected projects "offering the greatest potential in terms of creativity and benefit to the community".

Contact: Dulux Community Paints Projects Office, P O Box 343, London WC2E 8RJ (0171-836 6677). Closing date for application forms (stating the paint, quantity and colour required) is normally at the end of May each year.

Inchcape plc

St James's House, 23 King Street, London SW1Y 6QY

Tel: 0171-321 0110
Company activity: International marketing and services group

Sponsorship contact: Joanna Lavender, Corporate Affairs
Donations contact: Mary Maclennan, Corporate Affairs
Donations: £443,000 (31/12/94)
Policy: Arts support has been given to:
Glyndebourne Festival Opera;
Royal Academy of the Arts;
Royal Opera House.
Membership: ABSA

Jaguar Cars Ltd

Browns Lane, Allesley, Coventry CV5 9DR
Tel: 01203-402121
Company activity: Luxury car manufacturer
Sponsorship contact: Liz Baker, Promotions Manager
Donations contact: See above
Donations: £41,576 (31/12/94)
Policy: Sponsorship: The company seeks "association with British arts groups internationally that reflect the Jaguar image. It wants to make contact with potential customers through these associations and, in turn, help the arts cultivate new sponsorships".
In 1994/95 the company sponsored:
Edinburgh Festival;
Royal Ballet;
Royal College of Music;
Royal Shakespeare Company;
Royal Academy of Arts (corporate member);
Royal National Theatre (corporate member);
Welsh National Opera.
Its sponsorship budget in 1995 was £50,000 of which 95% was devoted to the arts.
Donations: The donations budget for the arts is very small, around £5,000. A grant has been given to the Arundel Festival.
Membership: ABSA

Johnson Matthey

2/4 Cockspur Street, Trafalgar Square, London SW1Y 5BQ
Tel: 0171-269 8400
Company activity: Precious metals and advanced materials technology
Sponsorship contact: Ian Godwin, Group

Public Relations Manager
Donations contact: I G Thorburn, Company Secretary
Donations: £254,000 (31/3/95)
Policy: Sponsorship: The company operates a limited programme of mainly opera/musical sponsorship including:
Glyndebourne Festival Opera;
Monteverdi Trust;
Royal Opera House;
National Gallery.
Membership: ABSA patron.

Johnson Wax

Frimley Green, Camberley. Surrey GU16 6AJ
Tel: 01276-852000
Company activity: Cleaning materials
Sponsorship contact: Claire Prior, Consumer Services Manager
Donations contact: see below
Donations: £214,000 (30/6/95)
Policy: The company's charitable support of over £200,000 in 1994/95 was spread over the following interests: social and medical projects (46%), environmental projects (15%) and cultural/entertainment (39%). Most of the 150 organisations supported are based in Surrey, Hampshire and Berkshire.
Beneficiaries have included:
Adonais Dance Company, for a new educational production;
Art & Craft Competition and Exhibition, for schools of Surrey Heath;
Newbury Spring Festival, for a choral concert;
Redgrave Theatre, Farnham, for a production of the Jungle Book;
Surrey Institute of Art & Design, for Chinese textiles exhibition.
Donations and sponsorship are handled jointly.

Kleinwort Benson

20 Fenchurch Street, London EC3P 3DB
Tel: 0171-623 8000
Company activity: Merchant bank
Sponsorship contact: Mrs Christine Willis, Financial Manager Creative Services

Donations contact: Philip J M Prain,
Kleinwort Benson Charitable Trust
Donations: £310,000 (31/12/94)
Policy: Sponsorship: Its arts sponsorship
ranges between £5,000 and £20,000. It is
mainly of events in the City of London, such
as the City of London Festival and
Spitalfields Festival, although major
organisations are also supported.
Charitable donations: The charitable trust,
which supports arts/culture within a very
wide range of interests, normally only
considers appeals from national charities.
Grants generally range between £250 ad
£1,000 and have included the Bach Choir
(£1,000) and the Foundation for Young
Musicians (£750).
Membership: ABSA patron.

Kodak Ltd

PO Box 66, Station Road, Hemel Hempstead
HP1 1JU

Tel: 01442-61122
Company activity: Photographic goods
manufacturer
Sponsorship contact: J G Richardson,
Public Relations Manager
Donations: £882,364 (31/12/94)
Policy: Sponsorship: Organisations which
have been supported include:
BAFTA;
Music for Youth;
National Trust Picture Library;
Royal Academy of Arts;
Royal Photographic Society.
Charitable donations: It prefers to support
local charities working in the local
communities where the company has a
presence and is particularly interested in:
medicine, conservation/environment, the
arts and young people.

KPMG

8 Salisbury Square, London EC4Y 8BB

Tel: 0171-311 1000
Company activity: Accountants and
management consultants.
Sponsorship contact: James Forte,
Director, Community Affairs

Donations contact: Bernard Clow, Partner
Policy: Generally support is given to major
national bodies such as:
Royal Opera House;
London Symphony Orchestra;
Royal National Theatre;
English National Opera.
Donations are also made to selected small
orchestras and theatre groups where a
member of staff has a direct involvement.
Membership: ABSA patron.

Laporte plc

Laporte House, PO Box 8, Kingsway, Luton
LU4 8EW

Tel: 01582-21212
Company activity: Chemical manufacture
Sponsorship contact: R D Ward, Head of
Public Affairs
Donations contact: See above
Donations: £82,000 (02/01/95)
Policy: Arts sponsorship and charitable
donations are handled together with
apparently no preference between either
kind of support. (Its industrial sites which
are mainly located in the Midlands and the
north of England.)
Arts sponsorship: "The company will
consider sponsoring individual concert
performances by youth and regionally-
based orchestras and musical ensembles at
concert halls in areas where it has major
manufacturing plants." The arts
sponsorship budget was £20,000 in 1995.
Recent arts sponsorship has included:
Royal Academy of Music Orchestra;
Liverpool Philharmonic Orchestra;
Buxton Festival.
Charitable donations: "We will assist
small semi-professional musical ensembles
with donations towards the cost of
mounting a concert in a concert venue in
centres where we have production plants."
Arts donations budget £12,000 in 1995.
Recent arts donations have included:
Royal Opera House (corporate membership);
Billingham Festival;
Brocket Consort.
Applications: A donations committee
meets quarterly.

LASMO plc

100 Liverpool Street, London EC2M 2BB

Tel: 0171-945 4500

Company activity: Oil & gas exploration

Sponsorship contact: Nina Hamilton, Public Affairs Advisor

Donations: £154,500 (31/12/94)

Policy: The company sponsors arts organisations, both nationally and locally (in areas of company presence), particularly music and theatre. Arts organisations supported include:

English National Opera;
Royal Shakespeare Company;
London Philharmonic Orchestra;
LASMO Arts Trust (music competition for
  advanced students only).

Legal & General plc

Temple Court, 11 Queen Victoria Street, London EC4N 4TP

Tel: 0171-528 6200

Company activity: Insurance

Sponsorship contact: Sue Green, Group Communications Director

Donations contact: See above

Donations: £477,750 (31/12/94)

Policy: Legal & General gives up to 1% of pre-tax profits to support activities which benefit the community. The long-term aim of the programme is to build a better quality of life. Legal & General believes that the best way to do this is to give significant long-term support to a small number of projects which are directly related to the group's core businesses. Local programmes are used to support the community in places where large numbers of employees live and work.

The company has an established, long-term programme which is run pro actively, in that the company looks for organisations that meet its criteria. Unsolicited appeals are not welcome, although information about organisations which work in the relevant areas is always useful. Local programmes fund a wide range of community activities in areas where employees live and work. Preference is given to projects in which employees are involved.

Local programmes are run in the following areas: Brighton and Hove; Reigate and Banstead.

The company supports the best of classical music, opera, ballet and theatre through a series of six to eight regional performance sponsorships selected annually. It is a supporter and corporate member of :

English National Opera;
Glyndebourne Festival Opera;
Royal Opera House.

Applications: National decisions are made by the Group Communications Division; local appeals are considered by individual offices. Appropriate local appeals should be sent to:

Reigate and Banstead: Rob Catt, Personnel Resources Officer, Legal & General, Legal & General House, St Monicas Road, Kingswood, Tadworth, Surrey KT20 6EU.

Enfield: Ed Christie, Managing Director, Legal & General, Southgate House, 15 Cannon Hill, Southgate, London N14 7DA.

Membership: ABSA, % Club, BITC

John Lewis Partnership plc

171 Victoria Street, London SW1E 5NN

Tel: 0171-828 1000

Company activity: Department stores & supermarkets

Sponsorship contact: n/a

Donations contact: Mrs D M Webster, Secretary to the Central Committee for Claims

Donations: £699,000 (29/01/95)

Policy: Donations: The Partnership's Central & Branch Councils are responsible for about half the total donations (£398,000 in 1994/95). They give to what can be broadly described as "welfare" organisations, generally with charitable status. Organisations at both national (Central Council) and local (Branch Councils) level are supported, preferring to give directly to the organisations concerned.

The chairman is responsible for about half the giving (£301,000 in 1994/95) and gives to organisations which, in broad terms, fall into the categories of the arts, education and the environment. Last year more than half was given in support of musical activities, the rest being divided among the other arts - drama, literature, painting etc., the conservation of buildings, and the countryside and teaching and research, including museums and natural history.

Beneficiaries have included a number of choirs, music festivals etc. including those at Ampthill, Cambridge, Chelsea, Cricklade, Newbury, the Aberdeen International Festival, and the Council for Music in Hospitals. The Partnership continues to support the National Children's Orchestra, as it has since 1979. Other support was given to the Royal Geographic Society to set up a Southern Region; Buckinghamshire County Museum Appeal towards a new art gallery; The Faceless Company, which explores social issues with young people through Theatre-in-Education projects.

Sponsorship: No sponsorship is arranged
Applications: In writing to the correspondent. Applications are discussed quarterly. Local charities should deal with their local Partnership department store, production unit or Waitrose branch.

Lex Service PLC

Lex House, 17 Connaught Place, London W2 2EL

Tel: 0171-705 1212
Company activity: Distribution & leasing of cars, trucks and lift trucks
Sponsorship contact: David Leibling, Head of Corporate Communications
Donations: £245,000 (26/12/94)
Policy: Sponsorship: The company has sponsored:
Royal National Theatre;
Royal Shakespeare Theatre Trust;
National Arts Collection Fund;
Royal Academy of Arts;
Royal Opera House;
English National Opera Company.
The typical sponsorship range is from £1,000 to £5,000.
Applications: In writing to the correspondent. Grant decisions are made by

a donations committee which meets every three months.
Membership: % Club, BITC

Lloyds Bank plc

Corporate Communications, 71 Lombard Street, London EC3P 3BS

Tel: 0171-626 1500
Company activity: Banking & finance
Sponsorship contact: David Goldesgeyme, Sponsorship Manager
Donations contact: Andy Finch, Manager, Community Affairs
Donations: £1,327,000 (31/12/94)
Policy: In December 1995 Lloyds Bank and the TSB Group merged. At the time this entry was prepared (Spring 1996) the separate public identities were still maintained, hence the two entries. Applicants should check the situation.
Sponsorship: The bank spends over £3 million world-wide on sponsorship each year. It sponsors both national and local events, with two main objectives: to promote the bank and its services to existing and potential customers, and to enhance the bank's image in the community at large. Its arts sponsorship policy is focused on the music, film and fashion linking sponsorship to the training and practical encouragement of young people. The national sponsorship programme is proactive and is handled centrally; local or regional sponsorships should be directed to regional executive officers.
The following events are sponsored:
Lloyds Bank Channel 4 Film Challenge for 11-25 year olds to submit short scripts and ideas for programmes. The chosen six are each assigned a director and broadcast in a showcase. Closing date mid December in 1995.)
BBC Young Musicians;
Lloyds Bank BAFTA awards;
Lloyds Bank British Fashion Awards;
Clothes Show Live;
Lloyds Bank Knebworth 1996.
Newport International Competition for Young Musicians.

The bank's regional activity also includes the following:
Brighton Festival;
Britten Sinfonia;
Cambridge University Orchestra & Choral Society;
Charleston Manor Festival;
Devon County Youth Orchestra;
Hallé Orchestra;
Minack Theatre;
New Shakespeare Company;
Northampton Royal Theatre;
Norwich Playhouse.
Applications: Local/regional requests for donations and sponsorship should be addressed to the relevant area directors office. Addresses can be obtained from local branches. All appeals should be properly addressed to the bank clearly setting out the organisation's aims, how much it wishes to raise and full details of the project for which support is required. The application should also include a copy of the report and accounts of the charity.
Membership: ABSA, % Club, BITC

Lloyds TSB Group (see separate entries under Lloyds and TSB)

London Electricity plc

Templar House, 81-87 High Holborn, London WC1V 6NU
Tel: 0171-242 9050
Company activity: Electricity supply
Sponsorship contact: Dorothy I Griffiths, Community Affairs Manager
Donations: £50,000 (31/03/95)
Policy: Total community contributions in 1995 were £547,000. Through sponsorships and charitable donations, the company supports projects which deal in particular with issues of direct concern to Londoners. Its main interests are education and training, urban regeneration and environmental projects. Arts projects which include these aspects are more likely to be considered. Recent arts support has included:
Royal National Theatre (corporate member);
London Schools Symphony Orchestra;

Theatre Royal Stratford East.
Operational managers are encouraged to develop relationships with local community groups including arts groups.
Membership: ABSA, BITC

London Stock Exchange

The Stock Exchange, London EC2N 1HP
Tel: 0171-797-1000
Sponsorship contact: Nick Micheals, Corporate Affairs Manager
Donations: £117,000 (31/3/95)
Policy: The Stock Exchange concentrates its charitable giving in six areas: arts, enterprise, local community, environment, medical and education.

Arts donations have been made to charities whose work focuses on creating access to the arts for disadvantaged groups, for example SHAPE (£10,000).
Applications: In writing to the correspondent.
Membership: ABSA patron

Manchester Airport

Manchester M90 1QK
Tel: 0161-489 3602
Company activity: International airport operator
Sponsorship contact: Sue Jones, Arts Sponsorship Manager, Corporate Affairs Directorate
Donations: £57,952 (31/3/93)
Policy: Arts sponsorship budget: £430,000 (1996/97). "Manchester Airport contributes 1% of gross operating profit to arts sponsorships as a minimum... We particularly value the cultural strength of the organisations in Greater Manchester and think it is important to support the centres of excellence in the area.

The company's portfolio includes: Music, Dance, Theatre, Museum and Opera and covers support for education and community projects, as well as production sponsorships. One of the aims of the airport's arts sponsorship is to make the city of Manchester more attractive to inbound tourism."

Recent sponsorships include:
Bolton Octagon;
Bury Met;
Contact Theatre;
Green Room;
Hallé Orchestra, to tour Japan;
Library Theatre;
Manchester Evening News Theatre Awards;
Manchester Museum of Science & Industry;
Opera North;
Rambert Dance Company;
Royal Exchange Theatre;
Tate Gallery;
*Skylights Circus Acts; Sandbach Arts
  Festival;*
*ABSA corporate sponsor award winner
  1993/94.*
Charitable donations: No arts donations
made.
Membership: ABSA

Manweb plc

Sealand Road, Chester CH1 4LR

Tel: 01244-652090
Company activity: Electricity supply
Sponsorship contact: Mrs Gaynor Kenyon,
Public Relations Officer
Donations contact: Mrs Jackie Unsworth,
Public Relations Officer
Donations: £85,638 (31/03/95)
Policy: Sponsorship: Arts sponsorship is
limited to two or three events a year,
planned well in advance.
Charitable donations: These are given to
organisations in its area of operations, and
its priorities include projects to help work
creation and new enterprises, projects
which help elderly and disabled people. In
1994/95 a major grant was given to Crewe
Lyceum Theatre (£30,000) and Live Music
Now! also received support.
Membership: ABSA, % Club, BITC

Marks and Spencer plc

Michael House, Baker Street, London
W1A 1DN

Tel: 0171-935 4422
Company activity: International retail
company

Sponsorship contact: Jane Leyland,
Assistant Manager, Arts, Heritage &
Community Arts
Donations contact: See above
Donations: £4,635,000 (31/03/95)
Policy: Marks & Spencer's corporate social
responsibility programme has two main
elements: donations and staff secondments.
Both include support for a variety of local
economic initiatives, with support
concentrated on deprived inner city and
rural areas, and projects in which company
staff and their families take an interest.

Community contributions in 1994/95
totalled £7,640,000 and were broken down
as follows:
Arts, heritage and community arts
£850,000
Health and care £1,885,000
Education, environment and community
£1,280,000
Matching funds and local support for stores
£620,000
Secondment £2,320,000
Departmental and support costs £685,000.

Arts sponsorship and donations are
treated together. Once a project is selected
for support a decision is made as to which
type of assistance is most appropriate. Its
programmes operate both nationally and
locally. Their regional programme not only
helps fund local arts activities but also
enables national companies to appear in
the provinces. Its support is wide-ranging
and covers all the traditional art forms
including design, crafts, the written word
and creative science. The company works
in institutions such as hospitals, day
centres and prisons and with particular
groups who would not easily have access
to the arts, for example elderly people and
those with special needs. Conservation of
heritage is supported by assisting the
training of young people in restoration
techniques. "We should avoid sponsorship
programmes that would only be accessible
to elite groups."

Store staff are asked to advise on appeals
in their local area and all stores are also
given a budget to be used for small local
appeals. The company will match on a £1

for £1 basis, monies raised by stores, distribution centres and head office department for specific projects.

In addition every year over 200 members of staff are seconded to projects in the community on either a full-time or part-time basis. Its staff offer specialist skills as business advisers through Business in the Arts (see Association of Business Sponsorship of the Arts).

The following list of arts sponsorships/donations shows that the widest range of activities is supported from the major national organisations to local community arts groups:
Royal Academy of Arts;
Aberdeen International Youth Festival;
Artlink, Edinburgh & Lothians;
Arvon Foundation;
Bedside Manners;
Blackpool Grand Theatre;
Broxbourne Midsummer Festival;
Canterbury Festival;
Central School of Ballet;
Chicken Shed Theatre Company;
City of Birmingham Symphony Orchestra (corporate member);
Council for Music in Hospitals;
Dolphin Opera;
East Molesey Textile Conservation Centre;
Edinburgh International Festival (corporate member);
Equal Arts;
Humberside Dance Agency;
Ipswich Museums Trust;
Kneehigh Theatre;
Ludus Dance Company;
Magic Lantern;
Norden Farm Community Arts Centre;
Paisley Art Institute;
Turtle Key Arts Centre;
Peterborough Storytelling Festival;
Poetry Society;
Share Music Courses;
Stand Magazine;
Raku Works Sculptural Arts;
Welsh Academy of Literature;
Yorkshire Sculpture Park.
The ABSA report 1994/95 lists 178 arts organisations supported by the company.
Applications: The programme is

administered from the London office by 9 staff. The department receives some 20,000 letters each year, about 10,000 are appeals. All applications should be in writing to the relevant contact at the address above.

Stores have a small budget for local initiatives, managed by the store charitable donations committee.
Membership: ABSA, % Club, BITC

Mars UK Ltd

3D Dundee Road, Slough, Berkshire SL1 4LG
Tel: 01753-693000
Company activity: Food manufacture
Sponsorship contact: Steve Clark, Event Marketing Manager
Donations contact: Jenny Ward
Donations: £541,980 (31/12/93)
Policy: The company sponsors national and local activities in the visual and performing arts. Recent support includes corporate membership of the following major organisations:
English National Opera;
London Symphony Orchestra;
Royal Academy of Arts;
Royal National Theatre.
Applications: Approaches by local charities should be made directly to operating companies.
Membership: ABSA

John Menzies plc

Hanover Buildings, Rose Street, Edinburgh EH2 2YQ
Tel: 0131-225 8555
Company activity: Newsagents, booksellers, stationers
Donations contact: C A Anderson, Company Secretary
Donations: £153,000 (30/04/95)
Policy: The company supports Scottish charities and those in areas of company presence. Recent examples of arts sponsorship and/or donations:
National Galleries of Scotland;
Pitlochry Festival Society;
Scottish National Orchestra;
Scottish Opera;

Scottish Theatre Company ;
St Andrews Festival Society.
Applications: In writing to the
correspondent.
Membership: % Club

Mercury Communications Ltd

New Mercury House, 26 Red Lion Square,
London WC1R 4HQ

Tel: 0171-528 2000
Company activity: Telecommunications
services
Sponsorship contact: Louise Gibson,
Sponsorship & Community Affairs Co-
ordinator
Donations contact: Sara Wagnall,
Manager, Corporate & Community Affairs
Donations: £801,000 (31/03/95)
Policy: Mercury supports the arts where
innovation and excellence are displayed in
order to reach specific target audiences.

Its community affairs programme focuses
on education, particularly in the areas of
communications, science and technology.
Support is provided to communications-
related projects that benefit disadvantaged
groups in communities local to its major
sites in London, Brentford, Manchester,
Birmingham, Bracknell, Milton Keynes, and
Glasgow.
Recent arts sponsorships/donations include:
Mercury Music Prize;
Donmar Warehouse;
Royal Court Theatre, for signed perform-
  ances;
Royal Exchange;
Youth & Music;
National Museum of Film, Photography and
  Television.
Applications: Although appeals are
considered continuously, the company's
existing and projected community affair
commitments will severely limit the number
of new appeals that can be successful.

Midland Bank plc

Poultry, London EC2P 2BX
Tel: 0171-260 8000
Company activity: Banking
Sponsorship contact: Ms B Furneaux-
Harris, Sponsorship & Donations Manager
Donations contact: See above
Donations: £1,000,000 (31/12/95)
Policy: The bank has carried out an entire
review of its community programme and has
decided to focus its support within three
areas: education, sport and popular culture,
urban/economic regeneration. By "popular
culture" is meant TV, music, film, dance and
leisure activities – all of which have a strong
orientation towards youth. It is "re-directing
its sponsorship from high-profile, televised
events to those that are more locally-based
and more closely linked with education and
training, the disadvantaged and deprived.
Midland is realistic about the objective it
hopes to achieve through the sponsorship –
projection of an image of responsibility,
contact with the community, a willingness to
give something back in return for business
gained, and a degree of favourable public
comment." Its philosophy for the arts is to
bring a variety of activities to the widest
number of people throughout the country.
Arts organisations sponsored include:
Midland Bank Proms at the Royal Opera
  House;
Royal Academy of Arts, outreach programme;
Birmingham Royal Ballet;
City Arts Trust;
Derby Playhouse;
Classical Christmas Festival;
Lichfield Festival;
Llangollen Eisteddfod;
Nottingham Youth Orchestra;
National Eisteddfod;
Hay Festival;
Mayflower Theatre;
University of York Orchestra:
Welsh Proms.
Applications: Local community project
contacts:
London area: Charity Liaison Officer,
Midland Bank plc, 2nd Floor, 27-32 Poultry,
London EC2P 2BX

Midlands area: Charity Liaison Officer, Midland Bank plc, PO Box 13, Exchange Buildings, 8 Stephenson Place, New Street, Birmingham B2 4NH
Northern area: Charity Liaison Officer, Midland Bank plc, PO Box 59, Midland Bank House, Bond Court, Leeds LS1 1LL
Southern area: Charity Liaison Officer, Midland Bank plc, Broadfield Park, Brighton Road, Crawley, West Sussex RH11 9FA
Wales: Charity Liaison Officer, Midland Bank plc, 8th Floor, Churchill House, Churchill Way, Cardiff CF1 4AX.
Membership: ABSA patron, % Club, BITC

Midlands Electricity plc

Mucklow Hill, Halesowen, West Midlands B62 8BP

Tel: 0121-423 2345
Company activity: Electricity supply
Sponsorship contact: Gail Wesley, Community Affairs Officer
Donations: £1,625,000 (31/03/95)
Policy: Recent sponsorships/donations have included:
Birmingham Readers and Writers Festival;
Birmingham Repertory Theatre;
Birmingham Symphony Hall;
City of Birmingham Symphony Orchestra;
City of Birmingham Symphony Orchestra
  Chorus;
Cheltenham International Music Festival;
English String Orchestra;
Welsh National Opera.
Membership: ABSA; BITC

Miller Group Ltd

Miller House, 18 South Groathill Avenue, Edinburgh EH4 2LW

Tel: 0131-332 2585
Company activity: Building & civil engineering
Donations contact: Janet Tully, Appeals Administrator
Donations: £59,000 (31/12/94)
Policy: Its policy is to help many causes in a small way, particularly those in the vicinity of the company's main offices ie. Colnbrook, Darlington, Dunfermline,

Edinburgh, Glasgow, Godalming, Lymm, Normanton, Rugby, Wakefield, Washington, Winchester. The company supports ballet, music and opera.
Membership: % Club

Mobil Oil Company Ltd

Mobil House, 500/600 Witan Gate, Central Milton Keynes MK9 1ES

Tel: 01908-853000
Sponsorship contact: Tracy Perrins, Manager Public Affairs Programme
Donations contact: See above
Policy: Sponsorship: The company prefers arts sponsorships to donations. Its sponsorship programme aims to: support its business objectives; enhance its reputation for excellence; play a part in the life of the local communities where it has employment centres, ie. Milton Keynes, Merseyside, Essex, Belfast and Dublin.
  Preferred artforms are: music, theatre, opera and youth programmes at national and regional level. Recent arts sponsorship include:
Birkenhead Arts Association;
Essex Youth Orchestra;
Greenwich Leisure Services;
Lichfield Festival;
PW Productions – Mobil Touring Theatre;
Southend Music Club;
Royal Exchange Theatre.
Donations: Not usually made to the arts.
Membership: ABSA

Morgan Crucible Company plc

Morgan House, Madeira Walk, Windsor, Berkshire SL4 1EP

Tel: 01753-837000 ext 222
Company activity: Materials & components for industry
Donations contact: D J Coker, Company Secretary
Donations: £99,566 (4/1/95)
Policy: The company states that its main support goes to relatively small "niche" charities in the fields of medical care and research. Grants range from £200 to £500, and are distributed by the Morgan Crucible

Charitable Trust. In 1994, the company gave £99,566 to UK charities and £44,423 to overseas charities. Grants are made nationally, but primarily in Wirral, Leeds, South Wales, South London, Worcester and Thames Valley. Some limited support for the arts in areas of company presence. Subsidiary companies have their own budgets for appeals, but no figures are available.

Applications: Grant decisions are made by a donations committee which meets quarterly.

Morgan Grenfell Group plc

23 Great Winchester Street, London EC2P 2AX

Tel: 0171-614 5298
Company activity: International merchant banking
Sponsorship contact: R P Elliston
Donations contact: Miss J White
Donations: £228,300 (31/12/94)
Policy: Charitable donations: All the group's charitable donations are distributed by head office mainly through the Charities Aid Foundation. Donations are only made to registered charities with support primarily given to national charities but local charities are supported if they are in, or for the benefit of, or have another connection with, the City of London. National charities donations usually range between £500 to £1,000.

Within these broad guidelines, the group supports organisations working in the areas of medical research/welfare, arts and music, social welfare, education, heritage and environment, disabled people, children and youth, religion, trades and professions, elderly people, armed forces and overseas aid. Support has been given to:

National Gallery, for complete illustrated catalogue in book and CD Rom form.
Membership: % Club, BITC

The National Grid Company plc

National Grid House, Kirby Corner Road, Coventry CV4 8JY

Tel: 01203-537777
Company activity: Electricity supply
Sponsorship contact: Tim Beaumont, Head of Public Relations
Donations contact: Sue Tyler, Donations Co-ordinator
Donations: £478,000 (31/03/95)
Policy: Community contributions in 1994 totalled £1,398,000 including £478,000 in charitable donations. In its developing community relations programme particular emphasis is given to environmental and educational initiatives.

Its charitable donations are made to national organisations and local charities in areas of company presence. The University of Warwick Arts Centre was a recent major beneficiary.

Sponsorship is undertaken on a local and national level including the arts, environment and education. Arts sponsorship covers music, theatre, festivals and galleries.
Applications: In writing to the correspondent. Local appeals should be made to regional offices.
Membership: ABSA, BITC

National Power plc

Windmill Hill Business Park, Whitehill Way, Swindon, Wiltshire SN2 6PB

Tel: 01793-877777
Company activity: Electricity generation & supply
Sponsorship contact: Philippa Calvert, Sponsorship Manager
Donations contact: John Hermans, Charitable Trust Officer
Donations: £500,000 (27/3/95)
Policy: Sponsorship: Arts, education and community initiatives are sponsored in areas of company presence. It looks for events which provide the right corporate entertaining opportunities.

Arts sponsorship includes;
English National Opera (corporate member);
Glyndebourne Festival Opera (corporate member);

*London International Piano Competition;
London Symphony Orchestra (corporate
member);
Philharmonia Orchestra;
Royal Opera House (corporate member).*
Membership: ABSA, % Club, BITC

National & Provincial Building Society

Provincial House, Bradford BD1 1NL

Tel: 01274-842503
Sponsorship contact: Sandra Cooper,
Sponsorship Manager
Donations contact: See above
Donations: £130,000 (31/12/94)
Policy: Arts Sponsorship and Donations
Budget: £200,000 (1995)

For both its donations and sponsorship
which are handled together the society has
developed a particular commitment to the
communities in which it operates, to the
socially disadvantaged and housing/homeless-
ness. In addition sponsorships must enhance
its image, offer visibility and opportunities for
corporate hospitality and, in some cases,
demonstrate its support for Bradford.
Recent sponsorships include:
*English Camerata;
Northern Broadsides;
National Trust Children's Concert;
Burnley Municipal Choir and Orchestra;
National Museum of Film, Photography and
Television.*
Recent donations include:
Bradford Festival.
Membership: ABSA

NatWest Group

41 Lothbury, London EC2P 2BP

Tel: 0171-726 1000
Company activity: Banking
Sponsorship contact: Amanda Jordan,
Head of Community Relations
Donations: £2,789,472 (31/12/94)
Policy: Arts sponsorship: The NatWest
Group has been undertaking a detailed
review of its arts sponsorship policy. The
NatWest Group seeks to be associated with
creativity, quality and excellence, particularly

amongst young people, making arts more
accessible to communities in which it
operates and offering corporate hospitality
opportunities.
Recent sponsorship includes:
*Garsington Opera (corporate member);
Glyndebourne Opera (corporate member);
Royal Academy of Arts;
Royal Opera (corporate member);
Royal Shakespeare Company (RSC NatWest
regional tour);*
NatWest 90s Prize for Art, open to artists
aged 35 years and under, including art
students. 1st Prize £20,000; 2nd Prize
£10,000; 3rd Prize £5,000. Special
additional Student Prize of £1,000. Entries
by 1 February (in 1996). Contact: PO Box
8926, London SW4 6ZA.
*The Business in the Arts/NatWest Board
Bank*, a register of middle and senior
business managers prepared to joint of the
of arts organisations, was launched in 1996.
Charitable donations: "The priority of the
NatWest Group Charitable Trust is to help
young people adjust to the changing world
of work. The trust funds projects in the
areas of volunteering and citizenship as well
as promoting new models of enterprise and
community development." Example of arts
donation: Haringey Arts Council.
Applications: Centrally, partnership funding
means that the group commits much of its
resources to long-term relationships. New
projects are agreed either through proactive
approaches or guidelines for applications are
developed and publicised amongst
appropriate organisations.

Applications for local projects only should
be made in writing to the nearest NatWest
branch.
Membership: ABSA, % Club, BITC

Nestlé UK Ltd

Community Relations Department, York
YO1 1XY

Tel: 01904-602233
Company activity: Food manufacturers &
distributors
Donations contact: Peter J Anderson,
Community Relations Manager

Donations: £864,000 (31/12/95)
Policy: The company considers donations in various fields which relate to arts and culture, community development, education, enterprise, environment, health (medical), or young peoples sport. Support is given to properly managed activities of high quality in their particular field. However, a relevant link or connection with the company's business is usually looked for, this may be geographic (within the catchment area of company factories, there are over 25 locations throughout the UK), related to the food industry or through connections with university departments or employee activities. Employees involved with local voluntary groups may apply for a grant of up to £1,500.

The Special Helper Award allows employees to nominate local organisations for a grant of £10,000. London Mozart Players once again received one of the largest donations in 1995.
Other recent sponsorship/donations include:
London Mozart Players;
York Theatre Royal;
York Early Music Festival;
Ryedale Festival.
Applications: Applications for support of local good causes should be made to the Manager of the nearest Nestlé location, but for large scale donations or national charities the request should be sent to Community Relations Department.
Membership: ABSA, % Club, BITC

News International plc

PO Box 495, Virginia Street, London E1 9XY

Tel: 0171-782 6995
Company activity: Printing & publishing
Sponsorship contact: a) Toby Constantine; b) Ellis Watson, a) Director of Marketing Times Newspapers Ltd; b) Director of Marketing News Group Newspapers Ltd
Donations contact: Andrew White, Deputy Director of Corporate Affairs
Donations: £800,000 (30/06/95)
Policy: Sponsorship: Arts sponsorship is undertaken, especially by the Times and Sunday Times. The Mozart Festival, London

art exhibitions and Blackheath Youth Theatre have been supported.
Charitable donations: "The company's policy does not give priority to the arts, unless the project concerned has a strong educational element."
Applications: In writing to the correspondent. The charities committee meets regularly. Unsuccessful applicants are given reasons and the corporate policy explained.

Appeals to subsidiary companies should be made to managing directors, managing editors or editors. In some cases larger requests are referred to the charities committee.

Sponsorship proposals to the group should be addressed to the Director of Marketing, News Group Newspapers or the Director of Marketing, Times Newspapers.

Northern Electric plc

Carliol House, Market Street, Newcastle-upon-Tyne NE1 6NE

Tel: 0191-221 2000
Company activity: Electricity distribution & supply
Sponsorship contact: Julian L Kenyon, Community Affairs Officer
Donations contact: See above
Donations: £229,000 (31/03/95)
Policy: Arts charitable donations/ sponsorship are focused entirely upon events and projects within the North East and North Yorkshire. The company is interested in region-wide projects and/or to spread its programme in a balanced way across the area, across all art forms and to interest all customer groups. There is a special emphasis on activities that bring opportunity to the disadvantaged and disabled. Sponsorship/charitable donations have included:
Northern Electric Arts Awards;
Architectural Design Award Prize;
Alnwick Festival;
Bede Foundation;
Dance City;
Drake Music Project;
Durham Street Studios;

First Act Theatre;
Live Music Now!;
Northern Screen Commission;
Northern Sights;
Royal Shakespeare Company in Newcastle;
Sunderland Empire;
Sunderland Festival of the Air;
Whitley Bay Jazz festival;
Japan Festival North.
Membership: ABSA, % Club, BITC

Northern Foods

Beverley House, St Stephen's Square, Hull
HU1 3XG

Tel: 01482-325432
Company activity: Food manufacturer
Donations contact: Secretary to Appeals
Committee
Donations: £695,000 (31/3/95)
Policy: Donations are the preferred type of
support for the arts. However the arts are a
relatively new category of charitable giving
by the company and only a small
percentage of the above figure is devoted
to the arts. Arts projects in locations near to
the company sites (spread throughout the
UK) are preferred, also projects which
introduce the arts to as wide an audience as
possible. Arts projects supported include:
Opera North, for work in schools;
Northern Broadside for its community-
based productions;
Humberside Dance Agency, for its work in
special schools;
Maltings Art Press, Hull, which introduces
young unemployed people to screen
printing.
Membership: ABSA; % Club, BITC

Northern Rock Building Society

Northern Rock House, Gosforth,
Newcastle-upon-Tyne NE3 4PL

Tel: 0191-285 7191
Company activity: Building society
converted to bank
Sponsorship contact: David Henderson,
Advertising & Public Relations Manager
Policy: Northern Rock is using its conversion
to a bank to set up a charitable foundation

to receive 5% of the bank's annual pre-tax
profits. This should generate about £7
million in its first year. The foundation should
be established in January 1998 after the
bank's flotation in Autumn 1997.
The foundation is expected to support
charitable causes mainly in the North East.
Membership: ABSA patron

NORWEB plc

Talbot Road, Manchester M16 0HQ

Tel: 0161-873 8000
Company activity: Electricity supply
Sponsorship contact: Paul Matley,
Marketing Department
Donations contact: G C Tong, Secretary to
the Charity Committee
Donations: £126,331 (31/03/95)
Policy: Sponsorship of arts/cultural events
has included:
17th Tameside Canals Festival;
Royal Exchange Theatre;
Hallé Orchestra.
Applications: In writing to the
correspondent.
Membership: % Club, BITC

Norwich Union Life Insurance Society

Surrey Street, Norwich NR1 3NG

Tel: 01603-622200
Company activity: Insurance
Sponsorship contact: Donna Barker, PR
Manager
Donations contact: David Barker, Head,
Secretary's Department
Donations: £257,000 (31/12/94)
Policy: Sponsorship: In March 1996 the PR
Manager wrote; "Norwich Union's
sponsorship policy is to sponsor events/
projects which:
♦ have a direct link with our core business
    ie. insurance, investment, healthcare
♦ are capable of sustained media coverage
♦ provide unique hospitality opportunities.
At present Norwich Union has no major arts
sponsorship and is not actively seeking one.
The group's most notable foray into arts
sponsorship was involvement with the

English National Ballet's production of 'The Nutcracker' (1990-1996)."
Donations: The group's charitable giving is currently being reviewed but concentrates primarily on charities with links to the business eg. health, safety, transport etc.
Membership: % Club, BITC

Pannell Kerr Forster

New Garden House, 78 Hatton Garden, London EC1N 8JA

Tel: 0171-831 7393
Company activity: Accountants
Sponsorship contact: Guy Bigland, National Marketing Director
Donations contact: Charles Cox, Audit Partner
Donations: £316,500 (1993) (30/4/94)
Policy: Donations and sponsorship have been given to:
Royal National Theatre;
Millstream Touring Theatre;
East of England Orchestra;
London Baroque Orchestra.
Membership: % Club, BITC

Pearson plc

3 Burlington Gardens, London W1X 1LE

Tel: 0171-411 2000
Company activity: News information & entertainment; UK businesses include: Financial Times; Longman Group; Penguin Publishing; the Economist (50% owned).
Sponsorship contact: Clare Peddell
Donations contact: Anette Lawless, Company Secretary
Donations: £486,000 (31/12/94)
Policy: Sponsorship: The company sponsors one major London-based visual arts exhibition a year:
Victoria & Albert Museum, W N Pugin
  exhibition, 1994;
Tate Gallery, Dynasties – Painting in Tudor
  and Jacobean England – exhibition, 1995.
V & A, William Morris, 1996.

It is a corporate member of:
Design Museum;
Dulwich Picture Gallery;
English Chamber Orchestra;

Friends of National Libraries;
Garsington Opera;
Glyndebourne Opera;
Monteverdi Choir;
National Art Collections Fund;
Royal Academy of Arts;
Student Design Awards;
Whitechapel Art Gallery.
Charitable donations: Most support is given in the fields of education and social welfare. Main beneficiaries in 1994 included:
British Library;
Oxford Bodleian Library (endowment for a
  New Media Librarian of £1 million over 10
  years).
Arts donations are generally not made.
Applications: Local and trade appeals should be sent directly to the relevant subsidiary company.

Lazard Brothers & Co Ltd has its own charity committee. The latest charitable donations figure available is £205,000 in 1989. The contact is the Secretary of the Charities Committee, Lazard Brothers 7 Co Ltd, 21 Moorfields, London EC2P 2HT (071-588 2721).
Membership: ABSA, % Club

Pilkington plc

Prescot Road, St Helens, Merseyside WA10 3TT

Tel: 01744-28882
Company activity: Glass manufacturing & processing
Sponsorship contact: Chris Moore, Corporate Affairs Manager
Donations contact: David Roycroft, Chairman, Grants Committee
Donations: £175,000 (31/03/96)
Policy: Charitable donations: "Pilkington supports local educational activities, employment programmes, the arts and charitable work in the communities where it operates." The company pays particular attention to the community of St Helens where its major site is located. Its grants committee gives donations ranging between £50 to £5,000. These donations totalled £175,000 in 1995/96. The donations list included:

Citadel Arts Centre (£7,500);
Council for Music in Hospital (£1,000);
Worshipful Company of Glaziers and
    Painters of Glass (£1,000).
Applications: In writing to the
correspondent. Decisions are made by the
grants committee which meets every two
months.
Membership: % Club, BITC

Post Office Group

148-166 Old Street, London EC1V 9HQ

Tel: 0171-250 2220
Company activity: Postal services. The
Group is managed as four businesses: Royal
Mail, Royal Mail Parcelforce, Post Office
Counters Ltd, and Subscription Services Ltd.
Sponsorship contact: Alan Williams,
Director of Communications and Corporate
Relations
Donations contact: Jim Common, Head of
Community Affairs
Donations: £1,820,000 (27/03/95)
Policy: Sponsorship: At its Old Street
office in London the company undertakes
"purely commercially motivated
sponsorship". It uses sponsorship for
corporate hospitality. Preference for classical
music, theatre and film. The Scottish, Welsh
and Northern Ireland Boards have
discretionary budgets to spend on
community activities. No commercial return
is expected and both spend a "small
proportion" on the arts.

The Welsh Post Office Board sponsorship
of the arts is a means of putting "some-
thing back into the community". The board
supports arts festivals within the principality
both regional and national. Sponsorship
budget £74,000 in 1994/95 of which 60%
devoted to the arts.
Recent examples of sponsorship:
Royal National Eisteddfod of Wales;
URDD (League of Youth) National Eisteddd-
    fod;
The Welsh Proms;
Swansea Festival;
North Wales Music Festival;
BBC National Orchestra of Wales concert,
    Bangor;

Lower Machen Music Festival.
The Scottish Post Office Board sponsors
arts including those which are community-
based. It is particularly interested in
activities which will generate positive media
coverage for the Post Office and/or provide
opinion-former hospitality opportunities.
Recent examples of sponsorship:
Edinburgh Book Festival;
Edinburgh International Film Festival;
Glasgow School of Art;
Scottish Amateur Music Association;
Northlands Festival;
Borders Festival.
Donations to the arts are rare.
Applications: Scottish Post Office Board,
102 West Port, Edinburgh EH3 9HS (0131-
2287274) Contact: Martin Cummins, Board
Secretary and Head of Public Relations.
Post Office Board Wales & the Marches,
Longcross Court, 47 Newport Road, Cardiff
CF2 1AW (01222-585 888) Contact:
Mr Moelwyn Jones, Public Relations.
Northern Ireland Post Office Board,
Queen's House, 14 Queen Street, Belfast
BT1 6ER (01243 2320) Contact: Jimmy
McClean, Board Secretary.
Royal Mail, 49 Feathersone Street, London
EC1Y 8SY (0171-320 4354) Contact: Laura
Baker, Sponsorship.
As one of the four businesses that make
up the Post Office Group, the Royal Mail
also conducts its own programme of art
sponsorship.
Membership: ABSA patron, BITC

PowerGen plc

Westwood Way, Westwood Business Park,
Coventry CV4 8LG

Tel: 01203-424000
Company activity: Generation and sale of
electricity, gas trading
Sponsorship contact: Dianne Long, Head
of Corporate Communications
Donations contact: See above
Donations: £339,000 (31/3/94)
Policy: Support mainly focuses on
education and the environment and
activities close to its operations. It "supports
excellence in the performing arts, and

encourages and supports new talent and young artists."
Organisations sponsored/grant-aided:
Birmingham Royal Ballet;
City of Birmingham Symphony Orchestra;
Dartington Festival;
Glyndebourne Festival Opera (corporate member);
Royal Opera House (corporate member);
Royal Shakespeare Company (corporate member);
Walton Trust.
Membership: ABSA, % Club

Price Waterhouse – United Kingdom

Southwark Towers, 32 London Bridge Street, London SE1 9SY

Tel: 0171-939 3000
Company activity: Chartered accountants
Sponsorship contact: Robert Sandry, Partner, Business Development Group
Donations contact: J Barrett, Secretary to the Charities Committee
Donations: £150,000 (30/06/95)
Policy: The company also sponsors music, theatre and art. Sponsorships have included:
City of Birmingham Symphony Orchestra;
Theatre Royal Windsor.
The company supports a wide range of charitable activities including the arts and heritage. Preference is given to organisations in which an employee is involved.
Applications: In writing to the correspondent. Donations are approved after consideration by a charities committee, made up of five appointed partners and the secretary.
Membership: % Club, BITC

Private Patients Plan Ltd

Tavistock House South, Tavistock Square, London WC1H 9LJ TN1 1BJ

Tel: 0171-380 0967
Company activity: Medical insurance company
Sponsorship contact: Jonathon Russell, Group Director of Public Relations

Donations: £300,000 (31/12/94)
Policy: The company concentrates its support on events and organisations in the vicinity of its head office in Tunbridge Wells. Organisations sponsored include:
Towner Art Gallery and Museum (Eastbourne);
Kent Youth Music Association;
West Kent Youth Theatre;
Trinity Arts Centre;
Monteverdi Choir.
Applications: The company did not wish to have an entry in this guide.
Membership: ABSA

Prudential Corporation plc

142 Holborn Bars, London EC1N 2NH
Tel: 0171-405 9222
Company activity: Life assurance, general insurance, financial services
Sponsorship contact: Dennis Martin, Sponsorship Manager
Donations contact: Mrs Jill Fowler, Community Affairs Manager
Donations: £1,224,000 (31/12/94)
Policy: Sponsorship: The arts sponsorship programme and budget is committed to the *Prudential Great Orchestra Series* – regional tours by four of London's major orchestras – and the *Prudential Awards for the Arts*, which encourage innovation and creativity, coupled with excellence and accessibility. There are category winners for dance, music, opera, theatre and visual arts, together with the overall Prudential Arts Award. Both events are arranged in conjunction with the Arts Council of Great Britain. Sponsorship/donations have also included:
Broomhill Trust;
Folkworks;
Glyndebourne Festival Opera (corporate member);
Hampstead Theatre;
Henry Moore Sculpture Trust;
Jonathan Burrows Group;
Mid-Wales Opera;
Northern Ballet Theatre;
Public Art Commissions Agency;
Royal National Theatre (corporate member);
Scarborough Theatre Trust;

Smith Quartet;
Tricycle Theatre.
Membership: ABSA, % Club, BITC

Reader's Digest Association Ltd

Berkeley Square House, Berkeley Square,
London W1X 6AB

Tel: 0171-629 8144
Company activity: Publishers
Sponsorship contact: n/a
Donations contact: Pamela Rowden,
Charities Administrator
Donations: £262,540 (30/06/94)
Policy: Charitable donations: These are
channelled through The Reader's Digest
Trust. The company favours donating to a
specific project rather than "blanket"
funding. Preference is given by the trust to
UK organisations which:

- foster a spirit of enterprise and self-help,
  particularly in the fields of education, arts/
  culture, environment or health education;
  and
- are involved in problem solving in the area
  of communications (eg. dyslexia, adult
  literacy, sub-titling, deafness, blindness,
  speech and learning difficulties). In
  addition, applications from charities
  connected with periodical, book or music
  publishing will be considered. The trustees
  are looking for: (a) the commitment of the
  people making the application to achieve
  their stated aims; (b) clear and realistic
  objectives; (c) a degree of volunteer
  involvement; (d) evidence of long term
  plans and future funding. The trust gives
  support to appeals from Swindon where it
  has a presence but otherwise local appeals
  are not generally supported. Projects in
  which members of staff are involved are
  more likely to receive support. Typical
  grants to national organisations range
  from £500 to £5,000, while local grants
  range from £250 to £2,500. Sponsorship:
  The company does not undertake
  sponsorships

Applications: In writing to the
correspondent. The trustees meet quarterly.
Local appeals should be made to head
office as local branches do not have an
independent policy or budget.
Other information: The company's main
gripes about appeals are that some are too
broad, are inadequately researched, are not
clear or are too lengthy. Too many appeals
are received each year so the following
advice should be taken into consideration:
appeals should be short summarising the
charity's aims, operations and revenue and
should specify a particular project (costed
out) where the trust might be associated.
Positive benefits for the company, where
these exist, should be spelled out clearly.

Really Useful Group Ltd

22 Tower Street, London WC2H 9NS

Tel: 0171-240 0880
Company activity: Development &
exploitation of copyright
Donations contact: Brigadier Adam
Gurdon
Donations: £70,000 (30/06/94)
Policy: The charities budget is about
£70,000 a year. Donations are usually to a
wide range of registered charities for up to
£500. There is a preference for children and
youth, medical and the arts. It is known
that support is given to some arts
educational schools. The company also
holds a monthly draw, giving free theatre
tickets to charitable causes.

Reed Elsevier

6 Chesterfield Gardens, London W1A 1EJ

Tel: 0171-499 4020
Company activity: Publishing
Sponsorship contact: Corporate Relations
Department
Donations contact: Jan Shawe, Chair of
the Charities Committee
Donations: £361,000 (31/12/94)
Policy: To receive the company's support an
arts event should be:

- nationally significant;
- appealing to business and political
  leaders;
- relevant to Reed's business;
- able to provide an elegant setting for
  receptions;

* directly beneficial to shareholders and employees;
* capable of being properly managed and marketed, with credit given, as appropriate, to the sponsor.

Sponsorships in 1993/94 included:
Music at Oxford;
National Art Collections Fund;
Royal Academy of Arts;
Royal Opera House;
Victoria and Albert Museum;
ABSA's Goodman & Garret Awards.
Applications: Sponsorship and donations are no longer being handled from head office.

Local appeals should be sent to one of the subsidiary companies or to a relevant local office. Addresses of principal locations can be found at the back of the company's annual report.

Applications for sponsorship should set out clearly and succinctly the project to be supported, the type and amount of assistance sought and the anticipated benefits to be secured by both the sponsored party and sponsor..
Membership: % Club, BITC

RIBA/BT Community Projects Awards

Community Architecture Resource Centre,
Royal Institute of British Architects,
66 Portland Place, London W1N 4AD

Tel: 0171-580 5533
Contact: Maureen Read
Grant Total: £100,000 (1994)
General: This fund provides grants for community and voluntary groups seeking professional help on the feasibility of building and environmental improvement projects. The fund's main sponsor is British Telecom (BT). Other supporters are the Tudor Trust and the Sports Council.

A feasibility study is a report which considers whether or not a scheme could go ahead. There is no one standard type of study. Normally the architect will make site visits and attend meetings with the community group and other interested parties. S/he will try to find out what is

required and will produce a report which may include a brief history of the project and its aims, alternative site options, an appraisal of the existing building, alternative sketch designs, lists of possible sources of funding, suggestions for project management and future action.

Successful applicants will receive a grant toward the cost of the feasibility study, usually up to a maximum of £1,000 inclusive of VAT. Occasionally grants of up to £3,000 are awarded to large-scale projects. The exact level of the grant is at the discretion of the Community Architecture Group assessors; under exceptional circumstances, a grant exceeding £1,000 may be offered. The grant is a contribution towards the cost of the architect/professional advisers fee, and it is left to the applicant to resolve the remaining balance of money with their architect/professional adviser.

Projects can include refurbishment, renovation, new building projects and associated landscape works. Applications are accepted from voluntary organisations who should be able to show that they are representative of the community. Projects funded must provide a wide community benefit, and show that they consult the wider community. There should be no personal gain for a small number of individuals involved.

A feasibility report has to be produced for each scheme containing a description of how the study was carried out and the methods used.

Examples of recent grants to arts-related projects:
Edwardian Music Hall, Derbyshire (refurbishment);
Development of a building as an arts in the community resource in Stroud;
Provision of a community building with arts and performance space for local people in Brighton;
Renovation of a building as a community arts resource in Liverpool.
Exclusions: Projects in Scotland and Northern Ireland. (Details of similar schemes in Scotland and Northern Ireland can be obtained from the addresses

below.) Basic repair work is not eligible. Work on the feasibility study should not have begun before the application is submitted to the RIBA. Grants will not be given to projects that have already started a feasibility study.

Applications: Applications are referred to regional co-ordinators who operate on a voluntary basis to give advice to voluntary groups. They may contact you regarding your project and they will then make a recommendation to the RIBA Community Architecture Group. You should also contact your co-ordinator if you have problems in completing the application form or if you need some guidance in finding professional help. A list of co-ordinators is attached.

The Community Architecture Group assessment panel (including architects and those with community work experience) will be looking to see that the project could not go ahead without support from the Community Projects Fund. They will aim to reach organisations and groups most in need of grant aid for professional assistance. Grants will be given to groups who can show that they are representative of the community and that they are constituted and managed in a representative way.

Regional Co-ordinators:
Eastern: Alan Wilkinson, Wilkinson Pratt Partnership (01473-288010)
East Midlands: Steve Banks, Groundworks Architects (0115-942 4388)
Northern: Michael Drage (01661-844300)
London: Will Hudson, Adakow Community design Aid (0181-833 9656)
South: Maureen Read, RIBA (0171-580 5533)
South West: Roger Deeming, Barlow Schofield (01326-563395)
"Wessex" and Avon: Hugh Nettlefield, Quattro Design Ltd (0117-929 9672)
South East: Mark Hills, Mark Hills Architects (01273-821169)
West Midlands: David Waites, Waites Architecture (0121-212 2123)
North West: Edmund Wood (01925-265657)
Yorkshire: Joe Ravetz (01706-816723)
North Wales: Bendicte Foo (01766-590320)
South Wales: Sue Barlow, Community

Design for Gwent (01633-250271)
Other National Schemes:
Scottish Community Projects Fund, The Royal Incorporation of Architects in Scotland, 15 Rutland Square, Edinburgh EH1 2BE; Tel: 0131-229 7545; Fax: 0131-228 2188; Contact: Joan Jackson

The Royal Bank of Scotland Group plc

36 St Andrew Square, Edinburgh EH2 2YE

Tel: 0131-556 8555
Company activity: Banking
Sponsorship contact: G P Fenton, Head of Sponsorship & Community Programme
Donations contact: See above
Donations: £977,000 (30/09/94)
Policy: Total Donations & Community sponsorship: £1.5 million (Sept 1995).
Sponsorship policy:
- The bank should have the potential to generate favourable public interest which should include clear and definite reference to the bank as sponsors.
- Ideally the event should be of broad general interest and there should be identifiable benefit to the bank. For example, the event might relate to a type of business or section of the community with which the bank wishes to be identified for business development purposes.
- Sponsorship of youth activities is of particular interest.
- Sponsorship which would attract adverse criticism are generally avoided.
- In general the bank is not keen on sharing events as this tends to detract from the public relations value of the involvement.
- Sponsorship proposals from organisations which should be self supporting are not encouraged.
- The bank does not wish to become involved in a sponsorship context with charitable fund-raising events. In these cases the bank prefers to consider whether or not they support such organisations on a national basis by way of charitable donation.

Current major projects:
Edinburgh International Festival;
Hallé Orchestra;
Scottish Chamber Orchestra;
Glyndebourne Touring Opera;
Royal Exchange Theatre;
Glasgow Museums on Tour;
*Monteverdi Choir and the Orchestre
    Revolutionnaire;*
Friends of the Royal Scottish Academy;
Dunfermline District Arts Festival;
European Theatre Company;
Galleries of Justice, Nottingham.
Donations: In addition through its
community programme the bank supports a
number of arts organisations through
corporate membership and/or charitable
donation.
Applications: All sponsorship proposals
must meet the criteria given above.
Requests for donations may be made in
writing to the correspondent, including
appropriate report and accounts or financial
statements. Grant decisions at head office
are made by a donations committee which
meets quarterly. Local appeals should be
sent to local branches.
Membership: ABSA, % Club, BITC

Royal Insurance Holdings plc

1 Cornhill, London EC3V 3QR
Tel: 0171-283 4300
Company activity: Insurance
Sponsorship contact: Betty E Hicks,
Assistant Manager, Corporate Relations
Donations contact: See above
Donations: £148,271 (31/12/94)
Policy: Sponsorship: "The main aims of
our sponsorship policy are to raise the
company's profile and show our
involvement in the communities in which
we operate." No particular artform is
preferred. Recent examples of arts
sponsorship include:
*RSC/ Royal Insurance Access to the Arts
    Programme;*
Royal Orchestral Exchange.
Donations: These mainly include corporate
memberships such as:
Glyndebourne Festival Opera;

Royal Academy of Arts.
Applications: Local appeals should be sent
to the nearest Royal Insurance office.
Membership: ABSA, % Club, BITC

RTZ Corporation PLC

6 St James's Square, London SW1Y 4LD
Tel: 0171-930 2399
Company activity: Mining
Sponsorship contact: Miss Karen Gorham,
Community Affairs Assistant
Donations contact: See above
Donations: £841,088 (31/12/95)
Policy: To support excellence in the arts
especially through training and nurturing
the talents of young people.
    Since 1992, RTZ's main initiative has been
to support five major arts training institu-
tions in London: the Centre for Young
Musicians, Guildhall School of Music and
Drama, Lilian Baylis Youth Dance Company
at Sadler's Wells, the Royal Academy
Schools and the Royal College of Art. In
1995 a sixth organisation, the Royal
Academy of Dramatic Art, was supported.
All six organisations have been represented
in the RTZ Arts Season (created by RTZ and
formerly called the RTZ Arts Festival which
was a dedicated week of performances at
St James's Church, Piccadilly). Other support
has been given to:
*International Early Music Network Young
    Artists' Competition;*
*RTZ Ensemble Prize at the Royal Over-Seas
    League Music Competition.*
The winners of these competitions are
invited to participate in the Arts Season.
Applications: In writing to the Community
Affairs Assistant. Applications which meet
the above criteria will be considered but the
ever increasing volume being received and
the current focused programme means RTZ
is unable to assist in many cases.
Membership: % Club, BITC, ABSA

J Sainsbury plc

Stamford House, Stamford Street, London SE1 9LL

Tel: 0171-921 6000
Company activity: Retail food distribution
Sponsorship contact: Miss Marah Winn-Moon, Sponsorship
Donations contact: Mrs S L Mercer, Community Investment
Donations: £1,400,000 (11/3/96)
Policy: Arts sponsorship: £800,000 (1996)"Through our sponsorship, we aim to make the arts more popular by presenting them in ways that are relevant and meaningful, allowing people of all ages contact and involvement. Support for the arts is nationwide and aims to make a real contribution to the many communities in which Sainsbury's has a presence."

Major sponsorships include:
Sainsbury's Choir of the Year;
Sainsbury's Pictures for Schools;
Sainsbury's Arts for All.

Recent sponsorship has also included:
Armadillo Theatre;
Bitesize Theatre Company;
Bournemoth Sinfonietta;
Contemporary Art Society;
English National Ballet;
English Touring Theatre;
Folkworks;
ITHACA;
Oxford Stage Company;
Phoenix Dance;
Sheffield Choir;
Sinfonia 21;
Suffolk Artlink;
Théatre de Complicité;
Welsh National Opera;
Wingfield Arts;
Woking Dance Umbrella.

Applications: Local appeals should be sent to the manager of local stores who will then approach the donations committees of Sainsbury Charitable Fund. This meets quarterly, but a sub-committee meets as and when necessary.
Membership: ABSA, % Club, BITC

Christian Salvesen plc

50 East Fettes Avenue, Edinburgh EH4 1EQ

Tel: 0131-559 3600
Company activity: Distribution, specialist hire and food services
Sponsorship contact: Peter O'Malley, Public Relations Manager
Donations contact: See above
Donations: £76,000 (UK) (31/03/95)
Policy: Sponsorship: The company is strongly supportive of the arts, particularly in Scotland. There is a preference for music. In 1994/95 organisations supported included:
Edinburgh Festival Theatre Trust;
National Library of Scotland (Salvesen RLS Award);
Scottish International Children's Festival;
National Association of Youth Orchestras - The Salvesen Baton for Young Conductors (Midlands);
Scottish Opera;
Scottish Chamber Orchestra.

Charitable donations: Support is given to education and youth activities, industrial training, community and environmental charities which are local to areas of company presence or in which a member of staff is involved. Grants in 1994/95 included the Edinburgh International Festival.
Applications: In writing to the correspondent. Grants are decided at head office by a donations board which meets quarterly. Smaller grants are decided by a member of the Community Affairs Department. Local appeals should be directed to the local branch.
Membership: ABSA

Scapa Group plc

Oakfield House, 93 Preston New Road, Blackburn, Lancashire BB2 6AY

Tel: 01254-580123
Company activity: Manufacture engineered fabrics & technical products
Donations contact: Mrs Marie Cockayne, Personal Secretary to the Chairman
Donations: £77,478 (31/03/95)
Policy: Grants are given mainly to

organisations with a local (Blackburn and the North West England), company or personnel connection. Preference for children and youth, medical research, hospices, the environment/heritage and the arts.

Grants to national organisations from £50 to £500. Grants to local organisations from £50 to £5,000.

Schroders plc

120 Cheapside, London EC2V 6DS

Tel: 0171-382 6000
Company activity: Merchant banking & investment
Sponsorship contact: see below
Donations contact: Brian Tew, Schroder Charity Trust
Donations: £505,000 (31/12/94)
Policy: Donations are channelled through the Schroder Charity Trust. Only registered charities are supported, with a tendency to support national appeals. Local branches of national charities also receive help, but very little money is given to purely local charities.

Within these broad areas of preference, each appeal is considered on its merits. Typical beneficiaries include organisations concerned with elderly people, health care, social welfare, education, medical, the environment, overseas and the arts. Currently particular attention is being given to the country's heritage and a substantial donation was made to the Oxford Bodleian Library campaign. Grants are usually for £500 to £2,000, larger donations may be spread over four or five years.

The company is a corporate member of:
Liverpool Philharmonic Orchestra;
Royal Opera House;
Glyndebourne Festival Society.
Applications: In writing to the correspondent. Grant decisions are made by a committee which meets monthly.
Membership: % Club, BITC, ABSA

Scottish Amicable

Amicable House, 150 St Vincent Street, Glasgow G2 5NQ

Tel: 0141-248 2323
Company activity: Financial services
Sponsorship contact: Ian Mackintosh, Marketing Controller
Donations contact: J C Mitchell, Secretary
Donations: £50,000 (31/12/94)
Policy: Community contributions totalled £113,000 including arts sponsorship, good-cause sponsorship and support for enterprise agencies (for youths), as well as charitable donations (£50,000 total). The company's support is split about half and half between local causes and national causes in Scotland. There is a preference for central Scotland, and mainly for organisations involved with youth, the arts and enterprise.

Support ranges from £100 for an advertisement at a local event to £10,000 sponsorship of a major Scottish arts body, with £250 being the typical grant to a charity. The largest arts sponsorships in 1995 were:
Scottish Opera;
Scottish Ballet;
Royal Scottish National Orchestra;
MacRobert Arts Centre, Stirling.

Scottish Hydro-Electric plc

10 Dunkeld Road, Perth PH1 5WA

Tel: 01738-455040
Company activity: Electricity supply
Sponsorship contact: Head of Corporate Communications
Donations contact: See above
Donations: £88,122 (31/03/95)
Policy: Sponsorship budget: £220,000, of which 45% to the arts (1995)

The company supports local charities in its area of operation, basically Scotland, with a particular interest in the north of Scotland. It prefers to support work with children and young people, social welfare, education, recreation, environment/heritage and the arts.

Recent examples of arts sponsorship:
National Youth Orchestra of Scotland
*   *Summer School and Tour and commission*
*   *of a piece of music;*
Scottish Opera Go Round Tour;
Traverse Theatre Tour;
Young Generators – Arts Programme in
*   Tayside.*
Donations: All types of activity relating to the community are considered but they must also adhere to the general sponsorship criteria above.
Recent arts donations include:
Magnus Photography Bus – Fotofeis;
Rediscovery;
Council for Music in Hospitals;
St Magnus Festival, Orkney;
Children's Music Foundation.
Membership: ABSA

Scottish & Newcastle Breweries plc

Abbey Brewery, Holyrood Road, Edinburgh
EH8 8YS

Tel: 0131-556 2591
Company activity: Brewing & leisure
Sponsorship contact: John Nicolson, Group Marketing Director
Donations contact: Cameron G Walker, Public Relations Manager
Donations: £375,000 (01/05/95)
Policy: Sponsorship: The company welcomes sponsorship proposals.
*   Corporate sponsorship is undertaken for Scottish and Newcastle plc.
*   Individual brands undertake their own sponsorship (eg. Beck's Biers).
*   regional breweries undertake their own sponsorship (eg. Newcastle Breweries).

Scottish Brewers
Sponsorship contact: Tony McGrath, Marketing Director (Address and telephone number as above)
Sponsorships have included;
Royal Lyceum Theatre, Edinburgh;
Tron Theatre, Glasgow;
Little Theatre, Island of Mull.

Beck's Biers
Contact: John Botia, Brand Manager
(Address and telephone number as above)

A "pioneering" sponsorship programme for contemporary visual arts often at the Tate and Hayward Galleries and for smaller scale touring theatre, notably Théatre de Complicité.

"Events must target key opinion-formers amongst Beck's Biers target audience, must be slightly out of the ordinary and avant-garde. Beck's Biers has a reputation for sponsoring productions which others shy away from!"

Its annual arts sponsorship programme recommended by Anthony Fawcett Sponsorship Consultants.

Newcastle Breweries Ltd
Sponsorship contact: Jim Merrington, Commercial Director, Newcastle Breweries Ltd, Tyne Brewery, Gallowgate, Newcastle NE99 1RA (0191-232 5091)

Events within the area of North Yorkshire and the Scottish borders are preferred. Sponsorships have included:
Theatre Royal, Newcastle;
Tyne Theatre and Opera House.
Charitable donations: The group gives preference to the arts and culture, social welfare, community services, health/medicine, conservation/environment, education, science and enterprise. Preference is given to projects in which a member of staff is involved. Grants to national organisations range from £50 to £1,000 (occasionally as high as £50,000) and grants to local organisations from £50 to 35,000 (occasionally as high as £10,000)
Applications: A donations committee meets quarterly. Local appeals should be directed to the regional office. Appeal mail is getting too large to deal with so appeals should be carefully researched and should fall into the company's donations categories. All appeals should be written. Information available: The company reports on its community involvement in its annual report, but do not have printed policy guidelines. Further information can be obtained from Cameron Walker on 0131-556 2591.
Membership: ABSA

Scottish Power plc

1 Atlantic Quay, Broomielaw, Glasgow
G2 8SP

Tel: 0141-248 8200
Company activity: Electricity supply
Sponsorship contact: Rachel Sherrard,
Corporate Affairs Manager
Donations contact: See above
Donations: £922,000 (31/03/95)
Policy: Sponsorship: The company
undertakes arts and good cause sponsorship
both nationally and locally. The typical
sponsorship range is from £500 to
£300,000. Arts sponsorship covers music,
orchestras and choirs. The company sponsors
its own pipe band – the Scottish Power Pipe
Band. Other recent sponsorships include:
*Edinburgh International Festival - the Mark
    Morris Dance Group;*
Mayfest:
Royal Scottish National Orchestra;
Scottish Opera.
Membership: ABSA

Sears plc

40 Duke Street, London W1A 2HP

Tel: 0171-200 5999
Company activity: Footwear (including
British Shoe Corporation) , stores (including
Selfridges, Wallis and Warehouse)
Donations contact: J D F Drum, Company
Secretary
Donations: £237,000 (31/01/95)
Policy: The company trust, the Sears
Foundation, has supported London City
Ballet, Glyndebourne Arts Trust and the
Royal Opera House Trust.
Applications: The correspondent states
that the funds of the Sears Foundation are
currently fully committed. The company
endeavours to develop projects in partner-
ship with a few major national charities so
its funds are committed in advance.
    British Shoe Corporation Holdings and
Freemans, subsidiaries of Sears plc, both
make donations totalling in the region of
£70,000, supporting charities in their areas
of operation.
Membership: BITC

Sedgwick Group plc

Sedgwick House, The Sedgwick Centre,
London E1 8DX

Tel: 0171-377 3456
Company activity: International insurance
& reinsurance broking
Sponsorship contact: Miss Julia Fish,
Director, Corporate Communications
Donations contact: Ms Victoria Secretan,
Community Programmes Manager
Donations: £159,000 (31/12/94)
Policy: Sedgwick does not undertake
commercial sponsorship but supports a
number of arts organisations and events
including;
Royal Academy;
Whitechapel Art Gallery;
City of London Symphonia;
Spitalfields Festival;
East End Festival;
Festival of Bangladesh;
Festivals in Norfolk and Norwich.
Where possible it chooses to support arts
organisations making an additional social
contribution to the community, such as
ADAPT, which facilitates access to arts
venues for people with disabilities, Artsline,
London's information and advice service for
disabled people on arts and entertainment,
the Council for Music in Hospitals and the
Geese Theatre Company which works in
prisons.
Applications: The group welcomes appeals
from charities, but advises applicants that
they should write rather than telephone
and that information should be concise.
Applications should include who benefits
from the work, what the charity/
organisation does, the aim of the project
and how Sedgwick's help could make a
difference, basic financial information and
an annual report.
    The company states "Remember that
Sedgwick may be able to offer time and
skills rather than money."
    Grants at head office are decided
quarterly by an appeals committee.
Applications should be addressed to the
correspondent. Local appeals in Norfolk,
Essex and East Anglia can be addressed to

Debbie Hilton, Public Relations Officer, Sedgwick Ltd, Victoria House, Queen's Road, Norwich N1 3QQ.

Local appeals may also be sent to regional offices – larger offices are in Birmingham, Bristol, Cardiff, Edinburgh, Glasgow, Leeds, Manchester, Norwich, Reading, Slough and Witham (Essex).

Membership: % Club, BITC

SEEBOARD plc

Forest Gate, Brighton Road, Crawley, West Sussex RH11 9BH

Tel: 01293-657295

Company activity: Electricity supply and distribution

Sponsorship contact: Julia Lynam, Public Relations Officer

Donations: £181,838 (31/03/95)

Policy: SEEBOARD sponsorship is confined mainly within its operating area: Kent, Sussex, Surrey and South London. The arts programme includes support for major arts festivals and small local projects.

Recent sponsorships include:

Hanover Band, a locally-based period orchestra for a programme of concerts and primary school projects Brighton & Hove Philharmonic Society;

Canterbury Festival;

Hove Festival of Music;

Lewes Festival;

New Sussex Opera;

The Opera Company;

Carousel Dance Group, Brighton.

Applications: Most awards are under £5,000. SEEBOARD makes a few major sponsorship awards – worth between £5,000 and £20,000 each – in each financial year. Applications for these must be made before the end of the previous December. In most cases these run for one year only, but longer programmes may be considered with an annual review.

Smaller awards are made on a rolling programme. These range from donations of small gifts for fundraising events, through donations of electrical appliances to financial support of up to £5,000. To apply please write, giving brief details of your organisation and your request to the correspondent.

The correspondent stated: "Seeboard makes every effort to reply to all appeals. We do, however, receive a large number of applications and can support only a small proportion of them."

Telephone and faxed applications cannot be considered.

Information available: The company reports on its community involvement in an annual publication, Links, available from the address above.

Membership: ABSA

Shell UK Ltd

Shell-Mex House, Strand, London WC2R 0DX

Tel: 0171-257 3425

Company activity: Oil industry

Sponsorship contact: Lesley Duncan, Arts & Environmental Sponsorship Manager

Donations contact: Janette Congdon, Programme Manager for Grants & Donations

Donations: £2,466,939 (31/12/94)

Policy: Shell UK's support of the arts at corporate level is confined to its long standing partnership with the London Symphony Orchestra, centred around the annual Shell LSO Music Scholarship for young instrumentalists and the biennial Shell LSO National Tour. The company also supports the Ulster Orchestra and Scottish Opera.

Support for the arts at regional level is on a small scale and confined to local partnerships with arts organisations in areas of the company's main sites eg. Grampian in Scotland and North West England.

Membership: ABSA, BITC

Slough Estates plc

234 Bath Road, Slough, Berkshire SL1 4EE

Tel: 01753-537171

Company activity: Industrial & commercial property development

Sponsorship contact: Brig N M White, General Manager External Affairs

Donations: £213,000 (31/12/94)
Policy: Charitable donations: The company gives support to a wide range of causes in the fields of art, music and culture; health research and care; youth; old age; education; relief of unemployment; environment and conservation; welfare and relief of poverty. All cases are considered on their merits. Preference is given to projects in areas where the company has a presence principally in Berkshire and Buckinghamshire and national charities. Typical grants range from £25 to £5,000.
Sponsorship: The company undertakes arts and good cause sponsorship on a national level. The main areas supported are art and music.
Applications: Decisions on donations are made by a committee which meets quarterly. Brigadier N M White should be contacted for donations and sponsorship.
Membership: % Club, BITC

W H Smith Group plc

Strand House, 7 Holbein Place, London SW1W 8NR

Tel: 0171-730 1200
Company activity: Retail & distribution group
Sponsorship contact: Lois Beeson, Sponsorship Manager
Donations contact: Valerie Evans, Donations Secretary
Donations: £172,000 (30/05/95)
Policy: The group supports a broad spectrum of activities connected with literature, music, the theatre, design, dance and opera. Through the W H Smith Arts in Schools Programme, the group has developed close partnerships with several organisations which seek to introduce young people to the arts. The typical sponsorship range is from £1,000 to £20,000. Three or four projects and activities receive £30,000 to £40,000. In 1993/94 the "Arts in Schools" sponsored projects reached 130,000 children from 9,000 schools.

Music is an important part of the arts programme. Sponsorships have included:

Music for Youth;
Urdd Eisteddfod Choral Competition;
Access to Music, Leicester for multi-cultural workshops;
Hallé Orchestra for gamelan workshops;
London Sinfonietta, "Explorations" workshops;
Children's Music Workshops.
In other fields of the arts the group has sponsored workshop projects for schools with:
Royal National Theatre, for "W H Smith Interact";
Poetry Society, for "Poets in Schools";
Rambert Ballet, for "Young Friends of Rambert";
English Shakespeare Company, teachers' workshops;
Glyndebourne Touring Company's school workshops;
IRIE! Dance Theatre, annual schools residency.
The company also runs the *Young Writer's Competition* and a *Literary Award.*
Applications: All appeals, including local appeals, should be addressed to the correspondent. Grant decisions are made by a donations committee which meets monthly, although smaller grants are sometimes made by a specialist staff member. Applicants are advised that they should make clear and concise applications in writing and not telephone. They should not submit multiple appeals.
Membership: ABSA patron, % Club, BITC

SmithKline Beecham plc

One New Horizons Court, Brentford, Middlesex TW8 9EP

Tel: 0181-975 2000
Company activity: Pharmaceutical & consumer healthcare products
Sponsorship contact: Director, Corporate Responsibility Programmes
Donations: £1,350,000 (31/12/95)
Policy: The company concentrates its support on the promotion and advancement of healthcare. Limited funds are available for exceptional, community-based projects located in areas where its

employers work and live. It has supported:

New Horizons Artswork Collection, a large international collection of work by disabled artists, a project undertaken in conjunction with its move to new headquarters;

Science Museum Permanent "Health Matters" Gallery;

Royal Academy of Arts (corporate member).

Sponsor of the 75th Anniversary of British Federation of Festivals.

From January 1996 the company has relaunched its Corporate Responsibility Programme with a healthcare focus. Major support for the arts will NOT form part of this programme.

Applications: "SB does not respond favourably to requests but proactively seeks partnerships with organisations which reflect a clear 'healthcare' theme."

Membership: ABSA, BITC

Sony United Kingdom Ltd

The Heights, Brooklands, Weybridge KT13 0XW

Tel: 01932-816000

Company activity: Manufacture & distribution of electronic goods

Sponsorship contact: W H Vestey, General Manager, Public Affairs Department

Donations contact: Rosemary Small, Public Affairs Department

Donations: £86,000 (31/3/95)

Policy: The company prefers to support local charities in areas of company presence (Weybridge, Thatcham, Basingstoke and South Wales), appeals relevant to company business and charities in which a member of staff is involved.

The company continues to encourage the arts by supporting and equipping the Music Performance Research Centre. Support has also been provided to:

Glyndebourne Festival Society;

Royal Opera House;

Design Museum;

Royal Academy of Arts.

Applications: All requests should, in the first instance, be made to Rosemary Small.

Membership: % Club, BITC

Sotheby's

34/35 New Bond Street, London W1A 2AA

Tel: 0171-408 5423

Company activity: Fine art auctioneers

Sponsorship contact: Luke Rittner, Head of Marketing

Policy: Sotheby's seeks to develop and secure its relationship with museums and galleries. Its sponsorship aims to develop awareness of the company with potential sellers and buyers. Visual and fine arts remain central, along with some sporting events.

Support in sponsorship/donations has included:

Courtauld Institute of Art (corporate member);

Dyson Perrins Museums;

Fitzwilliam Museum;

Historic Houses Association;

National Gallery (corporate member);

Petworth Festival;

Royal Academy of Arts (corporate member);

Tate St Ives;

Warburg Institute (corporate member);

York City Art Gallery.

Membership: ABSA

South Western Electricity plc

800 Park Avenue, Aztec West, Almondsbury, Bristol BS12 4SE

Tel: 01454-201101

Company activity: Electricity supply

Sponsorship contact: Jim Moir, Public Relations Manager

Donations: £148,000 (31/03/95)

Policy: Sponsorship: The company is particularly directed at young people through support of arts and sports events. Typical sponsorship range is from £500 to £12,000. The company has sponsored arts events in schools run by Bath Festival.

Applications: Approaches for charitable donations should be made between October and December. A committee considers all applications and a decision is based on (a) relevance locally (b) the nature of the application (c) geographical spread throughout the South West.

Membership: BITC

Robert Stephen Holdings Ltd

Lakeside House, Squires Lane, London
N3 2QL

Tel: 0181-346 2600
Company activity: General trading,
services & broking
Sponsorship contact: Stephen Rubin,
Chairman
Donations contact: Alison Mcmillan,
Chairman's Office
Donations: £510,000 (31/12/93)
Policy: In 1993, in addition to charitable
donations (see above) the company
contributed £22,000 in arts sponsorship.
Sponsorships have included:
Philharmonia Orchestra;
National Theatre;
Royal Academy of Arts.
Applications: The company's major
subsidiary, Pentland Industries plc, gave
donations of £207,000 in 1993.
Applications to Pentland Industries will
simply duplicate applications to Robert
Stephen Holdings.

Tarmac plc

Hilton Hall, Essington, Wolverhampton,
West Midlands WV11 2BQ

Tel: 01902-307407
Company activity: Road stone & civil
engineering
Sponsorship contact: Sean Bruen, Head of
Group Communications
Donations contact: A C Smith, Group
Secretary
Donations: £181,000 (31/12/94)
Policy: Subsidiary companies sponsor the
arts in their localities.
Membership: % Club, BITC

Tate & Lyle plc

Sugar Quay, Lower Thames Street, London
EC3R 6DQ

Tel: 0171-626 6525
Company activity: Sugar refiners,
commodity traders
Sponsorship contact: David Dale, Manager,
Group Corporate Communications

Donations contact: Geoff Down, Assistant
Company Secretary
Donations: £692,000 (UK) (24/09/95)
Policy: Sponsorship: "Art projects should
generally be of benefit, or relevant to, the
local community of our major UK refinery
ie. East London, and have a reasonable life
expectancy ie. not one-offs or short run
projects. Occasionally support for a national
project is considered."
Recent sponsorship has included:
Sinfonia 21, for their music for the elderly
  programme.
An estimated 15% of the sponsorship
  budget of £400,000 was devoted to the
  arts.
Charitable donations: Typical grants to
national organisations range from £250 to
£10,000, and to local organisations from
£250 to £5,000.
Membership: % Club, BITC

Tesco plc

Tesco House, Delamare Road, Cheshunt,
Hertfordshire EN8 9SL

Tel: 01992-632222
Company activity: Multiple retailing
Sponsorship contact: Bridget Burnham,·
Corporate Affairs
Donations contact: Linda Marsh, Secretary
to the Charitable Trust
Donations: £724,114 (26/02/95)
Policy: The company focuses its support on
the communities where its stores are
situated and on groups providing practical
help to disadvantaged people.
Arts sponsorship: Proposals likely to be well
received are linked with education projects
or targeted at children, women, the elderly
or disabled. Sponsorship has included:
Royal Opera House (corporate member);
Hereford Three Choirs Festival;
Hertford Choral Society.
Charitable donations: These are
channelled through the Tesco Charitable
Trust. Grants to national organisations are
£100 and over, with grants to local
organisations from £10 to £1,000. Each
Tesco store also holds a small community

budget to help local voluntary organisations in their fundraising activities.
Membership: ABSA, % Club, BITC

Texaco Ltd

1 Westferry Circus, Canary Wharf, London E14 4HA

Tel: 0171-719 3000
Company activity: Oil industry
Sponsorship contact: Paul Bray, Public Relations Manager
Donations: £142,500 in 1994 (31/12/93)
Policy: The company's arts policy is to provide help and support in those areas of the country where it has major operations (Aberdeen, Pembroke, Swindon, East London). Its main emphasis is on support for youth and arts education programmes which make a clear and long-term contribution to the local community. Sponsorships in 1994/95 included:
Glyndebourne Festival Opera (corporate member);
Aberdeen Texaco Theatre School;
Texaco Youth Dance Course at Thamesdown Dance Studio;
Royal Scottish Academy of Music & Drama;
Sinfonia 21, Texaco Music Workshops;
Texaco Art Summer School, Belfast;
Texaco Young Musicians of Wales Competition.
Membership: ABSA, BITC

Thames Water Utilities

Nugent House, Vastern Road, Reading RG1 8DB

Tel: 01734-593690
Company activity: Water & sewerage services
Sponsorship contact: Mrs Frances Scaddon
Donations contact: See above
Donations: £112,000 (31/03/95)
Policy: Arts sponsorship: "All requests are looked at, but concert performances and work with sick children are the norm."
Recent examples of arts sponsorship:
London Symphony Orchestra, ongoing;
St John's Smith Square;
Hexagon at Reading;
Wiltshire Music Festival.
About 25% of the 1996 sponsorship budget of £112,000 was devoted to the arts.
Charitable donations: Preference is given to appeals relevant to company business and those where a member of staff is involved. Most grants are to culture and recreation with support also to public health, heritage, education and the environment.
Membership: BITC

THORN EMI plc

4 Tenterden Street, Hanover Square, London W1A 2AY

Tel: 0171-355 4848
Company activity: Music, rental, retail
Sponsorship contact: Sally O'Grady, Communications Officer
Donations contact: Charities Committee, Corporate Affairs Department
Donations: £700,000 (31/03/95)
Policy: The company's worldwide community contributions totalled £9.5 million (It breakdown geographically showed 40% to UK and Europe, and by category showed 23 % to arts and culture).
Projects, events and charities are supported within the areas of: arts and music in the community, health and welfare; education; innovation and enterprise. In the UK there is a preference for national charities, local charities in areas where the company operates and appeals relevant to company business.
Arts and music in the community: The company is a corporate member of a number of major arts organisations including: Royal Albert Hall; Glyndebourne Festival Opera; English National Ballet; English National Opera; National Opera Studio; National Youth Theatre; Royal Opera House; Tate Gallery.
Projects receiving sponsorship/donations in 1994/95 included:
Music for Youth (£45,000);
Live Music Now (£15,000);
Hackney Youth Orchestras Trust (£5,000);
Artsline (£500).
Barbican Centre;

East London Late Starters Orchestra;
European Youth Orchestra;
Lake District Summer Festival;
New London Orchestra;
Royal Parks Summer Entertainments;
THORN EMI Prize for the Teaching of Music
   in School.

Support is not given for building/restoration programmes (unless for a specific reason such as being part of a project close to a company location).

Membership: ABSA, % Club, BITC

3i Group plc

91 Waterloo Road, London SE1 8XP

Tel: 0171-928 3131
Company activity: Provision of investment capital to unquoted businesses
Sponsorship contact: Adam Quarry, Marketing Director
Donations contact: Claire Bushay
Donations: £151,516 (6 mths) (31/3/1995)
Policy: Sponsorship: The company prefers to support national, innovative, forward-looking and high quality organisations and UK tours. Recent support has been given to:
Royal Academy of Music (Sinfonia
   Orchestra);
Chirlinginian String Quartet;
Barbican Arts Centre;
Royal Academy of the Arts.

Charitable donations: The company gives preference to local appeals for projects in areas of company presence and where a member of staff is involved. Local branches have an independent but small budget (around £3,000) for appeals. Over half the company's support is given in the field of education, with other main areas of support being the community, medical, drama and youth.

Membership: ABSA, % Club

TI Group plc

Lambourn Court, Abingdon Business Park, Abingdon, Oxon OX14 1UH

Tel: 01235-555570
Company activity: General engineers
Sponsorship contact: J B Hutchings,

Director of Public Affairs (see London address below)
Donations contact: D P Lillycrop, Company Secretary
Donations: £191,000 (31/12/93)
Policy: Charitable grants: These are channelled through the TI Charity Trust which assists a wide range of charitable interests including arts and culture. Preference is given to appeals from local and community organisations in areas where the company has a plant.

Sponsorship: The group has developed a scheme to support young artists. It sponsors the TI Group Scholarship at the Royal College of Art for painting students on a two-year Masters degree course and the college's annual Interim Exhibition for painting students entering their final year. It has also started its own art collection at its Abingdon headquarters with work from graduating or former students at the college. In 1994/95 the company has also sponsored/grant-aided;
Abingdon & District Music Society;
Floating Point Science Theatre;
Ironbridge Gorge Museum Development
   Trust;
Molecule Theatre Company;
Oxford Playhouse;
Museums & Galleries Commission.

Applications: All grant applications, including local appeals, should be sent to the correspondent. They should be concise giving an adequate description of their objects, activities and financial position. A donations committee makes quarterly grant decisions. Sponsorship requests should be directed to J B Hutchings at the head office in London: TI Group plc, 50 Curzon Street, London W1Y 7PN (0171-499 9131).

Membership: ABSA, % Club, BITC

Toyota (GB) Ltd /Lexus (GB) Ltd

The Quadrangle, Redhill, Surrey RH1 1PX

Tel: 01737-768585
Company activity: Vehicle import and distribution
Sponsorship contact: L I Bates, Promotions and Events Manager

Donations contact: See above
Donations: £62,000 (31/12/93)
Policy: Sponsorship: The company has a preference for arts sponsorship as opposed to donations.

Toyota (GB) Ltd supports the arts through its Lexus brand with the sponsorship of the National Youth Orchestra.

Toyota is also involved with support to a number of art-related projects in the area near its UK headquarters.
Membership: ABSA

TSB Bank plc

60 Lombard Street, London EC3V 9DN

Tel: 0171-398 3980
Company activity: Financial services
Sponsorship contact: Sally Tibbs (London/ national); Richard Ellis (Birmingham/regional)
Donations contact: See below
Donations: £1,150,753 (31/10/94)
Policy: *In December 1995 Lloyds Bank and the TSB Group merged. At the time this entry was prepared (Spring 1996) the separate public identities were still maintained, hence the two entries.*
Sponsorship: "The (former) TSB Group lends support to its business objectives, aims to enhance external perceptions of the company and fulfil its community involvement through, amongst other activities, its art sponsorship programme.

As well as local initiatives throughout Great Britain the (former) TSB Group, under the TSB Bank brand, has developed an arts sponsorship programme which provided educational opportunities for secondary school children to visit an arts institution for the first time." TSB Artsbound gives secondary school children the opportunity to experience the arts at first hand. Current schemes involve the London Symphony Orchestra (subsidised travel and tickets) and the National Gallery (subsidised travel, project packs related to the National Curriculum and teachers' courses).

In addition TSB sponsors the Royal Opera House Trust's "Chance to Dance" scheme.

On a local level, TSB sponsors mainly arts activities in areas of company presence, such as:
Birmingham Readers & Writers Festival;
Brighton, Andover and Edinburgh Festivals;
Birmingham Hippodrome Festival;
Andover based Art in Schools project.;
CBSO education project;
TSB Masterclasses at Symphony Hall Birmingham;
Royal Theatre Development Trust;
Whitechapel Gallery education programme;
Tate Gallery.
Charitable donations: See entries under "Trusts" for the various TSB Foundations, independent charitable trusts funded by the company.
Applications: Applicants should check the whether the Lloyds TSB Group merger has had a further effect on the policy and administration of its arts support. The address and telephone number are also likely to change.
Membership: ABSA, % Club, BITC

Unilever

Unilever House, Blackfriars, London EC4P 4BQ

Tel: 0171-822 6303
Company activity: Food, beverages, detergents & personal care products
Sponsorship contact: R A Harcourt
Donations: £2,000,000 (31/12/94)
Policy: Sponsorship: "Unilever considers support of cultural activities as important as that provided for other social needs. Because Unilever does not market any products using the corporate name, sponsorship has to be directed at very specific target audiences. This leads to a concentration on London, the Wirral and key university locations".

The company sponsors a wide range of artistic activities. Nationally, support is targeted at specific groups, and is based on long-term support for a number of organisations.

The company is a corporate member of several major arts organisations including: Barbican Art Gallery; British Museum; National Gallery; National Portrait Gallery;

Royal Academy of Arts; Royal National Theatre; Tate Gallery.

Recent sponsorships include:
Bach Choir;
Barbican Shakespeare Festival;
Castle Arts Week Durham;
City of London Festival;
Glyndebourne Festival Opera;
McLellan Gallery;
New Shakespeare Company;
Royal Shakespeare Company;
Three Choirs Festival;
English National Ballet;
Young Musicians' Symphony Orchestra;
Regent's Park Open Air Theatre.
Locally, operating companies are responsible for their own sponsorship programmes and encourage the arts in a variety of ways, from supporting school arts projects to sponsoring local festivals.

Charitable donations: Priorities include the national heritage, youth employment, child welfare, higher/further education. Preference is given to national charities and organisations in areas of company presence. About 70% of the donations budget is decided at head office. National grants range from £500 to £50,000 and local grants from £100 to £2,000. In 1994 the Globe Theatre was one of the main beneficiaries.

Subsidiaries make smaller grants independently.

Applications: R A Harcourt is responsible for corporate sponsorship while the individual company marketing directors are responsible for brand sponsorship. A donations committee meets more than once a month. Local appeals should be addressed to the local plant or branch. A J George is responsible for education liaison. Information available: A booklet 'Unilever in Partnership with the Community' gives an indication of the variety and number of projects with which the company is involved (available from external affairs department at head office).

Membership: ABSA, % Club, BITC

Unisys Ltd

Bakers Court, Bakers Road, Uxbridge UB8 1RG

Tel: 01895-237137
Company activity: Business machines, farm equipment
Sponsorship contact: Martin Sexton, Director, Corporate Communications
Donations: £89,108 (31/12/94)
Policy: Support is focused where the company has a major presence (main UK locations are Milton Keynes and Brent), and projects which enable client entertainment and foster public relations. The company has concentrated on music with recent support being given to:
City of Birmingham Symphony Orchestra;
Leeds Festival Chorus;
Milton Keynes Chamber Orchestra;
The Stables, Milton Keynes.
Membership: ABSA, % Club, BITC

United Biscuits (UK) Ltd

Church Road, West Drayton, Middlesex UB7 7PR

Tel: 01895-432142
Company activity: Biscuits, cakes, crisps, chocolates, frozen foods manufacture
Donations contact: Graham Parker, Secretary to the Appeals Committee
Donations: £681,000 (31/12/94)
Policy: United Biscuits supports arts activities on the basis of their educational, community and cultural links with business locations. The company prefers to donate to the arts rather than sponsor.

Operating companies have their own small budgets to allocate.

Sponsorship and/or donations were given in 1994/95 to:
Brouhaha;
Burnbake Trust;
English Chamber Orchestra (corporate member);
Edinburgh Theatre Trust;
New Shakespeare Company (corporate member);
Royal Academy of Arts (corporate member);
Royal Liverpool Philharmonic Orchestra;

*Royal Opera House (corporate member);
Salamander Theatre;
Teddington Theatre Club;
Watermans Arts Centre;
McVitie's Book Prize, for more information
see The Book Trust, Scotland (under
"Trusts").*
Applications: Grant decisions at head
office are made by a donations committee
which meets quarterly. Appeals should be
addressed to the Community Affairs
Department. Local appeals should be sent
to local branches where donations can be
made at the discretion of the local manager.
Membership: ABSA, % Club, BITC

Vauxhall Motors Ltd

Griffin House, PO Box No 3,
Osbourne Road, Luton LU1 3YT

Tel: 01582-21122
Company activity: Motor vehicle
manufacture
Sponsorship contact: Mike Nicholson,
Manager Motor Sport & Sponsorship
Donations contact: Elaine Cowley, Charity
& Community Affairs Administrator
Donations: £116,545 (1994) (31/12/94)
Policy: Charitable donations: The
company concentrates its support on
activities directly associated with the
industry and its employees' interests, and in
areas covered by its plants (i.e. Luton and
Ellesmere Port). The arts are included
amongst the wide range of organisations
supported.
Sponsorship: The company undertakes
some arts sponsorship.
Membership: BITC

Vodafone Group plc

Courtyard, 2-4 London Road, Newbury,
Berkshire RG13 1JL

Tel: 01635-33251
Company activity: Mobile
telecommunication services
Sponsorship contact: see below
Donations contact: Philip Williams,
Personnel Director/Trustee
Donations: £185,000 (31/3/95)

Policy: Charitable grants: The company
set up a charitable trust in 1992. About
70% of its budget is given to national
organisations and the remainder to charities
local to Newbury. It supports the arts and
education as well as social welfare, disability
and medical research.

The company has a clear preference for
giving arts donations rather than engaging
in sponsorship. (It has sponsored the
Newbury Festival).
Recent donations include:
*Southern Arts and Royal Society of Arts
(£1,000 each).*
Only 6% of its donations budget of
£185,000 for 1995/96 was given to the arts.

S G Warburg Group plc

1 Finsbury Avenue, London EC2M 2PA

Tel: 0171-606 1066
Company activity: Banking
Sponsorship contact: Anne Drew, Public
Relations
Donations contact: I B Marshall, Company
Secretary
Donations: £1,215,000 (31/03/95)
Policy: Sponsorship: The company has
sponsored the Chamber Orchestra of
Europe in 1990 and 1993.
Charitable donations: Grants are given to
a wide range of local, national and inter-
national charities with typical grants ranging
from £250 to £1,000 with the occasional
major grant of £150,000 or more.
Applications: The company was taken over
by the Swiss Banking Corporation and will
be revision its donations policy in due
course.
Membership: % Club, BITC

Whitbread plc

Chiswell Street, London EC1Y 4SD

Tel: 0171-606 4455
Company activity: Brewers
Sponsorship contact: Paul Vaughan,
Sponsorship Director
Donations contact: P D Patten, Charity
Co-ordinator
Donations: £482,963 (25/02/95)

Policy: Sponsorship: Whitbread's main commercial sponsorship is in sport and literary awards, eg. Whitbread Book of the Year.

In recent years the company's local community sponsorship programme has placed an emphasis on events outside London, particularly in areas where the company has a major presence. Beneficiaries have included:

English Shakespeare Company, for Maidstone Prison project;
Boddingtons Arts Festival, Manchester;
Heineken Free Music Festival;
North West Arts Festival;
Reading Children's Festival;
Tate Gallery, Liverpool.

Charitable donations: The company supports a wide range of charities with the emphasis on education, medical care and social welfare. Priority is given to appeals in areas of company presence and to charities in which employees are involved.

Applications: Approaches for arts sponsorship should be made to Paul Vaughan, Sponsorship Director, Whitbread plc, Porter Tun House, 500 Capability Green, Luton Beds LU1 3LS (01582-391166).

All appeals for charitable donations must be made in writing accompanied by a copy of the organisations current annual report and accounts and should be sent to: Paul Patten, Charities Co-ordinator.

The company has 10 regional Community Affairs Directors who are responsible for promoting and implementing the company's involvement with local communities.

Membership: % Club, BITC, ABSA

Willis Corroon Group plc

Ten Trinity Square, London EC3P 3AX
Tel: 0171-481 7066
Company activity: Insurance brokers
Sponsorship contact: see below
Donations contact: Janice Ashby, Charities Administrator
Donations: £238,000 (31/12/94)
Policy: Sponsorship: The main area of non-cash support was in arts sponsorship.

Due to the company having a poor trading year sponsorships have become more client based.

Charitable donations: Support is given to national charities and local charities in the London and Ipswich areas. Arts and heritage are amongst the activities supported.

Applications: The company provides further information/policy guidelines for grant applicants.

Membership: % Club

Woolwich Building Society

Watling Street, Bexleyheath, Kent DA6 7RR
Tel: 0181-298 5000
Company activity: Building society
Sponsorship contact: Paul Rogers, Group Public Relations Manager
Donations contact: David Blake, Group Head of Corporate Affairs
Donations: £259,000 (31/12/94)
Policy: Sponsorship: The company is particularly interested to support young artists in music, the visual and performing arts. Its long-term commitments are to:

Woolwich Young Radio Playwright's Competition, for writers of 25 and under, the 10 winning plays are produced and broadcast on London News Radio (formerly LBC), further information from 01206-299088);
Greenwich Festival;
Elgar Birthplace Appeal Concert in Birmingham. City of London Sinfonia;
English National Opera;
National Children's Orchestra.

Charitable donations: Support is directed primarily at disadvantaged people, appeals of national importance, building, housing and conservation causes. Arts organisations are amongst those supported. Sponsorship/donations have included:
Bexley Arts Bursaries;
Frenchstreet Opera;
Mayor of Dartford's Arts Bursaries;
Music at Oxford;
Orchard Theatre.

Membership: ABSA, % Club

Yorkshire Bank plc

20 Merrion Way, Leeds LS2 8NZ

Tel: 0113-247 2000
Company activity: Banking
Sponsorship contact: Corporate Communications Manager
Donations contact: The Secretary, Yorkshire Bank Charitable Trust
Donations: £119,000 (30/09/94)
Policy: The bank sponsors organisations and events throughout the UK. It has sponsored the following organisations and a distinct preference for activities in Yorkshire is apparent:
Leeds International Festival;
Harrogate International Festival;
Oldham Girls Choir;
Fauré Festival;
York Singing Day.
Applications: Grants decisions are made by a donations committee which meets twice a month; responses may take three or four weeks to process.

Yorkshire Electricity Group plc

Wetherby Road, Scarcroft, Leeds LS14 3HS

Tel: 0113-289 2123
Company activity: Electricity supply
Sponsorship contact: Mrs Angela Gault, Community Relations Manager
Donations: £160,353 (31/03/95)
Policy: Sponsorship: The company sponsors local events in its operating area. These have included:
Northern Ballet Theatre Schools Dance Programme;
Yorkshire & Humberside Museums Council;
Eureka Museum;
National Museum of Film, Photography and TV;
John Field Ballet Seminars;
Freehand Puppet Theatre;
Live Music Now;
Opera North.
Charitable donations: The company only supports: local charities in areas of company presence; national charities for work in the company's area of operation; appeals relevant to company business. Focus areas

are youth, elderly and disabled people, environment and economic development. The arts and heritage may also be supported provided they fit with the focus areas.

Previous support has been given to Grimsby International Jazz Festival, an annual three-day festival.
Applications: Written proposals/applications should be made in September/October for the following financial year budgets (April - March). The company has published a newsletter – Community Matters – which gives examples of its current community relations programmes. A copy of it's policy for sponsorship and donations is available on request.
Membership: ABSA patron, BITC

Yorkshire Water plc

2 The Embankment, Sovereign Street, Leeds LS1 4BG

Tel: 0113-234 3234
Company activity: Water and sewerage services
Sponsorship contact: Ken Auty, Community Support Manager
Donations contact: as above
Donations: £120,000 (31/3/96)
Policy: Support is given to activities in Yorkshire and North Humberside. The arts is one of the preferred areas, along with children and youth, the disadvantaged, social welfare, the environment and water-based sports. When an arts project links with one of the other areas of interest its chances of support are far greater. Both arts sponsorship and arts donations favour rural and community arts.
Sponsorship budget: £40,000 in 1995/96 of which 10% devoted to the arts.

Organisations which have received sponsorship/donations include:
Abbeydale Industrial Hamlet Museum;
Actors' Workshop Youth Theatre;
Bingley Little Theatre;
Bradford Festival Choral Society;
Chatterbox Theatre;
English Camerata;
Grassington Festival Society;
Ilkley Amateur Operatic Society;

Kirklees Theatre Trust;
Northern Aldborough Festival;
Opera North;
Skippo Arts Team;
Yorkshire Air Museum;
Pateley Bridge Dramatic Society.
Membership: ABSA

PART FOUR

FUNDING FROM CHARITABLE TRUSTS

INTRODUCTION

WHAT ARE CHARITABLE TRUSTS?

Charitable trusts are set by an individual or group to distribute money for charitable purposes and are registered with the Charity Commission. Usually the founder/s of a trust endows it with a capital sum, which is invested in stocks and shares or property and which benefits from charitable tax relief. The money available for grant-making comes from the income received from those investments.

Each grant making trust is established under a trust deed in which the wishes of the founder/s are set out. The most important parts determine how the money will be spent – the "objects" and where the money can be spent – the "beneficial area". Some trusts have tightly defined objects which only permit them to spend money on a very limited range of activities, whilst others have much wider objects and may even be permitted to support any charitable activity. Some trusts are permitted to spend their funds only to benefit people in a certain region, county, town or even parish, whereas others may be able to spend their money nationally or internationally. Each trust is controlled by a group of trustees who can determine the policy of the trust within what is permitted by the constitution. It is up to them how the money is spent within the confines of its objects.

Because of charity law, all charitable trusts can only support activities which are charitable and this normally means that they will only be prepared to give money to organisations that are established with charitable status. When an organisation which cannot, or has not become a charity, is seeking funds from charitable grant-making trusts, it is sensible for it to make an arrangement with another charity, (the regional arts board may be most appropriate) so that the grant can be paid over in the first instance to the charity, for forwarding to the arts organisation. Even where such an arrangement is made it should be remembered that money from charitable trusts can *only be spent for charitable purposes, ie. for work which is of some public and community benefit.*

RAISING MONEY FROM TRUSTS

Generalisations about trusts can be misleading. There are thousands of trusts in the UK and they vary greatly in their size and their styles of operation. Most of the largest employ professional staff, others use their lawyers or accountants to carry out their administrative work whilst many are run directly by the original donor trustee or his/her family.

A minority of the largest trusts are open about their policies and criteria for support – they publish annual reports, prepare guidelines to assist applicants and indicate the scale of grant they are most likely to accommodate. The majority do not do so. Hence the importance of using guides. Those published by the Directory of Social Change are based on a review of trusts' schedules of grants on public file at the Charity Commission. From this the actual preferences of individual trusts (where they are apparent) can be inferred. Some give money to the same organisations year after year, others give one-off grants. Some welcome applications, others decide their own interests and are likely to disregard unsolicited applications.

Consult the bibliography at the end of this book for a list of published guides. The services of local Charity Information Bureaux and local funding advice services may also be helpful. Contact your local council for voluntary service or rural community council to find out what services are available in your area. These often include access to Funderfinder, a computer programme which helps voluntary groups identify appropriate trusts for particular needs (see address within the bibliography).

THE IMPORTANCE OF RESEARCH

The importance of preliminary research cannot be overemphasised. Use the grant guides to make a list of selected trusts which seem to match your interests. Find out if a trust has policies and priorities, the size of its grants, its beneficial area, any restrictions, and so on. Obtain its annual report, any guidelines for applicants and application form if available. Don't start approaching trusts till you have identified a number of trusts which seem appropriate and then rank them in order of likelihood. Also don't trawl through only half a guidebook. Cover all entries. It is surprising the number of trusts near the end of the alphabet which get missed by fledgling fundraisers.

This is a highly competitive field. All trusts receive far more requests than they are able to fulfil. Do not spoil your chances of success by sending hasty and vague applications.

CONTACT WITH THE TRUST

Wherever possible try to develop a relationship with the trust in advance of any formal application. Telephone for advice, seek a meeting, invite administrators and trustees to performances, events and exhibitions, etc. Use personal contacts if at all possible. Where a trust is based far away from your work why not suggest with your invitation that they may like to choose someone more local to visit you "by proxy"? It's worth a try, you have nothing to lose. But remember to bear in mind the kind of administration used by the trust. Most will not be in a position to be receptive although they may appreciate your drive and that's another bonus.

Keep your letter of application as simple and concise as possible. Necessary details can be attached. Remember to state the obvious: what your organisation does and why its work is important/effective; who you are and what you have achieved.

If you are not a charity, identify those projects or parts of your work that are charitable.

THE PROJECT

Define your project and request for money clearly. Few trusts give support for general running costs. Identify an area of work which can be separately costed and which needs development. *Put the emphasis on the people who will benefit from this project, how many and for how long. Far more trusts are interested in supporting young people, people with disadvantage and the disabled rather than in supporting the arts. It is wise to concentrate on those aspects of your work which open up opportunities for these people whether as audiences or as participants.*

Draw up a fully budgeted proposal with a detailed breakdown. It is often an attractive "selling-point" to show how much the project costs per individual. Who will benefit. It emphasises the cost-effectiveness of the project, and often makes the cost of the project seem "smaller".

Pitch the size of your grant request to suit each trust. (Don't ask for £5,000 from a trust which generally gives grants of £500.)

Many larger trusts request a list of other sources of support being approached and may make a grant conditional on other support being obtained. Be sure to have a planned strategy.

If possible indicate the ways in which the project will be monitored and evaluated. This emphasises your efficiency and is also a request that more of the larger trusts are making of their beneficiaries.

TIMING

Be clear about the time-scale of your own project. You need to plan well in advance since you may have to wait several months to hear about the results of your application. Some trusts review their applications annually, some quarterly, some monthly. Try to find out when trustees next meet. Then keep a schedule so that you can check the progress of each if need be.

ATTACHMENTS WITH THE APPLICATION

Audited accounts, annual report, constitution, budget for the current year should be attached. Also attach clear background about your organisation, its aims and achievements and who is involved in the management.

Put together portfolio of reviews, endorsements of your work from well-known artists, previous funders, etc. Photographs, plans and maps often say far more than words. If you are working with young people remember that pictures by them may give your application greater "appeal" and far more immediacy.

MAINTAIN CONTACT

Maintain contact with a trust during the course of an application, inform of any successes, invite to functions, send newsletters, etc. Keep in touch if you receive a grant, send reports, invitations, latest reviews showing what is being done with their help.

N.B. Relatively few trusts give clear instructions about what they seek from applicants. It is useful to look at the application requirements of those major trusts with clear guidelines, whether of not you intend to apply to them. Suggested trusts include the City Parochial Foundation, the Paul Hamlyn Foundation, the Gulbenkian Foundation, and Henry Smith's (Kensington Estate) Charity.

CHARITABLE TRUSTS

The ADAPT Trust

The Alper Charitable Trust

The Anglo-Hong Kong Trust

The Milly Apthorp Charitable Trust

The Arts Foundation

The Arvon Foundation

The Ashden Charitable Trust (see also the Sainsbury Family Charitable Trusts)

Lord Ashdown Charitable Trust

The Ashe Charitable Foundation

The Laura Ashley Foundation

The Society of Authors

The Avenue Charitable Trust

The Nancy Balfour Trust

The Daphne Ballard Trust (see The Museums' Association)

The Barakat Trust

The Verity Bargate Award

The Baring Foundation

The Eleanor Barton Trust

The BBC Children in Need Appeal

The Beaverbrook Foundation

Beecroft Bequest (see The Museums' Association)

The Bernerd Foundation

The Charlotte Bonham-Carter Charitable Trust

The Book Trust

The Book Trust Scotland

The Bouverie Trust

The Bowerman Memorial Trust

The Brand Trust

The Bridge House Estates Trust Fund

The Britten-Pears Foundation

The Rosemary Bugden Charitable Trust

The Dorothy Burns Charity

The R M Burton Charitable Trust

The Barrow Cadbury Trust (incorporating the Barrow and Geraldine S Cadbury and Paul S Cadbury Trusts)

The Edward Cadbury Charitable Trust

Edward and Dorothy Cadbury Trust

The William Adlington Cadbury Charitable Trust

The Kathy Callow Trust (see the Museums' Association)

The David Canter Memorial Trust

Caritas (The James A de Rothschild's Charitable Settlement)

The Carlton Television Trust

The Carnegie Dunfermline Trust

The Carnegie United Kingdom Trust

Sir John Cass's Foundation

The Francis Chagrin Fund

The Chapman Charitable Trust

The Charities Aid Foundation

Charity Know How Fund

Charity Projects

The Charterhouse Charitable Trust

The Chase Charity

The Children's Film and Television Foundation

The Winston Churchill Memorial Trust

The City Parochial Foundation

J Anthony Clark Charitable Foundation

The Clore Foundation

The Clothworkers' Foundation

The John Coates Charitable Trust

The David Cohen Family Charitable Trust

The John S Cohen Foundation

The Cole Charitable Trust

The Joseph Collier Charitable Trust

The Ernest Cook Trust

The Duke of Cornwall's Benevolent Fund

The Cripplegate Foundation

The D'Oyly Carte Charitable Trust

The Daiwa Anglo-Japanese Foundation

The Dancers' Trust

The Delius Trust

The Djanogly Foundation

The Drapers' Charitable fund

The Ann Driver Trust

The Vivien Duffield Foundation

Gilbert and Eileen Edgar Foundation

The Elephant Trust

The John Ellerman Foundation (formerly The Moorgate Trust Fund and the New Moorgate Trust Fund)

The Elm Trust 11

The Elmgrant Trust

The Enkalon Foundation

The Equity Trust Fund

The Eranda Foundation

The Esmée Fairbairn Charitable Trust

The Federation of British Artists

The John Feeney Charitable Trust

The John Fernald Award Trust

The Finchcocks Charity

The First Film Foundation

The Sir John Fisher Foundation

The Joyce Fletcher Charitable Trust

The 42 Foundation

The Four Lanes Trust

The Gordon Fraser Charitable Trust

The Hugh Fraser Foundation

The Fulbright Commission

The Gane Charitable Trust

The Gannochy Trust

The Gatsby Charitable Foundation (see the Sainsbury Family Charitable Trusts also)

The Robert Gavron Charitable Trust

The German Academic Exchange Service (DAAD)

J Paul Getty Jr Charitable Trust

The Gibbs Charitable Trust

The Simon Gibson Charitable Trust

The Godinton Charitable Trust

The Golden Bottle Trust

The Goldsmiths' Company's Charities

The Gosling Foundation

The Granada Foundation

The Great Britain Sasakawa Foundation

The Greater Bristol Foundation

The Grocers' Charity

The Gulbenkian Foundation

The Hadrian Trust

J M Haldane's Charitable Trust

The Paul Hamlyn Foundation

Sue Hammerson's Charitable Trust

The Hampton Fuel Allotment Charity

The W A Handley Charity Trust

The Harding Trust

The Kenneth Hargreaves Trust

The R J Harris Charitable Settlement

The Headley Trust (see also the Sainsbury Family Charitable Trusts)

The Hellenic Foundation

The Myra Hess Trust

The Hilden Charitable Fund

The Hinrichsen Foundation

The Holst Foundation

The P H Holt Charitable Trust

The Hornton Trust

The John & Ruth Howard Charitable Trust

The Robin Howard Foundation

The Idlewild Trust

The INTACH (UK) Trust

The Inverforth Charitable Trust

The Ireland Funds

The Sir Barry Jackson County Fund

The John and Rhys Thomas James Foundation

The Japan Festival Fund

The John Jarrold Trust Ltd

The Jenour Foundation

The Jerusalem Trust (see also Sainsbury Family Charitable Trusts)

The Jerwood Foundation

The K C Charitable Trust

The Ilse and Michael Katz Foundation

The Robert Kiln Charitable Trust

The King's Fund (King Edward's Hospital Fund for London)

The Kingsmead Charitable Trust

The Dolly Knowles Charitable Trust

The John Kobal Foundation

The Kobler Trust

The Kreitman Foundation

The Kirby Laing Foundation

The Lady Artists Club Trust

The Langtree Trust

The Lankelly Foundation

The Leathersellers' Company Charitable Fund

The Leche Trust

The Morris Leigh Foundation

Lord Leverhulme's Charitable Trust

The Linbury Trust (see also Sainsbury Family Charitable Trusts)

The Lloyds Charities Trust

The Lyndhurst Settlement

The Sir Jack Lyons Charitable Trust

The Mackintosh Foundation

The MacRobert Trusts

The E D and F Man Charitable Trust

The Manifold Charitable Trust

The Michael Marks Charitable Trust

The Marsh Christian Trust

The Martin Musical Scholarship Fund

Sir George Martin Trust

The Catherine Martineau Trust

The Nancie Massey Charitable Trust

The Matthews Wrightson Charity Trust

The Mayfield Valley Arts Trust

The McKenna and Co Foundation

The Anthony and Elizabeth Mellows Charitable Settlement

The Mercers' Company Charitable Foundation

The Millichope Foundation

The James Milne Memorial Trust

The Milton Keynes Community Trust Ltd

Peter Minet Trust

The Esmé Mitchell Trust

The Monument Trust (see also under the Sainsbury Family Charitable Trusts)

The Henry Moore Foundation

The Moores Family Charity Foundation

The Peter Moores Foundation

The Theo Moorman Charitable Trust

The Movement for Christian Democracy Trust

The Munro Charitable Trust

The Countess of Munster Musical Trust

The Museums' Association

The Worshipful Company of Musicians

The Musicians' Benevolent Fund

The National Art Collections Fund

The Network Foundation

The Normanby Charitable Trust

The Northern Ireland Voluntary Trust

The Ofenheim Trust (including the former Cinderford Trust)

The Old Possums Practical Trust

The Oldham Foundation

The Oppenheim-John Downes Memorial Awards

The Oppenheimer Charitable Trust

The Orpheus Trust

The Ouseley Trust

The Rudolph Palumbo Charitable Foundation

The Paragon Concert Society

The Hon Charles Pearson Charity Trust

The PF Charitable Trust

The Stanley Picker Trust

The Pilgrim Trust

The Austin & Hope Pilkington Trust

The Poetry Society

The Porter Foundation

The Prince's Trust and the Royal Jubilee Trusts

Mr and Mrs J A Pye's Charitable Settlement

Dr Radcliffe's Trust

The Eleanor Rathbone Charitable Trust

The Rayne Foundation

The Richmond Parish Lands Charity

The Robertson Trust

The Helen Roll Charity

The Leopold de Rothschild Charitable Trust

The Roughley Charitable Trust

The Royal Victoria Hall Foundation

The RSA Art for Architecture Scheme

The Willy Russell Charitable Trust

The RVW Trust

The Audrey Sacher Charitable Trust

Dr Mortimer & Theresa Sackler Foundation

The Leonard Sainer Charitable Trust

The Alan and Babette Sainsbury Charitable Trust

The Sainsbury Family Charitable Trusts

The Basil Samuel Charitable Trust

The Coral Samuel Charitable Trust

The Save & Prosper Educational Trust

The Save & Prosper Foundation

The Francis Scott Charitable Trust

The Frieda Scott Charitable Trust

The Scouloudi Foundation

The Sears Foundation

The Skinners' Company Lady Neville Charity

The Henry Smith's (Kensington Estate) Charity

The Spitalfields Market Community Trust

The Foundation for Sport and the Arts

The Steel Charitable Trust

The Stevenson Family's Charitable Trust

The Stoll Moss Theatres Foundation (formerly the Robert Holmes à Court Foundation)

The Alexander Stone Foundation

The Summerfield Charitable Trust

The Bernard Sunley Charitable Foundation

The Swan Trust

The Theatres Trust Charitable Fund

The Thornton Foundation

The Tillett Trust

The Michael Tippett Musical Foundation

The Tory Family Foundation

The TSB Foundation for England and Wales

The TSB Foundation for Scotland

The TSB Foundation for Northern Ireland

The Tudor Trust

The Douglas Turner Trust

The 29th May 1961 Charitable Trust

The Tyne & Wear Foundation

The Lisa Ullman Travelling Scholarship Fund

The ULTACH Trust/Iontaobhas ULTACH

The Underwood Trust

The Charles Wallace India Trust

The Warbeck Fund Limited

The Ward Blenkinsop Trust

The Wates Foundation

The Weinberg Foundation

The Weinstock Fund

The Welsh Church Funds

The Welton Foundation

The Westminster Foundation

The Garfield Weston Foundation

Humphrey Whitbread's First Charitable Trust

The Harold Hyam Wingate Foundation

The Fred and Della Worms Charitable Trust

The Wolfson Family Charitable Trust (formerly the Edith and Isaac Wolfson Charitable Trust)

The Wolfson Foundation

The I A Ziff Charitable Foundation

The Zochonis Charitable Trust

The ADAPT Trust

Cameron House, Abbey Park Place, Dunfermline, Fife KY12 7PZ (address may change in 1996)

Tel: 01383-623 166; Fax: 01383-622 149
Contact: Gillian Dinsmore, Administrator
Trustees: Emma Nicholson MP (Chair), Dr Gillian Burrington, Robert F Donaldson, Gary Flather, Rachel Hurst, Lord Murray of Epping Forest, C Wycliffe Noble, Henry Wrong, Geoffrey Lord.
Grant total: £93,000 grants; £9,500 awards (1994)
Beneficial area: UK.
General: The ADAPT (Access for Disabled People to Arts Premises Today) Trust aims to improve accessibility for disabled and older people to primary arts venues.

Advisory Service: a network of honorary advisers throughout the UK undertake access surveys and assessments, particularly in venues wishing to apply for Lottery funding. Whilst general funds were fully committed during 1995, two special schemes were in operation:

Capital Access, sponsored by London Arts Board and designed to improve ground floor access to performing arts venues, museums and galleries in London. Grants are available up to a maximum of £10,000. Grants in 1995 included:
Union Chapel, Islington (£10,000);
Blackheath Concert Halls (£4,000).
Both were for ramps and accessible toilets.

Sightline, sponsored by Guide Dogs for the Blind Association, improves facilities in performing arts venues in the UK for visually impaired and blind people. Grants are available up to a maximum of £4,500. Grants in 1995 included:
Theatre Clwyd, Mold, for infrared system for audio described performances (£4,500);
Yorkshire Dance Centre, for improved signage, textured floor coverings, lift voice announcements (£4,500).
British Gas ADAPT Awards are made annually to the best adapted arts venues in the UK. Applications are invited from cinemas, arts centres, theatres, libraries,

concert halls, museums and galleries, heritage sites and historic houses which have facilities for disabled people which can be looked upon as role models.

ADAPT's Access Guidance Pack "ADAPTations to Accessibility" giving comprehensive guidelines on access to arts venues is available for £7. 50 incl p+p.

Exclusions: From grants (not the awards): stately homes, heritage centres, crafts centres; halls designed and used for other purposes such as church halls, hospitals or educational establishments even though they sometimes house the arts; festivals, unless at a permanent arts venue. Arts venues owned or managed by a local authority are excluded from ADAPT's general grants.

Applications: Applicants for grants have to demonstrate that all aspects of access have been considered, including parking, publicity and staff training. Application forms are available from the ADAPT office.

The Alper Charitable Trust

Chilford Hall, Linton, Cambridgeshire CB1 6LE

Contact: S Alper
Trustees: S Alper, Mrs I D Alper, T Yardley, J Horwood-Smart
Grant total: £9,000 (1983)
Beneficial area: National with preference for East Anglia.
General: Grants are generally limited to help for young musicians and other arts projects. Grants are usually one-off.
Applications: In writing to the correspondent enclosing an SAE for a reply.

The Anglo-Hong Kong Trust

58 St James' Street, London SW1A 1LD

Tel: 0171-493 8272
Contact: D Tang, Secretary
Trustees: John G Cluff, David J Davies, Simon Murray, David Tang.
Grant total: £105,000 approx. (1993/94)
Beneficial area: UK and Hong Kong
General: The aims of the trust are to promote the advancement of commerce

and industry for the mutual benefit of the communities in the UK and Hong Kong, and also to advance education. The trust was set up in 1989 as a charitable company by the current trustees including the multi millionaire businessman J G Cluff. Recent donations to the arts have included:

British Film Institute, for the London Film Festival (£4,000);
British Council, Hong Kong, for artist-in-residence (£8,000);
South Bank Centre (£8,000);
David Puttnam, the film producer, has received two grants totalling some £8,000, listed as "sponsorship for education".

The Milly Apthorp Charitable Trust

Grants Unit, Chief Executive's Department, London Borough of Barnet, Town Hall, The Burroughs, Hendon, London NW4 4BG

Tel: 0181-359 2092
Contact: Mrs Angela Corbett
Trustees: Lawrence Fenton, John Apthorp
Grant total: £595,000 (1994/95)
Beneficial area: London Borough of Barnet and its environs
General: The trust has general charitable objects. An eligible organisation must be a registered charity or non-profit making body which provides a service for residents of the borough and its environs and will normally be based in the Barnet area.

Eligible individuals must normally be resident in the borough and should be sponsored or recommended by an appropriate agency where possible.

Although applications can come from all sections of the community, priority will be given to those on behalf of people with special needs or with difficult social backgrounds, whose personal financial means are limited.

The trust divides its grant-making into five categories: young people, sports, illness/disability and health, elderly people, general community benefit. Arts projects are usually funded under the last of these categories.

Grants may be awarded for either capital

or revenue projects, which are designed to extend existing levels of provision or to develop new services, and which demonstrate a clearly defined benefit to local people. Services may be targeted towards the specific categories listed above, or to meet needs in other areas, so long as these are clearly explained. Awards will not generally be made to support existing activities alone.

The Apthrop Fund for Young Artists assists 18 to 30 year olds who are working or completing arts studies and living/working in the borough. They may submit three pieces of work to an annual competition. Selected items are purchased for between £500 and £2,000 and given to the borough for exhibition. In 1994 the fund spent £11,300 on purchases with £20,000 allocated for each of the following three years.

Arts grants in 1994/95 included:

Jigsaw, school/community arts festival (£5,000);

Live Music Now, for 22 concerts for special needs groups (£4,000);

Garden Suburb Theatre, scenery store (£2,500);

Artsreach, project for children with multiple disabilities (£2,000);

Flightways Photographic Group, outings (£1,600);

Indent Theatre Company, publicity (£220).

Applications: Application forms and explanatory leaflets for organisations and sponsored individuals are available from the above address for programmes run by the borough for the trust.

The Arts Foundation

Countess of Huntingdon Chapel, The Paragon, Bath BA1 5NA

Tel: 01225-315 775; Fax: 01225-317597
Contact: Prudence Skene, Director
Trustees: Lord Gowrie, Chairman, William Brown, Ed Victor, Tess Jaray, Terence Donovan, Mathew Prichard, Nelson Woo.
Grant total: £80,000 (1994/95)
General: The foundation was established in 1990 to serve the interest of the individual artist. In January 1993 the foundation announced that its policy would be to achieve this objective by funding artists living and working in England, Scotland or Wales, who have demonstrated commitment and proven their ability in their chosen art form.

The foundation awards a minimum of eight annual fellowships worth £10,000 each in eight specific art forms which change each year. Arts forms chosen have included Cross-Disciplinary Work, Installation, Jazz Composition, Music - General Composition, Painting, Photography, Screenwriting, Sculpture, and Theatre Design.

The programme is not open to application; a network of some 70 nominators (established artists and other professionals) name individual artists who are then invited to make an application.

Applications: No unsolicited applications are accepted.

The Arvon Foundation

Kilnhurst, Kilnhurst Road, Todmorden, Lancashire, OL14 6AX

Tel: 01706-816582; 01706-816359
Contact: David Pease, Director
Beneficial area: UK.
General: The foundation runs a major annual poetry competition. The Observer International Poetry Competition, supported also by the Arts Councils of England and Scotland, is open to writers resident in the British Isles and also to those resident elsewhere.

English poems of any length are eligible for an entry fee of £3. 50 each. In 1995 a first prize of £5,000 was awarded, five prizes of £500 each and 10 prizes of £250 each.

The foundation also runs four and a half day writing courses (poetry, narrative and drama) in its three centres throughout the year, at Lumb Bank, West Yorkshire, at Moniack Mhor, Scotland and at Totleigh Barton, Devon. A number of bursaries are available for those unable to afford the full fee for an Arvon writing course.

Applications: For full details about the competition and the bursaries contact the foundation. The closing date for the 1995 competition was 30th November.

The Ashden Charitable Trust

(see also the Sainsbury Family Charitable Trusts)

9 Red Lion Court, London EC4A 3EB

Contact: Michael Pattison
Trustees: Mrs S Butler-Sloss; R Butler-Sloss, Miss J SPortrait.
Grant total: £72,000 (1993)
Beneficial area: UK and overseas.
General: The trust supports: Homelessness; Green Issues; Urban Regeneration; Community Arts. In 1993/94 a total of £23,000 was allocated to Community Arts. Recipients included:
Ebony Steelband Trust (£6,000);
Cleveland Alzheimers Resource Centre, for a music worker for six months (£3,400);
Graeae Youth Theatre (£3,000);
Bridge Youth Theatre (£2,750);
Half Moon Young People's Theatre (£2,000);
Age Exchange Theatre (£1,200);
Stagefright Theatre Co, for a community play in Shrewsbury (£600).
Exclusions: No grants to individuals.
Applications: One application to the Sainsbury Family Charitable Trusts (see separate entry) is an application to all. See that entry for the names of the other trusts and application procedures.

Lord Ashdown Charitable Trust

c/o Clive Marks, 44a New Cavendish Street, London W1M 7LG

Tel: 0171-486 4663
Contact: C M Marks
Trustees: Clive Marks, George F Renwick, Richard Stone, Jonathan Silver.
Grant total: £1,326,000 (1992/93)
Beneficial area: UK.
General: In 1992/93 the trust made only five grants totalling £42,000 under its "Arts" category. The trust also supports: children; community; education; hospices

and aged; medical; preventative medicine; students. Many of the grants are made to Jewish charities. Information is not available with the 1992/93 accounts at the Charity Commission about its grants. The most recent information available relates to 1990/91. Several grants were then given under other categories as well as "Arts". Relevant grants in the "Community" category were:
Geese Theatre Company (£1,000);
Israel Folk Dance Institute (£1,000);
Tricycle Theatre Co Ltd (£500);
Carousel Arts for Learning Difficulties (£500);
Under the "Education" category:
Open College for the Arts (£10,000);
Amadeus Scholarship Fund (£3,250);
Grants under the "Arts" category included:
Yaa Asantewa Arts Centre (£10,000);
London College of Music (£7,500);
National Steel Band Co (£3,000).
Exclusions: No grants to individuals.
Applications: The trust's resources are already heavily committed and 'the chances of success for unsolicited applications are negligible'. For those undeterred, details of the project summarised on one sheet of A4 paper should be sent to the correspondent. Any supporting material should be cross-referenced to that sheet. Where possible, the trustees will want to see a budget for the forthcoming year, not exceeding one page.

The Ashe Charitable Foundation

c/o Messrs Binder Hamlyn, 17 Lansdowne Road, Croydon CR9 2PL

Tel: 0181-688 4422
Contact: F A M Akers-Douglas
Trustees: C J Heath, M J Heath, F A M Akers-Douglas.
Grant total: £15,000 (1993/94) but see below
Beneficial area: UK.
General: The foundation seems mainly to give to medically related and social welfare charities with some minor support for arts organisations. The foundation's giving

dropped to £15,000 in 1993/94 from £80,000 in 1990/91. In 1993/94 arts grants were given to:
Nordoff-Robins Music Therapy Centre (£2,000);
Royal Opera House (£900);
Chicken Shed Theatre (£200).
Applications: In writing to the correspondent.

The Laura Ashley Foundation

33 King Street, London WC2E 8JD

Tel: 0171-497 2503
Contact: Annabel Thompson
Trustees: Sir Bernard Ashley, David Ashley, Lord Hooson, Sir Richard Gaskell
Grant total: £231,000 to organisations; £172,000 to individuals (1993/94)
Beneficial area: UK
General: Most of the foundation's funds are allocated to second-chance education for individuals and for group projects. Funding is also given to colleges for distribution to students in fine art conservation, restoration and music. Examples of arts grants for part course fees and/or part maintenance (September 1993):
Camberwell College of Arts (£11,000);
City & Guilds of London Art School (£9,800);
London Cartoon Centre (£5,000);
Royal Northern College of Music (£2,625);
Guildhall School Foundation (£2,000);
Courtauld Institute, fresco painting, (£3,000);
Royal Academy of Music, for 5 students (£11,360);
Royal College of Music, for 7 students (£18,700).
Exclusions: No grants for running costs, expeditions, conferences, research, buildings, publications, exhibitions, dance or drama, graduates or undergraduates, materials, computers, childminding.
Applications: Applications for music conservatoires and conservation and restoration courses must come through a college, not from individuals. Send a SAE for an information sheet which gives examples of funding, exclusions, dates of trustees' meetings and an application form. The foundation replies only to applications which it wishes to consider further.

The Society of Authors

84 Drayton Gardens, London SW10 9SB

Tel: 0171-373 6642; Fax: 0171-373 5769
Beneficial area: UK.
General: The society administers some 23 schemes for prizes, awards or grants. Further information sheets are available from the society on request. Awards are also made for translations from French, Italian, Dutch, and German. The following is a selection of schemes administered by the society:
• Authors' Contingency Fund: grants for authors "in financial difficulties or for the financial relief of their dependants". An application form is available.
• Authors' Foundation: £70,000 in 1995, supported by the Arts Council, Mrs Isobel Dalziel and the Esmé Fairbairn Foundation: grants to authors needing funding additional to the advance when working on a book – fiction or non-fiction – commissioned by a British publisher. Applications in writing . Annual closing date 30 April.
• K Blundell Trust: £15,000 in 1994, grants to authors under the age of 40 to help with their next book. Their work, fiction not excluded, must contribute "to the greater understanding of existing social and economic organisation". Applications in writing enclosing their latest book by 30 April.
• Encore Award: £7,500 prize for second novels. The closing date for novels published in 1995 was 30 November.
• Eric Gregory Awards: £25,000+ annually for promising poets under the age of 30, decided on the strength of the work submitted and the means of each award winner. Closing date 31 October.
• McKitterick Prize: £5,000 for a first novel, published or unpublished, by authors over the age of 40. Closing date 16 December.
• Somerset Maugham Awards: £15,000 in total, for British authors under the age of

35 to enrich their writing by exposure to foreign countries. Given on the strength of a book, dramatic works excluded. Closing date 31 December.

* Betty Trask Prize and Awards: £25,000 in total for first novels published or unpublished, by writers under 35, for works of a romantic or traditional - not experimental - nature. Closing date 31 January (covering books published in the previous year).
* Travelling Scholarships: £6,000 annually to enable British writers to keep in touch with colleagues abroad. They are non-competitive.

The Avenue Charitable Trust

c/o Messrs Sayers Butterworth, 18 Bentinck Street, London W1M 5LR

Tel: 0171-935 8504
Contact: S G Kemp
Trustees: Hon F D L Astor, Mrs B A Astor, S G Kemp
Grant total: £210,000 (September 1995)
Beneficial area: UK and overseas.
General: The trust makes grants to a wide range of charitable work. In 1992 a far lower total of £91,000 was disbursed in 75 grants, most of which were either £1,000 or a few hundred pounds. Arts grants were given to:
Royal Academy of Arts of Africa (£3,000);
George Orwell Archive, National Portrait
  Gallery, Royal National Theatre (£1,000);
Dulwich Picture Gallery, Writers and
  Scholars Educational Trust (£500 each);
Chicken Shed Theatre Company (£200);
Commonweal Theatre Company,
  Garsington Opera, British Museum
  Society (£100).
Applications: It is understood that funds are already totally committed. No reply will received unless an SAE is sent.

The Nancy Balfour Trust

c/o Messrs Sayers Butterworth, 18 Bentinck Street, London W1M 5RL

Tel: 0171-935 8504
Contact: S G Kemp

Trustees: Kate Ashbrook, Karen Evans, Stuart Kemp
Grant total: £15,000 (1994/95)
Beneficial area: UK
General: The trust supports visual art, education and housing projects. Only national or London-based organisations are eligible. Funds are provided to certain college welfare officers for use as they think best; other student applications are seldom successful. Most grants are under £300.
Exclusions: No grants to religious or military bodies or schools.
Applications: In writing to the correspondent in January or July. Unsuccessful applications will not be acknowledged unless accompanied by an SAE. Telephone enquiries are not welcome.

The Daphne Ballard Trust (see The Museums' Association)

The Barakat Trust

c/o Penygon Systems Ltd, 2 Plantation Grove, Arnside, Carnforth, Lancs LA5 OH

Contact: G Swainbank
Trustees: Hamida Alireza, Tarik Alireza, Amir Alireza
Grant total: £48,000 (1993)
Beneficial area: UK
General: The trust gives grants for the "promotion of research into Islamic art and architecture, by assisting, by means of awards, various academics and students".
Applications: In writing to the correspondent.

The Verity Bargate Award

c/o The Soho Theatre Company, 24 Mortimer Street, London W1N 7RD

Tel: 0171-436 8833
General: An annual award, created as a memorial to the founder of the Soho Theatre Company, is made to the writer of a new and previously unperformed full-length play. The first prize of £1,500 represents an option on a full production by the Soho Theatre Company. Short-listed

plays are provided with workshop facilities to assist their further development.
Exclusions: Playwrights with three or more professional productions to their credit.
Applications: For full details write to the above address.

The Baring Foundation

60 London Wall, London EC2M 5TQ

Tel: 0171-767 1000
Contact: David Carrington, Director
Trustees: Lord Ashburton (Chariman), Nicolas Baring, Mrs Tessa Baring, Robin Broadley, Lord Howick, Lady Lloyd, Sir Crispin Tickell, Martin Tickell, Anthony Loehnis.
Grant total: around £2. 5 million
Beneficial area: UK, with a special interest in London, Merseyside and North East of England
General: The foundation has undergone a transformation as a result of the débacle of the Barings Bank. Its funding programmes have been severely reduced and its arts funding programmes curtailed. However the foundation will probably add to its programmes, which have concentrated on "Strengthening the Voluntary Sector".

A new programme of arts in education and the community is likely to be launched in Summer 1996. Please check with the foundation.
Applications: Obtain current policy information and guidelines for support.

The Eleanor Barton Trust

Ouvry Creed & Co Solicitors, Foresters House, Sherston, Malmesbury, Wiltshire SN16 OLQ

Tel: 01666-840 843
Contact: R D Creed
Trustees: C B Moynihan, R D Creed
Grant total: £16,000 (1994)
Beneficial area: UK, with a particular interest in Sherston.
General: "We have always looked for charities which help people to find a new dimension to their lives through artistic endeavour". The trust is particularly

interested in the arts as therapy for the disadvantaged. Most grants given on the basis that the charity concerned must raise an equivalent sum from other sources.
Grants in 1994 included:
Action Space London events (£2,238);
Goldsmith's College Trust, Brewery Arts Kendal, CARA, painting for those affected by HIV/AIDS (£1,000 each);
Dulwich Picture Gallery, Contagious Performance Co (£500 each);
Guildhall School of Music and Drama (£433);
Proper Job Theatre Projects, for people with learning difficulties (£250).
Exclusions: Organisations which are not registered charities.
Applications: In writing to the correspondent.

The BBC Children in Need Appeal

England & National: BBC Chilcren in Need, Admin Unit, PO Box 7, London W5 2GQ (0181-280 8057);

Northern Ireland: Broadcasting House, Ormeau, Avenue, Belfast BT2 8HQ (01232-338 221);

Scotland: Broadcasting House, Queen Street, Edinburgh EH2 IJF (0131-469 4225);

Wales: Broadcasting House, Llandaff, Cardiff CF5 2YQ (01222-572 383).

Contact: Julia Kaufmann, Director (at London address)
Trustees: Sir Kenneth Bloomfield (Chairman), Sir Robert Andrew, Jane Asher, Colin Browne, Mark Byford, David Carrington, Jonathan Clarke, Alison Reed, Elaine Ross, Michael Stevenson.
Grant total: £16. 2 million (1994/95)
Beneficial area: UK.
General: The appeal supports projects which seek to benefit children with mental, physical or sensory disabilities, children with behavioural or psychological disorders, children living in poverty or in situations of deprivation, children suffering through distress, abuse or neglect. It gives grants of all sizes for both one-off expenditure and

for up to three years for specified running costs. It assists with capital costs and equipment purchase but rarely with new buildings.

Its annual report states that in 1993/94 £2. 5 million was disbursed to projects involving children, many with physical or mental disabilities, in activities such as drama, music, sport and play.

Very clear and comprehensive grant guidelines are published and should be obtained by all potential applicants. It is worth mentioning that applications for minibuses or other vehicles must explain why it wouldn't make more sense to borrow, share or hire transport, to detail the running costs and show how these would be met.

Arts activities supported in 1994/95 included:

Midlands Arts Centre, for Saturday morning "Adventures in Art" (£8,000);

Carousel Project, Brighton, arts activities for people with learning difficulties to develop even more opportunities for young people (£7,828);

Nottingham Music Space working with disabled children through music therapy (£6,700);

Platform, disadvantaged young musicians are helped towards a professional career (£5,200);

Live Music Now!, for its work giving concerts in schools (£5,000);

Yorkshire Sculpture Park, sculpture work- shops for young people £4,150);

King's Music Centre, Macclesfield, to develop their Saturday morning music groups for special needs children (£2,000);

Sparks in the Dark, Northern Ireland, where young people, both able bodied and disabled, write, direct, compose, and perform their own dramas (as well as fundraise and promote). Funds will help them branch out into film making (£1,700).

Exclusions: The appeal does not consider applications from private individuals or the friends or families of individual children. In addition, grants will not be given for: trips and projects abroad; medical treatment or medical research; unspecified expenditure; deficit funding or repayment of loans; retrospective funding projects which will take place before applications can be processed (see note on closing dates below); projects which are unable to start within 12 months; the relief of statutory responsibilities; distribution to other organisations; general appeals; the relief of statutory responsibilities.

Applications: Application forms are available from the Appeal. There are two closing dates for applications - November 30 and March 30. Organisations may submit only one application and may apply to only one of these dates. Applicants should allow at least four months from each closing date for notification of a decision. (For summer projects applications must be submitted by the November closing date or be rejected because they cannot be processed in time.)

The Beaverbrook Foundation

11 Old Queen Street, London SW1H 9JA

Tel: 0171-222 7474

Contact: Michael Marshall, General Secretary

Trustees: Timoth M Aitken (Chair), Lady Violet Aitken, Lady Susan Beaverbrook, Laura Aitken, J E Kidd

Grant total: £332,000 (1992/93)

Beneficial area: UK, Nova Scotia and New Brunswick, Canada

General: The foundation's objects include the advancement of education in the UK and Canada, the improvement of churches, the relief of the sick, and the arts, specifically libraries, museums and art galleries. Grants in 1992/93 showed a particular interest in youth. Arts grants included:

Cartoon Art Trust (£10,000);

American Air Museum in Britain, British Aerial Museum (£5,000 each);

Royal Opera House Trust (£4,000);

Dulwich Picture Gallery (£3,000);

Applications: In writing.

Beecroft Bequest *(see The Museums' Association)*

The Bernerd Foundation

c/o Goodman Derrick, 90 Fetter Lane, London EC4 1EQ

Tel: 0171-404 0606; **Fax:** 0171-831 6407
Contact: Ian Montrose
Trustees: Ian Montrose, Kenneth Posner, Margaret Fielding
Grant total: £251,000 (1993/94)
Beneficial area: UK and overseas
General: The foundation makes grants to arts, medical and Jewish charities. Over 90% of grants are made to organisations known personally either to the trustees or to the founder, Elliott Bernerd, rather than in response to applications.

In 1993/94, out of a total or 13 grants, one major arts grant was given to London Philharmonic Orchestra (£167,000). The orchestra had already received regular grants with £25,000 and £75,000 in the two previous years.

In 1992/93 grants of £10,000 each had also been given to the Music Therapy Charity and the Jerusalem Music Centre.
Applications: In writing to the correspondent.

The Charlotte Bonham-Carter Charitable Trust

66 Lincoln's Inn Fields, London WC2A 3LH

Contact: Sir Matthew Farrer
Trustees: Sir C M Farrer, N A Bonham-Carter, N B Wickham-Irving.
Grant total: £53,000 (1993/94)
Beneficial area: UK and overseas.
General: The trust makes grants to charities with which Lady Charlotte Bonham-Carter was particularly associated during her life. There is also supposed to be a particular interest in Hampshire but this is not apparent in the grants awarded in 1993/94 when 21 grants were made ranging between £250 and £7,500. Arts grants were:
Royal Academy Trust (£7,500);
Tate Galley (£5,000);
Fitzwilliam Museum, Cambridge (£5,000);
Koestler Award Trust (£5,000);
Benesh Institute (£2,500);
Institute of Archaelogy (£1,000);
British Museum (£1,000).
Applications to assist with funding towards capital costs such as equipment purchase, building renovation or new buildings will be considered.
Exclusions: Only applications from registered charities are presently being considered.
Applications: In writing to the correspondent.

The Book Trust

Book House, 45 East Hill, London SW18 2QZ
Tel: 0181-870 9055; **Fax:** 0181-874 4790
Contact: Brian Perman, Executive Director
Trustees: Martyn Goff, Chairman.
Beneficial area: UK.
General: The Book Trust administers a portfolio of prizes which are for published works submitted via publishers: Booker Prize for Fiction, David Higham Prize; Sir Peter Kent Conservation Book Prize; The Mail on Sunday/John Llewellyn Rhys Prize; Kurt Maschler Award; Smarties Book Prize. In addition it organises:

The Saga Prize (£3,000 plus publication by Virago Press), for an unpublished novel in manuscript form written by a person born in the UK or the Republic of Ireland with black African ancestry. Sponsored by the Saga Group. Entrance fee £10.00.

The Book Trust Scotland

Scottish Book Centre, 137 Dundee Street, Edinburgh EH11 1BG

Tel: 0131-229 3663; **Fax:** 0131-228 4293
Contact: Lindsey Fraser
Beneficial area: UK, particularly Scotland.
General: Awards and prizes administered by the trust include the following:
• *McVitie's Prize for Scottish Writer of the Year:* £10,000 first prize, £1,000 to each short-listed writer. Annual awards for writing of all kinds, open to writers born in Scotland, or who have Scottish parents,

who are resident in Scotland, or who take Scotland as their inspiration. For work published/performed, etc in the previous 12 months. Closing date: 31 July.
- *Kathleen Fidler Award:* £1,000 plus publication. An annual award for an unpublished novel for children aged 8-12 years, to encourage writers new to this age group. The work should be their first attempt to write for this age range.

Exclusions: Further details should be obtained from the trust about the awards above and other prizes.

The Bouverie Trust

c/o Goodman Derrick, 90 Fetter Lane, London EC4A 1EQ

Tel: 0171-404 0606
Contact: The Trust Administrator
Grant total: £20,000 (1993/94)
Beneficial area: UK.
General: The grant-aid of this trust has been steadily dropping from a total of £100,000 in 1990/91. It is not known if the trust will continue its funding after the death of its main founder trustee, Lord Goodman. The trust supports a wide range of Jewish welfare and other charities as well as arts organisations. In 1993/94 the trust gave over 60 grants most of only a few hundred pounds and many for less. The largest grant was for £5,000. Arts grants in 1993/94 were given to:
Glyndebourne Arts (£500);
Jacqueline du Pré Music Building (£500);
English National Opera (£412 in 2 grants);
Oxford Playhouse Trust, (£150);
Poetry Society, Royal College of Music, British Music Society, British/Israel Arts Association (£100 each).

The Bowerman Memorial Trust

Champs Hill, Coldwaltham, Pulborough, West Sussex RH20 1LY

Tel: 01789-831205
Contact: D W Bowerman
Trustees: David W Bowerman, Clarice M Bowerman.
Grant total: £72,000 (1993/94)

Beneficial area: UK and with a particular interest in West Sussex.
General: The trust supports church activities, medical charities, youth work and charities concerned with relief of poverty and the resettlement of offenders in addition to arts organisations. Arts grants totalling £21,000 were given in 1993/94 to:
Music at Boxgrove;
Newbury Spring Festival;
Arundel Cathedral Organ Fund;
Arundel Festival Society.
Applications: This trust did not want an entry in this guide.

The Brand Trust

4 Montagu Square, London W1H 1RA

Tel: 0171-486 2573
Contact: M L Meyer
Trustees: M L Meyer, N Meyer, I Dunlop.
Grant total: £23,000 (1994)
Beneficial area: UK.
General: Grants are given to a wide range of charitable activities. Most grants are £100. Recent grants to the arts have been interesting since they have not included well known and established arts institutions. They have included: Burnbake Trust, London Prisons Creative Trust, Living Paintings Trust, Park Avenue Players, Manaton and East Dartmouth Theatre, Chicken Shed Theatre (£100 each).
Exclusions: No grants to individuals.
Applications: In writing to the correspondent.

The Bridge House Estates Trust Fund

Grants Unit, P O Box 270, Guildhall, London EC2P 2EJ

Tel: 0171-332 3710; Fax: 0171-332 3720
Contact: Clare Thomas, Chief Grants Officer
Grant total: £10 million approximately
Beneficial area: Greater London.
General: This fund was set up to mend and replace bridges over the Thames in the City of London. Its growth of funds over the years has far outstripped the demand on its

resources for bridging purposes. The Corporation of the City of London which controls the fund decided to put some of the surplus into a charitable fund for the benefit of Londoners. An income of £10 million a year is anticipated.

The fund has decided to concentrate on specific areas, none of which are specifically related solely to the arts but may be an important aspect of the educational and community work of an arts organisation. The main area of potential interest is:

• innovative projects for young people.

The other chosen areas are:

• transport and access to it for elderly and disabled people
• environmental conservation
• schemes which assist elderly people to stay within the community
• the provision of technical support to voluntary organisations. These priorities are to be reviewed periodically.

Exclusions: Individuals, schools or other educational establishments, academic research or religious purposes. Grants cannot be made to relieve any local authority or other statutory organisation of expenditure which they are under a duty to provide.

The trust does not normally fund organisations which have received a large proportion of their income from central or local government or the London Boroughs Grants Unit, unless the application relates to a new initiative.

Applications: Applicants should obtain the information leaflet and application form which must be completed fully. Applications should be accompanied by: a copy of the constitution; most recent annual report; latest audited accounts; current budget; any business plan for the proposed project.

The Britten-Pears Foundation

The Red House, Aldeburgh, Suffolk IP15 5PZ

Tel: 01372-466655
Contact: The Administrator
Trustees: Marion Thorpe (Chair), Dr Donald Mitchell, Dr Colin Matthews, Noel Periton, Hugh Cobbe, Peter Carter, David Drew, Sir John Tooley, Andrew Potter

Grant total: £173,000 (1992/93)
Beneficial area: UK
General: The foundation aims to promote the musical works and writings of Benjamin Britten and Peter Pears and the principles of musical education established by them. It also aims to promote the arts in general, particularly music. The foundation owns and finances the Britten-Pears Library. Typical grants were:

Britten-Pears School for Musical Studies (£95,000);
Britten Composition Award (£13,000);
Aldeburgh Festival (£11,500);
Society for the Promotion of New Music (£1,500);
Purcell Centenary Trust, Foundation for Young Musicians, Cambridge Boys' Choir, Westminister Cathedral Choir School (£1,000 each).

Exclusions: Support for festivals other than Aldeburgh, individual scholarships, bursaries and course grants other than for the Britten-Pears School, purchase or restoration of musical instruments or equipment.
Applications: In writing to the correspondent.

The Rosemary Bugden Charitable Trust

Osborne Clarke Solicitors, 30 Queen Charlotte Street, Bristol BS99 7QQ

Tel: 0117-923 0220
Contact: J W Sharpe
Trustees: J Sharpe, D Drew, Mrs A E Frimston
Grant total: £449,000 (1994/95)
Beneficial area: UK with a preference for the Avon area.
General: The arts, particularly music, in the Avon area are a priority for this trust. In 1993/94 it gave most of its grant-aid in eight grants to Bath and Wessex Opera (£305,000). The remainder of its funding was given to individuals.

In the preceding year grants were made to a wider number of musical organisations in the Avon area. In this case Bath City Opera was favoured with 11 grants totalling £83,474. Other grants were given to Bath Georgian Festival (£37,500), Bath Festival Society (£10,000), Great Elm Music Festival (£6,500).

Applications: In writing to the correspondent.

The Dorothy Burns Charity

Fladgate Fielder, Heron Place, 3 George Street, London W1H 6AD

Contact: A J M Baker
Trustees: Jane Morgan (Chairman), Christopher Campbell, Professor Bernard Cohen, Ann Minogue, Winifred Tumim.
Grant total: £175,000 (1993/94)
Beneficial area: UK and overseas particularly Jamaica.
General: The charity supports education, the arts, youth and Jamaica. It gives six travelling scholarships to students at Slade School of Art. Of its total of 28 grants to organisations, 11 were given to arts related work. Arts grants in 1993/94 included;
Scottish Museum Council (£10,000);
Music Space Trust (£5,000);
ENO Baylis programme (£4,000);
National Opera Studio (£2,500);
British Film Institute, British Friends of Art Museums of Israel, Live Music Now Wales (£2,000).
Applications: The charity did not wish to be included in this guide which indicates that unsolicited applications are unlikely to be successful.

The R M Burton Charitable Trust

c/o Trustee Management Ltd, 27 East Parade, Leeds LS1 5SX

Contact: R M Burton
Trustees: R M Burton, P N Burton, A J Burton
Grant total: £271,000 (1993/94)
Beneficial area: UK and Israel with a preference for Leeds and Yorkshire
General: The trustees prefer to give grants to smaller charities. They support health, education and social welfare projects. A few arts grants are also made. Grants range from under £100 to £30,000 and most

grants are small and for £100 or less.

Out of 250 grants made in 1993/94, 22 were given to arts organisations. The larger of these were to:
Royal Opera House Trust (£6,400 in 2 grants);
Yorkshire and Humberside Arts Association, Parnham Trust (£2,000 each);
Contemporary Dance Trust, Rydale Festival Trust, Glasgow School of Art, Chicken Shed Theatre Co, (£1,000 each);
Yorkshire Museum, Leeds City Arts Galleries, Royal College of Music (£500 each);
Leeds Festival Chorus, Richmondshire Museum, Friends of Courtauld Institute (£250 each).
The trust's position regarding capital grants is that consideration is given to approaches for conservation of important buildings and acquisition by museums and galleries.
Exclusions: No grants to individuals or local charities except in Yorkshire.
Applications: In writing to the correspondent.

The Barrow Cadbury Trust
(incorporating the Barrow and Geraldine S Cadbury and Paul S Cadbury Trusts)

2 College Walk, Selly Oak, Birmingham B29 6LQ

Tel: 0121-472 0417
Contact: Eric Adams, Director
Trustees: Charles L Cadbury (Chair), Catherine R. Hickinbotham, Geraldine M Cadbury, Edward P Cadbury, Philippa H Southall, Roger P Hickinbotham, Anna C Southall, Richard G Cadbury, Erica R Cadbury, Ruth M Cadbury, James E Cadbury
Grant total: £1,507,000 (1993/94)
Beneficial area: UK and overseas.
General: This trust has no arts programme as such and the director has stressed that *"any 'arts' grants are purely an off-shoot activity by organisations usually already known to trustees and only in pursuit of the goals of other programmes"*. Please be sure your programme/project is strongly grounded in the themes noted below and that you receive full details of the trust's

programme before making an application or other enquiries.

Grants are made for activities in the voluntary sector under the following headings: Civil Rights; Community Democracy; Disability; Gender; Penal Affairs; Racial Justice; Reconciliation. Support is also given to aspects of Quaker work. The trust supports activities in Northern Ireland relating to the above-named areas of interest. Particular attention is paid to activities in the West Midlands, but only local applications which come within the trustees' topic guidelines are considered.

Most grants made to arts organisations in l994/94 were in the West Midlands area. Arts grants in 1993/94 included:

Within the "Racial Justice" category
Community Radio Training (£20,000);
Kajans, black arts and cultural development centre (£10,000);
Birmingham Black Oral History Project (£850);
Play-In, training course for black artists (£500);
Shomari Productions, TV/film script writing course (£500);
West Midland Arts, costs of a resident storyteller (£500);
Within the "Disability" category
Kaleidescope Theatre, Walsall (£10,000);
Open Theatre Company (£500);
Within the "Civil Rights" category
Community Radio Association, research on a regional strategy for the Midlands (£750);
Within the "Other grant" category
City of Birmingham, Museum & Art Galleries (£10,000).
Exclusions: All fields outside the agreed policy areas. No grants to individuals.
Applications: In writing to the correspondent, giving only brief details initially. Trustees' meetings are normally held in March, late June, October and December. All applicants should first obtain the trust's guidelines.

The Edward Cadbury Charitable Trust

Elmfield, College Walk, Selly Oak, Birmingham B29 6LE

Tel: 0121-472 1838
Contact: Mrs M Walton, Secretary
Trustees: Charles E Gillett (Chairman), Christopher S Littleboy, Charles R Gillett, Andrew S Littleboy, Nigel R Cadbury.
Grant total: £545,000 (1993/94)
Beneficial area: UK and overseas, but with a special interest in the West Midlands.
General: The trust give in the following areas: the voluntary sector in the West Midlands; Christian mission, the ecumenical movement and interfaith relations; the oppressed and disadvantaged in this country and overseas; the arts and the environment. Examples of grants relevant to this guide:
In 1993/94
Avoncroft Museum of Buildings (£40,000 with £11,000 in the previous year);
Birmingham Museum and Art Gallery (£10,000 with £500 in the previous year).
In 1992/93
Ironbridge Gorge Museum Development Trust (£3,000);
Koestler Award Trust (£1,000).
Exclusions: No grants to individuals or organisations not registered as charities.
Applications: In writing at any time including clear details of the project with a budget. Trustees meet in May and November. Applications are not acknowledged unless an SAE is enclosed.

Edward and Dorothy Cadbury Trust

Elmfield, College Walk, Selly Oak, Birmingham B29 6LE

Tel: 0121-472 1838
Contact: Mrs M Walton, Secretary
Trustees: P A Gillett, Dr C M Elliot, Phillipa S Ward
Grant total: £81,000 (1993/94)
Beneficial area: UK and overseas with a preference for the West Midlands.
General: Grants are made to a wide range

of community and social welfare projects. Arts organisations are regularly represented among grant recipients. There seems to be a preference for music. Grants range between £50 and £3,000 with most falling between £50 and £500.

The most recent list of grants given with the trust's accounts on file at the Charity Commission is for 1992/93. In that year the trust gave 407 grants at least 23 of which were to arts organisations. They included:
Bromsgrove Festival (£3,000);
Bromsgrove Choral Society (£625);
Midland Youth Orchestra, Birmingham Contemporary Music Group, Birmingham Music Festival (£500 each);
St Albans Festival, Edinburgh Youth Orchestra Society, Bourneville Children's Choir, Ironbridge Gorge Museum, Welsh College of Music and Drama (£250 each).
Exclusions: No grants to individuals.
Applications: In writing to the correspondent, clearly giving relevant information concerning the project's aims and its benefits. Up-to-date accounts and annual reports where available would be helpful.

The William Adlington Cadbury Charitable Trust

2 College Walk, Selly Oak, Birmingham B29 6LE

Tel: 0121-472 1464
Contact: Mrs Christine Stober
Trustees: Brandon Cadbury, Hannah H Taylor, W James B Taylor, Rupert A Cadbury, Katherine M Hampton, C Margaret Salmon, Sarah Stafford, Adrian Thomas, John C Penny.
Grant total: £321,000 (1993/94)
Beneficial area: UK and overseas, but the main area of giving is the West Midlands
General: The trust's policy is to assist "charities working in the West Midlands, or where the projects have a national impact". The trust makes only about ten arts grants each year within a total of over 250. Recent grants to arts organisations have included:
Mid Wales Opera (£2,000);
Live Music Now, Wales (£1,000);

Bourneville Children's Choir, Birmingham Music Festival, Birmingham Balsall Heath Picture Palace (£200 each);
Birmingham Festival Choral Society (£100).
Grants were also made under its "preservation" category to:
Birmingham Museum (£15,000 in 2 grants);
Bunyan Free Church Museum Appeal (£2,000);
Sheepcote Street Project and Puppet Centre (£1,000);
Sheringham Museum Trust, Norfolk (£250).
The trust is prepared to assist with funding towards capital costs, including equipment, building renovation or new buildings.
Exclusions: No grants to individuals or to organisations which are not registered charities.
Applications: In writing to the correspondent. Applications should include clear details of the project together with a financial statement or budget. All applications, other than circulars, will be acknowledged if an SAE is enclosed. Trustees meet in May and September.

The Kathy Callow Trust (see the Museums' Association)

The David Canter Memorial Trust

PO Box 3, Ashburton, Devon TQ13 7UW

Contact: The Secretary
General: The fund gives financial assistance to craftspeople wishing to set up a workshop or for the purchase of materials and equipment, for education, research or travel or for special purposes. Grants of not less than £500 each are made annually, usually in the autumn. A different craft is chosen each year. In 1996 grants are for textile craftspersons.
Exclusions: No grants to students.
Applications: Guidelines and applications are available from the above address in April. An SAE must be enclosed. The deadline for applications is about June 11.

Caritas *(The James A de Rothschild's Charitable Settlement)*

c/o Saffery Champness, Fairfax House, Fulwood Place, Gray's Inn London WC1V 6UB

Contact: The Secretary
Trustees: Lord Rothschild, Lady Rothschild, M E Hatch.
Grant total: £114,000 (1991/92)
Beneficial area: UK and Israel.
General: The most recent information available about the trust's grants is for 1991/92 when 56 grants were given, half of them for £1,000 or more. The two largest grants were to arts organisations. Arts grants included:
National Gallery (£36,622);
Glyndebourne Productions Ltd (£15,000);
Glyndebourne Arts Trust (£3,200);
Ashmolean Museum, Oxford, Dulwich Picture Gallery (£5,000 each);
Royal Opera House (£2,102);
British Society of Theatre Designers (£2,000);
Royal Academy Trust, London Library Appeal (£1,000);
English Chamber Orchestra (£500);
Royal Academy of Dancing (£400);
Friends of the Courtauld Institute (£250);
Live Music Now! (£200).
Applications: In writing to the correspondent. An SAE must be included.

The Carlton Television Trust

101 St Martin's Lane London WC2N 4AZ

Tel: 0171-615 1641
Contact: Liz Delbarre, Administrator
Trustees: Nigel Walmsley (Chairman), Michael Green, Paul Corley, Jeremy Loyd, Colin Stanbridge, Karen McHugh, Sara Morrison, Winifred Tumim.
Grant total: £417,000 (1995)
Beneficial area: Greater London, and *part* of the counties of Bedfordshire, Berkshire, Buckinghamshire, East & West Sussex, Essex, Hertfordshire, Kent, Oxfordshire, Surrey.
General: The trust has a policy to concentrate its support on educational opportunities for children and young people with special needs or who are disadvantaged in other ways. It can only assist projects within its transmission region. A total of 106 grants were given in 1995. They ranged between £300 and £13,000 with most between £1,000 and £5,000. About 20% of applications were successful and too many were fruitless approaches from outside the transmission area.

The trust's grant-making decisions are made independently with the trustees assisted by assessors who may deal directly with the applicants.

In 1995 a total of £81,000 (19% of total grant-aid) was disbursed to 21 arts projects. These included:
Heritage Ceramics, African arts projects in special schools (£10,000);
Caught in the Act, marionette perform-ances re AIDS/health awareness in special schools (£8,000);
Drake Music Project, access to music activities for young people with severe physical disabilities (£5,000);
Rambert Dance Company, workshops in a special school (£5,000);
Shobana Jeyasingh Dance Company, workshops with young Asian girls and young people with hearing impairment (£4,280);
Caravanserai, performances in special schools (£1,080);
Corali Dance Company (a group of perform-ers with learning difficulties) workshops for children with learning difficulties (£1,000).
Capital costs: The trust is prepared to consider support towards building renovations and new buildings which meet its criteria for education/special needs. It has assisted with equipment purchase.
Exclusions: Projects OUTSIDE the Carlton transmission area (contact the trust if you are uncertain); trips abroad; conferences/seminars; general appeals; retrospective funding. ; ongoing salaries and running costs (but see note under "Applications"; relief of statutory responsibilities.
Applications: Funds are disbursed once a year only. Application forms are available

between April and June ONLY and an SAE (postage for 75 grammes) should be sent to Carlton Television Trust, PO Box 1, London W5 2GF. The closing date for receipt is shown on the form. Organisations may submit only one application per calendar year for projects due to take place from November onwards. Decisions will be made by 30th November. Applications must come from properly constituted non profit-making organisations. Grants are payable only to organisations registered as charities. Each application must be endorsed by a management committee member, and an independent referee (or the registered charity acting as a conduit for the funds).

Grants may be considered for individual children and young people if an organisa-tion, which can speak about the family's financial circumstances, applies on their behalf. (Private individuals, parents, teachers and other welfare professionals are not acceptable). Further details re equip-ment are given with the application form and guidelines.

Grants for 2 to 3 years are exceptional. Applicants for salary costs for up to three years must be registered charities and grants should establish new ways of meeting need or new levels of effective-ness.

The Carnegie Dunfermline Trust

Abbey Park House, Dunfermline, Fife KY12 7PB

Tel: 01383-723 638
Contact: William C Runciman, Secretary/ Treasurer
Trustees: 16 life Trustees, and a further six appointed by Dunfermline District Council and three by Fife Regional Council
Grant total: £116,000 (1994)
Beneficial area: Dunfermline and its immediate environs.
General: The trust's objects cover social, educational, cultural and recreational purposes in Dunfermline and its immediate environs. Each year the trustees allocate some of its funds for grant aid or other

support for local clubs and societies in arts and community activities. Support to the arts in 1994 included:
Royal Scottish National Orchestra, for performance in Dunfermline Abbey (£7,000 + £600 for school tickets); Brass Band Contest (£1,858); Council for Music in Hospitals (£1,000); Dunfermline District Arts Council, for minibus (£20,000).
Publications by local authors have been also supported and funds made available for purchase of musical instruments. The trust will fund equipment purchase but seldom any other type of capital cost.
Exclusions: Individuals; closed clubs; maintenance/running costs; projects which have already been started.
Applications: A simple application form, including a request re other funding sources, and guidelines are available. Applications are considered three times a year.

The Carnegie United Kingdom Trust

Comely Park House, 80 New Row, Dunfermline, Fife, Scotland KY12 7EJ

Tel: 01383-721445; **Fax:** 01383-620682
Contact: John Naylor
Trustees: The business of the trust is carried on by the members of the executive committee: Dame Gillian Wagner, Chair; George Atkinson; Linda Brown; Timothy Colman; Sherriff John Stuart Forbes; Walter Hutchison; Professor David Ingram; Joy Kinna; Professor Alexander Lawson; Paddy Lineker; Anthony Mould; Lord Murray; David Tudway Quilter; Sandy Saddler; Jessie Spittal; Sir Kenneth Stowe; David Stobie; William Thomson.
Grant total: £880,000 (1995)
Beneficial area: UK and Republic of Ireland
General: The trust's new policy guidelines for the quinquennium 1996-2000 were available from March 1996. The trust continues to work in the fields of amateur arts and community service. In community service the priorities will be parenting and young people. The parts of this policy

relevant to this guide are reprinted below.

General Guidance

Preference is given to proposals which are innovative and developmental, have potential to influence policy and practice more widely; and are undertaken in partnership with others. Grants usually range from £1,000 to £50,000. Grants may be for one year or phased over three years.

Arts

In recent years the trustees have concentrated on amateur activity. In 1988 they established the Voluntary Arts Network (VAN) to study the needs and structure of the amateur arts and crafts in Britain and to encourage high standards in amateur activity. VAN is now a separate organisation, still supported by the trust.

Young People: "Open to local, regional and national voluntary arts bodies to help young people participate in the arts outside and beyond formal education. Priority will be given to projects which develop links between voluntary arts bodies and educational establishments - schools, sixth form colleges, further education colleges, etc - to encourage a smooth transition for young people (aged 14-25) to enjoy continued involvement in the arts." Application by letter.

Multi-media: "Open to national, regional and significant local groups which work with electronic multi-media and the arts for creative purposes, not for management information. Priority will be given to initiatives outside the formal educational system for young people without other access to multi-media. Consideration will also be given to cross generational applications. Proposals with a wider community dimension or which link with libraries will be of particular interest.

"Recognising that work in this area at the time of writing is embryonic, other creative proposals, not aimed at professional artists, will be considered.

"As this field develops, this policy may be refined during the quinquennium, 1996-2000." Application by letter.

Voluntary Arts – Electronic Information: "Open to national and regional umbrella bodies for the voluntary arts. Hardware, software and training to electronically link with the Voluntary Arts Network information service, to access CD based reference material and to offer on line information services to groups will be considered.

"These grants are administered in conjunction with the Voluntary Arts Network." Application forms from the Carnegie UK Trust.

Voluntary Arts - Training: "Open to national, regional and major local voluntary arts organisations, eg. those with buildings or undergoing major developments. Training should be for key paid staff and volunteers and their cooperation to strengthen the management and administration of the arts organisation. Special consideration will be given to training which has a cascade effect, ie. those who receive the initial training passing it on to others." Application by letter.

Heritage

Independent Museums – Innovation in the Use of Information Technology: "Open to members of AIM (Association of Independent Museums) and registered with the Museums and Galleries Commission. For innovative use of technology in independent museums. Special consideration will be given to those who are prepared to share their success or difficulties with others and indicate how they will do it." Application by letter.

Independent Museums – Volunteer Development: "Open to members of AIM and registered with the Museums and Galleries Commission. Limited funding is available to enable volunteers to undertake structured training, preferably leading to a recognised qualification and for initiatives which improve volunteer management." Application forms from the trust.

Village Halls: "Open to village hall committees where the population is below 5,000. Grants of up to £5,000 are available to develop a new activity for equipment and relevant building alterations but not for general repairs and access. Between 1930 and 1949 the trustees assisted with the early development of village halls. Now they wish to assist the halls' development and growth by encouraging their use as multi-purpose village centres. These grants are administered in conjunction with ACRE (England), WCVA (Wales), SCVO (Scotland) and Foras Eireann (Ireland)." Application forms from the trust.

Community

Young People: During the quinquennium the trust, in collaboration with others will be initiating a project to "examine the social, economic and personal issues affecting young people, drawing mainly on existing knowledge but with some capacity for original research". An information leaflet with more detail is available.

In the meantime the trust retains its interest in young people from the previous quinquennium. "It will consider exceptional proposals which broaden constructive experience by involving disadvantaged young people in the community in ways that develop responsibility and possibly leadership potential. Preference will be shown to proposals which involve young people in their management. Application by letter.

Other areas of the Community pro-gramme are Parenting and the Third Age.

Unusual Initiatives

"Open to national, regional or local organisations. Creative initiatives which pioneer new ways forward across traditional boundaries will be considered by the trust. These may involve unusual collaborations, completely new ideas or the identification of gaps in provision which have emerged because they do not fit present institutional frameworks.

"The proposal should have significant ramifications, indicate what the wider impact might be and show how findings, approaches or ideas will be disseminated if the initiative is successful." Application by letter.

Exclusions: Individuals; general appeals; replacement of statutory funding; arts centres, professional arts companies and festivals, including performances and workshops; libraries; restoration, conversion or repair of buildings; pipe organs in churches or other buildings; research, publications and conferences (except the trustees' own initiatives).

Applications: Other applications should be composed having sent an A5 SAE for the policy guidelines. The annual report is lodged in all main libraries and can also be obtained for £6. 00, inclusive. Applications should include concise details of the organisation, its aims and achievements, a description of the project and its key practical features, needs and costs, proposals for monitoring, evaluation and dissemination. The letter of application should be no more than 2-3 typed pages with supplementary information such as budget, recent audited accounts, the constitution and committee membership.

Deadlines: 30 January for March meeting; 30 April for June meeting; 30 September for November meeting. Applications can be submitted at any time. Early preliminary discussions are welcome.

Sir John Cass's Foundation

31 Jewry Street, London EC3N 2EY

Tel: 0171-480 5884; Fax: 0171-481 3551
Contact: Michael Sparks, Clerk to the Governors
Trustees: G C H Lawson (Chairman), M Venn, Rev C Chessun, P Durrant, K M Everett, D Farrell, Canon G Greenwood, Mrs Joan Hanham, Revd G Heskins, D Hughes, Rev B J Lee, Mrs J Lomax, P D Minchin, Sir Peter Newsam, Revd J Osborn, J L Reed, D Smith, M R Streatfeild, P Wade.
Grant total: £292,000 for organisations; £118,000 for individuals (1993/94)
Beneficial area: Newham plus 13 former ILEA boroughs - Camden, City of London, Greenwich, Hackney, Hammersmith & Fulham, Islington, Kensington & Chelsea, Lambeth, Lewisham, Southwark, Tower Hamlets, Wandsworth, Westminster.
General: The foundation has programmes of support for organisations and individuals as well as funding "Cass" schools, a couple of Church of England schools, and London Guildhall University. It has a commitment to training in the arts and offers scholarships

at RADA, the London Contemporary Dance School, the Guildhall School of Music and Drama, the Courtauld Gallery, the Royal College of Art, the Central School of Ballet.

Individuals must be under 25 and must have lived in one of the beneficial areas (see above) for at least three years before beginning their course of study.

Applications from groups, schools and educational foundations must show they meet the educational needs of those under 25 who live within its beneficial area (see above). In its funding priorities for 1992/95 applications for both capital costs and short-term revenue funding would be considered. In particular:

- Projects which enrich or enhance the curriculum in educational institutions;
- Projects to improve literacy and numeracy and English as a second language;
- Projects promoting the study of the arts, science and mathematics;
- Projects improving the education and training of young offenders;
- Projects of strategic importance with policy-forming implications of more than a "local" significance.

In 1993/94 a total of 56 grants were given to 54 organisations - 21 of these were arts grants. Arts grants included:

Burnbake Trust, art materials for young offenders and ex-offenders (£8,000);

Royal Court Young People's Theatre, for youth programme in local schools (£6,500);

Vauxhall St Peter's Heritage, travelling museum for Lambeth school children (£6,000);

Lewisham Academy of Dance, to continue project for young people with learning difficulties (£5,000);

Clean Break Theatre Company, drama training for women ex-offenders (£4,000);

Film and Video Workshop, school workshops in 4 boroughs (£3,700);

Heart N' Soul, to establish youth performance group (£1,430);

Beckford Primary School, residency for storytellers and musicians (£1,000);

Montem Junior School, purchase of musical instruments (£720).

Exclusions: No grants to individuals over 25. No grants outside the beneficial area.

Applications: 1. There are several stages in the application process: an initial letter outlining your application should be addressed to the Clerk to the Governors. Please include some basic costings for your project and background details on your organisation, such as an annual report and the most recent set of audited accounts- if your project falls within our current policy and our basic criteria are satisfied, foundation staff will arrange to visit you- after a project visit, you may be invited to submit a formal application using a form we will provide-completed applications are then considered by our grants committee which meets quarterly. Applications for larger grants are also referred to our finance committee.

2. The deadlines for completed applications are: 10th February for the March meeting 11th May for the June meeting 17th August for the September meeting 16th November for the December meeting.

3. Decisions are usually conveyed to applicants in writing within seven days of a grants committee meeting.

4. Applicants must bear in mind that some proposals that appear to fit our declared priorities may still be unsuccessful. The award of a grant is entirely at the trustees' discretion.

5. Applicants are assessed in terms of their innovation, the extent of the need for support and the organisation's capacity to 'deliver the goods'.

Throughout the application process, the foundation's staff will be happy to clear up any questions you may have.

The Francis Chagrin Fund

Society for the Promotion of New Music, Francis House, Francis Street, London SW1P 1DE

Tel: 0171-828 9696

Contact: Elizabeth Webb, Administrator

Trustees: Anthony Graham Dixon (Chair), Michael Rubinstein, Murray Gordon, Gillian Newson, Sir John Tooley.

General: The fund provides grants for British composers and composers resident in the UK to help cover the costs that they have personally incurred by reproducing performance materials for works awaiting their first scheduled performance. The following costs are eligible for grant aid: reproduction of scores and parts (including vocal scores if appropriate) by photocopying or other reprographic means; covering and binding of scores and parts; reproduction of performance tapes.

The following costs are not eligible for grant aid: the production of a master set of materials, either by hand copying or computer data entry and printing, ie. copyists' fees, fees for entering data into a computer notation program or buying computer time for this purpose, printing a master set of materials from computer programs (though photocopies from such masters are eligible for consideration); studio and tape costs for the composition/ production of a master tape (though copies made from such a master are eligible for consideration).

Applications: Guidelines and application forms are available from the above address.

The Chapman Charitable Trust

Messrs Crouch Chapman, 62 Wilson Street, London EC2A 2BU

Tel: 0171-782 0007

Contact: Roger S Chapman

Trustees: Roger S Chapman, W John Chapman, Richard J Chapman, Bruce D Chapman.

Grant total: £147,000 (1994/95)

Beneficial area: UK.

General: In 1994/95 the trust made 80 grants ranging between £500 and £20,000. The majority of grants were for £1,000 or less. Most grants are given to organisations working for people with disabilities and other health needs, though a wide range of charitable interests are represented. Arts grants in 1994/95 included:

Aldeburgh Foundation (£20,000 and in the 2 previous years);

Kettle's Yard, Oily Cart Theatre Co (£1,000 each);

National Youth Orchestra of Great Britain (£500 with £2,000 in the previous year);

Artsline, Gregynog Festival, Ernest Read Music Association National Children's Orchestra (£500 each).

Exclusions: No grants to individuals.

Applications: In writing at any time. The trustees meet twice a year at the end of March and the end of September. The trustees receive so many applications that they do not acknowledge them. If no communication is received within six months the application has been unsuccessful.

The Charities Aid Foundation

Kings Hill, West Malling, Kent ME19 4TA

Tel: 01732-520 000; Fax: 01732-520 001

Contact: Mrs Judith McQuillan, Grants Administrator

Trustees: Grants Council: Sir Harold Haywood (Chairman), Rev Doctor Gordon Barritt, John Bateman, Gillian Crosby, Naomi Eisenstadt, Andrew Kingman, Jane Lewis, Lawrence Mackintosh, Mrs Leslie Marks, Professor Peter Quilliam, Michele Rigby, Ceridwen Roberts.

Grant total: £571,000 (1994/95)

Beneficial area: UK.

General: Grants are made to enable charities to improve their management and effectiveness. These help a charity to:

• improve its effectiveness in meeting its objectives

• improve its use of financial resources, facilities, members, staff or volunteers

• improve its stability or effectiveness

• to move into new areas of need.

Grants are normally made to made small or

medium-sized charities with a proven track record. Applications are encouraged from black and ethnic minority groups.

The maximum grant is £10,000. The average grant is less than £4,000 and only two thirds of applications are successful. Grants are seldom for the full amount requested. Arts grants in 1994/95 included:
National Association of Youth Theatres (£9,717);
Nottingham Musicspace (£6,983);
Northern Ireland Music Therapy Trust (£6,200);
East Midlands SHAPE (£4,400);
World Circuit Arts (£4,200);
Burnbake Trust (£4,000);
Yorkshire Film Archive (£3,500).

Exclusions: No grants to assist with Lottery bids. No grants to organisations which are not registered charities or approved for charitable status by the Inland Revenue. No grants to individuals, or for capital building projects, general appeals, general funds, debt clearance, start-up costs. Applications for retrospective funding are not considered.

Applications: In writing to the correspondent. The grants council meets quarterly to consider applications.

Charity Know How Fund

114/118 Southampton Row, London WC1B 5AA

Tel: 0171-400 2315; Fax: 071-404 1331
Contact: Claire Walters, Director
Trustees: Trustees of the Charities Aid Foundation; Grants Committee: Anne Engel, the Prince's Trust (Chair) and representatives from the fund contributors.
Grant total: £727,000 (1993/94)
Beneficial area: Albania, Bulgaria, Czech Republic, Estonia, Hungary, Latvia, Lithuania, Madedonia (FYROM), Poland, Republics of the former Soviet Union, Romania, Slovak Republic, Slovenia.
General: Charity Know How (CKH) was established in 1991 by a group of grantmaking trusts in conjunction with the Foreign Office which matches all donations. (Support additional to this arrangement was

given by the Foreign Office in 1993/94, a measure of its success.)

Total grant-aid has risen strongly over two years from £498,000 in 1991/92 to £727,000 in 1993/94. CKH supports initiatives, by partnerships between local and UK based charities, designed to promote the development of active voluntary sectors in the countries of central and eastern Europe. The fund is administered by the Charities Aid Foundation.

Grants can only be made to UK organisations with a partner organisation in the region or to organisations in the region with a partner in the UK. Awards can be considered for any of the following:

♦ Advice on the legal, fiscal and regulatory framework necessary for voluntary organisations to operate effectively.
♦ Advice and support for co-ordinating bodies seeking to promote and represent the voluntary sector.
♦ Study visits between voluntary organisations in the UK and their counterparts in the region.
♦ Training programmes for voluntary sector personnel, including seminars, workshops and, occasionally, conferences.
♦ Translation of training/information materials.

In 1993/94 there was a small increase in the number of grants, from 254 to 283. The grant range continues to be mainly between £500 and £5,000. In 1993/94 most of the grants (48%) were under £1,000, and 43% were between £1,000 and £2,000. Twenty grants (7%) were over £5,000 and under £10,000 and only seven grants (2%) were £10,000 and higher.

A pilot scheme of direct grants through trusted agencies in the region was started in March 1994. It is directed at charities unlikely to seek funding through CKH partnerships.

CKH's annual report for 1993/94 commented on its policy development: 'While maintaining its strong commitment to capacity building through partnership, Charity Know How is seeking to establish clearer priorities and stimulate greater activity in areas of particular need'. This is one initiative. East-East Grants is another whereby support is given to organisations in the region which are able to assist NGO development elsewhere in the region.

CKH is continuously developing its role as an information source and conduit across the spectrum of voluntary activity in different national situations. It makes introductions for potential partnerships and initiates briefing documents, seminars and workshops. All grant recipients are required to submit full reports of their projects. These can be consulted by other applicants and form a valuable advice/information resource.

Their support has covered a wide range of voluntary endeavour, from 'hospices to volunteer firemen, disability groups to environmental organisations, and street theatre to the boy scouts.' Grants have been given for study visits, training work-shops and other activities to support the emerging voluntary sector in Eastern and Central Europe.

CKH publishes a free quarterly bulletin "Update" which lists new grants awarded and gives details of workshops it organises. Arts organisations assisted in 1993/94 included:

Bulgaria:
Golden Key Children's Theatre/Unicorn Theatre for Children, for a visit to advise on budgeting and raising support, plus preparation of a joint production (£290);

Lithuania:
Open Society Fund, Lithuania/Community Music, training in running arts events for young people from minority groups in 3 countries (£4,948);

Open Society Fund/Royal National Theatre for 3 week placements in the UK followed by a 2 day debriefing and evaluation at the RNT (£3,393). Similar programmes were also supported for groups from Latvia and Estonia.

Poland:
Centrum Edukacjni Teatrainej/ Edinburgh Theatre Workshop, projects in Poland and Scotland to develop the skills of staff and volunteers at the centre (£3,000);

Slowaski Theatre/Stage International, workshops and conference on support to individual writers and artists (£3,080);

Romania:
Ion Creanga Theatre/London International Festival of Theatre, for 4 Romanians to visits the UK to learn different approaches to child centred theatre (£540);

Ion Creanga Theatre/Waterman's Arts Centre, for 2 Romanians to experience children' s theatre projects as a follow-up to the above grant (£610);

Casa de copii Prescolari/The Leaveners, a 4 week creative play training programme for staff, parents and volunteers at a Romanian school (£1,740).

Charity Know how is likely to review its policy on and emphasis towards support for cultural projects during 1996. This could lead to lesser support within this area for a period of time (it is not expected to be permanent). Potential applicants should contact Charity Know How direct.

Exclusions: Grants are not normally available for :

◆ Teaching English as a foreign language;
◆ The administration of schemes for UK volunteers (e. g. working volunteers);
◆ Core funding in the region, or the UK;
◆ Support towards offices or equipment;
◆ Full professional fees of any consultancy;
◆ The promotion of a particular creed or religion;
◆ Capital projects. Please check against new guidelines.

Applications: An application form and guidelines are available. New guidelines were to be announced in March 1996. The grants committee meets four times a year in March, June, September and December. All applications need to arrive six weeks earlier. Grants of under £1,000 can be considered at any time but a minimum of 4 weeks notice should be given.

Charity Projects

74 New Oxford Street, London WC1A 1EF

Tel: 0171-436 1122; Fax: 0171-436 1541

Contact: UK Grants Department

Trustees: Sir Tim Bell, President; Paul Jackson, Chair; Richard Curtis, Vice-Chair; Colin Howes, Secretary; Mike Harris, Treasurer; Paddy Coulter; Emma Freud; Lenny Henry; John Makinson; Firoze Manji; June McKerrow; Alan Parker.

Grant total: £4,615,000 for UK Grants (1993/94)

Beneficial area: UK and overseas (but see below)

General: Of the monies raised by Comic Relief, two thirds is distributed to UK aid agencies working in Africa, and one third is distributed to charities working in the UK. Four grant programmes operate in the UK and all applications must be for work with:

*   disabled young people aged 14-30;
*   young people aged 14-30 who use alcohol or drugs;
*   homeless young people aged 14-30;
*   people aged 55 and over.

Requests for both revenue and capital are considered. Applications for revenue support need to refer to a specific piece of work over a limited period of time. Grants are not normally for more than £10,000 in any one year. Grants for revenue funding are for a maximum of three years. *It is strongly recommended that the most up-to-date guidelines are obtained before making an application.*

UK Grants Programme: The following information is taken from its leaflet "Priorities for Grant-Making 1995-97'.

Types of organisations funded in the UK

Grants are given throughout the UK with priority to small organisations working directly with people at community level. Larger or national organisations will only be eligible for funding if they can demonstrate that the project will break new ground or will significantly help small community-based groups.

Equal Opportunities

Charity Projects believes it is important that everybody's needs are addressed, especially those who often miss out. It welcomes applications from all sections of the community including projects of specific benefit to: black and ethnic communities; women; lesbians and gay men; rural areas; towns and cities outside London. These applications must fall within one or more of the chosen grant-making programmes.

Young People's Disability Grants Programme

Aims to

*   to make sure that disabled young people have greater choices and rights and more influence over their lives and prospects
*   promote self-determination, self-representation and independence
*   encourage active participation of disabled young people in all aspects of life
*   support groups campaigning for adequate services in the community

Applications will only be considered from organisations which

*   are controlled by disabled people i. e. 51% of the managing body is disabled people
*   can show a commitment in moving towards such representation, or, until this is possible, giving as much say as possible in the running of the project by disabled users

Charity Projects recognises the some organisations may not have been involved in the Disability Movement's current fight for rights. It therefore provides funds to groups which:

*   offer relevant training to disabled young people to enable them to participate in the management of projects
*   offer Disability Equality Training to their own managers
*   support the exchange of information and collaboration between groups

Applications are particularly encouraged from groups concerned with: mental health issues; campaigning for adequate services in the community; self-advocacy or advocacy; people with learning difficulties; people with sensory disabilities.

Young People's Alcohol and Drugs Programme (for 14-30 year olds, particularly 14-21 year olds). Aims to:

• fund a broad range of projects addressing issues of drug and alcohol use with young people

• encourage work which is non-judgmental and responsive to users and open to all young people

• support work in providing accurate information, prevention and treatment options support organisations which include harm reduction in their pro-gramme

• support organisations which work, or are willing to, with a range of other services.

Young People's Homelessness Grants Programme (for young people aged between 14 and 30 who are homeless or in poor housing). Aims to:

• raise awareness of the difficulties facing homeless young people in securing appropriate housing and increase the options available to them

• make sure that young people have access to a range of services, responsive to the needs of users in order to help them address their housing and related needs

• address the needs of young people facing particular disadvantage and discrimination in their access to housing

• support young people in helping them solve their housing problems themselves

Applications are particularly welcomed from organisations working with: young people leaving care; 16 and 17 year olds; young people who have been sexually, physically or mentally abused; young people with HIV/AIDS; refugees; disabled people; current and former users of mental health services; homeless young families; young offenders and ex-offenders.

Older People's Grants Programme (for people aged 55 and over). Aims to:

• improve the social and economic status of older people in our society

• support the growth and development of organisations run by older people for older people

• enable older people to be actively involved in running their own lives and influencing the services they receive

• focus on groups who are especially disadvantaged and/or marginalised

• encourage the active involvement of older people in all aspects of the service.

Alongside the grant officers a network of regional advisers with an understanding of the local scene helps assess projects. An active committee gives its independent views on projects and makes funding decisions which are submitted to the board of trustees for final approval. Grants to arts organisations in 1993/94 included:

Under the Alcohol and Drugs Programme
Community Circus Initiative, South York-shire (£5,000);
Verbal Arts Centre, Londonderry (£1,000);

Under the Disability Programme
Half Moon Young People's Theatre (£102,700);
Artsline, London (£24,200);
Community Music Ltd (£20,000);
Graeae Theatre (£20,000);
Arts Disability, Wales (£18,000);
Avon Community Theatre Agency, Avon (£10,000);
Jackson's Lane Community Centre (£5,903);
London Deaf Visual Arts Forum (£1,500);

Under the Homelessness Programme
Bubble Theatre, London (£15,000);
Bhavan Ltd, London (£5,000);

Under the Older People Programme
Independent Arts, I o Wight (£21,212);
Theatre Venture, London (£16,275);
Women's Design Service (£1,870).

Exclusions: These include: academic research; general appeals; individuals; services run by publicly funded services; fundraising organisations.

Applications: Send a letter with brief details of your organisation and a short account of the project. You will then be contacted as to whether your project is suitable for funding. Those so considered will be sent further information to be able to make a full application. Applications for more than £3,000 will need to send more detailed information and may take up to six months to process. Please say how much you are applying for to be sent the correct information. All information is in large print, audiotape and in Braille. Applicants are encouraged to talk with a member of staff about their project prior to applying.

The Charterhouse Charitable Trust

I Paternoster Row, St Paul's, London EC4M 7DH

Contact: Miss S P Coatman, Secretary
Trustees: M V Blank, E G Cox.
Grant total: £98,000 (1992/93)
Beneficial area: UK.
General: In 1992/93 the trust made 75 grants, most of which (51) were under £1,000. Grants to arts organisations were:
Royal National Theatre (£7,500);
National Museums and Galleries of Merseyside (£500);
Council for Music in Hospital (£500);
National Art Collections Fund (£500);
London Schubert Players Trust (£250).

The Chase Charity

2 The Court, High Street, Harwell, Didcot, Oxon OX11 0EY

Tel: 01235-820044
Contact: Peter Kilgarriff, Secretary
Trustees: A Ramsay Hack (Chairman), Richard Mills, Gordon Halcrow, Mrs R A Moore, Mrs Claudia Flanders, Ann Stannard, Keith Grant.
Grant total: £214,000 (1994/95)
Beneficial area: UK.
General: The trust supports the arts, heritage, particularly churches, almshouses, and other buildings of historic interest and beauty, and social welfare projects.

In the field of the arts the trustees have their own schemes for young artists and musicians and have no further funds available for this purpose eg. the charity remains the main funder ot the Kirckman Concert Society which gives young professional musicians platform opportunities.

"A second aim is to further the arts in outlying areas. Small touring dance, theatre and opera groups are helped, mainly with one-off needs, eg. equipment. Grants are also made for theatre buildings, often conversions, and community arts centres outside London and other large cities. Help with production or running costs is rare.

The trustees are keen to encourage participation in the arts by those whose opportunities to do so are limited by geography or disability. Although they recognise the therapeutic value of such involvement, they lay great emphasis on quality of work and seek to promote excellence."

The charity's annual report for 1994/95 showed the following grants relevant to this guide:
Art/Community Arts £58,000 18 grants 27%
Historic Buildings £124,200 13 grants 11%
Conservation and Museums £5,000 grants 2%
Grants for arts-related activities are also made under other social welfare categories as is shown in the following list of examples of grants during 1994/95.

Under Arts/Community Arts
Bleddfa Trust, Powys for conversion of an ancient barn (£5,000);
Theatre Centre Limited, London towards new computer equipment;
Hoxton Hall, Hackney, London (£3,000 each);
Council for Music in Hospitals (£2,758);
Cumbria Arts Education for a dancer in residence, Rhayader & District Community Play Association (£2,000 each);
Portland Sculpture Trust, Dorset for a feasibilty study for the design and location of a building in Tout Quarry (£1,000);

Under Disibilities/Special Needs
BNI Visual Arts Project, Brighton for office equipment (£3,500);
Chapter, Cardiff, and Royal Court Young People's Theatre, London, both grants towards improving access for people with disabilities (£3,000 each);

Under Penal Affairs
Burnbake Trust, towards cost of artists materials for prisoners (£2,000).
Exclusions: No grants to individuals; organisations which are not registered charities; large appeals; conference, seminars, festivals or groups going to festivals; publications or films; formal education.
Applications: In writing to the correspondent. Preliminary enquiries may

be made by telephone or a short letter. Applications should include full supporting information including audited accounts. Summaries of all applications are sent to the trustees every four weeks. Applications listed for the trustees' consideration are carefully researched, normally visited, and presented to the trustees in a form of a report. There is usually a waiting list of cases for the trustees' quarterly meetings. A separate application needs to be made to the Lankelly Foundation (see separate entry) which shares the same administration.

The Children's Film and Television Foundation

Elstree Studios, Borehamwood, Herts WD6 1JG

Tel: 0181-953 0844; **Fax:** 0181-207 0860
Contact: Stanley Taylor, Director
Beneficial area: UK.
General: The foundation gives assistance to script development for eventual production by commercial companies for any suitable children's and family cinema or television production. Most of the work assisted is for television.
Exclusions: Animation and specifically educational programmes are not included

The Winston Churchill Memorial Trust

15 Queen's Gate Terrace, London SW7 5PR

Tel: 0171-584 9315: **Fax:** 0171-581 0410
Trustees: Lady Soames (Chairman) plus 11 other trustees.
Beneficial area: UK.
General: About 100 travelling fellowships are awarded annually. They "enable man and women from all walks of life to gain a better understanding of the lives and work of people in other countries overseas, and to acquire knowledge and experience which will make them more effective in their work and in the community when they return". All British citizens of any age and occupation are eligible. A lack of qualifications is not a bar.

Awards are offered in about ten different categories each year. One of these is usually in an arts-related area. In 1996 this category was for "Artists, craftsmen and technicians working in architecture".

The grant covers all fellowship expenses for an overseas stay of about eight weeks.
Exclusions: Attending courses and academic studies,
Applications: Return completed application form by late October (check for exact date as no applications received later will be considered); short-listed candidates are asked to give more details of their projects and their references are taken up by December; selected candidates from the short-list are interviewed in January; results known in February. Successful candidates are expected to start their travels within a year.

The City Parochial Foundation

6 Middle Street, London EC1A 7PH

Tel: 0171-606 6145; **Fax:** 0171-600 1866
Contact: Timothy Cook, Clerk
Trustees: 21 trustees nominated by 10 bodies including the Crown, the University of London, the Church Commissioners, the Bishopsgate Foundation and the Cripplegate Foundation.
Grant total: £3,640,000 (1995)
Beneficial area: London Metropolitan Police District, City of London
General: During 1991 the foundation undertook a major review of its grant-making policies. Such reviews have regularly been undertaken every five years. All applicants must satisfy the general criteria listed below and fit within one of the priority areas listed in the Grant-making Strategy."
General criteria for grant-making:
* all grants must benefit the poor inhabitants of London.
* all applicants must show how in practice they are developing services for all sections of the community.
* grants made should have an impact on a particular need or problem.
* applicants must show that they can tackle the problem realistically.

- wherever possible the users of services should be part of the designing, planning and delivery of services.
- partnerships with other funders are very welcome, and applications involving joint funding are encouraged.
- monitoring of work funded is important for both the beneficiary and the funder; the foundation will monitor grants made, and will require the cooperation of the beneficiaries."

"Grant-making strategy 1992-1996
Applications are invited which focus upon:
1. Training opportunities for staff and committees, especially in new areas such as community care developments, or providing services under contract.
2. Implementation of equal opportunity policies. Many organisations do not find it easy to move from written equal opportunity policies to practical implementation, despite every good intention; as cuts are made in statutory services, it is vital that all voluntary sector services are open to everyone at all levels.
3. Support structures for refugee communities. These are often lacking not least because of the speed with which people from some communities have arrived and been dispersed throughout all the boroughs.
4. Proposals which aim to help a group of voluntary organisations come together to develop a more coherent strategy in one borough, or to meet a particular need of one client group across several boroughs.
5. Proposals to address London-wide issues concerning the poor of London.
6. Disability - where the emphasis would be on support for organisations managed or led by people who themselves have disabilities.
7. Education and training - of particular interest, though not of exclusive concern, are services tackling under-achievement, supplementary education, English as a second language especially for women, and access provision to post-school education and training.
8. Elderly and frail people living in the community.

9. Homelessness affecting both families and single people: street work, outreach work, and work with homeless people with addictions being of special interest.
10. Young people - within this area, priorities are restricted to schemes providing after-school care, holiday care, work with young people with special needs, and daycare for young children.
11. Welfare rights work with special emphasis on money advice and debt counselling.
12. A major priority is to consider applications from some of the organisations recently grant-aided by the foundation. Further grants will not be given automatically, but staff will discuss with organisations what is required to continue the organisation's work.
13. Any charitable organisation can apply under the Small Grants Programme for grants up to £10,000, which will be a one-off grant."

Exceptional needs and interests
"The trustees will always be ready to consider exceptionally interesting proposals in any area of work helping the poor of London. A strong case would have to be made, amply supported by relevant experts in the field of concern. Any such applications should be submitted in the usual way."

Black and ethnic minority organisations
"The foundation wishes to encourage within the priorities applications from charitable organisations working within and managed by the black and ethnic minority communities, and is particularly aware of the opportunities to assist Section XI initiatives."

Small Grants Programme
Any London-based charitable organisation can apply under this programme for grants of up to £10,000 which will be made on a one-off basis.

Arts grants given in 1995:
These comprised 7% of the foundations's spending but at £254,000 this makes a substantial outlay. Grants were given to:
Roundabout (£28,000);
Blackheath Halls (£25,000);

Young People's Community Training Foundation (£22,000);
Oily Cart Company, Clean Break Theatre (£21,000 each);
London Contemporary School of Dance, Homerton Community Centre (£20,000 each);
Lewisham Academy of Music (£16,000);
Ealing Music Therapy (£15,000);
Music Works (£14,000);
Foundation for Young Musicians, Theatre Royal Stratford East, Tree House Multi Arts Centre, Prisons Video Trust (£10,000 each);
Action Space (£6,700);
Polyglot Theatre Company (£500).

Exclusions: Arts, open spaces, recreation, individuals, schools are amongst those areas of work excluded from receiving grants unless a "small grant or sustaining funds are being sought". Applicants normally have to be registered charities.

Applications: Applicants are advised to discuss in outline their proposed application with one of the staff. All applications are required to adopt the following format:
- Statement about the organisation; legal status, aims, history, staffing and management committee, current activities, previous grants from the foundation or the Trust for London;
- Financial position of the organisation and main sources of income;
- Full costing of the proposal;
- Other funding sources, particularly trusts;
- Monitoring of the proposed scheme.

This should not exceed three sides of A4 paper and should be accompanied by: copy of the constitution; most recent annual report and set of accounts; budget for the current financial year; equal opportunities policy; names and addresses of office holders; job description if the application concerns a post.

J Anthony Clark Charitable Foundation

Box 1704, Glastonbury, Somerset BA16 0YB

Contact: Mrs P Grant
Trustees: L P Clark, J C Clark, T A Clark, C Pym
Grant total: £153,000 (1993/94)
Beneficial area: UK.
General: The trustees support projects in health, education, peace, environment and the arts. Arts organisations supported in 1994 were:
Street Theatre Workshop Trust (£3,500 in 2 grants);
Leicestershire County Council Museum Arts Service (£2,000);
Northgate NHS Trust Arts Project (£1,500);
Quaker tapestry, Kendal (£1,000).
Exclusions: No grants to individuals.
Applications: In writing to the correspondent. It is understood that the trust does not seek unsolicited applications and does not reply to them.

The Clore Foundation

Unit 3, Chelsea Manor Studios, Flood Street, London SW3 5SR

Contact: Mrs Miriam Harris, Executive Director.
Trustees: Mrs Vivien Duffield (Chairman), David Harrel, Sir Mark Weinberg.
Grant total: £1,315,000 (1993)
Beneficial area: UK.
General: This foundation tends to make relatively few large grants, sometimes for projects which it sets up itself. It supports hospitals, medical, social welfare, Jewish and arts charities. It shares its director and administrative offices with the Vivien Duffield Foundation.

There is no information about the foundation's grants since 1991 when £2. 4 million was disbursed. Until recently the largest operation of the foundation has been the housing of the Turner Collection at the Tate Gallery giving some £6 million. A new project recently is Eureka! the Children's Museum in Halifax, £7 million of the cost of which will have come from the Clore and

Duffield Foundations. In 1991 about a quarter (£392,000) of total grant-aid went to 17 arts organisations. These included: *Eureka! Children's Museum (£910,554); Royal Opera House Trust, Natural History Museum, National Portrait Gallery (£50,000 each); National Gallery Trust (£46,742); Ashmolean Museum, Oxford (£30,000); Whitechapel Art Gallery (£10,000); Living Painting Trust (£6,000); British Israel Arts Foundation (£5,000); Jewish Literary Trust (£1,000).*

Exclusions: No grants to individuals or to organisations which are not registered charities.

Applications: Applications are neither sought nor acknowledged. No applications will be considered unless accompanied by a personal report from someone known to the trustees.

The Clothworkers' Foundation

Clothworkers' Hall, Dunster Court, Mincing Lane, London EC3R 7AH

Tel: 0171-623 7041
Contact: M G T Harris, Secretary
Trustees: The Governors of the Foundation.
Grant total: £2,150,000 (1994)
Beneficial area: UK.
General: "Preferential consideration is given to appeals received from self-help organisations and to charities requiring support to 'prime the pumps' for development and more extensive fundraising activities. Also to appeals related to Textiles and kindred activities."

Grants are made under the following categories: clothworking, medicine and health, relief in need and welfare, children and youth, education and the sciences, the arts, the church, heritage and environment, overseas.

In l994 a total of £62,000 was given to 13 organisations under the "Arts" category. However other grants relating to the arts were given from the "Clothworking" and "The Church" categories. This gives the far larger total of £202,000.

Grants given under "The Arts"
Florence Nightingale Museum Trust, National Youth Orchestra of Great Britain (£15,000 each); Cambridge Arts Theatre (£10,000); Oundle international Summer School for Young Organists, Shropshire Regimental Museum (£5,000 each); Dulwich Picture Gallery, Blackheath Concert Halls, Rose Theatre Company, (£2,000 each); Owton Fens Community Association, Whitechapel Art Gallery, Shape London, Bath Industrial Heritage Trust, Live Music Now! (£1,000 each).

Grants given under "The Church"
Royal School of Church Music (£2,000).

Grants given under "Clothworking"
Victoria and Albert Museum (£75,000); National Museum of Wales (£23,500); Textile Conservation Centre (£23,000); Royal School of Needlework apprenticeship scheme (£12,000); Bradford Textile Society, fabric design competition (£4,700).

Exclusions: Individuals; organisations which are not registered charities; support to activities which are the responsibility of statutory funding;

Applications: In writing to the correspondent having first obtained a copy of their guidelines for applicants. Detailed financial information including funding from other sources plus supporting documents is required. Telephone calls to discuss proposals are welcomed. Applications are processed continuously as meetings are held six times a year. Successful applicants are expected to provide periodic progress reports. A period of at least five years must elapse before further grant will be considered for an organisation receiving funds.

The John Coates Charitable Trust

Crockmore House, Fawley, Henley-on-Thames, Oxfordshire RG9 6HY

Tel: 01491-573367
Contact: Mrs P L Youngman
Trustees: Mrs V E Coates, Mrs G F McGregor, Mrs C Kesley, Mrs R G Lawes.
Grant total: £193,000 (1994/95)
Beneficial area: UK.
General: The trust gives grants to medical, environmental and educational organisations as well as a number of arts organisations. In 1994/95 when a total of £193,000 was disbursed the following arts grants were made:

Shakespeare Globe Trust, Royal Opera House, Ironbridge Gorge Museum (£10,000 each);
Purcell School of Music, Chichester Theatre Society (£5,000 each);
English National Opera (£1,000).

The trust is prepared to give grants for capital costs.
Exclusions: No grants to individuals.
Applications: In writing to the correspondent. Trustees' meetings are held in January and in July.

The David Cohen Family Charitable Trust

85 Albany Street, London NW1 4BT

Tel: 0171-486 1117
Contact: Duncan Haldane
Trustees: Dr David Cohen (Chairman), Veronica Cohen, Imogen Cohen, Olivia Cohen.
Grant total: £45,000 (1994)
Beneficial area: UK.
General: The trust gives exclusively to arts organisations and projects. It works in tandem with the John S Cohen Foundation (see following entry) on some of its grant-making. Grants range between £50 and £15,000. In 1994 the trust gave 20 grants. Its largest allocation was for the David Cohen British Literature Prize administered by the Arts Council of England (£15,000). Other projects supported included:

British Library organised Terezin Memorial Concert at Wigmore Hall (£5,000);
National Trust for guidebook of early musical instruments at Fenton House (£4,600);
South Bank Centre's Berio Festival, for a London Sinfonietta programme with life serving prisoners at Wormwood Scrubs (£4,000);
National Portrait Gallery, for "Put Yourself in the Picture" (£4,000);
Shared Experience Theatre for educational work (£2,500);
New MusICA 4 series of concerts (£2,500);
Signed Performances in Theatre (£1,500);
Poetry Society, for poetry map (£1,000);
Clonter Farm Opera, Covent Garden Festival (£1,000);
English National Opera for "New Stages" (£950);
London Masterclasses (£300).

Exclusions: No grants to individuals or to organisations which are not registered charities. No equipment costs.
Applications: In writing to the correspondent. There is no application form. Unsuccessful applications will not receive a reply.

The John S Cohen Foundation

85 Albany Street, London NW1 4BT

Tel: 0171-486 1117
Contact: Duncan Haldane
Trustees: Dr David Cohen (Chairman), Mrs Elizabeth Cohen, Richard Cohen
Grant total: £406,000 (1994/95)
Beneficial area: UK.
General: Grants were categorised in 1994/95 as follows: The arts £169,000 Academic and educational £66,000 Medical £35,000 Conservation £35,500 Environment £22,500 Jewish £31,000 The foundation's policy in the arts is to encourage innovative and contemporary work and young artists and musicians. Arts grants in 1994/95 included:

Glyndebourne Touring Opera for educational work (£25,000);
Bodleian Library (£20,000 5th and final grant totalling £100,000);

National Gallery (£16,000, 1st of 3 totalling £50,000);
Scarborough Theatre Development Trust, Tate Gallery of Modern Arts at Bankside (£10,000 each);
Royal Exchange Theatre Manchester (£7,500);
Museums and Galleries Commission, Handel House Museum Trust, Orchestra of the Age of Enlightenment, Almeida Opera, Mecklenburgh Opera (£5,000 each);
London Symphony Orchestra (£3,000);
Northern Centre for Contemporary Art (£2,500);
West Yorkshire Playhouse for Jewish cultural events and new Kops play (£1,000).
Koestler Award Trust (£500).
Exclusions: No grants to individuals or to organisations which are not registered charities. No equipment costs. No further medical support.
Applications: In writing to the correspondent. No response is made unless it is decided to make a grant.

The Cole Charitable Trust

11 Bracebridge Road, Four Oaks, Sutton Coldfield, Warwickshire B75 6DH

Contact: Dr J L Cole
Trustees: Mrs Joy Cole, G Cole, Dr T N Cole
Grant total: £40,000 (1993/94)
Beneficial area: Greater Birmingham
General: The trust gives a number of small grants to a wide range of charities, particularly local community organisations. Recent arts grants have been given to:
Midlands Arts Centre (£2,500);
Birmingham Conservatoire Association (£150).
Exclusions: No grants to individuals, large or national organisations or small organisations outside the Birmingham area.
Applications: In writing to the correspondent. No replies are sent to unsuccessful applicants. Applications are considered every two months.

The Joseph Collier Charitable Trust

c/o Binder Hamlyn, 17 Lansdowne Road, Croydon CR9 2PL

Contact: The Trust Administrator
Trustees: Mrs P H Maxwell, J A C Benthall.
Grant total: £35,000 (1992/93)
Beneficial area: UK.
General: Grants to arts organisations in 1992/93 included:
London Symphony Orchestra Endowment Trust (£5,740);
London Symphony Orchestra (£6,350);
Royal Opera House Trust (£2,500);
Hanover Band Trust (£500);
Live Music Now (£200).
Exclusions: No grants to individuals.
Applications: In writing to the correspondent. Only successful applications receive a reply.

The Ernest Cook Trust

Fairford Park, Fairford, Gloucestershire GL7 4JH

Tel: 01285-713273
Contact: Mrs J R Malleson, Awards Administrator
Trustees: Sir William Benyon (Chairman), Sir Jack Boles, C F Badcock, A M W Christie-Miller, M C Tuely.
Grant total: £406,000 (1994/95)
Beneficial area: UK, with a special interest in Gloucestershire and other areas where the trust owns land - Fairbridge, Slimbridge and Barnsley, Gloucestershire; Hartwell and Boarstall, Buckinghamshire; Little Dalby, Leicestershire; Trent, Dorset.
General: Although the major interest of this trust is with educational projects concerning conservation and appreciation of the countryside, the arts is one of its additional fields of interest. Support is given to programmes encouraging an appreciation of architecture and an interest in its conservation, although not to structural building and preservation programmes per se. Instruction in craft skills, with emphasis on practical rural skills, is supported, and help is given to programmes developing an

interest in music, though this is largely restricted to areas in the country where the trust holds land or in which it has some other specific interest. Community arts programmes are not supported. The trust has a particular interest in projects in the Gloucestershire area.

Over £35,000 was given within the "Arts, Crafts and Architecture" category in 1994/95. (This is a considerable drop from the previous year when £85,000 (21%) of its total grant-aid went to this category. It is not known if this reduction results from a policy decision or related to the calibre and relevance of applications.) Grants in 1994/95 included:

Institute of Archaeology, London University, for bursary scheme (£5,000);
Royal School of Church Music (£5,000);
Koestler Award Trust, for its competition and exhibition scheme for prisoners (£2,000);
Carousel, Brighton, for work with adults and children with severe communication problems.

Exclusions: General funding; building, restoration and conversion.
Applications: Applicants are advised to focus on a specific educational need within an overall programme as requests for general support are rarely successful. Applications should be restricted to four sides of A4 paper. Applicants are welcome to discuss a project on the telephone. Proposals may be submitted at any time. Trustees meet in Spring and Autumn but there are more frequent meetings for small requests. An SAE should be sent to ensure acknowledgement as only proposals to be forwarded to the trustees are otherwise acknowledged.

The Duke of Cornwall's Benevolent Fund

10 Buckingham Gate, London SW1E 6LA
Tel: 0171-834 7346
Contact: FAO Angela Wise
Trustees: Earl Cairns, J N C James.
Grant total: £152,000 (1992/93)
Beneficial area: South West England
General: In 1992/93 the fund gave

£18,000 in "annual subscriptions" and £134,000 in "donations". Arts grants were given to:
Royal Shakespeare Company (£6,000);
Wells Museum Development Trust (£2,000).
Applications: In writing to the correspondent. Applicants should give as much detail as possible, particularly on the amount of money raised to date, what the target is and how it will be achieved.

The Cripplegate Foundation

76 Central Street, London EC1V 8AG
Tel: 0171-336 8062; Fax: 0171-336 8201
Contact: David Green, Clerk to the Governors
Trustees: The Governors.
Grant total: £759,000 (1994)
Beneficial area: The Ancient Parish of St Giles, Cripplegate, an area extending from the Barbican in the City to the Angel, Islington.
General: The foundation's objects are to provide facilities and relief-in-need for people resident or employed in the beneficial areas. It supports a wide range of social welfare, educational and arts organisations in its beneficial area. In 1994 it supported nine organisations under its "Arts & Leisure" category totalling over £9,000. Other grants were given for arts work under other categories - "Young People" and "Education and Training". These grants raise the total given to arts activities to over £74,000.

Grants given under "The Arts & Leisure"
Bedside Manners (£3,000);
Islington International Festival, Islington Museum Trust, Shape Islington (£1,000);
Angel Canal Festival (£900);
Grants given under "Education & Training"
Guildhall School of Music & Drama, for bursaries (£30,000);
Islington Music Workshop, for tutor and programme in Islington schools (£20,000 in 2 grants);
Grants given under "Young People"
Acappella Music Workshop, for sound-proofing studios (£10,000);

*LEAP Confronting Conflict (£4,000);
Theatre Centre, for performances for
   children with special needs (£2,000).*
Applications: Preliminary enquiries by
telephone or letter are welcome to establish
eligibility. Application forms are now
available.

The D'Oyly Carte
Charitable Trust

1 Savoy Hill, London WC2R OBP

Tel: 0171-836 1533
Contact: Mrs Jane Thorne
Trustees: E J P Elliott (Chairman), J
McCracken, Sir Martyn Beckett, Sir John
Batten, Francesca Radcliffe, Julia Sibley.
Grant total: £100,000 (1993/94)
Beneficial area: UK.
General: The trust supports "causes
connected mainly with the arts, the
environment and medical welfare". In
1993/94 arts grants totalling £57,000 were
made most of which were between £250
and £1,000. Five major scholarships were
funded at "selected art establishments"
and 29 grants given to other organisations.
These included:
*Actors' Charitable Trust (£5,000 recurrent);
Crafts Council (£5,000 recurrent);
English National Ballet (£3,000);
Koestler Award Trust (£2,000);
British Youth Orchestra (£1,500);
London Mozart Players, Opera Factory
   (£1,000 each);
National Music and Disability Information
   Service, Pro Corda Young Chamber Music
   Players, Courtauld Institute, Black Shakes
   and Scenes Theatre, Mm Souhami Puppet
   Theatre (£500 each);
No Strings Attached - clarinet quintet
   (£250).*
Exclusions: No grants to individuals for
further education and training.
Applications: In writing to the
correspondent. There is no application
form. The trustees meet twice a year, in
June and December, to consider
applications. The list of applications for
consideration closes one month in advance
of each trustees' meeting.

The correspondent has declared that "the
resources of the trust are directed to
specific charities from year to year and the
trustees are restricted in considering new
applications".

The Daiwa Anglo-Japanese
Foundation

Japan House, 13-14 Cornwall Terrace,
London NW1 4QP

Tel: 0171-486 4348; Fax: 0171-486 2914
Contact: Christopher Everett, Director
General
Trustees: Lord Roll of Ipsden (Chair),
Yoshitoki Chino (Vice-Chair), Lord Adrian,
Lord Carrington, Nicholas Clegg, Akio
Morita.
Grant total: £475,000 (excluding
scholarships) 1993/94
Beneficial area: UK and Japan.
General: The trustees make grants to
organisations and individuals in order to
advance the education of Japanese and UK
citizens in each other's way of life. Within
this broad policy a number of arts grants
are made each year. Arts grants in 1993/94
included:
*Design Museum, education programme of
   exhibition (£35,000);
Roundabout Theatre Nottingham, performance at Okinawa 1994 International
   Festival of Young People's Theatre
   (£5,000);
National Youth Orchestra of Scotland,
   concert tour to Japan (£4,000);
The Wave Theatre, production of Japanese
   play at Battersea Arts Centre (£3,000);
The Small School, Devon, tour of "The
   Tempest" in Japan (£2,000).*
Applications: In writing to the
correspondent, including details of budget
and other sources of help available.
Applicants are interviewed before
recommendations are made to trustees.

The Dancers' Trust

Rooms 222-227 Africa House, 64 Kingsway, London WC2B 6BG

Tel: 0171-404 6141
Contact: Linda Yates
Beneficial area: UK.
General: Four bursaries of up to £5,000 each are offered for professional dancers in transition (applicants to be 30 years old or over and have been a professional dancer for at least 10 years and who are planning to change careers). This scheme is funded by the Arts Council, Equity Trust Fund and the Entertainment Charities Fund on an annual basis so interested readers should contact the trust to find out if it is still extant. The trust also gives small grants of up to £500 to assist independent dancers who are changing their careers.
Applications: Application forms are available for the bursaries. Contact the trust to find out more information.

The Delius Trust

16 Ogle Street, London W1P 8JB

Tel: 0171-436 4816
Contact: Marjorie Dickinson, Secretary
Trustees: Meredith Davies, Martin Williams, Musicians' Benevolent Fund (representative: Helen Faulkner). Advisory Panel: Dr Felix Aprahamian, Dr Lionel Carley, Robert Montgomery, Robert Threlfall
Grant total: £23,000 (1994)
Beneficial area: UK and overseas
General: The trust's objects are the advancement of the musical works of Frederick Delius by contributing towards the cost of performances, publications, recordings and the purchase of manuscripts. The trust does not assist with any capital funding such as equipment costs.
Applications: In writing to the secretary. Guidance notes are available.

The Djanogly Foundation

Serck House, 60-61 Trafalgar Square, London SC2N 5DS

Contact: Sir Harry Djanogly
Trustees: Sir Harry Djanogly, probably M S Djanogly
Grant total: £654,000 (1994/95)
Beneficial area: UK and overseas, with a special interest in Nottinghamshire.
General: The foundation donates to many charities including Jewish ones. It has been a major benefactor of Nottingham University and schools there. Arts grants totalling £72,000 in 1994/95 were given to:
Royal Academy of Art (£23,500);
Museum of Law, Nottingham (£20,000);
Chicken Shed Theatre (£12,500);
City and Guilds of London School of Art (£10,000);
National Theatre (£4,500);
Grassington Opera (£1,225);
Philharmonia Trust (£1,000).
Applications: In writing to the correspondent.

The Drapers' Charitable fund

Drapers' Hall, London EC2N 2DQ

Tel: 0171-588 5001; Fax: 0171-628 1988
Contact: Lisa Williams, Secretary
Trustees: Dr W B G Simmonds, A E Woodall, Rev Peter Taylor.
Grant total: £675,000 (1993/94)
Beneficial area: UK with a preference for the City of London
General: Eligibility has included a wide range of charitable organisations but the arts is not listed amongst those. It is likely that arts grants come under education/ training or children/youth. Organisations usually have a national remit or operate within the City of London. A connection or interest with the company, or in drapery or textiles would be considered. Funding is usually for capital rather than revenue. Most of the fund's income is committed for a number of years in the future. In 1995/96 about £100,000 was available for new grants. New grants range between £250 and £5,000, the average grants being

below £1,000 and one-off rather than recurrent. Grants are given towards the costs of equipment, buildings, projects and other needs but not generally for salaries or running costs. Arts related grants in 1993/94 were:

Friends of the Textile Conservation Centre (£5,000 last of 3);
Museum of Empire and Commonwealth Trust (£2,500);
Bodleian Library, Oxford (£2,000, 2nd of 5);
Incorporated Society of Designers (£1,000 1st of 2);
ADAPT, City and Guilds of London Art School (£500 each);
Aldeburgh Foundation (£400);
Blackheath Concert Halls, Museum of London, Fleet Air Arm Museum, Kent Institute of Arts and Design (£250 each).

Exclusions: Individuals.
Applications: Check current criteria by submitting a letter of application. A full budget and audited accounts and annual report are required. In some cases an application form will need to be completed. All applications are acknowledged. Applications are considered every two months.

The Ann Driver Trust

2nd Floor, St Dunstan's House, 2-4 Darey Lane, London EC2V 8AA

Contact: Kay Tyler
Trustees: Lady Elspeth Howe, Robert Pritchett, Charles Michell, Mrs Martin Neary, Sir Alan Triall
Grant total: £30,000 (1994/95)
General: The trust makes grants for education of youth in arts, particularly in music. The trust 's grants in 1994/95 funded scholarships for students at colleges for the arts, particularly for music and drama. The trust's grants for the 1994/95 academic year funded scholarships at the following colleges: Bodywork Company; Royal Scottish Academy of Music and Drama; Elmhurst Ballet School; Legat School of Classical Ballet; Musicians' Institute; Guildhall School of Music and Drama; Yehudi Menuhin School; Arts Educational

School; Dalcroze Institute; Central School of Ballet; Bristol University; Birmingham Conservatoire.
Applications: Application forms have to be submitted by April.

The Vivien Duffield Foundation

Unit 3, Chelsea Manor Studios, Flood Street, London SW3 5SR

Tel: 0171-351 6061
Contact: Miriam Harris, Executive Director.
Trustees: Vivien Duffield, David Harrel, Jocelyn Stevens, Maître Caroline Deletra, Michael Trask.
Grant total: £738,000 (1994)
Beneficial area: UK.
General: The foundation makes substantial grants to arts organisations as well as to children's social and medical welfare charities. It has the same director as the Clore Foundation and is run from the same offices. Both foundations have been involved in establishing the Eureka Children's Museum, for which very large sums have been given.

In 1993 the foundation announced a new award open to professional performing arts companies and arts centres with charitable status, to support innovative programmes aimed at developing audiences under the age of 25. For 1994 one or more awards within a total of £100,000 were available. This award was under review in late 1995.

In 1992, the most recent year for which detailed information about grants is available £1. 5 million was disbursed, the major part to arts organisations. Many grants are recurrent. Grants in 1994 included:

Eureka! The Children's Museum (£1,064,000);
Royal Opera House Trust (£116,844);
Glyndebourne Arts Trust (£50,000);
Dulwich Picture Gallery (£25,000);
Sir John Soane's Museum (£20,000);
Live Music Now! (£10,000);
Yorkshire and Humberside Arts - Yorkshire Ballet Seminars, Chicken Shed Theatre, Aldeburgh Foundation (£5,000 each);

Royal Ballet School (£3,510);
Jewish Film Foundation, Benesh Institute,
  English National Ballet School (£1,000
  each).

Exclusions: No grants to individuals.

Applications: As with the associated Clore Foundation applications are neither sought nor acknowledged. The trust says no application will be considered unless accompanied by a personal request from someone known to the trustees. This disheartening comment has been approved by the executive director although Mrs Duffield has said to the press that all applications are considered and prospective applicants have apparently received a more positive response.

Gilbert and Eileen Edgar Foundation

c/o Messrs Chantry Vellacott, 23-25 Castle Street, Reading, Berkshire RG1 7SB

Tel: 01734-595432

Contact: Avril Hallam, Secretary

Trustees: Mrs M Lloyd-Johnes, A Gentilli, J Matthews

Grant total: £104,000 (1994)

Beneficial area: UK.

General: The foundation has a preference for:

1. Promotion of medical and surgical sciences;
2. Helping of the young, the old and the needy;
3. Raising of artistic taste.

In 1994, 218 grants were made, mostly for £250 or £500. A large proportion of the grants appear to be recurrent. The arts do not seem to be a priority for the trustees at the moment and the number of arts grants has declined in recent years. Grants in 1993 were given to:
Royal National Theatre (£2,526);
Royal National Ballet (£1,150);
Shakespeare Globe Trust (£1,500);
Live Music Now (£250).

Applications: In writing to the correspondent.

The Elephant Trust

20 Furnival street, London EC4A 1BN

Contact: A A Forwood

Grant total: £44,000 (1993/94)

Beneficial area: UK.

General: The trust's objects are to develop, improve the knowledge, understanding and appreciation of the fine arts. Its policy is to extend the frontiers of creative endeavour and initiative. Both individuals and organisations may be supported. In 1993/94 ten grants were given to individuals. Other grants were given to:
Bankside Gallery (£3,000);
Camden Arts Centre, Chapter Arts Centre,
  Latin American Arts Association, Paintings
  in Hospitals, Royal West of England
  Academy, Tabernacle Cultural Centre,
  Women and Surrealism (£2,000 each);
Verso (£1,500);
Harris Museum and Art Galleries (£600);
Hastings Museum and Arts Gallery (£500).
The trustees also administer the George Melhuish Bequest which has similar objects. No further information is available about this.

Applications: In writing to the correspondent.

The John Ellerman Foundation
(formerly The Moorgate Trust Fund and the New Moorgate Trust Fund)

Suite 10, Aria House, 23 Craven Street, London WC2N 5NT

Tel: 0171-930 8566; **Fax:** 0171-839 3654

Contact: Peter C Pratt, Director and Secretary; Phyllis Hubbard, Administrator.

Trustees: Dennis G Parry, Angela Boschi, David Martin-Jenkins, Sir David Scott, R A Lloyd, Peter Strutt

Grant total: £3,338,000 (1994/95)

Beneficial area: UK and overseas.

General: This foundation gives mainly for "medical research, hospitals, the physically and mentally handicapped, the blind, the deaf, the arts, youth, the aged, charities associated with the sea, animals, the environment and special education" (trustees' report 1994/95).

The general policy is to give to ongoing support to the regular running costs of leading and established charities in a wide variety of fields. The foundation is willing to consider applications both for capital and revenue projects, for core running costs as well as for particular projects.

The foundation prefers to provide funding for central bodies or head offices rather than for local groups or branches, but would hope to encourage central bodies or head offices to distribute at least part of any funding provided by the foundation to such local groups or branches.

In 1994/95 the foundation made about 460 grants, most of which ranged between £1,000 and £10,000. A total of £203,000 was given to 29 arts organisations and included the following grants:
National Portrait Gallery (£25,000);
Royal College of Music (£15,000);
National Museums & Galleries on Mersey-side, National Museums of Scotland, National Opera Studio, Foundation for Young Musicians (£10,000 each);
New Shakespeare Company (£5,000);
Royal Academy of Arts, Royal Academy of Music (£6,000);
Burnbake Trust (£3,000);
Birmingham Museums and Art Gallery (£1,000).
Exclusions: No grants to individuals or to organisations which are not registered charities. The foundation is not permitted to make grants for any purpose related to areas in the continents of America south of the USA.
Applications: In writing to the correspondent, giving concise details of the charitable work undertaken, the funding requirement and the current financial position of the charity concerned. Applications may be made at any time.

The Elm Trust 11

Personal Financial Management,
12 Hans Road, London SW3 1RT

Tel: 0171-584 4277
Contact: P D Green
Trustees: R E Downhill, P D Green, Mrs C M Hawley.
Grant total: £79,000 (1991/92)
Beneficial area: UK.
General: Up-to-date information about this trust is not available. In 1991/92 the trust gave £79,000 (out of its income of £72,000) entirely to the National Portrait Gallery. In the previous year it gave two grants totalling £19,000 from an income of £87,000 to the National Portrait Gallery (£10,500); and the Victoria and Albert Museum (£8,500).
Applications: In writing to the correspondent.

The Elmgrant Trust

The Elmhirst Centre, Dartington Hall, Totnes, Devon TQ9 6EL

Tel: 01803-863160
Contact: Mrs M B Nicholson, Secretary
Trustees: Maurice Ash, Lord Young of Dartington, Claire Ash Wheeler, Sophie Young
Grant total: £138,000 (1994/95)
Beneficial area: UK, with a preference for Devon and Cornwall
General: The trust supports education, the arts and the social sciences, mainly in Devon and Cornwall. It grants are categorised as follows in its accounts:
Grants for education & educational research £53,000
Grants for arts & arts research £24,000
Grants for social sciences & scientific research £26,500
Pensions and compassionate grants £5,400
Donations £29,000.
Dartington College of Arts and associated activities are regularly supported. Arts beneficiaries in recent years have included: Falmouth College of Art; Lauderdale House Society; Beaford Arts Centre; Manaton & East Dartmoor Theatre. Applications for capital costs are considered.

Exclusions: No postgraduate, expedition or travel and other related applications.
Applications: In writing to the correspondent. Meetings are held in March, June, September and December.

The Enkalon Foundation

25 Randalstown Road, Antrim BT41 4LJ

Tel: 01849-463 535; Fax: 01849-465 733
Contact: J W Wallace, Secretary
Grant total: £100,000 a year
Beneficial area: Northern Ireland.
General: The foundation was established to improve the quality of life in Northern Ireland. Cross-community groups, self-help groups, community arts groups working to help the disadvantaged in a wide variety of ways may be considered for starter finance, single projects or capital projects. Grants are up to a maximum of £6,000.
Exclusions: No grants for projects or travel outside Northern Ireland. No grants to individuals with the possible exception of ex-employees of British Enkalon Ltd.
Applications: Guidelines for applicants are available. Applications are reviewed every four months.

The Equity Trust Fund

Suite 222, Africa House, 64 Kingsway, London WC2B 6AH

Tel: 0171-404 6041
Contact: Carla Hanreck, Secretary
Trustees: Jean Ainslie, Harvey Ashby, Colin Baker, John Barron, Derek Bond, Annie Bright, Nigel Davenport, Graham Hamilton, Barbara Hyslop, Milton Johns, John Johnson, Harry Landis, Louise Mahoney, Norman Mitchell, Frederick Pyne, Peter Plouviez, Gillian Raine, Hugh Manning, Ian McGarry, Jeffrey Wickham, Frank Williams.
Grant total: £220,000 (1993/94)
Beneficial area: UK.
General: This trust was established in 1989 with funds from British Actors Equity. The trust has made the following statement about the way it intends to fulfil its objects to support performances and the arts on which they depend:

* Assisting with the welfare of individual performers, and their dependants, in need of financial, medical or other assistance.
* Maintaining the arts upon which performers depend, in particular, the live theatre and live entertainment. It is not to be seen as an alternative source of state/local government funding, but as a complementary source.
* The Fund has a responsibility for the continuing education of members of the profession. Educational bursaries are available in cases of extreme financial hardship.
* To work with and complement - but not duplicate - the work undertaken by existing charities within the arts and entertainment field. It makes interest-free loans to organisations as well as substantial grants. It also has a small provision to help theatres with essential capital costs. Grants range between £500 to £250,000. In 1993/94 it gave 10 loans to theatres, totalling £82,000. The largest loan was given to the Theatre Royal, Margate (£30,000 with larger grants in the 2 previous years).

Grants were allocated as follows:
* Theatres £83,500
* Education £84,000
* Welfare/Benevolent £54,000.

Grants included:
Shakespeare's Globe Theatre (£15,000, 2nd of 2);
Watermill Theatre (£6,500);
British Performing Arts Medicine Trust (£12,500);
Artsline, the information service for diabled people (£2,000);
Exclusions: Revenue and production costs, including tour and production costs.
Applications: In writing to the correspondent enclosing an A5 SAE. Please telephone before submitting an application. Details should be presented no more than four sides of A4 paper, including a brief history of the organisation, its current funders, what the money is needed for and a concise breakdown of costs relevant to the application.

Applications for funds under £2,500 are considered by the executive committee, who meet approximately every six weeks. Applications for £2,500 and above are considered by the full board who meet approximately every three months.

The Eranda Foundation

New Court, St Swithin's Lane, London EC4P 4DU

Tel: 0171-280 5000
Trustees: Evelyn de Rothschild, Mrs Renée Robeson, Mrs Victoria de Rothschild, Leopold de Rothschild, Grahame Hearne
Grant total: £605,000 (1990/91)
Beneficial area: Mainly the UK.
General: The foundation gives grants in the fields of the arts; health, welfare and medical research; and education. In 1990/91 it gave a total of £348,500 in arts grants. This is the sum total of what is known about the work of this major foundation as at September 1995. The implementation of the Charities Act should alter this situation.
Applications: In writing to the correspondent.

The Esmée Fairbairn Charitable Trust

1 Birdcage Walk, London SW1H 9JJ

Tel: 0171-222 7041; Fax: 0171-233 0421
Contact: Margaret Hyde, Director
Trustees: J S Fairbairn (Chairman), A G Down (Treasurer), Sir Antony Acland, General Sir John Hackett, C J M Hardie, Mrs P Hughes-Hallett, Martin Lane-Fox, Mrs V Linklater, Lord Rees-Mogg, Andrew Tuckey.
Grant total: £9,142,000 (1994)
Beneficial area: UK.
General: The trust seeks to allocate its grants in the following proportions:

◆ Arts and Heritage 25%
◆ Education 27. 5%
◆ Social Welfare 25%
◆ Environment 10%
◆ Social and Economic Research 7. 5%

The trust says in its 1994 report that it is continuing its efforts to cover the whole of the UK and direct more of its resources to Northern Ireland, Scotland and Wales. Also that trustees are likely to bring "more shape and focus to their policies" in the arts and heritage field, taking account of the major lottery funding in these areas and the trust's newly published (1995) guidelines listing six priorities.

The trust's priorities in Arts and Heritage: "The trust wishes to help extend the artistic and business development of the performing and creative arts.

The trust is more likely to support organisations or projects less able to raise substantial funds from other sources. The trust's priorities are:

◆ The professional development of performers and other artists who have completed their formal training and are in the earlier stages of their careers. No grants are made to individuals.
◆ Initiatives which improve the management, artistic or business performance of arts organisations, or their financial independence.
◆ The public presentation or performance of contemporary work.
◆ Arts provision amongst groups or places less well served.
◆ Audience development.
◆ Arts education work involving local communities, particularly those less well served.

In the heritage field the trust supports:

◆ Significant acquisitions by provincial public museums and galleries (The trust provides only limited support directly, since it channels most of its funding in this area through another grant-giving body. Please consult the Secretary before applying.)
◆ The preservation of buildings of historic or architectural value where these are put to public use, and the conservation of artefacts.

In 1994 £2,074,000 was given to arts and heritage (43 grants of over £10,000 totalling £1,435,000, 110 grants of £10,000 or less totalling £640,000). No detail is available for grants of less than £2,500. The larger arts grants in 1994 were given to:

*Dulwich Picture Gallery, towards endow-
ment funding of its core costs (£250,000);*
*Tate Gallery, preliminary costs for its
Bankside gallery (£100,000);*
*Royal Northern College of Music, for its
major building (£100,000 over 2 years);*
*Royal Liverpool Philharmonic Society, for
relocation costs (£60,000);*

Because of the number and range of the
trust's grant-aid it is worth noting the areas
that the chairman draws attention to in the
1994 annual report: its support to a
number of smaller independent galleries
and museums (as well as to Dulwich see
above); the grants to literature via the Book
Trust, the Poetry Book Society for the T S
Eliot Poetry Prize and the South Bank
Centre for its education work with Poetry
International and Children's Book Week; the
support to conservation via specialist
teaching posts at the Courtauld Institute
and the new conservation centre for the
National Museums and Galleries on
Merseyside; the commitment to opera
extending to smaller ventures as well as to
the major national and regional companies.

It seems worthwhile also to give a sample
of the trust's smaller grants to display
further its range of giving:

Isle of Wight Oboe Competition (£7,500);
Laurence Stern Trust (£6,000);
Council for Music in Hospitals (£5,000);
Ebony Steelband Trust (£4,000);
Cumbria Arts in Education (£3,000);
Dance Umbrella (£5,000);
Gorbal Arts Project (£3,000);
London Suzuki Group Trust (£5,000);
*Manaton and East Dartmoor Theatre
(£3,000);*
Norfolk Contemporary Arts Society (£4,000);
Paines Plough (£5,000);
Phoenix Dance (£5,500);
*Weald and Downland Open Air Museum
(£5,000).*

Exclusions: These include individuals,
charities operating abroad, organisations
which are not registered charities. See
policy guidelines for the full list.

Applications: Prospective applicants should
first obtain the trust's latest policy
guidelines (send 9"x6" SAE). The annual

report is also available on request.
Applicants are advised to contact the
Secretary informally, Miss Judith Dunworth,
by telephone or letter, on the desirability of
making an application and the particular
information needed.

The Federation of British Artists

17 Carlton House Terrace, London
SW1Y 5BD

Tel: 0171-930-6844; **Fax:** 0171-839 7830
Trustees: John Walton, Ronald Maddox,
Brian Bennet, Tom Coates, Raymond
Spurrier, Daphne Todd.
General: The FBA is the umbrella
organisation for nine of the country's
leading art societies: Royal Institute of Oil
Painters; Royal Society of British Artists;
Royal Society of Portrait Painters; Royal
Institute of Painters in Water Colours; Royal
Society of Marine Artists; New English Art
Club; Pastel Society; Society of Wildlife
Artists; Hesketh Hubbard Art Society.

Annual exhibitions by each society are
held at the Mall Galleries. These are open to
all artists, not just members who are elected
on merit.

Artists' prizes are given at most exhibitions,
many of them specifically for younger artists.
Applications: For details of the exhibitions
and associated prizes, and how to submit
work, please send a large SAE to the Mall
Galleries at the above address.

The John Feeney Charitable Trust

Messrs Lee Crowder, 24 Harborne Road,
Edgbaston, Birmingham B15 3AD

Contact: M J Woodward, Secretary
Trustees: Hugh Kenrick, Maisie Smith,
Canon Ralph Stevens, Mollie Martineau,
Charles King-Farlow, Derek Lea, Jeremy
Martineau, Stephen Lloyd, Merryn Ford
Lloyd, Ranjit Sondhi, Patrick Welch
Grant total: £34,000 (1994)
Beneficial area: Birmingham and its
environs.
General: The trust's objects are to assist

public charities, the promotion of arts, and the acquisition and maintenance of open spaces in or near Birmingham. It currently prefers to support capital projects and does not give grants for maintenance expenses. Grants range between £200 and £5,000 but most are small and under £500. Two commissions have been arranged with Judith Weir and Thomas Ades . Grants in 1994 included:

Under the Arts
Lunar Society (£5,000);
Royal Birmingham Society of Artists (£2,000);
Hocus Pocus Theatre Group (£500);
Fox Hollies School (£250);

Under Music
Birmingham Bach Choir (£2,000);
Birmingham Festival Choral Society
  (£1,000);
City of Birmingham Brass Band, (£500);
Birmingham Early Music Festival, Rubery
  Youth Marching Band, (£250 each);
West Bromwich Operatic Society (£200).
Exclusions: Individuals, organisations which are not registered charities, objects which could possibly considered political or denominational.
Applications: In writing to the correspondent.

The John Fernald Award Trust

118 Victoria Drive, London SW19 6PS

Tel: 0171-229 6049
Contact: Frederick Pyne
Grant total: £5,000 (1991)
Beneficial area: UK.
General: The trust gives grants to trainee directors to get professional experience either through their own project or with an existing theatre company. Grants range between £1,000 and £3,000. In 1991 three awards totalling £5,000 were given for seasons with London theatres.
Exclusions: No grants for basic training, equipment or other capital costs.
Applications: In writing to the correspondent. Applicants must be affiliated to a professional theatre organisation. Applications are considered in December, January and February.

The Finchcocks Charity

Finchcocks, Goudhurst, Kent TN17 1HH

Tel: 01580-211702
Contact: Mrs K Burnett, Secretary
Trustees: Richard Burnett, Katrina Burnett. Council: Sir David Burnett, Katrina Burnett, Marion Dow, William Dow, Laurence Peskett, Theophilus Peters, Lord Wakehurst.
Grant total: £22,000 (1993/94)
Beneficial area: UK and overseas.
General: The trust is based at a museum of keyboard instruments and international music centre. It supports recitals, courses, competitions, provides bursaries for students and musicians, assists in paying for specialist performers and teachers and assists in the maintenance of instruments for educational events at the centre. Grants were categorised in 1993/94 as follows:
Finchcocks Festival (£17,852);
Broadwood Competition, prizes, fees
  (£3,200);
Subsidised visits to Finchcocks, tutorial fees,
  bursaries (£1,090).
Exclusions: Any person or event not connected with Finchcocks museum and music centre and the musical activities held there.
Applications: In writing to the correspondent.

The First Film Foundation

Canalot Studios, 222 Kensal Road, W10 5RN

Tel: 0181-969 5195; Fax: 0181-960 6302
Beneficial area: UK and Ireland.
General: This charity was set up in 1987 to create opportunities for new writers, producers and directors from the UK and Ireland. It does not provide funds itself but the services it offers are "worth their weight in gold". The foundation's work centres round projects submitted to it. All are read, given constructive feedback, advice on script rewrites, contacts and sources of funding.

Certain filmmakers are chosen for more intensive support including script editing, budgeting and scheduling, fundraising, team building. Most interestingly, the foundation has built up a network of established professionals who are attached to projects in an advisory capacity, as "godparents".

Applications: Submit one or more scripts or treatments, together with a CV and a covering letter outlining your current situation. Directors should submit examples of any previous work on VHS or U-Matic. Enclose an SAE if you need your material returned.

The Sir John Fisher Foundation

8-10 New Market Street, Ulverston, Cumbria LA12 7LW

Contact: R F Hart Jackson
Trustees: B G Robinson, R F Hart Jackson, Mrs D S Meacock.
Grant total: £172,000 (1993/94)
Beneficial area: UK with a preference for Cumbria, particularly south Cumbria.
General: The foundation has general charitable interests. It divides its grants into two schedules – Local and National. In 1993/94 local grant-aid totalling £105,000 was given in 40 grants ranging between £100 and £42,000. National grant-aid totalling £67,000 was given in 16 grants, the largest of which was for £30,000.

For many year the foundation has been a major funder of Brewery Arts Centre, Kendal (£25,000 in 1992/93). This agree-ment has now expired. Local arts grants in 1993/94 were given to:
Renaissance Theatre Trust (£4,250);
Cumbria Youth Orchestra (£2,000);
Lake District Summer Music (£500);
Cumbria Drama Festival (£200);
Cumbria Youth Brass Band, South Cumbria
   Music Festival (£100);

National arts grants included:
Actors' Benevolent Fund, Anglo-Austrian
   Music Society (£1,500 each and recurrent).
Applications: In writing to the correspondent.

The Joyce Fletcher Charitable Trust

17 Westmead Gardens, Upper Weston, Bath BA1 4EZ

Tel: 01225-314355
Contact: R A Fletcher
Trustees: R A Fletcher, W D R Fletcher, A V Fretwell.
Grant total: £17,000 (1995)
Beneficial area: UK, with a particular interest in the South West and the Bath area.
General: The trust gives "support to institutions and organisations specialising in music performance and education, and children's welfare, a particular interest being the role of music in the lives of the disabled and disadvantaged ".

Out of a total of 34 grants in 1995, 16 were clearly for music. Individuals are rarely considered. Most grants are between £250 and £500. Arts grants in 1995 were given to:
Live Music Now! SW (£4,000);
"Share Music" Courses (£1,500);
Off the Record (Bath); English Touring Opera,
   Theatre Royal Youth Theatre, Macintyre
   Charitable Trust, for music (£500 each);
Bath Festivals Trust, Bristol Cathedral Choir
   Tour, Leeds Youth Opera, Ernest Read
   Music Association, MusicSpace Trust,
   Rondo Trust for the Performing Arts,
   Royal Academy of Music, Wiltshire Music
   Centre (£250 each).
Exclusions: Professional performances with no community/outreach links.
Applications: In writing to the correspondent before 1 November each year. Replies are only sent to those enclosing an SAE, and those to whom a grant is made.

The 42 Foundation

Withers (Reference SGC), 2 Gough Square, London EC4 3DE

Tel: 0171-836 8400
Contact: The Administrator
Trustees: David Bralsford, Dr Brian Horne, Stephen Cooke

Grant total: £24,000 (1993/94)
Beneficial area: UK.
General: This new foundation set up in 1991 aims to support the performing arts, and in particular, to give "financial assistance to students in the performing arts on a one-off or continuing basis, according the availability of funds'. In 1993/94 the London Handel Society received £10,000 and seven grants, ranging between £60 and £7,000, given to individuals.
Applications: In writing to the correspondent, but the foundation has written that its "funds are fully committed... and the trustees think it is unlikely that sufficient donations will be received in the future to make the foundation viable".

The Four Lanes Trust

Beaurepaire House, Sherbourne St John, Basingstoke, Hants RG26 5EH

Contact: Dwight Makins
Trustees: D W Makins, V Shapiro, E I Roberts, L E A Evans, D Makins.
Grant total: £30,000 (1994/95
Beneficial area: Basingstoke and Deane Borough Council area.
General: The trust's objects are the advancement of education (including education in the arts) and the promotion of social welfare.

In 1993/94 38 grants were given, all but four of which were less than £1,000. Fifteen grants supported playgroups and schools. Arts grants were given to:
Arts Connection (£2,500);
Hampshire Dance Trust (£1,000);
North Hants Area Schools Band (£500);
Whitchurch Festival (£250). (In the previous year a larger grant of £14,000 had been given to the Proteus Theatre Company.)
Exclusions: No grants to individuals for their own benefit.
Applications: In writing to Len Treglown, 5 Caithness Close, Oakley, Basingstoke.

The Gordon Fraser Charitable Trust

Holmhurst, Westerton Drive, Bridge of Allan, Stirling FK9 4QL

Contact: Mrs M A Moss
Trustees: Mrs Margaret Moss, W F T Anderson
Grant total: £94,000 (1994)
Beneficial area: UK with a particular interest in Scotland.
General: The trust has general charitable objects. Its grant-list shows that it has a particular interest in arts, heritage and church conservation organisations. The trust states that "applications from and for Scotland will receive favourable consideration, but not to the exclusion of applications from elsewhere". The trust is prepared to assist with funding towards capital costs: equipment purchase, building renovation or new buildings.

Arts grants in 1994 comprised nearly a quarter of its grant-aid and included:
Scottish International Piano Competition (£4,000);
MacRobert Arts Centre, Scottish Museum Council, Museum of Scotland Projects (£3,000 each);
Smith Art Gallery and Museum, Artlink Central, Lincoln Cathedral Music Appeal, (£1,000 each);
Council for Music in Hospitals, National Appeal for Music Therapy, Northlands Festival, Paintings in Hospitals Scotland (£500 each);
French Film Festival, Glasgow Museums, National Association of Youth Orchestras (£250);
London Print Workshop, Theatre Cryptic, Borders Museum Forum, Grantown Museum and Heritage Trust, Textile Conservation Centre (£200 each);
Pilton Video Project, First Bite Theatre Education, Mull Little Theatre (£100 each).
Exclusions: No grants to individuals or to organisations which are not registered charities.
Applications: In writing to the correspondent. Applications are considered by the trustees in January, April, July and October.

The Hugh Fraser Foundation

c/o W & J Burness Solicitors, 16 Hope Street, Charlotte Square, Edinburgh EH2 4DD

Tel: 0131-226 2561
Trustees: Dr Kenneth Chrystie (Chairman), Lady Fraser of Allander, Ms A L Fraser, Ms P L Fraser, B Smith.
Grant total: £487,000 (1993/94)
Beneficial area: West Scotland and deprived areas of Scotland.
General: The foundation supports a wide range of concerns. Grants are made towards music and the arts, as well as medicine and health, social welfare, elderly people, education, development and training of young people. The trustees are prepared to consider applications for support towards capital costs.
Exclusions: Individuals. Major highly-publicised appeals are rarely supported.
Applications: In writing to the correspondent. The trustees meet quarterly.

The Fulbright Commission

Fulbright House, 62 Doughty Street, London WC1N 2LS

Tel: 0171-404 6880; Fax: 0171-404 6834
Contact: Programme Director
General: A series of academic awards are given for study and research in the United States. Applicants must be British citizens who are ordinarily resident in the UK. The following awards were available in 1995 and relevant to this guide:
Fulbright Postgraduate Student Awards, for candidates of academic or artistic excellence (25 for a minimum of 9 months);
Fulbright Calvin Klein - Harvey Nichols Award in Fashion Design (one award for 4 months);
Fulbright United Airlines Travel Only Awards (10 for a minimum of nine months);
Fulbright Scholarships Grants, for lecturers and post-doctoral research scholars of academic or artistic excellence, minimum 3 months;
Fulbright T E B Clarke Fellowship in Screenwriting, £18,000 plus travel and tuition fees for 9 months, preferably for applicants under 35.

Applications: Telephone the commission for further information. Requests for application forms and guidelines must be accompanied by a large SAE with 38p postage.

The Gane Charitable Trust

6 Sabrina Way, Stoke Bishop, Bristol BS9 1ST

Tel: 0117-968 4266
Contact: Mrs R J Fellows, Secretary
Trustees: Kenneth Stradling, Miss Barley Roscoe, Ben Barman, Miss June Lancaster
Grant total: £23,000 (1994)
Beneficial area: UK with a preference for Bristol and Newport and surrounding areas.
General: The trust's objects are:

1. Promotion of crafts
2. Further education in the crafts, architecture and design
3. Social welfare.

Grants are normally given to individuals rather than to organisations, but are rarely given for post-graduate courses. There is a bias towards craft-related studies, but against recurring operational expenditure. Grants range between £100 and £1,000. Arts grants in 1994 included:
Crafts Study Centre, Edward Barnsley Education Trust (£1,000 each);
Bristol Old Vic Theatre School (£600).
The trust is prepared to assist with capital costs such as equipment purchase.
Applications: In writing to the correspondent.

The Gannochy Trust

Kincarrathie House Drive, Pitcullen Crescent, Perth PH2 7HX

Tel: 01738-620653
Contact: Mrs Jean Gandhi, Secretary.
Trustees: Russell A Leather (Chairman), James Ross, Mark Webster, James A McCowan, Stewart Montgomery.
Grant total: £2,018,000 (1992/93)
Beneficial area: Scotland, with a preference for Perth and its environs.
General: Grants are given for capital costs of a wide range of charitable organisations with a preference for youth and recreation.

Apart from the £2 million+ distributed in 1992/93 a further £1. 4 million was set aside for allocation.

In 1992/93 the arts received 16% of total grant-aid. Only grants of over £70,000 are noted in the accounts. These included the following arts grants/provisions:
*Pitlochry Festival Society (£500,000);
Empire Theatre Trust (£250,000);
Scottish Museums Council (£100,000).*
The trust is prepared to consider applications for funding towards capital costs: equipment, renovation and new buildings.
Exclusions: No grants to individuals, or organisations not recognised as charitable by the Inland Revenue.
Applications: In writing to the correspondent including a copy of the latest accounts.

The Gatsby Charitable Foundation *(see the Sainsbury Family Charitable Trusts also)*

9 Red Lion Court, London EC4A 3EB

Tel: 0171-410 0330
Contact: Michael Pattison
Trustees: C T S Stone, Miss J SPortrait.
Grant total: £12 million (1993/94)
Beneficial area: UK and overseas.
General: The foundation funds projects in technical education, plant science, management development, disadvantaged children and the Third World but also has considerable leeway to donate to other interests.

In 1993/94 a total of some £838,000 was approved in grants to organisations relevant to this guide. A number of restoration projects in cathedrals were also supported. The foundation's annual report shows most of its arts grants under its "general" category but some have been classified within its other major interests eg. .

Under "Technical Education"
*National Museums & Galleries of Mersey-side (£30,000);
Floating Point Theatre (£8,000);*

Under "General"
*Sainsbury Centre for Visual Art, University of East Anglia (£537,000 plus £146,00 for a full-time display consultant);
Docklands Sinfonietta (£45,000);
Worcester Art Museum (£17,045);
Writers and Scholars Educational Trust (£14,500);
Wigmore Hall Chamber Players (£10,000);
Bath Festivals Trust (£15,000);
Ambache Chamber Ensemble, Cambridge Greek Play '95 (£5,000 each);
Shakespeare Link (£4,000);
Chicken Shed Theatre, British Friends of Art Museums of Israel (£1,000 each)*
Exclusions: No grants to individuals.
Applications: An application to one of the Sainsbury family trusts is an application to all. See the entry under "Sainsbury Family Charitable Trusts" for the names of the other trusts and the application procedure.

The Robert Gavron Charitable Trust

44 Eagle Street, London WC1R 4FS

Tel: 0171-400 4200
Contact: Susan Seigle-Morris
Trustees: Robert Gavron, Charles Corman, Katherine Gavron, Jessica Gavron, Sarah Gavron.
Grant total: £285,000 (1993/94)
Beneficial area: UK
General: The trust makes grants in the fields of health, welfare and the arts. A number of beneficiaries receive regular support.

The trust has been a major benefactor of the Open College of the Arts, providing significant annual grants and a loan (converted later to a grant). Arts grants in 1993/94 were made to:
*Open College of the Arts (£40,000);
Friends of Covent Garden (£10,040);
Highgate Literary and Scientific Institution (£5,000);
Royal Opera House (£2,900);
Opera Factory, Rambert Ballet, National Gallery (£1,000 each); ·
London Choral Society, Royal Court Theatre (£500 each);*

Friends of the Royal Academy (£250).
A forward commitment of £50,000 was made to the Royal Opera House Trust.
Applications: In writing only to the correspondent. The trust has stated that its funds are fully committed during 1996 and 1997.

The German Academic Exchange Service (DAAD)

17 Bloomsbury Square, London WC1A 2LP

Tel: 0171-404 4065; **Fax:** 0171-430 2634
Beneficial area: Germany
General: DAAD produces a brochure to draw attention to a variety of scholarships and funding schemes available for study and research in Germany. These are for academic staff, researchers and students at institutions of higher education and research institutes in the United Kingdom. These awards include:

* one-year grants for postgraduate studies (music and art students should have completed a full-time course of study in the subject they wish to study in German, and have gained a recognised qualifications which would entitle them to study at postgraduate level in the UK.
* Artists-in-Berlin programme. Each year about 20-25 artists of international repute (sculptors, painters, writers, composers and film makers) are invited to live and work in Berlin and to present their work to the Berlin public.

The booklet also refers to schemes run by other organisations as well as DAAD.

J Paul Getty Jr Charitable Trust

149 Harley Street, London W1N 2DH

Tel: 0171-486 1859
Contact: Ms Bridget O'Brien Twohig, Administrator
Trustees: J Paul Getty Jr KBE, Christopher Gibbs, James Ramsden, Vanni Treves
Grant total: £1,244,000 (1994)
Beneficial area: UK with a preference for less prosperous parts of the country.
General: "The trust aims to fund projects

to do with poverty and misery in general, and unpopular causes in particular. The emphasis is on self-help, building esteem, enabling people to reach their potential. The trustees favour small community and local projects which make good use of volunteers. Both revenue and capital grants are made... (but please see "Exclusions" below)... a particular aspect of your application rather than the general purpose of your organisation may be excluded."

"Priority is likely to be given to projects in the less prosperous parts of the country, and to those which cover more than one beneficial area.

"Grants are usually in the £5 - £10,000 range and those made for salaries or running costs are for a maximum of 3 years. Some small grants of up to £1,000 are also made.

1. Social Welfare
"**Mental Health** in a wide sense this includes projects for:

* mentally ill adults;
* mentally handicapped adults;
* drug, alcohol and other addictions, and related problems;
* support groups for people under stress, eg battered wives, victims of abuse, families in difficulties, etc;
* counselling, especially young people;
* mediation.

Offenders, both in and out of prison, men and women, young offenders, sexual offenders.

Communities which are clearly disadvantaged trying to improve their lot, and organisations enabling them, particularly projects to do with helping young people in the long-term.

Homelessness, particularly projects which help prevent people becoming homeless or resettle them.

Job Creation projects or ones aimed at making long-term constructive use of enforced leisure time, particularly ones set up by unemployed people.

Ethnic Minorities involved in above areas, including refugees, particularly projects aimed at integration."

2. Arts

* "therapeutic use of the arts for the long-term benefit of the groups under Social Welfare;
* projects which enable people in these groups to feel welcome in arts venues, or which enable them to make long-term constructive use of their leisure."

3. Conservation

"Conservation in the broadest sense, with emphasis on ensuring that fine building, landscapes and collections remain or become available to the general public or scholars. Training in conservation skills. Not general building repair work."

Arts grants in 1994 included:
Big Issue (£15,000 in 2 grants);
Clean Break Theatre Company, National Maritime Museum, Tricycle Theatre Company, Women's Playhouse Trust (£10,000 each);
Buck County Museum Art Gallery Appeal (£7,500);
Insight Arts Trust (£7,000);
Musicworks (£6,500);
National Museum of Wales, Yorkshire Film Archive (£5,000);
Artists' Agency (Brampton Comm Sculpture), Koestler Award Trust (£4,000 each);
Artlink (£500).

The administrator has emphasised that as far as the arts are concerned "the trust's primary interest really lies with the disadvantaged groups, not with the arts per se, hence the emphasis on long-term benefits. This means that short-term projects without a follow-up/continuing programme are unlikely to be considered, and successful applications are more likely to come from the organisation concerned with the disadvantaged group than from the arts organisation."

Exclusions: Music or drama (except therapeutically), the elderly, children, education, conferences/seminars, research, animals, churches, cathedrals, schools, national appeals, grant-giving trusts. Residential or large buildings projects are unlikely to be considered. No grants to individuals.

Applications: In writing to the correspondent. First obtain the trust's leaflet giving application guidelines. A full letter is all that is necessary at first, giving an outline and detailed costing of the project, existing sources of finance of the organisation, other applications, including those to statutory sources, applications to the trust. Annual accounts will be asked for if the application is going to be taken further. The project will be visited before consideration by the trustees.

Only about one tenth of applicants receive grants. There is often considerable delay between application and its consideration by the trustees who meet quarterly. Some small grants of up to £1,000 can be made more quickly but only for specific purposes.

The Gibbs Charitable Trust

1 Portland Place, Marine Parade, Penarth CF64 3DY

Tel: 01222-706304
Contact: Dr John N Gibbs (see below)
Trustees: Mrs S M N Gibbs, J M Gibbs, J N Gibbs, A G Gibbs, W M Gibbs, J Gibbs, S E Gibbs.
Grant total: £72,000 (1993/94)
Beneficial area: UK.
General: The trusts support Methodist churches and organisations, other Christian causes, wider charitable work especially creative arts. In 1993/93 arts grants were given to:
Charles Wesley Heritage Centre (£10,000);
National Museum of Wales (£2,000);
Riding Lights Christian Arts Centre (£2,000);
Farnham Maltings (£1,288);
Genesis Arts Trust (£250).
Applications: In writing to the correspondent: Dr John Gibbs, 3 Gardeners' Hill Road, Boundstone, Farnham GU10 4RL. The trustees meet three times a year: at Christmas, Easter and in August.

The Simon Gibson Charitable Trust

Touche Ross & Co, Hill House, 1 Little New Street, London EC4A 3TR

Contact: Bryan Marsh
Trustees: Bryan Marsh, Angela Homfray, George Gibson.
Grant total: £223,000 (1993/94)
Beneficial area: UK, with a particular interest in East Anglia, particularly the Newmarket area and Wales.
General: A wide range of charities are supported with grants ranging between £1,000 and £5,000. Arts grants in 1993/94 were given to:
Burnwell Museum Trust, London Welsh Chorale, National Horse Racing Museum, Royal Academy of Music (£2,000 each);
National Music for the Blind (£1,000).
In the previous year the Welsh College of Music and Drama received £10,000.
Exclusions: No grants to individuals.
Applications: In writing to the correspondent. Telephone calls should not be made. All applications are acknowledged but no further correspondence is carried out unless a grant is to be made. The trustees meet in April.

The Godinton Charitable Trust

Godinton House, Godinton Park, Ashford, Kent TN23 3BW

Tel: 01233-620773
Contact: A W Green
Trustees: J D Leigh-Pemberton, Moran Caplat, M F Jennings, G W Plumtre
Grant total: £157,000 (Oct 1994)
Beneficial area: UK.
General: The trust makes a large number of small grants to a wide range of causes including the arts where there is a discernible preference for music and opera. Most grants are under £1,000. Only 14 grants were higher, between £1,000 and £5,000. Arts grants were given to:
Glyndebourne Arts Trust (£5,000);
English National Opera (£2,000);
National Art Collections Fund (£1,000);

British Youth Opera, Blackheath Concert Halls, Kent Opera, Deal Summer Music Festival, Nomad Players, Artsline, Rehearsal Orchestra, English Chamber Orchestra & Music Society, Yehudi Menuhin School, Royal Academy of Music, British Federation of Festivals for Music, Dance and Speech, Artlink, Council for Music in Hospitals (£500).
Fifteen other arts grants of £250 each were given, all for music or opera. Individuals are supported.
Applications: In writing to the correspondent. The trustees meet a approximately 12 times a year.

The Golden Bottle Trust

37 Fleet Street, London EC4P 4DQ

Tel: 0171-353 4522
Contact: The Secretary
Trustees: Messrs Hoare Trustees
Grant total: £169,000 (1994)
Beneficial area: UK.
General: The trustees make a wide range of grants for medical, environmental, social welfare, arts and other causes.
In 1994 over 175 grants, ranging between £100 and £10,000, were made. The majority were small and under £1,000. Arts grants totalling £7,250 (4% of grant-aid) were given to:
Royal Academy of Music (£2,500);
Floating Point Science Theatre, Royal Albert Hall Trust (£1,000 each);
Natural History Museum Development Trust, Orchestra of Age of Enlightenment (£500 each);
Music Dept St Paul's Cathedral, International Animation Festival, North Kensington Video/Drama Project, Weald and Downland Open Air Museum, National Art Collections Fund, London Handel Society, Proms Charity Gala (£250 each).
Exclusions: No grants to individuals and organisations which are not registered charities.
Applications: In writing to the correspondent who has stated "Trustees meet on a monthly basis, but the funds are

already largely committed, and therefore, applications from sources not already known to the trustees are unlikely to be successful".

The Goldsmiths' Company's Charities

Goldsmiths' Hall, Foster Lane, London EC2V 6BN

Tel: 0171-606 7010
Contact: R D Buchanan-Dunlop, Clerk
Trustees: The Goldsmiths' Company
Grant total: £293,000 (1994)
Beneficial area: UK, with a special interest in London charities.
General: Its objects cover:

1. General support of goldsmiths, silver-smiths and jewellers;
2. Support of Greater London residents and charities;
3. General charitable purposes.

Preference for national or London-based charities. The charities support the Goldsmiths' Arts Trust Fund whose income is used mainly for the mounting of exhibitions. In 1994 arts grants were given to:
Goldsmiths' Arts Trust Fund (£100,000);
London International String Quartet
 Competition (£17,500);
City Music Society (£14,805);
Goldsmiths' Craft Council (£11,163);
Birmingham Museum and Art Gallery, British
 Museum, V & A Museum(£5,000 each);
National Museum of Wales (£4,000);
National Youth Orchestra (£3,000);
City of London Festival (£2,500);
Elgar Birthplace Appeal (£2,200);
Leeds City Art Galleries (£2,000);
Salisbury & South Wilts Museum (£1,500);
Brooklands Museum Trust, Council for
 Music in Hospitals (£1,000).
A number of grants of under £1,000 were also made. The company is prepared to consider applications towards capital costs: equipment purchase, building renovation and new buildings.
Exclusions: Students, provincial local appeals, endowment appeals.
Applications: In writing to the Clerk, including in the application: registered

charity number; latest annual report and full audited accounts; name of two independent referees (initial application only); object of the appeal; appeal target and amount needed to meet it; major grant-making organisations approached and results to date; preference for a single grant or for annual grants for up to three years.

No organisation, whether successful or not, will have more than one appeal considered every three years.

The Gosling Foundation

21 Bryanston Street, London W1A 4NH

Tel: 0171-499 7050
Contact: A E Broomfield, secretary
Trustees: Sir Donald Gosling, R F Hobson
Grant total: £1,533,000 (1993/94)
Beneficial area: UK.
General: The foundation makes grants to a range of charitable causes including social welfare, medical, and educational charities. The arts are clearly not a priority, but a few arts grants are made each year. No list of grants accompanied the foundation's accounts for 1993/94 on public file at the Charity Commission. These showed a large increase in grant-aid to £1.5 million from £634,000 in 1992/93.
Arts grants in 1992/93:
Bodleian Library (£75,000 with £100,000 in
 the previous year);
Entertainment Artistes Benevolent Fund
 (£2,000);
Liverpool School of Performing Arts
 (£1,000);
London City Ballet Trust (£700).
In 1991/92 the British Youth Orchestra
 received £20,000.
Applications: In writing to the correspondent.

The Granada Foundation

Granada Television Centre, Manchester M60 9EA

Tel: 0161-832 7211
Contact: Kathy Arundale
Trustees: Advisory Council: Sir Robert Scott (Chair), Professor F F Ridley, Margaret

Kenyon, Alexander Bernstein (trustee), Colin Hubbard (trustee), Professor Denis McCaldin, Professor T Husband, Carl Hawkins,

Grant total: £137,000 (1994/95)

Beneficial area: North-West England

General: The foundation's objects are:

1. To encourage the study and practice of the fine arts and sciences
2. To assist in provision of leisure facilities

gives a combination of one-off and recurrent grants to non-statutory projects.

General running costs are not usually covered and the foundation prefers to support registered charities. Grants range between £100 and £10,000 but most are of £1,000 or more. There is a clear preference for new projects.

In 1993/94 arts grants included:

Manchester, City of Drama (£50,000, 2nd of 2);

Chetham's Library, Manchester (£15,000, 1st of 2);

Greater Manchester Arts Centre for 2 exhibitions at the Cornerhouse (£10,000);

Royal Exchange Theatre, Brouhaha International Festival Liverpool, Manchester Camerata for "Myths & Masques" educational project (£5,000 each);

Octagon Theatre Trust, Bolton, equipment for studio development (£2,500);

Morecombe Youth Band for instrument purchase, Horse and Bamboo Theatre (£1,000 each);

Buxton Festival Fringe (£600);

North West Playwrights, for workshops (£500).

Exclusions: No grants to individuals or for courses of study, youth clubs, community associations, expeditions, overseas travel, general appeals.

Applications: In writing to the correspondent, giving brief details of the project. Application forms and guidelines are available. The advisory council meets quarterly to consider applications. all letters are acknowledged.

The Great Britain Sasakawa Foundation

43 North Audley Street, London W1Y 1WH

Tel: 0171-355 2229; **Fax:** 0171-355 2230

Contact: Peter Hand, Administrator

Trustees: Lord Butterfield (Chair), Baroness Brigstocke, Jeremy Brown, David Corsam, Brandon Gough, Dr Peter Mathias, The Earl of St Andrews, Baroness Park, Sir John Whitehead, Kazuo Chiba, Akira Iriyama, Professor Harumi Kimura, Professor Makoto Momoi, Yoshio Sakurauchi, Professor Shoichi Watanabe, Yohei Sasakawa.

Grant total: £579,000 (1994)

Beneficial area: Japan and the United Kingdom

General: The foundation aims to contribute to the education of British people about aspects of Japan and the Japanese about the United Kingdom. Approximately a quarter of grant money is given to cultural projects each year. In 1994 a total of 25 organisations received grants ranging between £500 and £50,000. Examples of arts grants in 1994:

Victoria & Albert Museum, exhibition of contemporary Japanese crafts (£50,000);

Horniman Museum, Japanese garden to surround the pavilion housing the 1910 model of the Taitokuin Museum (£50,000);

National Museums of Scotland, new Far Eastern Gallery in Edinburgh (£30,000);

Fitzwilliam Museum Trust, for post of curator of Japanese prints (£20,000);

Linc Productions, documentary film on Anglo-Japanese relations over the past 150 years (£10,000);

Artists' Agency, visit by Japanese musicians for an Anglo-Japanese music theatre project in Sunderland (£5,000);

Chetham's School of Music, Japanese tour by chamber orchestra (£4,500);

Edith Burge Educational Trust, classes in Japanese art for disabled and disadvantaged children (£2,500);

Gateshead Central Library, first visits of exchange programme with the twin city Komatsu by 2 ceramicists (£2,000);

Passe Partout, tour of Japanese schools by interactive theatre (£1,500);

Musicworks, project to introduce Japanese music to Vauxhall school children (£500).

Exclusions: Individual applications are not accepted, but applications by organisations on behalf of individuals may be considered. The beneficiary organisation must either be British or Japanese and any individual benefiting through grant must be a citizen of the UK or Japan.

Applications: In writing to the correspondent. The letter should outline the project and give full information on the total cost, what other funding may contribute to meet this, and what specific sum is requested of the foundation. The awards committee meets twice a year, in spring and autumn. The administrator can advise on deadlines for applications at these meetings as they are decided.

The Greater Bristol Foundation

PO Box 383, Bank of England Chambers, Wine Street, Bristol BS1 2AH

Tel: 0117-921 1311
Contact: Penny Johnstone, Director; Alice Berrisford, Grants Officer
Trustees: John Burke (Chair), Sir John Wills (Vice-chair), John Avery, Anthony Brown, Douglas Claisse, Stella Clarke, Chris Curling, George Ferguson, Marion Jackson, David Kenworthy, Lady Merrison, David S Norton, John Pontin, Hugh Pye, Andrew Thornhill, Rev Barry Rogerson Bishop of Bristol, Dereth Wood.
Grant total: £121,000 (1994/95)
Beneficial area: Greater Bristol, within ten miles of Bristol Bridge.
General: The foundation supports new and existing models of social and community work by voluntary organisations and encourages community involvement and self-help through the medium of voluntary organisations.

For the period 1996-2000 its "main concerns" are homeless people, disabled people, isolation, young people and safer communities. £5,000 is currently the largest grant made. In 1994/95 the following arts grants were made:

Under **"Isolation"**
Southmead Community Play (£1,000);

Under **"Young People"**
Live Music Now!, performances special schools by young musicians (£1,000 with £2,000 given in the previous year);

Under its small grants scheme of grants up to £500
CRE 8 Theatre Company, for a play written and performed by young people recovering from addiction (£500);
Oily Cart Co/Grimsbury Park School, for production in a school for children with learning difficulties (£250);
Red Ladder, theatre project with young people (£200).

Exclusions: No grants to individuals, general appeals, overseas travel, independent schools, direct replacement of government funds, organisations without permanent presence in Greater Bristol. Vehicles, conferences and exhibitions are unlikely to be funded.

Applications: Applicants should first obtain the foundation's booklet on grant-making policy and guidelines. All organisations are encouraged to talk to the director or grants officer before making a formal application. Application forms are available from the above address. Organisations are expected to show a commitment to equal opportunities. Grant committee meetings are held quarterly, in January, April, July and October. Application forms must be received at least one month before committee meetings.

The Grocers' Charity

Grocers' Hall, Princes Street, London EC2R 8AD

Tel: 0171-606 3113
Contact: Miss Anne Blanchard, Charity Administrator
Trustees: The Grocers' Trust Company Ltd.
Grant total: £221,000 (July 1995)
Beneficial area: UK.
General: The charity has general charitable objects and a national scope. "The Arts" are identified as a specific category of

grant-making but they are not given major support. Consideration is given to request for grants towards capital costs. In 1994/95 the charity gave 4. 5% (£10,000) out of a total of £221,000 to arts activities which included the following grants:

Shakespeare Globe Theatre (£5,000);
Live Music Now!, British Youth Opera
    (£1,500 each);
Royal School of Church Music (£750);
Theatre Royal Stratford East Education
    Department, Union Chapel Project (£500
    each);
Royal Shakespeare Theatre Trust (£300).

Exclusions: Organisations which are not registered charities. It is unusual for grants to be made to individuals.

Applications: In writing to the correspondent, accompanied by a copy of latest audited accounts. The trustees meet four times a year, in January, April, June and November. Informal enquiry by telephone is encouraged.

The Gulbenkian Foundation

98 Portland Place, London W1N 4ET

Tel: 0171-636 5313; Fax: 0171-637 3421
Contact: Ben Whitaker, Director
Trustees: The foundation's Board of Administration in Lisbon.
Grant total: £2,013,000 (1994)
Beneficial area: UK and Ireland.
General: Background: The Calouste Gulbenkian Foundation was established in 1956, a year after the death of the founder, Calouste Sarkis Gulbenkian, an Armenian who became a British citizen, but who eventually settled in Portugal. The UK branch of the foundation deals with grant applications for projects in the UK and the Republic of Ireland, and normally only with projects whose principal beneficiaries are people in these countries. (Other applications should be addressed to: The International Department, Calouste Gulbenkian Foundation, Avenida de Berna 45A, 1093 Lisbon, Portugal).
Policy: Readers should note that the policy priorities within each of the foundation's main sectors of giving can change in some respects each year. Applications should always ask for a free copy of the foundation's *'Advice for Applicants'*. The policy information given below concerns 1995 whilst the grant examples are for 1994.

Preference is given to original new developments, not yet a part of the regular running costs of an organisation; and to projects which are either strategic, such as practical initiatives directed to helping tackle the causes of problems; or seminal, because they seem likely to influence policy and practice elsewhere, and are projects which are of more than local significance.

Good applications from outlying rural areas, or from places outside London and south-east England, or which particularly assist women, are welcome.

The foundation particularly favours applications which include plans for an independent evaluation.

Arts
Assistant Director, Arts - Sian Ede
This programme deals with arts for adults. The Arts for Young People (up to the age of 25) priority is described under the Education Programme.
Practical Research and Development: support will be available for groups of professional artists to devise and experiment before they perfect a project. Priority will be given to applications which demonstrate some *genuine ground-breaking development for the art-form as a whole*, as well as being challenging for the artists involved;
Creative use of new technologies: applications are invited from arts organisations for projects which demonstrate a practical application of new multimedia technology in developing their art (applications for the use of new technology in arts administration will not be eligible);
Cultural equity: the foundation is interested in encouraging projects which help establish equity in the arts for people from Britain's diverse ethnic groups and disabled people, whether artists or audiences.

Education

Assistant Director, Education - Simon Richey

1. Arts for Young People (up to the age of 25)

Support for the arts in schools

* Governors: initiatives by governor training agencies, or groups of governing bodies, which promote the arts in schools;
* Self-Help: arts initiatives by self-help group of primary and secondary school teachers, including support for such local groups;
* Agencies: help with the establishment, or with the work of, agencies designed to assist schools in promoting the arts;
* Local Communities: arts-based initiatives designed to help primary schools engage more effectively with members of their local communities;
* Key Stage 4: initiatives that encourage young people to pursue the arts in the curriculum beyond the age of 14 and/or initiatives in this area concerned with the exchange of good practice.

Support for the arts 'out-of-school'

* projects initiated by young people, or voluntary/statutory agencies, where the emphasis is on popular culture and/or contemporary media (ie video, radio, film, electronic music, etc);
* projects initiated by the voluntary or statutory Youth Service, or by arts organisations for i) the needs of girls and young women; ii) training youth workers to develop arts activities within a youth work curriculum; iii) training artists to work in Youth Service settings.

2. Educational Innovations and Developments

a) Education for Family Life; b) The ethos of the school; c) Parental involvement in schools; d) Democracy in schools

Social Welfare

Deputy Director and in charge of Social Welfare - Paul Curno

Priority will be given to strategic national and regional proposals which focus on the needs and rights of children and young people (up to 18), and on parent education and support.

Anglo-Portuguese Cultural Relations

Director - Ben Whitaker

This programme aims to help Portuguese cultural projects in the UK and Ireland. (British cultural projects in Portugal are the responsibility of the British Council.)

'Cultural relations' are taken to include social welfare, as well as activities in the arts, crafts and education. The programme includes:

* activities in the UK and the Republic of Ireland concerned with Portugal - its language, culture, people - past and present;
* cultural and educational interaction between British or Irish or Portuguese people;
* the educational, cultural and social needs of the Portuguese immigrant communities (but not individual Portuguese immigrants or visitors) in the UK or the Republic of Ireland.

But grants are not normally given for projects focused on: sporting activities, tourism, holidays and individual exchanges; performances and tours (except sometimes in some educative context); full-time teaching or research posts or visiting fellowships; the maintenance, salary or supervision costs of researchers; attendance at conferences or similar gatherings; fees or expenses of individual students pursuing courses of education and training, or doing research; UK cultural visits to Portugal.

Ireland

The information leaflet does not include advice for the Republic of Ireland Programme which reflects the foundation's arts, education and social welfare priorities in a manner appropriate to the Irish context.

Director's grants may be given to interesting and potentially far reaching projects which fall outside the precise priorities of each of the three main programme areas. An interesting characteristic of this foundation, and one which gives it public influence greater than the scale of its grant-making, is its commissioning of reports and studies. Over the years some of these have been seminal eg the "Robinson Report" on arts and education The foundation also co-publishes with other organisations and occasionally assists an organisation to publish.

Grants in 1994

Arts £536,000 (86 grants)
Education £528,000 (88 grants)
Social Welfare £609,000 (82 grants)
Anglo-Portuguese Cultural Relations £180,000 (26 grants)
Republic of Ireland £160,000 (21 grants)
Total £2,013,000 (303 grants)

A selection from the grant list in the 1994 annual report follows. This is no substitute for obtaining a copy.

Under Cultural Equity

Modern Music Theatre Troupe, towards an opera project in Newham, East London, designed to bring more black Londoners to participate in a community opera production (£3,500);

Magdalena Project, towards their international workshops for women artists in Cardiff (£3,000);

Producers with Attitude (Hall Place Studio, Leeds) towards the first year's development of this black film and media group (£5,000);

Red Ladder Theatre Company, towards a training programme for female Asian arts administrators and stage managers to take (£9,580);

Arts in Rural Areas

The Beaford Coalition, Beaford Arts Centre, for the implementation of the foundation's rural arts policy in north Devon and North Cornwall (£6,000);

Gulbenkian Initiatives

The Arts Catalyst (Old Bull Arts Association, towards the development of a special programme of events designed to bring artists and scientists together to produce science-inspired art works (£10,000);

London School of Puppetry (London Puppet Centre Trust) towards a series of courses to introduce new skills and uses of puppetry to practising puppeteers (£5,000);

Arts for Young People

The Arts Connection, Hampshire, to encourage local schools for disaffected pupils to put drama on the curriculum (£1,225);

Pop-up Theatre, for video and print materials for their work in helping primary school children resolve personal difficulties and conflicts (£5,000);

Music Business Training (Interchange Trust) for a young people's training project music business and related skills (£5,000);

Skylight Circus in Education, training company members to work in youth centres (£1,860).

Exclusions: Individuals; buildings (construction or repair); equipment; performances or exhibitions; stage, film or television production costs; conferences/seminars; university or similar research; funds for scholarships/loans.

Applications: First obtain a copy of the foundation's "Advice to applicants" leaflet. This sets out clearly the information required in a written application (telephone, or in person calls are not encouraged). The majority of grants are for less than £5,000. The notional limit for any one grant of £10,000 is seldom exceeded.

The Hadrian Trust

36 Rectory Road, Gosforth, Newcastle-upon-Tyne NE3 1XP

Tel: 0191-285 9553
Contact: John Parker
Trustees: Richard Harbottle, Brian T Gillespie, John Parker.
Grant total: £156,000 (1993/94)
Beneficial area: Northumberland, Tyne & Wear, Durham.

General: Most grants go towards the running costs of social welfare organisations in the area. Applications for capital or revenue are treated equally. Most of the 162 grants given in 1993/94 were for either £500 or £1,000. Arts grants were given to:

Northern Sinfonia Development Appeal (£9,500);

People's Theatre Arts Group Newcastle, Garielli Trust for Brinkburn Priory Summer Festival, Northumberland Theatre Company, Tyne Theatre and Opera House (£1,000 each);

Hexham Abbey Festival (£500).
Exclusions: General appeals from large national organisations and smaller bodies working outside the beneficial area.
Applications: In writing to the correspondent. Meetings are usually held in October, January, March and July.

J M Haldane's Charitable Trust

Chiene & Tait, 3 Albyn Place, Edinburgh EH2 4NQ

Tel: 0131-225 7515
Contact: J M Haldane
Trustees: J M Haldane, Mrs Haldane.
Grant total: £6,000 (1993/94)
Beneficial area: UK and overseas, with a preference for Scotland and developing countries.
General: The trust generally makes small grants ranging between £50 and £250 to music groups, schools and development agencies. In 1993/94 an exceptional grant was given to the Edinburgh Festival Theatre Trust. Arts grants included:
Edinburgh Festival Theatre Trust (£5,000);
Scottish Opera (£100);
Music at Blair Atholl (£75).
Applications: In writing to the correspondent.

The Paul Hamlyn Foundation

Sussex House, 12 Upper Mall, London W6 9TA

Tel: 0181-741 2812/2847/2749;
Fax: 0181-741 2263
Contact: James Cornford, Director
Trustees: Paul Hamlyn, Helen Hamlyn, Michael Hamlyn, Jane Hamlyn, Robert Gavron.
Grant total: £2,907,000 (1994/95)
Beneficial area: UK and continental Europe, Third World
General: The foundation's support is concentrated on arts, education and book publishing projects in the UK and continental Europe, together with a number of projects in the Third World, mainly in the Indian subcontinent. The main emphasis is on supporting model projects and methodologies which have the potential for being adopted widely.

In 1994/95 a total of £897,000 was disbursed for arts activities. Grants ranged between under £500 to over £250,000. In the field of the arts the foundation is particularly interested in three areas:
Increasing awareness of the arts: At the moment projects funded are mostly those to bring new audiences to arts venues by, for example, subsidising ticket prices, new marketing schemes and effective outreach work. The foundation is interested in learning how far the development of experience and practice within arts venues can be extended to site-specific events outside. Grants in 1994/95 included:
Royal Opera House, for the Paul Hamlyn Westminster Week which will continue to run in 1996 and 1997 until its closure for redevelopment (£175,000 in 1995);
Cinemagic, International Film Festival for Young People (£15,000);
Scottish International Children's Festival, arts access scheme for school audiences (£12,500);
Opera North, audience development in Sunderland (£10,000);
SHAPE London for ticket scheme (£7,500);
Lyric Theatre Hammersmith, summer school for young people (£5,000);
Arts in Education: There are three priority areas: in-service training for teachers; after-school arts activity; collaboration between primary and secondary schools and other local agencies to promote the arts. There is also an on-going interest in developing new arts education agencies. Grants in 1994/95 included:
Tate Gallery Word and Image Programme (£35,000);
Talawa Theatre Company, long-term link-up scheme with schools and colleges (£14,500);
ADiTi, training plan for teachers and dancers (£12,800);
Youth Clubs Scotland, training workers in arts-based skills (£10,000);
Drake Music Project, after school music workshops for disabled children (£7,500);

Community Music, music tutor training course (£7,000);
Pedalling Art (Sustrans), sculptor in residence at a cluster of schools (£3,500).

Support for individual artists: The Paul Hamlyn Foundation Awards for Artists was established in 1993. Each year the foundation concentrates on a particular group of creative artists (in 1995/96 awards went to choreographers, in 1996/97 to visual artists - sculpture and installation). Five awards of £15,000 each are given.

The foundation also provides funds to a number of institutions to award bursaries for particular arts courses eg. Arvon Foundation, bursary scheme for black writers (£10,000). These grants were made for three years and will be reviewed in 1995/96. No other student bursaries are given. Some funding is available to projects supporting individual artists through the provision of information: for example, by the development of databases or through publications.

Exclusions: No grants for purchase or maintenance of property, general appeals, individuals in further education or study trips.

Applications: Guidelines are available from the above address. There is no application form. The relevant arts officers are Camilla Whitworth Jones and Manick Govinda.

Sue Hammerson's Charitable Trust

H W Fisher & Co, Acre House, 11-15 William Road, London NW1 3ER

Tel: 0171-388 7000
Contact: A J Bernstein
Trustees: Sir Gavin Lightman, Patricia Beecham, Richard Mordant, Sydney Mason.
Grant total: £146,000 (1993/94)
Beneficial area: UK.
General: The trust makes grants mainly in the fields of social welfare, medicine, Jewish charities and arts. Each year the Lewis W Hammerson Memorial Home is the major beneficiary receiving the lion's share of grant-aid (£120,000 in 1993/94). The arts organisations supported in 1993/94 are regular beneficiaries:

Royal National Theatre (£2,500);
Royal Opera House (£1,500);
New Shakespeare Company, English National Opera (£1,000 each).

Exclusions: No grants to individuals or organisations which are not registered charities.

Applications: In writing to the correspondent but applications are not encouraged by the correspondent because the funds are heavily committed for the foreseeable future.

The Hampton Fuel Allotment Charity

15 Hurst Mount, High Street, Hampton, Middlesex TW12 2SA

Tel: 0181-941 7866
Contact: A W Goode, Clerk
Trustees: J Webb (Chairman), A Cavan, Mrs J Woodriff, A Wood, H Severn, Dr D Lister, Mrs M Martin, P Simon, A Smith, Rev W D F Vanstone.
Grant total: £2,092,000 (1993/94)
Beneficial area: Hampton, the former borough of Twickenham, and the borough of Richmond
General: Grants are given for relief-in-need, the mentally ill and handicapped, social and medical welfare, housing; schools projects and other council related matters, youth work, community work, recreation and leisure time occupation, education.

Total grant-aid rose by over £1 million between 1993 and 1994. Arts grants may be few but can include some substantial awards. Arts grants in 1993/94:
Teddington Theatre Club (£90,000 approved);
Richmond Music Trust (£12,500);
Hampton Choral Society (£4,500);
Richmond Concert Society (£1,500).

Applications: Application forms are available from the correspondent.

The W A Handley Charity Trust

c/o Ryecroft, Glenton & Co., 27 Portland Terrace, Newcastle-upon-Tyne NE2 lQP

Contact: The Secretaries
Trustees: A E Glenton, D W Errington, D Milligan.
Grant total: £204,000 (1993/94)
Beneficial area: UK, with a preference for Northumberland and Tyneside.
General: The trust has recently stated that grants will normally be restricted to applicants from within the Northumberland and Tyneside area and to national charities operating within or benefiting this area. Grants will be directed in particular towards crisis funding, pump priming finance, operating expenses, alleviation of distress.

Grants range between £250 and £25,000. Most grants are recurrent but a number of one-off payments are also made each years. These totalled £67,000 in 1993/94 and only one arts grant was given. The trust gives to a regular list of four arts organisations. Arts grants in 1993/94:
Northern Opera*, Royal Academy of Arts Trust* (£1,250 each);
Northern Sinfonia*, (£750);
Literary and Philosophical Society*, Newcastle (£600);
People's Theatre Art Group (£500).
* Regularly supported.
Exclusions: No grants to individuals or to organisations which are not registered charities.
Applications: In writing and quoting charity registration number. Trustees meet at the end of March, June, September and December. Applications need to be received by the preceding month.

The Harding Trust

c/o Messrs Lace Mawer, Castle Chambers, 43 Castle Street, Liverpool L2 9SU

Tel: 0151-236 2002
Contact: Peter O'Rourke
Trustees: M E Harding, W F Glazebrook, J S McAllester, G G Wall.
Grant total: £21,000 (1994/5))
Beneficial area: North Staffordshire and surrounding areas.

General: The trust's interests are mainly music and arts-based charities. Some local welfare charities are being given support and consideration will be given to national charities if there is a special reason for doing so. Arts grants in 1994/95:
Stoke & Newcastle Music (£4,000 recurrent);
Lichfield Festival (£3,000);
BBC Philharmonic Education Project, Stoke on Trent (£2,500);
Staffordshire Youth Orchestra, Dudley Piano Competition, Lindsay Quartet, English Haydn Festival at Bridgnorth (£1,000 each);
Keele Concert Society, Orchestra de Camera, Stoke on Trent Young Musicians' Competition (£500 each).
Applications: In writing to the correspondent.

The Kenneth Hargreaves Trust

Bridge End Cottage, Linton, Wetherby, West Yorkshire LS22 4JB

Contact: Mrs Sheila Holbrook
Trustees: Dr Ingrid Roscoe, Mrs Sheila Holbrook, P Chadwick, Mrs Margaret Hargreaves-Allen.
Grant total: £30,000 (1994)
Beneficial area: UK, with a particular interest in West Yorkshire.
General: The trust has a preference for local projects and includes the arts and community amongst its areas of interest along with medical research, education and the environment.

There is no up-to-date information on file at the Charity Commission. Previous information showed a special interest in the Selby Abbey Trust and a payment for a Janet Baker concert there as well as grants to music event in Leeds and to the RSC and Snape Maltings.
Exclusions: No grants to individuals.
Applications: In writing to the correspondent. Trustees meet quarterly.

The R J Harris Charitable Settlement

c/o Messrs Thring & Long, Solicitors, Midland Bridge Road, Bath, Avon BAl 2HQ

Tel: 01225-448494
Contact: J Thring
Trustees: T C Stock, H M Newton-Clare, J L Rogers, A M Pitt.
Grant total: £48,000 (1993/94)
Beneficial area: UK, but with preference for Wiltshire, North Somerset and South Gloucestershire
General: The trust makes grants primarily in the fields of medicine, mental health, social welfare and education, but a few arts grants are made each year. In 1993/94 34 grants were given, 16 of which were to individuals. Arts grants in 1993/94:
Theatre Royal, Bath (£4,000);
Bristol Old Vic Theatre School (£3,000);
Bristol Old Vic (£1,000);
Parnham Trust (£500).
Applications: In writing to the correspondent. Applications are considered at four-monthly intervals.

The Headley Trust (see also the Sainsbury Family Charitable Trusts)

9 Red Lion Court, London EC4A 3EB

Tel: 0171-410-0330
Contact: Michael Pattison
Trustees: Hon Tim Sainsbury MP, Lady Susan Sainsbury, T J Sainsbury, J R Benson, Miss J S Portrait.
Grant total: £1,865,000 (1994)
Beneficial area: UK and overseas.
General: The trust holds a separate Museums, Galleries and Libraries Fund which approved support in 1994 to the National Museums and Galleries on Merseyside (£100,000).

The trustees consider proposals under the following headings (approvals in 1994 shown in brackets):
Arts and the Environment (Home) £501,000;
Arts and the Environment (Overseas) £140,000;
Medical £53,000;
Developing Countries £199,000;

Health and Social Welfare £636,000; Education £235,000.

No information is given by the trust about the size of its grants. The following are a selection of arts organisations supported:

Under "Arts & Environment (Home)"
Dyson Perrins Museum Trust;
Hackney Youth Orchestra;
Lambeth Palace Library;
Manchester City of Drama;
Parnham Trust;
Pimlico Arts and Media Scheme

Under "Education"
North Kensington Video/Drama Project;
Architectural Association School of Architecture

Under "Health & Social Welfare"
Music Therapy Charity Ltd.
Exclusions: No grants to individuals.
Applications: An application to one of the "Sainsbury Family Charitable Trusts" is an application to all. See separate entry for the names of the other trusts and the application procedures.

The Hellenic Foundation

St Paul's House, Warwick Lane, London EC4P 4BN

Contact: S J Fafalios, Honorary Secretary
Trustees: George Lemos (Chairman), C M Frantzis, S J Fafalios, M S Moschos, T E Kedros, G A Tsavliris.
Grant total: £47,000 (1994)
Beneficial area: UK.
General: The foundation supports "education and learning in Great Britain in the cultural tradition and heritage of Greece, particularly education, arts, philosophy and science". Arts grants in 1994:
British Museum Byzantine Exhibition (£7,500);
Cambridge Greek Play (£2,500);
Shoestring Theatre Company, Gate Theatre for "After the Trojan War" (£2,000 each);
Actors Touring company £1,000);
Warburg Institute Library (£1,000 over 4 years);
Teatro Technis (£1,000, annual grant).

Applications: In writing to the correspondent. *All prospective applicants should have projects concerned with the culture and heritage of GREECE only. The foundation receives far too many totally inappropriate approaches.*

The Myra Hess Trust

16 Ogle Street, London W1P 7LG

Tel: 0171-636 4481
Contact: Martin Williams, Secretary
Trustees: Musicians' Benevolent Fund; Management Committee: Professor Yfrah Neaman, Professor Denis Matthews, Susan Bradshaw, Anthony Payne, Roger Vignoles
Grant total: £6,000 (1992)
Beneficial area: UK.
General: To help outstanding young instrumentalists by assistance with purchase of musical instruments, with tuition fees, the cost of first recitals, maintenance at music college. The trust's policy is currently not to make grants for 5th and further years of study, nor for the purchase of instruments for students in the first four years at college. The average grant is £850.
Exclusions: Grants given only to individuals between ages 18-30.
Applications: In writing to the correspondent. The committee meets twice a year to consider applications. Up to eight applicants are auditioned.

The Hilden Charitable Fund

34 North End Road, London W14 0SH

Tel: 0181-603 1525
Contact: Rodney Hedley, Secretary
Trustees: Mrs G J S Rampton, J R A Rampton, Dr D S Rampton, Mrs H M C Rampton, Dr M B H Rampton, Mrs A M A Rampton, Professor C H Rodeck, Elizabeth Rodeck, Marianne Duncan, C H Younger.
Grant total: £466,000 (1993/94)
Beneficial area: UK and overseas.
General: The trustees' main interests are race relations, minorities, penal affairs, homelessness and Third World countries. The fund makes about 150 grants a year, ranging in 1993/94 from £500 to £20,000..

A few arts grants are given each year to organisations working in areas related to the above priorities.
Arts grants in 1993/94:
Under "Penal Affairs"
Clean Break Theatre Company, London Prison Counselling and Creative Trust (£3,000 each);
CAST Creative and Supportive Trust (£2,500);
Burnbake Trust (£1,500);
Brixton Prison/English National Opera (£1,000);
Under "Minorities"
Community Arts Workshop (£2,500).
Exclusions: No grants to individuals or to organisations which are not registered charities.
Applications: Applicants should contact the office for application forms and guidelines. Applicants are requested to complete a short "summary form" (one side of A4) with their request and support their application with further details together with their latest report and accounts and names of other trusts which have been approached. Meetings take place at four-monthly intervals.

The Hinrichsen Foundation

10-12 Baches Street, London N1 6DN

Tel: 0171-253 1638
Contact: Lesley Adamson, Secretary
Trustees: Professor Arnold Whittel (Chairman), Mrs C Hinrichsen, P Strang, K Potter, M Davies, P Standford, Ian Horsbrugh, Stephen Walsh.
Beneficial area: UK.
General: Grants are given to assist composition and performance of new music and for music research. The foundation has recently decided to concentrate on the "written areas" of music. In 1994 50 grants were awarded, nine of which were to individuals. Grants included:
Huddersfield Contemporary Music Festival (£6,000);
MusICA, Park Lane Group (£3,000 each);
Bromsgrove Concerts, Rainbow over Bath (£2,500 each);

Ensemble of the Centre of Microtonal Music, Bath Festival, Composers Guild of GB (£2,000 each);
Scottish Chamber Orchestra, Coull Quartet (£1,500 each);
Shiva Nova, Lontano, Almeida Festival, London Mozart Players (£1,000 each).
Exclusions: No grants for commissioning new works, recordings, degree courses, purchase of musical instruments and equipment. No retrospective grants.
Applications: In writing to the correspondent. Guidance notes on application procedures are available.

The Holst Foundation

43 Alderbrook Road, London SW12 8AD
Tel: 0181-673 4215; Fax: 0171-228 2358
Contact: Colin Matthew, Executive Administrator; Anna Cuddon, Grants Administrator
Trustees: Rosamund Strode (Chair), Andrew Clements, Noel Periton, Bayan Northcott (Consultant), Professor Arnold Whittall, Peter Carter.
Grant total: £244,000 (1993/94)
Beneficial area: Mainly UK.
General: The foundation's objects are the promotion and encouragement of new music, together with the promotion of public knowledge and appreciation of the musical works of Gustav and Imogen Holst, and the study, knowledge and practice of the arts.

The foundation tends to be pro-active rather than reactive. Funds are available almost exclusively for the performance of music by living composers. An awards scheme is offered in most years to performing groups who wish to commission new work. The foundation has historical links with Aldeburgh in Suffolk and is a major funder of new music at the annual Aldeburgh Festival.

There is no list of grants with the foundation's accounts for 1993/94 on file at the Charity Commission so more detailed information has been taken from 1992/93. Grants were then broadly categorised as follows:

General £85,000
NMC £116,000
Holst Awards £10,000.

About 100 grants were given ranging between £200 and £8,000. Examples were:
Aldeburgh Foundation (£8,000);
Huddersfield Festival, SPNM (£4,000 each);
ECAT, Singcircle, Platform 2, Kingdom Records (£2,000 each);
Rainbow over Bath, Women's Playhouse Trust (£1,500 each);
Opus 20, Community Arts Studio, ICA (£1,000 each);
Ebony Steelband Trust, Sonic Arts Network (£500 each);
English Tuba Consort (£400);
Artsline (£100).
In 1991/1992 approximately 100 grants were offered totalling around £90,000. In addition the Foundation has funded the establishment of the recording label NMC Ltd, which received £130,000 during the same year.
Exclusions: No support for recordings or performances of the works of Gustav and Imogen Holst that are already well supported. No funding towards capital costs. No support for postgraduate research, travel or instrument purchase.
Applications: In writing to the correspondent.

The P H Holt Charitable Trust

India Buildings, Liverpool, Merseyside L2 0RB
Tel: 0151-473 4693: Fax: 0151-473 4663
Contact: Roger Morris, Secretary
Trustees: D T Ash, N C Barber, H B Chrimes, I C Laurie, P I Marshall, H J Smeeton, J T Utley, K Wright
Grant total: £338,000 (1993/94)
Beneficial area: Unrestricted, with a preference for Merseyside.
General: The trust supports community, educational, arts, health and maritime charities. Grants are given in the form of recurrent subscriptions, one-off donations and grants spread of a limited period, eg. three years.

In 1993/94 the trust made 318 grants most of them for less than £1,000. About

£230,000 was given to Merseyside organisations and £90,000 elsewhere. Three exceptional period grants of £100,000 each have been made to the Tate Gallery in Liverpool, the National Museums and Galleries on Merseyside and the Royal Philharmonic Orchestra to be paid over a number of years. Other recent arts grants have been given to:

Bluecoat Arts Centre (£20,000);
Brouhaha International, Centre for Arts
    Development Training, Liverpool Play-
    house, Music for Youth (£5,000 each);
Unity Theatre (£1,500);
Africa Oyé, Ariel Trust, Boat Museum,
    Clonter Farm Music Festival, National
    Children's Orchestra, Vivat Trust, North
    West Museums Service (£1,000 each);
Merseyside Youth Dance Forum, Health
    through Arts Charity (£300 each).

Exclusions: No grants to individuals.
Applications: In writing to the correspondent.

The Hornton Trust

Price Waterhouse, Cornwall House, 19 Cornwall Street, Birmingham B3 2DT

Tel: 0121-200 3000
Contact: B Taylor
Trustees: A C Hordern, S M Wall, S W Landale, A R Collins
Grant total: £61,000 (1993/94)
Beneficial area: UK, with preference for the Midlands.
General: The trust gives to a wide range of charitable causes particularly in the Midlands and every year gives a number of arts grants. Arts grants in 1993/94:

New English Orchestra (£2,000);
Birmingham Repertory Theatre (£1,750,
    also given in the previous year);
Dudley Pianoforte Competition (£1,000);
Ironbridge Gorge Museum, Stedfast Band,
    Mid Wales Opera (£500 each).

Exclusions: No grants to individuals.
Applications: In writing to the correspondent.

The John & Ruth Howard Charitable Trust

c/o 93 High Road, London NW10 2TB

Tel: 0181-459 1125
Contact: A S Atchison, Secretary
Trustees: A S Atchison, N O Feldman, J H Hillier, R N Hobson.
Grant total: £50,000 approx (1995/96)
Beneficial area: England and Wales.
General: The trust's grants were categorised as follows in its accounts for 1992/93 when £70,000 was disbursed: Archaeology £19,700; Preservation/ protection of public buildings £30,800; Choral, choir school and associated music £6,500; General £13,900. There was no grant-list. Examples of arts grants from the previous year were:

Chelmsford Cathedral, for music (£5,000);
Questors Ltd (£4,000);
Royal School of Church Music (£3,000);
Historic Churches Preservation Trust
    (£2,500).

Exclusions: Individuals, national charities.
Applications: In writing to the correspondent.

The Robin Howard Foundation

The Place, 17 Duke's Road, London WC1H 9AB

Contact: Ms J Eager, Secretary
Trustees: Robert Cohan (Chair), R Alston, Janet Eager, Emma Russell, Baron Russell of Liverpool, Peter Lumsden, David Burnie.
Beneficial area: UK.
General: The foundation promotes education in all aspects of dance, and in particular:

♦ makes grants to individual dance artists to enable them to carry out new projects or further their artistic development;

♦ presents public performances and events;

♦ encourages artists, especially dance artists, to carry out contemporary and innovative projects and to provide them with opportunities to perform publicly.

In November 1995 the foundation presented a special performance of work by the choreographer Charles Lineham at The

Place, intended as the first of an annual event for a choreographer.
Exclusions: No capital grants.

The Idlewild Trust

54 Knatchbull Road, London SE5 9QY

Tel: 0171-274 2266
Contact: Ms Lyn Roberts, Administrator
Trustees: Dr G Beard (Chair), Mrs P Minet, H J Parratt, Mrs F Morrison-Jones, Mrs A Grellier, M H Davenport, J Goodison.
Grant total: £148,000 (1994)
Beneficial area: UK.
General: The trust's objects are:
1. Advancement of education and learning and encouragement of music, drama and the fine arts.
2. Preservation for the benefit of the public of lands, buildings and other objects of beauty or historic interest of national importance.
The funding and number of grants was broken down in 1994 as follows:
Performing Arts £42,800 21 (31%)
Preservation £71,450 34 (49%)
Museums & Galleries £10,000 2 (3%)
Fine Arts £17,000 6 (9%)
Conservation £2,500 2 (3%)
Miscellaneous £4,035 4 (5%)

Examples of arts grants in 1994:
National Youth Orchestra (£10,000);
Museum of Empire & Commonwealth (£8,000);
Voices Foundation (£6,000);
Central School of Ballet, Hallé Concert Society (£3,000 each);
Circus Space, Musicworks Music Resource Centre, Sir John Soane's Museum (£2,500);
Oxford Bach Choir, Oxford Playhouse (£2,000 each);
Royal Northern College of Music, Malvern Festival (£1,500);
Clonter Music Farm Trust, Gregynog Festival, South West Jazz (£1,000 each);
Pop-up Theatre (£750);
Plain Clothes Productions (£500).
Exclusions: No grants to individuals or to organisations which are not registered charities.

Applications: In writing to the correspondent, enclosing audited accounts. Unsuccessful applications will not be acknowledged unless SAE has been enclosed. Trustees' meetings are usually held in April, August and December.

The INTACH (UK) Trust

10 Barley Mow Passage, London W4 9PH

Tel: 0181-994 6477
Contact: The Secretary
Trustees: B K Thapar (Chairman), J B Dadachanji, Dame J Jenkins, Sir B M Fielden, Sir J Thomson, S W Skelton.
Grant total: £48,000 (1993)
General: The trust was created by a transfer of over £1 million from the Indian National Trust for Art and Cultural Heritage (INTACH). It is concerned with preserving India's art both inside and outside India and concentrates on history, art and literature. Its funding in 1993 covered:
Stipends and travel of students and scholars (£20,000);
Grants to INTACH conservation (£18,000);
Documentation of British Library/Indian art objects in UK (£10,000).
Applications: In writing to the correspondent.

The Inverforth Charitable Trust

The Farm, Northington, Alresford, Hampshire SO24 9TH

Tel: 01962-732205 (emergencies only)
Contact: E A M Lee, Treasurer and Secretary
Trustees: Elizabeth Lady Inverforth, Lord Inverforth, Mrs Jonathan Kane, Michael Gee
Grant total: £208,000 (1994)
Beneficial area: UK.
General: The trust's emphasis is on care, in the areas of physical and mental health, hospices, youth and education, disabled and elderly people, and specialist caring charities (£148,000 - 71% of total in 1994). Music, opera and other performing arts (£48,000 - 23%) and heritage (£12,500 - 6%) make up the balance.
The trustees like to support smaller

national charities and are willing to make grants towards administrative costs as well as for projects. Most grants are for £500 or £1,000, with a few larger grants deriving from long-standing connections, from a list of about 60 "core" charities. The majority of grants are to previous recipients. However no commitments for more than a year are made to any charity. Each has to apply every year.

The 33 arts grants in 1994 included:
Aldeburgh Festival (£20,000);
Spitalfields Festival (£2,500);
Rehearsal Orchestra (£2,000);
Live Music Now! (£1,500);
Bucks County Museum, Cambridge Arts Theatre, Centre for Young Musicians, City of London Festival, Clonter Farm Music Trust, Ernest Read Music Association, Guildhall School of Music and Drama, Lincoln Cathedral Music Appeal, London Sinfonietta, London Handel Society, Molecule Theatre, Music for Youth, National Youth Orchestra, Opera Factory, Salisbury Festival, Sixteen Choir and Orchestra, Tricycle Theatre, Welsh National Opera (£1,000 each);
The OPERAting Theatre, British Youth Opera, Park Lane Group, Young Vic (£500 each).

Exclusions: No grants to individuals or to organisations which are not registered charities. Small localised charities are also excluded.

Applications: In writing to the correspondent, including accounts, at least a month before meetings. . A summary is prepared for the trustees, who meet quarterly, in March, June, September and early December. Replies are normally sent to all applicants. Allow up to four months for answer. "The correspondent receives about 1,000 applications a year, and advises of a very high failure rate for new applicants."

The Ireland Funds

20-22 College Green, Dublin 2
Tel: 003531-679 2743;
Fax: 003531-677 1850
Trustees: Dr Maurice Hayes (Chairman).
Grant total: £1. 5 million
Beneficial area: Ireland.
General: At present there are nine independent funds in America, Australia, Canada, Great Britain, France, Germany, Japan, South Africa and New Zealand. The purpose of the funds is to raise money for the promotion of peace, culture and charity throughout Ireland. "From 1993 to 1995 inclusive resources are being targeted on programmes which are specifically designed to develop positive responses to conflict in Northern Ireland, unemployment, inner city disadvantage and rural depopulation. In particular the funds are interested in stimulating local leadership, fostering self-help, promoting women's contribution to society, encouraging young people's creativity and generally promoting renewal, rejuvenation and regeneration."

During 1993 to 1995 the funds focused on three programme areas: reconciliation; arts development; community development/enterprise/leadership. Where a project involved more than one of the areas, the advisory council decided the heading it should come under.

Grants ranged in size from £5,000 to £30,000. Most grants were one-off. However, a project may receive support over three years if the need is clearly demonstrated.

At the time of compiling this guide the funds had not decided whether the support for the arts would continue as in the past or whether a totally new policy should overtake it. Interested organisations should contact the office for up-to-date information.

Exclusions: Grants are not given for general appeals, purchase of buildings or land, capital costs for equipment, major construction or repairs to buildings, individuals, purchase of vehicles, travel or transport costs, choirs or bands, projects

not based in Ireland, replacement of statutory funding, general administration of national or provincial organisations.
Applications: Detailed guidelines and application forms are available from the above address. All applications are centrally processed through the Dublin office of the Ireland Funds and are considered three times a year.

The Sir Barry Jackson County Fund

7 Sir Harry's Road, Birmingham B15 2UY
Tel: 0121-440 2572
Contact: C R Graham Winteringham
Trustees: C R G Winteringham (Chairman), R S Burman (Hon Secretary), I A King (Hon Treasurer), plus 10 other trustees.
Grant total: £63,000 (1993/94)
Beneficial area: West Midlands
General: The trust gives grants for drama and theatrical production (including all manual, technical and artistic skills associated with theatre production). Its major support over many years has been to Birmingham Repertory Theatre. In 1993/94 it made seven grants to:
Birmingham Repertory Theatre Company (£50,000 with £47,000 in the previous year);
Theatre Absolute (£2,200);
Banner Theatre Co Ltd (£2,000);
Foursight Theatre Ltd, Round Midnight Theatre Company (£1,000 each);
Music theatre (£600).
Exclusions: No funding of buildings or equipment.
Applications: In writing to the correspondent.

The John and Rhys Thomas James Foundation

Pantyfedwen, 9 Market Street, Aberystwyth SY23 1DL
Tel: 01970-612806
Contact: Richard H Morgan, Executive Secretary
Trustees: Professor G L Rees (Chairman) plus 24 other trustees.

Grant total: £40,000 (1994/95)
Beneficial area: Wales.
General: The foundation mainly makes awards to eisteddfodau (88% of total grant-aid in 1994/95). Other grants are given to churches to buy overhead projects and to Sunday Schools for the purchase of resource materials.

The foundation may amalgamate with its larger sister organisation, the Catherine, Lady Grace James Foundation which disbursed £205,000 in 1994/95.
Exclusions: Organisations which are not registered charities.
Applications: Application forms are available. Trustees meet in March, May, August and December.

The Japan Festival Fund

6th Floor, Morley House, 314 Regent Street, London W1R 5AH
Tel: 0171-580 8149; Fax: 0171-636 3089
Contact: Anne Kanedo, Executive Director
Trustees: Directors: Sir Kit McMahon (Chairman), Sir High Cortazzi, Graham McCallum, Sir Peter Parker.
Grant total: Awards: £37,000 (1995)
Beneficial area: UK
General: The Japan Festival Awards were established as a lasting reminder of the Japan Festival 1991. Each year awards are made for recent outstanding achievements in furthering the understanding of Japanese culture in the United Kingdom. Both organisations and individuals are eligible. For the purpose of the award the term "culture" covers the visual and performing arts, music, literature, sports, media and education.

The number and value of prizes each year is entirely at the discretion of the directors who judge the entries. The 1995 awards included:
Artangel, for Tatsuo Miyajima's installation "Running Time" at the Queen's House, Greenwich (£10,000);
Case TV, for a series of geography pro-grammes for secondary schools for BBC Schools (£5,000);

Yorkshire Sculpture Park, for exhibition of Kan Yasada's sculptures (£5,000);
Butoh Kinoko and Chisenhale Dance Space for their "East Winds Festival of New Butoh" (£2,000);
UK-Japan Music Society (£1,000).
Applications: Candidates may be nominated by an independent or may nominate themselves. In either case their application must be supported by two referees (one of whom may be their nominator). The event/project must have taken place, for a 1996 award, between 1st April 1995 and 31st March 1996. Entries for the 1996 awards had to be received no later than 1st April 1996.

Application forms must be used. The finalists are selected in May with the winners announced in June.

The John Jarrold Trust Ltd

Messrs Jarrold & Sons Ltd, Whitefriars, Norwich, Norfolk NR3 1SH

Tel: 01603-660211
Contact: G. Bloxsom, Secretary
Trustees: Directors: R E Jarrold, A C Jarrold, P J Jarrold, Mrs D J Jarrold, Mrs J Jarrold, Mrs A G Jarrold, Mrs W A Jarrold
Grant total: £153,000 (1993/94)
Beneficial area: UK and overseas but with a strong preference for East Anglia
General: The trust makes grants to a wide range of charities in Norwich and East Anglia. About 200 grants are made ranging generally between £100 and £10,000. It has a particular interest in education and research in the natural sciences.

In 1993/94 arts grants totalling some £32,000 were given to:
Norwich Cathedral Choir Endowment, Norwich Arts Centre, Norwich Playhouse (£5,000 each);
Norfolk & Norwich Festival (£4,000);
Norfolk Museums (Norman Exhibition), Sewell Barn Theatre (£2,500 each);
Museum of the Broads, UEA School of Music Concert (£2,000);
Norfolk Opera Players (£1,000);
Maddermarket Theatre, Opera de Camera, Music at Georges, Norfolk & Norwich

Music Club, Tiebreak Touring Theatre (£500 each);
Nutmeg Theatre, Adam and Eve's Theatre (grants under £500).
Exclusions: Organisations which are not registered charities.
Applications: In writing to the correspondent.

The Jenour Foundation

Fitzalan Court, Newport Road, Cardiff CF2 ITS

Tel: 01222-481111
Contact: Karen Griffin
Trustees: P J Phillips, G R Camfield.
Grant total: £51,000 (1993/94)
Beneficial area: UK, with a particular interest in Wales.
General: The trust gives to a wide range of causes in Wales particularly those working in the fields of health and disability. In 1993/94 31 grants were given ranging between £500 and £5,000. A small number of arts grants are given each year. In 1993/94 these were:
Welsh National Opera (£2,500 and in the previous year);
Vale of Glamorgan Festival, Welsh St Donat's Art (£500 each and in the previous year);
Old Library Fundraising Project (£250).
There seems to be little leeway for new projects as many grants are recurrent.
Applications: In writing to the correspondent.

The Jerusalem Trust *(see also Sainsbury Family Charitable Trusts)*

9 Red Lion Court, London EC4A 3EB

Tel: 0171-410 0330
Contact: Michael Pattison
Trustees: Hon Tim Sainsbury MP, Lady Sainsbury, V E H Booth MP, Rev T Dudley-Smith, Mrs Diana Wainman.
Grant total: £2, 408,000 (1994)
Beneficial area: UK And overseas.
General: The trust supports Christian work in evangelism and relief work (at home and overseas), media, education and art.

In 1994 six art grants were approved totalling £87,000 were agreed for the following organisations (no information was given about the grant sizes):
Art Christian Enquiry Trust
Two publishers for Christian art books
Greenbelt
New Art CentreSt Paul's Harringay.
Exclusions: No grants to individuals.
Applications: An application to one of the "Sainsbury Family Charitable Trusts" is an application to all. See the separate entry under "Sainsbury" for the address and guidelines.

The Jerwood Foundation

22 Fitzroy Square, London W1P 5HQ

Tel: 0171-388 6287
Contact: Dr Patricia Morison, Development Executive
Trustees: Alan Grieve (Chairman), Dr Peter Marxer, Dr Walter Kieber.
General: The foundation is registered in Liechtenstein rather than in the UK but has its representative office in London and makes grants principally in the fields of the arts, further education, conservation (of artefacts rather than the natural environment), and medicine. The foundation awards the Jerwood Painting Prize "to celebrate the excellence of living British painters" (£30,000). Recent arts support includes:
Sole sponsor of the National Art Collections
  Fund Prizes;
The Conservation Awards, in association
  with the Conservation Unit of the
  Museums & Galleries Commission;
National Youth Chamber Orchestra,
  principal sponsor;
Young Documentary Film Makers Awards,
  with the National Film and Television
  School;
Young Choreographers Awards;
Jerwood Foundation Prize for the Applied
  Arts, in association with the Crafts
  Council (£15,000);
Royal Court Season of Young Writers. The acknowledgement by the Royal Court Theatre says that the foundation "from its

inception in 1977 has been concerned with the welfare of young people and supported excellence and achievement.
The foundation has a strong commitment to the visual and performing arts and to the support and encouragement of young artists and through them to contribute to the education and culture of a wide audience".
Exclusions: Individuals, building or capital equipment projects, religion, sport, projects with a specifically local application.
Applications: In writing to the correspondent. There is no application form.

The K C Charitable Trust

c/o Kleinwort Benson Private Bank, PO Box 191, 10 Fenchurch Street, London EC3M 3LB

Contact: Mr N Kerr-Sheppard
Trustees: Kleinwort Benson Trustees Ltd
Grant total: £8,000 (1994)
Beneficial area: Principally Scotland and in particular the Edinburgh area.
General: Preference for small local charities concerned with drug abuse, medical research, children/youth, the unemployed and the aged. Arts organisations are regularly represented in the annual lists of grants. Regular and one-off grants are offered and range between £10 and £2,000.
In 1994 the trust gave all its grant-aid to the Brook Advisory Centres. However in the previous year when £45,000 was disbursed, five arts grants were made to:
Scottish Opera (£5,000);
Traverse Theatre (£2,000);
Scottish Chamber Orchestra, Scottish
  National Orchestra Endowment (£1,000
  each);
Royal Scottish Orchestra (£500).
Exclusions: No grants to individuals.
Applications: In writing to the correspondent. Applications are considered half-yearly.

The Ilse and Michael Katz Foundation

New Garden House, 78 Hatton Gardens, London EC1N 8JA

Tel: 0171-831 7393
Contact: A D Foreman, Trustees' Accountant
Trustees: Norris Gilbert, Osman Azis.
Grant total: £145,000 (1990/91)
Beneficial area: UK and overseas.
General: In 1990/91, the most recent year for which information is available, the foundation gave 60 grants mostly to Jewish charities with over half its grant-aid allocated to the Federation of Jewish Relief Organisations. Many grants were small. Arts grants totalled some £29,000 (20% of total grant-aid) and were given to:
Glyndebourne Productions Ltd (£20,000);
Glyndebourne Festival Society (£2,500);
Western Orchestral Society (£6,000);
Anna Scher Children's Theatre (£150);
Northern Ballet Theatre (£100).

The Robert Kiln Charitable Trust

15a Bull Plain, Hertford, Herts SG14 1DX

Contact: Mrs Margaret Archer, Secretary to the trustees
Trustees: Mrs S F Chappell, S W Kiln, Mrs B Kiln, Dr N P Akers, Mrs J E Akers
Grant total: £48,000 (1993/94)
Beneficial area: UK and overseas with a particular interest in Hertfordshire and Bedfordshire.
General: The trustees give preference to archaeology, environmental conservation and musical education, but also supports a wide range of other charitable activities. Grants are usually one-off or instalments for particular projects. Salaries are not considered. Grants generally range from £100 to £1,000. In 1993/94 it gave 57 grants totalling £48,000, the largest being £5,000.

The trust states that arts grants are now given only to organisations in Hertfordshire and Bedfordshire. Grants in 1993/94 included:

Hertford Museum (£5,000);
East Sussex Archaeological Museums Project, Hatfield Philharmonia Orchestra, Hertford Symphony Orchestra (£1,000 - £2,000 each);
Avoncroft Museums Development Trust (under £1,000).
Exclusions: No grants to individuals for degree or other educational courses, churches, schools, artistic projects (eg. theatre groups).
Applications: In writing to the correspondent with full details including costings and information about any other support. Receipt of applications is not acknowledged. Trustees meet in January/ February and July/August.

The King's Fund (King Edward's Hospital Fund for London)

11-13 Cavendish Square, London W1M 0AN

Tel: 0171-307 2495; Fax: 0171-307 2801
Contact: Susan Elizabeth, Grants Director
Trustees: The Management Committee (Chairman, S M Gray) under the authority of the President and General Council.
Grant total: £1,879,000 (1994)
Beneficial area: Mainly London.
General: The fund has reorganised its grantmaking. It will continue to make grants of all sizes, some one-off, some spread over a number of years, in the following priority areas:
♦ Equal access to health care
♦ Innovations in primary and community care
♦ Developing quality in London's acute health services
♦ Strengthening the voice of the user
♦ Arts and health
♦ Open category
This organisation was set up nearly a century ago. It takes the widest view of its responsibilities, believing that the future of London's hospitals cannot be separated from that of the NHS generally, or indeed of health care everywhere. Grantmaking is only part of its activity. It is involved in many kinds of development, training and

evaluation in the field of health care, but it does not get involved in clinical research. The fund states that "Projects outside London are only supported under specific grant programmes which are initiated by the fund, usually on an annual basis". Grantmaking is the responsibility of the Grants Committee.

Projects that link the arts and health (priorities for 1994/1997)

"The problem: In recent years there has been a growing interest in the 'holistic' approach to health. While the traditional approach to health looks at the individual and their illness, the holistic approach looks at the whole person and at their relationships with their family, the community and the environment. Within the holistic approach, there is growing evidence that the arts can improve health, both in individuals and in the wider community.

We have limited sums available for applications that want to show the impact of the arts on better health. "Our priorities: We look for applications that:

* will explore, or show, how art and design can create positive surroundings for effective health care; or
* will use the creative arts to improve the health of individuals or communities.

"Grants for arts projects were given in 1994 to:

Public Art Development Trust (£50,000);
Celebratory Arts for Primary Health Care (£7,500);
Theatre in Health Education Trust (£1,000);
Art Money (£500).

Exclusions: Individuals, capital projects (buildings and equipment), general appeals, local work outside London.

Applications: In writing after obtaining the detailed guidelines. Applications are considered at least five times a year, but they need to be submitted three months before the meeting concerned and at least four months before the project starts. The fund suggests that prospective applicants first contact the Grants Department to make sure the project fits the priority areas.

The Kingsmead Charitable Trust

Enigma Productions, Pinewood Studios, Pinewood Road, Iver, Bucks SLO ONH

Tel: 01753-849577
Contact: S A Norris, Administrator
Trustees: David Puttnam, Patricia Puttnam.
Grant total: £22,000 (1992/93)
Beneficial area: UK.
General: This new trust was established by David Puttnam, the film producer, in 1991. Its grants are directed at a variety of causes with a preference for medical charities and the arts evident at this stage. Arts grants have included:

National Film and Television School, Walter Powell School (£5,000 each);
RADA, Live Music Now! (£1,000 each).

Applications: Donations are rarely made to any charity with which the trustees are not directly involved.

The Dolly Knowles Charitable Trust

Hays Allan Chartered Accountants, Southampton House, 317 High Holborn, London WC1V 7NL

Tel: 0171-831 6233
Contact: The Secretary
Trustees: M E Demetriadi, Miss B R Masters J D Marnham, Miss S E Stowell.
Grant total: £7,000 (1994/95)
Beneficial area: UK and Southern England.
General: Support for drama, music and dancing as well as animal welfare. Most grants are around £500. Each year the trustees support a list of charities which rarely changes. This trust has the same trustees and correspondence address as The Scouloudi Foundation (see separate entry). Grants in 1994/95 were given to:

Ballet Rambert, Kent Youth Music Associa-tion, National Folk Music Fund, National Youth Orchestra, Rehearsal Orchestra, St Albans Chamber Choir, Young Concert Artists' Trust (£500 each).

Exclusions: No grants to individuals, or for music and drama festivals.

Applications: The trust states that 'no new applicants will be considered for funding in the foreseeable future'.

The John Kobal Foundation

PO Box 3838, London NW1 3JF

Tel: 0171-383 2939
Contact: Simon Crocker and Angela Grant
Trustees: Simon Crocker (Chairman), Zelda Cheatle, Angela Flowers, Rupert Grey, Jenny Hall, Monika Kobal, Liz Jobey, Sir Eduardo Paolozzi, Terence Pepper, Bill Rowlinson, John Russell Taylor, Yolanda Sonnabend, June Stanier.
General: The foundation exists to increase awareness of photographic portraiture. It funds the John Kobal Photographic Portrait Award and Exhibition at the National Portrait Gallery, London and a subsequent tour to Bath and Edinburgh.

Funding is also available for photographers, educationalists, gallery owners and art centres to mount exhibitions or publish publications promoting portrait photography. No single grant is in excess of £2,000.
Applications: Funding is only given to projects directly relevant to portrait photography. Applicants must be 18 years or older. Fuller criteria are available with an SAE.

The Kobler Trust

Stoy Hayward, 8 Baker Street, London W1M 1DA

Tel: 0171-486 5888
Contact: Alfred Davis
Trustees: A Davis, A Xuereb, A H Stone
Grant total: £234,000 (1992/93)
Beneficial area: UK.
General: This trust appears to give for a wide range of charities, including a number of Jewish ones. Its arts grants are not many but interestingly varied. In 1992/93 three arts grants were given to:
Royal Academy of Music (£10,000);
Mountview Theatre School (£2,000 and in the previous year);
Adventures in Motion Pictures (£1,000).

In the previous year grants had been given to Theatre Venture, Tower Hamlets (£8,000) and the Courtauld Institute (£1,000).
Exclusions: No grants to individuals.
Applications: In writing to the correspondent.

The Kreitman Foundation

Citroen Wells, Chartered Accountants, 1 Deveonshire Street, London W1N 2DR

Tel: 0171-637 2841
Contact: Eric Charles
Trustees: Hyman Kreitman, Mrs Irene Kreitman, Eric Charles.
Grant total: £819,000 (1994/95)
Beneficial area: UK and Israel.
General: The foundation supports Jewish charities and the arts. In 1994/95 it gave £684,000 to the Ben Gurion Foundation, 50 grants were under £1,000, 15 grants (seven to the arts) were between £1,000 and £9,999 and five grants between £10,000 and £20,000. Arts grants were given to:
Royal National Theatre (£10,399);
British Friends of Arts Museums in Israel (£4,150);
Tate Gallery (£3,500);
Royal Opera House Trust (£2,500);
British Museum Society, Chicken Shed Theatre, Tricycle Theatre, Friends of the LSO (£1,000 each);
Royal College of Art (£823);
British Israel Arts Foundation (£750);
Friends of Israel Philharmonic (£750).
Exclusions: No grants to individuals.
Applications: In writing to the correspondent. It is understood the foundation does not seek applications.

The Kirby Laing Foundation

Box 1, 133 Page Street, London NW7 2ER

Tel: 0181-906 5200
Contact: R M Harley
Trustees: Sir Kirby Laing, Lady Isobel Laing, David E Laing, Simon Webley
Grant total: £1,322,000 (1994)
Beneficial area: UK and overseas.
General: The foundation makes over 60

grants a year in almost all charity areas with a current interest in medical welfare. The majority of grants are given on a one-off basis and normally range between £2,500 and £60,000 though larger grants may be awarded. The arts are not seen as a main area of giving. In 1994 the foundation gave grants relevant to this guide under a series of categories as follows:

Under "Cultural and Environmental"
Mary Rose Trust (£10,000);
National Art Collections Fund (£5,000 and in the previous year);
Glyndebourne Art Trust (£960);

Under "Children and Youth"
Chicken Shed Theatre (£25,000 and in the previous year);

Under "Education"
British Library (£20,000);
Floating Point Science Theatre, Wimbledon School of Art (£5,000 each and in the previous year);

Exclusions: No grants for individuals, travel or running costs.
Applications: In writing to the correspondent. Only successful applicants will receive a reply. The foundation says that unsolicited appeals are unlikely to be successful.

The Lady Artists Club Trust

c/o McGrigor Donald Solicitors (Reference ENVK), 70 Wellington Street, Glasgow G2 6SB

Tel: 0141-248 6677
Grant total: £1,000 approx (1995)
Beneficial area: Glasgow and the surrounding area.
General: The trust supports the work of women visual artists born, educated, trained or residing within 35 miles of George Square, Glasgow. Each year the trustees give an award to one or more woman artists who, in their opinion, makes a real contribution to the promotion of the visual arts in the West of Scotland.
Exclusions: No awards to students.
Applications: Application forms and further details available from the above

address. The trustees consider completed work and, in particular, future projects

The Langtree Trust

c/o Randall & Payne, Rodborough Court, Stroud, Gloucestershire GL5 3LR

Contact: The Secretary
Trustees: R H Mann, Col P Haslam, E J Coode, Mrs J Humpidge, G J Yates, Mrs A M Shepherd.
Grant total: £40,000 (1994)
Beneficial area: Gloucestershire only.
General: The trust gives to a wide range of causes. All its grants, except one, in 1994 were under £1,000. Arts grants were given to:
Festival Players Gloucester, Five Valley Sounds, Nailsworth Festival, National Waterways Museum, Stroud Museum Association (£250 each);
Gloucester Music Society (£200);
Painswick Music Society, Stroud Festival (£100 each).
Two grants were given to individuals for the purchase of a musical instrument.
Exclusions: Occasional grants for individuals but none for training for higher qualifications. No grants to general appeals from national organisations.
Applications: In writing to the correspondent. Meetings are held every three months.

The Lankelly Foundation

2 The Court, High Street, Harwell, Didcot, Oxfordshire OX11 0EY

Tel: Tel & Fax: 01235-820044
Contact: Peter Kilgarriff
Trustees: Cecil Heather (Chairman), Leo Fraser-Mackenzie, A Ramsay Hack, Mrs Georgina Linton, Wallace Mackenzie, Lady Merlyn-Rees. Mrs Shirley Turner.
Grant total: £2,606,000 (1994/95)
Beneficial area: UK.
General: Arts are not a main priority but the trustees will consider applications which involve and encourage participation, particularly amongst those who get little opportunity to be so involved. The trustees

are working to achieve an equitable geographical balance in their grant-making. At their 1995 policy review they decided to exclude all projects in Greater London until a further review in early 1998.

They retain an interest in innovative programmes of residencies or workshops which bring professional excellence to people isolated by disability or location. Priority is given to small agencies or projects, especially those whose work or location severely limit possible financial support. Grants are aimed primarily at groups or communities who are disadvantaged by poverty or disability, or isolated by age, location or culture. They are made for specific purposes, but may be for capital or revenue needs. They are not made to replace funds which have been withdrawn from other sources.

Grants agreed in 1994/95 and relevant to this guide were:

Under "Arts/Community Arts"

The Blackie - Great George's Cultural Community Project, towards improving disabled access (£47,000 in 2 grants);

Contemporary Dance Trust, workshops in schools (£24,000);

Tobermory Centre, Isle of Mull, towards converting former school to an arts centre (£20,000);

Village Arts, Loftus, Cleveland towards renovation of a building into a community arts centre (£15,000);

Pat Keysall Mime, Scotland, for a residency in Lochilpead (£5,000).

Under "Heritage & Conservation"

National Maritime Museum, Greenwich (£40,000);

National Museums & Galleries on Merseyside Development Trust (£50,000);

Under "Penal Affairs"

Koestler Award Trust (£15,000);

Under "People with Disabilities & Special Needs

ADAPT Trust to help establish a full—time office in Edinburgh (£45,000);

North Yorkshire Music Therapy Centre (£33,000).

Exclusions: No grants for individuals; festivals or theatre productions; research or feasibility studies; conferences/seminars; publications or films.

Applications: The foundation plans well in advance and waiting lists are long. Applicants should include the following information with their initial letter: brief information about origins and present company/charitable status; recent annual report; a description of what you do and/or plan to do; an explanation of why you are seeking our help; a description of what you need and, where necessary, your development plans to meet that need, including information about timescale; detailed up-to-date financial information, including audited accounts and estimates, which covers both your general work and particular need.

One of the staff visits a project prior to preparing a formal submission to the trustees. Applicants are notified of decisions as soon as possible and, if a grant is agreed, of any conditions attached to its release. Groups in receipt of more than one year's funding will be subject to a yearly review which will include a written report and a self-assessment of progress.

A separate application needs to be made to the Chase Charity (see entry) which shares the same administration, but it is rare for both trusts to support the same appeal.

The Leathersellers' Company Charitable Fund

15 St Helen's Place, London EC3A 6DQ

Tel: 0171-588 4615
Contact: The Clerk
Trustees: The Worshipful Company of Leathersellers and the Clerk.
Grant total: £1,250,000 (1992/93)
Beneficial area: UK.
General: The fund supports a wide range of charities under the following categories: Children and youth, medicine and health, education and the sciences, relief of those in need, the arts, the church, the environment, national and international

disasters. Awards are subject to the following criteria:

- Appeals
- Grants must not relieve public funds
- There must be positive evidence of financial need
- Wherever possible there should be proof of a measure of self-help
- Applicants must be able to prove economic use of their resources.

No information about its grants is given with its accounts at the Charity Commission so it is not possible to give more details about the size of grants, the beneficiaries and the likely measure of interest in the arts.

Exclusions: No grants to organisations which are not registered charities.

Applications: In writing to the correspondent. A charity is investigated and visited before an award is made.

The Leche Trust

84 Cicada Road, London SW18 2NZ

Tel: 0181-870 6233
Contact: Mrs Louisa Lawson, Secretary
Trustees: Gillian Wagner (Chair), Primrose Arnander, Ian Bristow, Simon Jervis, John Porteous, Diana Hanbury, Sir John Riddell.
Grant total: £155,000 (1993/94)
Beneficial area: UK.
General: Grants are normally made in the following categories:

1. Preservation of buildings and their contents, primarily of the Georgian period;
2. Repair and conservation of church furniture, including such items as bells or monuments, but not for structural repairs to the fabric - preference is given to objects of the Georgian period;
3. Assistance to the arts and for conservation, including museums;
4. Assistance to organisations concerned with music and drama;
5. Assistance to students from overseas during the last six months of their doctoral postgraduate studies in the UK.

In 1993/94 34% of total funds were given to the Arts. These grants included "£3,606 to the Garsington Opera... several festivals throughout the country, including the Highbury Festival in London and the Presteigne Festival in Wales. Several theatrical productions were also supported with grants". Grants are one-off rather than recurrent and range mainly between £200 and £5,000.

Exclusions: No grants to religious bodies, overseas missions, schools or school buildings, social welfare, animals, medicine, expeditions, British students other than postgraduate music students.

Applications: In writing to the correspondent. Trustees meet three times a year.

The Morris Leigh Foundation

Bouverie House, 154 Fleet Street, London EC4A 2DQ

Tel: 0171-353 0299
Contact: M D Paisner
Trustees: M Leigh, Sir Geoffrey Leigh, A A Davis, Mrs M Leigh, Mrs E C Greenbury, M D Paisner.
Grant total: £109,000 (1992/93)
Beneficial area: UK and overseas.
General: In 1993 about half the grants, including most of the larger ones were given to Jewish charities, with the remainder given to health, welfare and arts causes. Of the 61 grants only 16 were for £1,000 or higher. The great majority were for £500 or less. Arts grants were given to:
British Friends of the Arts Museums (£5,900);
Chicken Shed Theatre (£5,700);
London Philharmonic Orchestra (£2,985);
Royal Northern College of Music (£2,536);
Royal College of Music (£600);
Jerusalem Rubin Academy of Music (£565);
LSO Benjamin Britten Festival (£500);
Friends of the Royal Academy, Glyndebourne Arts Trust (under £500 each).

Applications: In writing to the correspondent.

Lord Leverhulme's Charitable Trust

Coopers & Lybrand Deloitte, Plumtree Court, Farringdon Street, London EC4A 4HT

Tel: 0171-583 5000
Contact: The Joint Secretary
Trustees: R W Neve, Director, The Barbinder Trust.
Grant total: £705,000 (1994/95)
Beneficial area: UK, especially Cheshire and Merseyside.
General: The trust was set up in 1957 by the 3rd Viscount Leverhulme for general charitable purposes. There are two funds within the trust. One generates £30,000 a year which is paid to the Merseyside County Council, the trustees of the Lady Lever Art Gallery. The second is the Lord Leverhulme's Youth Enterprise Scheme: the income from this sponsors young people in the Wirral and Cheshire areas who receive support from the Prince's Youth Business Trust.

In 1992/93 when a total of £439,000 was disbursed about 140 other grants were given, eight of which were large, between £10,000 to £50,000. Fifty grants were between £1,000 and £5,000, 30 grants were between £100 and £999 and 49 minor grants of under £100 were also given. The trust gives to major national appeals and charities in Cheshire and Merseyside. Arts grants in 1992/93 were given to:
National Museums and Galleries of Merseyside (£50,000);
Bluecoat Society of Arts (£20,000 with £2,500 in the previous year);
Bristol Old Vic Theatre School, Little Singers of St Joseph (£1,000 each).
Exclusions: Individuals; organisations not registered as charities.
Applications: In writing.

The Linbury Trust *(see also Sainsbury Family Charitable Trusts)*

9 Red Lion Court, London EC4A 3EB

Tel: 0171-410 0330
Contact: Michael Pattison
Trustees: Lord Sainsbury of Preston Candover, Lady Sainsbury, Miss J S Portrait.
Grant total: £4,919,000 (1993/94)
Beneficial area: UK and overseas.
General: This trust helped with major finance for the Sainsbury extension of the National Gallery. Its other grant-making activities are more difficult to trace. Only a very broad breakdown of its approved grant-aid in categories is given about its actual giving. No information is available about beneficiaries or the size of their grants. Grants *approved* in 1993/94:
Major capital projects £4,550,000
Overseas/third world £1,175,000
Social welfare (including children and young people) £391,000
Arts and arts education £328,000
Chronic fatigue syndrome £291,000
Other medical £222,000
Drugs £174,000
Environment £146,000
Old people £119,000
Education £101,000
Miscellaneous £52,000
Exclusions: No grants to individuals.
Applications: An application to one of the Sainsbury family trusts is an application to all. See address under the Sainsbury Family Charitable Trusts for names of the other trusts and application procedures.

The Lloyds Charities Trust

Lloyds of London, Lime Street, London EC3M 7HL

Tel: 0171-327 5925
Contact: Mrs Linda Harper, Secretary
Trustees: H R Dobinson (Chair), D J Barham, P Barnes, David Beck, Lady Delves Broughton, A W Drysdale, R J R Keeling, M J Wade.
Grant total: £310,000 (1994)
Beneficial area: UK.
General: This trust, established by Lloyds Insurance Brokers, gives a large number of

small grants, mostly of £500 or less, to a wide variety of causes with a particular concern shown for social welfare and the disadvantaged and disabled. The arts are not a priority but a number of arts grants are given each year. In 1994 only eight arts grants were given. These included:
Natural History Museum (£1,000);
National Youth Orchestra of Great Britain (£700);
Artsline (£250).
Exclusions: No grants to individuals.
Applications: In writing to the secretary enclosing a copy of the latest annual report and accounts. Trustee meetings are held in March, June, September and December.

The Lyndhurst Settlement

c/o Bowker Orford & Co, Chartered Accountants, 15-19 Cavendish Place, London WIM ODD

Contact: Michael Isaacs
Trustees: Michael Isaacs, Peter Schofield, Anthony Skyrne
Grant total: £140,000 (1994/95)
Beneficial area: UK and overseas.
General: The settlement has a particular interest in social problems, especially civil liberties, the rights of minorities and protecting the environment. The arts are not a priority but a number of grants, relative to the above interests, are made each year. In 1994/95 these were:
Writers and Scholars Educational Trust (£3,000);
Public Arts, Black Country Museum Development Trust, Colne Valley Museum, Ironbridge Gorge Museum (£2,000 each);
Studio 3 Arts (£1,000).
Grants are usually made for the general purposes of the organisation supported.
Exclusions: Individuals; organisations which are not registered charities. Individuals.
Applications: In writing to the correspondent. (Do not telephone.) An SAE should be enclosed.

The Sir Jack Lyons Charitable Trust

Sagar Croudson, Elizabeth House, Queen Street, Leeds LS1 2TW

Tel: 0113-243 5402
Contact: M J Friedman
Trustees: Sir Jack Lyons, Lady R M Lyons, M J Friedman, J E Lyons.
Grant total: £40,000 (1993/94)
Beneficial area: UK and overseas.
General: The trust makes grants to non-sectarian and Jewish arts and educational projects. Its total grant expenditure has dropped considerably in the past few years. In the field of the arts it is particularly interested in music. Grants ranged between under £100 to £7,600 in 1993/94. Some 50 grants were made most of which were under £1,000.

In 1993/94 nine arts grants totalled over £15,000 and included:
London Symphony Orchestra (£7,600);
Royal Academy of Music (£5,000);
Jewish Music Festival Trust (£3,550);
University of York Music Dept, York Early Music Festival (£500 each);
Chicken Shed Building Fund (£450).
Exclusions: No grants to individuals.
Applications: In writing to the correspondent. 'However, in view of pressure for funds, unsolicited appeals are unlikely to receive a favourable response.'

The Mackintosh Foundation

1 Bedford Square, London WC1B 3RA

Tel: 0171-637 8866
Contact: Sherry Dennehy, Appeals Secretary
Trustees: Sir Cameron Mackintosh, Martin McCallum, Nicholas Allott, D Michael Rose, Patricia MacNaughton, Alain Boubil.
Grant total: £1,183,000 (1994/95)
Beneficial area: UK and overseas.
General: The foundation supports the arts (principally theatre), and charities concerned with AIDS, refugees, medicine, homeless people, education and children and drama training.

The foundation has endowed the study of

contemporary theatre at Oxford University (£1. 25 million) and committed £1 million to the Royal National Theatre Musical Fund for musical revivals (£500,000 still to be paid).

A Drama School Bursary Scheme was set up in 1992. Annual auditions are held. In 1994/95 a total of 226 grants were made. These broke down by size as follows:

£150,000 +	1
£20,000 - £50,000	12
£10,000 - £19,999	25
£5,000 - £9,999	43
£1,000 - £4,999	79
less than £1,000	66

Arts grants included:

Alliance for New American Musical (£187,000);
New Musicals Alliance (£25,000);
Bristol Old Vic Theatre (£30,000);
Actors' Charitable Trust (£20,000);
Children's Musical Theatre of London, Glasgow City Council Dept of Performing Arts (£2,000 each);
Polka Theatre, Sign Dance Theatre (£1,500 each);
Thames TV Theatre Training Scheme Trust, and Theatre Writers' Trust (£1,250 each);
Midnight Theatre Co, Tricycle Theatre, Drama Centre, the Operating Theatre, Tom Allen Arts Centre (£1,000 each).

Exclusions: Religious or political activities.

Applications: In writing to the correspondent. Trustees meet in March and November, but "procedures are in place for grant approval without necessarily having to wait to the half-yearly plenary meetings of the trustees".

The MacRobert Trusts

Balmuir, Tarland Aboyne, Aberdeenshire AB3 4UA

Tel: 013398-81444; Fax: 013398-81676
Contact: The Administrator
Trustees: I G Booth, Air Vice-Marshall G A Chesworth, D M Heughan, A S MacDonald, Dr J Paterson-Brown, A M Scrimgeour; R M Sheriff, A M Summers, Cromar Nominees Ltd
Grant total: £686,000 (1994/95)
Beneficial area: UK, mainly Scotland.

General: There are four MacRobert Trusts which, for the purposes of application, can be treated as one. The trusts support a wide variety of charities. Their main interests are services and sea, ex-servicemen's hospitals and homes. Other interests include education and youth. The arts and music are a regularly supported, though minor area, of the trusts' giving: £25,000 (4%) in 1994/95. The largest grant was: Haddo House Arts Trust (£5,000 pa x 2 years).

Exclusions: Individuals; general appeals.

Applications: In writing including evidence of charity status; clear description of the organisation; its key people; project details with costings, funds raised and promised; latest audited accounts and annual report.

The E D and F Man Charitable Trust

E D & F Man Ltd, Sugar Quay, Lower Thames Street, London EC3R 6DU

Tel: 0171-285 3000
Contact: Ms Anne Cuttill
Grant total: £165,000 (1994/95)
Beneficial area: UK.

General: This company trust has supported a range of causes including social welfare, medical research and art charities. It reviewed its donations policy in 1995 and decided to make fewer, larger donations. Half the available money will go to about 10 selected charities. Grants (totalling 35% of available funds) will be for more than one year. Organisations where staff and pensioners have an involvement will continue to be supported.

The arts in London are expected to receive about 15% of available funds. In 1994/95 some £24,000 was disbursed to arts organisations. These included:

Royal Academy Trust (£5,875);
Royal National Theatre Enterprises (£5,287);
Royal Opera House Trust (£4,500);
London Philharmonic Orchestra (£2,526);
New London Orchestra (£2,000);
Orchestra of the Age of Enlightenment (£1,762);
Westminster Abbey Choir School Foundation (£1,000);

St Paul's Cathedral Choir School Foundation (£750).
Applications: In writing to the correspondent.

The Manifold Charitable Trust

Shottesbrooke House, Maidenhead SL6 3SW

Tel: 01628-825660
Contact: Miss C Gilbertson
Trustees: Sir John Smith, Lady Smith
Grant total: £850,000 (1993)
Beneficial area: UK.
General: The trust makes grants for the preservation of historic buildings, the environment, education, including museums, music, the arts and social causes. The trust's sister charity, the Landmark Trust, restores and organises holiday lettings of historically and architecturally unusual buildings. The 1993 grant to the Landmark Trust (£458,000) absorbed nearly half its grant-aid.

In 1993 its 142 grants were categorised in its annual report as follows:

Preservation	£	%
Historic Buildings	489,200	58
Churches	172,180	20
Education, including museums	53,200	6
Environment	68,000	8
Music, arts, social causes	67,500	8

Exclusions: Organisations not registered as charities.
Applications: In writing to the correspondent, preferably on a single sheet of paper, with details of the project, the amount needed and the amount already raised. If the application is for repair to an historic building, a photograph of it, and a note on its history, should be enclosed. The trust says it is unable to reply to all unsuccessful applicants.

The Michael Marks Charitable Trust

c/o H W Fisher & Co, Acre House, 11-15 William Road, London NW1 3ER

Tel: 0171-388 7000: Fax: 0171-380 4900
Contact: The Secretary
Trustees: Lord Marks of Broughton, Lady Marks, Dr Enis User
Grant total: £171,000 (1994)
Beneficial area: UK.
General: No information is available about its actual grants since 1992 when 15 grants were made ranging between £600 and £56,000. Since it first started making grants in 1967 it has regularly supported Potheinos Ltd, the company of the Little Angel Marionette Theatre in Islington, London. Arts grants in 1992:
National Gallery (£56,000);
Potheinos Ltd (£32,655);
Ashmolean Museum, Oxford (£30,000);
Hellenic Community Trust (£25,000);
Folklore Society (£10,000);
London Library (£2,000);
York Early Music Festival, Malt House Trust (£1,000 each),
Exclusions: No grants to individuals.
Applications: In writing to the correspondent.

The Marsh Christian Trust

Granville House, 132-135 Sloane Street, London SW1X 9AX

Tel: 0171-730 2626; Fax: 0171-823 5225
Contact: The Secretary
Trustees: B P Marsh, M Litchfield, A B Marsh, R J Marsh, N C Marsh.
Grant total: £118,000 (1992/93)
Beneficial area: UK.
General: Support is given to charities working in the fields of social welfare, the environment, animal welfare, healthcare and medical research, education and training, arts and heritage, and overseas appeals. The trust prefers to give long-term core funding to established charities. Project work is not supported. Many grants are recurrent. In 1992/93 over £22,000 was

given to art projects (about one fifth of the total grant-aid. Arts grants in 1992/93:
V & A Museum (£5,000);
Authors' Club Literary Awards Scheme
(£4,514);
National Portrait Gallery (£3,000);
Royal College of Music (£1,490, 2 grants);
Natural History Museum (£1,175);
Slade School of Fine Art (£1,250);
British Museum (£1,000);
Arvon Foundation (£750);
Fan Museum, St Anne's Music Society
(£500 each);
St John's Smith Square London, Live Music
Now!, Friends of the Royal Academy
(£250 each).
Exclusions: No grants to individuals.
Applications: In writing to the correspondent, including a copy of the most recent accounts. The trustees meet every two weeks.

The Martin Musical Scholarship Fund

76 Great Portland Street, London WIN 5AL

Tel: 0171-580 9961; Fax: 0171-436 5517
Contact: Mrs Vivienne Dimant, Administrator
Trustees: Council of Management of the Philharmonia Orchestra Ltd
Grant total: £40,000 (1995)
Beneficial area: UK and overseas.
General: The broad aim of this fund is to assist exceptional young musical talent with specialist and advanced study and to help in bridging the gap between study and fully professional status. In certain cases younger candidates will also be considered. The upper age limit is 25, except for the *Pierre Fournier Award*.

The fund supports individuals and preference is given to United Kingdom citizens; practising musicians as well as students are eligible but these should be instrumental performers, including pianists, preparing for a career on the concert platform either as a soloist or orchestral player. It is not the present policy of the fund to support: organists, singers, conductors, composers, academic students.

Two types of Martin Fund award are made; tuition fees and/or maintenance grants while studying, both in this country and abroad.

An award in the name of the Trevor Snoad Memorial Trust is granted annually to an outstanding viola player under the aegis of the Martin Fund. An award is valid for two years and must be taken up within that time. There is no limit to the number of times unsuccessful candidates may apply. Each candidate is eligible to apply for two awards. *The Pierre Fournier Award* is made biennially to a promising postgraduate 'cellist to assist with the cost of a debut recital. The age limit for this award is 28. Selection of candidates is by audition.
Exclusions: No grants to individuals over the age of 25.
Applications: Selection of candidates is by audition. Application forms are sent to prospective candidates during Summer. Application forms must be submitted by Autumn for consideration for an award for the following financial year beginning in April. Preliminary auditions are held in October or November. Final auditions are held in March. Awards to successful candidates are payable from April. These details do not apply to the Pierre Fournier Award for which there are no set audition periods.

Sir George Martin Trust

Netherwood House, Ilkley, Yorkshire LS29 9RP

Tel: 01943-831019
Contact: Peter Marshall, Secretary
Trustees: T D Coates (Chair), M Bethel, R F Marshall, P D Taylor
Grant total: £267,000 (1992/93)
Beneficial area: UK, with preference for Yorkshire, particularly Leeds and Bradford.
General: The trust principally supports education and social welfare projects. It gives preference to capital rather than to revenue projects, and usually makes one-off grants. In 1992/93 227 grants were given. The trust stated that "many small initiatives were supported particularly in the inner cities of Leeds and Bradford". The arts are

not a priority, but a few arts grants are usually made each year. In 1992/93 they totalled some £25,000 (9%) of grant-aid. Arts grants included:

Brewery Arts Centre Kendal, Eureka
    Museum Halifax (£5,000 each);
Yorkshire Ballet Seminars (£4,000);
Hebden Bridge Little Theatre, Ryedale Folk
    Museum (£2,000 each);
Cook Museum Trust, Harrogate Choral
    Society, Harrogate International Festival
    (£1,500 each);
Leeds Festival Chorus, Live Music Now
    (£750 each).

Exclusions: Individuals; postgraduate courses; publications; seminars; organisations which are not registered charities. The trust does not like to fund projects which were formerly statutorily funded.

Applications: In writing to the correspondent. The trustees meet in June and December each year. Only applications qualifying for consideration by the trustees will be acknowledged. Telephone calls are not encouraged.

The Catherine Martineau Trust

Jock Farm, Little Henham, Saffron Walden, Essex CB11 3XR

Contact: Mr C E M Martineau
Trustees: Charles Martineau, Jane Martineau, Susan Martineau
Grant total: £8,000 (1993/94)
Beneficial area: UK.
General: The trust gives support for relief of poverty and distress, advancement of education and conservation of the national heritage. In 1993/94 eight grants of £1,000 each were given including: Music in Hospitals and the Royal Academy of Music. In the previous year when a similar total of grant-aid was disbursed grants of £1,000 each were given to Cambridge Arts Theatre Trust, Prior's Field Music Appeal and the London Library.
Exclusions: Grants made only to registered charities.
Applications: In writing to the correspondent. The trustees meet in November each year.

The Nancie Massey Charitable Trust

3 Albyn Place, Edinburgh EH2 4NQ

Contact: J G Morton
Trustees: J G Morton, C A Crole, E K Cameron
Grant total: £150,000 (1994/95)
Beneficial area: Scotland, particularly Edinburgh and Leith
General: The trust fund "exists to assist bodies helping the elderly, children, the arts, medicine and education. Assistance is normally only given to projects established in the Edinburgh and Leith areas". It states that in general donations range from £2,000 to £5,000, though larger donations are made on the basis that the trustees may wish to verify how the donation has been spent.

In 1992/93 grants between £300 and £25,000 and were fairly evenly spread over its charitable interests. The largest arts grants given to:

Edinburgh International Festival, Empire
    Theatre Project (£10,000 each);
National Gallery of Scotland (£7,000).

Exclusions: Individuals.
Applications: "All applications must be in writing setting out in detail why an application for assistance is being made, how the donation would be spent and the overall cost of the project. Applications will be acknowledged, confirming whether they will be considered".

The Matthews Wrightson Charity Trust

The Farm, Northington, Alresford, Hampshire SO24 9TH

Contact: Adam Lee, Secretary
Trustees: Miss P W Wrightson, A H Isaacs, G D G Wrightson
Grant total: £58,000 (1994)
Beneficial area: UK.
General: The trustees favour smaller charities seeking to raise under £250,000, and particularly under £25,000, with an emphasis on caring and Christian charities. The largest grant is to the Royal College of

Art for student bursaries. Donations are occasionally made to individuals and students. In 1994 its 142 grants were categorised as follows:

Arts & arts welfare 19%
Homeless & handicapped 21%
Youth 16%
Individuals 10%
Rehabilitation 9%
Medical 7%
International 4%
Others 5%

Grants are mostly recurrent and are made in small amounts (a "unit" is £250) with a few larger grants for long-standing connections. It is understood that in the arts field grants are given only to organisations already known to the trustees. The secretary stated in late 1995 "no new arts organisations are being considered at present".

1994 arts grants:
Royal College of Art, bursaries for students in need (£7,000);
Genesis Arts Trust (£1,000);
Arts Centre Group (£900);
Touchdown Dance (£300);
Witt Library Courtauld Institute, Live Music Now!, Park Lane Group, Rehearsal Orchestra (£250 each).

Exclusions: No support for unconnected churches, village halls, schools, etc. Non-qualifying applications are not reported to the trustees.

Applications: In writing to the correspondent including latest report and accounts. The trustees are sent covering letters only (1-2 pages) monthly, and meet at six-monthly intervals for policy and administrative decisions. Replies are only sent to successful applicants or if a SAE is enclosed. Allow up to two months for this answer.

The Mayfield Valley Arts Trust

65 Rawcliffe Lane, York YO3 6SJ

Tel: 01904-645738
Contact: Delma Tomlin, Administrative Director
Trustees: A Thornton, R J Thornton, Priscilla Thornton, D Whelton
Grant total: £34,000 (1992/93)

General: This trust primarily supports the arts, particularly music. It is understood that grants are offered to individual music students, and for musicians in need as well as to organisations. Grants in 1992/93 were given to:
Sheffield Chamber Music Festival (£22,000 in 4 grants including £1,000 for a children's opera);
York Early Music Festival (£5,000);
Lindsay String Quartet (£4,500);
Live Music Now! (£2,000).
Applications: The trust states that no unsolicited applications are considered.

The McKenna and Co Foundation

McKenna & Co Solicitors, Mitre House, 160 Aldersgate Street, London EC1A 4DD

Tel: 0171-606 9000
Contact: C B Powell-Smith
Trustees: R S Derry-Evans, C B Powell-Smith, Mrs C F Woolf.
Grant total: £61,000 (1993/94)
Beneficial area: UK.
General: The foundation supports a range of charities, particularly those concerned with children, the environment, medical research and social welfare. A few arts grants are also made, some of which are recurrent. There seems to be a preference for music and opera projects, most of them London-based. In 1993/94 a total of 57 grants were given ranging between £100 and £5,000 (apart from one exceptional grant of £18,000 to the City Solicitors Educational Trust). Fifteen arts grants were made, most for under £1,000.

Arts grants were given to:
London Concert Choir, Glyndebourne Opera (£1,000 each);
Aldeburgh Foundation (£750);
London Welsh Male Voice Choir (£600);
Richmond Parish Organ Appeal, Salisbury Cathedral Girl Choristers, Council for Music in Hospitals, Chelsea Opera Group, Shakespeare Globe Trust (£500 each);
Opera Factory (£400);
Royal Shakespeare Company, English National Opera, National Theatre,

London Symphony Orchestra (£250 each).

Applications: The foundation did not wish to have an entry in this guide. It is understood the foundation does not consider unsolicited applications.

The Anthony and Elizabeth Mellows Charitable Settlement

22 Devereux Court, Temple Bar, London WC2R 3JJ

Contact: Professor A R Mellows
Trustees: Professor Anthony Mellows, Mrs Elizabeth Mellows
Grant total: £54,000 (1993/94)
Beneficial area: UK.
General: This trust supports the arts and national heritage; churches of the Church of England; hospitals and hospices; and training and development of children and young people. In 1993/94 only two grants were given under "Arts & Heritage":
Royal Opera House Trust (£11,000 with £12,400 in the previous year);
Royal Academy Trust, for gallery refurbishment (£5,000 with £750 in the previous year);
In the previous year grants were also given to Glyndebourne Festival Trust (£3,200); Dr Johnson's House Appeal (£500).
Applications: Only accepted from national bodies with whom the trustees are in contact.

The Mercers' Company Charitable Foundation

Mercers' Hall, Ironmonger Lane, London EC2V 8ME

Tel: 0171-726 4991
Contact: The Charities' Administrator
Trustees: The Mercers' Company
Grant total: £1,092,000 (1994)
General: The foundation makes grants to a very wide range of charities. The major grants go to five schools connected with the company and for medical research, capital housing and educational building schemes. In 1994 the foundation only listed

its 16 grants of £10,000 and over. Two of these were for arts organisations:
English National Opera (£25,000); Parnham Trust (£10,000).
There were no details about the remainder of its grant-aid (£444,000). In 1992, when £1,177,000 was distributed, about 180 grants were then given. The majority of these (120) were under £1,000. A total of £139,000 (12%) was given to 27 arts organisations:
English National Opera (£35,000);
Arts Council (£13,000);
Royal Academy Trust (£10,000);
Royal Opera House Trust (£9,000);
Textile Conservation Centre (£7,500);
Guildhall School of Dramatic Art, Royal Academy of Art (£6,000 each);
Ashmolean Museum, Florence Nightingale Museum, Glyndebourne New Opera House, Glyndebourne Opera (£5,000 each);
Courtauld Institute, Tate at St Ives (£3,000 each);
National Art Collections Fund, National Portrait Gallery Whitechapel Art Gallery (£2,500);
D'Oyly Carte Opera (£2,000);
Birmingham Royal Ballet, Cambridge Arts Theatre, Friends of the Courtauld, Friends of the National Library, Milton's Cottage, Royal School of Music, Sir John Soane's Museum, Women's Playhouse Trust (£1,000 each).
Exclusions: Circular appeals and unsolicited general appeals. Grants are made to individuals only in the form of educational support.
Applications: In writing to the correspondent. The trustees meet every month, the educational trustees every quarter.

The Millichope Foundation

c/o Murray Johnstone Ltd, 1 Cornwall Street, Birmingham B3 2DT

Tel: 0121-236 1222
Contact: Mrs Linda Collins
Trustees: M L Ingall, S A Bury, L C N Bury, Mrs B Marshall.

Grant total: £155,000 (1993/94)
Beneficial area: UK, especially Birmingham and Shropshire.
General: The foundation makes grants to a wide range of charitable purposes including medical research, disability, the environment, the arts (especially music), youth and social welfare. Occasional 'one-off' donations are made in response to appeals.

Grants are usually given for five-year periods, in order that beneficiaries can plan ahead. Most grants range between £250 and £3,000 a year. The foundation moni-tors all grants, and if a grant has been given for a specific purpose and the money is then used for some other purpose without the foundation's prior knowledge, then the trustees may see fit to stop future grants.

In 1993/94 about 174 donations ranging from £50 to £10,000 were given. Most grants were between £500 and £1,000. Arts grants (half of them to music and opera) were given to:
City of Birmingham Touring Opera (£10,000);
Royal Opera House Trust (£2,500);
English National Opera (£2,000);
City of Birmingham Orchestral Endowment (£1,500);
Malvern Festival of Visual Arts, Musicians' Benevolent Fund, English Chamber Music Society, National Gallery, Performing Arts Laboratory, Welsh National Opera, Royal Academy of Music, Birmingham Hippo-drome Theatre Development Trust (£1,000 each);
Opera 80, Avoncroft Museum of Buildings, City of Birmingham Symphony Orchestra, Royal Academy of Arts, Live Music Now Scotland, Parnham Trust, Midlands Arts Centre, Shropshire Youth Arts Network (£500 each);
Ludlow Festival Society (£400);
Ludlow Music Society (£250).
Exclusions: Individuals or organisations which are not registered charities.
Applications: In writing to the correspondent, stating why money is required, how much has been raised already, if any grants have been given or applied for, other methods being used to raise money. Trustees meet twice a year. Applicants are asked not to follow up written requests by phone. Replies will be sent only to those who enclose a SAE.

The James Milne Memorial Trust

Scottish Trades Union Congress, Middleton House, 16 Woodlands Terrace, Glasgow G3 6DF

Tel: 0141-332 4946
Contact: Mary Picken, Arts Officer
Trustees: Sir Kenneth Alexander, H Morrison, J Airlie, Alex Clark, Campbell Christie, Harry Rae, Dr Tom Johnston, Dr Rita McAllister, Simpson Stevenson.
Grant total: £7,000 (1995)
Beneficial area: Scotland.
General: The trustees make awards to young talented Scots for overseas study in the arts discipline of their choice.

In deciding whether to make an award, trustees consider: if other organisations are assisting, if the person will return to Scotland with their talent developed and their career enhanced, if the person will be a good ambassador for Scotland and the trade union movement, the possibilities for developing international friendship and understanding. Grants range between £500 and £2,000. Examples of recent grants include:
One year's study in Berklee, USA, for a jazz pianist;
One year's study in Holland for a young composer;
One year's visit to a drama school in Sweden.
Exclusions: Only individuals are eligible.
Applications: In writing to the correspondent. The trustees consider applications twice a year. Main awards are offered in late March.

The Milton Keynes Community Trust Ltd

Acorn House, 381 Midsummer Boulevard, Central Milton Keynes MK9 3HP

Tel: 01908-690276
Contact: Maggie Nevitt, Arts Fund Consultant
Trustees: Jim Barnes, Richard Bentley, Robert de Grey, Naomi Eisenstadt, Rob Gifford, Bob Hill, Brian Hocken, Chris Hopkinson, Simon Ingram, Andrew Jones, Peter Kara, Bob King, Juliet Murray, Michael Murray, Stephen Norrish, Francesca Skelton, Ken Taylor, Sir Peter Thompson, Lady Tudor-Price, Dr Tony Walton.
Grant total: £110,000 (1993/94)
Beneficial area: The borough of Milton Keynes.
General: The trust runs the Community Trust Arts fund which was created when the Milton Keynes Foundation (for the Arts) merged with the Community Trust. Its current priorities are quoted below but as there were under review in late 1995, potential applicants are advised to contact the trust to seek guidance:

* support, where appropriate, of existing arts organisations in Milton Keynes where they offer projects of city-wide significance;
* identification of innovative arts projects from any source which could have citywide impact and significance;
* encouragement of arts provision for young people;
* commissioning of new works.

Grants are for a minimum of £1,000.
Applications: Application forms can be obtained from and projects discussed before submission with Maggie Nevitt, the Arts Fund Consultant, direct line: 01908-563349. Deadlines for applications are: 15 January, 15 May, 15 September.

Peter Minet Trust

54 Knatchbull Road, London SE5 9QY

Tel: 0171-274 2266
Contact: Ms Lyn Roberts, Administrator
Trustees: J C South (Chair), N McGregor-Wood, H J Parratt, Mrs Peter Minet, Mrs R L Rowan, Mrs S P Dunn, Miss P Jones
Grant total: £199,000 (1993/94)
Beneficial area: UK, with a particular interest in Lambeth and Southwark, London.
General: The trust gives priority to registered charities in the London boroughs of Lambeth and Southwark, particularly those working with young people, the sick and disabled, the disadvantaged, the elderly, the arts and the environment. Occasional support is given to capital projects by national charities working in the same fields. Grants in 1993/94 included:
National Listening Library (£3,377);
Weald and Downland Open Air Museum (£2,500);
Chethams School for Music (£2,200);
Arts Dyslexia Trust (£2,000);
Chamber Music Competition for Schools (£1,000).
In the previous year Artsline, the arts information service for disabled people, received (£1,500).
Exclusions: No grants to individuals, or to organisations which are not registered charities, large nationwide appeals.
Applications: In writing to the correspondent, including audited accounts. Unsolicited applications will not be acknowledged unless an SAE is enclosed. Meetings are usually held in January, April, July and October.

The Esmé Mitchell Trust

PO Box 800, Donegall Square West, Belfast BT2 7EB

Tel: 01232-245277
Contact: The Northern Bank Executor & Trustee Co Ltd
Trustees: P J Rankin, D J Maxwell, R P Blakiston-Houston.
Grant total: £80,000 (1994/95)

Beneficial area: Northern Ireland and Eire
General: The objects of the trust are general charitable purposes in Ireland as a whole but principally in Northern Ireland with a particular interest in culture and the arts. The trust states that about a third of its total grant-aid is only available to a limited number of heritage bodies. No information has been made available about its grants.
Exclusions: Individuals wishing to undertake further education or voluntary service are most unlikely to be successful.
Applications: Applicants should submit: a description of the proposed project, a recent statement of accounts and balance sheet, a copy of the constitution, details of tax and legal or charitable status (including the Inland Revenue Charities Division reference number, a copy of the latest annual report, a list of committee officers, information on other sources of finance).

The Monument Trust (see also under the Sainsbury Family Charitable Trusts)

9 Red Lion Court, London EC4A 3EB

Tel: 0171-410 0330
Contact: Michael Pattison
Trustees: R H Gurney, Sir Anthony Tennant, S Grimshaw.
Grant total: £4,282,000 (1993/94)
Beneficial area: UK and overseas.
General: This major trust gives grants for health and community care, environment and the arts. The size of individual grants is not given with their annual report but several are likely to be large - a major capital grant of £5 million over several years has been agreed. In 1993/94 a total of £625,000 was allocated in the arts category to 17 organisations (an average grant of some £37,000). These grants were given to: *Arts Theatre Cambridge, Attingham Summer School, Benesh Institute, Fitzwilliam Museum Cambridge, Friends of the Textile Conservation Centre, Georgian Group, Heritage Conservation Trust, National Art Collections Fund, National Youth Orchestra, Royal Opera House Trust, Space (Arts Services Grants Ltd), Topsham*

Museum Society, Cambridge University Development Appeal, Wallace Collection, West Dean College, Whitechapel Art Gallery, Women's Playhouse Trust.

Other relevant grants were given in the "General" category: *British Youth Opera, Burlington Magazine.*

The correspondent has noted that the trust concentrates its support within the UK although its beneficial area includes "overseas".
Exclusions: No grants to individuals.
Applications: An application to one of the Sainsbury family trusts is an applications to all; see the entry under "Sainsbury Family Charitable Trusts" for the names of the other trusts and the application procedures.

The Henry Moore Foundation

Dane Tree House, Perry Green, Much Hadham, Herts SGl0 6EE

Tel: 01279-843333; Fax: 01279-843647
Contact: Timothy Llewellyn, Director
Trustees: Sir Rex Richards (Chairman), Sir Alan Bowness, Dr Andrew Causey, Joanna Drew, Patrick Gaynor, Miss Margaret McLeod, Lord Rayne, David Sylvester, Henry Wrong.
Grant total: £793,000 (1994/95)
Beneficial area: UK.
General: The foundation promotes both nationally and internationally exhibitions and publications about Henry Moore, drawing on its own resources of both works of art and archival material. The foundation has a wholly owned trading subsidiary, HMF Enterprises (formerly the Raymond Spencer Company Ltd), whose principal activity has been selling works of art by Henry Moore for the benefit of the foundation.

In addition to these activities, the foundation makes grants towards exhibitions, acquisitions, conservation and publications which encourage public interest in sculpture and, to a lesser extent, in other visual arts. Occasional small capital grants are made.

In 1988 the foundation established the Henry Moore Sculpture Trust, based in Leeds, with its own committee of trustees and director. This trust is actively promoting public interest in sculpture with exhibitions at a gallery in Leeds and at Dean Clough Studios, Halifax. It received a grant of £644,000 from the foundation in 1994/95. Recent grants have included:

Tate Gallery Liverpool (£30,000);
MOMA Oxford (£20,000);
Kettle's Yard Cambridge (£15,000);
Centre for Contemporary Arts (£8,000).

Exclusions: Grants are not made to individual artists, but fellowships and scholarships have been provided at universities and colleges.

Applications: In writing to the correspondent, from whom guidelines are available. The trustees meet in January, April, July and October for which applications need to be sent two months in advance.

The Moores Family Charity Foundation

PO Box 28, Crosby, Liverpool L23 0XJ

Tel: 0151-949 0117
Contact: Mrs Patricia Caton
Trustees: John Moores, Peter Moores, Lady Grantchester, James Svenson-Taylor.
Grant total: £920,000 (1993)
Beneficial area: UK, with a preference for Merseyside.
General: The foundation makes annual payments to other Moores Family trusts. In 1993 £211,000 was given to the John Moores Foundation, £165,000 in two grants, one extraordinary, to the Peter Moores Foundation, £62,730 to The Fairway Trust, £40,850 to the Janatha Stubbs Foundation.

Apart from these major allocations the foundation made over 300 grants, mostly of £250 or less (only 42 were for £1,000 or more). Arts grants were given in 1993 to:

John Moores Exhibition Trust (£60,000);
John Moores University Liverpool, Dept of Graphic Design (£1,500);
Dept of Fine Art and Dept of Textiles & Fashion (£1,000 each);
Ironbridge Gorge Museum (£1,000 recurrent support);
National Music for the Blind, Kings Head Theatre London (£250 each);
Oily Cart Company (£400);
Everyman Youth Theatre, Mockbeggar Theatre company (£200);
Musical Keys (£150);
National Art Collections Fund (£100).

Exclusions: No grants to individuals, salaries, purchase or repair of vehicles, research, organ restoration, statutory projects or conservation. Buildings and building work have a very low priority.

Applications: In writing to the correspondent including details of charitable status, most recent accounts, budget, funding raised or which has been applied for. Applications are considered on a continuing basis. The foundation gives preference to applications from Merseyside. Currently (1996) it is not inviting applications from organisations working in other geographical areas although applications from organisations which have received grants in the past will be considered.

The foundation's grant-giving rarely support the arts. The annual grant to the John Moores Exhibition Trust is one of the few exceptions. Other arts grants are historical and would not now be eligible for consideration. Most have been given because they also fall into another area supported by the trustees, ie projects which benefit disabled people.

The Peter Moores Foundation

c/o Messrs Wallwork Nelson and Johnson, Derby House, Lytham Road, Fulwood, Preston PR2 4JF

Contact: Peter Saunders
Trustees: Mrs B D Johnstone, T Conway, P Egerton-Warburton, Donatella Moores, A G Swerdlow.
Grant total: £4,478,000 (1993/94)
Beneficial area: UK and Barbados.
General: The foundation was established by Peter Moores, a director of Littlewoods Organisation, the pools and mail order company. He remains a patron of the foundation which supports activities

reflecting many of his personal interests. He received musical training at university and then worked in opera production at Glyndebourne and the Vienna State Opera. He has sponsored many complete recordings in English of a wide range of operas, been a trustee of the Tate Gallery and a governor of the BBC.

The objects of the foundation are stated in its report as:

* Raising the artistic taste of the public whether in relation to music, drama, opera, painting, sculpture or otherwise in connection with the fine arts;
* Provision of education in the fine arts;
* Promotion of academic education;
* Promotion of Christian religion;
* Provision of facilities for recreation or other leisure time occupation.

The 1992/93 report noted that over half its grant-aid was given to increase public interest in or access to opera and associated activities. The foundation has not provided a schedule of its grants for many years. It split up its total allocation for 1993/94 as follows:

Creative £3,074,000

Sociological £421,000

Barbados £460,000

One-off project £523,000

In 1991/92 arts grants included:

Royal Northern College of Music, for bursaries;

Wexford Festival, for opera production;

English National Opera;

Royal Liverpool Philharmonic Society, for capital work on its hall;

British Museum, for purchase of ancient Chinese bronzes;

Welsh National Opera;

Great Georges Community Cultural Project, for a loan.

The 1992/93 report noted that "over half (of its grant-aid was given) to increase public interest in or access to opera and associated activities. Substantial sums were also allocated to the visual arts, to community projects and to education".

Applications: In writing to the correspondent.

The Theo Moorman Charitable Trust

33 Smithies Avenue, Sully, South Glamorgan CF64 5SS

Tel: 01222-530125
Contact: Margaret Hansford
Trustees: M Davis, Miss E Chadwick, Mrs B Cox
Grant total: £9,000 (1994/95)
General: This trust was set up "to enable all weavers to enjoy artistic freedom in order to contribute to the development of the craft and education of future crafts people". In 1994/95 six awards ranging between £300 and £3,000 were made. The largest grant was for a sabbatical, others were for materials, a loom, research for a book, and studio rent.
Exclusions: All applicants who are not weavers, and also applicants who are still studying weaving, or who have worked for less than two years following a course of study.
Applications: Application forms and guidelines are available from the above address. Applications are considered in *even-numbered years*, deadline February 28.

The Movement for Christian Democracy Trust

14 Rockstone Place, Southampton SO1 2EQ

Contact: Francis Davis
Grant total: £50,000 approx (1992/93)
General: This new trust, registered in 1992, is targeting public arts, development work in Romania and projects in UK urban priority areas in it first year of operation. The fund for public arts, which totalled about £5,000 in 1993, was allocated in a number of small grants to community arts bodies including several theatre companies that involve people with disabilities.

The Munro Charitable Trust

c/o Drummond Bank, 49 Charing Cross
Road, London SW1A 2DX

Contact: The Secretary
Trustees: Sir Alan Munro, N G Munro
Grant total: £8,000 (Oct 1994)
Beneficial area: UK with a particular
interest in south and south west London
and West Sussex
General: The trust's first priority is to
"bodies offering an activity or experience to
people not normally able to enjoy it as a
result of disability or deprivation". In 1994
arts grants were given to:
Actors' Centre (£500);
Artsline, National Listening Library (£250);
*Lyric Theatre Hammersmith, Richmond
   Theatre (£200).*
Exclusions: Individuals.
Applications: Only successful applicants
will be contacted. Trustees meet twice a
year.

The Countess of Munster Musical Trust

Wormley Hill, Godalming, Surrey GU8 5SG

Tel: 01428-685427
Contact: The Secretary
Trustees: Leopold de Rothschild, Mrs P
Arnander, Dame Janet Baker, Mrs A
Cantacuzino, Sir George Christie, Mrs C
Erskine, Dr J Glover, I Horsburgh, P Jones,
Sir John Manduell, Bernard Richards, Dr J
Ritterman.
Grant total: £235,000 (1995/96)
Beneficial area: UK and overseas.
General: The trust supports education in
classical music in any part of the world. The
focus is on the provision of educational
grants to assist students with the cost of
relevant courses and the provision of
musical instrument loans. About 80 to 100
educational grants are made each year,
open to British and Commonwealth
students only. The grant-aid in 1995/96:
Educational grants £181,000
Recital scheme £45,000.
Age limits: Over 18 years and under 25 for
instrumentalists, 27 for female singers, 28
for male singers. Upper age limit for
instrument loans, 28 years.
Applications: Contact the secretary for
detailed guidance notes and an application
form. Awards are made for one year at a
time. Auditions take place in Spring and
early Summer each year for which
applications have to be submitted between
1st November and 31st January. Awards
commence in the following September.

The Museums' Association

42 Clerkenwell Close, London EC1R OPA

Tel: 0171-608 2933/625 1836
Contact: Heather Kelly
General: The association administers a
number of funds designed to enhance
collections.

   The Beecroft Bequest was formed in
1961 for the purchase of pictures and
works of art (furniture and textiles can be
considered) not later than the eighteenth
century in date. Grant-aid is restricted to
smaller galleries and museums and the
maximum for any one grant is £2,000.
Items in auction sales are eligible but
applicants should try to give at least five
working days notice. Applicants should
obtain the additional information about
grant provisions and an application form.

   The Daphne Bullard Trust was set up
in 1973 to promote the work of dress and
costume conservation, display and
publication. Applicants can be either
students or persons engaged in the
conservation and study of dress and
textiles of any period and their display.
Grants are up to approximately £300
annually and are not normally made to
assist with living costs or fees. Further
guidelines and an application form are
available. The closing date is 1st May.

   The Kathy Callow Trust was founded in
1994 to make awards to small museums
for the purposes of assisting with the costs
of a conservation project. Such projects
might include an exhibition, improving
stored collections or running workshops
for people connected with museums. The
maximum size of grant is about £300

annually. Applications are particularly welcomed on the following aspects of social history conservation: the disadvantaged, women, the sea, industrialisation, small localities. The closing date is 1st May. Further details and an application form are available.

The Worshipful Company of Musicians

2nd Floor, St Dunstan House, 2-4 Carey Lane, London EC4V 8AA

Tel: 0171-600 4636
Contact: S N Waley
Beneficial area: UK.
General: The company administers a number of funds and awards to support musicians:

The **Cornwath Fund Trust** (which gives a supplementary prize to the Maggie Teyte Singing competition and a scholarship for an advanced pianoforte student);

The **Maisie Lewis Young Artists' Fund** (to assist young artists who could not otherwise afford the expense of attending concerts);

The **Allcard Fund**. Further details about these funds and how to apply can be obtained from the correspondent.

The Musicians' Benevolent Fund

16 Ogle Street, London W1P 7LG

Tel: 0171-636 4481
Contact: Valerie Beale, Trust Administrator
Grant total: £130,000 (1994)
Beneficial area: UK.
General: The Awards & Trusts Department of the MBF administers a number of schemes to assist musicians with musical education, postgraduate studies, and with specific projects eg. the Courtauld Trust for the Advancement of Music. Support is also available towards the purchase of instruments.

During 1994 the committee decided to help fund performance opportunities for young professional instrumentalists with assistance to Live Music Now and the London Symphony Orchestra String Experience.
Applications: Contact the administrator for further details.

The National Art Collections Fund

Millais House, 7 Cromwell Place, London SW7 2JN

Tel: 0171- 225 4800; Fax: 0171-225 4848
Contact: Mary Yule, Assistant Director and Head of Grants
Trustees: Committee: Sir Nicholas Goodison, Chairman; Cavid Barrie, Director and 16 others.
Grant total: £2,500,000 (1994)
Beneficial area: UK.
General: The purpose of this fundraising charity, set up by charter in 1903, is to make grants to museums and galleries to help them acquire works of art for public exhibition. It receives no government funding and is entirely dependent on the support of its members. Since its launch the fund has helped hundreds of galleries, museums and historic houses to buy more than 10,000 works of art. these have included treasures such as the Velazquez's "Rokeby Venus" and the Leonardo cartoon. The fund is dedicated to making art accessible to everyone. It has been at the forefront of many successful campaigns to save major works of art from British Collections from going overseas.

In 1994 the fund gave 128 grants to 80 museums in all four countries of the UK. Some of the larger grants were given as contributions towards purchases.

The fund publishes a magnificent annual 'Review' with its report and accounts, including articles on selected acquisitions accompanying a full illustrated catalogue and 'The Art Quarterly' magazine four times a year.
Exclusions: No support for capital costs.
Applications: Apply in writing to Mary Yule, Assistant Director and Head of Grants.

The Network Foundation

BM Box 2063, London WC1 3XX

Contact: Vanessa Adams, Administrator
Trustees: Patrick Boase (Chair), John S
Broad, Ingrid Broad, Samuel Clark, C Gillett,
Manning Goodwin, Sara Robin, Hugh
MacPherson, Oliver Gillie
Grant total: £254,000 (1993)
Beneficial area: UK and overseas.
General: The income of this foundation
comes from "a community of wealthy
individuals seeking to realise their visions in
ways that enable others". The foundation
supports projects in the fields of
environment, human rights, peace and the
arts which are chosen and supported by its
members. They develop programmes of
activities in a form of partnership.
Applications which are unsolicited and arise
from outside the Network are not
considered.
Applications: See above. Unsolicited
applications are not considered.

The Normanby Charitable Trust

c/o Touche Ross & Co, 10-12 East Parade,
Leeds LS1 2AJ

Tel: 0113-243 9021
Contact: Mr Taylor
Trustees: The Dowager Marchioness of
Normanby, the Marquis of Normanby, Lady
Lepel Kornicka, Lady Evelyn Phipps Buchan,
Lady Peronel Phipps de Cruz, Lady Henrietta
Sedgwick.
Grant total: £375,000 (1994/95)
Beneficial area: UK and overseas, with a
special interest in Yorkshire
General: Grants generally range from
under £100 to £50,000. About a third of
the grants were given to organisations in
North Yorkshire, especially in Whitby. Arts
grants in 1994/95:
*British Museum, Haynes Memorial Lecture
(£20,000);*
*Royal Academy of Art Scholarship Appeal
(£5,000);*
*Bury St Edmunds Arts Gallery Trust
(£3,737);*
Dulwich Picture Gallery (£1,500);
Thomas More Picture Trust (£500);
Fylindales Museum Trust (£200).
Applications: In writing to the
correspondent. Only successful applications
are acknowledged. Telephone calls are not
encouraged.

The Northern Ireland Voluntary Trust

22 Mount Charles, Belfast BT7 INZ

Tel: 01232-245927; Fax: 01232-329839
Contact: Avila Kilmurray, Director
Trustees: David Cook (Chair), Vivienne
Anderson, Mary Black, Mark Conway,
Eamonn Deane, Sammy Douglas, Mari
Fitzduff, Sheelagh Flanagan, Jim Flynn, Sam
McCready, Philip McDonagh, Aideen
McGinley, Angela Paisley, Ben Wilson.
Grant total: £446,000 (1994/95)
Beneficial area: Northern Ireland.
General: The trust has a detailed Strategic
Plan for 1995/97 and Guidelines for Grant
Seekers which are available on request. The
trust prioritises funding for projects which
support: community development;
initiatives to combat poverty and
disadvantage; the promotion of equity and
social justice. It also aims to maintain and
develop certain specific programmes. Of
these the Community Arts Award Scheme
and Telecommunity could be also of
particular interest to users of this guide.
Community and Arts Education: 25
grants totalling £20,000. Grants ranged
between £150 and £3,000. They included:
Belfast Community Circus (£3,000);
East Belfast Festival (£1,000);
Armagh Together Writers' Group (£300);
*Claudy Apple Group, West Belfast Commu-
nity festival (£200 each).*
Community Arts Award Scheme: 84
grants totalling £33,000. All grants were
£800 or less.
*Derry Travellers' Support Group, for
photography (£750);*
*Simon Community Hostel, for painting
(£550);*
Youth Initiatives, for music (£500);
Horizons Drama Group (£250);

Banbridge Storytellers (£150).
Telecommunity: 12 grants totalling £61,500. Grants ranged between £2,500 and £10,000. Exceptional grants of £20,000 can be made. This partnership with BT Northern Ireland and British Telecom Union Committee funds locally-based self-help groups involving young, elderly or disabled people. Priority is given to those in areas of particular disadvantage. A phased commitment over three years is possible and a contribution towards the salary of a key worker may also be considered. A wide range of projects can be considered including: creativity and self-expression through drama, music or a range of arts activities; community education and training; out of school projects for young people. Major capital building programmes, ongoing running costs, individuals, travel, vehicles are amongst the exclusions.
Examples of beneficiaries:
Foyle Film Centre/The Nerve Centre, interactive multi-media project and outreach programme (£10,000 1st of 2);
The Playhouse, Derry, creative workshops with the young, the old and people with special needs (£10,000, 2nd of 2).
Exclusions: The trust does not normally give grants to individuals, support the ongoing running costs of organisations, fund major capital building programmes, make grants for travel, vehicles, pay off debts, make retrospective grants, respond to general appeals, fund projects where there is a statutory responsibility or respond to cutbacks in statutory funding.
Applications: There are no formal application forms. Potential applicants should obtain copies of the trust's 'Guidelines for Grant Seekers'. Trustees meet every two months to consider applications, but requests for less than £1,500 can be considered at any time.

The Ofenheim Trust *(including the former Cinderford Trust)*

Messrs Baker Tilly & Co, Iveco Ford House, Station Road, Watford, Herts WD1 1TG

Tel: 01923-816400
Contact: G Wright
Trustees: R J Clark, R Fitzherbert-Brockholes, R McLeod
Grant total: £89,000 (1993/94)
Beneficial area: UK.
General: The trusts support nationally known and well-established organisations of personal interest to the trustees. Most grants are made in the fields of health and the environment and many are recurrent. Arts grants in 1993/94 were given to:
Musicians' Benevolent Fund (£4,900);
National Youth Orchestra (£2,800);
Glyndebourne Arts Trust (£1,400);
National Art Collections Fund (£700).
Each grant had also been made in the previous two years.
Applications: Applications: In writing to the correspondent. Unsuccessful applications will not be acknowledged.

The Old Possums Practical Trust

Baker Tilly, Iveco Ford House, Station Road, Watford WD1 1TG

Tel: 01923-816400
Contact: The Secretary
Trustees: Esmé Eliot, Charles Willett, Brian Stevens
Grant total: £70,000 (1992/93)
Beneficial area: UK and overseas.
General: The trust supports medical research and education of the public in the literary history of England. In 1992/93 the trust made 15 grants including:
September Press (£7,000);
British Library, London Library, Poetry Book Society, Royal National Theatre (£5,000 each);
Garsington Opera Trust (£500);
Opera Factory (£300).
Applications: In writing to the correspondent.

The Oldham Foundation

King's Well, Douro Road, Cheltenham, Gloucestershire GL50 2PF

Contact: Mrs D Oldham
Trustees: O Oldham, J Bodden, Mrs D Oldham, J H Oldham, S T Roberts, Professor R E Thomas.
Grant total: £65,000 (1994/95)
Beneficial area: South West and North West of England.
General: The trust gives to a wide range of causes. Its main grants are for former employees of Oldham Batteries. Each year a few arts organisations are supported. The size of grants varies a great deal from year to year. In 1991/92 two grants of £10,000 were given. Arts grants in 1993/94:
Bath and West Opera (£1,000);
Cheltenham Literature Festival (£250 with £1,800 in 1995/96);
Festival of Music (£250);
Cheltenham Violin Course, Parnham Trust, Fleet Air Arm Museum (£100 each).
Exclusions: Individuals; general appeals from national bodies.
Applications: In writing, only, to the correspondent.

The Oppenheim-John Downes Memorial Awards

36 Whitefriars Street, London EC4Y 8BH

General: Awards are made to "deserving artists of any kind whether writers, painters, sculptors, musicians, dancers, craftsmen or inventors who are unable to pursue their vocation by reason of their poverty". Applicants must be over 30 years of age and natural born British subjects of parents both of whom are British subjects.
Applications: Application forms are available from the trust and must be returned no later than the last day of October each year.

The Oppenheimer Charitable Trust

17 Charterhouse Street, London EC1N 6RA

Tel: 0171-404 4444
Contact: J J Hawkins
Trustees: T W Capon (Chair), E G Dawe, S P Shoesmith, Sir Christopher Collett, J J Hawkins.
Grant total: £103,000 (Oct 1994)
Beneficial area: UK.
General: The trust gives to a very wide range of charitable activities. 130 grants were made in 1994 ranging between £100 and £8,000. Of these 16 grants were to arts organisations and totalled over £18,000. Many of the larger arts grants were recurrent and to national organisations. Arts grants in 1994 included:
Victoria & Albert Museum (£5,000);
Royal Opera House Trust (£4,500);
Royal Albert Hall Trust (£2,000);
Royal Academy Trust, British Museum, Contemporary Art Society (£1,000 each);
Council for Music in Hospitals, Actors' Centre Building Development Appeal (£500 each);
Artsline, British Federation of Festivals (£250 each).
Exclusions: Individuals for education; organisations which are not registered charities.
Applications: In writing. The trustees meet in January, April, July and October each year.

The Orpheus Trust

Trevereux Manor, Limpsfield Chart, Oxted, Surrey RH8 OTL

Contact: Richard Stilgoe
Trustees: Rev Donald Reeves, Dr Michael Smith, Esther Rantzen, Alex Armitage, Andrew Murison.
Grant total: £117,000 (1995/95)
Beneficial area: UK.
General: The trust aims to "relieve mentally and physically handicapped adults and children... particularly with music and musical entertainment". Its 1994/95 report stated that "three courses were run with SHARE Music. In addition we have

supported music and drama projects at the Royal Hospital, Putney, helped Music and the Deaf, the Drake Research Project and Strathclyde Orchestral Productions. We have funded projects in Aberdeen and helped individual teachers and music therapists in the general needs field".
Several of the above-named projects have received support from the trust in previous years.
Applications: In writing to the correspondent.

The Ouseley Trust

74 Sweet Briar, Welwyn Garden City, Herts AL7 3EA

Tel: 01707-322132
Contact: K B Lyndon, Clerk to the Trustees
Trustees: H G Pitt (Chairman), Dr J A Birch, Dr L F Dakers, Prof B W Harvey, Sir John Margetson, Dr J H H Oliver, C J Robinson, R J Shephard, N E Walker, Rev A F Walters, Rev A G Wedderspoon, Sir David Willcocks.
Grant total: £106,000 (1995)
Beneficial area: UK and Ireland.
General: Every application must have a direct bearing on promoting and maintaining a high standard of choral service. Grants tend to fall into six categories: *Courses, instruction* (only awarded where an already acceptable standard has been reached and will be raised); *Endowment grants*; *Individual fees*; *Music*, replacement or purchase of new instrument; *Organs*, only for an instrument of particular significance and integral to high standard choral service; *Other*.

In 1995 grants totalled 35, 23 of which were choristers' fees and chorister scholarship endowments at various cathedrals. Grants included:
Westminster Abbey Choir School for choral bursaries (£15,000);
Hexham Abbey for its music foundation (£2,000);
Parish of the Claydons, Bucks, for music (£590).
Exclusions: Buildings, commissions, recordings, furniture, outside vocal tuition, pianos, robes, tours or visits. Grants to

individuals are only made through an institution.
Applications: Guidelines and application forms are available. Closing dates are 31st January and 30th June. The trustees usually meet in March and September/October.

The Rudolph Palumbo Charitable Foundation

37a Walbrook, London EC4N 8BS

Contact: T H Tharby
Trustees: Lord Mishcon, Sir Matthew Farrer, Lady Palumbo, T H Tharby, J G Underwood.
Grant total: £434,000 (1992/93)
Beneficial area: UK and overseas.
General: The foundation has classified its grants under the following headings which indicates its priorities: Advancement of Education; Conservation of the Environment; Relief of Poverty, General Purposes. In 1992/93 a total of 40 grants were made, two very large including Painshill Park Trust (£100,000). Only a small number of other arts grants were made:
Chicken Shed, Glyndebourne Productions (£25,000 each);
Natural History Museum (£20,000);
English National Ballet School (£250).
Applications: In writing to the correspondent.

The Paragon Concert Society

13 St Edwards Road, Clifton Wood, Bristol BS8 4TS

Contact: C J Brisley
Trustees: D Gibbs (Chair), Mrs V Pritchard, Ms L Leschke, A Tyrell.
Grant total: £9,000 (1994)
Beneficial area: Avon area.
General: The society's objects are to promote the knowledge and performance of serious music for small combinations of instruments, for string orchestras, with or without voices and instrumental soloists, and its choice of work for performance shall at all times be consistent with its purpose of educating its members and the general public in music of the highest standard. Twenty grants, mostly between £100 and

400   The Arts Funding Guide

£500, were given in 1994 and included:
*Bristol Opera Company (£1,750 regularly
   supported);*
*Avon Music School/Centre (£1,250 regularly
   supported);*
St George Lunchtime Concert (£750);
Amici (£642);
Music box (£500);
Opera Project (£450);
Chantry Singers (£446);
Chipping Sodbury Music society (£200).
Exclusions: No grants for tuition fees.
Applications: In writing to the
correspondent.

The Hon Charles Pearson Charity Trust

Pollen House, 10-12 Cork Street, London
W1X 1PD

Tel: 0171-439 9061
Contact: The Secretary
Trustees: The Cowdray Trust Ltd.
Grant total: £55,000 (1993/94)
Beneficial area: UK
General: In 1993/94 the trust made 11
grants ranging between £1,000 and
£10,000. The following grants relevant to
this guide were made:
*Gordon Highlanders Museum Campaign
   (£5,000);*
Gordon Forum for the Arts (£2,000).
Exclusions: Individuals.
Applications: In writing to the
correspondent. Applications from registered
charities only. No acknowledgement unless
"a donation" sent.

The PF Charitable Trust

25 Copthall Avenue EC2R 7DR

Tel: 0171-638 5858
Contact: The Secretary
Trustees: Robert Fleming, Rory D Fleming,
Valentine P Fleming, Philip Fleming.
Grant total: £731,000 (1993/94)
Beneficial area: UK, with apparent special
interest in Oxfordshire area and Scotland.
General: The trust gives about 500 grants a
year over a wide range of charitable
interests. It lists its grants in categories.

Over half its grant-aid is given to medical
research and hospitals and associated
organisations. It also gives for conservation,
youth, old people, welfare, housing and
education. In 1993/94 £28,000 was given
in 21 grants under its category "Music, art
and theatre"; of these seven grants were to
Scottish organisations and nine for music
and opera. Arts grants included:
Royal Academy of Arts (£10,000);
*Edinburgh International Festival Endowment
   Fund (£4,000);*
*Scottish Museums Council, Scottish
   Sculpture Workshop (£2,500 each);*
*Scottish Music Information Centre, Serpen-
   tine Trust, London Symphony Orchestra
   (£1,000 each);*
*National Youth Orchestra of Scotland,
   British Youth Orchestra, Rehearsal
   Orchestra, ADAPT Trust, Cambridge Arts
   Theatre (£500 each);*
Music Therapy Trust (£250).
Applications: To the correspondent at any
time. Replies will be sent to unsuccessful
applicants if an SAE is enclosed.

The Stanley Picker Trust

c/o Wilsons Solicitors, Steynings House,
Chapel Place, Fisherton Street, Salisbury,
Wiltshire SP2 7RJ

Tel: 01722-412412
Contact: Peter Lawson
Trustees: Peter Lawson, Anthony Edwards.
Grant total: £79,000 (June 1994)
Beneficial area: UK, with a preference for
Kingston, Surrey and the South East.
General: The trust mainly supports the arts,
giving annual grants and fellowships to the
Kingston School of Fine Arts. It also gives
grants in the fields of music, writing, acting,
printing and sculpture and a few grants to
arts organisations. Grants in 1994 were
given to:
*British Friends of Art Museums of Israel
   (£14,000);*
Park Lane Group (£2,000);
Salisbury Girl Choristers Fund (£1,000);
*Whitechapel Art Gallery for 2 open tutorials
   by Eric Fischl and William Tucker (£1,500
   each);*

14 general education grants (£32,400);
6 Kingston University lectureships
(£12,000);
2 Picker Fellows (£9,775).
Applications: In writing to the
correspondent.

The Pilgrim Trust

Fielden House, Little College Street, London
SW1P 3SH

Tel: 0171-222 4723
Contact: Alastair Hoyer Millar, Secretary
Trustees: Mrs Mary Moore (Chairman),
Lord Jenkins of Hillhead, Lord Thomson of
Monifieth, Nicolas Barker, Lady Anglesey, Sir
Claus Moser, Lord Armstrong, Neil
MacGregor, Sir Thomas Bingham, Eugenie
Turton, Lord Cobbold.
Grant total: £1,497,000 (1994)
Beneficial area: UK.
General: The trust makes grants,
sometimes large and spread over a number
of years, but seldom recurrent and usually
for amounts between £3,000 and £10,000,
in the fields of preservation, art and
learning, and social welfare. In 1993 the
largest grant was for £25,000. Grants are
for capital and specific project purposes,
rather than revenue funding. No detailed
information on grants is available about
1994. In 1993 grants divided as follows:
Art and learning (Conservation of
collections of national importance,
improvement to theatre facilities, acquisitions
for local galleries): £322,000 in 52 grants
Preservation (Preservation of building of
architectural or historic importance,
occasionally, preservation of the
countryside): £322,000 in 49 grants
Social welfare (Homelessness, penal
reform, alcohol and drug addiction,
rehabilitation of the mentally ill,
unemployment): £351,000 in 47 grants.

The following are examples of arts grants
given in 1994:

Under "Preservation"
Blackheath Concert Halls, renovation of
dressing rooms (£10,000);
The "Hotties" Science and Arts Centre Ltd,
restoration (£5,000);

Under "Art and Learning"
Buckinghamshire Archaeological Society, for
a new art gallery in Aylesbury (£15,000);
Cambridge Arts Theatre Trust, dressing
room facilities, Norwich Playhouse Trust.
for conversion to theatre (£10,000);
Ryedale Folk Museum (£7,500);
Fruitmarket Gallery, for galley development,
Gloucestershire Everyman Theatre,
refurbishment of theatre workshop,
Kendal Brewery Arts Centre Trust,
extension to theatre, St Donat's Arts
Centre, improved facilities (£5,000 each);
English Touring Opera, for CCTV system,
Ipswich Borough Council for purchase of
painting (£3,000).
Exclusions: Individuals, underwriting or
sponsoring of exhibitions, seminars,
festivals, theatrical and musical production,
the commissioning of new works of art and
"mega appeals" from national or non-
national museums.
Applications: In writing to the
correspondent including: name, address
and telephone number of the charity;
charity number and date of registration;
name and designation of contact; aims of
the organisation; subject of the appeal;
timescales for phases of the work and dates
for completion, as appropriate; financial
details of the project with total cost and
amount already raised or promised, any
contribution from statutory sources, major
contributors; sum requested from Pilgrim
Trust; latest report and accounts.

The Austin & Hope Pilkington Trust

c/o Messrs Coopers & Lybrand, 9 Greyfriars
Road, Reading RG11JG

Tel: 01734-597111
Contact: The Secretary
Trustees: Dr L H A Pilkington,
Mrs J M Jones, Mrs P S Shankar.
Grant total: £294,000 (Nov 1994)
Beneficial area: UK with a preference for
Merseyside
General: The trust gives to a wide range of
charities with an interest shown in
organisations working for the disabled, the

environment and overseas aid as well as the arts. In 1994 the trust made 40 grants totalling £294,000 and ranging between £500 and £60,000. Nine grants were for £10,000 or more. The arts received £86,000 (29%) of funding, a higher proportion than in previous years because of the exceptional grant to the Purcell School of Music. The grants were almost entirely for music. Examples of grants were:

Purcell School of Music (£60,000);
Royal Academy of Music (£10,000);
London Philharmonic (£5,000);
National Music for the Blind, Clonter Opera for All (£2,000 each);
National Children's Orchestra, Living Paintings Trust, Live Music Now (£1,000 each).

Exclusions: No grants to individuals or to local organisations except those in the St Helen's area.
Applications: In writing.

The Poetry Society

22 Betterton Street, London WC2H 9BU

Tel: 0171-240 4810; Fax: 0171-240 4818
Beneficial area: UK.
General: The society runs the annual National Poetry Competition in association with BBC Radio 4 and support also from Holt Jackson and the Arts Council for England. Entries can be from anyone aged 18 and over, for poems in English, on any subject, and of not more than 100 lines. The winning poems are published in an anthology and may be broadcast. In 1995 prizes of £4,000, £1,000 and £500 were awarded.
Applications: Full details and an application form are available from the society. In 1995 each poem submitted cost £5. 00 and the closing date was October 30th.

The Porter Foundation

Dolphin House, St Peter Street, Winchester, Hants SO23 8BU

Tel: 01962-877691; Fax: 01962-866116
Contact: Paul Wiliams, Director
Trustees: Dame Shirley Porter, Sir Leslie Porter, David Brecher, Steven Porter.
Grant total: £478,000 (1994/95)
Beneficial area: UK and Israel.
General: The foundation's policy is that the majority of its funding be given towards projects in "education, the environment, cultural activity, and health, welfare and humanitarian assistance". Grants can be made for capital projects or for specific programmes.

The foundation has given the bulk of its grants to Jewish organisations but this is "not through deliberate policy and could change". In 1994/95 a total of 35 grants were made. Arts grants were given to:

National Portrait Gallery, where the Porter Gallery houses new acquisitions (£25,000, 1 of 3);
Royal Opera House Trust (£6,000);
Imperial War Museum Appeal (£5,000);
Friends of Israel Opera (£2,000);
Englsih National Opera, London Philharmonic (£1,000 each).

Exclusions: General running costs.
Applications: Guidelines for applicants are available. An initial letter summarising the application should include basic costings and background details of the organisation such as annual report and accounts. A mass of documentation at this stage is not encouraged. Suitable proposals falling within the foundation's current interests will be contacted for further information and, perhaps, a staff visit. Trustees meet in March, July and November. Short-listed applications will be informed within a week. However the foundation does not answer unsolicited requests for funding unless they are successful.

The Prince's Trust and the Royal Jubilee Trusts

18 Park Square East, London NW1 4LH

Tel: 0171-543 1234; Fax: 0171-831 7280
Contact: Hussein Syed, Grants Administrator
Trustees: The Prince's Trust: J J Gardner; E G Pratt; Dr J Paterson-Brown; R G Beckett; A R Kenney; P D C Collins. The Royal Jubilee Trusts: Lord Wardington; Lord Ashburton; Sir Peter Studd; Lord Remnant.
Grant total: £5,246,000 (1993/94)
Beneficial area: UK and the Commonwealth.
General: Some 8,000 grants a year are made by the trusts to both individuals and organisations. In 1989/90 a policy was adopted for most grants to be one off, with some for two years. Grants for more than two years are extremely rare. Most grants are distributed locally, to a maximum of £2,500. National grants may be for as much as £24,000.

The trusts aim to enable young people, particularly the most disadvantaged, to develop themselves and to help them be of service to others. They operate as 'pump primers' and are keen to fund new initiatives, even from established organisations.

Local committee grants
The major part of the trusts' grant-aid comes from this sector of its activities - £1.9 million in 1993/94. (The Foundation for Sport and the Arts gives over £1 million to this local programme.) The trust have attempted to reach individuals, local organisations and ad hoc groups by devolving most of their administration and decision-making to committees of local people. "Each committee has its own budget, and seeks out potential applications and helps them to apply. Every applicant is visited allowing us to do away with application forms and almost all paperwork. " This system relies on volunteers who are themselves regularly trained. Local contacts can either be found in the local telephone book under "Prince's Trust" or by calling (or writing to) the national office in Bedford Row. Local grants

have a maximum of £800 for an individual and £2,500 for groups or organisations. If a local organisation is requesting more than this, their application will be assessed by the local committee, and passed on if suitable to the national office.

National and Commonwealth grants
In 1993/94 the trusts' gave £352,000 in national and commonwealth grants ranging between £1,500 and £24,000.

"National grants are intended to support innovative and pioneering approaches to work with young people undertaken by national and regional organisations. Our priority is to support work for disadvantaged young people and to enable and encourage young people to help others. "Commonwealth grants arose from the Queen's 1977 Silver Jubilee Appeal to establish a fund encouraging people throughout the Commonwealth to undertake projects of value to themselves and others. Since then, the trust "has helped many thousands of young people from the UK to travel to Commonwealth countries often undertaking long periods of community service for the benefit of local communities. " The trust is aiming to increase the applications from Commonwealth countries other than Britain, and is developing a system of local representatives, modelled on the local UK committee system.

Programmes initiated by the trusts
The trusts have their own programme of research and development. Each initiative has its own budget, but initiatives do change. To receive an award from these budgets, an organisation simply applies to the national office, which decides where the money will come from.

Partners in Europe
This programme, launched in 1989 and run with the Prince's Youth Business Trust, aims to develop opportunities for young people to create partnerships across the continent (in both Europe and the former Soviet Union) either to provide them with real business opportunities or to put them in contact with those in other countries who can help them develop projects. Joint

publishing ventures, conservation and environmental projects and trans-European training programmes have been developing from this investment. The backbone of this programme is the provision of 'Go and See' grants enabling young people to establish links with their potential partners. 111 grants of a few hundred pounds each were given in 1992/93 and nine 'Go Ahead' grants (for follow-up support to ideas generated by the initial contacts) have been awarded so far.

Three *Richard Mills Travel Fellowships* worth about £1,000 each are awarded annually to community artists under the age of 35 for travel to mainland European countries. The closing date for applications (in writing, no application form) is in January.

Exclusions: Core costs or capital projects.

Applications: Only national organisations must fill in an application form. Contact your regional Prince's Trust Committee (see local telephone directory) or write to head office.

Mr and Mrs J A Pye's Charitable Settlement

c/o Messrs Darby's, 50 New Inn Hall Street, Oxford OX1 2DN

Tel: 01865-247294
Contact: The Trust Administrator
Trustees: R H Langton-Davies, G W F Archer, G C Pye.
Grant total: £289,000 (1994/95)
Beneficial area: UK, particularly the Oxford area.
General: The settlement was created by Jack A Pye, an estate developer from Oxford. Its particular interests are "nutritional and medical research, mental health and education, child welfare, conservation and the arts as well as national and local needs in various fields". Grants between £500 to over £50,000. Many grants particularly the larger ones are recurrent.

Interest free loans were given in 1994 to the Parnham Trust (£185,000) and Music at Oxford (£20,000). The scale of these may

account in part for the drop in grant-aid over the past two years (£539,000 was allocated in 1992/93). It seems that the lower grant range offers greater opportunities for new applicants. Arts grants in 1994/95:

Parnham Trust (£10,000, regularly supported);
Reading Foundation for Art (£3,000);
Oxford Youth Music Trust (£1,500);
Oxford Playhouse Trust, Sixteen Choir & Orchestra (£1,000 each);
Hallé Endowment Trust Appeal, Young Person's Concert Foundation (£500 each);
St Edmund's School Organ Scholarship (£250);
Chipping Norton Theatre (£200).

Only one of these grants was recurrent. In the previous year arts grants included:

Music at Oxford (£15,000);
Ashmolean Museum (£4,000);
RADA, Royal Academy Trust (£1,000 each).

Exclusions: No payments to individuals.

Applications: In writing to the correspondent.

Dr Radcliffe's Trust

5 Lincoln's Inn Fields, London WC2A 3BT

Tel: 0171-242 9231
Contact: Ivor F Guest
Trustees: Sir Ralph Verney, Lord Wilberforce, Sir Edgar Williams, Lord Quinton, Lord Balfour of Burleigh, Lord Cottesloe.
Grant total: £253,000 (1993/94)
Beneficial area: UK.
General: The trust gives its grants within three categories: crafts; music and miscellaneous.
Crafts: £72,000 in 30 grants were given ranging between £750 and £7,000. In this area the trust mainly supports apprentices, mostly, but not exclusively at cathedral workshops (10 cathedrals received grants in 1993/94). For other grants the trust looks to support excellence in crafts particularly in conservation. Grants for the repair and conservation of church furniture, including bells and monuments, are made through the Council for the Care of Churches. Direct

applications are not accepted. Grants in 1993/94 included:
Council for the Care of Churches (£7,000);
Textile Conservation Centre (£6,500);
Museum of Modern Art, Oxford (£3,000);
Devon Guild of Craftsmen (£2,800);
Courtauld Institute (£2,000);
St Donat's Arts Centre (£1,500).

Music: £85,000 in 24 grants ranging between £200 and £17,000In this area the trust regularly supports the Allegri Quartet's visits to universities and other centres giving concerts, masterclasses and teaching sessions. It also sponsors the Radcliffe Composer-in-Residence with the City of Birmingham Symphony Orchestra. Its grants show a particular interest in supporting the musical education of young people in classical music:
Allegri String Quartet (£17,771);
Royal Northern College of Music (£15,179);
National Youth Orchestra (£10,000);
City of Birmingham Symphony Orchestra
  (£7,500);
Loan Fund for Musical Instruments
  (£5,000);
Music for Youth (£1,000).

Miscellaneous: £79,000 in 23 grants ranging between £100 and £12,000. Grants in 1993/94 included:
Parnham Trust, Royal Academy of Dancing
  (£3,000 each);
National Maritime Museum (£300).

Exclusions: Construction, conversion, repair or maintenance of buildings; individuals for education fees or maintenance; musical and theatrical performances; to clear deficits.

Applications: In writing before the end of March and September each year. Music applicants need to apply by 1 February and ! August since a music panel meets in March and October to short-list applications and makes recommendations to the trustees. Trustees meet in June and December.

The Eleanor Rathbone Charitable Trust

Rathbone Bros & Co, 4th Floor, Port of Liverpool Building, Pier Head, Liverpool L3 INW

Tel: 0151-236 8674
Contact: Barbara Pedersen
Trustees: Dr B L Rathbone, W Rathbone, Ms Jenny Rathbone, P W Rathbone.
Grant total: £172,000 (1992/93)
Beneficial area: UK, with a most particular interest in Merseyside.
General: Up-to-date information is not available about this trust. It is known to have had a particular interest in women's projects, improving race relations and public arts. Most grants ranged between £100 and £10,000.
Exclusions: No grants to individuals, church buildings, major national appeals or appeals outside Merseyside.
Applications: In writing to the correspondent.

The Rayne Foundation

33 Robert Adam Street, London W1M 5AH

Tel: 0171-935 3555
Contact: R D Lindsay-Rea
Trustees: E L George, Lord Greenhill, F M Milligan, Lord Rayne, R A Rayne.
Grant total: £1,546,000 (1994)
Beneficial area: UK and overseas.
General: This large foundation operates without published policies or application guidelines. It gives a very large number of grants (700) to a very wide range of organisations which are not listed in any particular order.

In 1994 a small number of beneficiaries received major payments eg Darwin College, Cambridge (£200,000), but only 31 grants were £10,000 or higher; some 80 were between £1,000 and £9,999; the majority were under £1,000.

In 1994 120 arts grants were given. The predominant support was given to the Chicken Shed Theatre Company (£26,500 in five grants) which has also received substantial support in previous years. It is difficult to discern any specific pattern in its arts interests. Major national organisations in all art forms are represented along with many others. Other arts grants given in 1994 included:

National Art Collections Fund;
Royal Academy of Arts;
Courtauld Institute (£5,000 each);
Royal Opera House Trust (£4,000);
Friends of the Textile Conservation Centre (£3,000);
Mountview Theatre School, European Stage Company, Shape London, Birmingham Conservatoire (£1,000 each);
Chamber Music Competition for Schools (£750);
Contemporary Art Society (£500);
Florence Nightingale Museum (£200).

Exclusions: No grants to individuals.

Applications: In writing to the correspondent at any time.

The Richmond Parish Lands Charity

The Vestry House, 21 Paradise Road, Richmond, Surrey TW9 1SA

Tel: 0181-948 5701
Contact: Andrew Ayling, Clerk to the Trustees
Trustees: The mayor of Richmond (ex-officio), three nominated by the borough of Richmond, five nominated by local voluntary organisations, four co-opted.
Grant total: £576,000 (1994/95)
Beneficial area: Richmond, Kew and North Sheen.
General: In 1994/95 only 2%, some £9,000, was allocated to the category Music and the Arts, according to its annual report. Of the ten grants the larger ones were given to:
Richmond Arts Council (£3,500);
Richmond Music Festival, Richmond Orchestra (£1,000 each).
However other relevant grants were also given under other categories or which the following are some examples:

Under Youth/Community
St Matthias Arts Festival (£2,000);
Heatham House Music Group (£500);

Under Education
Orange Tree Theatre, schools programme (£6,000).
Support was also given to the Disability Arts Forum and to projects concerned with music and dance therapy.

Exclusions: Residents or organisations outside the beneficial area.

Applications: An application form is obtainable. Applications should be accompanied by the latest annual report and accounts and a detailed statement of the purposes for which a grant is requested. Grants for capital outlay should be described separately. Meetings of the trustees are normally held every five weeks (except in August). Applications should be received at least one week before the meeting. Telephone enquiries are welcome.

The Robertson Trust

50 West Nile Street, Glasgow G12 ND

Tel: 0141-248 4296; Fax: 0141-242 5333
Contact: Sir Lachlan Maclean, Secretary
Trustees: J A R Macphail (Chairman), J J G Good, K D M Cameron, B McNeil, T M Lawrie.
Grant total: £3,200,000 (1993/94)
Beneficial area: UK with a particular interest in Scotland.
General: The trust supports a wide range of charitable activity. It shows a particular interest in medical research, education and the welfare of people in need. The arts and the national heritage are also amongst its interests.

In 1992/93, the most recent year for which detailed information about individual grants is known, seven arts grants were given, all of which were for music. An exceptional grant of £150,000 was given to the Piping Trust with a further £11,750 to six beneficiaries which included:
Glasgow Royal Concert Hall (£5,000);
Council for Music in Hospitals, Live Music Now! (£1,000 each)

Applications: In writing to the correspondent including a copy of the accounts and charity number. The trustees meet six times a year.

The Helen Roll Charity

Morrell Peel and Gamlen, 1 St Giles, Oxford OX1 3JR

Contact: F R Williamson
Trustees: Jennifer Williamson, Dick Williamson, Paul Strang, Christine Chapman, Terry Jones.
Grant total: £139,000 (1993/94)
Beneficial area: UK, with a particular interest in Oxford
General: The charity gives grants, ranging from £250 to £10,000, to quite a wide range of charities. Arts grants in 1993/94 were given to:
Playhouse Theatre Trust, Oxford (£10,000 and in the previous year);
Bodleian Library, Oxford (£7,000 and in the previous year);
Purcell School of Music (£6,000 with £9,000 in the previous year);
Ashmolean Museum, Oxford (£6,000 with £5,000 in the previous year);
Songmakers Almanac (£1,500).
Hackney Empire Preservation Trust received £1,000 in 1990/91.
A number of grants are recurrent and there seems little leeway for new applicants.
Applications: In writing to the correspondent.

The Leopold de Rothschild Charitable Trust

Rothschild Trustee Corporation, New Court, St Swithin's Lane, London EC4P 4DU

Tel: 0171-280 5000
Contact: The Secretary
Trustees: Rothschild Executor & Trustee Co Ltd.
Grant total: £45,000 (1994)
Beneficial area: UK.
General: The trust supports a wide range of causes including the arts. It gives a large number of grants (150) most of which are under £1,000. Arts grants in 1994 were given to:
English Chamber Orchestra and Music Society (£700 with £3,000 and £5,000 in the previous years);
Bournemouth Orchestras Foundation (£500);
Royal Opera House (£300);
Bach Choir (£300 with £5,000 in the previous year);
Sir John Soane's Museum, Music Space Trust, Evin Arts Centre (£250);
Lincoln Cathedral Music Appeal, English National Ballet (£200 each);
Oily Cart Company, Wiener Library, Nuffield Theatre Appeal, Museum of Garden History (£100 each).
Applications: In writing to the correspondent.

The Roughley Charitable Trust

2B Bracebridge Road, Sutton Coldfield, West Midlands B74 2SB

Contact: Mrs M K Smith
Trustees: Mrs M K Smith, G W L Smith, Mrs D M Newton, M C G Smith, J R L Smith.
Grant total: £66,000 (1994/95)
Beneficial area: UK and overseas, with a particular interest in the West Midlands.
General: Grants are given to a wide range of charities. In 1994/95 these included the following arts grants:
Midlands Arts Centre (£8,000 with grants in the 2 previous years);
Highbury Centre Theatre (£500);
National Youth Music Theatre (£100).
Exclusions: The trust says its funds are fully committed and it does not welcome unsolicited applications.

The Royal Victoria Hall Foundation

111 Green Street, Sunbury on Thames, Middlesex TW16 6QX

Tel: 01932-782341
Contact: Carol Cooper, Clerk to the Trustees
Trustees: Dilys Gane (Chair), Professor David Bradby, Yvonne Brewster, Valerie Colgan, Peter Hiley, Jonathan, Michael Reddington, David Russell Anne Stanesby.
Grant total: £22,000 (1994/95)
Beneficial area: Greater London area only.
General: The foundation supports drama only. It makes two categories of award:

a) Eleven annual Lilian Baylis Awards totalling £11,000, to one student in each accredited drama school in London, on the recommendation of the drama school only.
b) Grants to support theatrical groups and to encourage experience of the theatre. Grants are one-off and mainly for capital expenditure. Grants in 1994/95 included:
Midnight Theatre Company, Battersea Arts Centre (£1,000);
Paines Plough (£750);
Weekend Arts College (£600);
Logos, Modern Music Theatre Troupe, Framework Children's Theatre, Red Shift, Lyric Theatre, Open Air Theatre, National Youth Music Theatre, Tricycle Theatre, Camberwell Pocket Opera, New Playwrights Trust (£500 each).
Exclusions: Individuals. Retrospective grants, dance projects which are not in a theatrical context. No repeat applications within three years.
Applications: In writing by 1 February and 1 August prior to trustees' meetings. No replies without an SAE.

The RSA Art for Architecture Scheme

8 John Adam Street, London WC2N 6EZ
Tel: 0171-930 5115; **Fax:** 0171-839 5805
Contact: Michaela Crimmin, Project Manager, Art for Architecture
Trustees: Panel Members: Sir Andrew Derbyshire, Paul Bonaventura, Sherban Cantacuzino, Dr John Gibbons, Michael Keatinge, Morris Latham, Sandra Percival.
Grant total: £72,000 (1994/95)
Beneficial area: UK.
General: This scheme, managed by the RSA (The Royal Society of Arts, Manufactures & Commerce) is a collaborative initiative with the Department of National Heritage, supported by the Scottish Office, the Welsh Office and a number of private sponsors including Marks & Spencer and British Airways plc.

It aims to create a visually stimulating urban environment by providing funds for artists to work with architects and other design professionals at the initial stages of a projects's development. ("Architect" includes landscape architects, engineers, planners etc and "artist" includes craftspeople.) The emphasis is on collaboration.

In 1994/95 the scheme supported 13 artists with grant-aid totalling £72,000. The largest grant paid to date has been £12,000. Recent grants have included:
Tania Kovats working with Axel Burrough from Levitt Bernstein Associates on the design of the refurbishment and conversion of the new Ikon Gallery, Birmingham;
Simon Patterson and Langlands & Bell working on the design of the parklands and new laboratory facilities of Hinxton Hall Medical Research Campus, Cambridgeshire.

The scheme is being extended to include Publications Awards to further the dialogue in this area of activity. Publications may include documentation and records of case studies, lectures, conferences and discussions between artists and design professionals. Applications are now also being invited from temporary as well as permanent projects. Temporary projects must contribute to a longer term development.
Applications: Applications may be made by any of the partners involved in the project including the artist. Full details of criteria for Incentive Awards are available from the RSA. The projects must be accessible to the general public. The Advisory Panel meets four times a year. The final dates for submissions in 1996 are 22 March, 21 June, 20 September. Payment (not subject to VAT) is made direct to the artist in 3 equal instalments on receipt of: a copy of a contract or letter of intent between the artist and the client; a progress report and artist's invoice from the applicant on behalf of the artist half way through the contract; proof that the artist's employment is complete as per contract.

Successful applicants are required to include the Art for Architecture funding mark in their publicity material.

The Willy Russell Charitable Trust

Malthouse & Co, Chartered Accountants, America House, Rumford Court, Rumford Place, Liverpool L3 9DD

Tel: 0151-284 2000
Contact: J Malthouse
Trustees: Willy Russell, Ann Russell, John Malthouse.
Grant total: £24,000 (1992/93)
Beneficial area: UK.
General: In 1992/93, its first full year of operation, this trust, set up by the well-known playwright, gave over £6,000 in two student sponsorships, one for theatre school and the other for university. The remaining £18,000 was given amongst 11 causes, five of which were arts organisations. Arts grants have included:
Unity Theatre (£3,000);
Acorn Gallery (£1,000);
National Youth Music Theatre, Raw Cotton Theatre Co, International Drama in Education Association (£500 each).
Applications: In writing to the correspondent.

The RVW Trust

7th Floor, Mansfield House, 376-379 Strand, London WC2R OLR

Tel: 0171-370 6547
Contact: Bernard Benoliel, Administrator
Trustees: Michael Kennedy (Chairman), John Alldis, Lord Armstrong of Ilminster, Lord Chelmer, Eric Downing, Eva Hornstein, Bruce Roberts, Jeremy Dale Roberts, Michael Tippett, UK. Mrs Ralph Vaughan Williams, Miss Muriel Williams.
Grant total: £254,000 (1993)
Beneficial area: UK.
General: The trust's objects include support to the public performance of musical works (including opera and concerts), copying and music festivals.

In 1993 £37,000 was set aside for five Electro-Acoustic Music Scholarships of up to £7,500 each. Each of the four royal colleges of music received £25,000 to encourage the study and performance of contempo-rary British music. Grants were given for young composers to study for first perform-ances and to performing organisations. These included:
English Folk Dance and Song Society (£17,500);
Music Space Trust (£8,000);
National Opera Studio (£7,000);
Haddo House Choral and Operatic Society (£3,000);
Mayer-Lismann Opera Centre (£2,000);
Piano Circus, Luton Music Club, Soundpool, Huddersfield Contemporary Music Festival (£1,000 each).
Applications: In writing to the correspondent. Meetings are held three times a year - November, February/ March and June/July (the latter is mainly devoted to composition students).

The Audrey Sacher Charitable Trust

c/o Marks & Spencer plc, Michael House, 47 Baker Street, London W1A IDN

Tel: 0171-935 4422
Contact: Mrs I Bailey
Trustees: Simon Sacher, Jeremy Sacher, Michael Sacher.
Grant total: £96,000 (1994/95)
Beneficial area: UK.
General: The trust states its main areas of interest are the arts, medicine and care. It is understood that grants are only made to charities known personally to the trustees. In 1994/95 arts grants included:
English National Ballet (£25,000);
Royal Opera House Trust (£25,000 with large grants in the previous year);
Glyndebourne Productions (£10,000 and in the previous year);
Anna Freud Centre (£2,000 with £12,000 and £17,000 in the 2 previous years);
Contemporary Dance Trust, Courtauld Institute (£5,000 each);
Royal College of Music (£4,000 in 2 grants);
London masterclasses, Parnham Trust (£1,000 each).
Several small grants of under £1,000 were given to organisations such as the Royal Ballet School and the Almeida Theatre.

Exclusions: Individuals, organisations not registered as charities.
Applications: In writing to the correspondent, but see above.

Dr Mortimer & Theresa Sackler Foundation

66 Chester Square, London SW1W 9DU

Contact: Mrs Helen Bonneaus
Trustees: Mortimer Sackler, Thereas Sackler, Christopher Mitchell, Robin Stormonth-Darling, Raymond Smith.
Grant total: £400,000 (1993)
Beneficial area: UK.
General: The foundation's interests are the arts, science and medical research. Arts grants in 1993:
Tate Gallery (£125,000 and in the previous year);
National Gallery (£120,000);
Ashmolean Museum, Oxford (£13,650);
National Maritime Museum (£50,000 with £37,500 in the previous year);
Young Musicians' Symphony Orchestra (£10,000);
London Library Appeal (£4,000 with £1,000 in the previous year);
Royal Opera House (£400 with £2,400 in the previous year);
London Suzuki Group (£250).
The foundation has major commitments to the National Galley, Ashmolean, the Tate and the National Maritime Museum. Since the foundation's income seems likely to fall the prospect for new initiatives is not great.
Applications: In writing to the correspondent, but note above.

The Leonard Sainer Charitable Trust

Titmus Sainer Dechent, 2 Serjeant's Inn, London EC4Y ILT

Tel: 0171-583 5353
Contact: The Secretary
Trustees: Silas Krendal, Edward Footring, A P Sainer, C L Corman.
Grant total: £29,000 (1994/95)
Beneficial area: UK.
General: This trust gives to Jewish, the arts and welfare charities. It total grant-aid has fallen markedly (£163,000 in 1991/92; £71,000 in 1993/94). Arts grants in 1994/95 were given to:
British Israel Arts Foundation (£2,000);
Royal Opera House (£1,761).
Grants under £1,000 were given to the Chicken Shed Theatre and the Royal Opera House Trust.
Applications: In writing to the correspondent.

The Alan and Babette Sainsbury Charitable Trust

c/o Clark Whitehill, 25 New Street Square, London EC4A 3LN

Tel: 0171-353 1577
Contact: D J Walker
Trustees: Lord Sainsbury, Iimon Sainsbury, Miss J S Portrait,
Grant total: £340,000 (1993/94)
Beneficial area: UK and overseas.
General: The fund gives many recurrent grants and is notable for its support to organisations addressing the most intractable social problems. Its accounts show its grant-aid categorised under major headings, giving the names of organisations supported without any information about the size of individual grants. These categories were: Education; Health and Social Welfare; Overseas; Scientific and Medical Research; Religion; Environment; The Arts.

In 1993/94 five arts grants were given to organisations each of which had be supported in the previous two years: *Anna Freud Centre; English Stage Company; Weiner Library Endowment Trust; Young Concert Artists' Trust; Youth and Music.* The Education category included a grant to the *Writers' and Scholars' Education Trust.* In the previous year the *Braintree Museum,* the *Soho Theatre Fund* had also been supported.
Exclusions: Individuals.
Applications: In writing to the correspondent.

The Sainsbury Family Charitable Trusts

9 Red Lion Court, London EC4A 3EB

Tel: 0171-410 0330
Contact: Michael Pattison
General: The Sainsbury Family Charitable Trusts included in this guide are:
The Gatsby Charitable Foundation
The Monument Trust
The Linbury Trust
The Headley Trust
The Jerusalem Trust
The Ashden Trust.
All these trusts have a common administration and one letter will ensure that an application is considered by whichever trust is the most appropriate. Each trust has different policies and priorities although there are overlapping interests, and often overlapping trustees. All are prepared to consider applications for capital costs.
Exclusions: None of the Sainsbury Family Charitable Trusts listed here gives grants direct to individuals.
Applications: The trusts do not provide any guidelines for applicants or application forms. Applicants should apply in writing including details of the organisation, its project, costs and planned outcomes.

The Basil Samuel Charitable Trust

c/o Ernst & Young, Beckett House, 1 Lambeth Palace Toad, London SE17EU

Tel: 0171-580 3040
Contact: George Howkins
Trustees: Coral Samuel, Richard Perkins.
Grant total: £564,000 (1993/94)
Beneficial area: UK and overseas.
General: The trust gives mainly to Jewish charities, medical work and the arts. in 1993/94 it gave only 22 grants, the largest of which was to Jewish Care (£100,000). The trust seems to favour giving substantial grants and half were £20,000 or more. Arts grants were given to:
Royal Academy of Arts (£75,000);
London Historic House Museum Trust (£50,000);
National Gallery Trust (£50,000 and in the previous year);
Prince of Wales's Institute of Architecture (£20,000 and in the previous year).
Large grants have been given in the previous year to the English National Opera, Dulwich Picture Gallery, Chelsea Physic Garden and the Natural History Museum.
Applications: In writing to the correspondent.

The Coral Samuel Charitable Trust

c/o Ernst & Young, Beckett House, 1 Lambeth Palace Road, London SE1 7EU

Tel: 0171-580 3040
Contact: George Howkins
Trustees: Coral Samuel, P Fineman.
Grant total: £235,000 (1993. 94)
Beneficial area: UK.
General: The trust gives to health, the art and a wide range of other charities. It tends to make a few substantial grants, many of which are recurrent, and a considerable number of small grants of under £1,000. In 1993/94 when 33 grants were given, arts grants included:
Glyndebourne Productions (£25,000);
Chelsea Physic Garden (£15,000 and in the previous year);
Royal Opera House Trust (£13,000 with £5,000 in the previous year);
Anna Freud Centre (£10,500);
Natural History Museum Development Trust (£10,000 and in the previous Year);
Royal National Theatre (£3,000);
Chicken Shed Theatre (£1,000).
Grants under £1,000 included the Hampstead Theatre Trust and the North West London Orchestra.
Applications: In writing to the correspondent.

The Save & Prosper Educational Trust

Finsbury Dials, 20 Finsbury Street, London EC2Y 9AY

Tel: 0171-417 2332
Contact: Duncan Grant, Director
Trustees: Save & Prosper Group Limited has appointed the following Managing Committee: C J Rye, D Grant, I W Lindsey, J G Tregoning.
Grant total: £1,155,000 (1994/95)
Beneficial area: UK.
General: The trust supports educational projects which "generally fit into one of the following categories:

* support for primary and secondary schools, tertiary educational establishments such as universities as well as research bodies and museums.

* Community projects, particularly those relating to children and young people in inner-cities. We aim to improve the education and training of these people, particularly in information technology, and to widen the opportunities open to them, giving them prospects of a more rewarding adult life.

* Arts education, with the emphasis on helping more people gain access to the arts and to better appreciate them. Support for performing, fine and decorative arts is usually directed at school-age children and students.

* Education for the disadvantaged. This covers special needs, inner cities, ethnic minorities and, more recently, the rural disadvantaged.

* Scholarships and bursaries to organisations for educational fees and maintenance. Generally, direct support is not given to individuals.

* New and innovative ways of advancing education in the UK".

It is the usual policy of the trust to establish, where possible and appropriate, a relationship with successful applicants, particularly those of larger grants. Although the general policy of the trust is not to make firm commitments for longer than two years, support can be continued in exceptional cases on a year to year basis without a commitment to any definite period.

In 1994/95 a total of 250 grants were given ranging between £100 and £33,000. Over £240,000 was allocated to arts interests. Arts grants included:
Museum of Scotland (£33,000);
National Maritime Museum, Royal Opera House (£20,000 each);
National Gallery, Interchange Trust for Weekend Arts College, Oval House, Welsh National Opera (£15,000 each);
Crafts Council (£14,000);
Purcell School (£10,000);
Queen's Theatre Trust (£8,000);
Traverse Theatre, Foundation for Young Musicians, Saturday Arts Scheme (£6,000 each);
Hullaballoo Theatre Company (£5,200);
Byam Shaw School of Art, Central School of Ballet, Contemporary Dance Trust, English National Ballet, National Youth Orchestra, Offstage Community Art Resource, Scottish Opera, Spitalfields Festival (£5,000 each);
Dulwich Picture Gallery (£3,000);
Actors' Centre Building Appeal, Contemporary Applied Arts, Light Opera (£2,500 each);
Manchester Dance Trust, Kettles Yard (£2,000);
London Suzuki Group (£1,500);
Royal Academy of Music (£1,300);
Community Music East, Northern Junior Philharmonic Orchestra (£1,000);
Fruitmarket Gallery, Havering College for Conundrum Arts (£500 each).
A handful of other small grants of £500 and less were also given.
Exclusions: Open appeals from national charities; charity gala nights and similar events; appeals by individuals ; building appeals.
Applications: In writing (a brief letter of not more than two A4 sides) enclosing any relevant publicity material and accounts. Applications are always acknowledged. Those supported by a member of Save and Prosper's staff may be particularly welcome. Unsuccessful applicants should wait a year before reapplying. Trustees meet in March, May, July, September and December.

The Save & Prosper Foundation

Finsbury Dials, 20 Findsbury Street, London EC2Y 9AY

Tel: 0171-417 2332
Contact: Duncan Grant, Director
Trustees: Save & Prosper Group Limited has appointed the following Managing Committee: C J Rye, D Grant, I W Lindsey, P J Roney.
Grant total: £192,000 (1994/95)
Beneficial area: UK.
General: The foundation supports a range of charitable activities, compared with its sister organisation the Save and Prosper Educational Trust which operates from the same building with the same administration but with a solely educational brief, including arts education.

In 1994/95 the foundation made 76 grants ranging between £100 and £20,000, half of which were small and of a few hundred pounds. Arts grants were given to:
Royal Academy of Arts (£7,000);
Barbican Art Gallery (£5,000);
Royal Opera House Trust (£4,500);
English National Opera (£4,000);
Brereton Int Music Symposium (£3,000);
Royal Academy Trust Ltd (£2,938);
London Philharmonic Orchestra (£2,526);
ABSA (£1,623);
English Chamber Orchestra and Music Society (£1,175).

Applications: See advice for the Save and Prosper Educational Trust. One application will suffice to both charities which share a common administration.

The Francis Scott Charitable Trust

Sand Aire House, Kendal, Cumbria LA9 4BE
Tel: 01539-723415
Contact: Donald Harding, Director
Trustees: R W Sykes (Chair), W A Willink, A G Thompson, Lord Cavendish of Furness, Miss M M Scott, F A Scott, Dr R A Hanham, W Dobie, I H Pirnie.
Grant total: £812,000 (1994/95)
Beneficial area: UK, but in effect Cumbria and Lancashire only.

General: The trust gives a large number of relatively small grants in Cumbria and Lancashire. Its first geographical priority is Cumbria and North Lancashire as far south as Lancaster and Including Morecambe and Heysham. Its second geographical priority is to the area within the county boundary of Lancashire. Beneficiaries should be registered charities involved with work with/ for under privileged or disadvantaged people. It is within this context that arts activities would receive support. Grants may be given for either capital or revenue purposes and range from under £1,000 to £5,000 with occasional larger sums where there is a particular interest in the work of the charity concerned. Arts grants in 1994/ 95 included:
Kendal Brewery Arts Centre (£15,000 plus £10,000 loan write-off);
Prism Arts, Carlisle (£3,000);
Community Arts Mobile Workshop Team, Contact Theatre Company Manchester, Cartwheel Community Arts, Lancs CC Summer Arts Project Rossendale (£1,000 each);
Actors Workshop Youth Theatre, Halton Youth Roadshow (£750 each);
Disability Arts Magazine Publishing Ltd Grimsby, Friends of Knowsley Youth Performing Arts, Live Music Now, Multi-Asian Arts Rochdale, Oily Cart Co (£500 each).

Exclusions: Individuals; organisations not registered as charities; projects formerly statutorily funded; church restoration; exhibitions.
Applications: An application form has to be returned with the latest set of accounts. The trustees meet three times a year around March, June and October. Applications need to arrive two months before each meeting. The director is happy to discuss requirements with potential applicants over the telephone.

The Frieda Scott Charitable Trust

Sand Aire House, Kendal, Cumbria LA9 4BE

Tel: 01539-723415
Contact: Donald Harding, Secretary
Trustees: Mrs C Brookbank (Chair), Mrs O Clarke, Mrs C R Scott, O Turnbull, R A Hunter, P R Hensman, D Y Mitchell.
Grant total: £139,000 (1994/95)
Beneficial area: The Westmoreland and Lonsdale constituency area as well as the area covered by the South Lakeland District Council.
General: The trust shares the same correspondent and address, though not the same trustees, as the Francis Scott Charitable Trust (see separate entry). In 1994/95 about 60 grants were given. Eight arts organisations received grants totalling over £70,000, several having received help in the previous year. Arts grants were given to:
Brewery Arts Centre (£60,000);
Westmoreland Music Council (£3,750);
Mary Wakefield Music Festival (£2,000);
Friends of Cumbria Youth Orchestra,
Westmoreland Orchestra (£1,000 each);
Renaissance Theatre, Ulverston (£850);
Kendal Mid-day Concert Society (£750).
Applications: In writing. Applications are considered three times a year and applicants are notified of the trustees' action. Applicants are welcome to telephone for an informal discussion before making a formal approach.

The Scouloudi Foundation

c/o Hays Allan, Southampton House, 317 High Holborn, London WC1V 7NL

Tel: 0171-831 6233
Contact: The Administrator
Trustees: J M Carr, A J Parr, M E Demtriadi, Miss B R Masters, J D Marnham, Miss S E Stowell.
Grant total: £131,000 (1994/95)
Beneficial area: UK, but not for activities of a purely local nature
General: The trust splits its donations into three categories - "regular", "special" and "historical awards". These awards totalled £60,000 in 1994/95 and are given to individuals for historical research. "Regular" donations are made each year to a basic list of some 110 national charities, which is unlikely to be extended (£60,000 in 1994/95) "Special" donations absorb the remainder. Most of these grants are not recurrent, are of £1,000 or less, and for special appeals.
Arts grants in 1994/95 were given to:
British Museum Society (£1,000);
Friends of the National Libraries, National Art Collections Fund, Historic Churches Preservation Trust (£800 each);
Architectural Heritage Fund (£400).
Exclusions: Except for the historical awards, grants are only made to registered charities and not to individuals. No grants to purely local causes.
Applications: Only a small proportion of the funds are uncommitted. Applications with full but concise details should be sent to the correspondent. These applications are considered once a year in March.

The Sears Foundation

Sears plc, 40 Duke Street, London W1A 2HP

Tel: 0171-200 5999
Contact: D Drum
Trustees: Sir Bob Reid, Liam Strong, David Defty, Rod Taylor, David Drum.
Grant total: £117,000 (1994/95)
Beneficial area: UK.
General: Whilst it is understood the arts are not a priority, a number of arts grants are given each year. In 1993/94 when £42,000 was disbursed these were:
Glyndebourne Festival Society (£3,200);
RSA Student Design Awards, British Museum Society (£1,000 each);
Edinburgh International Festival, Almeida Theatre (£500 each);
National Youth Ballet (£300);
British Youth Orchestra (£250);
Joe Loss Concert (£200).
Applications: In writing to the correspondent.

The Skinners' Company Lady Neville Charity

Skinners' Hall, 8 Dowgate Hill, London EC1R 2SP

Tel: 0171-236 5629
Contact: The Clerk
Trustees: The Master and Wardens of the Worshipful Company of Skinners.
Grant total: £162,000 (1993/94)
Beneficial area: UK.
General: This charity almost entirely funds the company schools. However a sum of about £30,000 is also available to assist about 100 charities with small grants. Arts grants in 1993/94 included:
City and Guilds of London Art School
    (£600);
Museum of London (£500);
Molecule Theatre, Guildhall School of Music
    and Drama Foundation (£250 each);
Foundation for Young Musicians (£200);
Whitechapel Art Gallery, London Symphony
    Orchestra (£150 each);
Shape London, Salisbury Cathedral Girl
    Choristers Trust, Live Music Now! (£100
    each).
Exclusions: Charities which are not registered; schools other than Company schools; purely local charities outside London.
Applications: By letter to the Clerk by the end of March and the end of September enclosing a copy of the latest accounts, Acknowledgements are not normally made.

The Henry Smith's (Kensington Estate) Charity

5 Chancery Lane, Clifford's Lane, London EC4A IBU

Tel: 0171-242 1212
Contact: Brian McGeough, Treasurer
Trustees: Lord Kindersley (Chairman), Mrs A E Allen, Lord Ashcombe, Lord Crawshaw, T E Egerton, Lord Egremont, Lady Euston, Lord Gage, J D Hambro, Lord Hamilton of Dazell, T D Holland-Martin, T F Jones, Lord Kingsdown, Major E J de Lisle, J N C James, Ronnie Norman, J J Sheffield, J F Smith, G E Lee-Steere.

Grant total: £12,520,000 (1994)
Beneficial area: UK, but a high proportion of the charity's local grants are made in London, East or West Sussex, Kent, Surrey, Hampshire, Gloucestershire, Leicestershire and Suffolk.
General: This large trust supports medicine, disability and social welfare. It is included in this guide not because it has any arts interests per se, but because it supports arts organisations working with the disabled and the disadvantaged. The charity makes three kinds of donations:

* one-off grants in response to applications received for specific projects;

* annual grants, subject to re-application every three years;

* grants to organisations in the counties of Gloucester, Hampshire, Kent, Leicestershire, Suffolk, Surrey and East and West Sussex.

The County lists: Each county list is the responsibility of an individual trustee or other person who is normally resident in the county concerned. Applications are made both through the offices of the charity and direct to the trustees concerned. The appointed trustees are as follows:
Gloucestershire: T D Holland-Martin, The Overbury Estate, Near Tewkesbury, Gloucestershire.
Hampshire: J J L G Sheffield, Laverstoke Mill House, Whitchurch, Hampshire.
Kent: Ronnie Norman, St. Clere Estates, St. Clere, Kemsing, Sevenoaks, Kent.
Leicestershire: Major E J R M D de Lisle, Stockerston Hall, Uppingham, Leicestershire.
Suffolk: The Countess of Euston, The Racing Stables, Euston, Thetford, Suffolk.
Surrey: G E Lee-Steere, Jayes Park, Ockley, Surrey.
East Sussex: T F Jones, The Old Rectory, Berwick, Polegate, East Sussex
West Sussex: J F E Smith, The Old Rectory, Slaugham, Haywards Heath, West Sussex.

Every year a major and specific programme of work in a particular field or geographical area is undertaken, funded with £1. 5 million over the following three years.

Grants for arts activities in 1994 were given to:

North Kensington Video/Drama Project, London, for young people at risk (£20,000, 2nd of 3);

Community Music East, Norfolk, towards its Young Offender programme (£10,000, 3rd of 3);

Artsline Limited, London, salary and costs of an Asian Outreach Worker (£14,000, 2nd of 3);

Council for Music in Hospitals, (£7,000, 2nd of 3);

Oily Cart Co Ltd, London, for a project for children with severe learning difficulties (£7,000, 3rd of 3);

SHAPE, London, towards the training of young disabled students (£6,000);

Painshill Park Trust, Surrey (£3,500);

West Kent Youth Theatre (£1,000);

Kingswood Arts Umbrella, Gloucestershire (£500);

Snowball Arts, Hampshire (£500);

Stoneligh Youth Orchestra, Surrey (£200).

Exclusions: Individuals, care or restoration of buildings.

Applications: In writing to the correspondent. The Chief Visitor is Virginia Graham. The charity does not use application forms but offers the following guidelines to applicants for grants:

1. Applications should be no longer than four A4 sides (plus budget and accounts) and should incorporate a short (half page) summary.

2. Applications should:

a. state clearly who the applicant is, what it does and whom it seeks to help.

b. give the applicant's status (eg. registered charity).

c. describe the project for which a grant is sought clearly and succinctly; explain the need for it; say what practical results it is expected to produce; state the number of people who will benefit from it; show how it will be cost effective and say what stage the project has so far reached.

d. enclose a detailed budget for the project together with a copy of the applicant's most recent audited accounts. (If those accounts show a significant surplus or deficit of income, please explain how this has arisen).

e. name the applicant's trustees/patrons and describe the people who will actually be in charge of the project giving details of their qualifications for the job.

f. describe the applicant's track record and, where possible, give the names and addresses of two independent referees to whom Henry Smith's Charity may apply for a recommendation if it wishes to do so.

g. state what funds have already been raised for the project and name any other sources of funding to whom the applicant has applied.

h. explain where the on-going funding (if required) will be obtained when the charity's grant has been used.

i. state what plans have been made to monitor the project and wherever possible to evaluate it and, where appropriate, to make its results known to others.

j. ask, where possible, for a specific amount.

3. Please keep the application as simple as possible and avoid the use of technical terms and jargon.

The Spitalfields Market Community Trust

Attlee House, 28 Commercial Street, London E1 6LR

Tel: 0171-247 6689; Fax: 0171-247 8748
Contact: Ms Sandra Davidson, Grants Administrator
Trustees: Rev Christopher Bedford (Chairman), K B Appiah, Dr G R Cruickshank, Miss S E M Currie, N F Smith.
Grant total: £730,000 (1993/94)
Beneficial area: The London Borough of Tower Hamlets, and specifically Bethnal Green.

General: The trust was established as part of the "planning gain" arrangements with the development of Spitalfields market. The trust has general charitable objects with a particular interest in job opportunities, training, environmental improvements and sheltered housing. The arts organisations in its area which received support in 1993/94 were:

Whitechapel Art Gallery (£30,590);
Spitalfields Festival Education & Community
   Programme (£19,110);
Spitalfields Market Opera (£5,000);
Chisenhale Art Education Programme
   (£2,900);
East London Late Starter Orchestra (£960).
Exclusions: Organisations outside Tower
Hamlets.
Applications: To the grants administrator
on its application form accompanied by the
latest annual report and accounts,
governing documents, copy of all leases,
and equal opportunities statement. The
trust meets twice a year to consider
applications in March and September and
completed applications must be received by
the end of January for the March meeting
and the end of July for the September
meeting.

The Foundation for Sport and the Arts

PO Box 20, Liverpool L13 1HB

Tel: 0151-259 5505; Fax: 0151-230 0664
Contact: Grattan Endicott, Secretary
Trustees: Sir Tim Rice (Chairman), Lord
Brabazon of Tara, Nicholas Allott, Lord
Attenborough, Dame Janet Baker, Sir
Christopher Chataway, Clive Lloyd, Rebecca
Stephens, Malcolm Davidson, Michael
Smith, Paul Zetter.
Grant total: £56,875,000 (1994/95)
Beneficial area: UK.
General: This huge foundation is "an
independent discretionary trust... funded via
the football pools and this is made possible,
in part, by a reduction in pool betting duty...
While the pursuit of excellence is not
ignored... Its main objective is to support
measures to increase participation in, and
enjoyment of, sport and the arts by the
whole community, regardless of levels of
competence... The foundation "ring-fences"
60% of its disposable funds for medium and
small bids. The purpose is to safeguard the
shares enjoyed by smaller schemes. These
are often the cases that are closest to the
ground, local to the towns and villages
throughout the UK. We help a lot of larger

projects, but only after we have set money
aside for those who ask little." (1995 Annual
Report).

The foundation aims to give a third of its
funding to arts projects, with two-thirds
given to sports and related activities.

The foundation sends out monthly lists of
all its grants to the media giving the name
of the organisation, its address plus a brief
note on the purpose of the grant and its
size. The arts grants are arranged in the
following groups: Dance, Drama, Literature,
Festivals, Multidisciplinary, Music including
Opera, Visual Arts, Museums and Galleries,
Film and Television, Crafts, Theatres. A few
individual artists received grants.

Its 1994/95 annual report analysed
approvals by county in both sports and the
arts and showed every county in the UK
apportioned funds. These provided, for
example, the following totals of *approved*
arts grants:
Scotland £1,704,000
Northern Ireland £1,085,000
Wales £2,065,000
Greater London £4,636,000
The introduction of the National Lottery has
had a considerable effect on the income of
the pools companies and it seems unlikely
that the foundation will be able to maintain
this scale of grant-making.

Grants made in 1994/95 showed
allocations to mainstream arts organisations
such as the Royal Opera, Royal Scottish
National Orchestra, Welsh National Opera.
The following sample list shows the wide
range of organisations supported:
Belfast Civic Arts Theatre (£149,000);
Glasgow Film Theatre (£100,000);
Brixton Academy (£80,000);
Royal Court Theatre, London (£75,000);
Women's Radio Group (£15,206);
Small Bones Dance Company (£13,000);
Swansea Little Theatre (£12,000);
Antrim Camera Club (£9,030);
Lancaster Literature Festival (£8,880);
No Fit State Theatre (£7,420);
Banbridge Pipe Band (£5,000);
Country Music Festival, Scotland (£5,000);
Pontypridd Male Choir (£1,600);
Skye Arts Guild (£500);
An upper limit of £150,000 to any one

grant has been agreed. Small grants are made to individuals from time to time. The foundation considers all types of request - project-based, revenue and capital requests.

Applications: The Arts Team comprises: Carole McGiveron (Leader), Carla Sinners, Sue Connor, Charles Adebayo, Lyn Fitzgerald. Applications should give background, stating the purpose of the organisation's existence and a brief note of its history and affiliations. They should also include:

- completed questionnaire (available from the foundation).
- latest financial statements;
- purposes for the grant, backed up, as appropriate, with reports by consultants and professional advisers;
- total cost of the project and the amount requested from the foundation.
- information on other money which will, or may, be committed
- In particular: How many people will benefit from the proposal? What numbers of people will be accommodated? Who owns the club, society premises etc. (eg. is it a charity?) and who runs it - board of governors, trustees, members' committee or the like.
- Information about who may/will be involved in the realisation of the plan eg. suppliers and contractors
- Any expressions or support from noteworthy sources.

The trustees would prefer that your detailed application should be accompanied by a synopsis of the key elements set out on a single sheet of A4 paper.

The application will be submitted to the relevant working party, followed by further contact with the applicant to whom the reaction of the working party will be made known. Further information may be requested and professional advisors to the foundation may seek a meeting with the applicant. (The trustees do not make themselves available for presentation of cases in person.) The working party obtains any further reports before making a recommendation to trustees.

Organisations offered grants must await the formal letter of offer before committing the money in order to ensure that they know the precise terms on which the grants are offered and the exact objects for which they are given. Cases approved for grants are held in a queue and offers released each week as fresh funds arrive from the pools firms.

The Steel Charitable Trust

Messrs Bullimores, 3 Boutport Street, Barnstaple, Devon EX31 1RH

Tel: 01271-75257
Contact: The Secretary
Trustees: Mrs M M Steel, N E W Wright, A W Hawkins, H M Hay.
Grant total: £799,000 (1994)
Beneficial area: UK, with some preference for Bedfordshire.
General: The trust's grants in 1994 were categorised as follows:
Culture & recreation £52,500 7%
Medical research £120,000 15%
Health £138,000 17%
Social services £328,500 41%
Environment/preservation £144,500 18%
International aid £15,000 2%
About 60 grants were given ranging between £1,000 and £100,000 with most for £10,000+. Arts grants included:
Royal Academy of Music (£20,000 and in the previous year);
Queens Theatre Trust, Salisbury Cathedral Girls' Choir (£10,000 each);
Friends of Luton Museum (£8,000).
Applications: In writing. Applications are not acknowledged.

The Stevenson Family's Charitable Trust

33 King William Street, London EC4R 9AS

Tel: 0171-280 2840
Contact: H A Stevenson
Trustees: H A Stevenson, Mrs C M Stevenson, J F Lever.
Grant total: £58,000 (1993/94)
Beneficial area: UK and overseas.
General: The trust gives to a wide range of

causes. It has recently given large grants to arts organisations. In 1993/94 these were:

Shakespeare's Globe Theatre (£16,000 with £1,000 in the previous year);

Glyndebourne (£100 with £24,316 in the previous year to its building fund);

British Museum Society (£1,000 also given in the previous year).

The assets of this trust not large and these exceptional gifts have been possible because of a Gift Aid payment of over £150,000 in 1992/93.

Exclusions: The trust has written "As the charity's funds are required to support purposes chosen by the trustees, no unsolicited applications can be considered".

Applications: In writing to the correspondent.

The Stoll Moss Theatres Foundation *(formerly the Robert Holmes à Court Foundation)*

21 Soho Square, London W1V 5FD

Tel: 0171-494 5200

Contact: Richard Johnston, Chief Executive

Trustees: Mrs Janet Homes á Court, Sir Michael Clapham, Derek Williams, Richard Johnston.

Grant total: £37,000 (1994)

Beneficial area: UK.

General: The primary focus of the foundation has been the development of theatrical arts. Grants in 1994 were given to:

Black Swan Theatre Co (£20,000);

Zenana Theatre Co (£4,000);

Royal Academy of Dance (£2,500);

Shape London (£2,000);

Mercury Workshop, Sarah Esdaile Productions, Fin de Siecle, Talawa Theatre Trust (£1,000 each);

Gate Theatre (£428).

Exclusions: No funding for capital costs.

Applications: The foundation has written that it "maintains a limited programme of support for projects of its own initiation and does not provide funding in response to applications".

The Alexander Stone Foundation

36 Renfield Street, Glasgow G2 1LU

Tel: 0141-226 4431

Contact: Robert B Black, Administrator

Beneficial area: UK with a particular interest in Scotland, especially Glasgow.

General: It is understood that the trust is mainly interested in the promotion of arts and education. Whilst grants are mainly given in Scotland, applications from the rest of the UK are also considered. Grants have ranged from less than £100 and £150,000.

Exclusions: Organisations not registered as charities.

Applications: In writing, enclosing the report and accounts and charity number. The trustees meet at the end of March, June, September and December.

The Summerfield Charitable Trust

PO Box 4, Winchcombe, Cheltenham, Gloucestershire GL54 5ZD

Tel: 01242-676774

Contact: Mrs Lavinia Sidgwick, Administrator

Trustees: The Earl Fortescue, Martin Davis.

Grant total: £310,000 (1994)

Beneficial area: UK, but particularly Gloucestershire.

General: In 1994 the trust gave 141 grants, eight of which were £10,000 and higher, 11 between £5,000 and £9,900, 55 under £1,000 and the majority – 89 – between £1,000 and £4,900. Grants were given in the following categories:

Arts £44,900 (16)

Museums £12,214 (5)

Conservation and environment £20,00 (11)

Disabled and chronically sick £62,550 (26)

Elderly £44,750 (13)

Education £34,950 (15)

Recreation, community work, sport £29,600 (15)

Other categories were homeless, counselling and youth. Causes in Gloucestershire attract most attention. Applicants outside the county are only likely to receive relatively small grants. In 1994 grants relevant to this guide were:

Under "Arts"

Cheltenham Arts Festivals Ltd (£16,500);
Everyman Theatre (£11,000);
Art Shape Ltd (£4,000);
Langley House Trust, a conversion to make an art therapy room in a home for ex-offenders (£2,500);
Cirencester Workshops Trust (£1,000);
Solango, for dance course by Nigerian dancer, Disability Art Magazine, Charlton Kings Choral Society (£500 each);
Cheltenham Choral Society (£400).

Exclusions: London-based projects; national charities where the trust has already supported a local branch. Private organisations and individuals are only very rarely supported.

Applications: The trustees prefer to award one-off grants to help fund specific projects. Meetings are held quarterly in February, April, July and October when all applications received before the end of the preceding month are considered. All new applications are acknowledged. An SAE is welcomed.

The Bernard Sunley Charitable Foundation

53 Grosvenor Street, London W1X 9FH

Tel: 0171-409 1199; Fax: 0171-409 7373
Contact: D C Macdiarmid, Director
Trustees: John B Sunley, Sir William Shapland, Mrs Joan M Tice, Mrs Bella Sunley, Sir Donald Gosling.
Grant total: £3,941,000 (1994/95)
Beneficial area: UK and overseas.
General: In 1994/95 grants were made to 325 charities. The main categories of giving were as follows:
The arts, museums etc - £291,000
Universities, colleges, schools - £297,000
Community aid & recreation - £603,000
Youth clubs, training - £287,000
Churches, chapels - £138,000
Hospitals & medical schools - £400,000
General Medicine - £137,000
The elderly including housing - £1,453,000

Additional support was also given to service charities, professional bodies, wildlife/environment and overseas. Applications for capital funding given consideration. Arts grants in 1994/95 included:

National Gallery (£60,000);
Fleet Air Arm Museum, Liverpool National Conservation Centre (£50,000 each);
Glyndebourne Arts Trust (£23,200);
Sixteen Choir and Orchestra London (£10,000);
Bar Convent Museum Trust, Birmingham Central Library for James Watt papers (£5,000 each);
Royal Opera House Trust (£4,000);
Young Concert Artists Trust (£3,000);
Dundee Heritage Trust, Living Paintings Trust, Pitlochry Festival Trust (£2,500 each);
Natural History Museum Development Trust (£2,000);
National Horseracing Museum (£1,500);
Harry Simpson Memorial Library appeal, Museum of Garden History, Young Persons Concert Foundation (£1,000 each).

Exclusions: No grants to individuals.
Applications: In writing to the director, with latest audited accounts. Regret no reply to unsuccessful applicants.

The Swan Trust

Pollen House, 10-12 Cork Street, London W1X 1PD

Tel: 0171-439 9061
Contact: The Secretary
Trustees: The Cowdray Trust Ltd.
Grant total: £23,000 (1993/94)
Beneficial area: UK.
General: In 1993/94 the trust which has general charitable objects gave some £5,000 (22% of its grant-aid) to arts organisations. These included:
Live Music Now! (£1,500);
Royal National Theatre (£600);
Tate Gallery Foundation (£575);
Music at Oxford, London Library, British Museum Society (£500 each);
Royal Academy Trust, St John's Smith Square (£250 each);

The Maltings, Farnham (£100).
Exclusions: Individuals. Organisations not registered as charities.
Applications: In writing to the correspondent. Acknowledgement will only be made if an SAE is sent.

The Theatres Trust Charitable Fund

22 Charing Cross Road, London WC2H OHR
Tel: 0171-836 8591
Contact: Peter Longman, Director
Trustees: G Laurence Harbottle (Chairman), Peter Plouviez, Ian Albery, Baroness Birk, Yvonne Brewster, Sir Geoffrey Cass, Sir John Drummond, Gayle Hunnicutt, Sir Eddie Kulukundis, Jonathan Lane, Sir Michael Marshall, John Muir, Cob Stenham.
Grant total: £8,000 (1994/95)
Beneficial area: UK.
General: The trust was established by Parliament in 1976 and its 15 expert trustees are appointed by the Secretary of State for the National Heritage. Its main function is to advise on all planning applications affecting land on which there is a theatre. It also gives information and advice to central and local government, theatre managements and theatre preservation groups. It conducts the "Curtains!" survey of theatres throughout the country.

Occasional small grants are given to theatres and charities working to preserve theatres.
Exclusions: Routine repairs, running costs or the elimination of deficits.
Applications: In writing to the correspondent, with cost schedules of work, as well as descriptive and illustrative material. Applicants should demonstrate how any grant made will be used to raise additional funds.

The Thornton Foundation

Saffrey Champness, Fairfax House, Fulwood Place, Gray's Inn, London WC1V 6UB
Tel: 0171-405 2828
Contact: G J Holbourn
Trustees: A H Isaacs, G Powell, H D C Thornton, R C Thornton, S J Thornton.
Grant total: £143,000 (1989/90)
Beneficial area: UK.
General: No up-to-date information about the grants made about this foundation are available. In 1989/90 the trust's main beneficiary was the Astrid Trust to which it also made loans. Arts grants in 1989/90 were:
Cheltenham Young People's Orchestra (£9,000 also supported in the previous year);
Oxted & Limpsfield Choral Society (£2,500 also in the previous year);
Ealing Chamber Orchestra (£1,500);
Parnham Trust, Beethoven Fund for Deaf Children (£1,000 each).
The Hallé Concert Society received £10,000 in the preceding year.
Applications: In writing to the correspondent.

The Tillett Trust

4 Alwyne Road, London W7 3EN
Tel: 0171-579 2911
Contact: Wilfred Stiff, Secretary and Treasurer
Trustees: Paul Strang (Chairman), David L Booth, Simon J Foster, Fiona M Grant, Wilfred C Stiff, Lady Patricia Tooley.
Grant total: £36,000 (Sept 1994)
Beneficial area: UK.
General: The trust's objects are to support education, "particularly musical education and encourage the arts, including the arts of music, drama, mime, dancing and singing". Most of its grants (44) were given to individuals and ranged between £1,500 and under £100. Four grants were given to organisations, all musical:
YCAT (£13,910);
Young Songmakers' Almanac (masterclasses) £3,000;

Moriarty Quartet (£1,400);
Wigmore Hall Concerts (Young Artists
Platforms) £1,080).
Applications: In writing to the
correspondent.

The Michael Tippett Musical Foundation

1 Dean Farrar Street, London SW1 ODY

Contact: Miss G Rhydderch
Trustees: Peter Makings (Chair), Meiron
Bowen, Ian Kemp, David Cairns, Professor
John Casken, Paul Crossley, Robert
Ponsonby, Veronica Slater, Elizabeth
Thurston, Judith Weir.
Grant total: £20,000 (July 1994)
Beneficial area: UK.
General: The trustees give priority to help
bring live and, especially contemporary
music, to audiences and participants
through performance and educational
means. The main part of the trust's
support is given to projects "although the
trust will always be sympathetic to the
needs of individuals in the music
profession". The foundation does not exist
to further the works of Sir Michael Tippett
and has no financial involvement in such
projects.

Commission fees, music copying costs,
recording projects, research or study fees
and expenses are not among the trustees'
priorities, though from time to time they
are prepared to see whether there is an
exceptional case.

In 1993/94 a total of 39 grants were
made ranging between £150 and £1,000.
Sixteen were guarantees against loss (g).
Examples of 1993/94 grants:
Huddersfield Contemporary Music Festival
(g), Electric Concerts (£1,000 each);
Strike Out Summer School ((£750);
Vocem (g) (£600);
Rare Music Club (g), Chamber Group of
Scotland (g), Shiva Nova (g), Spitalfields
Festival, Women's Playhouse Trust (£500
each);
Saltburn Music Festival (£400).
Applications: In writing to the
correspondent. A guidance leaflet is

available which applicants are advised to
obtain in advance. The trustees meet three
times a year.

The Tory Family Foundation

Five Badger, Ridgehill farm, Etchinghill,
Folkestone, Kent CT18 8NR

Contact: P N Tory
Trustees: P N Tory, J N Tory, Mrs S A Rice.
Grant total: £60,000 (1994/95)
Beneficial area: International and Kent.
General: The major part of the trust's
giving is in Kent which has included a small
number of arts grants, for instance in 1993/
94:
Folkestone & Hythe Operatic & Dramatic
Society, expansion appeal (£5,000)
Metropole Arts Centre, Folkestone for
music concerts (£4,250 with £3,500 in
the previous year).
Exclusions: Applications outside Kent are
unlikely to be considered.
Applications: In writing to the
correspondent. Only successful applications
are answered.

The TSB Foundation for England and Wales

PO Box 140, St Mary's Court, 100 Lower
Thames Street, London EC3R 6HX

Tel: 0171-204 5272; **Fax:** 0171-204 5275
Contact: Kathleen Duncan, Director
General
Trustees: The Duke of Westminster
(Chairman), Joanna Foster, P D Allen, Lord
Edward Fitzroy, D A Hinton, Lady Mary
Holborow, J P R Holt, Christine Kenrick,
L E Linaker, J W Robertson, H W E Thompson,
R D Wood.
Grant total: £819,000 (1994)
Beneficial area: England and Wales.
General: The merger which has formed the
Lloyds TSB Group will lead to a considerable
increase in the funds available to all the TSB
Foundations since the new group will be
giving 1% of pre-tax profit calculated over a
three-year period to them. The foundations
are likely to change their names to the Lloyds
TSB Foundations in 1997.

The foundation gives support to voluntary organisations assisting disabled and disadvantaged people and youth projects. It supports the arts insofar as they improve participation in and access to the arts and the national heritage, particularly for disabled people.

The majority of its income is allocated to eight regional areas with representative trustees. Over 500 grants a year are made, ranging between £250 and £10,000+. Most are on a one-off basis, with very few commitments made over two or more years. Arts grants in 1994 included:

Between £3,001 - £5,000
Wimbledon School of Arts Trust Fund, for wheelchair ramp

Between £1,001 - £2,000
Aldeburgh Foundation, to install hearing system at Snape Maltings; Bath Abbey Trust, access ramps; Artsline, London, towards access guide for elderly disabled people;
Footprints Theatre Company, Nottinghamshire, for primary school tour; Skippko Community Arts Team, Leeds, equipment for project in a hospital;
Path Productions, London, teaching materials for disabled arts group.

Exclusions: No grants to organisations not recognised as charities, individuals, general appeals, restoration of buildings.

Applications: Applicants should obtain a copy of the foundation's guidelines leaflet. Application forms are available and can be returned at any time as they are reviewed on a continuing basis. Information required includes report and audited accounts, project budget, funds already raised etc. The trustees prefer to make donations towards specific items and not to make contributions to large appeals for eg. building costs, or general running costs. For local or regional projects the average grant is rarely in excess of £2,500.

The TSB Foundation for Scotland

Henry Duncan House, 120 George Street, Edinburgh EH2 4TS
Tel: 0131-225 4555
Contact: Andrew Muirhead
Trustees: Dame Mary D Corsar, Chairman; J W Cradock, Mrs A Denholm, C D Donald, A D Foulis, P C Paisley, R G E Peggie, J D M Robertson.
Grant total: £600,000 (1994/95)
Beneficial area: Scotland.
General: This foundation is one of four set up 'to preserve... the TSB's traditional role of contributing to the life of the community' when the Trustee Savings Bank was converted into a public limited company. Although it is legally independent, the foundation works in close association with the bank. The foundation gives a good general description of its grantmaking.

The trustees' interests are therefore directed to activities at local level. Appeals of a national or general nature should therefore be broken down into specific local or regional projects.

"The majority of donations are made on a one-off basis with very few commitments made over two or more years. Successful applicants should leave at least two years before applying for further support. "For local or regional projects the average grant is currently approximately £3,000 and applicants should bear this in mind when considering an appeal."

The foundation states that its overall policy is to support underfunded voluntary organisations which enable disabled people and those who are disadvantaged through social or economic circumstances to make a contribution to the community. Its main areas of interest are stated as follows: *Education and training; Scientific and medical research; Social and community needs.* These include a number of areas of potential interest to arts organisations, including:

♦ Cultural enrichment through improving participation in and access to the arts and national heritage for disadvantaged and disabled people.

In 1994/95 grants included:
Edinburgh Festival Theatre Trust, for disabled access (over £5,000);
Artlink (£2,500-£4,999);
Council for Music in Hospitals (between £1,000-£2,499 each);
Lung Ha Theatre Company (between £100-£999 each).

The foundation will assist with funding towards capital costs providing there is a clear benefit to disadvantaged/disabled people.

Exclusions: Recognised charities only, individuals including students, activities primarily the responsibility of central or local government, general appeals, endowment funds, loans, overseas travel, recurring costs.

Applications: Application forms are available from the secretary and can be returned at any time.

The TSB Foundation for Northern Ireland

PO Box 4, 4 Queen's Square, Belfast BT1 3DJ

Tel: 01232-225599
Contact: T T T Thompson, Secretary
Grant total: £65,000 (1993)
Beneficial area: Northern Ireland.
General: The foundation mainly concentrates on social and community welfare.
Exclusions: Individuals, capital costs, general appeals.
Applications: In writing to the correspondent.

The Tudor Trust

7 Ladbroke Grove, London W11 3BD

Tel: 0171-727 8522; Fax: 0171-221 8522
Contact: Jill Powell, Grants Administrator
Trustees: Grove Charity Management Ltd - Directors: Mrs M K Graves, Mrs H M Dunwell, Dr D J T Graves, A A Grimwade, Mrs P J Buckler, C J M Graves (Director of the trust), Mrs C M Antcliff, Sir James

Swaffield, R W Anstice, Mrs L K Collins, Mrs E H Crawshaw, M S Dunwell, J W L Long.
Grant total: £17,848,000 (1994/95)
Beneficial area: Mainly UK.
General: The trust did not wish to be included in this specialist guide as they felt their inclusion was misleading and could lead to many inappropriate applications. **The trust only funds arts activities serving particular disadvantaged groups (see below). It does not support arts organisations as such.** The scale of its funding to arts activities is a small proportion (under 1%) of its total funding however, in view of the size of this trust compared with smaller trusts an entry is included.

The trust reviews its strategy every three years and adopted the following strategy in April 1994: "The Tudor Trust assists organisations with charitable objectives in promoting practical projects benefiting communities throughout the United Kingdom. It particularly welcomes applications from groups working within a rural or urban setting where need is especially great, current provision is inadequate and resources are scarce or potential is unrealised. The active involvement of local people in projects is considered important.

"At present the trust places an emphasis on projects offering support and opportunities to people who are:

• homeless or in other severe housing need
• at risk of offending, already involved in the penal system or offenders' families
• frail elderly
• carers needing support and respite
• vulnerable or who have a history of mental illness
• abusers of drugs and alcohol.

"The following information applies to grants approved in 1994/95 (as opposed to actually paid). A total of 1,372 grants were approved to a very wide range of organisations. Of these the trust's annual report noted that 14 grants totalling over £52,000 were allocated to the "Arts". However additional grants allocated under other headings (see below) increased the total given to arts by a further £109,000 in grants to six organisations.

Arts organisations receiving assistance in 1994/95 were:

Under "Arts"
Carousel (£20,000 over 2 years);
Pedalling Arts Ltd (£10,000 over 2 years);
Soft Touch Co-operative Ltd (£3,000);
Community Music Wales, Islington Arts Factory, Theatre Venture (£2,000 each);
Ithaca Ltd (£1,350);
Community Music, Manchester Young People's Theatre, North Tyneside Art Studio, Raku Works Sculptural Arts (£1,000 each);

Under "Arts: Mental Disability/Handicap"
Prism Arts (£1,000);
Under "Arts: Mental Illness"
Art Studio, Sunderland (£4,000);

Under "Arts: Offenders/Probation"
Theatre in Prisons and Probation Care (£3,000);

Under "Crime - Women's Organisations"
Creative and Supportive Trust (£40,000);
Clean Break Theatre Company (£50,000 in 2 grants);

Under "Health - Alcoholism"
Roundabout (£5,000);

Under "Welfare"
Project Ability Ltd (£5,000);
Bermondsey Village Arts Project (£3,000);
Framework Theatre Company (£1,000).

Exclusions: No grants to individuals "or arts organisations per se".

Applications: All potential applicants are strongly advised to obtain the guidelines for applicants before proceeding further. Applications may be made in writing at any time to Jill Powell, Grants Administrator. The information supplied should include:

- Latest annual accounts (or a copy of a recent financial/bank statement if the organisation is too new to have annual accounts);
- A description of the project/proposals/ area of work for which funding is required; An indication of the numbers benefiting from/involved in the project;

- A breakdown of costs (for capital works, these might be building costs, VAT, fees, furniture and equipment; for revenue they might be salaries, premises, training, publicity, expenses);
- Details of funding raised or committed to date and steps being taken to raise the balance other than the approach to the Tudor Trust;
- Any other relevant information such as the catchment area served, numbers attending existing activities per month or per annum, how revenue implications of capital proposals will be met. For new buildings or major refurbishment schemes, drawings/ plans are usually helpful.

After approval of applications a letter is sent giving the trustees' decision and explaining any conditions attached to the grant. Organisations are asked not to publicise funding they receive from the trust.

The Douglas Turner Trust

1 The Yew Trees, High Street, Henley in Arden, Solihull, West Midlands B95 5BN

Tel: 01564-793085
Contact: J E Dyke, Trust Administrator
Trustees: Roger D Turner, W S Ellis, J R Clemishaw, D P Pearson.
Grant total: £345,000 (1993/94)
Beneficial area: UK, with a strong preference for West Midlands particularly Birmingham.
General: The trust has wide charitable interests and most recently has given large grants for organisations working with old people in Birmingham. Grants to the arts in 1993/94 totalled some £21,000 (6% of total grant-aid) and were given to:
Royal Academy of Arts Gallery Appeal (£10,000);
Birmingham Museums & Art Gallery (£5,000 with £10,000 in the previous year);
Birmingham Conservatoire Junior School, Birmingham Hippodrome Development Trust (£2,000 each);
Birmingham Rep Foundation (£1,500);
Birmingham Music Festival (£100 and in the

previous year).
Exclusions: No grants to individuals.
Applications: Registered charities only. Telephone enquiries before formal applications are welcomed. Trustees meet in April, July, October and December.

The 29th May 1961 Charitable Trust

c/o Macfarlanes, 10 Norwich Street, London EC4A 1BD

Tel: 0171-831 9222; **Fax:** 0171-831 9607
Contact: Fiona Brown, The Secretary
Trustees: V E Treves, J H Cattell, P Varney, A J Mead.
Grant total: £2,969,000 (1994/95)
Beneficial area: UK with a particular interest in Warwickshire and Coventry.
General: The trust makes grants to a wide range of charities particularly in the social welfare field. Most grants are to national bodies or organisations in the London or Coventry area. A large number of regular annual payments are made. The trust states that it gives grants in three categories:
"a) Capital grants for projects in process of development or which are instigated by the trustees.
b) Recurrent grants to help ensure the viability of such projects, usually for no more than three years.
c) Recurrent grants to assist the general finance of institutions in need, usually for no more than three years."
Over 300 grants given in 1994/95, 7 were £100,000 and over, 28 between £20,000 and £65,000, 40 between £10,000 and £15,000, and nearly 200 between £1,000 and £5,000, with some 40 less than £1,000. Arts grants in 1994/95 amounted to some £205,000 (7% of total grant-aid) and were given to:
Martin Musical Scholarship Fund* (£54,500);
Museum of Scotland, National Portrait Gallery Development Appeal* (£25,000 each);
Philharmonic Orchestra Ltd* (£20,000);
Geffrye Museum Trust, Tate Gallery (£15,000 each);
Music Therapy Centre, National Art

Collections Fund* (£10,000 each);
Live Music Now* (£5,000);
Albatross Arts Project, Framework Children's Theatre, SHAPE London (£3,000 each);
Living Paintings Trust, London Mozart Players* (£2,500 each);
Musicspace Trust (£1,000);
ArtLink of West Midlands, Warwick Arts Society (£500 each);
Spencer Industrial Arts Trust (£250).
*Recurrent grants.

Exclusions: No grants to individuals.
Applications: In writing to the correspondent.

The Tyne & Wear Foundation

MEA House, Ellison Place, Newcastle upon Tyne NE1 8XS

Tel: 0191-222 0945; **Fax:** 0191-230 0689
Contact: Carol Meredith, Assistant Director
Trustees: Alastair Balls, Alan Brown, Alma Caldwell, Sir Tom Cowie, Hilary Florek, John Hamilton, Richard Harbottle, Carole Howells, Brian Latham, Parmjit Mattu, Sylvia Murray, Pauline Nelson, Lord Ralph Percy, Brian Roycroft, Alan Share, John Squire, Alan Wardropper, Anthony winder, Michael Worthington.
Grant total: £795,000 (1994/95)
Beneficial area: Tyne & Wear, Northumberland.
General: The foundation both fundraises to build up a permanent and growing endowment as well as makes grants to support the "changing needs and opportunities" of the communities of Tyneside, Wearside and Northumberland. It makes grants to groups representing all sections of the community including children, people with disabilities, the elderly, and areas of high social need.
Some major donations are held in special funds for charitable purposes nominated by the donor. In addition the foundation is administering £1.5 million allocated by Henry Smith's Charity for work in the North East. One of the seven projects selected was: Dance in Action, an innovatory programme of work with young people and

special needs groups in Newcastle and Cleveland, organised by Dance City (£200,000).

Another outstanding development of 1994/95 was "The Royal Shakespeare Company's work with the deaf community and with disabled people, at the invitation of the foundation and funded jointly with two other trusts. The project... included special workshops on Twelfth Night and A Midsummer Night's Dream (and) culminated in a trip to the Theatre Royal during the RSC Newcastle Season" (Annual Report). Arts grants in 1994/95:
South Tyneside Art Studio (£6,000);
Equal Arts (£5,000);
Headway Theatre (£4,000);
Wansbeck Hospital Arts Trust* (£3,000);
Felling Male Voice Choir*, Whitburn
  Jazzliners* (£2,000 each);
Let's Make Music Project (£600);
Winlaton Mill Community Festival Group*
  (£500);
Bede Wind Philharmonic (£500);
Buddle Arts Centre (£200).
*From donor-advised funds.

The foundation makes grants as outlined above when art is the medium through which people can be supported. Its main focus is social welfare and grants for arts related work are limited,
Exclusions: No grants to individuals, for capital projects, equipment, to large scale appeals or for formal research.
Applications: Preliminary enquiries to Carol Meredith, Assistant Director. Major grants over £2,000 are awarded in Autumn and Spring. Applicants are advised to discuss their work before completing an application form. Requests are responded to within two months and the foundation informs applicants whether their project will go forward to the next meeting for consideration. Small grants are awarded every quarter and such requests need to be on an application form. Preliminary enquiries are welcomed for both kinds of grant.

The Lisa Ullman Travelling Scholarship Fund

56 Salisbury Road, Carshalton Beeches, Surrey SM5 3HD

Tel: 0181-669 6608
Contact: Mary Wilkinson
Trustees: A G Crombie, Anthony Knapp, Dr Marion North.
Grant total: £11,000 (1994/95)
General: Funds for travel in the UK or abroad to attend a conference, course of study or to pursue a research project in the field of movement or dance.
Exclusions: Grants are not usually awarded to applicants in their first years of training. No funding for capital costs.
Applications: Application forms are available.

The ULTACH Trust/Iontaobhas ULTACH

Room 202, Fountain House, 19 Donegall Place, Belfast BT1 5AB

Tel: 01232-230749; Fax: 01232-321245
Contact: Aodan Mac Poilin, Rosie Ni Bhaoill
Trustees: Ruairi O Bleine, Leslie Burnett, Sean O Coinn, Barry Kinghan, Ferdia Mac an Fhailigh, Risteard Mac Gabhann, Sue MacGeown, Christopher McGimpsey, Seamus de Napier, Maolcholaim Scott.
Grant total: about £100,000 a year
Beneficial area: Northern Ireland.
General: The trust aims to widen appreciation of the Irish language and culture throughout the entire community in Northern Ireland. The trust normally funds new or established groups based in Northern Ireland. Particular consideration is given to groups developing inter-community Irish language activities. Grants do not usually exceed £5,000 and are for specific projects rather than on-going costs.
Exclusions: Only Irish language activities are funded. Grants are not normally made to individuals, to support running costs, fund major capital programmes support travel expenses, publications or videos.
Applications: An application form is available.

The Underwood Trust

32 Haymarket, London SW1Y 4TP

Contact: Antony P Cox, Manager
Trustees: C Clark, R Clark, Mrs P A H Clark.
Grant total: £334,000 (1993/94)
Beneficial area: UK.
General: The trust gives in the following
categories: medicine and health; general
welfare; education, sciences, humanities
and religion; environmental resources. The
most recent information available about
grants is for 1991/92 when £306,000 was
disbursed in 52 donations, many recurrent.
Most grants were for £1,000 or £5,000
whilst six were for £10,000 or more. Arts
grants totalling £30,000 were given to;
London Library, Organ Appeal St Andrew's
*   Frognal (£10,000 each);*
International Musicians' Seminar, Scottish
*   Opera (£5,000).*
Exclusions: No grants to individuals.
Applications: New applications are very
unlikely to be considered and cannot expect
an acknowledgement.

The Charles Wallace India Trust

9 Shaftesbury Road, Richmond, Surrey
TW9 2TD

Tel: 0181-940 9295
Contact: Dr F H Taylor
Trustees: Sir David Orr, Lord Briggs,
R Cavaliero.
Grant total: £217,000 (1994/95)
Beneficial area: UK and India.
General: The trust gives awards for
"training and professional attachments in
Britain of Indian postgraduate students,
scholars and professionals concerned with
the arts and humanities". In 1994/95, 105
awards were given including grants for
creative artists and for people concerned
with architectural conservation and
museum conservation.
Exclusions: No grants towards capital
costs.
Applications: In writing to the
correspondent.

The Warbeck Fund Limited

32 Featherstone Street, London EC1Y 8QX

Tel: 0171-490 1922
Contact: The Secretary
Trustees: Directors: Michael David, Neil
Sinclair, Jonathan Gestetner
Grant total: £146,000 (1994/95)
Beneficial area: UK and overseas
General: This fund gave considerably less in
1994/95 than in previous years (£703,000
in 1993/94 and £691,000 in 1992/93). This
seems to be because the fund did not carry
out its usual practice of giving one, and
sometimes more, very large grants, eg
£500,000 to Bristol University in 1993/94.

In 1994/95 the fund gave around 150
grants ranging from less than £100 to
£19,000. The majority of grants were small
with only five grants of £10,000 or more
and 19 grants between £1,000 and £9,999.
Over 22 arts grants were given totalling
over £31,000 (21% of total grant-aid). They
included:
Royal National Theatre (£16,250);
London Symphony Orchestre Trust (£2,500);
Chichester Festival Theatre Productions
*   (£2,050);*
Chicken Shed Theatre (£1,615);
Friends of the Royal Academy (£1,407);
British Museum Society (£1,020);
Shakespeare Globe Theatre (£1,060);
Hampstead Theatre (£1,000);
Almeida Theatre (£405);
Writers & Scholars Educational Trust (£135).
Exclusions: Individuals; organisations not
registered as charities.
Applications: In writing.

The Ward Blenkinsop Trust

Broxbury, Codmore Hill, Pulborough,
West Sussex RH20 2HY

Contact: J H Awdry
Trustees: A M Blenkinsop, J H Awdry,
T R Tilling.
Grant total: £186,000 (1993/94)
Beneficial area: UK with a special interest
in the Cheshire, Merseyside area.
General: In 1993/94 the trust gave some
100 grants to a wide range of charitable

interests particularly health and social welfare. Grants ranged from under £100 to £25,000, with most of its grants for £1,000 or less. Only six grants were given to arts organisations but they were amongst the largest in size and totalled over £62,000, a third of total giving. Arts grants in 1993/94:

Cheshire County Council, Youth Arts
   Initiative (£25,000 with £6,250 in the
   previous year);
Cheshire County Council, Year of Culture
   (£12,500 with £6,250 in the previous
   year);
Royal Academy of Dancing (£8,190 with
   £15,750 in the previous year);
Manchester Youth Theatre (£7,800 with a
   similar grant in the previous year);
Bristol Old Vic Theatre School (£5,970 with
   a similar grant in the previous year);
Andante Theatre Company (£3,000).

Exclusions: Individuals and organisations not registered as charities.

Applications: In writing to the correspondent.

The Wates Foundation

1260 London Road, Norbury, London
SW16 4EG

Tel: 0181-764 5000
Contact: Sir Martin Berthoud, Director
Trustees: Ann Ritchie (Chair), Andrew Wates, David Wates, Jane Wates, John Wates, Susan Wates. (The grants committee also includes other members of the Wates family.)
Grant total: Around £1. 1 million
Beneficial area: UK but with a special emphasis on London, especially south London, and with specific but limited attention for Merseyside, Tyne and Wear and Northern Ireland.
General: The foundation's primary aims are the alleviation of distress and the improvement of the quality of life. There is emphasis on the physical, mental and spiritual welfare of the young and disadvantaged with a concentration on the field of addiction and criminality between 1994 and 1997.

The foundation gives over 200 grants a

year, normally between £1,000 and £25,0000 with a maximum length of support of three years. Around 75% of the money is given to community projects and help for disadvantaged people. Over half of the money goes to the London areas, particularly south London. **Arts projects are only funded where there is a strong social welfare aspect**.

In 1994/95 grants to arts activities totalled £34,000 (4% of total grant-aid):

Under "Community"
Euro Gallery, Waterloo, towards the work
   of this halfway house rehabilitating ex-
   offenders through the arts (£3,000);
North Kensington Video/Drama Project,
   salary costs for a trainer (£7,500);
Sidings Community Centre, purchase of
   video camcorder to train young people in
   video production (£850);

Under "Arts"
Camberwell Choir School (£5,000);
Roundabout, drama and movement therapy
   group working with the elderly (£3,356);
Orchestra of St John's Smith Square, to help
   for access for elderly and inform (£3,000);
Live Music Now!, to help establish an office
   in Northern Ireland (£3,000);
London Symphony Orchestra, to expand
   recital scheme for elderly and retired
   people in Greater London (£2,000);
Royal Academy Trust (£1,000);
Croydon Philharmonic Choir (£500);
Mansfield Eagles Band, purchase of
   instruments (£200);

Under "Northern Ireland"
Suffolk Community Arts Programme, video
   equipment for community theatre project
   (£1,500).

Exclusions: No grants to individuals, general appeals from well-established organisations, large building projects.
Applications: Recipients must have charitable status. Apply in writing at any time to the director including a description of the project and latest accounts.

The Weinberg Foundation

Spencer house, 27 St James' Street, London SW1A 1NR

Tel: 0171-493 8111
Contact: Maria Torok
Trustees: Neville Ablitt, Freddie Mauwer.
Grant total: £41,000 (1993/94)
Beneficial area: UK.
General: The assets of this foundation are decreasing as it continues to give out more in grants than it receives in income. The foundation mainly supports Jewish, medical and welfare charities with a number of arts grants are given each year. In 1993/94 these included:
Royal Opera House Trust (£4,800);
Market Theatre (£1,000);
Almeida Theatre (£250).
Applications: In writing to the correspondent but applicants should realise that there is little leeway for new appeals.

The Weinstock Fund

1 Stanhope Gate, London WIA 1EH

Tel: 0171-493 8484
Contact: Ms Jacqueline Elstone
Trustees: Simon Weinstock, Michael Lester.
Grant total: £366,000 (1993/94)
Beneficial area: UK.
General: The fund gives its grants widely with support to disability, social welfare, medicine, children as well as to the arts. Arts grants totalling over £60,000 were given to 24 organisations in 1993/94. Arts grants were given to:
Friends of Ravenna Festival (£15,875);
Opera Comique (£10,000);
Newbury Spring Festival (£8,000);
Friends of Vienna Philharmonic (£5,700);
Royal Opera House (£5,000);
London Bach Society (£2,000);
English National Ballet (£1,500);
Academy of London, British Friends of Arts Museums of Israel, Chicken Shed Theatre, Friends of St John's Smith Square, Jewish Museum, Music at Oxford, National Gallery Trust, Royal Academy Trust, Women's Playhouse Trust (£1,000 each);

Benesh Institute, Centre for Music in Hospitals, Live Music Now!, Young Concert Artists Trust, Youth & Music (£500 each).
Exclusions: No grants to individuals or organisations not registered as charities.
Applications: In writing to the correspondent including the charity registration number.

The Welsh Church Funds

see separate addresses below

Grant total: £660,000 (1993/94)
General: The Welsh Church Funds are charitable trusts currently administered by each county council applying funds released by the disestablishment of the Church of Wales. Each has its own criteria and application procedure. All can support education, libraries, museums, art galleries and recreational activities. the measure to which each does so varies.

After 1st April 1996 the funds will be administered by the new unitary authorities under a variety of arrangements. After this date all applicants should ask their local authorities about the new arrangements.
Clwyd: The Chief Executive's Department, Clywd County Council, Shire Hall, Mold, Clwyd CH7 6NR (01352-702406);
Dyfed: The County Secretary, Dyfed County Council, County Hall, Carmarthen, Dyfed (01267-233333);
Gwent: M J Perry, Secretary to the Trustees, Gwent County Council, County Hall, Cwmbran, Gwent NP44 2XH (01633-832841);
Gwynedd: The County Secretary, County Offices, Caernarfon, Gwynedd LL5 1SH (01286-672255);
Powys: The Chief Executive, Powys County Council, Powys County Hall, Llandrindod Wells, Powys LD1 5LG (01597-826000);
South Glamorgan: Barbara Lees, South Glamorgan County Council, County Hall, Atlantic Wharf, Cardiff CF1 5UW (01222-872423);
West Glamorgan: The County Clerk, West Glamorgan County Council, Guildhall, West Glamorgan SA1 4PA (01792-471111).

The Welton Foundation

2 Finsbury Avenue, London EC2M 2PP

Tel: 0171-236 8000
Contact: R R Jessel, Secretary
Trustees: G C Seligman, Sir Ronald Leach, D B Vaughan, H A Stevenson.
Grant total: £718,000 (1992/93)
Beneficial area: UK, including Jersey
General: The foundation gives particularly to hospitals and medical research as well as to the arts and a more general range of charities.

Eleven arts grants totalling over £91,000 were given in 1992/93. This does not include small grants of less than £1,000 which are not listed. They included:
Contemporary Dance Trust (£24,000 with £22,500 in the previous year);
Goldberg Ensemble (£22,000 with £10,000 in the previous year);
Molecule Theatre of Science (£10,000);
National Art Collections Fund (£7,000);
Bodleian Library, Milton's Cottage Trust, Monteverdi Trust, National Portrait Gallery, Young Concert Artists Trust (£5,000 each);
British Youth Opera (£2,000);
Royal Academy of Music (£1,531).
Exclusions: Orgnaisations not registered as charities. General appeals.
Applications: In writing to the secretary with full details about the charity, the project, its budget and other sources of funding. Because of the large number of approaches it receives, the foundation cannot acknowledge all applications.

The Westminster Foundation

53 Davies Street, London WIY 1FH

Tel: 0171-408 0988
Contact: J E Hok
Trustees: The Duke of Westminster, J H M Newsum, B A J Radcliffe.
Grant total: £1,071,000 (1993/94)
Beneficial area: North West of England, Central London particularly Westminster.
General: The foundation categorised its 1993/94 grant-aid showing that 4% (£42,000) was given to The Arts. The main area of support as Social Welfare (51%), followed by Medical (14%), Youth (11%); Conservation (9%) and the Church (4%). The arts are never a priority and have received less in previous years eg. only 2% in 1991 when total grant-aid was also much lower (£674,000).

Five arts grants were given in 1993/94, four of which had been given in the previous year. They included:
Chester in Concert (£20,000);
Northern Ballet Theatre*, Thomas Cubitt Memorial Fund* (£10,000);
Chester Summer Music Festival* (£1,000).
* previously supported.

Exclusions: Individuals; organisations not registered as charities. Unsolicited applications from arts and theatre projects are not considered.
Applications: Applications can be made in writing. Trustees meet in February, May, September and November,

The Garfield Weston Foundation

c/o G Weston Centre, Bowater House, 68 Knightsbridge, London SW1X 7LR

Tel: 0171-589 6363
Contact: Harold W Bailey
Trustees: Garfield Weston, Chairman; Guy Weston; Galen Weston; Grainger Weston; Miriam Burnett; Barbara Mitchell; Nancy Baron; Wendy Rebanks; Gretchen Bauta; Camilla Dalglish.
Grant total: £7,917,000 (1993/94)
Beneficial area: UK and overseas.
General: The foundation sketches its policy in a brief annual report attached to its accounts. The foundation was created with general charitable objectives. The aims of the trustees are to support a broad range of activities in the field of religion, education, the environment, the arts, health (including research) and other areas of general benefit to the community in the United Kingdom.

"The size and scope of donation depends on the nature of the appeals under consideration. The trustees endeavour to support appeals across the broad spectrum, including causes and projects having a substantial impact within the community or of significant national importance through to requests from small charitable funds or individuals applying on behalf of causes deemed worthy of support... All appeals under consideration are reviewed by a committee of the trustees and the policy is to give proper consideration and a prompt response to all applicants."

The foundation's largest grants (£100,000 to £1 million) are to well-established institutions, especially, but not exclusively, to hospitals, universities, and medical research. This means that the major part of its annual expenditure is devoted to a relatively small number of organisations. Its smaller grants, mostly between £100 and £5,000, cover a very wide range of types of activity.

In 1993/94 the foundation gave nearly 700 grants totalling £7,917,000. The trust allocated close on £600,000 to arts and museums in this year. Arts grants in 1993/94 included:

Science Museum (£250,000);
Royal Academy of Arts (£101,000 and in the previous year);
Bodleian Library, Oxford, Welsh National Opera (£50,000 each);
London Library Anniversary Appeal (£25,000);
Blackheath Concert Halls, Painshill Park Trust (£20,000 each);
Cambridge Arts Theatre, Lyric Theatre, Hammersmith, London Contemporary Dance School, Rambert Dance Company (£10,000 each);
Fruitmarket Gallery, Royal Academy of Music, Young Vic (£5,000 each);
Koestler Award Trust, National Youth Orchestra (£2,500 each);
British Friends of Gdansk Theatre Trust, Glyndebourne Festival Opera, Glasgow Cathedral Organ Restoration, York Early Music Festival (£2,000 each);
Tron Theatre (£1,500);
British Museum, Chamber Music Competition for Schools, English Chamber Music Orchestra and Music Society, Hackney Youth Orchestras, Honiton Festival,
Leicester Philharmonic Youth Choir, Market Harborough Drama Society, Purcell School, Monmoth Choral Society (£1,000 each).

Exclusions: No grants to individuals.
Applications: To the correspondent. Miss S Weston fields enquiries by potential applicants on behalf of Mr Bailey.

Humphrey Whitbread's First Charitable Trust

34 Bryanston Square, London W1H 7LQ
Tel: 0171-402 0052
Contact: Mary Scallan, Secretary
Trustees: H Whitbread, S C Whitbread, H C Whitbread, C R Skottowe.
Grant total: £60,000 (1993/94)
Beneficial area: UK.
General: The trust makes a large number of very small grants to a wide range of charities including churches. In 1993/94 a total of 360 grants were given, many of which were under £100 and seemed more like membership subscriptions. Arts grants included:

Cambridge Arts Theatre Trust (£3,000);
Royal College of Music, Women's Playhouse Trust (£500 each);
Gregynog Festival (£250);
Arts Educational School (£230);
Rehearsal Orchestra, Royal Ballet School (£100 each);
Live Music Now!, Glyndebourne Arts, London Library, Park Lane Group (£100 each).

Smaller grants under £100 were given to a wide range of arts organisations including Choral Music In Hospitals, and the Contemporary Dance Trust.
Applications: In writing to the correspondent.

The Harold Hyam Wingate Foundation

38 Curzon Street, London W1Y 7AF

Tel: 0171-465 0565
Contact: Karen Cohen
Trustees: Mrs M Wingate, R C Wingate, A J Wingate.
Grant total: £195,000 (1993/94)
Beneficial area: UK and Israel.
General: The foundation was set up for the general advancement of Jewish and other charitable objects. In 1993/94 the foundation gave 77 grants totalling £195,000. The majority (45) were between £1,000 and £10,000 with 30 lower than £1,000. At least 21 grants totalling £74,000 were given to Jewish organisations. Grants were given to medical research and health care, education (particularly Jewish studies) and arts particularly music and opera. Arts grants totalling £34,000 (18% of grant-aid) in 1993/94:
Wingate Literary Prize, organised by the Jewish Quarterly (£8,000);
English Touring Opera (£7,500);
Jewish Museum of London (£6,500);
Guildhall School of Music and Drama (£6,000);
English Chamber Orchestra and Music Society (£1,175);
British Youth Opera, Path Productions, Shakespeare Globe Trust (£1,000 each);
Magical Experiences Arts Co Ltd, Molecule Theatre Company (£500 each).
The foundation also operates the *Wingate Scholarship Fund* for students over the age of 24. Details may be obtained from Jane Reid at the above address. In 1993/94 scholarship payments totalled £294,000.
Exclusions: No grants for capital costs. No grants to individuals except via the Scholarship Fund. No funds to support individual productions.
Applications: In writing to the correspondent. Applications, which must be from a registered charity, are considered every three months. The scholarship scheme has an annual closing date of 1st February. Please include an SAE to receive an acknowledgement.

The Fred and Della Worms Charitable Trust

Frederick House, 58a Crewys Road, London NW2 2AD

Tel: 0181-458 1181
Contact: F S Worms
Trustees: F S Worms, Mrs D Worms, M Paisner.
Grant total: £72,000 (1993/94)
Beneficial area: UK.
General: This trust's grant-aid has dropped consistently in the past few years from £203,000 in 1991/92. It gives mainly to Jewish charities. Arts grants included:
European Jewish Publication Society (£5,000);
British Friends of Art Museums in Israel (£2,590);
Royal National Theatre (£600);
Jewish Literary Trust, Tate Gallery, Israeli Music Foundation (£500 each);
Jewish Book Council, Royal Academy, Northern Centre for Contemporary Art, Ben Uri Art Society, Jewish Museum (grants under £500 each).
Applications: In writing to the correspondent.

The Wolfson Family Charitable Trust *(formerly the Edith and Isaac Wolfson Charitable Trust)*

18-22 The Haymarket, London SW1Y 4DQ

Tel: 0171-930 1057; Fax: 0171-930 1036
Contact: Dr Barbara Rashbass
Trustees: Lord Wolfson; Lady Wolfson; Janet Wolfson de Botton; Laura Wolfson Townsley; Martin D Paisner; Dr Martin Gilbert; Lord Finsberg; Professor Barrie Jay.
Grant total: £4,829,000 (1994/95)
Beneficial area: UK and overseas.
General: The trust, which is administered alongside the Wolfson Foundation, supports a relatively small number of organisations, so its grants are large. The charity's forward commitments to projects in Israel are extensive, so its capacity to make new awards is much more limited than the grant total might suggest.

Grants were categorised in the 1994/95 annual accounts as follows:
Science, Technology & Medicine £2,196,000
Education £887,000
Medical Care and Welfare £1,231,000
Arts and Humanities £521,000
Arts grants in 1994/95 included eight grants of £25,000 and more:
British Museum (£62,000);
Imperial War Museum (£41,000);
Theatre Royal Plymouth (£37,000);
Lyceum Theatre Crewe, Fleet Air Arm
  Museum, Miners' Institute Theatre
  (£25,000 each).
A further 33 grants under £25,000 each and totalling £251,000 were also allocated.

The Wolfson Foundation

18-22 The Haymarket, London SW1Y 4DQ
Tel: 0171-930 1057: Fax: 0171-930 1036
Contact: Dr Barbara Rashbass, Director and Secretary
Trustees: Lord Wolfson; Lady Wolfson; Lord Quirk; Lord Quinton; Professor Sir Eric Ash; Lord Phillips; Lord McColl; Mrs Janet Wolfson de Botton; Mrs Laura Wolfson Townsley, Professor Sir Leslie Turnberg.
Grant total: £10,071,000 (1994/95)
Beneficial area: Mainly UK and Israel.
General: The foundation's principal aims are "to advance the progress of health, education, the arts and humanities". The trustees meet biannually and are advised by specialist panels who meet before the main board meetings. The foundation's guidelines state that the areas supported under "Arts and the Humanities" include libraries, museums, galleries, theatres, academies and historic buildings. Several types of grants are made which are not necessarily independent of each other.

• Capital projects towards the cost of erecting a new building or extension, or of renovating and refurbishing existing buildings.
• Equipment grants to cover the supply of equipment for specific purposes, and/or furnishings and fittings.

"Eligible applications from registered charities for contributions to appeals will normally be considered only when at least 50% of that appeal has already been raised".

Recurrent costs are not normally provided unless they are part of the foundation's designated competitive programmes of grants to universities for research and scholarship.

The foundation established a Museums & Galleries Improvement Fund which operated for five years from 1990. In 1994 grants from this fund totalled more than £3 million matched by a similar amount from government. This programme has now ended.

The trustees continue to emphasise the importance of maintaining the fabric of historic buildings and made more than 30 such grants totalling over £155,000 in 1994/95.

Within its "Education" programme the foundation gives support to music. Grants were awarded in 1994/95 to:
Wolfson College, Oxford (£20,000);
Wigmore Hall Trust (£6,000).
Six music colleges received grants totalling £48,000 for singing prizes and four grants totalling £20,688 were given for instruments to the four main music colleges.

Exclusions: Individuals; costs of attending or running meetings, conferences, exhibitions, concerts, lectures; general appeals; endowment funds; making of films and videos; overheads, running or administrative costs, VAT or professional fees; purchase of buildings.

Applications: Guidelines should be obtained. The following information covers the main points. Prospective applicants are encouraged to explore the eligibility of their project by submitting a brief outline with a copy of the most recent audited accounts. Detailed proposals (preferably no longer than 1,000 words excluding appendices) should be in the following format:

• In lay terms a brief summary of the immediate and longer term objectives of the project. For historic buildings, please specify: the category of building (Grade, Listed building); date of current building; enclose a recent photograph.

- The proposal describing in non-specialist language the need or the problem, and justifying the approach proposed to satisfy this need or to solve the problem.
- An illustration of the benefits which could accrue to individuals, organisations, commerce or society at large from a successful project.
- Two independent, professional referees with full names and addresses.
- A detailed financial breakdown of the grant requested and any other financial information such as, for capital works the architects' or surveyors' costings of the planned building work, together with explanatory sketch and floor plans (A4 only); for student accommodation the cost per room and a detailed breakdown of the building costs.
- Proposals for funding the entire project.
- Estimates of subsequent running and maintenance costs of the complete new development and how these costs will be met.
- The application must come from the Chairman or equivalent person of the applying organisation.
- Eleven copies are requested with one copy of the audited accounts for the most recent two years.

The I A Ziff Charitable Foundation

Town Centre House, The Merrion Centre, Leeds LS2 8LY

Tel: 0113-245 9172
Contact: K N Riley, Secretary to the Trustees
Trustees: I Arnold Ziff, Marjorie Ziff, Michael Ziff, Edward Ziff, Ann Manning.
Grant total: £109,000 (1992/93)
Beneficial area: UK with a special interest in Yorkshire.
General: Half the grant-aid in 1992/93 was given to the University of Leeds. The trust made some 90 grants of less than £500 supporting a wide range of interests. Arts grants included:
Israel Philharmonic Orchestra (£3,000);
Royal College of Music (£250);

Live Music Now! (£200);
Harrogate Arts & Mercer Gallery Development Trust, Scottish International Piano Competition (£100 each).
Applications: In writing to the correspondent.

The Zochonis Charitable Trust

Touche Ross & Co, PO Box 500, 74 Mosley Street, Manchester M60 2AT

Tel: 0161-228 3456
Contact: The Secretary
Trustees: John Zochonis, Richard James, Alan Whittaker.
Grant total: £995,000 (1994/95)
Beneficial area: UK but most particularly Manchester
General: The trust supports a wide range of organisations. Its expenditure has risen considerably (by over £300,000) from £663,000 in the previous year. There is a strong preference for activities in the Manchester area. Grants relevant to this guide were given in 1994/95 to:
Chetham's Library Appeal (£50,000);
Manchester Youth Theatre (£15,000 in 2 grants);
Northern Chamber Orchestra (£10,000);
City of Drama, Royal Marines Museum Heritage Appeal (£5,000 each).
Manchester Chamber Concert Society (£3,000).
Exclusions: No grants to individuals, or organisations not registered as charities. *No unsolicited requests or appeals.*
Applications: In writing to the correspondent.

APPENDICES & INDEXES

APPENDIX 1
AWARDS FOR INDIVIDUAL ARTISTS

The awards for individual artists covered in this guide include support for individuals from the main arts funding organisations, (the national arts councils, crafts council and regional arts boards, etc), plus the trusts and companies. A list of the organisations and trusts which support individuals (apart from the national arts councils and regional arts boards) is to be found in the index.

Awards for individual artists are legion, far too many to be tackled fully in this guide which concentrates on giving an overview of the key funding sources for groups and organisations. Many are one-off or short-term PR ventures by companies; others commemorate individuals and so on.

Certain key organisations which administer a number of permanent schemes for individual artists are also listed in this guide. These organisations should be a useful advice point about further sources of funding. They are noted below along with a few magazines/journals which are helpful sources of information and should be regularly scanned by those seeking funding.

LITERATURE

Arvon Foundation;

Book Trust;

Book Trust Scotland;

Poetry Society;

Society of Authors

Details of awards for novels, short stories and works of non-fiction are found in journals such as:

"The Author", the Society of Authors, London, quarterly;

"Writers" and Artists' Yearbook" contains a very useful section on Prizes and Awards; A & C Black, London

"Guide to Literary Prizes, Grants and Awards", Book Trust, Book House, 45 East Hill, Wandsworth, London SW18 2QZ (Tel: 0181-870 9055; Fax: 0181-8744 4790) £6.99

MUSIC

Musicians' Benevolent Fund

"Classical Music", Rhinegold Publishing, London

"Handbook of Music Awards and Scholarships", Musicians' Benevolent Fund £3.50

DANCE

"Dance Now", Dance Books, London Quarterly

"Dancing Times", Dancing Times Ltd, London, monthly

VISUAL ARTS/CRAFTS

Federation of British Artists

Museums Association

"Crafts". Crafts Council, London, bi-monthly (see entry for address)

"Artists' Newsletter", AN Publications, Sunderland, monthly

"British Journal of Photography", Henry Greenwood & Co Ltd, London, weekly

APPENDIX 2
TRAINING COURSES

A number of organisations around Britain provide training in fundraising and management for voluntary organisations, some of which are particularly geared to the needs of arts organisations. The following list gives a selection. Also check with your national Arts Council or Regional Arts Board for services they give, or can recommend, in your vicinity.

Administration Research Training Services
8 The Maltings, East Tyndall Street,
Cardiff CF1 5EA
Tel: 01222-495387;
Fax: 01222-455031
Short courses on sponsorship, production management, customer care etc.

Arts Training North West
(previously Centre for Arts Management)
Institute of Public Administration and Management, University of Liverpool,
2 Abercrombie Square,
Liverpool L69 3BX
Tel: 0151-794 2916/8;
Fax: 0151-794 2909
One- and two-day courses on strategies for financing the arts, marketing, management, planning etc.

Arts Training Programme
De Montfort University,
Scraptoft Campus, Scraptoft,
Leicester LE7 9SU
Tel: 0116-257 7804;
Fax: 0116-257 8804
Short courses for arts workers on a wide range of topics including fundraising, sponsorship, financial administration, marketing, publicity, applying to trusts.

Arts Training South
Centre for Continuing Education,
University of Sussex, Falmer,
Brighton BN1 9RG
Tel: 01273-606755 x 3602;
Fax: 01273-678466
Short courses on arts fundraising and management.

Arts Training South West
Melville House, 12 Middle Street,
Taunton TA1 1SH
Tel: 01823-334767;
Fax: 01823-334768
Information on training only.

Directory of Social Change
The Charity Centre, 24 Stephenson Way, London NW1 2DP
For Courses:
Tel: 0171-209 4949
Fax: 0171-209 4130
For Books:
Tel: 0171-209 515
Fax: 0171-209209 5049

Directory of Social Change, Northern Office
Federation House, Hope Street,
Liverpool L1 9BW
Tel: 0151-708 0117;
Fax: 0151-708 0139
One-day and two-day seminars on a wide range of subjects such as basic

fundraising, applying to trusts, applying to companies, sponsorship, accounting and financial management. The Northern Office arranges conferences in the regions.

Interchange Training
Interchange Studios, Dalby Street, London NW5 3NQ
Tel: 0171-267 5220;
Fax: 0171-482 5292
Short courses on fundraising, management skills, marketing, printing layout and design.

Independent Theatre Council
12 The Leathermarket, Weston Street, London SE1 3ER
Tel: 0171-403 6698;
Fax: 0171-403 1745
One and two day courses in regional centres for managers and would-be managers of small-scale professional performing arts companies and arts centres. Subjects include Starting a Performing Arts Company, Contracts and Copyright, Finance and Accounts, Booking Tours, Co-productions, Employment Procedures, Programming.

The Management Centre
65 Westgate Road, Newcastle upon Tyne NE1 1SG
Tel: 0191-221 1177;
Fax: 0191-261 7002
Runs the National Arts Fundraising School (5 and a half days) in Spring and Autumn each year.

The Volunteer Centre
Carriage Row, 183 Eversholt Street, London NW1 BU
Tel: 0171-388 9888 x 214;
Fax: 0171-383 0448
Short courses on Training Volunteers, Project Management, Working with

Volunteers (useful for those planning to enlist regular volunteers to help in fundraising and administrative work).

ABSA/Business in the Arts run advice sessions and courses at their regional offices (see Association for Business Sponsorship of the Arts entry for addresses, etc.).

The Arts Councils and some **Regional Arts Boards** run short training courses for arts administrators on subjects such as Marketing, Sponsorship, Financial administration.

The Arts Councils offer a range of training grant opportunities such as individual bursaries, short-term training project grants and Group Training Scheme grants. These are open to administrators as well as professional artists.

APPENDIX 3
BIBLIOGRAPHY OF FUNDING/ SPONSORSHIP GUIDES

GENERAL
The Complete Fundraising Handbook by Sam Clarke, published by the Directory of Social Change in association with the Institute of Charity Fundraising Managers, 2nd edition 1993, 3rd edition forthcoming.

Capital Grants for the Arts, published by the Arts Council of England, 1994

TRUSTS
Directory of Grantmaking Trusts, basic information on over 3,000 trusts, published by the Charities Aid Foundation

A Guide to the Major Trusts, Volume 1, 1995-96 edition, The top 300 trusts disbursing 80% of charitable trust funding, with details of their grant-making practice and examples of grant-aid, published by the Directory of Social Change

A Guide to the Major Trusts, Volume 2, a further 700 trusts, published by the Directory of Social Change

The Scottish Trusts Guide, details of 350 trusts, published by the Directory of Social Change 1996

Guides to Local Trusts, published by the Directory of Social Change; four volumes: *London; Midlands; North; South* 1996

Trust Monitor, 3 times a year, general news about the trust world including information on new trusts, 32 pages, published by the Directory of Social Change

Also:
Funderfinder, the computer programme which helps voluntary groups identify appropriate charitable trusts. For further information: 65 Raglan Road, Leeds LS2 9DZ (Tel: 0113-243 3008; Fax: 0113-243 2966)

COMPANIES
The Major Companies Guide, the charitable and community support of the UK's 400 leading corporate donors, 1996/97 edition, published by the Directory of Social Change

A Guide to Company Giving, Facts, Figures and Contacts for the giving of 1,400 Companies, 1995/96 edition, published by the Directory of Social Change

The Arts Sponsorship Handbook by David Fishel, published by the Directory of Social Change, 1993

ABSA/W H Smith Sponsorship Manual, published by Association for Business Sponsorship for the Arts

ABSA/Arthur Andersen Tax Guide, published by Association for Business Sponsorship for the Arts

Principles for Good Practice in Arts Sponsorship, published by Association for Business Sponsorship for the Arts

Evaluating Arts Sponsorship – Finding Your Way, published by Association for Business Sponsorship for the Arts

ABSA Annual Report,

See ABSA entry for address to obtain publications

INTERNATIONAL

More Bread and Circuses, Who does What for the Arts in Europe? published by IETM and the Arts Council of England 1995, available from the Arts Council and the International Arts Bureau (see entries for addresses)

International Arts Digest, quarterly, produced by the International Arts Bureau for the Arts Council of England and available with "Arts Council News" (see entries for addresses)

Communication, bimonthly information update, produced by the International Cultural Desk (see entry for address)

The Directory of Social Change *publishes a wide range of general fundraising books which could be most useful eg. "Organising Local Events" and "Tried and Tested Ideas for Raising Money Locally" and DIY Guides to Marketing and Public Relations.*

Further enquiries and a full book list available from The Publications Department, DSC, 24 Stephenson Way, London NW1 2DP Tel 0171-209 5151; Fax: 0171-209 5049

Geographical Index of Charitable Trusts

The following lists indicate those charitable trusts which have shown a particular interest in supporting activities within these geographical areas. This does not necessarily mean these are the *only* areas within which the trust will give support (though that may be the case with a few). Neither does it mean these are the only trusts to give support in these areas. Most trusts are able to donate widely in the UK.

Eastern

East Anglia
Alper Charitable Trust, 310
Simon Gibson Charitable Trust, 356
John Jarrold Trust Ltd, 373

Bedfordshire
Carlton Television Trust, 323
Robert Kiln Charitable Trust, 375
Steel Charitable Trust, 418

Suffolk
Henry Smith's (Kensington Estate) Charity, 415

Newmarket
Simon Gibson Charitable Trust, 356

East Midlands

Hornton Trust, 369

Leicestershire
Henry Smith's (Kensington Estate) Charity, 415

Nottinghamshire
Djanogly Foundation, 342

London

Baring Foundation, 315
Carlton Television Trust, 323
Royal Victoria Hall Foundation, 407

Central London
Westminster Foundation, 431

Barnet
Milly Apthrop Charitable Trust, 310

City
Drapers' Charitable Fund, 342

Lambeth
Peter Minet Trust, 390

Southwark
Peter Minet Trust, 390

Tower Hamlets
Spitalfields Market Community Trust, 416

Twickenham
Hampton Fuel Allotment Charity, 364

Westminster
Westminster Foundation, 431

North

Cumbria
Sir John Fisher Foundation, 350
Francis Scott Charitable Trust, 413
Frieda Scott Charitable Trust, 414

Northumberland
W A Handley Charity Trust, 365
Tyne & Wear Foundation, 426

North East
Baring Foundation, 315
Oldham Foundation, 398

Tyneside/Tyne & Wear
W A Handley Charity Trust, 365
Tyne & Wear Foundation, 426
Wates Foundation, 429

North West

Granada Foundation, 357

Cheshire
Lord Leverhulme's Charitable Trust, 381
Ward Blenkinsop Trust, 428

Lancashire
Francis Scott Charitable Trust, 413

Merseyside
Baring Foundation, 315

SUBJECT INDEX

Do not confine your use of the guide to these indexes alone. To do so would severely reduce its usefulness.

The following indexes *exclude* individual references to the National Arts Councils and Regional Arts Boards. These entries should be consulted for their support to all artforms, and specific types of activity whether touring, international initiatives, or marketing/business support.

Users will also be helped by the grouping into sections of other sources of official support (listed in the Contents Page). These sources are *not* listed again in the following lists.

These indexes mainly direct users to those charitable trusts which display a *clear interest in the specific heading*. This does not mean that other trusts may not have the potential to assist this area.

Particular artforms and interest areas are only listed where a definite interest is shown. Some artforms are not listed . This does not necessarily mean that support may not be forthcoming from a number of official sources and certain charitable trusts.

YOUNG PEOPLE

*(see also the sections of Official Sources:
Education and Youth; Visiting Arts and
Exchange Visits)*

Charitable Trusts

INTERNATIONAL:
TRAVEL/EXCHANGE, ETC

*(see also International section under Official
Sources)*

Charitable Trusts

BUSINESS/MANAGEMENT
SUPPORT

The Association for Business Sponsorship of
   the Arts (ABSA), 228
Business in the Arts, (see ABSA)

Charitable Trusts

SUPPORT FOR
INDIVIDUAL ARTISTS

Official Sources
*(in addition to the Arts Councils and
Regional Arts Boards)*

Charitable Trusts

ALPHABETICAL LISTS

OFFICIAL SOURCES OF ARTS FUNDING IN THE UK & EUROPE

COMPANIES

CHARITABLE TRUSTS

US FOUNDATIONS